Unless Re...   ...or
    DA...

History of the American Economy

SEVENTH EDITION

History of the American Economy

SEVENTH EDITION

Gary M. Walton
University of California, Davis
Foundation for Teaching Economics

Hugh Rockoff
Rutgers, The State University of New Jersey

The Dryden Press
Harcourt Brace College Publishers

Fort Worth Philadelphia San Diego New York Orlando Austin San Antonio
Toronto Montreal London Sydney Tokyo

Publisher	Liz Widdicombe
Acquisitions Editor	Rick Hammonds
Developmental Editor	Stacey Fry
Project Editor	Doug Smith
Production Manager	Keith Gregg
Art Director	Beverly Baker
Photo Editor	Steve Lunetta
Copy Editor	Dan Hammer
Indexer	Leslie Leland Frank
Compositor	GTS Graphics
Text Type	Adobe Caslon
Cover Image	*The Lackawanna Valley,* © 1993 National Gallery of Art.

Address for Editorial Correspondence
The Dryden Press, 301 Commerce Street, Suite 3700, Fort Worth, TX 76102

Address for Orders
The Dryden Press, 6277 Sea Harbor Drive, Orlando, FL 32887
1-800-782-4479, or 1-800-433-0001 (in Florida)

ISBN: 0-03-097633-2

Library of Congress Catalog Card Number: 93-071382

Printed in the United States of America

3 4 5 6 7 8 9 0 1 2   048   9 8 7 6 5 4 3 2 1

The Dryden Press
Harcourt Brace College Publishers

In honor of our dissertation advisors,
Douglas C. North and Robert W. Fogel,
Nobel laureates in Economics, 1993.

THE DRYDEN PRESS SERIES IN ECONOMICS

Landsburg
Price Theory and Applications
Second Edition

Link, Miller, and Bergman
EconoGraph II: Interactive Software for Principles of Economics

Lott and Ray
Applied Econometrics with Data Sets

Nicholson
Intermediate Microeconomics and Its Application
Fifth Edition

Nicholson
Microeconomic Theory: Basic Principles and Extensions
Fifth Edition

Ormiston
Intermediate Microeconomics

Oser and Brue
The Evolution of Economic Thought
Fourth Edition

Puth
American Economic History
Third Edition

Ramanathan
Introductory Econometrics with Applications
Second Edition

Rukstad
Corporate Decision Making in the World Economy: Company Case Studies

Rukstad
Macroeconomic Decision Making in the World Economy: Text and Cases
Third Edition

Samuelson and Marks
Managerial Economics

Scarth
Macroeconomics: An Introduction to Advanced Methods
Third Edition

Smith and Spudeck
Interest Rates: Principles and Applications

Thomas
Economics: Principles and Applications
(Also available in micro and macro paperbacks)

Wachtel
Labor and the Economy
Third Edition

Walton and Rockoff
History of the American Economy
Seventh Edition

Welch and Welch
Economics: Theory and Practice
Fourth Edition

Yarbrough and Yarbrough
The World Economy: Trade and Finance
Third Edition

Zimbalist, Sherman, and Brown
Comparing Economic Systems: A Political-Economic Approach
Second Edition

THE HARCOURT BRACE COLLEGE OUTLINE SERIES

Emery
Principles of Economics: Macroeconomics

Emery
Principles of Economics: Microeconomics

Emery
Intermediate Microeconomics

PREFACE

The appearance of the Seventh Edition of *History of the American Economy* attests to the continued brisk advance of research in the field of economic history, and to the rapid changes unfolding in the world economy today. Indeed, the collapse of communism throughout much of the world since 1989 and the conversion from centrally planned to market led economies urges a reconsideration of the American economic record. Hence, new evidence and revised interpretations of our economic past have been the most compelling reasons for offering this new edition. Each chapter has been substantially revised and several are almost entirely new. In addition new pedagogical features have been introduced in this edition, and greater emphasis has been given to the twentieth century.

To realize our primary purpose, the teaching of American economic history, we have retained the presentation of material in chronological order, albeit not rigidly. This edition retains the multi-part structure that users have found so useful. Part 1, "The Colonial Era, 1607–1776," has been shortened, but the critical issues and legacies of that era have been highlighted to stimulate appreciation and understanding of this colorful period. Part 2, "The Revolutionary, Early National, and Antebellum Eras, 1776–1860," and Part 3, "The Reunification Era, 1860–1920," each begin with a chapter on the impact of war and its aftermath. The other chapters in these sections follow a parallel sequence of discussion topics—land, agriculture, and natural resources; transportation; product markets and structural change; conditions of labor; and money, banking, and economic fluctuations. Each of these sections closes with a chapter on an issue of special importance to the period: Part 1, the causes of the American Revolution; Part 2, slavery; and Part 3, domestic markets and foreign trade. The most dramatic change from the sixth edition is in Part 4, previously labeled "The Modern Era, 1920 to the Present." This section has been divided into two parts, Part 4, "The Interwar Era," and Part 5, the "Postwar Era." In combination they contain eleven chapters, many of them new, and all of them expanded and updated.

All five sections explicitly emphasize and illustrate five grand themes that provide the foundation of the book: (1) economic growth, (2) markets and the role of government, (3) the quest for security, (4) competitiveness and international comparisons, and (5) demographic forces. These themes reflect the research interests of scholars, past and present, who have contributed to the revision of the historical record. We have purposely stressed these themes to excite the readers' interest in economic history and, we hope, to place the American economic experience in a clearer current-day perspective. We firmly believe that presenting specific policy issues in their web of economic, political, and demographic forces provides convincing evidence of the relevance of economic history to contemporary events and to our personal lives.

The Seventh Edition retains a strong emphasis on the importance of institutions and the influence, both positive and negative, of government policies. It gives special note to the economic consequences of legal change and of government intervention and regulation of business practices and markets, especially in the past 100 years. The book provides evidence on the distributions of income prevailing in each of the major periods. This should encourage students to draw their own conclusions on matters of economic justice and to appreciate that economic change produces both winners and losers, at least relatively. Similarly, key legacies from the past, such as slavery and the failures of Reconstruction, are highlighted to add focus to the circumstances and issues we face today.

Finally, the Seventh Edition further develops the pedagogical features used in earlier editions. A list of historical and economic perspectives still precedes each of the five parts of the book, providing a brief summary of key characteristics and vital events that gave special historical distinction to each unfolding era. Furthermore, each chapter still ends with a reference list of articles and books. Each list is at once the basis of much of the scholarship underlying the chapter and a source of suggested additional readings. In addition to these pedagogical aids, each chapter begins with a brief over-view and summary of the key lesson objectives and issues. Each chapter also includes an economic insight section. These economic insights utilize explicit economic analysis to reveal the power of economic analysis in explaining the past and to show economic forces at work on specific issues raised in the chapters.

This and earlier editions have been sustained and supported by many individuals whose influence has surely filtered through or directly benefited this one. We remain especially indebted to Hugh G. J. Aitken, Paul Uselding, and Stewart Lee, who offered critical comments and advice on the entire fourth edition, and similarly to George Green, Gavin Wright, and Richard Winkelman for their suggestions and criticism of drafts of the fifth edition, and Michael R. Haines and Paul Rhode for their comments on the Seventh Edition. We are grateful for the continued advice and encouragement of Lee Alston, Terry Anderson, Fred Bateman, Diane Betts, Stuart Bruchey, Susan Carter, Philip Coelho, Paul A. David, Lance Davis, Richard A. Easterlin, Barry Eichengreen, Stanley L. Engerman, Albert Fishlow, Robert W. Fogel, Robert Gall-man, Claudia Goldin, Phil Graves, Robert Higgs, Gary Libecap, James Mak, Russell Menard, Lloyd Mercer, Donald N. McCloskey, Douglass C. North, Edwin Perkins, Jack Purdum, Roger L. Ransom, Joseph D. Reid, Jr., Don Schaefer, R. L. Sexton, James Shepherd, Austin Spencer, Jeffrey Williamson, and Mary Yeager.

Gary Walton is grateful to the Foundation for Teaching Economics for research assistance and clerical support, and to his colleagues at the University of California, Davis, for advice and encouragement, especially Alan Olmstead, Greg Clark, and Peter Lindert.

Hugh Rockoff thanks his colleagues at Rutgers who stood willing and able to answer all manner of questions. His fellow economic historian, Eugene White, patiently shared his extensive knowledge of the 1920s and 1930s. Hugh owes his largest debt to his wife, Hope Corman, who provided instruction in the subtleties of labor economics and unflagging encouragement for the whole project. To all of them Hugh expresses his deepfelt thanks.

Our greatest personal and professional debt remains to Ross M. Robertson.

Gary Walton
Hugh Rockoff

BRIEF TABLE OF
CONTENTS

TABLE OF CONTENTS

CHAPTER ONE

ECONOMIC HISTORY

A STUDY WITH A PURPOSE

Demographers inform us that in the United States 1-year-olds today will live long lives, one-fifth reaching the age of 100. In 1990, the U.S. Census counted 35,888 Americans as centenarians. Even the relatively young, say 80-year-olds, can recall and tell tales of their youth, when automobiles were a rare novelty, the airplane was for daring stunts only, the radio was the center of home entertainment, and the outhouse was as common as the flush toilet in most neighborhoods. How will Americans live 100 years from now? How will you live 50 years from now?

One hundred years ago, citizens of Great Britain enjoyed the highest standards of living in the world and the British Empire was the leading world power. In 1892 the dominant European powers upgraded the rank of their diplomats in Washington, D.C., from ministers to ambassadors, thereby elevating the United States to first-division status among nations. In 1950 the United States was the most powerful nation in the world and Americans enjoyed standards of living higher, by far, than any other people. Throughout most of the post–World War II period, the Soviet Union maintained levels of economic, technological, and military strength to rival the United States as a world power. By the early 1990s that strength had largely dissolved, and Russia was in desperate need of aid just to feed its people.

Such swings in international power, status, and relative well-being are sobering reminders that the present is forever changing and slipping into the past. Are the changes that each of us will see and experience in our lifetimes inevitable, or can destinies be steered? How did we get to where we are today?

It is unfortunate that history is often presented in forms that seem irrelevant to our everyday lives. Memorizing long lists of dates and places, generals and wars, presidents and legislative acts too often misdirects our attention to what happened to whom and when rather than the more useful focus on how and why events happened. One of the special virtues of the study of economic history is its focus on how and why. It provides us with a deeper understanding of how we developed as a nation, how different segments of the population have fared, what principal policies or compelling forces brought about differential progress, or regress, among regions and people. In short, the study of economic history holds great promise and enrichment for us. Not only does it enrich our intellectual development and provide essential perspective on contemporary affairs, but it also offers practical analytical guidance on matters of policy. The study of economic history is best suited for those who care about the next one to one thousand years and who want to make the future better than the past.

This is no empty claim! Surely one of the major reasons students major in economics or American history is ultimately to enhance the operation and performance of the American economy. Certainly instructors hope their students will be better informed citizens and more productive businesspeople, politicians, and professionals. "If this is so," as Gavin Wright recently properly chastised his economic colleagues, "if the whole operation has something to do with improving the performance of the U.S. economy, then it is perfectly scandalous that the majority of economics students complete their studies with no knowledge whatsoever about how the United States became the leading economy in the world, as of the first half of the twentieth century. What sort of doctor would diagnose and prescribe without taking a medical history?"[1]

Too often students are victims of economics textbooks that convey no information on the rise and development of the U.S. economy. Rather textbooks convey the status quo of American preeminence as if it just happened, that there was no puzzle to it, as if growth was more or less an automatic, year-by-year, self-sustained process. Authors of such textbooks need an eye-opening sabbatical in Greece, Russia, or Zaire.

Economic history is a longitudinal study, but not so long and slow as, say, geology, in which only imperceptible changes occur in one's lifetime. In contrast, the pace of modern economic change is fast and accelerating in many dimensions. Within living memory of most Americans, nations have risen from minor economic significance to world prominence (Hong Kong, Japan, South Korea), while others have fallen from first-position powers to stagnation (Russia). Whole new systems of international economic trade and payments have been developed (North American Free Trade Agreement, European Economic Community). New institutions, regulations, and laws (Clean Air Act) have swiftly emerged, which sometimes expand and sometimes constrain our range of economic choices. The role of government in the economy is vastly different from what it was just 60 or 70 years ago; undoubtedly it will be strikingly different 50 years from now. The study of economic history stresses the role of institutional change and how certain groups brought about economic change and why. One important topic, for example, is how late nineteenth-century midwestern farmers enacted Granger laws that ultimately led to the formation of the Interstate Commerce Commission, which influences our lives daily but silently through regulations. Another vital topic is the legacy of slavery and the policies and circumstances that have sustained poverty disproportionately among American blacks. Another is the rise and impact of labor unions and their stagnation and decline in the United States in recent years. The Great Depression, banking regulations, and the savings and loan crisis are others, and on goes the list.

Consider the following questions: Should we have free trade or raise tariffs? Who wins and who loses? Are mergers of firms in the public interest? Can the Great Depression recur? Are U.S. firms more poorly managed and organized than Japanese firms? Are we losing our status as the leader in technology and innovation? If we are,

---

[1] Gavin Wright, "History and the Future of Economics," in *Economic History and the Modern Economics*, ed. William Parker (New York: Basil Blackwell, 1986), p. 81.

how are we losing it? How did we get it? Should incomes be more equally distributed? What makes them so unequal? Do past patterns of immigration and assimilation have any relevance for Hispanic, Asian, and other immigrants today? What is the basis for our rights to own and use property and to assure contracts? Should government bail out poorly managed banks, savings and loan institutions, and other businesses, or should they be allowed to fail?

The study of history, then, is more than an activity to amuse or sharpen our wits. History is a vast body of information essential to a wide spectrum of public policy decisions. It is a basis for testing the soundness of opinions. This is especially true of economic history because of its quantitative features and because economic theory can give useful organization to historical facts. In combination, these enhance our ability to test (refute or support) particular propositions and policy recommendations. Consider, for instance, a recommendation for mandatory wage and price controls as a means to combat inflation. Figure 1-1 traces a decade of inflation and reveals our experience with wage and price controls during the Nixon years. President Nixon's opinion at the time was that the controls would benefit the economy.

As shown in Figure 1-1, Nixon's controls were imposed in August 1971, when the inflation rate was 4.5 percent. The precontrol rate of inflation was 6 percent in early 1970 and was actually falling at the time controls were imposed. The rate of inflation continued to drift down and remained around 3 percent throughout 1972; it started to rise in 1973, and by the time the controls were completely lifted in early 1974 the rate was 10 percent and rising.

On the face of it, controls did little to stop inflation. But what explains this dismal record? Were controls themselves to blame, or were other factors at work? Only a careful study of the period can identify the role of controls in the acceleration of inflation. A contrast between Nixon's price controls and those during the Korean War

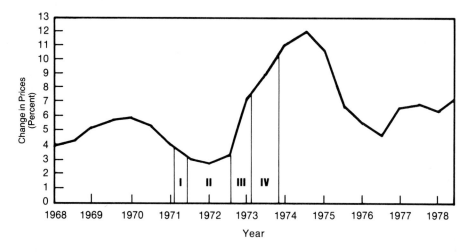

FIGURE 1-1 INFLATION AND NIXON'S PRICE CONTROLS

SOURCE: U.S. DEPARTMENT OF COMMERCE STATISTICAL ABSTRACT, 1978, P. 483.

(which were not followed by a price explosion after controls were lifted) suggests two important things to look at: monetary and fiscal policies.

Price controls, moreover, disrupted the smooth functioning of the economic system. For example, to circumvent the Nixon controls, the lumber industry regularly exported lumber from the United States to Canada, then reimported it for sale at higher prices. As it became more profitable to sell fertilizers and chemical pesticides abroad than at home, agricultural production suffered for want of these essential inputs. These and many other similar disruptions to production made the growth rate of goods and services less and therefore the inflation worse than it would have been otherwise. We cannot explore this issue in depth here. Our point is simply that to evaluate policy proposals we must inevitably turn to the historical record.[2]

The use of wage and price controls during World War II provides another example adding to our understanding of their effectiveness. One important lesson this episode teaches is about the need to supplement quantitative studies with historical research. An economist cannot naively assume that price statistics always tell the truth. During the war, controls were evaded in numerous ways that were only partly reflected in the official numbers despite valiant efforts by the Bureau of Labor Statistics. One form of evasion was quality deterioration. Fat was added to hamburger, candy bars were made smaller and inferior ingredients were substituted, coarser fabrics were used in making clothes, maintenance on rental properties was reduced, and so on. Sometimes whole lines of low-markup, low-quality merchandise were eliminated, forcing even poor consumers to trade up to high-markup, high-quality lines. And, of course, black markets developed, like illegal markets in drugs today. It is the job of the economic historian to try to assess the overall effect of these activities.[3]

Many students ask the following question: Granted that economic history is important to the professional economist or economic policymaker, is there any practical reason for studying it if I have other long-term goals? The answer is yes. The skills developed in studying economic history—critically analyzing the economic record, drawing conclusions from it based on economic theory, and writing up the results in clear English—are valuable skills in many lines of everyday work. The lawyer who reviews banking statutes to determine the intent of the law, the investment banker who studies past stock market crashes to find clues on how to foretell a possible crash, the owner-operator of a small business who thinks about what happened to other small businesses that were sold to larger firms—all are taking on the role of economic historian. It will help them if they can do it well.

Besides the importance of historical study for its vital role in deliberating private and public policy recommendations, knowledge of history has other merits. For one thing, history can be fun—especially as we get older and try to recapture parts of our lives in nostalgic reminiscence. For another, history entertains as well as enriches our

[2]An attempt to compare and contrast American experiences with wage and price controls is presented in Hugh Rockoff, *Drastic Measures: A History of Wage and Price Controls in the United States* (New York: Cambridge University Press, 1984).

[3]For one exploration of this issue see Hugh Rockoff, "Indirect Price Increases and Real Wages in World War II," *Explorations in Economic History* 15 (1978): 407–420.

self-consciousness and oftentimes, because of TV, the historical account is provided almost instantly (for example, during the Persian Gulf War). A sense of history is really a sense of participation in high drama—a sense of having a part in the great flow of events that link us with people of earlier times and with those yet to be born.

THE MERGING OF ECONOMICS AND HISTORY

The marriage of history and economics is not contrived or forced; the two disciplines are based on the common use of *both* theory and empirical information. This similarity is not always fully appreciated, but like any organized body of knowledge, both economics and history summarize events and reality. Without such aid, the human mind cannot comprehend the complexity of our economic system. Because there are too many "facts," we cannot simply look at the facts or the interrelationships among economic variables and make sense out of them. It is equally apparent that history must be selective—that any attempt to record the whole of the past would be an exercise in futility. Economists and historians make their respective subjects manageable by prudently selecting relevant information and disregarding irrelevant information. Which data and information are relevant is largely, indeed some would claim solely, determined by theoretical considerations. The theoretical underpinnings of a story or argument may often be implicit, but theory is being used whenever cause and effect are stated or implied. Economics enhances history by making explicit the use of theory, and history serves as the essential testing ground for economic theory. As William Parker reminds us, "Without theory, history becomes undisciplined and disorganized, shaping its material by whim, or purely by rhetoric. Without history, theory loses any grounding in the actual course of human events."[4] Together history and economics stand stronger than either does alone. Still it is useful to understand and appreciate their separate domains and differences of scope, style, and approach.

HISTORY

History, as a study, is the narrative statement of happenings in the past. So the historian, like the economist, is confronted with a jumble of facts that must be collected and molded into an intelligible, significant narrative. We can better understand the difficulty of the task when we realize that the historical event has happened in the unalterable past and can never be observed again. It can only be reconstructed from remaining evidence, chiefly in the form of documents of one kind or another, and much of the evidence is fragmentary and unreliable. But whatever difficulties historians encounter, they must collect and organize the facts, interpret them in the light of modern interests, and present them in usable form. It is important to emphasize that sound

[4] See William N. Parker, ed., *Economic History and the Modern Economists* (New York: Basil Blackwell, 1986), p. 99.

Winston Churchill, whose writings of history matched the significance of his contributions as a leader and statesman to history.

historical arguments are more than mere opinions; they are informed, persuasive opinions, consistent with evidence organized in convincing form.

It has been said that there are three phrases of historical procedure. With caution, so that we do not jump to any conclusions about separating the historian's work into neat compartments, we may still find it useful to consider these steps:

1. *Reconstruction of the historical facts—"the science of history."* Historical facts can be reconstructed by people who do not write history at all—basic researchers who search through attics and cellars, courthouses, and business records and who publish their material in the form of collected letters, papers, memoirs, and journals. But no one has a monopoly on fact collection, and many historians who write at highly generalized levels enlist the aid of scholars in sociology, political science, and anthropology who often contribute to our knowledge of historical events.

2. *Writing the historical narrative—"the art of history."* Because the facts must be assembled to form a significant written record, the historian must make a literary effort. Sometimes this effort is so successful that the result is a high art form. Historians from Herodotus to Churchill to McCloskey have become famous as a result of their literary abilities as well as their substantive contributions. Macaulay is still assigned in English literature classes, and readers even today are moved by Gibbon. For some time, the nineteenth-century emphasis on literary quality in historical works may have disappeared, but in recent years, first-

class historians have revived it. The monograph of a young scholar, whose aim is to exhaust a subject of limited range, can afford perhaps to be both technical and unexciting. But general histories, including popularizations, that do not cast their spell will be quickly usurped by a TV program or the latest best-seller.

3. *Interpretation of history—"the philosophy of history."* After the facts have been gathered and the historical narrative has been written, the record should be explained in terms of general principles that govern human conduct. Older historians sought to explain the flow of events by some grand central motivation; they exhibited an essentially *monistic* philosophy in opposition to the *pluralistic* philosophy of modern writers. The most common and best-known monistic theme was that history centered around political activity—around governments and the major phenomena of governments, such as wars, legislative acts, and changes in rulers. College students can hardly escape another monistic approach—the "great man" interpretation of Thomas Carlyle, who held that a few highly gifted people constituted the determining force in human affairs.[5] Alternatively, in the nineteenth century, the economic determinism or materialistic view of Karl Marx emphasized the economic determinants of the cultural, social, and political values of life.[6] There have been many other attempts to find a single wellspring of human motivation centered on strict economic determination, psychology, spirituality, science or technology, the "creative mind," and geography. Gradually, however, modern historians have come to believe that the vast sweep of history cannot be explained in terms of one aspect of human activity and have adapted the pluralistic view that in a physical environment more and more shaped and dominated by people, the human race progresses or retrogresses for a variety of reasons.

But if historical writing is only the result of a drastic sifting of evidence, can we ever be sure that the history we are reading is absolutely true? To this question, we must answer that we can never be certain. From a tangled web of facts, the historian must select some and discard others. Foremost historical scholars used to contend that this selection could be made on an "objective" basis. But one historian's objectivity is another historian's bias. No individual historian, however honorable or gifted, can write outside the context of his or her own experience and philosophy. We must include in our narrative those facts that we think are important in explaining changes and show that they do the explaining. Whether we like it or not, history involves implicit theorizing.

Progress in historical argument and knowledge is persistent. History is constantly moving toward greater clarification—toward a deeper, fuller knowledge of what has happened and how and why it has occurred. This progress is possible because a succession of historians, dedicated to the job of seeking new insights into and more logical explanations of events, endlessly rewrite history. It is this compulsion to take another

---

[5] For some examples of men and women who made a difference, written elegantly with charm and style, see Jonathan R. T. Hughes, *The Vital Few,* 2d ed. (New York and London: Oxford University Press, 1986).

[6] The tradition and contributions of the "Marxist school" are outlined in Jon S. Cohen, "The Achievements of Economic History: The Marxist School," *Journal of Economic History* 38 (1978): 29–57.

Donald N. McCloskey, the John F. Murray Professor of Economics and Professor of History at the University of Iowa, writes in both history and economics with insight, charm, and wit.

look, to ask one more question, to perceive something a little more clearly, that makes history in the sense of the narrative a changing and vital subject—a progressive science.

ECONOMICS

Economics is the study of how scarce resources are allocated among alternative competing uses to satisfy unlimited individual and social wants. It is also a study in social cooperation through markets or by central planning. The scarcity of a nation's resources, its people (human capital including knowledge and skills), its natural endowments (land, water, minerals) and its stock of produced goods (physical capital), and the levels of utilized technology—all set limits on total output. Because of the conflict between scarcity and wide-ranging, unlimited wants, economic choices must be made. Producing more wine imposes costs, such as producing less bread perhaps, as land and labor must be shifted from wheat to grapes.

Any economic system must address the following questions:

1. How much and what kind of productive (factor) services should be provided? Specifically, how many clerks, managers, doctors, teachers, and other types of workers are required to manufacture goods and furnish services?

2. Which enterprises should obtain the different productive services?

3. How much of the total output of the economy should be relegated to households

for immediate use (consumption), and how much should be added to the stock of real capital (tools, machinery, and so on) that will be needed for future productive effort?

4. How should consumer goods be distributed (rationed) among consumers, and how should additions to the stock of capital be parceled out among various enterprises?

These four questions are explicitly addressed in centrally planned economies. For example, in the old Soviet Union, in the 1980s and before, government planners made decisions on the output mix. They allocated resources among competing uses and monitored production activities to coordinate production units and distribute goods and services to firms and people.

In contrast, in a market economic system, no one person or agency asks and answers these questions. Nevertheless they do get answered. Markets are networks of people exchanging services and things. Suppliers and demanders acting in their own interests are coordinated by markets. Prices provide signals and incentives for people, helping them decide what, when, and where to buy (or produce and sell), where to live, what career to choose, when to change jobs, and on and on.

In action, the American economic system is one of the most fascinating and complex mechanisms ever devised by Western civilization. Even in its most trivial manifestations, the system ordinarily provides goods and services from all parts of the world, as if by magic, exactly when and where they are needed. The everyday items that we all take for granted—our morning coffee and our evening newspaper, our ride to work and our favorite television program, a telephone call to a friend, or a FAX to an office in New York—require the cooperative efforts of hundreds or thousands of people and the equipment with which they work. And when we wish to describe the system in all its intricate detail, the task seems formidable to the point of impossibility.

At this point, economists must resort to theory; that is, they must abstractly summarize the reality of the world about them to see the fundamental forces. In effect, they must construct models like the illustration, which is seen on page 11, of the circular flow model. Insofar as they abstract from reality to discover principles, economists are theorists.

But what do economists theorize about? First, they examine markets and the workings of the principal mechanism used to allocate resources—the *pricing* system, which (1) establishes the order of priority in which producers obtain resources and (2) rations goods among consumers. For a long time, the central inquiry of economic theory was to discover how the prices and quantities of goods were determined. This inquiry led to the discovery of the laws of supply and demand. Since the 1930s and even earlier, other problems—such as periods of widespread unemployment of resources—have increasingly occupied the attention of economists, and a body of theory has developed to explain how unfulfilled wants can exist side by side with idle workers and idle equipment. Another problem of economic stabilization has been one of inflation, and another area of study is economic growth. To the classical theory of price, then, economists appended the theory of income and employment, an analysis that complements the theory of price determination.

A market economy is a decentralized price system involving the interactions of millions of individuals. A circular flow, as illustrated in Figure 1-2, simplifies these interactions and allows assessment of the basic characteristics of market systems.

In our model people live in *households* and earn income in two ways: by selling their labor services or by selling use of their property (capital, land, or natural resources). They sell these in *input markets*, where the resources of production are exchanged. Money flows are generated by these exchanges as households receive income from the businesses that pay out money to obtain the productive factors. This selling and buying involves quantities (hours worked, square footage of space rented, acres of land, machine hours used) and prices (hourly wages, monthly rents, interest paid for capital, and profits).

Households are also confronted by a variety of prices in *output markets*, where goods and services are exchanged. The flow of goods and services from businesses to households (consumers) is matched by a flow of money in return. Similarly, these exchanges are made in terms of quantities (bicycles, haircuts, tacos, or textbooks) and prices. (This model of markets is incomplete because government is not included, although it reveals the basic features of market exchange.)

Both the input and output markets combine to form the *circular flow model* of market exchange. This model shows the money flows between households and businesses and the interdependent relationship between the input and output markets of a market economy. The relationship between incomes and prices determines the standards of living for individuals and for the society. As prices for goods and services fall relative to wages and other earnings, households become better off; if wages rise relative to prices for goods and services, households are better off. They can buy more with their income from the input market. In any economy, choices are continuously being registered in both input and output markets. As Figure 1-2 illustrates, these markets are interdependent. The choices households make are telegraphed to businesses by price and quantity changes through sales or inventory fluctuations. Businesses respond to these shifting messages from households by changing their purchases of productive resources in the input markets. These changes, in turn, influence households' incomes and expenditures.

It would be a mistake, however, to suppose that the price system performs its functions simply by sending impulses from consumers to business. The business sector is constantly introducing new products and innovating low-cost ways of making old ones, with resulting changes in consumer outlays. Moreover, through advertising, the business community constantly strives to sway consumer preferences among goods and services and also between making consumption expenditures and saving.

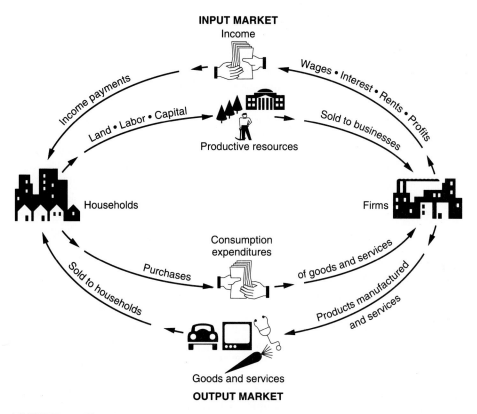

INPUT MARKET
Income

Income payments

Wages • Interest • Rents • Profits

Land • Labor • Capital

Productive resources

Sold to businesses

Households

Firms

Consumption expenditures

Purchases

of goods and services

Sold to households

Products manufactured and services

Goods and services
OUTPUT MARKET

FIGURE 1-2 THE CIRCULAR FLOW MODEL OF MARKET EXCHANGE *The input and output markets are connected and interdependent. The circular flow model diagrams the flow of money from businesses to households in exchange for the productive resources of land, labor, and capital. The money flow in the opposite direction from households to businesses represents consumption expenditures made in exchange for goods and services.*

Indeed, because the choices registered by both business managers and consumers are often made *simultaneously*, it is hard to say which decisions are causes and which are effects. The important point is that through the pricing mechanism, consumer and producer choices are translated into ultimate decisions about how resources should be allocated. More explicitly, prices perform three principal functions in a market system: an information function, an incentive function, and a rationing function. Because prices are so vitally important, their study and observation is the chief preoccupation of businesspeople and economists.

The broad subject of economics has been subdivided into a number of specialties. Some economists specialize in the theory of the firm, with its recent emphasis on problems of strategy and conflict. Others devote their full time to the study of monetary theory or to the perfection of social accounting systems. Still others investigate the principles by which international trade is regulated and the intricate theory of the determination of international exchange rates and many other areas including economic history, labor, law, and public finance fill out the field. But in whatever way economists specialize or break down the job of analysis, the fact remains that there are two basic theoretical questions in economics: (1) How are resources allocated? and (2) What forces determine the level of a nation's income?

Whenever a subject has a body of theory, it also has a body of applied knowledge. Thus, we often speak of "applied" economics, that part of economics that deals with more "practical" matters. The applied economist, like the theorist, can specialize in many areas. An economic statistician compiles, organizes, and interprets current quantitative information. An economic historian is concerned largely with the perception of *change* in economic phenomena. A practicing economic consultant furnishes executives who formulate policies with business forecasts to guide in their decision making.

Economists are fond of saying that economics is not an exact science. But neither is it guesswork. By and large, economists rely on an almost universally accepted theoretical apparatus. Social goals are subject to debate among economists just as they are among other occupational groups. But once they are furnished with a consensus about objectives—about ends—economists can offer, within tolerable limits of error, policy prescriptions calculated to achieve those objectives. In a word, economics is a way of thinking about the "unrelated confusion" of prices, production, and incomes to make these phenomena intelligible and sufficiently well ordered to permit scientific prediction.

Like any scientist working in an applied field, the economist must ultimately answer the question, what *action* should be taken? To return to our earlier discussion, for example, is a policy of wage and price controls the best alternative to end inflation? Here an appeal must be made both to theory and to the lessons of experience.[7] Advisers to government officials and other decision makers cannot reason through real-world problems without some means of eliminating the least relevant facts—without applying the principles of the theoretical economist. But any adviser with good sense must inevitably return to a reading of the record. We must turn finally to economic history to check faults of reasoning and to illuminate paths of action.

In the pages that follow, the history of the American economy is written once again. There would be no excuse for just another recounting of the same old facts and figures, updated by a few years that all too rapidly recede into the past. There is a solid reason, though, for recasting the record to further relieve it of its mythological overburden and to bear witness to the strengths and shortcomings of a democracy that operates within the discipline of markets constrained by laws and institutions.

---

[7] For further insight into the relationship between economics and history provided by two outstanding economic historians, see Donald N. McCloskey, "Does the Past Have Useful Economics?" *Journal of Economic Literature* 14 (1976): 434–461; and 1993 Noble Laureate Douglass C. North, "Structure and Performance: The Task of Economic History," *Journal of Economic Literature* 16 (1978): 963–978.

PART ONE

THE COLONIAL ERA

1607–1776

ECONOMIC AND HISTORICAL
PERSPECTIVES
1607–1776

1. The American colonial period was a time when poverty was the norm throughout the world and wars among nations were frequent. The earliest settlements in North America were costly in terms of great human suffering and capital losses.

2. The nation-states of western Europe that emerged from the long, relatively stagnant period of feudalism rose to prominence in wealth and power relative to earlier leading centers in the Mediterranean and the Orient.

3. Spain, Portugal, Holland, England, and France each built international empires, and England and France especially further advanced their relative economic and military strength by successfully applying mercantilist policies. Great Britain ultimately dominated the colonization of North America and was the first nation to launch the Industrial Revolution, beginning in the second half of the eighteenth century.

4. Innovations in trade and commerce, the spread of practical learning, new and expanding settlements that added land and adapted it to best-uses, and falling risks in trade and frontier life raised living standards in the New World. By the time of the American Revolution, the material standards of living in the colonies were among the highest in the world and comparable to those in England. However, the distribution of wealth and human rights among the sexes, races, and among free citizens was vastly unequal.

5. Although Americans sustained their long English heritage even after independence, their strong economic rise ultimately placed them in a position of rivalry with the mother country. The period from 1763 to 1776 was one of confrontation, growing distrust, and ultimately rebellion.

CHAPTER TWO

FOUNDING THE COLONIES

CHAPTER THEME "For the pleasing entertainment of the Polite part of Mankind, I have printed the most Beautiful Poems of Mr. Stephen Duck, the famous Wiltshire Poet," announced "Fry, Stationer, Bookseller, Paper-Maker, and Rag Merchant, late of the City of London and now located in Boston." The advertisement, which appeared in the Boston *Gazette* of May 1–8, 1732, was not an introductory offer, for the notice continued, "It is a full demonstration to me that the People of New England have a fine taste for Good Sense and Polite Learning, having already sold 1,200 of these Poems."

Colonial merchant shops, like the one depicted in this painting, served in large part as a cultural tie with Great Britain.

No doubt Fry was anxious to please and entertain the "Polite part of Mankind," possibly at a profit. But his advertisement contained another, somewhat plainer matter. It was "the common Method of the most curious merchants of Boston, to Procure their (account) Books from London," and Fry, for business reasons, took exception to the practice. He addressed the notice to all gentlemen, merchants, and tradesmen. "This," he declared, "is to acquaint those Gentlemen, that I, said Fry, will sell all sorts of Accompt-Books, done after the most accurate manner, for 20 percent cheaper than they can have them from London."

The fact that prepared "accompt" books "done after the most accurate manner" were offered for sale at such an early date should have occasioned no more surprise than that the polite part of New England was entertained by the poems of Mr. Stephen Duck of Wiltshire. *For in the beginning, the American colonies were only a small part of a greatly expanded Europe—a western frontier, so to speak.* The culture of the colonists, including double-entry bookkeeping and poetic preferences, was in many respects the culture of their former associates on the other side of the Atlantic. These ties were primarily to Great Britain. For in the race for empire among the European nation-states, it was ultimately Britain that prevailed in North America. Britain dominated because of its liberal policies of migration and colonization. Accordingly our legacy as Americans is principally English—if not in blood, at least in language, law, and custom.

EUROPEAN BACKGROUND
TO THE VOYAGES OF DISCOVERY

More than ten centuries passed from the fall of Rome to the voyages of discovery leading to the European expansion to the "New World." Toward the end of that period the feudal age had passed, and by the late 1300s many nation-states had emerged throughout Europe. In Russia, Sweden, England, France, and Spain, national rulers held the allegiance of large citizenries, and sizable groups of German-speaking peoples were ruled by their own kings and nobles.

The center of European wealth and commerce rested in the Mediterranean. That economic concentration was based primarily on long-distance trades between Asia (mainly Persia), the Middle East, and Europe. Because of their locational advantage and superior production and commercial skills and knowledge, the Italian city-states of Milan, Florence, Genoa, and Venice had dominated most of the Old World's long-distance trade for centuries.

EUROPEAN ROOTS AND
EXPANDING EMPIRES

By the end of the fifteenth century, however, northern Europe had experienced substantial commercial growth, especially in the Hanse cities bordering the North Sea and the Baltic. Greater security of persons and property, established in law and enforced through courts and recognized political entities, spurred commerce and economic investments. Growing security in exchanges and transactions opened up whole new trades and routes of commerce, especially in the north and west regions of Europe. This rise often augmented the old trades in the Mediterranean, but the new trades grew faster than the old.

Noteworthy as well was the rapid increase in Europe's population, which was recovering from the famines of the early fourteenth century and most importantly from the Black Death of 1347 and 1348. In England, for example, the population had fallen from 3.7 million in 1348 to less than 2.2 million in the 1370s; France probably lost 40 percent of its population; and losses elsewhere vary in estimates from 30 to 50 percent. During the fifteenth and sixteenth centuries, the demographic revival from that catastrophe added to the commercial growth and shifting concentrations of economic activity. The rapid growth of populations and growing commercialization of Europe's economies were significant building blocks in the strengthening of Europe's fledgling nation-states. Expansion in Europe and elsewhere—including ultimately America—was also part of the nation-building process.

It is important to emphasize that for centuries Catholic Europe had been pitted in war against the Muslim armies of Islam with one Crusade following another. By the fifteenth century, the age of Renaissance, Europe forged ahead in many political, commercial (and seagoing), and military areas. This century was a turning point, speeding the pace of an arms race among competing nations and empires. Fourteen ninety-two

COMMERCIAL SPLENDOR: *Venice (rendered here by Caneletto) was almost as much an Eastern as a Western city, and for hundreds of years its commercial and naval power was a great sustaining force of Western civilization.*

is as celebrated in Christian Spain for its capture of Granada from the Moors, ending seven centuries of Muslim rule there, as for Christopher Columbus's voyage to America.

PORTUGAL AND THE FIRST DISCOVERIES

It was somewhat of a historical accident that Christopher Columbus—a Genoese sailor in the employ of Spain—made the most vital and celebrated of the landfalls. Neither Spain nor the great Italian city-states were the world's leaders in long-distance exploration. Tiny, seafaring Portugal was the great Atlantic pioneer, and by the time Columbus embarked, Portugal could claim more than seven decades of ocean discoveries.

Having already driven the Muslims off Portuguese soil in the twelfth century, Portugal initiated Europe's overseas expansion in 1415 by capturing Cuenta in North Africa. Under the vigorous and imaginative leadership of Prince Henry the Navigator, whose naval arsenal at Sagres was a fifteenth-century Cape Canaveral, Portugal—from 1415 to 1460—sent one expedition after another down the western coast of Africa. The island of Madeira was taken in 1419 and the Canary Islands shortly thereafter. The Portuguese colonized the Azores from 1439 to 1453 and populated most of these islands

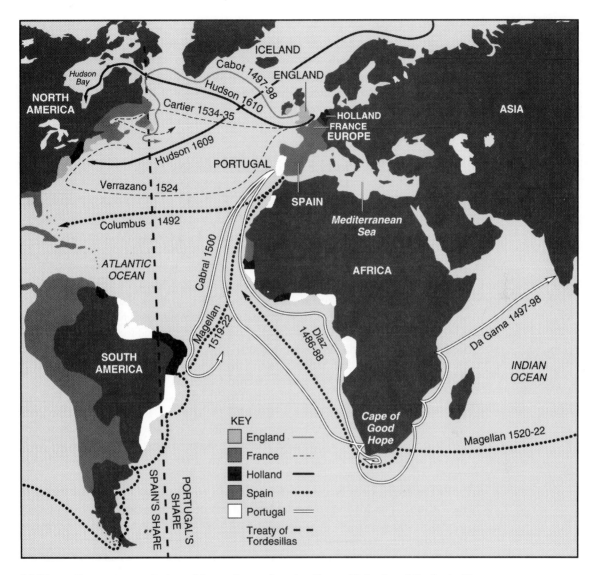

MAP 2-1 EXPLORATION: *Spain and Portugal came first; then France, Holland, and England. All of these nations explored vast amounts of territory in North America, giving rise to new economic opportunities, but England's explorations gave rise to the most extensive permanent settlements in the New World.*

with slaves imported from Africa to grow sugar. There were commercial as well as military aims to these ventures. Europeans had first become familiar with sugar during the early Crusades, and the Mediterranean islands of Cypress, Crete, and Sicily had long been major sugar-producing areas. The commercial development and sugar plantations of the Iberian-owned islands reflected the fifteenth-century western shift of economic strength and activity. In addition, the Portuguese and others sought to circumvent the Muslim blockade of the eastern Mediterranean trade routes. Europeans hungered for Asian goods, especially spices. In an age before refrigeration, pepper, cloves, ginger, nutmeg, and cinnamon were used with almost unbelievable liberality by medieval cooks, whose fashion it was to conceal the taste of tainted meat and embellish the flavor of monotonous food.

PORTUGAL AND SPAIN: EXPANDING EMPIRES

The greatest of the sea explorations from Europe took place within a little less than 35 years. The historical scope of it is astonishing. In 1488, Bartholomeu Dias of Portugal rounded the Cape of Good Hope and would have reached India if his mutinous crew had not forced him to return home. In September 1522, the *Vittoria*—last of Ferdinand Magellan's fleet of five ships—put in at Seville; in a spectacular achievement, 18 Europeans had circumnavigated the globe. Between these two dates, there were two other voyages of no less importance. Columbus, certain that no more than 2,500 miles separated the Canary Islands from Japan, persuaded the Spanish sovereigns Ferdinand and Isabella to finance his first trip. On October 12, 1492, his lookout sighted the little island of San Salvador in the Bahamas. Only a few years later, Vasco da Gama, sailing for the Portuguese, reached Calicut in India via the Cape of Good Hope, returning home in 1499. Following Dias's and Columbus's discoveries, Portugal and Spain, with the Pope's blessing, agreed in the treaty of Tordezillas (1494) to grant Spain all lands more than 370 leagues west of the Cape Verde Islands (a measurement accident that ultimately established Portugal's claim to Brazil). Thus, the sea lanes opened with Portugal dominant in the East (to East Africa, Persian Gulf, Indian Ocean, China, and beyond) and Spain supreme in the West.

By the early sixteenth century, the wealth and commerce of Europe had shifted to the Atlantic. The Mediterranean leaders did not decline absolutely; they were simply overtaken and passed by. In an international context this was a critical first phase in the relative rise and eventual supremacy of key western nation-states.

After Spain's conquest of Mexico by Hernando Cortés in 1521, American silver and gold flowed into Spain in ever-increasing quantities. When the Spanish king Philip II made good his claim to the throne of Portugal in 1580, Spanish prestige reached its zenith. By royal decree Spain simply swallowed Portugal, and two great empires, strong in the Orient and unchallenged in the Americas, were now joined. When we reflect that no other country had as yet established a single permanent settlement in the New World, it seems astonishing that the decline of Spanish power was so imminent.

Although Spain was a colonizer, Spanish attempts to settle in the Americas lacked a solid foundation. Spain's main interests, for both the conquistadors and the rulers at home, were treasures from America's mines (especially silver) and Christianity for the conquered. To be sure, attempts were made to extend agriculture and to establish man-

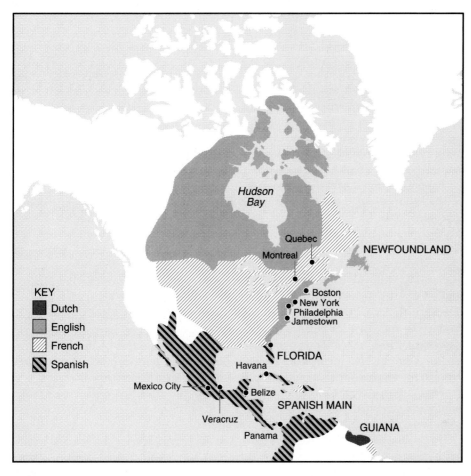

MAP 2-2 *European possessions and claims in America fluctuated. Shown here are those territories and the major cities toward the end of the seventeenth century.*

ufacturing operations in the New World, but the Spaniards remained a ruling caste, dominating the natives who did the work and holding them in political and economic bondage. Their religious, administrative, military, and legal institutions were strong and lasting, but the Spanish were more like occupying rulers than permanent settlers.

Meanwhile the Protestant Reformation radically altered the nature of European nation-building and warfare. When, toward the end of the sixteenth century, Spain became involved in war with the English and began to dissipate its energies in a futile attempt to bring the Low Countries (Holland and Belgium) under complete subjection, Spain lost the advantage of being the first nation to expand through explorations in America. Also harmful to Spain was the decline in gold and silver imports after 1600 as the mines of better-grade ores became exhausted.

THE LATECOMERS: HOLLAND, FRANCE, AND ENGLAND

Like Spain, Holland, France, and England all ultimately vied for supremacy in the New World. English and Dutch successes represented the commercial revolution sweeping across northern and western Europe in the 1600s. Amsterdam in particular rose to preeminence in shipping, finance, and trade by midcentury. But Holland's claim in North America was limited to New York (based economically on furs), and for the most part its interest lay more in the Far East than in the West. Moreover, the Dutch placed too much emphasis on the establishment of trading posts and too little on colonization to firmly establish their overseas empire.

As it turned out, France and England became the chief competitors in the centuries-long race for supremacy. From 1608, when Samuel de Champlain established Québec, France successfully undertook explorations in America westward to the Great Lakes area and had pushed southward down the Mississippi Valley to Louisiana by the end of the century. And in the Orient, France, though a latecomer, competed successfully with the English for a time after the establishment of the French East India Company in 1664. In less than a century, however, the English defeated the French in India, as they would one day do in America. The English triumphed in both India and America because they had established the most extensive permanent settlements. It is not without significance that at the beginning of the French and Indian War in 1756, there were some 60,000 French settlers in Canada and the Caribbean compared with 2 million in the English North American colonies.

For our purposes, the most important feature of the expansion of Europe was the steady and persistent growth of settlements in the British colonies of North America. Why were the English such successful colonizers?

To be sure, the English, like the French and the Dutch, coveted the colonial wealth of the Spanish and the Portuguese, and English sailors and traders acted for a time as if their struggling outposts in the wilderness of North America were merely temporary. They traded in Latin America, while privateers like Francis Drake and Thomas Cavendish plundered Spanish galleons for their treasures as they sailed the Spanish Main. English venturers, probing the East for profitable outposts, gained successive footholds in India as the seventeenth century progressed. Yet, unlike the leaders of some western European countries, Englishmen like Richard Hakluyt advocated permanent colonization and settlement in the New World, perceiving that true colonies would eventually become important markets for manufactured products from the mother country as well as sources of raw materials.

It was not enough, however, for merchants and heads of states to reap the advantages of the thriving colonies: commoners had to be persuaded of the benefits to themselves and their families of emigrating to the New World. The greatest motivations to emigrate were a desire to own land—still the European symbol of status and economic security—and to strive for a higher level of living than could be attained at home by any but the best-paid artisans. These economic motivations were often accompanied by a religious motivation. Given the exorbitant costs of the transatlantic

THE DUTCH TRADE FOR FURS ~ 1640

Initially, the Dutch were active fur traders as well as shippers in early America. Their key settlement was New Amsterdam, lost to the English in 1664, and renamed New York. Note the Dutch-built windmill in the distance.

voyage (more than an average person's yearly income), the problem remained how to pay for and move people to the New World.

FIRST BRITISH SETTLEMENTS IN NORTH AMERICA

PERILOUS BEGINNINGS

Two half brothers, Sir Humphrey Gilbert and Sir Walter Raleigh, were the first Englishmen to undertake serious ventures in America. Gilbert, one of the more earnest seekers of the Northwest Passage, went to Newfoundland in 1578 and again in 1583 but failed to colonize the territory either time and lost his life on the return voyage to England after the second attempt. Raleigh, in turn, was granted the right to settle in "Virginia" and to have control of the land within a radius of 200 leagues from any colony that he might successfully establish. Raleigh actually brought two groups of colonists to the new continent. The first landed on the island of Roanoke off the coast of what is now North Carolina and stayed less than a year; anything but enthusiastic about their new home, these first colonists returned to England with Sir Francis Drake in the summer of 1586. Undaunted, Raleigh solicited the financial aid of a group of wealthy Londoners and, in the following year, sent a second contingent of 150 people under the leadership of Governor John White. Raleigh had given explicit instructions that this colony was to be planted somewhere on the Chesapeake Bay, but Governor White disregarded the order and landed at Roanoke. White went back to England for supplies; when he returned after much delay in 1590, the settlers had vanished. Not a single member of the famed "lost colony" was ever found, not even a tooth.

After a long war between England and Spain from 1588 to 1603, England renewed attempts to colonize North America. In 1606, two charters were granted—one to a group of Londoners, the other to merchants of Plymouth and other western port towns. The London Company was given the right to settle the southern part of the English territory in America; the Plymouth Company was given jurisdiction over the northern part.

So two widely separated colonies were established in 1607: one at Sagadahoc, near the mouth of the Kennebec River, in Maine; the other in modern Virginia.[1] Those who survived the winter in the northern colony gave up and went home, and the colony established at Jamestown won the hard-earned honor of being the first permanent English settlement in America.

Hard indeed! When the London Company landed three tiny vessels at the mouth of the Chesapeake Bay in 1607, 105 people disembarked to found the Jamestown Colony. Easily distracted by futile "get rich quick" schemes, they actually sent shiploads of mica and yellow ore back to England in 1607 and 1608. Before the news reached their ears that their treasure was worthless "fool's gold," disease, starvation, and misadventure had taken a heavy toll: 67 of the original 105 Jamestown settlers died in the first year.

The few remaining survivors (one of whom was convicted of cannibalism) were joined in 1609 by 800 new arrivals, sent over by the reorganized and renamed Virginia Company. By the following spring, frontier hardships had cut their number from 838 to 60. That summer, those who remained were found fleeing down river to return home to England by new settlers with fresh supplies who encouraged them to reconsider. This was Virginia's "starving time," to use Charles Andrews's vivid label.

Inadequately supplied and untutored in the art of colonization, the earliest frontier pioneers routinely suffered and died. In 1623, a royal investigation of the Virginia experience was launched in the wake of an Indian attack that took the lives of 500 settlers. The investigation reported that of the 6,000 who had migrated to Virginia since 1607, 4,000 had died. The life expectancy of these hardy settlers upon arriving was two years.

The heavy human costs of first settlement were accompanied by substantial capital losses. Without exception, the earliest colonial ventures were unprofitable. Indeed, they were financial disasters. Neither the principal nor the interest on the Virginia Company's accumulated investments of more than £200,000 were ever repaid (approxi-

---

[1]At this time, the name *Virginia* referred to all the territory claimed by the English on the North American continent. Early charters indicate that the area lay between the thirty-fourth and the forty-fifth parallels, roughly between the southern portion of the Carolinas and the northernmost boundary of New York.

any other could use, and saved him a great deall of trouble, and gave farr better contente. The women now wente willingly into the feild, and tooke their litle-ons with them to set corne, which before would aledg weaknes, and inabilitie; whom to have compelled would have bene thought great tiranie and oppression. The experience that was had in this commone course and condition, tried sun-drie years, and that amongst godly and sober men, may well evince the vanitie of that conceite of Platos & other ancients, applauded by some of later times;—that the taking away of propertie, and bringing in communitie into a comone wealth, would make them happy and flourishing; as if they were wiser then God. For this comunitie (so farr as it was) was found to breed much confusion & discontent. . . . For the yong-men that were most able and fitte for labour & service did repine that they should spend their time & streingth to worke for other mens wives and children, with out any recompence. The strong, or man of parts, had no more in devission of victails & cloaths, then he that was weake and not able to doe a quarter the other could; this was thought injuestice. . . . Let none objecte this is men's corruption, and nothing to the course it selfe. I answer, seeing all men have this corruption in them, God in his wisdome saw another course fiter for them.[2]

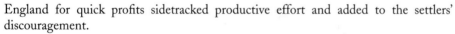

England for quick profits sidetracked productive effort and added to the settlers' discouragement.

Jamestown residents gained greater control over local matters in 1609 when small garden plots of land were given to individuals and again in 1612 when various insti-tutional reforms were undertaken. To generate more flexible leadership and local autonomy in that hostile environment, a deputy governor was stationed in Virginia. Steadily thereafter, centralized direction from England became less and less frequent.

As private landholdings replaced common ownership, work incentives improved; the full return for individual effort became a reality, superseding output sharing arrangements. In 1614, private landholdings of three acres were allowed. A second and more significant step toward private property came in 1618 with the establishment of the *headright* system. Under this system, any settler who paid his own way to Virginia was given 50 acres and another 50 acres for anyone else whose transportation he paid. In 1623—only 16 years after the first Jamestown settlers had arrived—all landholdings were converted to private ownership. The royal investigation of that year also ushered in the dissolutions of the corporate form of the colony. In 1625, Virginia was converted to a Crown colony.

Many of the difficulties experienced in early Jamestown were also felt elsewhere in the colonies. But the Puritan settlements of New England, first at Plymouth (the Plymouth Company, 1620) and then at Boston (the Massachusetts Bay Company,

[2] *William Bradford, of Plymouth Plantation* (New York: Capricorn Books, 1962) pp. 90–91.

1630), avoided some of the problems faced by the Jamestown settlers. For instance, because the Massachusetts Bay Company actually carried its own charter to the New World, it avoided costly direction and absentee control from England. Stronger social and cultural cohesion and more homogeneous religious beliefs may have contributed to a greater success of communal arrangements there, but as noted in the foregoing Economic Insight, the Plymouth colonies also reverted to private holdings. Town corporations prolonged the use of common landholdings, but private landholdings steadily replaced land held in common. By 1650, privately owned family farms were predominant in New England.

Another noteworthy colony established by a joint-stock venture was New York, first settled by the Dutch West India Company (1620) but taken in a bloodless confrontation in 1664 by the British. Maryland and Pennsylvania were initiated through proprietary grants, respectively to Lord Baltimore in 1634 and to William Penn in 1681. The former's desire was to create a haven for Roman Catholics, profitably if possible, and the latter's was the same for Quakers and other persecuted religious groups. Rhode Island's settlement was also religiously motivated due to Roger Williams's banishment from Puritan Massachusetts in 1644. These, the Carolinas, and the last mainland colony to be settled, Georgia (1733), benefited from the many hardships and lessons provided by the earlier settlements. Despite each colony's organizational form, the Crown assured all settlers except slaves the rights due English citizens. The British empire in North America extended from French Canada to Spanish Florida and through to the sugar plantation islands of the Caribbean.

BRINGING IN SETTLERS

The Atlantic Ocean posed a great barrier to settlement in North America. In the early seventeenth century, the cost of the Atlantic passage was £9 to £10 per person, more than an average English person's yearly income. Throughout most of the later colonial period, the peacetime costs of passage were £5 to £6. Consequently, in the seventeenth century, a majority of British or European newcomers could not and did not pay their own way to America. By 1775, however, more than half a million English, Scotch, Irish, German, and other Europeans had made the transatlantic voyage. More than 350,000 of them paid their way by borrowing and signing a unique IOU, an indenture contract.

The *indenture contract* was a device that enabled people to pay for their passage to America by selling their labor to someone in the New World for a specified period of time. These contracts were written in a variety of forms, but law and custom made them similar. Generally speaking, prospective immigrants would sign articles of indenture binding them to a period of service that varied from three to seven years, although four years was probably the most common term. Typically, an indenturer signed with a shipowner or a recruiting agent in England. As soon as the servant was delivered alive at an American port, the contract was sold to a planter or merchant. These contracts typically sold for £10 to £11 in the eighteenth century, nearly double the cost of passage. Indentured servants, thus bound, performed any work their "employers" demanded in exchange for room, board, and certain "freedom dues" of money or land that were received at the end of the period of indenture. This provided an active trade in human talent, and the indentured system should be viewed as an investment in migration as well as in job training (or apprenticeship).

The first indentures were sent to Jamestown and sold by the Virginia Company: about 100 children in their early teens in 1618, a like number of young women in 1619 for marital purposes, and a young group of workers in 1620. Soon thereafter private agents scoured the ports, taverns, and countryside to sign on workers as indentures. The indentured servants were drawn from a wide spectrum of European society, from the ranks of farmers and unskilled workers, artisans, domestic servants, and others. Most came without specialized skills, but they came to America voluntarily because the likelihood of rising to the status of landowner was very low in Britain or on the Continent. They were also willing to sign indentures because their opportunity cost, the next best use of their time, was typically very low—room and board and low wages as a rural English farm worker, a "servant in husbandry." Children born in English cottages usually went to work at the age of 10, moving among families and farms until good fortune (often inheritance or gifts) allowed them to marry. For many, a period of bondage for the trip to America seemed worth the risk.

Whether the life of a servant was hard or easy depended primarily on the temperament of the taskmaster; the courts usually protected indentured servants from extreme cruelty, but the law could also be applied quickly to apprehend and return servants who ran away. The usual punishment for runaways was an extension of the contract period.

Studies by David Galenson, Robert Heavener, and Farley Grubb reveal many of the intricacies of this market in bonded labor. For example, the indentured period for women was originally shorter than for men because of the greater scarcity of women in the colonies, but by the eighteenth century the periods of service were comparable for both sexes. The indentures' work conditions and duration of service also depended on location. Generally, the less-healthful living areas such as the islands of the Caribbean offered shorter contractual periods of work than did the mainland colonies. Skilled and literate workers also obtained shorter contracts, as a rule. Overall it was a highly competitive labor market system steeped in rational conduct.

Immigrants from continental Europe, mainly Germans, usually came as *redemptioners,* immigrants brought over on credit provided by ship captains. After arrival they were allowed a short period of time to repay the captain, either by borrowing from a relative or a friend or by self-contracting for their services. Because they usually arrived with no ready contacts and typically could not speak English, their contract period was sometimes longer, up to seven years. In addition, German immigrants usually came over in families whereas English migrants were typically single and more likely to enter into indentured servitude. The longer period of service for German redemptioners also was in part a consequence of their preference to be very selective in choosing their master-employer, a right indentured servants did not have. Migrating in family groups encouraged this preference, and most Germans settled in Pennsylvania. Alternatively, when the families had paid a portion of their passage costs before disembarking, their redemptioners' time could be much shorter.

As the decades passed, the percentage of European immigrants arriving as indentures or redemptioners declined. By the end of the eighteenth century, this market for indentures had disappeared. It did so by economic forces rather than legislation. The costs of passage slowly fell over time, and the earnings of workers in Europe rose. In addition, slavery was a viable cost-cutting labor source compared to indentures.

The counterpoint to white servitude—slavery—did not become an important source of labor until after 1650, although slaves were imported in increasing numbers after 1620. By 1700, slavery had become a firmly established institution from Maryland southward. Slaveholding was not unknown in New England and the Middle colonies, but it was less positive there for several reasons.

Rarely was a slave in the South unable to work due to the rigors of bad weather, whereas working outdoors in the North could be impossible for days at a time. Also important was the fact that tobacco, then rice, and finally indigo were the staple crops of the South. Because they required much unskilled labor that could be performed under limited supervision in work groups, these cash crops were especially suited to cultivation by slaves. Although not nearly as large as the huge sugar plantations of the Caribbean islands, large-scale farm units made slavery particularly profitable, and the size of farms became much larger in the South than in the Middle or New England colonies. The crops, especially rice and indigo, and the slave system itself generated *economies of scale* and fostered larger production units of team labor under supervision. Economies of scale occur when output expands relative to inputs (land, labor, and capital) as the production unit gets larger. Also *primogeniture,* a form of inheritance in which the land is transferred to the oldest son, prevailed in the southern colonies. In the Middle and New England colonies (except in Rhode Island and New York), multigeniture was typically followed, with an equal division among the sons. Over time, primogeniture perpetuated and built comparatively larger estates. Also, the purchase of imported slaves in the South triggered the headright to land of 50 acres per slave purchased, reinforcing the growth in the size of farm units there. Finally, the mere momentum of the growth of slavery in the South was accompanied by moral and institutional adaptations to strengthen and sustain it.

Unlike the indentured whites, African slaves were not protected in the colonies as British subjects. Terms of service were for life, and children of female slaves were born slaves regardless of who fathered the child. Only by self-purchase or benevolence could a slave become free. In 1774, there were nearly 500,000 blacks in the colonies, 18,000 of whom were free.

As we have emphasized, those coming to America on their own resources received 50 acres of land from headright land grants in most colonies. However, not only land but relatively high wages as well attracted workers to the colonies. Especially in the seaports, craftsmen and artisans of all sorts, merchants and seamen, even scholars gave vibrance to the commercial life on western Atlantic shores. Finally prisoners too, perhaps as many as 30,000, avoided the death sentence or indefinite imprisonment in England by voluntarily transporting themselves to the New World. After 1718 it was customary for convicts to serve 7 years of indenture for minor crimes and 14 years for major ones.

DEMOGRAPHIC CHANGE

UNDERPOPULATION DESPITE HIGH RATES OF POPULATION GROWTH

One major fact of American economic life—underpopulation and labor scarcity—persisted throughout the entire colonial period. Another extremely important aspect of British colonization and a crucial factor in securing and maintaining Britain's hold on the North American frontier was the extremely high rate of population growth in the colonies. What generated the characteristic of apparent underpopulation was the vast amount of available land, which "thinned" the population spatially and established high population densities in only a few major port towns. This occurred despite the exceptionally high rate of growth, which was so high—the population approximately doubled every 25 years—that Thomas Malthus worrisomely referred to it as "a rapidity of increase, probably without parallel in history." Malthus and others pointed to the American colonies as a prime example of virtually unchecked population growth. Wouldn't such a rate of increase, which was twice the population growth rate in Europe, ultimately lead to famine, pestilence, and doom? Wasn't it an obvious truism that the aggregate supply of land—essential to food production—was fixed in amount?

Yes, but these European polemics were far from the minds of the colonists. Indeed, Benjamin Franklin wrote an essay in 1751 extolling the virtues of rapid population increases in the colonies. Overpopulation never occurred in the colonies, despite the various methods that were used to encourage or force (in the case of African captives) population relocation to the New World. Nor did the high natural rate of population increase create population pressures in the colonies; population growth was generally viewed as a sign of progress and a means of reducing the uncertainties, risks, and hazards of a sparsely populated frontier region.

POPULATION GROWTH IN BRITISH NORTH AMERICA

The population growth from both migration and natural causes is illustrated by region and race in Table 2-1 on the following pages. Note that there is a remarkable similarity in the timing, rise, and levels of the total populations in New England and the Upper South. The latecomers—the Middle colonies and the Lower South—displayed somewhat higher growth rates, which allowed them to catch up somewhat. The rate of population expansion was quite steady for the colonies as a whole, slightly over 3 percent per year. By 1770 there were 1.7 million people of European origin and half a million of African origin in the thirteen colonies.

The period of greatest absolute migration occurred in the eighteenth century—particularly after 1720, when between 100,000 and 125,000 Scotch-Irish and about 100,000 Germans arrived in North America. Most immigrants in the seventeenth century were British, and there was another strong surge of British migration between

TABLE 2-1   POPULATION BY REGION FOR THE THIRTEEN NORTH AMERICAN COLONIES (IN THOUSANDS)

New England				Middle Colonies			
Year	Whites	Blacks	Total	Year	Whites	Blacks	Total
1610	0.0	0.0	0.0	1610	0.0	0.0	0.0
1620	0.1	0.0	0.1	1620	0.0	0.0	0.0
1630	1.8	0.0	1.8	1630	0.4	0.0	0.4
1640	13.5	0.2	13.7	1640	1.7	0.2	1.9
1650	22.5	0.4	22.9	1650	3.8	0.5	4.3
1660	32.6	0.6	33.2	1660	4.8	0.6	5.4
1670	51.5	0.4	51.9	1670	6.7	0.8	7.4
1680	68.0	0.5	68.5	1680	13.4	1.5	14.9
1690	86.0	1.0	87.0	1690	32.4	2.5	34.8
1700	90.7	1.7	92.4	1700	49.9	3.7	53.5
1710	112.5	2.6	115.1	1710	63.4	6.2	69.6
1720	166.9	4.0	170.9	1720	92.3	10.8	103.1
1730	211.2	6.1	217.3	1730	135.3	11.7	147.0
1740	281.2	8.5	289.7	1740	204.1	16.5	220.5
1750	349.0	11.0	360.0	1750	275.7	20.7	296.4
1760	436.9	12.7	449.6	1760	398.9	29.0	427.9
1770	565.7	15.4	581.1	1770	521.0	34.9	555.9
1780	698.4	14.4	712.8	1780	680.5	42.4	722.9

1768 and 1775. Perhaps as many as 300,000 white immigrants came to the New World between 1700 and 1775, and a somewhat smaller number of blacks came as well. Plenty of highly fertile land and a favorable climate attracted Europeans and provided motives for securing African slaves. Nevertheless, migration was the dominant source of population growth in only the first decades of settlement in each region.

In New England immigration virtually halted in the late 1640s, and natural causes became the source of population growth after 1650. For areas settled later, such as Pennsylvania, the forces of migration remained dominant later, but natural forces swiftly took over even there. Even the enslaved black population grew swiftly and predominantly from natural sources after 1700. On the eve of the Revolution, only one white in ten was foreign born; the figure for blacks was between two and three in ten.

Commercial successes, favorable economic circumstances, and the high value of labor powered a high rate of reproduction in the colonies. White birthrates in North America per 1,000 women ranged between 45 and 50 per year, compared to near 30 in Europe or 12 per 1,000 in the United States today. The colonial population was exceptionally young. By the 1770s, 57 percent were under the age of 21. Moreover, a higher percentage of its population was of childbearing age. Typically, colonial women tended to marry rather early—between the ages of 20 and 23, which was a couple of years younger than the average European. The cheapness of land encouraged early marriage in the colonies, and it was generally easier for colonists than for Europeans to strike out on their own, acquire land, and set up a household. Childbearing was a major cause of death for women, and many men remarried to sustain their families. The average European married man produced four or five children, but earlier mar-

TABLE 2-1 POPULATION BY REGION FOR THE THIRTEEN NORTH AMERICAN COLONIES (IN THOUSANDS) *continued*

Upper South				Lower South				Total of Thirteen Colonies			
Year	Whites	Blacks	Total	Year	Whites	Blacks	Total	Year	Whites	Blacks	Total
1610	0.3	0.0	0.3	1610	0.0	0.0	0.0	1610	0.3	0.0	0.3
1620	0.9	0.0	0.9	1620	0.0	0.0	0.0	1620	1.0	0.0	1.0
1630	2.4	0.1	2.5	1630	0.0	0.0	0.0	1630	4.6	0.1	4.7
1640	8.0	0.1	8.1	1640	0.0	0.0	0.0	1640	23.2	0.5	23.7
1650	12.4	0.3	12.7	1650	0.0	0.0	0.0	1650	38.7	1.2	39.9
1660	24.0	0.9	24.9	1660	1.0	0.0	1.0	1660	62.4	2.1	64.6
1670	38.5	2.5	41.0	1670	3.8	0.2	4.0	1670	100.5	3.9	104.3
1680	55.6	4.3	59.9	1680	6.2	0.4	6.6	1680	143.2	6.7	149.9
1690	68.2	7.3	75.5	1690	9.7	1.8	11.5	1690	196.3	12.6	208.8
1700	85.2	12.9	98.1	1700	13.6	2.9	16.4	1700	239.4	21.2	260.4
1710	101.3	22.4	123.7	1710	18.8	6.6	25.4	1710	296.0	37.8	333.8
1720	128.0	30.6	158.6	1720	24.8	14.8	39.6	1720	412.0	60.2	472.2
1730	171.4	53.2	224.6	1730	34.0	26.0	60.0	1730	551.9	97.0	648.9
1740	212.5	84.0	296.5	1740	57.8	50.2	108.0	1740	755.6	159.2	914.7
1750	227.2	150.6	377.8	1750	82.4	59.8	142.2	1750	934.3	242.1	1,176.5
1760	312.4	189.6	502.0	1760	119.6	94.5	214.1	1760	1,267.8	325.8	1,593.6
1770	398.2	251.4	649.6	1770	189.4	155.4	344.8	1770	1,674.3	457.1	2,131.4
1780	482.4	303.6	786.0	1780	297.4	208.8	506.2	1780	2,158.7	569.2	2,727.9

SOURCE: COMPILED FROM TABLES 5.1, 9.4, 6.4, AND 8.1 ON THE RESPECTIVE REGIONS IN JOHN J. MCCUSKER AND RUSSELL R. MENARD, *THE ECONOMY OF BRITISH AMERICA 1607–1789* (CHAPEL HILL: UNIVERSITY OF NORTH CAROLINA PRESS, 1985), PP. 103, 203, 136, AND 172.

riages and higher proportions of mothers in their childbearing years resulted in an average colonial family of about seven to eight children. Greater emphasis on rural economic activity also encouraged higher birthrates in the colonies. Children were more costly to raise in urban areas, and their labor contribution tended to be less there.

Also of great significance was the fact that once the first few years of starvation had passed, the colonies experienced rather low mortality rates. The annual death rate in Europe was about 40 per 1,000 people; in the colonies, it was 20 to 25 per 1,000.

The lower age structure of the colonial population accounts in part for this, but the exceptionally low rate of child mortality was an even more impressive statistic. On the average, white mothers in the colonies were better fed and housed than mothers in Europe. Consequently, colonial babies were healthier. The harsh winters of North America and the inferior medical technology of the frontier were more than offset by plentiful food supplies, fuel, and housing. And because the population was predominantly rural, epidemics were rare in the colonies.

Once past infancy, white colonial males typically lived to be 60 or more. Due to the hazards of childbirth, however, the comparable age for early colonial women was normally slightly over 40.[3]

---

[3] Although perhaps atypical, evidence presented by Philip Graven in "Family Structure in Seventeenth Century Andover, Massachusetts," *William and Mary Quarterly* (April 1966): 234–256, shows women also living into their sixties in that area.

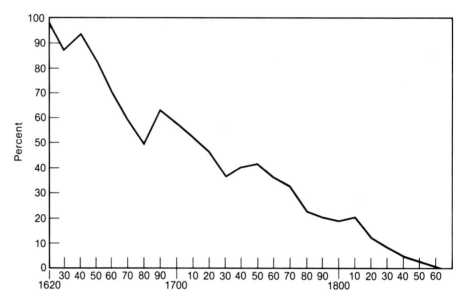

FIGURE 2-1 FOREIGN-BORN BLACKS AS A PERCENTAGE OF THE U.S. BLACK POPULATION, 1620–1860

SOURCE: ROBERT W. FOGEL AND STANLEY L. ENGERMAN, *TIME ON THE CROSS* (BOSTON: LITTLE, BROWN, 1974) P. 23.

THE RACIAL PROFILE

Six percent of all slaves imported into the New World came to areas that became the United States. As shown in Figure 2-1, migration was the initiating force of population growth of blacks. By the eighteenth century, however, natural forces dominated the growth of the black population. By midcentury the birthrate of blacks, like that of whites, was near the biological maximum. Death rates were also similar to those of whites in North America. Because the natural rate of increase was comparable for both races—which resulted in a doubling of the population nearly every 20 to 25 years—and because the actual number of imported slaves practically equaled the number of white immigrants, the proportion of the total population that was black increased significantly after 1700. We see from Table 2-1 (pages 32 and 33) that in 1670, only about 4 percent of the total population was black. A century later, this proportion had increased to about 20 percent, and the black population was near one-half million.

Of course, regional differences were great, and more than 90 percent of the slaves resided in southern regions. As Figure 2-2 indicates, however, relatively small proportions of the total population of the mainland colonies were composed of blacks, compared to the Caribbean islands. In New England the proportion of blacks was in the neighborhood of 2 percent; in the Middle colonies, 5 percent. In Maryland in the late colonial years, blacks comprised 32 percent of the total population; in Virginia, 42 percent. The more limited commercial development in North Carolina, due to inadequate harbors, generated a black population proportion of only 35 percent. In contrast,

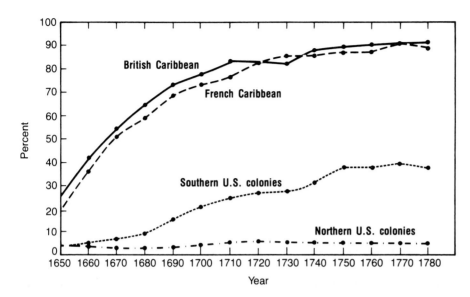

FIGURE 2-2 BLACKS AS A PERCENTAGE OF THE TOTAL POPULATION, 1650–1780: *The population profile was much different on the North American continent from the islands of the Caribbean. Only in South Carolina did the black population outnumber the resident white population.*

SOURCE: ROBERT W. FOGEL AND STANLEY L. ENGERMAN, *TIME ON THE CROSS* (BOSTON: LITTLE, BROWN, 1974), P. 21.

South Carolina contained the largest concentration of blacks—60 percent. This especially high proportion in South Carolina resulted from the special advantages of slave labor and economies of scale in rice and indigo production. Consequently, the social profile of South Carolina suggested by its high concentration of enslaved blacks was similar to the profiles of the British and French West Indies sugar islands. Although Virginia's population profile did approach this proportion, South Carolina's profile of a majority of slaves controlled by a minority of plantation owners was unique among the mainland colonies. In contrast to their Caribbean counterparts, blacks typically remained a minority race on the mainland of North America.

Finally, the pattern of change for the Native American population was in sharp contrast to that of whites and blacks. At the time Jamestown was founded, it was likely that as many as 300,000 Indians lived within 150 miles of the Atlantic seaboard. By the mid-eighteenth century the impact of battle, and especially the devastation of communicable diseases such as smallpox and measles, against which the natives had developed no immunity, reduced their population to between 50,000 and 100,000. This depopulation aspect was unique among North Americans, whatever their origin.

SPATIAL DISTRIBUTION OF THE POPULATION

Though the settlement of British North America continued steadily after Jamestown's founding, most of the population remained clustered around a few Atlantic ports. It took 50 years to secure a firm hold on the new continent, and at the end of the first century of colonial history, settlement of the eastern seaboard was far from complete. By 1660, Virginia, Maryland, and Massachusetts were established commonwealths, but the first settlers in Georgia did not move there for almost another 75 years. In 1640, about 24,000 people inhabited the English colonies on the mainland. By 1660, there were 65,000 colonists; by 1700, 260,000. From one-third of a million people in 1710, the colonial population had increased to nearly 2.5 million at the time of the Revolution.

Map 2-3 shows the extent of settlement as of 1660, 1700, and 1760. Before 1660, there was nothing to speak of south of Norfolk, and at the turn of the century a wilderness still separated Charleston and its environs from the major inhabited area in upper North Carolina. By 1760, the land-hungry rich and poor had spread over nearly all of the coastal plain and into the Piedmont areas. As early as 1726, Germans and Scotch-Irish had begun moving into the Shenandoah Valley, and down this and the other great valleys in ever-increasing numbers, settlers sought the cheap land to the west. Through gaps in the mountains some turned east into the Piedmont area of Virginia and the Carolinas; only a few years later pioneers began to trickle to the west, particularly through the Cumberland Gap into Kentucky and Tennessee.

IMPERIAL RIVALRIES IN NORTH AMERICA

The rivalry of empires persisted for a long time and the growth of population and the colonization of new territory were not restricted to the eastern coast of North America. During the sixteenth century, Spain had occupied northern Mexico and Florida, and while English settlement was taking place, the Spanish were moving northward into Texas, southern Arizona, and southern California. As we have already mentioned, in the seventeenth century, France established bases in the Lesser Antilles and in Canada; from Canada, French explorers and traders pushed into the Mississippi Valley and on to the Gulf of Mexico. The three rival states were bound to clash in America, even if they had not been enemies in other parts of the world. To the general historian we must leave the descriptions of these bitter rivalries and of the resulting complex, if small-scale, wars. Following intermittent conflict between the French and the English in the northeast and along most of the western frontier, the French and Indian War resulted in the temporary downfall of the French in North America. By the Treaty of Paris in 1763, only Spain and England were left in possession of the North American continent. Spain took all the territory west of the Mississippi, and England secured everything to the east, with the exception of certain fishing rights and small islands retained by the French off Newfoundland. According to this agreement, England acquired all of Florida, thereby settling perennial disputes with Spain that had long disturbed the colonies of South Carolina and Georgia. It is difficult to remember that Spain, not France, harassed the pioneers who moved out of the original thirteen colonies and into the old Southwest. Not until 1800 did France again own

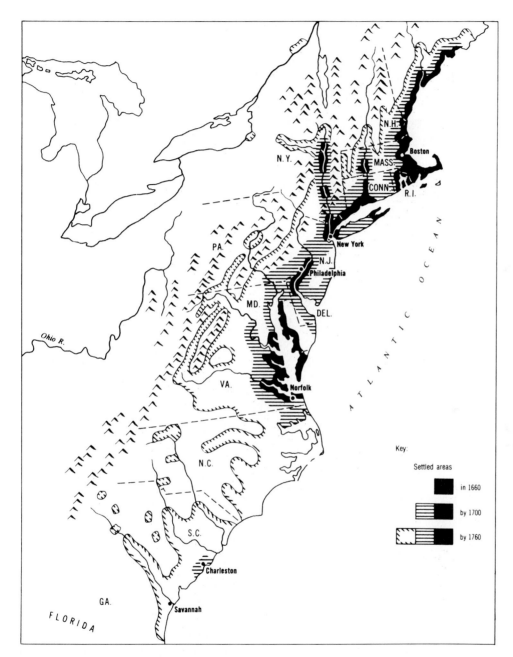

MAP 2-3 SETTLEMENT: *Easily accessible coastal regions and river valleys provided the first sites for settlements, but settlers soon moved into the Piedmont areas, the great valleys of the Appalachians, and the inviting country of the mountains.*

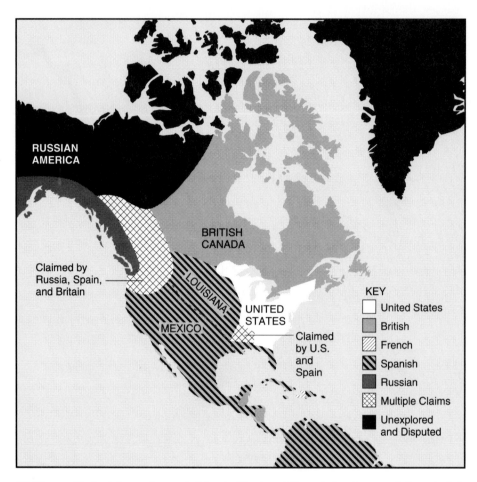

MAP 2-4 *Territorial possessions and claims in North and Central America toward the end of the eighteenth century.*

the Territory of Louisiana and its vital port of New Orleans, and that control did not last long.

Two institutional arrangements particularly favored British dominance in North America. First was the open labor market of indentured servitude, used by the British but not the Spanish or French to facilitate migration. Second was the establishment of permanent British settlements, which fostered farms and families and ultimately towns. Thanks largely to these two institutions, British settlers in North America outnumbered the French nearly twenty to one by 1750. High levels of English migration, encouraged by wide-ranging economic opportunities, forged the beginnings of an American identity cloaked in English law, language, and customs.

SELECTED REFERENCES
AND SUGGESTED READINGS

Alston, Lee J., and Morton O. Shapiro. "Inheritance Laws Across the Colonies: Causes and Consequences." *Journal of Economic History* 44 (1984): 277–287.

Anderson, Terry, and Robert P. Thomas. "The Growth of Population and Labor Force in the 17th-Century Chesapeake." *Explorations in Economic History* 15 (1978): 290–312.

————. "White Population, Labor Force, and Extensive Growth of the New England Economy in the Seventeenth Century." *Journal of Economic History* 33 (1973): 634–667.

Andrews, Charles M. *The Colonial Period of American History.* New Haven: Yale University Press, 1934.

Bancroft, George. *History of the United States of America from the Discovery of the Continent.* Boston: Little, Brown, 1879, 6 vols.

Boorstin, Daniel. *The Americans: The Colonial Experience.* New York: Vintage Books, 1958.

Bruce, Philip A. *Economic History of Virginia in the Seventeenth Century.* New York: Macmillan, 1896, 2 vols.

Bruchey, Stuart. *The Roots of American Economic Growth 1607–1861: An Essay in Social Causation.* London: Hutchinson University Library, 1965.

Curtin, Philip. *The Atlantic Slave Trade: A Census.* Madison: University of Wisconsin Press, 1969.

Earle, Carville. *The Evolution of a Tidewater Settlement System: All Hallow's Parish, 1650–1783.* Chicago: University of Chicago Press, 1975.

Fogel, Robert, and Stanley Engerman. *Time on the Cross: The Economics of American Negro Slavery.* Boston: Little, Brown, 1974, Chapter 1.

Franklin, Benjamin. "Observations Concerning the Increase of Mankind." Philadelphia, 1751. In *The Papers of Ben Franklin,* ed. Leonard Laberee. New Haven: Yale University Press, 1961.

Galenson, David W. "British Servants and the Colonial Indenture System in the Eighteenth Century." *Journal of Southern History* 44 (1978): 41–66.

————. "Immigration and the Colonial Labor System: An Analysis of the Length of Indenture." *Explorations in Economic History* 14 (1977): 361–377.

————. "The Market Evaluation of Human Capital: The Case of Indentured Servitude." *Journal of Political Economy* 89 (1981): 446–467.

————. "The Rise and Fall of Indentured Servitude in the Americas: An Economic Analysis." *Journal of Economic History* 44 (1984): 1–26.

————. *White Servitude in Colonial America.* Cambridge: Cambridge University Press, 1981.

Gemery, Henry. "Emigration from the British Isles to the New World, 1630–1700." In *Research in Economic History,* ed. Paul Uselding. New York: Johnson, 1980, 5: 179–232.

Grubb, Farley. "Colonial Labor Markets and the Length of Indenture: Further Evidence." *Explorations in Economic History* 24 (1987): 101–106.

————. "Immigrant Servant Labor: Their Occupational and Geographic Distribution in the Late Eighteenth-Century Mid-Atlantic Economy." *Social Science History* 9 (1985): 249–275.

————. "The Incidence of Servitude in Trans-Atlantic Migration, 1771–1804." *Explorations in Economic History* 22 (1985): 316–339.

————. "The Market for Indentured Immigrants: Evidence on the Efficiency of Forward-Labor Contracting in Philadelphia, 1745–1773." *Journal of Economic History* 45 (1985): 855–868.

————. "Redemptioner Immigration to Pennsylvania: Evidence on Contract Choice and Profitability." *Journal of Economic History* 46 (1986): 407–418.

Heavener, Robert. "Indentured Servitude: The Philadelphia Market, 1771–1773." *Journal of Economic History* 38 (1978): 701–713.

Higgs, Robert, and Louis Stettler. "Colonial New England Demography: A Sampling Approach." *William and Mary Quarterly* 27, no. 2 (1970): 282–294.

Hughes, Jonathan R. T. "William Penn and the Holy Experiment." In *The Vital Few: American Economic History and Its Protagonists.* New York: Oxford University Press, 1973 (reprint), Chapter 2.

Kulikoff, Allan. "A 'Prolifick' People: Black Population Growth in the Chesapeake Colonies, 1700–1790." *Southern Studies* (1977): 391–428.

Lemon, James. *The Best Poor Man's Country: A Geographical Study of Early Southeastern Pennsylvania.* Baltimore: Johns Hopkins University Press, 1972.

Menard, Russell. "From Servants to Slaves: The Transformation of the Chesapeake Labor System." *Southern Studies* (1977): 355–390.

Morgan, Edmund S. *American Slavery, American Freedom: The Ordeal of Colonial Virginia.* New York: W. W. Norton, 1975.

————. "The First American Boom: Virginia 1618 to 1630." *William and Mary Quarterly* 28 (1971).

————. *The Puritan Family: Religion and Domestic Relations in Seventeenth-Century New England.* New York: Harper & Row, 1966.

Morison, Samuel E. *The Oxford History of the American People.* New York: Oxford University Press, 1964.

Morris, Richard. *Government and Labor in Early America.* New York: Columbia University Press, 1946.

Nash, Gary. *Red, White, and Black: The Peoples of Early America.* Englewood Cliffs, New Jersey: Prentice-Hall, 1974.

North, Douglass C., and R. P. Thomas. *The Rise of the Western World.* New York: Cambridge University Press, 1973.

Perkins, Edwin J. *The Economy of Colonial America.* 2d ed. New York: Columbia University Press, 1988, Chapter 1.

Potter, Jim. "The Growth of Population in America, 1700–1860." In *Population in History: Essays in Historical Demography,* eds. D. V. Glass and B. E. C. Eaversley. Chicago: Aldine, 1960.

Powell, Sumner C. *Puritan Village: The Formation of a New England Town.* Middletown, Connecticut: Wesleyan University Press, 1963.

Rink, Oliver. *Holland on the Hudson: An Economic and Social History of New York.* Ithaca, New York: Cornell University Press, 1986.

Rosenberg, Nathan, and L. E. Birdzell, Jr. *How the West Grew Rich.* New York: Basic Books, 1986, Chapter 3.

Smith, Abbot E. *Colonists in Bondage: White Servitude and Convict Labor in America, 1607–1776.* Chapel Hill: University of North Carolina Press, 1947.

Smith, Billy G. "Death and Life in a Colonial Immigrant City: A Demographic Analysis of Philadelphia." *Journal of Economic History* 38 (1977): 863–889.

Smith, Daniel S. "The Demographic History of Colonial New England." *Journal of Economic History* 32 (1972): 165–183.

————. "The Estimates of Early American Historical Demographers: Two Steps Forward, One Step Back, What Steps in the Future." *Historical Methods* (1979): 24–38.

Thomas, Robert P., and Richard Bean. "The Adoption of Slave Labor in British America." In *The Uncommon Market: Essays in the Economic History of the Atlantic Slave Trade,* eds. H. Genery and J. Hogendorn. New York: Academic Press, 1978.

Ver Steeg, Clarence. *The Formative Years, 1607–1763.* New York: Hill & Wang, 1964.

Walton, Gary M., and James F. Shepherd. *The Economic Rise of Early America.* Cambridge: Cambridge University Press, 1979, Chapter 2.

Weeden, William B. *Economic and Social History of New England, 1620–1789.* Boston: Houghton Mifflin, 1890, 2 vols.

Wells, Robert V. *The Population of the British Colonies in America before 1776: A Survey of Census Data.* Princeton: Princeton University Press, 1975.

William Bradford, of Plymouth Plantation (New York: Capricorn Books, 1962), pp. 90–91.

CHAPTER THREE

COLONIAL ECONOMIC ACTIVITIES

CHAPTER THEME After the discovery of "cash crops" such as tobacco, market production and trade grew rapidly and gave permanent features to the English settlements in North America. The economic activities of the colonists are shown here in terms of their regional and occupational specializations.

These specializations were fundamentally determined by comparative advantages in production, and these varied significantly among the colonies. Those colonial specializations, for market trade in particular, allowed the young economy to grow and fit itself into the British imperial economy and the world economy.

SOCIAL ENGINEERING
AND ECONOMIC CONSTRAINTS

It is merely a coincidence that in 1732, when Mr. Fry was selling his accounting books and poetry books in Boston, plans for the last British colony to be settled in North America were being made. The colonization of Georgia provides a vivid example of good intentions pitted against the economic realities of opportunities and restraints.

Like Pennsylvania and Massachusetts, Georgia was founded to assist those who had been beset with troubles in the Old World. Dr. Thomas Bray, an Anglican clergyman noted for his good works, was persuaded by General James Edward Oglethorpe to attempt a project for the relief of people condemned to prison for debt. This particular social evil of eighteenth-century England cried out to be remedied, because debtors could spend years in prison without hope of escape except through organized charitable institutions. As long as individuals were incarcerated, they were unable to earn any money to pay their debts, and even if they were eventually released, years of imprisonment could make them unfit for work. It was Oglethorpe's idea to encourage debtors to come to America, where they might become responsible and even substantial citizens.

In addition to their wish to aid the "urban wretches" of England, Bray, Oglethorpe, and their associates had another primary motivation: to secure a military buffer zone between the prosperous northern English settlements and Spanish Florida. Besides their moral repugnance to slavery, they believed that an all-white population was needed for security reasons. It was doubtful that slaves could be depended on to fight, and with slavery, rebellion was always a possibility. Therefore slavery was prohibited in Georgia—initially.

In 1732, King George II obligingly granted Dr. Bray and his associates the land between the Savannah and Altamaha rivers; the original tract included considerably less territory than the modern state of Georgia. By royal charter, a corporation was created that was to be governed by a group of trustees; after 21 years, the territory was to revert to the Crown. Financed by both private and public funds, the venture had an auspicious beginning. Oglethorpe himself led the first contingent of several hundred immigrants—mostly debtors—to the new country, where a 50-acre farm awaited each colonist. Substantially larger grants were available to free settlers with families, and determined efforts were made, both on the Continent and in the British Isles, to secure colonists.

Unfortunately, the ideals and hopes of the trustees clashed with economic reality. Although "the Georgia experiment" was a modest success as a philanthropic enterprise, its economic development was to prove disappointing for many decades. The climate in the low coastal country—where the fertile land lay—was unhealthy and generated higher death rates than in areas farther north. As the work of Ralph Gray and Betty Wood has shown, it was impossible without slavery to introduce the rice and indigo plantations in Georgia that were so profitable in South Carolina, and the 50-acre tracts given the charity immigrants were too small to achieve economies of scale and competitive levels of efficiency for commercial production.

Failing to attract without continuous subsidy a sufficient number of whites to secure a military buffer zone and given the attractive potential profits of slave-operated plantation enterprises, the trustees eventually bowed to economic forces. By midcentury, slavery was legalized and slaves were pouring into Georgia, which was converted to a Crown colony in 1751. By 1770, 45 percent of the population there was black.

This particular example of social-economic engineering reveals a wider truth: colonial economic freedoms were severely restrained, not so much by man-made laws or ordinances but by the scarcity conditions of nature and production potential. Colonial production capabilities were determined and limited by the available factors of production—land and natural resources, capital, and labor—by the technology of the period, and by other influences such as economic organization and frontier hazards. The most distinctive characteristic of production in the colonies throughout the entire colonial period is that land and natural resources were plentiful but labor and capital were exceedingly scarce, both relative to land and natural resources and compared to the input proportions in Britain and in Continental Europe. This relationship among the factors of production explains many institutional arrangements and patterns of regional development in the colonies.

LAND AND NATURAL RESOURCE ABUNDANCE, LABOR SHORTAGE

Throughout the colonial period, most people depended on the land for a livelihood. From New Hampshire to Georgia, agriculture was the chief occupation, and what industrial and commercial activity there was revolved almost entirely around materials extracted from the land, the forests, and the ocean. Where soil and climate were unfavorable to the cultivation of commercial crops, it was often possible to turn to fishing or trapping and to the production of ships, ship timbers, pitch, tar, turpentine, and other forest products. Land was seemingly limitless in extent and therefore not highly priced, but almost every colonist wanted to be a landholder. When we remember that ownership of land signified wealth and position to the European, this is not hard to understand. The ever-present desire for land explains why for the first century and a half of our history, many immigrants who might have been successful artisans or laborers in someone else's employ tended instead to turn to agriculture, thereby aggravating the persistent scarcity of labor in the New World. A shortage of workers with highly developed skills was most notable, because artisans and trained craftsmen in great demand in Europe were too content at home to be tempted even by substantially higher wages into a life of hardship at the very bounds of civilization. But all types of labor were generally scarce, because the high ratio of land to labor assured independent farmers fairly comfortable material standards of living once many of the early frontier hazards had been overcome.

CAPITAL SHORTAGES

Items of physical capital for production were in limited supply in the aggregate, especially during the first century of settlement. Particular forms of capital goods that could be obtained from natural resources with simple tools were in apparent abundance. For instance, so much wood was available that it was fairly easy to build houses, barns, and workshops. Wagons and carriages were largely made of wood, as were farm implements, wheels, gears, and shafts. Shipyards and shipwares were also constructed from timber, and ships were built in quantity from an early date.

Alternatively, finished metal products were especially scarce, and mills and other industrial facilities remained few and small. Improvements of roads and harbors lagged far behind European standards until the end of the colonial period. Capital formation was a primary challenge to the colonists, and the colonies always needed much more capital than was ever available to them. English political leaders promoted legislation that hindered the export of tools and machinery from the home country. Commercial banks were nonexistent, and English or colonials who had savings to invest often preferred the safer investment in British firms. Nevertheless, as we shall see in Chapter 5, residents of the developing American colonies lived better lives in the eighteenth century than most other people, even those living in the most advanced nations of the time.

THE DOMINANCE OF AGRICULTURE

At the end of the eighteenth century, approximately 90 percent of the American people earned a major portion of their living by farming (compared to about 3 percent today). Generally, high ratios of land and other natural resources to labor generated exceptionally high levels of output per worker in the colonies. Most production in the New World was for the colonists' own consumption, but sizable proportions of colonial goods and services were produced for commercial exchange. In time, each region became increasingly specialized in the production of particular goods and services. Areas of specialization were largely determined by particular soil types, climate, and natural bounties of the forests and ocean.

THE SOUTHERN COLONIES

In terms of value of output, southern agriculture was dominant throughout the colonial period and well into the nineteenth century. The southern colonies present us with a good example of the comparative advantage that fertile new land can offer. Almost at the outset, southern colonials grew tobacco that was both cheaper to produce and of better quality than the tobacco grown in most other parts of the world. Later the South began to produce two other staples, rice and indigo (a blue dye, native to India). For nearly two centuries, the southern economy was to revolve around these few export staples, because the region's soil and climate gave the South a pronounced advantage in the cultivation of crops that were in great demand in the populous industrializing areas of Europe.[1]

---

[1] There were failures, too. For example, every effort was made to encourage the production of wines then being imported from France and Spain, but the quality of American wines was so poor that serious attempts to compete with established wine-producing areas were abandoned. Similarly, it was hoped that silk and hemp could be produced in quantity, and bounties and premiums were offered for their production; but again quality was inferior, and high wage rates resulted in a high-cost product.

TOBACCO. Tobacco was exported from Virginia to England within a decade after the settlement of Jamestown. The weed had been known in Europe for over a century; sailors on the first voyages of exploration had brought back samples and descriptions of the ways in which natives had used it. Despite much opposition on moral grounds, smoking had increased in popularity during the sixteenth century; thus, even though James I viewed it "so vile and stinking a custom," it was a relief to the English to find a source of supply so that tobacco importation from the Spanish would be unnecessary. Tobacco needed a long growing season and fertile soil. Furthermore, it could be cultivated in small areas, on only partly cleared fields, and with the most rudimentary implements. All this suited the primitive Virginia community. But there were two additional advantages to tobacco production in the colonies: as successive plantings exhausted the original fertility of a particular plot, new land was readily available, and ships could move up the rivers of the Virginia coast to load their cargoes at the plantation docks. One marked disadvantage that lingered for most of the seventeenth century was that the colonists had much to learn about the proper curing, handling, and shipping of tobacco, and for many years the American product was inferior to tobacco produced in Spain. Nevertheless, colonial tobacco was protected in the English market, and the fact that it was cheaper led to steady increases in its portion of the tobacco trade. The culture of tobacco spread northward around the Chesapeake Bay and moved up the many river valleys. By the end of the seventeenth century, there was some production in North Carolina.

During the early years of the seventeenth century, Spanish tobacco sold in England for an average retail price of about 40 pence per pound. When Virginia tobacco was first marketed, it commanded 4 to 8 pence per pound, and until 1627 the consensus was that a price of around 3 pence per pound could be maintained. At that price, the production of tobacco was so profitable that colonists could scarcely be persuaded to grow anything else, and a mining-camp spirit pervaded the Virginia colony.[2]

All too soon, however, the tobacco growers of Virginia encountered the problem of volatile prices that forever besets agricultural producers. By 1630, Governor Harvey complained that tobacco was fetching less than a penny a pound. And although prices in the following years had their ups as well as their downs, colonists resorted to all kinds of devices, including burning half of one year's crop, to raise their incomes.[3] An especially difficult period ensued with the increased English immigration to the colonies between the outbreak of the English Civil War and the Restoration; only the intervention of devastating weather in 1667, which greatly reduced output, rescued the growers from desperately low prices.

Then, as now, restrictions on production led to disappointing and frustrating results. Planters who were limited to a specific number of plants per farm responded by moving more rapidly to new fertile fields. If Virginia tried to limit the number of

---

[2] Lewis C. Gray, *History of Agriculture in the Southern United States to 1860*, Vol. I (Washington, D.C.: Carnegie Institution of Washington, 1933), pp. 259–260. Also see Russell Menard, "A Note on Chesapeake Tobacco Prices 1618–1660," *Virginia Magazine of History and Biography* (1976): 401–410.

[3] It should be emphasized that crop destruction would have raised incomes only if the price elasticity of demand was *inelastic;* that is, if the percentage increase in price due to the lower quantity supplied was greater than the percentage reduction in the quantity marketed.

pounds of tobacco exported, it was unlikely that Maryland and North Carolina would cooperate. Marketing of tobacco by consignment to merchants resulted in uncertainties about the prices to be received, and in any case, individual planters knew that they could increase their own incomes by increasing their outputs. Overall, the absence of effective coercion and cooperation doomed the restrictive policies.

During the latter part of the seventeenth century and the first half of the eighteenth, there were some years of relative prosperity, but the days in which tobacco was a profitable crop for every producer were gone. It slowly became apparent that the competition would be won by large plantations and that if the small planters were to succeed at all, they would have to specialize in high-quality tobacco or in the production of food and other crops. From the work of David Klingaman we have learned that in the eighteenth century, substantial areas around the Chesapeake (especially in Maryland) turned to the production of wheat.

Larger production units were favored in tobacco cultivation because slaves could be worked in groups very effectively. To achieve the best results, a plantation owner had to have enough slaves to assure the economical use of a plantation manager. Supervision costs did not grow in proportion to the number of slaves owned and used; therefore, per unit costs fell as plantations grew in size (at least up to a point). A plantation with less than ten slaves intermittently prospered, but only larger units earned substantial returns above cost, provided they were properly managed and contained sufficient acreage to avoid soil exhaustion. Thus, the wealthy or those who were able to secure adequate credit from English and Scottish merchants attained more efficient scales of tobacco production and, in so doing, became even wealthier and improved their credit standing further. In short, bigness fostered bigness, and wealth led to wealth. We should not conclude that slaves were held only by the largest plantation owners, however; the crude statistics available today indicate that in pre-Revolutionary times, as later, large numbers of planters owned fewer than ten slaves. Nonetheless, there was persistent pressure in the tobacco colonies to develop large-sized farms favored by lower per unit costs.

RICE. About 1695, the second of the great southern staples was introduced. Early Virginia colonists had experimented with rice production and South Carolina had tried to cultivate the staple in the first two years after settlement, but success awaited the introduction of new varieties of the grain.[4]

By the early 1700s, rice was an established crop in the area around Charleston, although problems of irrigation still remained. It is possible to grow rice without intermittent flooding and draining, but the quality of the grain suffers. Rice was first cultivated in the inland swamps that could be flooded periodically from the rivers, but the flooding was dependent on uncertain stream flows. Besides, such a growing method could not be used on the extremely flat land that lay along the coast itself. Before long, a system of flooding was devised that enabled producers to utilize the force of tide flows. Water control, originally a Dutch specialty, had grown in impor-

---

[4]Lewis C. Gray, *History of Agriculture in the Southern United States to 1860,* p. 278.

tance and sophistication in England (to drain marshes). These learnings were transferred to America. Dikes were built along the lower reaches of the rivers, and as the tide pushed back the fresh water, it could be let through gates into irrigation ditches crossing the fields.

Proper flooding remained unpredictable because no salt water could be let in, and proper drainage demanded painstaking engineering. But the heavy investment of capital was worthwhile, because proper engineering permitted the two major tide-propelled floodings to occur at precisely the right time and the water could be removed just as accurately. Much labor was needed, and slaves were imported at a great rate during the eighteenth century for this purpose. The "task" system of working slaves, which gave each slave a particular piece of ground to cultivate, was utilized. The work was back-breaking and was carried out in hot, mosquito-infested swamps; although contemporary opinion held that Africans were better able to withstand the ravages of disease and the effects of overexertion than Europeans, the mortality rate among blacks in this region was high. Despite production difficulties, rice output steadily increased until the end of the colonial period, its culture finally extending from below Savannah up into North Carolina.

INDIGO. To the profits from rice were added those of another staple—indigo, so named from a plant native to India. The indigo plant was first successfully introduced in 1743 by Eliza Lucas, a young woman who had come from the West Indies to live on a plantation near Charleston. Indigo almost certainly could not have been grown in the colonies without special assistance, because its culture was demanding and the preparation of the deep blue dye required exceptional skill. As a supplement to rice, however, it was an ideal crop, both because the plant could be grown on high ground

Colonial agriculture depended heavily on such cash crops as indigo—shown above being processed in South Carolina from fresh-cut sheaves to final drying—and rice, shown on the next page in a plantation setting.

The cultivation of rice required advanced engineering techniques and much slave labor, but it remained a profitable crop for South Carolina and Georgia during the colonial period.

where rice would not grow and because the peak work loads in processing indigo came at a time when the slaves were not busy in the rice fields. Indigo production, fostered by a British subsidy of sixpence a pound, added considerably to the profits of plantation owners, thereby attracting resources to the area.

In emphasizing the importance of tobacco, rice, and indigo, we are in danger of overlooking the production of other commodities in the southern colonies. Deerskins and naval stores were exported from the Carolinas, and iron in quantity was shipped from the Chesapeake region. Throughout the South, there was a substantial output of hay and animal products and of Indian corn, wheat, and other grains. These items, like a wide variety of fruits and vegetables, were grown mostly to make the agricultural units as self-sufficient as possible. Yet upland farmers, especially in the Carolinas and Virginia, grew livestock for commercial sale and exported meat, either on the hoof or in cured form, in quantity to other colonies. In all the colonies, food for home consumption was a main economic activity.

THE MIDDLE COLONIES

The land between the Potomac and the Hudson rivers was on the whole fertile and readily tillable and therefore enjoyed a comparative advantage in the production of grains and other foodstuffs. As the seventeenth century elapsed, two distinct types of agricultural operations developed there. To the west, on the cutting edge of the frontier, succeeding generations continued to encounter many of the difficulties that had beset the first settlers. The trees in the forests—an ever-present obstacle—had to be felled, usually after they had been girdled and allowed to die. The felled trees were burned and their stumps were removed to allow for the use of horse-drawn plows. The soil was worked with tools that did not differ much from the implements used by medieval Europeans. A living had literally to be wrested from the earth. At the same time, a stable and reasonably advanced agriculture began to develop to the east of the frontier. The Dutch in New York and the Germans in Pennsylvania, who brought skills and farming methods from areas with soils similar to those in this region, were encouraged from the first to cultivate crops for sale in the small but growing cities of New York, Philadelphia, and Baltimore. Gradually, a commercial agriculture developed. Wheat became the important staple, and although there was also a considerable output of corn, rye, oats, and barley, the economy of the region was based on the great bread grain. During the latter part of the seventeenth century, a sufficient quantity of wheat and flour was produced to permit the export of these products, particularly to the West Indies.

The kind of agricultural unit that evolved in the Middle colonies later became typical of the great food belts of the midwestern United States. Individual farms, which were considerably smaller in acreage than the average plantation to the south, could be operated by the farmer and his family with little hired help. Slaveholding was rare, because wheat production was labor-intensive only during planting and harvest periods and because there were no apparent economies of large-scale production in wheat, corn, or generalized farming as in the southern plantation staples of tobacco or rice. It was normally preferable to acquire an indentured servant as a hand; the original outlay was not great, and the productivity of even a young and inexperienced servant was soon sufficient to return the owner's investment. The more limited growing season in the north also lowered the economic gains of slave labor in the fields.

NEW ENGLAND

Vital as the agriculture of New England was to the people of the area, it constituted a relatively unimportant part of commercial output for sale. Poor soils, uneven terrain, and a severe climate led to typical "subsistence" farming, the growth of only those crops necessary for family maintenance. Because it could be produced almost anywhere and because its yield even on poor land was satisfactory, Indian corn was the chief crop. Wheat and the other cereal grains, along with the hardier vegetables, were grown for family use. Due partly to climate and partly to the protection from wild predators that natural barriers furnished, the Narragansett region, including the large islands off its coast, became a cattle- and sheep-raising center. By the eve of the Revolution, however, New England was a net importer of food and fiber. Its destiny lay in another kind of economic endeavor, and from a very early date, many New Englanders combined farming with other work, thereby living better lives than they would have if they had been confined to the resources of their own farms. Homecraft employments of all varieties were common features of rural life in all the colonies, but especially in New England. Shipping and fishing were also major economic activities of this region.

THE EXTRACTIVE INDUSTRIES

Although most colonial Americans made their living from agriculture, many earned their livelihood indirectly from the land in what we will call *extractive* pursuits. From the forest came the furs and wild animal skins, lumber, and naval stores. From the coastal waters came fish and that strange mammal, the whale. From the ground came minerals, though only in small quantities during the early colonial years. From the various industries that were built around these products arose an output second in value only to that of agriculture.

FURS, FORESTS, AND ORES

The original thirteen colonies were a second-rate source of furs by the late colonial period, because the finest furs along the seaboard were processed quickly and the most lucrative catches were made long before the frontier moved into the interior. It was the French, not the English, who were the principal furriers in North America. Nonetheless, farmers trapped furs as a sideline to obtain cash, although they caught primarily muskrats and raccoons, whose pelts were less desirable then, as now.

The forest itself, more than its denizens, became an economically significant object of exploitation. The colonials lived in an age of wood. Wood, rather than minerals and metals, was their chief fuel and their basic construction material. Almost without exception, the agricultural population engaged in some form of lumbering. Pioneers had to fell trees to clear ground, and wood was used to build houses, barns, furniture, and sometimes fences. Frequently, the timber was burned and the ashes were scattered, but enterprising farmers eventually discovered that they could use simple equipment to produce potash and the more highly refined pearlash. These chemicals were needed to manufacture glass, soap, and other products and provided cash earnings to many households throughout the colonies.

Along the fall line of the northern and Middle colonies, small sawmills sprang up in the earliest settlements. Using stream water as both a source of power and a means of transportation, sawmill operators tended to locate in areas that boasted the best combination of virgin timber and accessible rivers. The commercial manufacture of basic wood shapes—boards, planks, cooperage materials, and so forth—began in Maine and New Hampshire and was a common occupation as far south as North Carolina by the end of the colonial period.

Some sawmills were totally devoted to the manufacture of materials for shipbuilding and ship repair. White pine was unmatched as a building material for the masts and yards of sailing ships, and white and red oak provided ship timbers (for ribbing) of the same high quality. The pine trees that grew abundantly throughout the colonies furnished the raw material for the manufacture of naval stores: pitch, tar, and resin. In the days of wooden vessels, naval stores were indispensable in the shipyard and were used mostly for protecting surfaces and caulking seams. These materials were in great demand in both the domestic and British shipbuilding industries. Considerable skilled labor was required to produce naval stores, and only in North Carolina, where slaves were especially trained to perform the required tasks, could these materials be produced profitably without British subsidy.

The only mineral obtained by the colonials in any significant quantity was iron. The methods used in the colonial iron industry did not differ greatly from those developed in the late Middle Ages, although by the time of the Revolution furnace sizes had increased greatly. In the seventeenth century, the chief source of iron was bog ore, a sediment taken from swamps and ponds. When this sediment was treated with charcoal in a bloomery or forge until the charcoal absorbed the oxygen in the ore, an incandescent sponge of metal resulted. The glowing ball of iron was removed from the forge and in a white-hot condition was hammered to remove the slag and leave a substantial piece of wrought iron.

Rich rock ores were discovered as the population moved inward, and during the eighteenth century, a large number of furnaces were built for the reduction of these ores. Pig iron could then be produced in quantity. A mixture of rock ore, charcoal, and oyster shells or limestone was placed in a square or conical furnace and then ignited. Under a draft of air from bellows worked by water power, the iron ore was reduced to a spongy metal, which as it settled to the bottom of the furnace alloyed itself with large amounts of carbon, thereby becoming what we call cast iron. Poured into molds called "pigs" or "sows," the resulting metal could be either remelted and cast into final form later or further refined and reworked in a mill or blacksmith shop.

The discussion of these rudimentary processes provides us with an important background that will help us understand the later development in the American iron and steel industry. It is also worth noting that because of the simple processing required and an abundance of charcoal, the colonial iron industry was able to compete with that of the British Isles in the sale of bars and pigs. There is agreement that the number of forges and furnaces in the colonies just before the Revolution probably exceeded the number in England and Wales combined, and the annual output of wrought and cast iron by then was in the neighborhood of 30,000 tons, or about one-seventh of the world's output. But the colonies remained heavy net importers of finished iron products.

SEA PRODUCTS

Although restricted primarily to the northern colonies, the occupations of fishing and whaling were of major importance in the development of the entire early colonial economy. The sea provided New Englanders with a commodity for which there was

Whaling was a hazardous but profitable industry in early America and an important part of New England's seafaring tradition. New Bedford, where Captain Ahab started his quest for Moby Dick, and Nantuckett were the main whaling centers of New England.

a ready market and also furnished a stimulus for shipbuilding. When Jacques Cartier sailed up the St. Lawrence River in 1534, fishermen from many European countries were already at work near the mouth of the river and had probably been making the hazardous journey across the North Atlantic for a long time. Originally, these pioneers had operated a "wet fishery"—that is, the catch was partly cleaned, salted down, and returned to the home country for drying. The quality of the product was much better, however, if a "shore fishery" could be established to dry fish at a nearby land base, and during the sixteenth century, fishermen from Spain, Portugal, France, and England attached themselves temporarily to the northern coastal country.

When a permanent settlement was at last made not far from the banks that extended from Long Island to Newfoundland, the settlers there naturally turned to deep-sea fishing. There were many splendid harbors to house small fishing vessels and plenty of timber with which to build them. But more importantly, there was a great market for the magnificent cod. The large, fat, hard-to-cure cod were consumed at home. The best cod were exported to Catholic Europe; the poorer grades were sent to the West Indies, where they were fed to slaves. Gloucester, Salem, Boston, and Marblehead became the chief home ports for the great fishing fleets.

In colonial times, whale oil was highly prized as both an illuminant and a lubricant, ambergris as a base for perfumes, and whalebone as a material for stays. Whaling was therefore a profitable and vigorous, if small, industry. Before 1700, whalers operated near the New England coast, but their take was small. During the eighteenth century, however, whalers ranged far and wide, and by 1775, more than 300 vessels of all sizes sailed from the Massachusetts ports, of which Nantucket was the great whaling center.

THE MANUFACTURING INDUSTRIES

It is convenient for us to distinguish between the colonial extractive and manufacturing industries, even though these activities overlapped in actual practice. Included under the heading of manufacturing are the processes by which the crude or primary materials produced by the extractive industries became finished products. We should also realize that the word *industry* is ordinarily used rather loosely to describe any colonial activity, because the "firms" that comprised an industry were frequently heterogeneous units that could range from a household to a fairly large shop or mill. Nevertheless, the output of each of the major categories of commodities *tended* to be produced by only one of three major types of colonial organizations: households, craftshops, or mills and yards.

HOUSEHOLD MANUFACTURE AND CRAFTSHOPS

The first concerns of the colonial household were the manufacture of food and clothing. Finer items were imported, but household manufacture actually created a marketable surplus of some commodities. Cured or pickled meats, leather, and lard were essentials that only the well-to-do could afford to buy; most colonial families had to produce their own, working together at the first sign of winter to make these and other animal products. Wheat, rye, or Indian corn grown on the farm was ground into flour at the local gristmill, but the women of the family made plentiful weekly rations of bread and hardtack. Jellies and jams were made with enough sweetening from honey, molasses, or maple syrup to preserve them for indefinite periods in open crocks. The men of the family were rarely teetotalers, and the contracts signed by indentured servants indicate that nearly a third of the feeding costs of indentures was for alcoholic beverages. Beer, rum, and whiskey were easiest to make, but wines, mead, and an assortment of brandies and cordials were specialties of some households.

Making clothing—from preparing the raw fiber to sewing the finished garment— kept the women and children busy. Knit goods such as stockings, mittens, and sweaters were the major items of homemade apparel. Linsey-woolsey (made of flax and wool) and jeans (a combination of wool and cotton) were the standard textiles of the North and of the pioneer West. Equally indestructible, though perhaps a little easier on the skin, was fustian, a blend of cotton and flax used mostly in the South. Dress goods and fine suitings had to be imported from England, and even for the city dweller, the purchase of such luxuries was usually a rare and exciting occasion.

Early Americans who had special talents produced everything from nails and kitchen utensils to exquisite cabinets. Everywhere the men of the family participated in the construction of their own homes, although exacting woodwork and any necessary masonry might be done by a specialist. Such specialists, of widely varying abilities, could be found both in cities and at country crossroads. Urban centers especially

The spinning wheel was a common utensil in the homes of colonial America, the starting tool for homemade clothing.

exhibited a great variety of skills, even at a rather early date. In 1697, for example, 51 manufacturing handicrafts, in addition to the building trades, were represented in Philadelphia.

The distinction between the specialized craftsman and the household worker, however, was not always clear in colonial America. Skilled slaves on southern plantations might devote all their time to manufacture; this made them artisans, even though their output was considered a part of the household. On the other hand, the itinerant jack-of-all-trades, who moved from village to village selling reasonably expert services, was certainly not a skilled craftsman in the European sense. Because of the scarcity of skilled labor, individual workers often performed functions more varied than they would have undertaken in their native country; a colonial tanner, for example, might also be a currier (leather preparer) and a shoemaker. Furthermore, because of the small local markets and consequent geographic dispersal of nearly all types of production, few workers in the same trade were united in any particular locality. For this reason, there were not many guilds or associations of craftsmen of the same skill. As an exception, however, we note that as early as 1648 there were enough shoemakers in Boston to enable the General Court to incorporate them as a guild, and by 1718 tailors and cordwainers were so numerous in Philadelphia that they too applied for incorporation.[5]

MILLS AND YARDS

In our discussion of the extractive industries, we observed that even rudimentary manufacture required somewhat more complex organizations than were found in the household or the craftshop. The basic form of commercial manufacture was the mill. To colonials, a mill was a device for grinding or a machine driven by animal, wind, or water power. Mills, for example, turned out the basic wood shapes and the wrought-iron bars and iron pigs.

Until around the middle of the eighteenth century, most mills were crude affairs, run by water power that was furnished by the small streams found all along the middle and north Atlantic coast. Throughout most of this period, primitive mechanisms were used; the cranks of sawmills and gristmills were almost always made of iron, but the wheels themselves and the cogs of the mill wheel were made of wood, preferably hickory. So little was understood about power transmission at this time that a separate water wheel was built to power each article of machinery. Shortly before the Revolution, improvements were made in the application of power to milling processes, and the mills along the Delaware River and the Chesapeake Bay were probably the finest in the world at that time. In 1770, a fair-sized gristmill would grind 100 bushels a day; the largest mills, with several pairs of stones, might convert 75,000 bushels of grain into flour annually.

We can only suggest the variety of the mill industries. Tanneries with bark mills were found in the North and the South. Paper-making establishments, common in Pennsylvania and not unusual in New England, were called mills because machinery was required to grind the linen rags into pulp. Textiles were essentially household products, but in Massachusetts, eastern New York, and Pennsylvania, a substantial number of mills were constructed to perform the more complicated processes of weaving and finishing. The rum distilleries of New England provided a major product for both foreign and domestic trade, and breweries everywhere ministered to convivial needs. The gristmill, like the sawmill, was found everywhere in the colonies, but the largest ones eventually developed in Pennsylvania, Delaware, and New Jersey.

---

[5]Carl Bridenbaugh, *Cities in the Wilderness* (New York: Oxford University Press, 1971), pp. 43, 191.

SHIPBUILDING

Although large-scale manufacturing was not characteristic of colonial economic activity, shipbuilding was an important exception. As early as 1631, barely a decade after the Pilgrims landed at Plymouth, a 30-ton sloop was completed in Boston. During the seventeenth century, shipyards sprang up all along the New England coast, with Boston and Newport leading the way. New York was a strong competitor until the Navigation Act of 1651 (see Chapter 4) dealt its Dutch-dominated industry a crippling blow, but the shipbuilding industry in New York again grew rapidly after 1720. By this time, Philadelphia boasted a dozen large shipyards along the banks of the Delaware River, and of the five major towns, only Charleston relied on ships produced by others. In the first half of the eighteenth century, the output of colonial shipyards reached its peak.

By 1700, the New England fleet exceeded 2,000, exclusive of fishing boats. American industry not only furnished the vessels for a large domestic merchant fleet, it also sold a considerable number of ships abroad, chiefly to the English. An uncontradicted estimate attributes nearly one-third of the ships in the British Merchant Marine in 1775 to American manufacture.[6]

Many of the ships constructed were small. But whether they were building a square-rigged, three-masted vessel of several hundred tons or a fishing boat of ten tons, Americans had a marked and persistent advantage. The basis for success in colonial shipbuilding was the proximity of raw materials, mainly lumber. Although labor and capital costs were lower in England, the high costs of transport of bulky materials from the Baltic—or the colonies—made shipbuilding more expensive in England. Higher wages encouraged sufficient numbers of shipwrights and artisans to migrate from Holland and England to the colonies, where they built colonial vessels with low-cost materials at about two-thirds of British costs. Consequently, shipbuilding in the colonies was exceptional: Though other manufacturers did not generate raw material cost savings enough to offset the much higher labor costs in the colonies, in this case the high costs of transport of the bulky raw materials assured the comparative advantage of production in favor of the colonies. In addition, the Navigation Acts (discussed in Chapter 4) equally encouraged shipbuilding both in the colonies and in England. There was, however, an important distinction between England and North America in the first century of manufacturing development. In England raw materials were typically imported or brought to the craftsman, but in the New World workers located near raw materials.

THE MERCHANT MARINE

Finally, as the sizable New England fleet suggests, shipping services and other distribution services associated with the transportation, handling, and merchandising of goods were important commercial activities in the colonies. The merchant marines in

---

[6]Jacob Price, "A Note on the Value of Colonial Exports of Shipping," *Journal of Economic History* 36 (1976): 704–724.

Thanks to their ready supplies of first-class timber and naval stores, colonial shipbuilders enjoyed an early comparative advantage in shipbuilding.

New England and the Middle colonies, which employed thousands of men, were as efficient as the Dutch and English merchants in many trades throughout the world. Indeed, by the end of the colonial period, the colonies could boast of a sizable commercial sector, and as a source of foreign exchange earnings, the sale of shipping services was second only to tobacco exports. Shipping and overseas trade as commercial activities were vital to the colonial economy.

OCCUPATIONAL GROUPS

Although the colonies established a rich diversity of economic activities, from a functional occupational standpoint, daily life was fairly stable. Occupational roles changed little over the years in settled areas; from today's perspective, occupational opportunities remained narrow and rigid. Most people expected the future to replicate the past, and most young people followed the employment footsteps of their parents.

The male population generally fit into one of several employment categories, the most predominant being family farmers. Other significant categories or classes were slave, indentured servant, unskilled laborer, and seaman. Upper middle classes included artisans, merchants, and landowning farmers, but the richest occupational groups included merchants in New England and the Middle colonies and large land-holding planters in the South. As Edwin Perkins and Alice Jones inform us, the very wealthy were classified as esquires, gentlemen, or officials.

Most women participated in work to complement that of the male head of the household. Women's duties were dominated by child care, domestic service, livestock tending, and household production. Family farm life in particular, the most typical lifestyle of the period, had women and children engaged in handicraft production within the home. During harvest times, they usually turned to outdoor work to help the men. In seventeenth-century Maryland, for instance, Louis G. Carr and Lorna Welsh have shown that wives routinely spent the spring and summer months in the tobacco fields. In the Middle colonies, according to Joan Jensen, women typically helped in the easier tasks of spreading hay to dry, digging for potatoes, gathering flax, and picking fruit. Most away-from-home work for women, especially younger women, was in other people's homes. Such domestic service for extra income was common for women under the age of 25.

It is important, as Alice Hansen Jones reminds us, to emphasize the inferior legal and political status of women and the fact of male dominance and patriarchal authority within the family. A woman was expected to be obedient to her husband, and marriage was accepted unquestioningly as her proper destiny, regardless of class or status. For those who did not marry, the outlook for work was bleak. To spin fiber or help in the household tasks of parents or relatives was likely for an unmarried woman (hence the term "spinster" meaning an unmarried woman). Some, with education and special connections, might teach music, reading, or other skills.

Children began helping their parents at about the age of 7 or 8; by the age of 12 they were usually important apprentice-type workers in the home or fields. Child labor was very important, and maintaining the allegiance of children to labor on behalf of parents was a special problem for parents in the nonslave areas. Indeed, the problem was even reflected in the law. The laws of inheritance varied among the colonies, but were consistent with the goals of economic efficiency and the maintenance of a reliable rural labor force.

The scarcity of labor, as we have seen, manifested itself in many forms in the colonies. Thanks to the work of Lee Alston and Morton Shapiro, we now have even greater insight into the methods colonists used to solve their labor scarcity problems.

Table 3-1 shows the inheritance laws in force for each colony.[7] The geographical distinction is sharp. Why did the New England and Middle colonies rely primarily

---

[7] Estates and property could also be transferred by will, but this practice was rare because of the high legal costs involved.

TABLE 3-1 Intestate Inheritance Laws

Location	Inheritance Law
New England Colonies	
Maine	multigeniture
New Hampshire	multigeniture
Vermont	multigeniture
Massachusetts	multigeniture
Plymouth	multigeniture
Rhode Island	primogeniture until 1798 (except for 1718–1728)
Connecticut	multigeniture
Middle Colonies	
New York	primogeniture until 1786
New Jersey	multigeniture
Pennsylvania	multigeniture
Delaware	multigeniture
Southern Colonies	
Maryland	primogeniture until 1786
Virginia	primogeniture until 1785
North Carolina	primogeniture until 1784
South Carolina	primogeniture until 1791
Georgia	primogeniture until 1777

SOURCE: Robert B. Morris, "Primogeniture and Entailed Estates in America," *Columbia Law Review* 27 (January 1927): 24–51.

on multigeniture (equal division among the sons), whereas the southern colonies all used primogeniture (no division; entire estate to the eldest son)? The prevailing law in England (except for the county of Kent) was primogeniture. Consequently primogeniture automatically prevailed in the colonies through the common law, unless special legislation was passed to establish multigeniture. Any colony wanting multigeniture had to pass a special law through legislative act.

The legislative power in the South rested primarily in the hands of wealthy plantation owners. It was in their economic interests to maintain and foster efficiencies from the economics of large-scale production, and they were loathe to divide the plantations into smaller units. Their labor supply problem was solved by the market for slaves plus a son for supervision responsibilities.

The legislative power in the North rested primarily with the urban merchants and secondarily with propertied family farmers. The merchants had no strong stake in the matter, but the family farmer had a keen vested interest in multigeniture. By this legal form of inheritance, each son was motivated to stay at home (or nearby) longer and work (with less supervision) more diligently to maintain and expand the family farm. Clearing wooded lands for future farming was a key part of each parent's promise to their sons, to secure their labor loyalty.[8]

---

[8] Doweries served the same purpose in part for daughters, although daughters had far fewer economic options than sons did.

In this way, the law bent to reflect the special labor scarcity circumstances of each of the colonies. Note that New York was a special case; this is attributed to the powerful Dutch estates that utilized platoonships of at least 50 indentures and often ample slaves to provide labor on them. As Table 3-1 on the preceding page suggests, the spirit of revolution changed the law even in the South despite bitter protests and actions taken by large plantation owners to sustain primogeniture. They failed, but in England primogeniture lasted until 1926.

SELECTED REFERENCES AND SUGGESTED READINGS

Adams, Donald. "Prices and Wages in Maryland 1750–1850." *Journal of Economic History* 46 (1986): 625–645.

Alston, Lee, and Morton Owen Shapiro. "Inheritance Laws Across Colonies: Causes and Consequences." *Journal of Economic History* 44 (1984): 277–287.

Bailyn, Bernard. *The New England Merchants in the Seventeenth Century.* Cambridge: Harvard University Press, 1955.

Bridenbaugh, Carl. *Cities in the Wilderness: The First Century of Urban Life in America, 1625–1742.* New York: Oxford University Press, 1971.

————. *The Colonial Craftsman.* New York: New York University Press, 1950.

Bruchey, Stuart. *The Colonial Merchant: Sources and Readings.* New York: Harcourt, Brace & World, 1966.

Carr, Lars G., and Lorna Walsh. "The Planting Wife: The Experience of White Women in Seventeenth Century Maryland." *William and Mary Quarterly* 34 (1977): 542–571.

Carroll, Charles. *The Timber Economy of Puritan New England.* Providence, Rhode Island: Brown University Press, 1973.

Clark, Victor S. *History of Manufacturers in the United States 1607–1860.* Washington, D.C.: Carnegie Institution of Washington, 1916.

Coon, David. "Eliza Lucas Pinckney and the Reintroduction of Indigo Culture in South Carolina." *Journal of Southern History* (1976): 61–76.

Doerflinger, Thomas. "Commercial Specialization in Philadelphia's Merchant Community 1750–1791." *Business History Review* 57 (1983): 20–49.

Goldenberg, Joseph. *Shipbuilding in Colonial America.* Charlottesville: University Press of Virginia, 1976.

Gray, Lewis C. *History of Agriculture in the Southern United States to 1860.* Washington, D.C.: Carnegie Institution of Washington, 1933.

Gray, Ralph, and Betty Wood. "The Transition from Indentured Servant to Involuntary Servitude in Colonial Georgia." *Explorations in Economic History* 13 (October 1976): 353–370.

Greenberg, Michael. "William Byrd II and the World of the Market." *Southern Studies* (1977): 429–456.

Hedges, James. *The Browns of Providence Plantation: The Colonial Years.* Cambridge: Harvard University Press, 1952.

Henretta, James. "Economic Development and Social Structure in Colonial Boston." *William and Mary Quarterly* 22 (1965).

Jensen, Joan. *Loosening the Bonds: Mid-Atlantic Farm Women 1750–1850.* New Haven, Connecticut: Yale University Press, 1986.

Jones, Alice Hansen. "The Wealth of Women, 1774." In *Strategic Factors in Nineteenth Century American Economic History,* eds. Clauda Goldin and Hugh Rockoff. Chicago: University of Chicago Press, 1992.

Klingaman, David. "The Significance of Grain in the Development of the Tobacco Colonies." *Journal of Economic History* (1969): 267–278.

McCusker, J. J., and R. R. Menard. *The Economy of British America, 1607–1789.* Chapel Hill: University of North Carolina Press, 1985. Part II and Ch. 14 and 15.

McManis, Douglas. *Colonial New England: A Historical Geography.* New York: Oxford University Press, 1975.

Norton, Thomas. *The Fur Trade in Colonial New York, 1686–1766.* Madison: University of Wisconsin Press, 1974.

Paskoff, Paul. *Industrial Evolution: Organization, Structure, and Growth of the Pennsylvania Iron Industry, 1750–1860.* Baltimore: Johns Hopkins University Press, 1983.

Perkins, E. J. *The Economy of Colonial America.* 2d ed. New York: Columbia University Press, 1988. Section 1.

Price, Jacob. "A Note on the Colonial Exports of Shipping." *Journal of Economic History* 36 (1976): 704–724.

Schweitzer, Mary. *Custom and Contract: Household Government, and the Economy in Colonial Pennsylvania.* New York: Columbia University Press, 1987.

Shammas, Carol. "The Female Social Structure of Philadelphia in 1775." *Pennsylvania Magazine of History and Biography* (1983): 69–138.

Stackpole, Edward. *The Sea-Hunters: The New England Whalemen during Two Centuries, 1635–1835.* Philadelphia: Lippincott, 1953.

Vickers, Daniel. "The First Whalemen of Nantucket." *William and Mary Quarterly* 40 (1983): 560–583.

CHAPTER
FOUR

THE ECONOMIC RELATIONS OF
THE COLONIES

CHAPTER THEME The economic relations of the colonies to England and to other overseas areas are a central part of the story of economic progress in the colonies. Overseas areas were economically important as markets for colonial products, as sources of manufactured goods and other items demanded by American consumers, and as sources of labor and capital. Additional investment came from England for provision of defense. This chapter analyzes the commercial relations and commodity exchanges of the colonies, the legal and business aspects of their shipping and trade, and the special problems of money, capital, and debt in overseas and domestic commerce. It shows how the colonies fit into the world economy and into the English trading realm.

ENGLISH MERCANTILISM AND
THE COLONIES

In the long period from 1500 to 1800, western European nation-states were all influenced by a set of ideas known as the *mercantile system* or *mercantilism*. Mercantilist doctrine was not created by a particular group of thinkers, nor was it ever set forth in systematic fashion by a "school" of economists, but the ideas were important because they were held by practical businesspeople and heads of state who—at different times in different countries—strongly influenced public policy.

The primary aim of mercantilists was to achieve power and wealth for the state. Spain's experience in the sixteenth century had led most observers to conclude that an inflow of gold and silver was a potent help in attaining needed goods and services and in prosecuting wars. To generate an inflow of gold or silver through trade, the value of exports should exceed the value of imports. The gold or silver paid for the differences between exports and imports. With such additions to amounts of money, called *specie*, domestic trade would be more brisk and tax revenues higher. It was further held that the state could attain great power only if political and economic *unity* became a fact. In a day when productivity depended so greatly on the skills and knowledge of workers, it was crucial to keep artisans at home. If all the materials necessary to domestic industry were not available, they could best be obtained by establishing colonies or friendly foreign trading posts from which such goods could be imported. A strong merchant marine could carry foreign goods, thereby helping to secure favorable trade balances, and merchant ships could be converted for war if the need arose.

Mercantilists believed that these means of achieving national power could be made effective by the passage and strict enforcement of legislation regulating economic life. England had begun to pass such laws by the end of the fifteenth century, but its mercantilist efforts did not fully flower until after the British, together with the Dutch, had successfully turned back Spanish power. Indeed, it was largely a consequence of England's desire to surpass Holland—a nation that had reached the zenith of its power during the first half of the seventeenth century—that British legislation was passed marking the beginning of an organized and consistent effort to regulate colonial trade.

Adherence to mercantilist principles was implicit in the colonizing activity that the English began in the early 1600s. Almost as soon as Virginia tobacco began to be shipped in commercial quantities to England, King James I levied a tax on it while agreeing to prohibit the growth of competing tobacco in England. Taxes, regulation, and subsidies were all used as mercantile policies, but the main ones affecting the colonies were the Navigation Acts.

THE EARLY NAVIGATION ACTS

During the English Civil War, which began in 1642 and ended in 1649, the British had too many troubles of their own to pay much attention to regulating trade with the colonies. In this period, Americans had slipped into the habit of shipping their goods directly to continental ports, and the Dutch made great inroads into the carrying trade of the colonies. In 1651, Parliament passed the first of the so-called Navigation Acts, directed primarily at prohibiting the shipping of American products in Dutch vessels. Not until after the Restoration, however, was England in a position to enforce a strict commercial policy, beginning with the Navigation Acts of 1660 and 1663.

These acts were modified from time to time by hundreds of policy changes; at this point it is sufficient to note the three primary categories of trade restriction:

1. All trade of the colonies was to be carried in vessels that were English built and owned, commanded by an English captain, and manned by a crew of whom three-quarters were English. *English* was defined as "only his Majesty's subjects of England, Ireland, and the Plantations." Of great importance to colonists was the fact that colonists and colonial ships were both considered "English" under the law.

2. All foreign merchants were excluded from dealing directly in the commerce of the English colonies. They could engage in colonial trade only through England and merchants resident there.

3. Certain commodities produced in the colonies could be exported only to England (or Wales, Berwick-on-Tweed, or other English colonies—essentially any destination within the Empire). These "enumerated" goods included sugar, tobacco, cotton, indigo, ginger, and various dyewoods (fustic, logwood, and braziletto). The list was later amended and lengthened, and Scotland was added as a legal destination after 1707.

It is important to keep these three categories of restrictions firmly in mind. Although they were the cause of occasional protests on the part of the colonists, they caused practically no disruption of established trade patterns during the remaining decades of the seventeenth century. When, in 1696, a system of admiralty courts was established to enforce the Navigation Acts, their impact became somewhat more pronounced. Indeed, from the beginning of the eighteenth century, most spheres of colonial commercial activity were regulated.

EXPORTS, IMPORTS, AND MARKETS

The enumeration of certain products requiring their direct shipment to England suggests their special importance from the perspective of the mother country. Table 4-1 on the next page confirms this importance also from the perspective of the colonies. Tobacco, rice, and indigo accounted for more than half the value of the top ten exports, and these were predominantly from southern soils. The dominance of the southern staples as a proportion of total colonial exports was greater in the seventeenth century than in the eighteenth, but their lead and importance were maintained right up to the decade of independence. These top ten exports comprised 77 percent of the total commodity exports on average between 1768 and 1772.

Miscellaneous manufacturers of all varieties composed the lion's share of imports from England; a Philadelphia merchant provided a contemporary description of his import trade from Britain:

TABLE 4-1   TOP TEN COMMODITY EXPORTS FROM THE THIRTEEN COLONIES
(AVERAGE ANNUAL VALUES, 1768–1772, IN THOUSANDS OF POUNDS
STERLING)

Tobacco	£766
Bread and flour	410
Rice	312
Fish	154
Wheat	115
Indigo	113
Corn	83
Pine boards	70
Staves and headings	65
Horses	60

SOURCE: DERIVED FROM GARY M. WALTON AND JAMES F. SHEPHERD, *THE ECONOMIC RISE OF EARLY AMERICA* (CAMBRIDGE: CAMBRIDGE UNIVERSITY PRESS, 1975), TABLE 21, PP. 194–195.

. . . all kinds of British manufactories in great abundance and India goods, etc. In the last of the winter or early spring [we] choose to import our linens and other things fit for summer, the latter end of which we should have our woolen goods of all kinds ready for fall sale to use in winter. The spring is the best time for iron mongery, cutleryware, furniture for furnishing houses, and all other brass and iron work. Our imports of those articles are very large, the people being much employed in agriculture, husbandry, clearing and improving lands, but slow progress is made in the manufactories here.[1]

Wine and salt came from southern Europe, and sugar, molasses, and rum imports from the West Indies.

A useful summary of the relative importance of the various trading partners of the colonies is shown in Figure 4-1. Great Britain was the main overseas region to receive colonial exports (56 percent of the total) and to supply colonial imports (80 percent of the total).[2] Nevertheless, the West Indies and southern Europe were important trading partners, especially as markets for American exports.

Another feature of colonial trade is revealed in Figure 4-2 (page 68). Here we see the sharp difference among the regions' ties to various overseas markets. Commerce in the southern regions was overwhelmingly dominated by the trades to Great Britain. Alternatively, the trades of the Middle colonies were more evenly balanced among Great Britain, southern Europe, and the West Indies. New England's most important trading partner was the West Indies. Colonial imports in each region arrived predominantly by way of Great Britain. Few products were imported from southern Europe, and commodity trade with Africa was insignificant.

---

[1]Letter from Thomas Clifford, Philadelphia, to Abel Chapman, Whitby, England, July 25, 1767, as quoted from Ann Bezanson et al., *Prices in Colonial Pennsylvania* (Philadelphia: University of Pennsylvania Press, 1935), p. 263.

[2]Because of reshipment allowed by the Navigation Acts, not all of these amounts were actually consumed or produced in the British Isles.

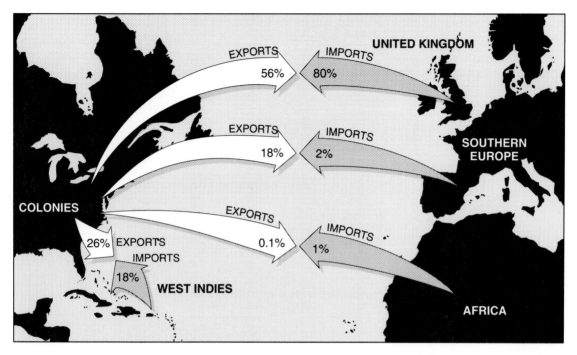

FIGURE 4-1 PERCENTAGE DISTRIBUTION OF TOTAL COLONIAL TRADE *The United Kingdom was colonial America's dominant trading partner in exports and imports, followed by the West Indies and southern Europe.*

SOURCE: JAMES F. SHEPHERD AND GARY M. WALTON, *SHIPPING, MARITIME TRADE, AND THE ECONOMIC DEVELOPMENT OF NORTH AMERICA* (CAMBRIDGE: CAMBRIDGE UNIVERSITY PRESS, 1972), PP. 160–161.

OVERSEAS SHIPPING AND TRADE

Although urban residents numbered little more than 5 percent of the total population in the late colonial period, the major port towns with safe harbors and accessible productive hinterlands became key locations for trade and commerce. Table 4-2 (page 69) shows the ten most populated towns and reminds us that Philadelphia, at that time, was second only to London in population within the Empire, slightly less in number than Davis, California, or Iowa City, Iowa, today. All of the top ten urban centers were port towns. Because these were both readily accessible and points of change in transportation modes, from sea to river craft or to land vehicles and animals, they were greatly advantaged as trade centers. In an age when bluff-bowed sailing ships typically took six weeks to cross the Atlantic and relaying news to the interior took additional weeks, the port towns also had a special communication advantage. Lastly, travel and shipment were always much less expensive by water than by land, especially for bulky, weighty items typical of the colonies. Landlocked cities were a rarity in history before the railroad age.

Advantages of location and communication also went far in determining overseas shipping and trade patterns. For example, British ships almost completely dominated

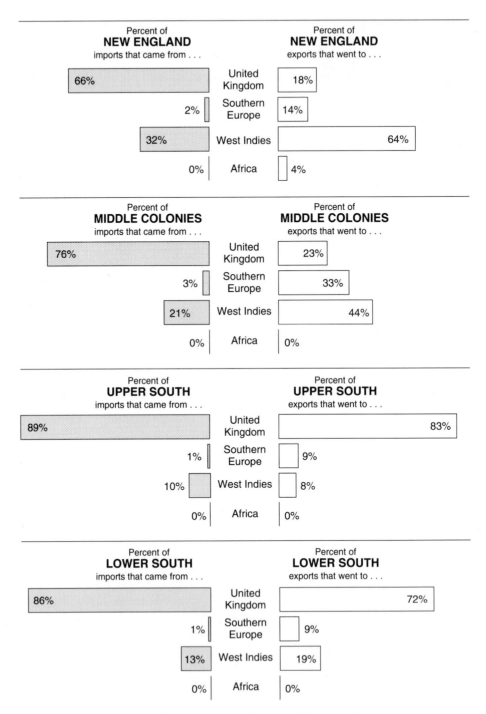

FIGURE 4-2 PERCENTAGE DISTRIBUTION OF COLONIAL TRADE BY REGION

SOURCE: FIGURE 4-1 (SEE PAGE 67).

TABLE 4-2   TOP TEN COLONIAL URBAN CENTERS, 1775

Town/City	Population
Philadelphia	40,000
New York City	25,000
Boston	16,000
Charleston	12,000
Newport	11,000
Providence	9,000
New Haven	8,300
Norwich	7,000
Norfolk	6,200
Baltimore	6,000

SOURCE: CARL BRIDENBAUGH, *CITIES IN THE WILDERNESS AND CITIES IN REVOLT* (NEW YORK: OXFORD UNIVERSITY PRESS, 1971).

the trades of the southern colonial regions, whereas New England shippers dominated the New England–West Indies trade route.

Table 4-3 shows ownership proportions of shipping on several key routes of commerce. It is clear that neither British nor colonial shippers dominated, or had a comparative advantage in shipping, on all routes. For example, colonists owned 96 percent of the tonnage clearing New England to the West Indies and 85 percent to Great Britain, but only 12 percent of the tonnage clearing the Upper South to Great Britain. Why did British shippers dominate the southern trades to England but get left behind in the trades between New England and Great Britain, and between New England and the West Indies? Three critical factors provide the answer: (1) the high risks of

TABLE 4-3   MID-EIGHTEENTH CENTURY OWNERSHIP, PROPORTIONS OF SHIPPING

	Colonial Owned	British Owned	West Indian Owned	Colonial Owned	British Owned	West Indian Owned	Colonial Owned	British Owned	West Indian Owned
Ships Clearing	To Great Britain			To Southern Europe			To West Indies		
From New England	85	15	0	93	7	0	96	3	1
From Middle Colonies	72	28	0	75	25	0	80	20	0
From Upper South	12	88	0	88	12	0	85	0	15
From Lower South	23	77	0	0	100	0	51	23	26
Ships Entering	From Great Britain			From Southern Europe			From West Indies		
Into New England	68	12	0	84	16	0	96	1	3
Into Middle Colonies	63	37	0	76	24	0	84	16	0
Into Upper South	9	91	1	33	67	0	61	23	16
Into Lower South	12	88	0	20	80	0	30	43	27

SOURCE: GARY M. WALTON, "NEW EVIDENCE ON COLONIAL COMMERCE," *JOURNAL OF ECONOMIC HISTORY* 28, 3 (SEPTEMBER 1968): 368.

Safe harbors and productive hinterlands were the conditions favoring these ten leading urban centers in the colonies.

maritime trade; (2) the problems of acquiring and responding to information about markets (prices and trade opportunities); and (3) the opportunities to lower labor costs by discharging crews in home ports.

Consider first the problem of trading and marketing goods. New England and other colonial merchants typically consigned their goods either to ship captains or selling agents, called *factors*, who were stationed in overseas markets and took delivery of the goods. Since these relationships necessitated placing a high degree of trust in a third party, it is not surprising that colonial merchants favored colonial ship captains. After all, greater familiarity and more frequent contact between merchant and agent lowered the risks of trade. So colonial merchants most often favored colonial shippers, to gain trust and better assure higher revenues in their exchanges.

Due to the rudimentary forms of communication and transportation at the time, geographical closeness to a market was an important advantage. For example, British shippers and merchants in the tobacco trade could acquire information about changing market conditions in the Chesapeake Bay area and in Europe more easily than New England shippers could. However, in trades to and from the West Indies, colonial shippers and merchants were nearer to their markets and could respond more quickly to fluctuations in them. Being close to a market reduced the time and cost of obtaining market information, allowing merchants to respond with more timely cargo arrivals and reduce the risks of trade. As British shipowner Michael Atkins stated in a 1751 letter to his colonial colleague: "Traders at the Northern Colonies have all the West India business to themselves, Europeans can have no encouragement for mixing with them in the commodities of provisions and lumber. You time things better than we and go to market cheaper."[3]

Finally, the efficient use of labor time was always an important factor. It was general practice in colonial times for crews to be paid while a vessel was docked in foreign ports, and crews were normally discharged only at the end of the voyage in the home port. This meant that British crews in the tobacco trade were paid for the time they spent at sea and in southern colonial ports, but not for their port time in England. Therefore, New England shippers were at a disadvantage on this trade route, because they paid wages both in British ports and in the Chesapeake Bay. Conversely, colonial shippers faced lower labor costs on trade routes between their home ports and the Caribbean.

These same considerations played a large role in determining the routes of trade. It was not too long ago that students of American colonial history were taught that shuttle routes (out and direct return) were common and typical of the southern colonial trades—mainly to England—but that the New England and Middle colonial shippers usually engaged in triangular and other more complex patterns.[4] It has been shown, however, that shuttle patterns were the dominant pattern for *all* of the colonial regions.[5] For most trades, shuttle patterns cut costs. Although the desire to keep vessels as fully loaded as possible encouraged "tramping" from port to port to take advantage of differences in demand and cargo availability, such a practice often incurred major offsetting costs. For example, a New England ship captain in the West Indies trade, acting on behalf of his merchant, would attempt to locate the best markets for the commodities he carried. This might require several voyages among the islands before agreeing on prices, the medium of exchange, and even the question of past debts.

---

[3] See Richard Pares, *Yankees and Creoles* (Cambridge: Harvard University Press, 1956), p. 8.

[4] American history textbooks in the 1960s and before commonly emphasized these descriptions. Famous triangles included New England–Africa–West Indies (to New England); New England–Southern Europe–England (to New England); and New England–West Indies–England (to New England). For examples, see Dudley Dillard, *Economic Development of the North Atlantic Community* (Englewood Cliffs, New Jersey: Prentice-Hall, 1967), pp. 197–198; Ross M. Robertson, *History of the American Economy*, 2d. ed. (New York: Harcourt, Brace & World, 1964), pp. 80–81; Harold F. Williamson, ed., *The Growth of the American Economy*, 2d. ed. (Englewood Cliffs, New Jersey: Prentice-Hall, 1951), pp. 50–51; Edward Kirkland, *A History of American Economic Life* (New York: Appleton-Century-Crofts, 1960), pp. 111–112; and Chester W. Wright, *Economic History of the United States* (New York: McGraw-Hill, 1941), pp. 153–154.

[5] See Table 4-3 (page 69) and its source (Gary M. Walton, "New Evidence on Colonial Commerce").

Transactions were often complex, even when the merchants and captains were acquainted with one another. Of course, in unfamiliar markets, poor communications, credit limitations, and other vexatious details compounded the difficulties. For all these reasons, arrivals at strange ports often resulted in delays and costly extensions of port times; therefore, captains usually maintained regular runs between a limited number of familiar destinations. The practice of discharging crews only in their home ports further supported the growth of shuttle trade routes, because such routes increased the percentage of total port time that was home port (wage free) time.

INTERCOLONIAL COMMERCE

For similar reasons, colonials dominated the great volume of coastwise commerce. Early in the seventeenth century, the Dutch of New Amsterdam had anticipated the profit potential in distributing European products along the colonial coast in exchange for tobacco, furs, grain, and fish, which were then sent to Holland. After the Dutch lost power in North America in 1664, their hold on these trades declined, and New Englanders—together with enterprising merchants in New York and Philadelphia—dominated the coastal trades of North America.

In terms of the money value of products exchanged, coastal commerce was less than overseas trade with either Britain or the West Indies, but it was equal to each of these major trade branches in physical volume. As James Shepherd and Samuel Williamson have shown, just before the Revolution coastwise trade comprised about one-third of the volume of total overseas trade. Compared to the North, the coastwise commerce of the South was much less important, but even there it comprised perhaps one-fifth of the tonnage that entered and cleared southern ports.[6]

With regard to commerce within the interior and between the countryside and towns, we can say little in quantitative terms. Thanks to recent work by a host of scholars including James A. Henretta, Winifred B. Rothenberg, and Thomas M. Doerflinger, much of it based on probates, tax lists, and other original sources, we know much more about the rich diversity of rural trade and activity.[7] Statistical estimates of volume still elude us, however. Back-country people traded their small agricultural surpluses for goods they could not produce themselves—salt, medicines, ammunition, cotton yarn, tea or coffee, and the like. In the villages and towns, households were less self-sufficient, although even the wealthiest homes produced some goods for everyday consumption.

In the complex of colonial domestic trade between country and town, it became common practice for the town merchant to extend credit to farmers, either directly or through the so-called country traders who served as intermediaries. Advances were made for the purposes of obtaining both capital equipment, such as tools and building

---

[6]E. R. Johnson et al., *History of Domestic and Foreign Commerce of the United States* (Washington, D.C.: Carnegie Institution of Washington, 1915), pp. 171–172.

[7]For examples, see their papers in Ronald Hoffman et al., eds., *The Economy of Early America: The Revolutionary Period, 1763–1790* (Charlottesville: University Press of Virginia, 1988).

Boston's natural endowments helped the city attain a place of prominence as a trading and shipping center, but the mountains to the west inhibited access to the hinterland, and Boston ultimately fell behind New York in the commercial rivalry between these two great ports.

hardware, and the supplies necessary for day-to-day existence. At the end of the growing season, farmers brought their produce to town to discharge their debts. In times of seriously depressed agricultural prices, farmers might be substantially in debt by the end of the year, and two or three bad years in a row could result in foreclosure and the loss of a farm with its improvements. The outcome was that many farmers gave up and moved farther west, and merchants or other propertied people who were able to withstand the vicissitudes of crop failures and wide swings in agricultural prices took the titles to these farms. As we will learn in Chapter 5, this changed the distribution of wealth in colonial times in some important ways.

MONEY AND TRADE

One of the most persistent problems in the colonies was establishing and maintaining an acceptable currency. Among friends and acquaintances especially, barter trade and exchanges on account were common. Money was needed for general commerce, however, to facilitate exchange among merchants and farmers. Money also served as a unit of account and as a liquid form of wealth.

COMMODITY MONEY

One of the earliest solutions, borrowed from the Indians by the first New England settlers, was to use wampum for money. The black and white polished beads made from clam shells, which circulated for several decades after the founding of the colonies, were legal tender for private debts in Massachusetts until 1661 and were used as money in New York as late as 1701.

In Maryland and Virginia, tobacco remained the principal medium of exchange long after its value had declined from three shillings to a penny or two a pound; indeed, the monetization of tobacco actually stimulated its production and thereby furthered its depreciation in value.

Other colonies designated as "country pay" (acceptable for taxes) such items as hides, furs, tallow, cows, corn, wheat, beans, pork, fish, brandy, whiskey, and musket balls. Harried public officials were often swindled into receiving a poor quality of "country pay"; just as serious were the cost of transporting the commodities received for taxes and loss through shrinkage and deterioration.[8] What public treasuries would accept, private merchants could not refuse. Until his death in 1764, Thomas Hancock, John's uncle, in conducting business with the country merchants of New England, had to accept commodities and pass them on to reluctant creditors in turn.

Clearly, one of the major problems in using commodity money, besides inconvenience, spoilage, and storage difficulties, was quality control. Gresham's law—that bad money (low quality) drives out good (high quality)—applied because it was in an individual's self-interest to make payments whenever possible with low-quality goods.

One of the earliest domestically initiated regulations, the Maryland Tobacco Inspection Act of 1747, addressed the issue of quality control. The act was designed to increase the value of tobacco exports from Maryland, and came in response to a 1730 tobacco inspection law in Virginia. After 1730, British importers had been discounting Maryland tobacco relative to Virginia tobacco because Virginia's new inspection system eliminated the widespread practice of including damaged or "trash" tobacco in its shipments. Marylanders, however, continued this practice, and the prices of Maryland tobacco slipped relatively. The adoption of the 1747 act reversed that trend, and closed the price gap abruptly.[9]

Not only did this move to quality control raise the value of Maryland's tobacco exports, but it also set firm standards of quality control for tobacco as money. In fact, because paper certificates called inspection notes were given on inspected tobacco, the circulation of money became easier, thus increasing the velocity of money. One planter from Virginia commented in 1747 in the *Maryland Gazette:* "The very circulation of the inspection notes in the country is a great advantage to the people, for perhaps they will pass from one to another fifty times before they return to the Inspector again."[10]

---

[8] Charles J. Bullock, *Essays on the Monetary History of the United States* (New York: Macmillan, 1900), p. 11.

[9] For an excellent analysis of the impact of the act and evidence on tobacco prices, see Mary McKinney Schweitzer, "Economic Regulation and the Colonial Economy: The Maryland Tobacco Inspection Act of 1747," *Journal of Economic History* 40 (1980): 551–570.

[10] *Maryland Gazette*, May 1747, as reported in Schweitzer, pp. 563–564.

A Maryland planter in 1753 reported on "the Advantage of having Tobacco Notes in my pocket, as giving me credit for the quantity mentioned in them wherever I went, and that I was thereby at large to dispose of them when, to whom, and where I pleased; whereas, before this Act, my credit could not be expected to go beyond my own Neighborhood, or at farthest, where I might be known."[11]

Despite the problems it entailed, commodity money was extensively used in the colonies, especially in the seventeenth century whenever specie and paper substitutes were scarce. But by the early eighteenth century, both specie (gold or silver) and paper currency were common in the major seaboard cities, and by the end of the colonial period, commodities—particularly furs—were accepted as a medium of exchange only in communities along the western frontier.

COINS, SPECIE, AND PAPER MONEY

Because of the sizable colonial trades with many overseas areas, the gold and silver coins of all the important commercial countries of Europe and their dependencies in the Western Hemisphere were freely exchanged throughout the eastern seaboard. More important than English coins, which could not be legally exported from Britain to the colonies, were the silver coins of the Spanish mint. These were struck for the most part in Mexico City and Lima and introduced into the colonial economy via vigorous trading with the Spanish colonies. English-speaking people referred to the "piece of eight" (as the old Spanish peso was called) as a "dollar," probably because it was about the size of the German *thaler*. Spanish dollars were so common in the colonies that the coin was eventually adopted as the monetary unit of the United States. The fractional coin, known as the "real" or "bit," was worth about 12$\frac{1}{2}$¢, or one-eighth of a Spanish dollar, and was important in making change.[12]

Although Massachusetts first attempted to mint coins of low bullion content as early as 1652, it is not surprising that the colonies turned to paper to increase their meager and undependable money supply, and settlers became accustomed to paper money at an early date. The promissory notes of well-known individuals often exchanged hands for several months. Bills of exchange drawn on English merchants or various government officials in London also circulated widely. Treasurers of the various colonies began to issue promissory notes in advance of tax collection and issue written orders to town officers requiring the payment of obligations from local stores; like other negotiable instruments, these pieces of paper were exchanged on endorsement as money.[13]

In 1690, Massachusetts issued the first bills of credit to pay soldiers who had returned from an unsuccessful military expedition. During the next 65 years, at least

---

[11] *Maryland Gazette,* April 5, 1753, as reported in Schweitzer, p. 564.

[12] The "piece of eight" was so called in colloquial language because of the numeral *VIII* impressed on one side to indicate its value of eight *reales*. In many parts of the United States, the expressions *two bits, four bits,* and *six bits* are still used today.

[13] See Curtis P. Nettels, *The Money Supply of the American Colonies Before 1720* (Madison: University of Wisconsin Press, 1934), pp. 250–251.

eight other colonies followed this example to meet financial emergencies, especially payments of war-related efforts. Bills of credit were issued with the proviso that they were to be redeemed in specie at some future date; in the meantime, they were accepted for taxes by the issuing colony. Such redemption provisions, although restricted, facilitated the free circulation of these bills as money. In some states—notably Rhode Island, Massachusetts, Connecticut, and South Carolina—the bills were commonly overissued, thereby depreciating their value relative to specie. The same difficulty was encountered with the paper of the publicly owned "banks" established by colonial governments. These institutions, unlike anything we call a bank today, issued "loan bills" to individuals, usually based on the security of land or houses. Borrowers used the bills to meet their obligations and were usually required to repay the debt, with interest, in annual installments.

Occasionally, despite public issues of paper, private remedies were still undertaken, as exemplified by one merchant's April 1761 announcement in the *Maryland Gazette:*

> As I daily suffer much inconvenience in my Business for Want of small Change, which indeed is a universal Complaint of almost everybody in any Sort of Business, I intend . . . to Print . . . a Parcel of small Notes, from Three Pence to Two Shillings and Six Pence each, to pass Current at the same Rate as the Money under the Inspecting Law, and to be Exchanged by me . . . for good Spanish Dollars at Seven Shillings and Six Pence each Dollar.[14]

In this fashion, transaction costs were lowered, especially on retail and small-lot exchanges.

MONEY, DEBTS, AND CREDITORS

During the eighteenth century, there was continuing conflict—especially in New England—over the currency question. As in communities throughout recorded history, there were advocates of "sound" money, who took the position that efforts to increase the money supply beyond the quantity of coin in circulation were both unethical and dangerous. On the whole, however, American colonists were disposed toward an expansive supply of money. Primarily farmers and exporters of raw materials, most Americans wanted prices to rise to increase money incomes and to provide relief from debt. Farmers clearly favored the establishment of banks so that they could obtain money at low interest rates by offering their land as security. And many merchants, themselves debtors, joined with the agrarians to urge continuing issuances of paper.

Historically, most paper issues in the colonies invited little attention from England, but over time debtors more frequently attempted to pay off old obligations with depreciated paper. To use paper currency as legal tender, not just in tax payments but in

---

[14] From Joseph A. Ernst, *Money and Politics in America, 1755–1775* (Chapel Hill: University of North Carolina Press, 1973), pp. 154–155. For more on this issue, see John R. Hanson II, "Small Notes in the American Colonies," *Explorations in Economic History* 17 (1980): 411–420.

Crowded prisons in seventeenth-century England held many debtors. The colonization of Georgia, in part, had a purpose of relieving debtor-filled jails.

private transactions as well, became well established by custom and law in New England.

Figure 4-3 on the next page illustrates the problem and traces the exchange rate of Pennsylvania paper currency for English sterling in London. In the late 1740s, nearly £180 Pennsylvania currency was needed to equal £100 sterling. The discrepancy between the currency's face value and its market value was the source of the conflict between colonial debtors and English creditors. English merchants were normally willing to accept currency at market value, but debtors pointed to colonial laws stating that creditors had to accept paper money at face value (£1 currency for £1 debt in sterling). Ultimately the Crown and Parliament were forced into the controversy. In response to complaints by British creditors, the Currency Act of 1751 prohibited the New England colonies from issuing further bills of credit and from organizing new public banks. Furthermore, existing paper note issues, which because of depreciation normally did not exceed 5 percent of New England's purchasing power of money, were to be retired as they fell due. More important, from the point of view of its ultimate political consequences, was the Currency Restraining Act of 1764, which extended the

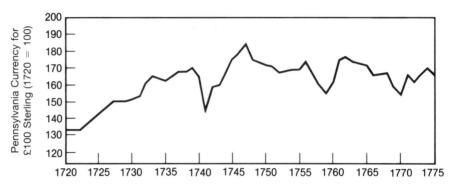

FIGURE 4-3 ANNUAL RATE OF EXCHANGE IN LONDON FOR PENNSYLVANIA CURRENCY *The exchange rates between English sterling and Pennsylvania's paper currency moved upward between 1720 and 1739, taking more Pennsylvania money to buy an English pound. Later there were periods when the sterling rate fell.*

SOURCE: *HISTORICAL STATISTICS* (WASHINGTON, D.C.: GOVERNMENT PRINTING OFFICE, 1976), SERIES Z585.

provisions of the Currency Act of 1751 to all the colonies. Precipitated by events in Virginia, which after 1755 had issued £250,000 in bills of credit with full legal tender provisions, the act brought loud protests from residents in the southern colonies. Meanwhile British merchants, who objected that debts due in specie were being paid in paper money issued in great quantity during the French and Indian War, nodded approval. Coming as it did during a postwar recession, the Currency Restraining Act aroused much animosity. By 1773, amidst growing antagonism, Parliament relented and permitted the colonies to use currency issues as legal tender at face value for public payments, but not for private ones.

It is important to emphasize that paper money at that time was uniquely American. Although invented and used in ancient China, paper money was not used anywhere in the world after 1500 until reintroduced by the mainland colonists. A paper currency that was widely acceptable stands as one of the great legacies of the colonists.

TRADE DEFICITS WITH ENGLAND

It is important to reemphasize that mercantilist measures were implemented by the Crown to regulate trade and to generate favorable trade balances for England. In addition, because European manufactured goods were in great demand in the New World, colonists faced chronic deficits, especially in their trade with England. Trade deficits in the colonies resulted in a continual drain of specie from colonial shores and encouraged the use of paper money substitutes. Table 4-4 shows the size and trend of these trade deficits with England over much of the eighteenth century. As highlighted in

TABLE 4-4   VALUES AND BALANCES OF COMMODITY TRADE BETWEEN ENGLAND
AND THE AMERICAN COLONIES (ANNUAL AVERAGES BY DECADE, IN
THOUSANDS OF POUNDS STERLING)

	Imports	Exports	Deficit
1721–1730	£ 509	£ 442	£ 67
1731–1740	698	559	139
1741–1750	923	599	324
1751–1760	1,704	808	896
1761–1770	1,942	1,203	739

SOURCE: JAMES F. SHEPHERD AND GARY M. WALTON, *SHIPPING, MARITIME TRADE, AND THE ECO-
NOMIC DEVELOPMENT OF NORTH AMERICA* (CAMBRIDGE: CAMBRIDGE UNIVERSITY PRESS, 1972), P. 42.

Table 4-5, most of these deficits were incurred by New England and the Middle colonies, but even the southern colonies frequently faced deficits in their commodity trade
with England.

How did the colonists pay for their trade deficits? Benjamin Franklin's reply to a
Parliamentary committee in 1760 explaining Pennsylvania's payment of its trade deficit
with England was,

The balance is paid by our produce carried to the West Indies, and sold in our
own islands, or to the French, Spaniards, Danes, and Dutch; by the same carried
to other colonies in North America, as to New England, Nova Scotia, Newfoundland, Carolina, and Georgia; by the same carried to different parts of
Europe, as Spain, Portugal and Italy: In all which places we receive either money,
bills of exchange, or commodities that suit for remittance to Britain; which,
together with all the profits of the industry of our merchants and mariners arising in those circuitous voyages and the freights made by their ships, center finally
in Britain to discharge the balance and pay for British manufactures continually
used in the province or sold to foreigners by our traders.[15]

As emphasized by the esteemed Franklin, colonial trade deficits to Britain could be
paid by surpluses earned in trades to other overseas areas as well as by earnings from
shipping and other mercantile services.

Other sources of foreign exchange, such as payments by the British forces stationed
in the colonies, also affected the inflow of sterling. To determine the relative importance of these and other sources of exchange earnings (and losses), we need to assess
the various components of the colonies' overall balance of payments.

[15] Quoted in Harold U. Faulkner, *American Economic History*, 8th ed. (New York: Harper & Row, 1960),
p. 81.

A BALANCE OF PAYMENTS FOR THE THIRTEEN COLONIES

A balance of payments study clarifies many critical issues. It can determine how the deficits to England were paid and show the size of net specie drains from the colonies or indicate the magnitude of growing indebtedness of colonists to British creditors. It can show the inflows of capital into the colonies and suggest the magnitude of possible British subsidization of colonial economic development. A balance of payments is an accounting framework in which debits and credits always balance. In short, one way or another, things get paid for, with goods, money, or IOUs (debt). This is true for people and true for nations (and colonies) as well.

Surviving information on the myriad of exchanges for the years from 1768 to 1772 gives us a reasonably clear picture of the colonies' balance of payments in the late colonial period. A breakdown of the colonies' commodity trade balances with the major overseas areas during this period is provided in Table 4-5. These data confirm the findings presented earlier in Table 4-4, indicating that sizable deficits were incurred in the English trade, especially by New England and the Middle colonies. Somewhat surprisingly, even the colonies' commodity trade to the West Indies was unfavorable

TABLE 4-5   AVERAGE ANNUAL COMMODITY TRADE BALANCES OF THE THIRTEEN AMERICAN COLONIES, 1768–1772 (IN THOUSANDS OF POUNDS STERLING)

	Great Britain and Ireland	Southern Europe	West Indies	Africa	All Trades
New England	− 609	+ 48	−36	+19	− 577
Middle Colonies	− 786	+153	−10	+ 1	− 643
Upper South	− 50	+ 90	− 9	0	+ 30
Lower South	− 23	+ 48	+44	0	+ 69
Total	−1,468	+339	−11	+20	−1,121

SOURCE: JAMES F. SHEPHERD AND GARY M. WALTON, *SHIPPING, MARITIME TRADE, AND THE ECONOMIC DEVELOPMENT OF NORTH AMERICA* (CAMBRIDGE: CAMBRIDGE UNIVERSITY PRESS, 1972), P. 115.

NOTES: (1) A plus sign denotes a surplus (exports exceed imports); a minus sign, a deficit (imports exceed exports).
(2) Values are expressed in prices in the mainland colonies; thus, import values include the costs of transportation, commissions, and other handling costs. Export values are also expressed in colonial prices and therefore do not include these distribution costs.

(except for the trade of the Lower South). However, trades to southern Europe generated significant surpluses (augmented slightly by the African trades), which were sufficient to raise the southern colonial regions to a surplus position in their overall commodity exchanges.

Although commodity exchanges made up the lion's share of total colonial exchanges, the colonies did have other sources of foreign exchange earnings (and losses) as well. Table 4-6 begins with colonial commodity exchanges indicating the £1,120 aggregate deficit in that category.

The most important source of foreign exchange earnings to offset that average deficit was the sale of colonial shipping services. Shipping earnings totaled approximately £600,000 per year in the late colonial period. In addition, colonial merchants earned more than £200,000 annually through insurance charges and commissions. Together, these "invisible" earnings offset more than 60 percent of the overall colonial commodity trade deficit. Almost 80 percent of these invisible earnings reverted to residents of New England and the Middle colonies. Thus, the mercantile activities of New

TABLE 4-6 BALANCE OF PAYMENTS FOR THE THIRTEEN COLONIES, 1768–1772
(IN THOUSANDS OF POUNDS STERLING)

	Debits	Credits
Commodities		
Export earnings		2,800
Imports	3,920	
Trade deficit	1,120	
Ship sales to foreigners		140
Invisible earnings		
Shipping cargoes		600
Merchant commissions, insurance, etc.		220
Payments for human beings		
Indentured servants	80	
Slaves	200	
British collections and expenditures		
Taxes and duties	40	
Military and civil expenditures[a]		440–460
Payments deficit financed by specie flows and/or increased indebtedness		20–40

SOURCES: DATA COMPILED FROM GARY M. WALTON AND JAMES F. SHEPHERD, *THE ECONOMIC RISE OF EARLY AMERICA* (CAMBRIDGE: CAMBRIDGE UNIVERSITY PRESS, 1979), TABLE 9, P. 101; JULIAN GWYN, "BRITISH GOVERNMENT SPENDING AND THE NORTH AMERICAN COLONIES, 1740–1775," IN *THE ATLANTIC EMPIRE BEFORE THE AMERICAN REVOLUTION,* EDS. PETER MARSHALL AND GLYN WILLIAMS (LONDON: FRANK CASS, 1980), PP. 74–84, FN. 7, AND ALSO IN *JOURNAL OF IMPERIAL AND COMMONWEALTH HISTORY* (1980): 74–87, FN. 7; AND PETER D. G. THOMAS, "THE COST OF THE BRITISH ARMY IN NORTH AMERICA, 1763–1775," *WILLIAM AND MARY QUARTERLY* (1988): 510–516.

[a] Gwyn's estimates of total expenditures for military and civil purposes for 1768–1772 are £365, but Thomas's study suggests higher arms payments by nearly £100,000 yearly for the same period. Neither account for savings by men stationed in the colonies who returned some of their earnings home; thus the £440–460 range. £460 assumes no savings sent home.

Englanders and Middle colonists, especially in the West Indian trade, enabled the colonies to import large quantities of manufactured goods from Great Britain. When all thirteen colonies are considered together, invisible earnings exceeded earnings from tobacco exports—the single most important colonial staple export.

Another aspect of seafaring, the sale of ships, also became a persistent credit item in the colonies' balance of payments. As Jacob Price has shown, colonial ship sales averaged at least £140,000 annually from 1763 to 1775, primarily to England. Again, the lion's share of these earnings went to New England shipbuilders, but the Middle colonies also received a portion of the profits from ship sales. Taken together, ship sales and "invisible" earnings reduced the colonies' negative balance of payments to only £160,000.

In contrast to these earning sources, funds for the trade of human beings were continually lost to foreign markets. An average of approximately £80,000 sterling was spent annually for the 5,000 to 10,000 indentured servants who arrived each year during the late colonial period. Most of these servants were sent to Pennsylvania and the Chesapeake Bay area. A more sizable amount was the nearly £200,000 spent each year to purchase approximately 5,000 slaves. Over 90 percent of these slaves were sent to the Southern colonies, especially to the Lower South in the later colonial period.

Finally, expenditures made by the British government in the colonies on defense, civil administration, and justice notably offset the remaining deficits in the colonists' current account of trade. Table 4-6 does not indicate the total amount of these costs to Great Britain. Instead, it shows how much British currency was used to purchase goods and services in the colonies and how much was paid to men stationed there. The net inflow for these expenditures averaged between £440,000 and £460,000 from 1768 to 1772, reducing the net deficit in the colonial balance of payments for these years to £40,000 per year at most, and probably less.

INTERPRETATIONS: MONEY, DEBT, AND CAPITAL

Having assessed the colonies' balance of payments, we turn now to its impact on the colonial economy. The estimated remaining annual colonial deficit of £20,000 to £40,000 was paid either by an outflow of specie or by growing indebtedness to Britain. Temporary net outflows of specie undoubtedly did occur, thereby straining trade and prices in the colonies. Certainly contemporary complaints of money scarcity, especially specie, indicate that this often happened. But no significant part of this normal deficit could have been paid with precious metals. The colonists could not sustain a permanent net outflow of specie because gold and silver mines were not developed in colonial North America. Typically, then, the outflow of specie to England was matched by an inflow from various sources of colonial exchange earnings. Nevertheless, the erratic pattern of specie movement and the issuance of paper money of uncertain value caused monetary disturbances, as reflected in price movements and alterations in rates of exchange among the currencies. But most colonists preferred to spend rather than to accumulate a stock of specie. After all, limited specie was simply another manifestation of a capital-scarce economy. To the colonists, it was more desirable to receive additional imports—especially manufactures—than to maintain a growing stock of specie.

The final remaining colonial deficits were normally financed on short-term credit, and American merchants usually purchased goods from England on one-year credit. This was so customary, in fact, that British merchants included a normal 5 percent interest charge in their prices and granted a rebate to accounts that were paid before the year ended. And in Virginia, Scottish firms generally established representatives in stores to sell or trade British wares for tobacco and other products. Short-term credit was a normal part of day-to-day colonial exchanges in these instances.

The growth of short-term credit reflected the expanding Atlantic trades and represented a modest amount of increasing colonial indebtedness to Britain. Sizable claims against southern planters by British merchants after the Revolution[16] have encouraged some historians to argue that the relationship between London merchants and southern planters was disastrous at that time and even to argue that increasing colonial indebtedness to Britain provided impetus for the Revolution. But was this, in fact, so?

By adding the "invisible" earnings and ship sales to the regional commodity trade deficits (and surpluses), we obtain these rough averages of the regional deficits ($-$) and surpluses ($+$) in the colonies:[17]

New England	$-£$ 50,000
Middle Colonies	$-$ 350,000
Southern Colonies	$+$ 240,000

Clearly, the major deficit regions were north of the Chesapeake Bay area, primarily in the Middle colonies. The southern regions were favored with more than a sufficient surplus in their current accounts of trade to pay for their purchases of slaves and indentured servants.

A fair number of planters availed themselves of greater credit from abroad, according to separate studies by Timothy Breen, Jacob Price, and Allan Kulikoff. Nevertheless, it appears there was no growing indebtedness on average in the South at this time, and British expenditures for military and administrative purposes eliminated the

---

[16]Of the approximately £5,000,000 claimed by British merchants in 1791, more than £2,300,000 was owed by Virginia, nearly £570,000 by Maryland, £690,000 by South Carolina, £380,000 by North Carolina, and £250,000 by Georgia. However, nearly one-half of these amounts represented accumulated interest on deficits that had been in effect since 1776. Moreover, Aubrey Land argues that these claims were exaggerated by as much as 800 percent and that the Americans honored only one-eighth of such claims. See Aubrey C. Land, "Economic Behavior in a Planting Society: The Eighteenth Century Chesapeake," *Journal of Southern History* 32 (1967): 482–483.

[17]The regional division of shipping earnings and other "invisibles" is derived from Shepherd and Walton, *Shipping, Maritime Trade, and the Economic Development of North America*, Chapter 7. Because the ownership of vessels is not given separately for the Upper South and the Lower South, we have combined these two regions here, but undoubtedly the Upper South earned the greater portion of the combined £240,000 surplus. All ship sales have been credited to the northern regions; £100,000 to New England and £40,000 to the Middle colonies.

negative New England balance and reduced most of the Middle colonies' balances as well.[18]

Nevertheless, England's claims were real enough, even if exaggerated. But remember that British merchants and their colonial representatives normally extended credit to southern planters and accepted their potential harvests as collateral. Usually, of course, the harvests came in, and the colonists' outstanding debts were paid. But with the outbreak of the Revolution, this picture changed radically. Colonial credit normally extended throughout the year was still outstanding at the end of the year, because agents or partners of British firms had retreated home before the crops were harvested and the debts were paid. But the mere existence of these debts did not indicate growing indebtedness—nor did it provide motivation for colonial revolt.

The capital inflows that did occur were rarely channeled directly into long-term investments in the colonies, and British merchants held few claims on such investments. Nevertheless, it is important to realize that because commercial short-term credit was furnished by the British, colonial savings were freed for other uses: to make long-term investments in land improvement, roads, and such physical capital as ships, warehouses, and public buildings. For the purposes of colonial development, British short-term credit represented a helping hand, and its form was much less important than its amount.

However, with the highly important exception of military and civil defense, the colonies apparently were not subsidized by Britain to any great extent. For the most part, the formation of capital in the New World was dependent on the steady accretion of savings and investment from the pockets of the colonists themselves. It is impossible to determine precisely how much was annually saved and invested in the late colonial period. According to our estimates, which will be elaborated in Chapter 5, annual incomes probably averaged at least £11 sterling per person in the colonies. Since nearly 2.5 million people were living in the colonies on the eve of the Revolution, if we assume a savings rate of not less than 9 percent (£1 out of £11), total capital accumulation per year would have exceeded £2.5 million at that time. Thus, the capital inflow from Britain probably accounted for 1 or 2 percent of capital formation in the colonies.

The sizable estimates of British military expenditures in North America between 1763 and 1775 (by Peter Thomas) and of civil and military expenditures for the longer period from 1740 to 1775 (by Julian Gwyn) support these general conclusions of small net deficits in the colonies' balance of payments throughout much of the late colonial period. Only the substantial British expenditures for military and administrative purposes reveal a form of British subsidization or colonial dependency in the decades just prior to the Revolution.

---

[18] Further alteration of the regional deficits and surpluses would have resulted from coastal trade among the regions. Surprisingly, however, the major regions in the thirteen colonies appear to have earned surpluses in coastal trade. Florida, the Bahamas, and the Bermuda Islands and the northern colonies of Newfoundland, Nova Scotia, and Quebec were the deficit areas in coastal trade. See James F. Shepherd and Samuel H. Williamson, "The Coastal Trade of the British North American Colonies, 1768–1772," *Journal of Economic History* 32 (1972): 803.

SELECTED REFERENCES
AND SUGGESTED READINGS

Andrews, Charles M. *The Colonial Period of American History.* Vol. 4 of *England's Commercial and Colonial Policy.* New Haven: Yale University Press, 1938.

Barrow, Thomas. *Trade and Empire: The British Customs Service in Colonial America, 1660–1775.* Cambridge: Harvard University Press, 1967.

Becker, Robert A. *Revolution, Reform, and the Politics of Taxation in America: 1763–1783.* Baton Rouge: Louisiana State University Press, 1980.

Beer, George L. *British Colonial Policy, 1754–1765.* Gloucester: Peter Smith, 1958.

Breen, Timothy H. *Tobacco Culture: The Mentality of the Great Tidewater Planters on the Eve of the Revolution.* Princeton: Princeton University Press, 1985.

Brock, Leslie. *The Currency System of the American Colonies, 1700–1764.* New York: Arno Press, 1975.

Bruchey, Stuart. *The Colonial Merchant: Sources and Readings.* New York: Harcourt, Brace & World, 1966.

———. *The Roots of American Economic Growth 1607–1861: An Essay in Social Causation.* London: Hutchinson University Library, 1965.

Burnstein, M. L. "Colonial and Contemporary Monetary Theory." *Explorations in Entrepreneurial History* 3, no. 3, 2d series (Spring 1966).

Coleman, D. C., ed. *Revisions in Mercantilism.* London: Methuen, 1969.

Dickerson, Oliver M. *American Colonial Government 1696–1765.* Cleveland: Arthur H. Clark, 1912.

———. *The Navigation Acts and the American Revolution.* Philadelphia: University of Pennsylvania Press, 1951.

Ernst, Joseph. *Money and Politics in America, 1755–1775.* Chapel Hill: University of North Carolina Press, 1973.

Evans, Emory. "Planter Indebtedness and the Coming of the Revolution in Virginia, 1776 to 1796." *William and Mary Quarterly* 19, 2d series (1962): 511–533.

Greene, Jack P., and Richard M. Jellison. "The Currency Act of 1764 in Imperial-Colonial Relations, 1764–1776." *William and Mary Quarterly* 18, no. 4, 2d series (October 1961).

Gwyn, Julian. "British Government Spending and the North American Colonies, 1740–1775." *Journal of Imperial and Commonwealth History* 8 (1984): 74–84.

Hacker, Louis M. "The First American Revolution." *Columbia University Quarterly,* part 1 (September 1935). Reprinted in Gerald D. Nash. *Issues in American Economic History.* New York: D. C. Heath, 1972.

Hanson, John R. "Money in the Colonial American Economy: An Extension." *Economic Inquiry* (1979): 281–286.

———. "Small Notes in the American Economy." *Explorations in Economic History* 21 (1984): 411–420.

Harper, Lawrence A. *The English Navigation Laws.* New York: Columbia University Press, 1939.

———. "Mercantilism and the American Revolution." *Canadian Historical Review* (March 1942). Reprinted in Gerald D. Nash. *Issues in American Economic History.* New York: D. C. Heath, 1972.

Hughes, J. R. T. *Social Control in the Colonial Economy.* Charlottesville: University Press of Virginia, 1976.

Kulikoff, Allan. "The Economic Growth of the Eighteenth-Century Chesapeake Colonies." *Journal of Economic History* 39 (1979): 275–288.

Lester, Richard A. "Currency Issues to Overcome Depressions in Pennsylvania, 1723 and 1729." *Journal of Political Economy* 71 (1963): 324–375.

———. *Monetary Experiments: Early American and Recent Scandinavian.* Princeton: Princeton University Press, 1939.

Neal, Larry. "Interpreting Power and Profit in Economic History: A Case Study of the Seven Years' War." *Journal of Economic History* 37 (1977): 20–35.

Nettels, Curtis C. "British Policy and Colonial Money Supply." *Economic History Review* 3 (1931).

———. *The Money Supply of the American Colonies Before 1720.* Madison: University of Wisconsin Press, 1934.

Perkins, Edwin J. *The Economy of Colonial America.* 2d ed. New York: Columbia University Press, 1988. Chapters 2 and 7.

Price, Jacob. *Capital and Credit in British Overseas Trade: The View from the Chesapeake, 1700–1776.* Cambridge: Harvard University Press, 1980.

———. "Economic Function and the Growth of American Port Towns in the Eighteenth Century." In *Perspectives in American History,* vol. 8, eds. D. Fleming and B. Bailyn. Cambridge: Harvard University Press, 1974.

———. "The Economic Growth of the Chesapeake and the European Market, 1697–1775." *Journal of Economic History* 24 (1964): 496–511.

———. "A Note on the Value of Colonial Exports of Shipping." *Journal of Economic History* 36 (1976): 704–724.

Rosenberg, Nathan, and L. E. Birdzell, Jr. *How the West Grew Rich.* New York: Basic Books, 1986. Chapter 4.

Schweitzer, Mary McKinney. "Economic Regulation and the Colonial Economy: The Maryland Tobacco Inspection Act of 1747." *Journal of Economic History* 40 (1980): 551–570.

Shepherd, James F., and Gary M. Walton. *Shipping, Maritime Trade and the Economic Development of Colonial North America.* Cambridge: Cambridge University Press, 1972.

Shepherd, James F., and Samuel Williamson. "The Coastal Trade of the British North American Colonies 1768–1772." *Journal of Economic History* 32 (1972): 783–810.

Smith, Bruce. "Some Colonial Evidence on Two Theories of Money: Maryland and the Carolinas." *Journal of Political Economy* 93 (1985): 1178–1211.

Studenski, Paul, and Herman Krooss. *Financial History of the United States.* New York: McGraw-Hill, 1952.

Thomas, Peter A. G. "The Cost of the British Army in North America, 1763–1775." *William and Mary Quarterly* 45 (1988): 510–516.

Ver Steeg, Clarence. *The Formative Years, 1607–1763.* New York: Hill & Wang, 1964.

Walton, Gary M., and James F. Shepherd. *The Economic Rise of Early America.* Cambridge: Cambridge University Press, 1979.

Weiss, Roger. "The Colonial Monetary Standards of Massachusetts." *Economic History Review* 27, no. 4, 2d series (November 1974).

———. "The Issue of Paper Money in the American Colonies, 1720–1774." *Journal of Economic History* 30 (1970): 770–785.

Wicker, Elmer. "Colonial Monetary Standards Contrasted: Evidence from the Seven Years' War." *Journal of Economic History* 45 (1985): 860–884.

CHAPTER FIVE

ECONOMIC PROGRESS AND WEALTH

CHAPTER THEME Because of high levels of migration and rapid population growth, total output in the colonies grew at high rates throughout the colonial period. Standards of living for the average colonist also grew at rates that were high by contemporary standards and comparable to gains in Britain, Holland, and France. The sources of growth of per capita income form an important part of the story of economic development, as these sources of progress lifted the colonial economy to a position where it could become independent from England. These sources are found principally in case (or sectoral) studies of productivity change. Although the economy grew and prospered, people and regions did not gain equally, and there was already substantial inequality of wealth (and income) among people and places as settlements in the wilderness grew into towns and centers of trade.

GROWTH AND CHANGE IN THE COLONIAL ECONOMY

The many local and regional economies that comprised the total colonial economy were always in a state of flux. Because the colonies began literally as settlements in the wilderness, and because war and other frontier disturbances were frequent, it is particularly difficult to systematically portray the economic growth of the colonies. The data are simply too scant to provide any systematic and comprehensive measures of economic growth.

Economic growth, of course, refers to the rate at which a society's material standard of living advances over an extended period of time. It implies more than a mere increase in inputs that enlarge output. Economic growth means an advance in output relative to population in the long run. This can be accomplished by an increase in the labor-population ratio, by the movement of inputs from lower- to higher-value uses, by other productivity gains (such as technological change, economies of scale, improvements in business organization, and economic institutions), and by skill-enhancing investments (such as education and on-the-job training). In addition, labor productivity (output per unit of labor input) can be increased by raising the capital-labor ratio or the land-labor ratio. As any or all of these sources of productivity advance, they in turn raise the standard of living for the total population.

In 1964, George R. Taylor triggered a debate that has not yet run its course. In his presidential address to the Economic History Association, Taylor argued that before 1710 very little economic growth occurred in the colonies (it was "slow and irregular"), but then between 1710 and 1775 it averaged "slightly more than one percent per annum."[1] There is a handy rule-of-thumb calculation to show the impact of annual growth rates. If r is the rate of growth in percentage terms and t is the number of years that the growing quantity takes to double, then $r \times t = 70$. Taylor's assertion of 1 percent implies a doubling of income per capita in 70 years: $t = 70/1$, or 70 years. Did Taylor's claim of an early eighteenth-century acceleration really take place, and did per capita incomes really almost double between 1710 and 1775 as the 1-percent rate implies? Did such economic advances continue indefinitely thereafter, or did periods of stagnation reappear?

Because of data limitations on real per capita income, firm answers elude us.[2] Through recent scholarly efforts, however, fragments of information have appeared to significantly advance our understanding of the pace and main sources of growth in the colonies.

---

[1]George R. Taylor, "American Economic Growth Before 1840: An Exploratory Essay," *Journal of Economic History* 24 (1964): 437.

[2]It is important to remember that in measuring changes of income, we often neglect other factors that affect the quality of life, such as the amount of leisure time enjoyed, conditions of health, environment, personal attributes, even the distribution of wealth.

appears that total productivity advanced approximately 10 percent during these decades. Expressed in terms of rates of change, total productivity expanded by 0.1 to 0.2 percent per year, with the most rapid change (0.3 percent) occurring in the first decades of the eighteenth century. Finally, the growth of output per worker was somewhat higher (approximately 0.2 to 0.3 percent per year) over the first three-quarters of the century.[4]

Specific evidence on the precise sources of these advances is almost entirely lacking. The low measured rate of advance, however, does reinforce historical descriptions. For instance, in their classic study of agriculture, Bidwell and Falconer assert that in the colonies north of the Chesapeake, "The eighteenth century farmers showed little advance over the first settlers in their care of livestock," and "little if any improvement had been made in farm implements until the very close of the eighteenth century."[5] Another study of Pennsylvania agriculture specifically concludes that "economic conditions throughout the century prohibited major changes and encouraged a reasonably stable and uniform type of mixed farming that involved fairly extensive use or superficial working of the land."[6] It seems reasonable to conclude that farmers were probably beginning to learn to use the soil and their implements more effectively. But there is little indication of input savings, either from technological improvements or from economies of scale in terms of larger farms. Better organized and more widespread market participation, however, may have contributed somewhat to gains in agricultural productivity.

These findings and conclusions come as no surprise when examined in the light of agricultural developments in later periods. For instance, investigations by Robert Gallman indicate total productivity gains of approximately 0.5 percent per year over the nineteenth century.[7] However, in the first half of the century, combined output per unit of land, labor, and capital advanced at a rate of 0.1 to 0.2 percent. In the second half of the century, the productivity rate rose to 0.8 percent. Undoubtedly, the lower-paced first half of the nineteenth century—before the transition to animal power and increased mechanization—would have been more suggestive of the eighteenth-century experience. In short, agricultural progress throughout most of the colonial period was sporadic, limited, and slow-paced.

---

[4] It should be noted that labor productivity (output per worker) increased more than total productivity (output per total combined input), because the amounts of capital and cleared land per worker increased during this period. Increases in these other inputs enabled labor to produce more.

[5] P. W. Bidwell and J. I. Falconer, *History of Agriculture in the Northern United States, 1620–1860* (Washington, D.C.: Carnegie Institution of Washington, 1925), pp. 107, 123.

[6] James T. Lemon, *Best Poor Man's Country: A Geographical Study of Early Southwestern Pennsylvania* (Baltimore: Johns Hopkins University Press, 1972), pp. 150–151.

[7] See Robert E. Gallman, "Changes in Total U.S. Agricultural Factor Productivity in the Nineteenth Century," *Agricultural History* 46 (1972): 191–210; and Gallman, "The Agricultural Sector and the Pace of Economic Growth: U.S. Experience in the Nineteenth Century," in *Essays in Nineteenth Century Economic History*, eds. David C. Klingaman and Richard K. Vedder (Athens: Ohio University Press, 1975), pp. 35–76.

PRODUCTIVITY GAINS IN TRANSPORTATION AND DISTRIBUTION

Although productivity advances in agriculture were slow and gradual, substantially higher gains were registered in the handling and transportation of goods. Such gains were extremely important because transportation and other distribution costs comprised a large portion of the final market price of products. This was especially true of the bulky colonial products, which were normally low in value relative to their weight or volume (displaced cargo space). For example, transportation and handling costs would double the value of a barrel of pitch between Maryland and London. Even the distribution costs of expensive lightwares represented a significant fraction of their value.

During the eighteenth century, the differential between English and colonial prices for manufactures shipped to the colonies was declining at a fairly steady rate. In the early decades of the century, it was not uncommon for English goods to sell for 80 to 140 percent more in the colonies than in England. By midcentury, prices on British wares were 45 to 75 percent higher in the colonies. Finally, just prior to the Revolution, this price spread had been reduced to a range of only 15 to 25 percent. However, as late as the 1770s, colonial staples such as pitch, tar, lumber, rice, and other space-consuming exports were still commanding more than double their domestic price in normal English and European markets.

Evidence of improvements in the marketing and distribution of transatlantic tobacco shipments reveals the declining average differential between the Amsterdam price and the colonial price of tobacco (given as a percentage of the Amsterdam price):[8]

Years	Price Differences
1720–1724	82%
1725–1729	76
1730–1734	82
1735–1739	77
1740–1744	77
1745–1749	76
1750–1754	67
1755–1759	72
1760–1764	70
1765–1769	65
1770–1774	51

A series of advances in transatlantic tobacco distribution stemmed from improvements in packaging and merchandising, from declining costs of information on prices and markets, and from reductions in risk in trade. However, by far the most important improvements were in shipping. Although freight rates fluctuated and varied according to route, the long-run trend was persistently downward. During the 100 years preceding the Revolution, the real costs of shipping were almost halved. Expressed in terms of productivity gains, shipping advanced at a rate of approximately 0.8 percent per year.

---

[8]James F. Shepherd and Gary M. Walton, *Shipping, Maritime Trade, and the Economic Development of Colonial North America* (Cambridge: Cambridge University Press, 1972), p. 60.

For that period—and specifically compared to changes in agriculture—these increases suggest that shipping was a strategic factor in the overall economic advance of the colonies.

SOURCES OF PRODUCTIVITY CHANGE IN SHIPPING.

What caused these productivity gains? Where trades were well organized and markets reasonably large and safe, economies of scale in shipping were usually realized. In the Baltic timber trades, for instance, the use of larger vessels generated labor savings per ton shipped. Although larger ships necessitated larger crews, the increased cargo capacity more than compensated for the additional labor costs. As vessels increased in size, their carrying capacity per unit of labor also increased. In other words, on larger ships, fewer men were needed to transport a given volume of goods.

Despite these possibilities, the average size of vessels employed in the western Atlantic and in the Caribbean failed to increase significantly over the 100-year period. The potential labor savings of the larger ships were offset by greater occurrences of low utilization in these waters. In fact, in those numerous small and scattered markets, the port times of large vessels were usually as much as twice as long as those for small vessels. Therefore, in colonial waters, schooners and sloops normally traveled a greater number of miles per ton than large ships or brigs did.

Nevertheless, the number of tons per man increased because crew sizes decreased as vessels remained unchanged in size. For example, a Boston vessel of 50 tons employed an average of seven men early in the eighteenth century, but by the late colonial period the same ship required only five crew members. Over this same time span, the crew size of a typical New York vessel of 50 tons decreased from eleven to seven members. Paralleling this reduction in labor was the reduction or elimination of armaments on vessels that traded in colonial waters. Guns had been commonplace on seventeenth-century vessels trading in the western Atlantic, but cannons had all but disappeared on ships there by the end of the colonial period.

Although the average useful life of vessels changed little over the period, insurance rates decreased due to the declining risks in ocean travel. In contrast to earlier times, insurance rates for most one-way transatlantic passages had reached the rock-bottom common peacetime level of 2 percent by 1720. Of course, rates for voyages into pirate-infested waters were quite another matter. Between New York and Jamaica, for example, the prevailing rate of 5 percent in 1720 had dropped to 4 percent by the 1770s. On routes from New England to various other islands in the West Indies, peacetime insurance rates were halved between 1700 and 1775.

Faster ship speed was not a positive force in raising productivity. Vessels from New England and the Middle colonies that sailed to the West Indies and back showed no gains in speed on either leg of the journey over this period, as shown in Figure 5-2 on the next page. Nevertheless, round-trip voyage times declined from 1700 to 1775. As Figure 5-3 (see page 97) shows, with the single exception of Boston, layover times fell markedly in many key ports in the New World. Because a very large portion of a sailing ship's life was spent in port, such declines contributed greatly to higher productivity. For example, in the Chesapeake trade, vessels were in port more than twice as long at the end of the seventeenth century as they were in the 1760s. An important

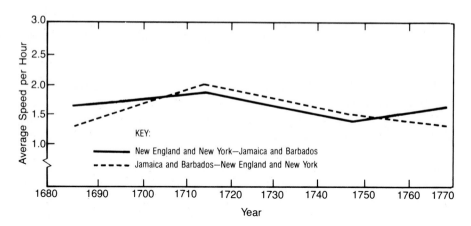

FIGURE 5-2 Average Ship Speeds (knots)

SOURCE: Gary M. Walton, "Sources of Productivity Change in American Colonial Shipping," *Economic History Review* 20 (April 1967): 74.

contributor to this change was the introduction of Scottish *factors* (representatives of Scottish merchant firms) into the Chesapeake Bay area after 1707. Undoubtedly their methods of gathering and inventorying the tobacco crop in barns and warehouses for quick loading significantly shortened port times in the Chesapeake Bay.

Similarly, port times in Barbados were halved during this period. In the early colonial days, port times were extraordinarily long because exchanges were costly to transact. The many scattered markets were small and remote, and prices varied widely among islands and even within the same island. The shipmaster, acting on behalf of a merchant, might have to visit several islands on one trip to find the best market for his cargo. Difficulties in negotiating prices and determining the medium of exchange, as well as possibly settling past debts, all tended to lengthen the transaction period. Often bartering was practiced, but even when money was used, prices were not easy to determine because different currencies and bills of exchange (with varying degrees of risk) were afforded no set value. Finally, the problem of collecting cargoes extended port times, especially when harvests were poor.[9] As a more systematic market economy evolved, long layovers in the Caribbean became less common.

It should be emphasized that decreasing port times produced savings not only in capital but also in labor costs, since crews were customarily fed and paid while they were in foreign ports.

Such savings more than offset other sources of cost increases. Although wages and ship repair costs remained fairly constant over the period, the costs of shipbuilding and victualing (obtaining food for the crew) increased. Overall, however, the productivity gains countervailed, and freight costs were cut in half between 1675 and 1775.

---

[9] As discussed in Chapter 4, many of these factors also explain the generality of shuttle patterns of shipping and of route dominance by the colonists vis-à-vis the British on particular routes.

SPECULATIONS ON GROWTH TRENDS

All such measures of productivity advance suggest that while improvements in colonial standards of material well-being occurred, the pace was slow and irregular, as George Taylor proposed. However, they do not support his assertion of an acceleration of growth of real income per capita to 1 percent annually between 1710 and 1775. Before the modern age of rapid technological change and widespread investments in schooling to generate a highly skilled and adaptive labor force, the effective sources of growth were much more limited. This is revealed in the analysis of sources of productivity advance, emphasizing the importance of learning by doing, adapting and utilizing economies of scale where possible, and the diffusion of existing technologies.

WEALTH HOLDINGS

Additional evidence, based on probated wealth holdings of deceased colonists, also portrays slow and irregular growth rates throughout the period from 1630 to 1775. Per capita wealth included land, buildings, physical possessions, money, debts receivable minus debts owed, and often slaves and indentured contracts. Allan Kulikoff's analysis of wealth holdings in Maryland over the eighteenth century suggests a long-run trend rate of growth of 0.4 percent per year.[15] His evidence shows contrasting periods: a slight fall in the first quarter of the century, a sharper decline in the second, and a very strong advance in the third quarter. Recalling the strong productivity growth period of 1630 to 1670 in the tobacco colonies, with little or no change in the late seventeenth century, it appears that most of the growth bracketed a long period of no growth (or possibly some decline) in per capita well-being in the Upper South. Work by Terry Anderson on New England also shows very strong advances in wealth holdings per person from 1650 to 1680, then very little growth up to 1710. The trend from 1650 to 1710 was unusually high, perhaps 1.6 percent per year.

Recent evidence provided by Gloria and Jackson Main on southern New England between 1640 and 1774 is shown in Table 5-2 on the next page. This evidence of growth in total wealth per male indicates a trend in yearly average income advance of 0.35 percent in this region. Note, however, the spurt following the 1638–1654 period, relative stagnation until the turn of the century, then another 20-year spurt followed by another 20-year flat period, and finally another rapid spurt. This evidence further supports the view that regions differed greatly in the timing of their growth phases. Over a very long period, however, the trend growth rates of regions were probably fairly similar.

---

[15] Deceased people's wealth exceeded average wealth per capita substantially, and not everyone who died had their estates probated. However, if the distribution of wealth did not change dramatically over the period, trends of probated wealth holdings probably reflected the trend in wealth holdings per person. Further, if the ratio of output (or income) to physical non-human wealth (capital) stayed fairly consistent, trends in such wealth per person would mirror trends in income per person.

TABLE 5-2   COMPONENTS OF MALE PER CAPITA PROBATE WEALTH IN
SOUTHERN NEW ENGLAND, 1638–1774

Years	Total Wealth
1638–1654	£227.3
1655–1674	251.9
1675–1694	263.5
1695–1714	248.9
1715–1734	272.4
1735–1754	275.8
1765–1774	364.7

SOURCE: ADAPTED FROM GLORIA L. MAIN AND JACKSON T. MAIN, "ECONOMIC GROWTH AND THE STANDARD OF LIVING IN SOUTHERN NEW ENGLAND, 1642–1774," JOURNAL OF ECONOMIC HISTORY 48 (1988): 27–46.

NOTE: For estates of males only; weighted for age and area. Estates from 1755–1764 were not included due to incomplete sample for area weighting.

It seems reasonable to conclude that over the last 100 to 150 years of the colonial period, the growth rate trend was slightly below 0.5 percent per year. Based on evidence of wealth gathered from samples of probated estates for all the colonial regions, Alice Hanson Jones concluded:

> Despite possible local or regional spurts or lags or even declines in some subperiods after 1650, it seems likely that, for all regions combined, fairly steady intensive growth accompanied accumulating experience in the New World, learning by doing, increasing knowhow in shipping within the Atlantic community, and the enlargement in size of the market that came with growth of population and trade.[16]

By her calculations, Jones suggests growth rates for three distinct periods that are 0.3 percent, 1650–1725; 0.4 percent, 1725–1750; and 0.5 percent, 1750–1775.[17] Although the acceleration of growth implied by her figures may be challenged, the range seems reasonable in light of the improvements we have already noted and also in light of England's estimated annual economic growth rate of 0.3 percent throughout most of the eighteenth century.[18]

PER CAPITA WEALTH AND INCOME, 1774

Reflecting upon the ordeals of first settlement, such as "the lost colony" at Roanoke and the "starving time" in early Jamestown, projects stark contrast to the economic

---

[16] Alice Hanson Jones, *Wealth of a Nation to Be* (New York: Columbia University Press, 1980), p. 305.

[17] Jones, p. 78.

[18] See Phyllis Deane and W. A. Cole, *British Economic Growth, 1688–1959: Trends and Structure* (London: Cambridge University Press, 1964), p. 80.

conditions of colonial life on the eve of the Revolution. From distant Scotland in 1776, Adam Smith declared in his *Wealth of Nations:*

> There are no colonies of which the progress has been more rapid than that of the English in North America. Plenty of good land, and liberty to manage their affairs their own way, seem to be the two great causes of the prosperity.

Contemporaries in the colonies also supported this view. As early as 1663, the Reverend John Higginson of Boston could observe, "We live in a more plentifull and comfortable manner than ever we did expect." And by the 1740s Benjamin Franklin could remark, "The first drudgery of settling new colonies, which confines the attention of people to mere necessities, is now pretty well over; and there are many in every province in circumstances that set them at ease . . ."[19] Indeed, by most any standards of comparison, the quality of life and standards of material well-being were extraordinarily high for free Americans by the end of the colonial period. They lived longer and better than populations of other nations and places at the time, and better than most people throughout the world today.

The quantitative basis for accepting the sweeping conclusions reported above also stems from the work of Alice Jones. Her wealth estimates for 1774 are shown in Table 5-3. These are nonhuman physical wealth holdings (excluding financial debts and slavery and indenture contracts) per capita and per free person in the separate regions. Table 5-4 on the next page shows several income estimates per capita and per free

TABLE 5-3   PRIVATE NONHUMAN PHYSICAL WEALTH, 1774 (IN POUNDS STERLING)

Region	Per Capita	Per Free Capita
New England	36.4	38.0
Middle Colonies	40.2	44.1
Southern Colonies	36.4	61.6
Thirteen Colonies	37.4	48.4

SOURCE: ADAPTED FROM ALICE HANSON JONES, *WEALTH OF A NATION TO BE* (NEW YORK: COLUMBIA UNIVERSITY PRESS, 1980), PP. 54, 58.

[19] Stuart Bruchey, ed., *The Colonial Merchant: Sources and Readings* (New York: Harcourt Brace Jovanovich, 1966), p. 1.

TABLE 5-4   ESTIMATES OF REGIONAL INCOMES, 1774 (IN POUNDS STERLING)

| | Capital Output Ratios | | | | | |
| | Per Capita | | | Per Free Capita | | |
Region	(3:1)	(3.5:1)	(4:1)	(3:1)	(3.5:1)	(4:1)
New England	12.1	10.4	9.1	12.7	10.9	9.5
Middle Colonies	13.4	11.5	10.0	14.7	12.6	11.0
Southern Colonies	12.1	10.4	9.1	20.5	17.6	15.4
Thirteen Colonies	12.5	10.7	9.4	16.1	13.8	12.1

SOURCE: ADAPTED FROM ALICE HANSON JONES, *WEALTH OF A NATION TO BE* (NEW YORK: COLUMBIA UNIVERSITY PRESS, 1980), P. 63.

NOTE: These estimates of income per capita and for the free population are derived from Alice Hanson Jones's wealth estimates by using her assumption of a capital-to-income ratio of 3.5:1 and two others (3:1 and 4:1) to widen the analysis somewhat. It bears remembering that these income estimates are only approximate. Estimates of wealth stocks can be converted into income flows by dividing the wealth estimates by a capital-output ratio, but the relationship between capital and output (the capital-output ratio) is influenced by many different factors and varies both over time and among countries and regions. Nevertheless, under normal peacetime conditions, the capital-output ratio is seldom lower than 3 or higher than 5.

person derived from the wealth figures in Table 5-3 by using capital-output ratios. Actual incomes estimated from wealth holdings would depend on the prevailing ratio of capital to output, but the range of ratios (3 to 1, 3.5 to 1, and 4 to 1) used likely brackets the true incomes earned in 1774.

Using a capital-output ratio of 3.5:1 generates an estimate of income per free person in 1774 of £13.8, or £12.1 if the ratio was 4:1. These estimates compare approximately to $1,400 and $1,200 in 1993 prices, slightly less than half the 1993 official U.S. poverty level, but obviously the range of goods and other conditions of life and errors of estimation make any such comparisons extremely crude. Nevertheless, we can safely guess that free colonials enjoyed surprisingly high standards of living for the world at that time. Because taxes in the colonies were much less than in England, after-tax incomes of free persons in the colonies were probably above those in the mother country on the eve of the Revolution.

Even today, relatively few countries generate average income levels that approach the earnings of free Americans on the eve of the Revolution. In fact, more than one-half of the present world population lives in countries where the average income is below the level of the typical free American's income of over 200 years ago. This is true of most people of the "Third World," including mainland China, India, Pakistan, Indonesia, and large parts of Africa and South America. Relatively speaking, free colonial Americans lived very well, both by today's standards in many areas of the world and in comparison to the most advanced areas of the world in the late eighteenth century.

THE DISTRIBUTION OF INCOME AND WEALTH

As Tables 5-3 and 5-4 illustrate, the high levels of material well-being for colonial Americans were not equally distributed regionally. By far the richest area was the South, where wealth and incomes per free capita were far above those in the Middle colonies and in New England.

Evidence from probate records of the times also permits us to estimate the distribution of wealth among individuals. It is widely believed that wealth and income in North America were fairly equitably distributed until the onset of industrialization in the early nineteenth century. However, the estimates in Table 5-5 (which includes holdings in slaves and indentured contracts) suggest that widespread inequalities of wealth and income existed much earlier. For instance, the wealthiest 20 percent of all New Englanders owned 66 percent of the total wealth there. In the Middle colonies, the wealthiest 20 percent held 53 percent of the total wealth. In the South, 70 percent of the wealth was held by the top fifth. In short, the South had the most concentrated distribution of wealth, the Middle colonies had the least. The greater southern concentration was due primarily to the dominance of wealthy plantations enjoying advantages of economies of scale in production. Slavery also added to the South's high concentrations of wealth, but note that New England had concentrations almost as high, and wealth inequalities were notably high in the port towns.

Thanks to the pioneering efforts of Jackson T. Main and James Henretta, we have learned that a growing inequality in wealth and income accompanied the very process of colonial settlement and economic maturity. As development proceeded, frontier areas were transformed into subsistence farming areas, then into commercial farming,

TABLE 5-5 TOTAL PHYSICAL WEALTH, 1774: ESTATE SIZES AND COMPOSITION FOR FREE WEALTH HOLDERS (IN POUNDS STERLING)

	All Colonies	New England	Middle Colonies	South
Mean average	£252.0	£161.2	£189.2	£394.7
Median Average	108.7	74.4	152.5	144.5
Distribution				
Bottom 20%	0.8%	1.0%	1.2%	0.7%
Top 20%	67.3	65.9	52.7	69.6
Composition				
Land	53.0%	71.4%	60.5%	45.9%
Slaves and servants	22.1	0.5	4.1	33.6
Livestock	9.2	7.5	11.3	8.8
Consumer-personal	6.7	11.2	8.4	5.1

SOURCE: ADAPTED FROM ALICE HANSON JONES, *AMERICAN COLONIAL WEALTH: DOCUMENTS AND METHODS*, 2D ED., 3 VOLS. (NEW YORK: ARNO PRESS, 1978); PRESENTED IN EDWIN PERKINS, *THE ECONOMY OF COLONIAL AMERICA*, 2D ED. (NEW YORK: COLUMBIA UNIVERSITY PRESS, 1988), P. 219.

and finally, in some instances, into urban areas. In Main's opinion, this increasing commercialization resulted in greater inequality in the distribution of colonial wealth and income.[20]

Other studies by James Henretta and Bruce D. Daniels also suggest a growth in the inequality of colonial wealth distribution within regions over time.[21] Comparing two Boston tax lists, Henretta found that the top 10 percent of Boston's taxpayers owned 42 percent of its wealth in 1687, whereas they owned 57 percent in 1771.[22] Daniels surveyed many New England probate records and therefore was able to tentatively confirm Main's contention that as economic activity grew more complex in the colonies it tended to produce a greater concentration of wealth. Apparently, as subsistence production gave way to market production, the interdependence among colonial producers generated (or at least was accompanied by) a greater disparity in wealth. This was true both in older and in more recently settled agricultural areas. Alternatively, large established urban areas such as Boston and Hartford exhibited a fairly stable distribution of wealth throughout the eighteenth century until 1776. These urban centers also reflected the greatest degree of wealth inequality in the colonies. Smaller towns showed less inequality, but as towns grew, their inequality also increased.

Particularly high levels of affluence were observed in the port towns and cities where merchant classes were forming and gaining an economic hold. Especially influential were the merchant shipowners, who were engaged in the export-import trade and were considered to be in the upper class of society. In addition, urbanization and industrialization produced another class group: a free labor force that owned little or no property.

Probably one-third of the free population possessed few assets (according to estate records and tax rolls), but as Jackson Main has argued and Mary Schweitzer's work supports, these were not a permanent underclass of free poor people. These were mostly young people in their twenties, still dependent on parents or relatives. Through gifts and savings and other sources, marriage usually tripled household wealth almost immediately. There were also wandering poor, but their numbers grew more slowly than the total population.

Not only occupation, marriage, and property ownership but also circumstances determined by birth greatly influenced a person's social standing. Race and sex were major factors. Some women were wealthy, but typically they owned far less property than men and very few owned land. The rise of slave labor after 1675 furthered the overall rise of wealth inequality in the colonies.

---

[20]Jackson T. Main, *The Social Structure of Revolutionary America* (Princeton, New Jersey: Princeton University Press, 1965).

[21]James Henretta, "Economic Development and Social Structure in Colonial Boston," *William and Mary Quarterly* 22 (1965): 93–105; and Bruce D. Daniels, "Long-range Trends of Wealth Distribution in Eighteenth-Century New England," *Explorations in Economic History* 11 (1973–1974): 123–135.

[22]Henretta's 1771 estimate was later revised downward to 48 percent by Gerard Warden, who found historical inconsistencies in the evaluation of assets in the tax lists on which Henretta's study was based. This adjustment modifies substantially the argument for rapidly rising inequality in Boston, but not the overall picture of substantial inequality of wealthy holdings there.

The urban wealth portrayed here stands in stark contrast to the mud huts of Virginia's first English settlers.

It is a statistical curiosity, however, that throughout most of the colonial period up to 1775, growing wealth concentration did not occur among free whites in the thirteen colonies as a whole. Although growing inequality occurred within specific regions and localities, this did not occur in the aggregate. This is because the lower wealth concentration areas, the rural and especially the new frontier areas, contained over 90 percent of the population. These grew as fast or faster than the urban areas, therefore offsetting the modest growth of inequality of the urban centers.[23] As an added statistical oddity, although rural wealth holdings (per free person) were less than urban holdings within each region, in the aggregate rural wealth holdings averaged above urban holdings. This reversal in order happened because of the very high wealth holdings per free person in the South, which actually exceeded the average wealth holdings of northern urban residents. In any case, despite these peculiarities of aggregation, substantial wealth inequality was a fact of economic life long before the age of industrialization and the period of rapid and sustained economic growth that occurred in the

---

[23]Jeffrey G. Williamson and Peter H. Lindert, *American Inequality: A Macroeconomic History* (New York: Academic Press, 1980), pp. 21–31.

nineteenth century. The absence of growing inequality of wealth among free Americans implies that the growth of per capita income and wealth was shared widely among these nearly 1.8 million people.

On the eve of the Revolution, their sense of well-being and economic outlook was undoubtedly positive. British interference and changing taxation policies were threats that a powerful young emerging nation was willing and able to overcome.

SELECTED REFERENCES AND SUGGESTED READINGS

Anderson, Terry. "Economic Growth in Colonial New England: 'Statistical Renaissance.' " *Journal of Economic History* 39 (1979): 243–257.

_____. *The Economic Growth of Seventeenth-Century New England: A Measurement of Regional Income.* New York: Arno Press, 1975.

Anderson, Terry, and Robert Paul Thomas. "Economic Growth in the Seventeenth Century Colonies." *Explorations in Economic History* 15 (1978): 368–387.

_____. "White Population, Labor Force, and Extensive Growth of the New England Economy in the Seventeenth Century." *Journal of Economic History* 33 (1973): 634–661.

Ball, Duane, and Gary M. Walton. "Agricultural Productivity Change in Eighteenth-Century Pennsylvania." *Journal of Economic History* 36 (1976): 102–117.

Carr, Lois G., and Lorena S. Walsh. "Changing Life Styles in Colonial St. Mary's County." In *Economic Change in Chesapeake Colonies,* eds. G. Porter and W. Mulligan. Greenville, Delaware: Regional Economic History Research Center, 1978.

Daniels, Bruce. "Economic Development in Colonial and Revolutionary Connecticut: An Overview." *William and Mary Quarterly* 37 (1980): 427–450.

_____. "Long Range Trends of Wealth Distribution in Eighteenth-Century New England." *Explorations in Economic History* 11 (1973–1974): 123–135.

Doerflinger, Thomas. *A Vigorous Spirit of Enterprise: Merchants and Economic Development in Revolutionary Philadelphia.* Chapel Hill: University of North Carolina Press, 1986.

Egnal, Marc. "The Economic Development of the Thirteen Continental Colonies, 1720 to 1775." *William and Mary Quarterly* 32 (1975): 191–222.

Galenson, David, and Russell Menard. "Economics and Early American History." *Newberry Papers,* No. 77-4E. Chicago, 1978.

Hanson, John R. "The Economic Development of the Thirteen Colonies, 1720 to 1775: A Critique." *William and Mary Quarterly* 37 (1980): 165–172.

Jones, Alice H. *American Colonial Wealth: Documents and Methods.* New York: Arno Press, 1978, 3 vols.

_____. *Wealth of a Nation to Be: The American Colonies on the Eve of the Revolution.* New York: Columbia University Press, 1980.

Jones, Douglas L. "The Strolling Poor: Transiency in Eighteenth-Century Massachusetts." *Journal of Social History* (1975): 28–54.

Kulikoff, Allan. *Tobacco and Slaves: The Development of Southern Cultures in the Chesapeake, 1680–1800.* Chapel Hill: University of North Carolina Press, 1986.

_____. "The Economic Growth of the Eighteenth-Century Chesapeake Colonies." *Journal of Economic History* 39 (1979): 275–288.

Maddison, Angus. "A Comparison of Levels of GDP Per Capita in Developed and Developing Countries, 1700–1980." *Journal of Economic History* 43 (1983): 27–41.

Main, Gloria. "The Standard of Living in Colonial Massachusetts." *Journal of Economic History* 43 (1983): 101–108.

_____. *Tobacco Colony: Life in Early Maryland.* Princeton, New Jersey: Princeton University Press, 1982.

Main, Gloria, and Jackson T. Main. "Economic Growth and the Standard of Living in Southern New England, 1640–1774." *Journal of Economic History* 48 (1988): 27–46.

Main, Jackson T. "Standard of Living and Life Cycle in Colonial Connecticut." *Journal of Economic History* 43 (1983): 159–165.

McCusker, John J., and Russell R. Menard. *The Economy of British America, 1607–1789.* Chapel Hill: University of North Carolina Press, 1985. Chapters 3 and 12.

Paskoff, Paul. "Labor Productivity and Managerial Efficiency against a Static Technology: The Pennsylvania Iron Industry, 1750–1800." *Journal of Economic History* 40 (1980): 129–135.

Pencak, William. "The Social Structure of Revolutionary Boston: Evidence from the Great Fire of 1760." *Journal of Interdisciplinary History* (1979): 267–278.

Perkins, Edwin. *The Economy of Colonial America,* 2d ed. New York: Columbia University Press, 1988. Chapter 9.

_____. "The Material Lives of Laboring Philadelphians, 1750 to 1800." *William and Mary Quarterly* 38 (1981): 163–202.

Schweitzer, Mary. *Custom and Contract: Household Government and the Economy in Colonial Pennsylvania.* New York: Columbia University Press, 1987.

Smith, Billy G. "Inequality in Late Colonial Philadelphia: A Note on Its Nature and Growth." *William and Mary Quarterly* 41 (1984): 629–645.

Walsh, Lorena S. "Urban Amenities and Rural Sufficiency: Living Standards and Consumer Behavior in the Colonial Chesapeake, 1643–1777." *Journal of Economic History* 43 (1983): 109–117.

CHAPTER SIX

THREE CRISES AND REVOLT

CHAPTER THEME At the close of the French and Indian War (also called the Seven Years' War), when the French were eliminated as a rival power in North America, Britain's mainland colonies were on the brink of another wave of economic growth and rising prosperity. In accordance with British practices of colonization, the colonists remained English citizens with all rights due the King's subjects under the laws of England. For financial, administrative, and political reasons, the Crown and Parliament in 1763 launched a "new order." Misguided policies, mismanagement, and ill timing from England added political will to the economic circumstances of the colonies to steer an independent course. The American Revolution was the outcome.

THE OLD COLONIAL POLICY

Being part of the British Empire, and in accord with English laws and institutions, colonial governments were patterned after England's governmental organization. Although originally there were corporate colonies (Connecticut and Rhode Island) and proprietary colonies (Pennsylvania and Maryland), most eventually became Crown colonies and all had similar governing organizations. For example, after 1625, Virginia was a characteristic Crown colony, and both its governor and council (the upper house) were appointed by the Crown. But only the lower house could initiate fiscal legislation, and this body was elected by the propertied adult males within the colony.

Although all laws could be vetoed by the governor and the Crown, power gradually shifted to the lower houses as colonial legislative bodies increasingly tended to imitate the House of Commons in England. The colonists controlled the lower houses—and therefore the purse strings—thereby generating a climate of political freedom and independence in the colonies. Governors, who were generally expected to represent the will of the Empire and to veto legislation contrary to British interests, were often not only sympathetic to the colonists but also dependent on the legislatures for their salaries (which were frequently in arrears). Consequently, the actual control of civil affairs generally rested with the colonists themselves, through their representatives.

Of course, the power that permitted this state of affairs to exist rested in England, and the extent of local autonomy was officially limited. After the shift in power in England from the Crown to Parliament in 1690, the Privy Council reviewed all laws passed in the colonies as a matter of common procedure. According to official procedure, colonial laws were not in effect until the Privy Council granted its approval, and sometimes the council vetoed legislation passed in the colonies. Time, distance, and bureaucratic apathy, however, often permitted colonial laws and actions to become effective before they were even reviewed in England; and if a vetoed piece of legislation was highly desired by the colonists, it could be reworded and resubmitted.

In short, day-to-day events in the colonies were influenced only modestly by British directives. Indeed, government activity—whether British or colonial—was a relatively minor aspect of colonial affairs. The burdens of defense, for example, fell on the shoulders of those in Britain, not on those in the colonies, and colonists were among the most lightly taxed people in the world. Furthermore, the colonists themselves held the power to resolve issues of a local nature. They had no central or unifying government,[1] but the colonial governments had organized themselves to the point in the early eighteenth century where they appointed officials, granted western lands, negotiated with the Indians, raised taxes, provided poor relief, and the like. In this way, British subjects in the New World enjoyed extensive freedom of self-determination throughout most of the colonial period.

The main provisions of the early Navigation Acts, which imposed the most important restrictions on colonial economic freedom, formed the basis of the old colonial policy. Recall that these laws epitomized British mercantilism, and that their aim was

---

[1] In 1754 Ben Franklin had proposed a new unified colonial administration, but his idea was rejected.

threefold: (1) to protect and encourage English and colonial shipping; (2) to ensure that major colonial imports from Europe were shipped from British ports; and (3) to make sure that the bulk of desired colonial products—the enumerated articles—were shipped to England.

The first Acts of Trade and Navigation (in 1651, 1660, and 1663) introduced these concepts concerning the colonies' relationship with the Empire. Colonial settlers and investors had always been aware of the restrictions on their economic activities. Rules were changed gradually and, until 1763, in such a way that American colonists voiced no serious complaints. Articles were added to the enumerated list over a long period of time. At first, the list consisted entirely of southern continental and West Indian products, most importantly tobacco, sugar, cotton, dyewood, and indigo. Rice and molasses were not added until 1704, naval stores until 1705 and 1729, and furs and skins until 1721. Whenever enumeration resulted in obvious and unreasonable hardship, relief might be granted. For example, the requirement that rice be sent to England added so much to shipping and handling costs that the American product, despite its superior quality, was priced out of southern European markets. Consequently, laws passed in the 1730s allowed rice to be shipped directly to ports south of Cape Finisterre, a promontory in northwestern Spain.

Commodities were enumerated if they were especially important to English manufacturers or were expected to yield substantial customs revenue. However, the requirements of shipping listed items to English ports were less onerous than we might initially suppose. First, because the Americans and the English shared general ties of blood and language (and, more specifically, because their credit contacts were more easily established), the colonists would have dealt primarily with English merchants anyway. Second, duties charged on commodities that were largely reexported, such as tobacco, were remitted entirely or in large part to the colonies. Third, bounties were paid on some of the enumerated articles. Fourth, it was permissible to ship certain items on the list directly from one colony to another for the purpose of furnishing essential supplies. Finally, the laws could be evaded through smuggling; with the exception of molasses, such evasion was probably neither more nor less common in the colonies than it was in Europe during the seventeenth and eighteenth centuries.

With respect to colonial imports, the effect of the Navigation Acts was to distort somewhat—but not to influence materially—the flows of trade. The fact that goods had to be funneled through England added to costs and restricted trade to the colonists. Again, however, traditional ties would have made Americans the best customers of British merchants anyway. Furthermore, hardship cases were relieved by providing direct shipment of commodities like salt and wine to America from ports south of Cape Finisterre.

If English manufacturers were to be granted special advantages over other European manufacturers in British American markets, should restrictions also be placed on competing colonial manufacturers? Many British manufacturers felt that such "duplicate production" should be prohibited and tried to convince Parliament that colonial manufacturing was not in the best interest of the Empire. In 1699, a law made it illegal to export colonial wool, wool yarn, and finished wool products to any foreign country or even to other colonies. Later, Americans (many of Dutch origin) were forbidden to export hats made of beaver fur. Toward midcentury, a controversy arose in England over the regulation of iron manufactures; after 1750, pig and bar iron were admitted into England duty free and the colonial manufacture of finished iron products was expressly forbidden. The fact that these were the only prohibitive laws directed at colonial manufacturing indicates Britain's lack of fear of American competition.

After all, England enjoyed a distinct comparative advantage in manufacturing, and the colonies' comparative advantage in production lay overwhelmingly in agriculture and other resource-intensive products from the seas and forests. Note that the important shipbuilding industry in the colonies was not curtailed by British legislation; indeed, it was supported by Parliament. Therefore, any piecemeal actions to prevent colonial manufacturing activities appear to have been taken largely to favor particular vested interests in England, especially those with influence and effective lobbying practices.

The laws prohibiting colonial manufactures were loosely enforced; they were restrictive and a cause of annoyance, but they did not seriously affect the course of early American industrial development or the colonial quest for independence. Also, the economic controls that England imposed on the colonies were less strict than the colonial controls other European countries imposed, and these controls were less harsh for Americans than for Ireland and other colonies within the Empire. We should not, however, misapprehend the trend of enforcement of the old colonial policy. Regulation of external colonial trade was progressively strengthened. Beginning in 1675, governors were supplied with staffs of officials to aid in enforcing trade regulations; after the general reorganization of 1696, the powers of these officials were sufficient to provide considerable surveillance and commercial regulation.

The only trade law flaunted with impunity was the Molasses Act of 1733—an act that, if enforced, would have disrupted one of the major colonial trades and resulted in serious repercussions, especially in New England. Before 1700, New England had traded primarily with the British possessions in the West Indies. In time, however, British planters failed to provide a sufficient market for northern colonial goods, and sugar and molasses from the increasingly productive French islands became cheaper than the English staples. During the same period, British planters in the sugar islands were hurt by the requirement that cane products be shipped to England before being reexported. In an effort to protect British West Indian holdings, Parliament imposed high duties on foreign (predominantly French) sugar, molasses, and rum imported to the English colonies. The strict levying of these duties and the prevention of smuggling would have suppressed the market of northern staples in the West Indies and would have seriously curtailed all trade involving rum. New Englanders felt they had no feasible alternative, because they had to sell their fish, provisions, lumber, and rum to pay for their imports. Rather than accept such hardships, the New Englanders continued to trade as usual; instead of facing the issue resolutely, English officials, many of whom were routinely bribed (10 percent being the custom for "looking the other way"), made no serious attempts to enforce trade regulations. Some 30 years later, after the matter had been raised time after time, the Sugar Act of 1764 ruled against the American colonists in favor of the British West Indian planters. This decision to impose and collect the tax was a key factor in bringing on the first crisis leading to revolution.

THE NEW COLONIAL POLICY AND THE FIRST CRISIS

The events that led to the American Revolution are more clear if we repeat and keep in mind its central underlying theme: new and rapid changes in the old colonial policy that had been established and imposed on an essentially self-governing people for 150 years precipitated a series of crises and, ultimately, war. These crises were essentially political, but the stresses and strains that led to colonial fear and hatred of British authority had economic origins. Britain's "new" colonial policy was only an extension of the old, with one difference: the new enactments were adopted by a Parliament and enforced by bureaucratic oversight that had every intention of enforcing them to the letter of the law, thereby sharply changing the atmosphere of freedom in the colonies. Furthermore, high British officials insisted—at almost precisely the wrong moments—on taking punitive actions that only compounded the bitterness they had already stirred up in the colonies.

The series of critical events that generated the first crisis began with the English victory over the French in 1763. The Seven Years' War had been a struggle for empire, of course, but it had also been a fight for the protection of the American colonies. And the colonials had only been of limited help in furnishing England with either troops or materials—to say nothing of the hurtful trade they intermittently carried on with the French in both Canada and the West Indies. The English were in no mood to spare the feelings of an upstart people who had committed the cardinal sin of ingratitude. Besides, the war had placed a heavy burden on the English treasury, and British taxes per capita in the mid-1760s were probably the highest in the world.[2] Interest on the national debt had soared to £5 million annually (nearly $500 million in today's values), and land taxes in England had doubled during the war. To many Englishmen, especially taxpayers, it seemed only fair that American colonists be asked to contribute to the support of the garrisons still required on their frontier.

Despite their substantial wealth, the colonists at this time were still free riders of protection, receiving British defense at almost no cost. Taxes per capita in the colonies were among the lowest in the world, just 20 to 25 percent of taxes paid by the average English resident.

George Grenville, England's Prime Minister, proposed stationing a British force of some 10,000 men in the North American possessions. Although the actual number realized was closer to 6,000, their costs were over £350,000 annually. To help meet these costs, Parliament passed two laws to generate approximately one-tenth of this revenue. Of the two laws, the Sugar Act of 1764 had more far-reaching economic implications for the colonists, because it contained provisions that served the ends of all major English economic interests and threatened many American businesses in the colonies. But the Stamp Act of 1765, although really much less inclusive, incited political tempers to a boil that in a very real sense started the first step towards rebellion.

---

[2]Lance E. Davis and Robert A. Huttenback, "The Cost of Empire," in *Explorations in the New Economic History*, eds. Roger L. Ransom, Richard Sutch, and Gary M. Walton (New York: Academic Press, 1982), p. 42.

The most important clauses of the Sugar Act levied taxes on imports of non-British products of the West Indies. Although the duty on foreign molasses was actually lowered from 6d. to 3d. a gallon—a marked reduction from the rate set by the old Molasses Act—provision was made for strict collection of the tax in the belief that the smaller tax, if strictly enforced, would produce a larger revenue. (A similar argument is characteristic of today's supply-side economics.) A more important goal, however, was the protection of British West Indian planters—who were well represented in Parliament—from the competition of New England rum makers. Actually, more than half of the molasses imported by colonials was used in homes to make Boston baked beans, shoofly pie, apple pandowdy, and molasses jack (a kind of home-brewed beer); but the chief fear of the English sugar planters was that cheap molasses imports from the French West Indies would enable the New England rum distilleries to capture the rum market on the mainland as well as in the non-British islands.[3] And their concern was probably justified, despite the alleged inferiority of the New England product. Moreover, the Sugar Act added to the list of enumerated articles several raw materials demanded by British manufacturers, including some important exports of the northern and Middle colonies. Finally, this comprehensive law removed most of the tariff rebates (drawbacks) previously allowed on European goods that passed through English ports and even placed new duties on foreign textiles that competed with English products. Nevertheless, the Sugar Act, in form and substance, was just like earlier acts passed to restrict and control trade.

The Stamp Act, on the other hand, was simply designed to raise revenue and served no ends of mercantile policy. The law required that stamps varying in cost from half a penny to several pounds be affixed to legal documents, contracts, newspapers and pamphlets, and even playing cards and dice.

According to Benjamin Franklin's argument to Parliament against the tax, the colonists objected on the grounds that the act levied an "internal" tax, as distinguished from the traditional "external" taxes or duties collected on goods imported to the colonies. When English ministers refused to recognize this distinction, the colonists further objected that the tax had been levied by a distant Parliament that did not contain a single colonial representative. Thus was born the colonial rallying cry, "no taxation without representation!" Colonists complained that both the Sugar Act and the Stamp Act required the tax revenues to be remitted to England for disbursement, a procedure that further drained the colonies of precious specie and constantly reduced the amount of goods that could be imported to America. When it became apparent that strict enforcement would accompany such measures, severe resistance arose in the colonies. Lawyers and printers—who were especially infuriated by the Stamp Act—furnished articulate, able leadership and communication for anti-British agitation.

The decade of trouble that followed was characterized by alternating periods of colonial insubordination, British concession, renewed attempts to raise revenues, further colonial resistance, and, at last, punitive action—taken by the British in anger at

---

[3]For the details of this controversy, see Gilman M. Ostrander, "The Colonial Molasses Trade," *Agricultural History* 30 (1956): 77–84. See also Stuart Bruchey, *The Colonial Merchant* (New York: Harcourt Brace Jovanovich, 1966), pp. 67–78.

what was felt to be rank disloyalty. The so-called Stamp Act Congress met in New York in 1765, passed resolutions of fealty, and organized a boycott of English goods. "Nonimportation associations" were established throughout the colonies, and the volume of imports from Britain declined dramatically as docks and warehouses bulged with unsold British goods.

A concerted effort to boycott English goods did not develop in all regions. The Middle colonies—where the boycotts first centered—exhibited the greatest decrease in trade with England. The Upper South contributed effectively to the boycott, largely because of the Restraining Act of 1764 curtailing Virginia's paper money issues (see Chapter 4). New England gave only slight support to these first nonimport agreements, and the lower South failed to join in the boycott. Yet overall, colonial efforts to boycott British imports were very effective. In fact, English merchants were so sharply affected that they demanded the repeal of the Stamp Act. They were joined by such political leaders as Edmund Burke and William Pitt, whose sympathies lay with the colonists. Parliament promptly responded, repealing the Stamp Act and reducing the duty on foreign molasses from 3d. to 1d. per gallon. Thus the first major confrontation between America and England ended peacefully, and a profound lesson had been learned. In the mercantilist scheme of things, the Empire had tilted. The American mainland colonies ultimately had become as important a market for English wares as they and the West Indian planters were a source of raw materials. Americans as consumers had found a new and powerful economic weapon—the boycott.

MORE CHANGES AND THE SECOND CRISIS

Although Parliament had responded to economic pressure from America by repealing the Stamp Act, England angrily and obstinately maintained its *right* to tax the colonies. The other sugar duties remained, and the Declaratory Act of 1766 affirmed the right of Parliament to legislate in all matters concerning Americans. Nevertheless, there was rejoicing both in the colonies and in England, and it was generally believed that their differences would be reconciled. But even then, the Quartering Act of 1765 had been on the statute books a year, with its stipulations that the colonial assemblies provide barracks, some provisions, and part of the costs of military transport for British troops stationed within the colonies. This law was to prove especially problematic in New York, where soldiers were to be concentrated on their way to the West. Much worse was to come, however. George Grenville had been dismissed from the British ministry in 1765, largely because King George III (aged 25) disliked him. Grenville was replaced as Chancellor of the Exchequer by Charles Townshend. Because the great English landowners were persistently clamoring for relief from their heavy property taxes, Townshend tried once again to raise revenues in America. He felt that if the colonials objected to "internal" taxes, he would provide them with some "external" duties levied on such important articles of consumption as tea, glass, paper, and red and white lead (pigments for paint). By 1767, the Townshend duties were imposed.

Although these dutied items were definitely important to colonial life, the colonists might have accepted their taxation calmly if the British had not adopted measures to put real teeth into the law. One of the Townshend Acts provided for an American Customs Board, another for the issuance by colonial courts of the hated general search warrants known as *writs of assistance,* and another for admiralty courts in Halifax, Boston, Philadelphia, and Charleston to try smuggling cases. With a single stroke, the British ministry succeeded once again in antagonizing a wide cross-section of the American populace, and again resistance flared—this time in the form of both peaceful petitions and mob violence, culminating in the 1770 Boston Massacre, which left five colonials dead. Once more the nonimportation agreements, especially effective in the port towns, were imposed. Only in the Chesapeake colonies—the one major colonial region spared a court of admiralty—was this boycott fairly unsuccessful.[4] Nevertheless, by late 1769, American imports had declined to perhaps one-third of their normal level. The value of lost English sales in the colonies exceeded £1 million in 1768 and 1769 combined, and once again English merchants exerted pressure to change trade policy. For the second time, Parliament appeared to acquiesce to colonial demands. In 1770, all the Townshend duties except the duty on tea were repealed, and although some of the most distasteful acts remained on the books, everyone except a few colonial hotheads felt that a peaceful settlement was possible. Trade was resumed, and a new level of prosperity was reached in 1771.

THE THIRD CRISIS AND REBELLION

Reasonable calm prevailed until 1773, when resistance flared up again over what now seems to have been an inconsequential matter. The English East India Company, in which many politically powerful people owned an interest, was experiencing financial difficulties. Parliament had granted the company a loan of public funds (like Congress gave the Chrysler Corporation in 1981) and had also passed the Tea Act of 1773, which permitted the company to handle tea sales in a new way. Until this time, the company, which enjoyed a monopoly on the trade from India, had sold tea to English wholesalers, who in turn sold it to jobbers, who sent it to America. There the tea was turned over to colonial wholesalers, who at last distributed it to American retailers. Overall, many people had received income from this series of transactions; besides, duties had been collected on the product when it reached English ports and again when it arrived in America. The new Tea Act allowed the East India Company to ship tea directly to the colonies, thereby eliminating the British duty and reducing handling costs. Consumers were to benefit by paying less for tea, the company would presumably sell more tea at a lower price, and everybody would be happy. Only everybody was not happy. Smugglers of Dutch tea were now undersold, the colonial tax was still collected (a real sore point), and most importantly, the American importer was removed from the picture, thus alarming American merchants. If the colonial tea wholesaler could be

---

[4]Another contributing factor may have been that trade in the Chesapeake region was relatively decentralized, thereby reducing the possibility of blacklisting or boycotting colonial importers and others who failed to join the effort.

Angered colonists disguised as Indians, invited themselves to a "tea party" to show the British how they felt about English mercantile policies. The damage to property was nearly £9,000 (about $900,000 in 1993 values).

bypassed, couldn't the business of other merchants also be undercut? Couldn't other companies in Great Britain be granted monopoly control of other commodities, until eventually Americans were reduced to keeping small shops and selling at retail what their foreign masters imported for them? Wouldn't just a few pro-British agents who would handle the necessary distribution processes grow rich while staunch Americans grew poor? The list of rhetorical questions grew, and the answers seemed clear to almost every colonist engaged in business. From wealthy merchants in Boston to shopkeepers in the hamlets, there was a swift and violent reaction. Tea in the port towns was sent back to England or destroyed in various ways—the most spectacular of which was the Boston Tea Party, a well-executed three-hour affair involving 30 to 40 men. Many colonists were shocked at this wanton destruction of private property, estimated at nearly £9,000 (or nearly $900,000 in 1993 prices), but their reaction was mild compared with the indignation that swelled in Britain.

The result was the bitter and punitive legislation known as the Intolerable Acts. Passed in the early summer of 1774, the Intolerable Acts (1) closed the port of Boston to all shipping until the colonists paid the East India Company for its tea, (2) permitted British officials charged with crimes committed in an American colony while enforcing British laws to be tried in another colony or in Britain, (3) revised the charter of Massachusetts to make certain cherished rights dependent on the arbitrary decision

This illustration emphasizes the political antagonisms launched by the Intolerable Acts in 1774.

of the Crown-appointed governor, and (4) provided for the quartering of troops in the city of Boston, which was especially obnoxious to the citizens after the events of the Boston Massacre four years earlier. In the ensuing months, political agitation reached new heights of violence, and economic sanctions were again invoked. For the third time, nonimportation agreements were imposed, and the delegates to the First Continental Congress voted not to trade with England or the British West Indies unless concessions were made. On October 14, 1774, the Continental Congress provided a list of grievances:

1. Taxes had been imposed upon the colonies by the "British" Parliament.
2. Parliament had claimed the right to legislate for the colonies.
3. Commissioners were set up in the colonies to collect taxes.
4. Admiralty court jurisdictions had been extended into the interior.
5. Judges' tenures had been put at the pleasure of the Crown.
6. A standing army had been imposed upon the colonies.
7. Persons could be transported out of the colonies for trials.
8. The port of Boston had been closed.

long-run perspective, such conjectures defy empirical testing. After all, how can we judge whether independence or British rule offered more promise for economic progress in North America?

Of course, the short-run consequences of independence can be assessed—a task that awaits us in Chapter 7. But at this point, it is important to reconsider the question of colonial exploitation as a motive for revolt. Did British trade restrictions drain the colonial economy?

First, manufacturing restrictions had been placed on woolens, hats, and finished iron products. Woolen production in the colonies was limited to personal use or local trade, so this imposed no significant hardship. The colonists were quite satisfied to purchase manufactures from England at the lower costs made possible by the large-scale production methods employed there. This situation continued even after independence was achieved, and American woolens provided no competition for imported English fabrics until the nineteenth century.

A small portion of colonial manufacturing activity (predominantly New York producers) was hurt by the passage of the Hat Act in 1732. This one-sided legislation benefited London hatters by prohibiting the colonial export of beaver hats. For the overall American economy, however, the effects of the Hat Act were negligible. Similarly, parliamentary restrictions on iron proved moderately harmless. Actually the colonial production of raw pig and bar iron was encouraged, but the finishing of iron and steel and the use of certain types of equipment were forbidden after 1750. Nevertheless, like the Molasses Act of 1733, restrictions on the manufacture of colonial iron were ignored with impunity: 25 iron mills were established between 1750 and 1775 in Pennsylvania and Delaware alone. Furthermore, the legislative freedom enjoyed by the colonists was amply displayed when the Pennsylvania assembly, in open defiance of the law, appropriated financial aid for a new slitting mill (nail factory). No matter how distasteful these British regulations were to the colonists, they were either superfluous (woolen restrictions), ignored (the slitting mill), or inconsequential (hat production).

The generally liberal British land policy was designed to encourage rapid settlement. Only after the war with Chief Pontiac and the resulting Royal Proclamation of 1763 did land policy suddenly become less flexible. When land controls were tightened again by the Quebec Act of 1774, important political issues emerged. Western lands claimed by Massachusetts, Connecticut, and Virginia were redistributed to the Province of Quebec, and land was made less accessible. Territorial governments were placed entirely in the hands of British officials, and trials there were conducted without juries.

We have already assessed the economic implications of these land policies. Some people gained; others lost. But clearly the climate of freedom changed swiftly, and the political implications of these new policies were hard for the colonists to accept. The major issue appears to have been who was to determine the policy, rather than what the policy itself was to be. In fact, the British land policies proved to be largely necessary, and the same basic restraints were prescribed and adopted by the federal government after American independence was achieved. It seems unlikely that the new government would have adopted these restraints if they had been economically burdensome.

The same thing was true of currency restrictions. After independence, the new government adopted measures similar to those England had imposed earlier. For instance,
in 1751, Parliament passed the Currency Act, which prohibited New England from
establishing new public banks and from issuing more paper money. A similar and sup-
plemental Restraining Act appeared in 1764, in the wake of events in the Chesapeake
area. Planters there were heavily in debt because they had continued to import goods
during the Seven Years' War even though their own exports had declined. When Virginia issued £250,000 in bills of credit, to be used as legal tender in private transactions
as well as for public sector payments (mainly taxes), British creditors stood to lose.
When the planters began to use cheap money to repay debts they had incurred in hard
sterling, Britain countered by extending the original Currency Act to all the colonies.
This enactment certainly hurt the hard-pressed Chesapeake region and stimulated its
unusual support for the boycott of English imports in 1765. But the adoption of similar
controls after independence indicates that the economic burden of currency restriction
could not have been oppressive overall. The real point at issue was simply whether
England or the colonists themselves should hold the reins of monetary control.

It appears that only with respect to the Navigation Acts was there any significant
exploitation in a strict economic sense. In the words of Lawrence A. Harper:

> The enumeration of key colonial exports in various Acts from 1660 to 1766 and
> the Staple Act of 1663 hit at colonial trade both coming and going. The Acts
> required the colonies to allow English middlemen to distribute such crops as
> tobacco and rice and stipulated that if the colonies would not buy English man-
> ufactures, at least they should purchase their European goods in England. The
> greatest element in the burden laid upon the colonies was not the taxes assessed.
> It consisted in the increased costs of shipment, transshipment, and middleman's
> profits arising out of the requirement that England be used as an entrepôt.[8]

While these burdens of more costly imports and less remunerative colonial exports
amounted to nearly 1 percent of total colonial income, there were also benefits to the
colonies: they were provided with bounties and other benefits such as naval protection
and military defense at British expense.

In any case, the colonists had lived with these restrictions for over a century. Even
those hardest hit—the producers of tobacco and other enumerated products—almost
never mentioned them in their lists of grievances against England. It is especially noteworthy that *the acts of trade are not even mentioned in the Declaration of Independence.*

Rather than exploitation, it was the rapidly changing and severely administered new
colonial policies that precipitated the American Revolution. Before 1763, the colonists
had been free to do pretty much as they pleased. An occasional new enactment or a
veto of colonial legislation by Britain had caused little or no discord. After the Seven
Years' War, however, conditions suddenly changed. A host of new taxes and regulations
were effected and strictly enforced by Britain. The new taxes were light, but their

---

[8]Lawrence A. Harper, "The Effect of the Navigation Acts on the Thirteen Colonies," in *The Era of the
American Revolution*, ed. Richard B. Morris (New York: Columbia University Press, 1939).

Supply and demand analysis is useful to illustrate explicitly the burdens on the colonists caused by the Navigation Acts. The requirement that England be used as an "entrepôt" burdened the colonists with extra handling and shipping costs—costs over and above those that would have occurred if commodities had been shipped directly from (and to) continental Europe. A graph using supply and demand curves illustrates the case for imports:

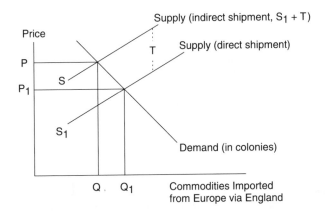

Let T represent these extra indirect routing costs on colonial imports from continental Europe. These extra costs may be viewed as a shift in the supply curve from S_1 to S. The effect of the higher transport costs is to cause prices of the affected imports to be higher in the colonies, at P rather than P_1, and quantities to be less, Q rather than Q_1.

The change in price $(P - P_1)$ times the quantities traded (Q) gives a lower bound to the burden on colonial imports from Europe. $(P - P_1)$ (Q_1) gives an upper-bound measure. A similar approach can illustrate the burdens of the laws on colonial exports to continental Europe. In this case the export price in the colonies is lower because of the law. As the work of Roger Ransom has shown, these burdens were disproportionately large on southerners. Overall, however, the burdens on imports and exports from indirect routing were less than 1 percent of colonial income.[9]

---

[9]For an assessment of the several studies and estimates of these costs, see Gary M. Walton, "The New Economic History and the Burdens of the Navigation Acts," *Economic History Review* 24, 2d series (1971): 533–542.

methods of collection bore heavily.[10] Collectively the acts after 1763 gave almost every colonist a grievance: debtors objected to the Currency Act; shippers and merchants to the Sugar Act; pioneers to the Quebec Act; politicians, printers, and gamblers to the Stamp Act; retailers and smugglers to the Tea Act. As colonial resentments flared, Committees of Correspondence pressed forward to formally claim the rights they had long held de facto before 1763.

In many ways, it appears that the growing economic maturity of the colonies would soon have made American independence inevitable. Indeed, the gross product of the colonies was nearly £25 million at the time, or nearly one-third of England's gross national product, as compared to only about 4 percent at the beginning of the eighteenth century. Clearly the colonies had matured economically to a point where an independent course was feasible.

But was Revolution necessary to break away from the Empire? After all, other English colonies subsequently gained independence without resorting to armed warfare. By 1775, according to Charles Andrews, the colonies had reached a point where they were

> qualified to cooperate with the mother country on terms similar to those of a brotherhood of free nations, such as the British world is becoming today (1926). But England was unable to see this fact, or to recognize it, and consequently America became the scene of a political unrest which might have been controlled by a compromise, but was turned to revolt by coercion. The situation is a very interesting one, for England is famous for her ability to compromise at critical times in her history. For once, at least, she failed.[11]

The nature of that "failure" is nicely summarized by Lawrence Harper:

> As a mother country, Britain had much to learn. Any modern parents' magazine could have told George III's ministers that the one mistake not to make is to take a stand and then to yield to howls of anguish. It was a mistake which the British government made repeatedly. It placed a duty of 3d. per gallon on molasses, and when it encountered opposition, reduced it to 1d. It provided for a Stamp Act and withdrew it in the face of temper tantrums. It provided for external taxes to meet the colonial objections and then yielded again by removing all except one. When finally it attempted to enforce discipline, it was too late. Under the circumstances, no self-respecting child—or colonist—would be willing to yield.[12]

---

[10]As noted by Ed Perkins, "From 1792 to 1811 U.S. per capita tax rates were over 10 times higher than the imperial taxes levied by the British from 1765 to 1775." See Perkins, *The Economics of Colonial America*, 2d ed. (New York: Columbia University Press, 1988), p. 208; again, it wasn't the weight of the financial burden but how and by whom it was imposed that mattered most.

[11]Charles Andrews, "The American Revolution: An Interpretation," *American Historical Review* 31 (1926): 232.

[12]Lawrence A. Harper, "Mercantilism and the American Revolution," *Canadian Historical Review* 25 (1942): 14.

It would appear that the lessons the English learned from their failures with the American colonies served them well in later periods, because other English colonies subsequently won their independence without widescale bloodshed. This colonial legacy was of paramount importance in the centuries to follow.

SELECTED REFERENCES
AND SUGGESTED READINGS

Barrow, Thomas. *Trade and Empire: The British Customs Service in Colonial America, 1660–1775.* Cambridge: Harvard University Press, 1967.

Becker, Robert A. *Revolution, Reform, and the Politics of Taxation in America: 1763–1783.* Baton Rouge: Louisiana State University Press, 1980.

Beer, George L. *The Old Colonial System 1660–1754.* New York: Macmillan, 1912.

Davis, Lance E., and Robert A. Huttanbeck. "The Cost of Empire." In *Explorations in the New Economic History,* eds. Roger L. Ransom, Richard Sutch, and Gary M. Walton. New York: Academic Press, 1982.

Ernst, Joseph, and Marc Egnal. "An Economic Interpretation of the American Revolution." *William and Mary Quarterly* 29 (1972): 3–32.

Hacker, Louis M. "The First American Revolution." *Columbia University Quarterly,* part 1 (September 1935). Reprinted in Gerald D. Nash. *Issues in American Economic History.* New York: D. C. Heath, 1972.

Harper, Lawrence. "The Effects of the Navigation Acts on the Thirteen Colonies." In *The Era of the American Revolution,* ed. Richard Morris. New York: Columbia University Press, 1939.

———. "Mercantilism and the American Revolution." *Canadian Historical Review* (March 1942). Reprinted in Gerald D. Nash. *Issues in American Economic History.* New York: D. C. Heath, 1972.

McClelland, Peter D. "The Cost to America of British Imperial Policy." *American Economic Review: Papers and Proceedings* 59, no. 7 (May 1969): 370–381.

Miller, John C. *Origins of the American Revolution.* Stanford, California: Stanford University Press, 1959.

Morgan, Edmund S. *The American Revolution: A Review of Changing Interpretations.* Washington, D.C.: Service Center for Teachers of History, 1958.

Morgan, Edmund, and Helen Morgan. *The Stamp Act Crisis: Prologue to Revolution.* Chapel Hill: University of North Carolina Press, 1963.

Nash, Gary. *The Urban Crucible.* Cambridge: Harvard University Press, 1979.

Nettels, Curtis P. "British Mercantilism and the Economic Development of the Thirteen Colonies." *Journal of Economic History* 12 (1952): 105–114.

Ostrander, Gilman M. "The Colonial Molasses Trade." *Agricultural History* 30 (1956): 77–84.

Perkins, Edwin J. *The Economy of Colonial America.* 2d ed. New York: Columbia University Press, 1988. Chs. 7 and 8.

Ransom, Roger. "British Policy and Colonial Growth: Some Implications of the Burdens of the Navigation Acts." *Journal of Economic History* 27 (1968): 427–435.

Reid, Joseph D. "Economic Burdens: Spark to the American Revolution?" *Journal of Economic History* 38 (1978): 81–120.

———. "On Navigating the Navigation Acts with Peter D. McClelland." *American Economic Review* 60 (1970): 949–955.

Thomas, Robert P. "British Imperial Policy and the Economic Interpretation of the American Revolution." *Journal of Economic History* 28 (1968): 436–440.

————. "A Quantitative Approach to the Study of the Effects of British Imperial Policy on Colonial Welfare: Some Preliminary Findings." *Journal of Economic History* 25 (1965): 615–638.

Tucker, Robert W., and David Hendrickson. *The Fall of the British Empire: Origins and the Fall of the British Empire.* Baltimore: Johns Hopkins University Press, 1982.

Ver Steeg, Clarence. "The American Revolutionary Movement Considered as an Economic Movement." *Huntington Library Journal* 20 (1957).

Walton, Gary M. "The New Economic History and the Burdens of the Navigation Acts." *Economic History Review* 24, 2d series, no. 4 (1971): 533–542.

Walton, Gary M., and James F. Shepherd. *The Economic Rise of Early America.* Cambridge: Cambridge University Press, 1979. Ch. 8.

PART TWO

THE REVOLUTIONARY, EARLY NATIONAL, AND ANTEBELLUM ERAS

1776–1860

ECONOMIC AND HISTORICAL
PERSPECTIVES
1776–1860

1. Industrializing Great Britain and the newly revolutionized France under Napoleon stood as the world's two leading powers. Britain was dominant in naval forces and led in per capita income; France was dominant in land forces and strong in total output, and had a larger population.

2. War broke out between Britain and France in 1793 and lasted until 1815. To help finance his war, Napoleon sold the Louisiana Territory to the United States in 1803, doubling the land size of the new nation. Trade and commerce soared in American ports as U.S. shippers served as neutrals to the belligerents. The suppression of U.S. shipping entangled the United States into a second war with Britain in 1812.

3. The Northwest Land Ordinances of 1785 and 1787 assured that new U.S. territories could progress toward statehood and enter the Union having full equality with the older states.

4. The U.S. Constitution adopted in 1789 is a landmark document, historically unprecedented for its scope and simplicity, for its constraint on government power, and as a model of political compromise. It provided assurances of protection of property consistent with individual freedoms (with the telling exception of slavery, which persisted in the South).

5. The cotton gin, invented in 1793 by Eli Whitney, allowed the seeds of short staple cotton to be economically removed. Thereafter, U.S. cotton production as a share of world production increased from 0.5 percent in 1791 to 68 percent in 1850. Southern slavery became increasingly entrenched and a growing threat to the Union as western migrations brought the proslavery and antislavery forces into continual dispute.

6. As the Industrial Revolution spread from England to the United States in the early nineteenth century, a transportation revolution also unfolded to create a strong national market linking the industrializing Northeast with the agrarian Midwest and the southern cotton kingdom.

7. By 1860 the United States was the second leading industrial power in the world.

CHAPTER SEVEN

HARD REALITIES FOR A NEW NATION

CHAPTER THEME The years from 1776 to 1815 consisted of four distinct periods: first war (the Revolution), then peace and independence, followed by war again (Napoleonic wars) with the new United States as a neutral, and finally the young nation's second war with England. These events caused economic fluctuations and imposed significant shocks on the economy, pressing resources into new areas of production as trade lanes opened and closed. Years of war generally reduced American trade and economic activity. However, during the years of war when U.S. neutrality gave American shipping and commerce the opportunities to fill the void of others who were engaged in combat, times were especially prosperous.

Even during peacetime there were great economic adjustments, because the new nation was now outside the British Empire; severe peacetime trade restrictions added to the nation's difficulties.

Finally, there were the problems of paying the debts accumulated during the Revolutionary War years and of forging agreements among the states on how to form a government based on constitutional limitations.

THE WAR AND THE ECONOMY

The Revolutionary War, which began officially on April 19, 1775, dragged on for more than six bitter years. From a vantage point two centuries later, we can see that the war foreshadowed a massive upheaval in the Western world—a chain reaction of revolutions, great and small, that would transform the world. But to the embattled colonials, it was simply a conflict fought for the righteous cause of securing freedom from intolerable British intervention in American affairs. Paradoxically, the Revolution was never supported by the substantial popular majority. Perhaps one-third of the colonists remained loyal to England; another third did little or nothing to help the cause, often trafficking with the enemy and selling provisions and supplies to American troops at profitable prices. In varying numbers and in widely scattered theaters, foot soldiers slogged wearily back and forth in heartbreaking campaigns that produced no military gains. Although there were relatively few seamen, and sea battles were for the most part militarily indecisive, it is an irony of history that the Revolutionary War was finally won with naval strength, as the French fleet under its admiral, the Comte de Grasse, drove off the British men-of-war and bottled up Cornwallis at Yorktown.

Of course, maritime commerce was always an important factor in the war effort, and trade linkages were vital to the supply of arms and ammunitions. When legal restrictions were implemented by both the British and the colonists in 1775, nearly all American overseas commerce abruptly ceased. By mid-1775, the colonies faced acute shortages in such military essentials as powder, flints, muskets, and knives. Even salt, shoes, woolens, and linens were in short supply. Late in 1775, Congress authorized limited trade with the West Indies, mainly to procure arms and ammunitions, and trade with other non-British areas was on an unrestricted basis by the spring of 1776.

Nevertheless, the British maintained a fairly effective naval blockade of American ports, especially during the first two years of the war. Boston was pried open late in 1776, but most of the other major ports in New England and the Middle colonies were tightly sealed until 1778. As the British relaxed their grip on the North, they tightened it on the South. Savannah was taken late in 1778, Charleston in 1780.

Yet the colonies engaged in international trade despite the blockade. Formal treaties of commerce—with France in 1778 and with Holland and Spain shortly thereafter—stimulated the flows of overseas trade. Between 1778 and early 1782, American wartime commerce was at its zenith. During those years, France, Holland, and Spain and their possessions all actively traded with the colonies. Even so, the flow of goods in and out of the colonies remained well below prewar levels. Smuggling, privateering, and legal trade with overseas partners only partially offset the drastic trade reductions with Britain. Even the coastal trades were curtailed by a lack of vessels, by blockades, and by wartime freight rates. British-occupied ports, such as New York, generated some import activity but little or nothing in the way of exports.

As exports and imports fell, import substitution abounded and the colonial economy became considerably more self-sufficient. In Philadelphia, for instance, nearly 4,000 women were employed to spin materials in their homes for the newly established textile plants. There was also a sharp increase in the number of artisan workshops and a similar stimulus to the production of beer, whiskey, and other domestic alcoholic beverages. The rechanneling of American resources into import-competing industries was especially strong along the coast and in the major port cities. Only the least-commercialized rural areas remained little affected by the serpentine path of war and the sporadic flows of wartime commerce.

Overall, the war imposed a distinct economic hardship on the new nation. Most goods rose in cost and were more difficult to obtain. High prices and severe commercial difficulties encouraged some investors to turn from commerce to manufacturing. Then once the trade lanes reopened with the coming of peace, even those who profited from the war were stung by the tide of imports that swept into American ports and sharply lowered prices. Although many Americans escaped the direct ordeals of war, few Americans were untouched by it—at least indirectly.

The strains of war and economic decline were complemented by the critical problem of forming a government. The thirteen colonies were bound together by the Articles of Confederation; established initially for the pressing issue of uniting to engage the enemy, it took from 1777 to 1781 for the individual states to ratify them. The Articles had merit and were effective as a source of early political agreement among the colonies, but they were inadequate as a permanent framework for national government. For example, the power to tax was left to the individual states, thus allowing any state to free-ride on revenues supplied by others. Furthermore, after independence was won, the great powers treated the new nation with a disdain that bordered on contempt. Britain, annoyed because Americans refused to pay prewar British creditors or restore confiscated Tory property as provided in the peace treaty, excluded the United States from valuable commercial privileges and refused to withdraw troops from its frontier posts on American soil. Spain tried to close the lower Mississippi to American traffic. Even France refused to extend the courtesies traditionally offered a sovereign government. These and other problems too great to be surmounted by the states acting individually pressed inexorably for a strong rather than weak union. Under the Articles, the national government appeared too weak to negotiate improvements in its economic or military relations.

Internally, the most pressing problems were financial. Between 1775 and 1781, the war was financed by the issue of paper money in amounts great enough to result in a galloping inflation—the only one ever experienced in America except in the Confederate South. Nearly $400 million (at face value) in continental money, quartermaster and commissary certificates of the central government, and paper money of the states was issued to defray wartime expenses. For all practical purposes, these various issues were repudiated by the middle of 1783, the effect being a tax on those who held the depreciating currency while it declined in value. Only a relatively small foreign and domestic debt totaling less than $40 million remained, but the question of responsibility for its repayment remained a thorny issue because political leaders assumed that the states that paid the debt would ultimately hold the balance of power politically. More important was the fact that Congress had no independent income and had to rely for funds on catch-as-catch-can contributions from the states, made roughly in proportion to their individual populations. Nor were the states without their own fiscal problems. By 1786, no less than seven states were issuing their own paper, and debtor groups in the other six states were clamoring for similar issues. Although the issuing states (except Rhode Island) acted responsibly, perhaps no other course of events so frightened conservatives as the control of the money supply by the states. Indeed the legacy of hyperinflation left a general distrust of government monetary management.[1]

American leaders remained divided over what kind of government should ultimately be adopted. One group wanted no stronger central government than the Articles provided, preferring to cast its lot and fortune with the individual states. Another group, made up on the whole of less-fiery revolutionaries, took the view that a strong central government, with power to coerce the states, should be quickly established. Until the end of the war, those who preferred a strong government were largely in control of the nation's affairs; but when news of a favorable peace arrived in 1783, many of the strongest leaders went home to their own pursuits, leaving the administration largely in the charge of weak-government advocates.

Even as early as 1783, however, supporters of a weak central government had begun to make concessions that would strengthen the power of Congress, and by 1786 most of the vehement opponents of a strong central government knew that genuine union was inevitable. That year Virginia called the Annapolis Convention, ostensibly to settle questions of trade regulations among the states; however, the only action taken by the delegates was to recommend to Congress that another convention be called to examine a broader range of problems.

It was clear that American leadership was moving toward unity. The convention that met in Philadelphia in 1787 was able to ignore its instructions to amend the Articles of Confederation and to create a new government instead only because the great constitutional questions debated so heatedly since 1775 were at least settled in the minds of the majority. In a little over four months from the first meeting of the delegates, George Washington, president of the convention, sent the completed document to the states for ratification.[2] Delaware ratified it almost immediately, on December 7, 1787; on June 21, 1788, New Hampshire cast the crucial ninth vote in favor. Congress declared the Constitution in effect beginning March 4, 1789, and two years later the Bill of Rights was passed and put in effect.

THE CONSTITUTION

With the adoption of the Constitution, the power to tax was firmly delegated to the federal government, which was empowered to pay off past debts, even those incurred by the states. The assurance that public debts will be honored has proven critical to the development of a sound capital market in the United States. There have been failings—as in the late 1830s, when several states defaulted on loans—but even today, the United States benefits from this heritage and is viewed as a haven by major investors seeking safety for their capital.

---

[1] See Charles W. Calomiris, "Institutional Failure, Monetary Scarcity, and the Depreciation of the Continental," *Journal of Economic History* 48 (1988): 47–68.

[2] For an analysis assessing the economic vested interests of the delegates, see Robert A. McGuire and Robert L. Ohsfeldt, "An Economic Model of Voting Behavior over Specific Issues at the Constitutional Convention of 1787," *Journal of Economic History* 46 (1986): 79–82.

The Constitution also gave the central government the sole right to mint coins and regulate the money supply. Such rights were not allowed the states. Having just emerged from monetary chaos and hyperinflation, a stable dollar was highly desired and viewed as an answer to the conflicting interests of creditors and debtors.

Both of these powers, to tax and to regulate money, brought into sharp focus the founders' concerns over conflicting factions, the limits of majority rule, and the ability to redistribute wealth and income by government means.[3] Consequently, federal taxes had to be uniform among all the states and, of course, U.S. dollars had to be exchangeable throughout the states. The concerns urging barriers to prevent significant and radical changes in the distribution of wealth through government formed the basis for a major section of the Fifth Amendment: "nor shall any person . . . be deprived of life, liberty, or property, without due process of law; nor shall private property be taken for public use without just compensation."

Another matter of great political and economic significance was the regulation of trade among the states. Although no substantial barriers to interstate commerce had emerged in the 1780s, the possibility for them was evident. Under the Constitution the states were forbidden to enact tariffs—the toll-free movement of goods was thus assured. The important "interstate clause" established a great national common market; in later decades, it also permitted the extension of federal authority to many areas of interstate economic activity.

The Constitution promoted trade and economic specialization in other ways. It authorized the federal government to maintain an army and navy, establish post offices and roads, fix standards of weights and measures, and establish uniform bankruptcy laws. It also gave Congress the authority to set laws on patents: "To promote the progress of science and useful arts by securing for limited times to authors and inventors the exclusive right to their respective writings and discoveries." With greater assurances to the gains of their own ideas and creations, creative people would hasten technical change.

---

[3]In Paper 10 of the Federalist Papers, James Madison demonstrates his preoccupation with these important matters:

> The most common and durable source of factions has been the various and unequal distribution of property. Those who hold and those who are without property have ever formed distinct interests in society. Those who are creditors, and those who are debtors, fall under a like discrimination. A landed interest, a manufacturing interest, a mercantile interest, a money interest, with many lesser interests, grow up of necessity in civilized nations, and divide them into different classes, actuated by different sentiments and views. The regulation of these various and interfering interests forms the principal task of modern legislation, and involves the spirit of party and faction in the necessary and ordinary operations of the government. . . . The inference to which we are brought is, that the causes of faction cannot be removed, and that relief is only to be sought in the means of controlling its effects.
>
> If a faction consists of less than a majority, relief is supplied by the republican principle, which enables the majority to defeat its sinister views by regular vote. It may clog the administration, it may convulse the society; but it will be unable to execute and mask its violence under the forms of the Constitution. When a majority is included in a faction, the form of popular government, on the other hand, enables it to sacrifice to its ruling passion or interest both the public good and the rights of other citizens. To secure the public good and private rights against the danger of such a faction, and at the same time to preserve the spirit and the form of popular government, is then the great object to which our inquiries are directed.

This painting of the formal closing of the Philadelphia convention and sending of the Constitution to the states for ratification highlights the hot work of the delegates through the months of late July, August, and September before the age of air conditioning.

Another transfer of authority to the federal government was foreign affairs. It alone could negotiate treaties or set tariffs. The power to regulate tariffs became a powerful lever in negotiations with foreign nations to reduce or eliminate duties on American goods abroad, as it remains today in the global negotiations on the General Agreement on Tariffs and Trade (GATT). Before this shift of power, competition among the states minimized the possibility of this leverage, and U.S. tariffs were very low. Once they were centralized, however, tariffs became the chief source of federal revenues throughout most of the nineteenth century.

For the delegates at the Philadelphia convention (and the individual states) to voluntarily release such powers to the central government was unprecedented—made possible only through compromise, which was epitomized in the question of slavery. The Constitutional compromise allowed slavery to continue but limited the importation of slaves to only 20 years, ending in 1808. A tax of up to $10 per imported slave was allowed. Furthermore, each state was ordered to recognize the laws and court orders of other states; thus runaway slaves escaping to another state were to be returned, like stolen property. Was a slave merely property, or a person? Oddly, the

Constitution viewed slaves in two respects: first and foremost as property, just as in colonial times; secondly, each slave was counted as three-fifths of a person for the purpose of determining each state's membership in the House of Representatives, which was based on population.

The debates of the convention focused carefully on the question of state versus national interests, and it was temporarily left implicit that powers not delegated to the federal government, or forbidden to the states, were reserved to the states (or the people). To strengthen these reserved rights, the Tenth Amendment was added to the Bill of Rights, ensuring the states' powers to set local and state laws such as licensing, regulation of business, taxes, zoning laws, civil conduct, and the like, and to use police powers to enforce them.

In respect to relations among people, the new nation preserved the treasured English Common Law. This long string of rules based on court decisions had worked well for centuries, and the First Continental Congress of 1774 had formally proclaimed the Common Law of England as the right of Americans.[4] Many states repeated this claim, and legal interpretations were left to the states as long as their legal statutes and interpretations were consistent with the Constitution, the supreme law of the land. Any conflict or challenge was to be adjudicated by the courts and, if necessary, ultimately by the Supreme Court.

The Constitution laid the foundation of private property rights we enjoy today. It curbed the arbitrary powers of government and fostered personal security required for the pursuit of all varieties of productivity-enhancing activities. Amazingly brief and clear, the Constitution has proven flexible through court interpretation and, on 16 occasions since the Bill of Rights, through amendment.

There probably was no single original source from which the essential concepts of the Constitution were derived. And yet, in 1776, the same year that the Declaration of Independence rang its message of political freedom around the world, an odd-looking Scot, whose professorial mien belied his vast knowledge of economic affairs, offered a clarion rationale of economic freedom. *The Wealth of Nations* ultimately became a best-seller, and Adam Smith became admired and famous. Educated people everywhere, including American leaders, read his great work, marveling at the lucid language and its castigation of mercantilist constraints on economic processes. It does not diminish Adam Smith's great influence to say that he was the articulate commentator on forces that existed long before he began to write. Chief among these forces were a growing regard for the advantages of private property arrangements and an abiding conviction that law and order were essential to the preservation of property rights and to the opportunity for all people to acquire the things of this world. It follows, therefore, that matching the political guarantees of the Constitution, with their ultimate assurance of personal freedoms, would be fundamental economic guarantees of protection of private property and enforcement of contracts, essential to a viable market economy. The United States was especially well tailored to Smith's concept of an economic order, directed by self-interest, which limited governmental rules

---

[4] For the origins, development, and significance of the Common Law, and trial by jury, as contrasted to Roman law, see Winston S. Churchill, *A History of the English-Speaking Peoples, Volume I, The Birth of Britain* (New York: Dorset Press, 1990), Chapter 13.

and regulations but assured the domestic tranquility and freedom from foreign interference that only a strong central government could provide.

AMERICAN INDEPENDENCE AND ECONOMIC CHANGE

The adoption of the Constitution in 1789 and the emergence of a stronger federal
government did not have dramatic immediate effects. The crucial political decisions
of that time were matched by challenging economic problems. The central problem
was independence itself. All at once the young nation found itself outside the walls of
the British Empire, and soon even the wartime trade alliances with France and Spain
began to crumble.

In the Caribbean, U.S. ships were excluded from direct trade with the British West
Indies. American merchants who tried to evade the law faced possible seizure by offi-
cials. Spain added to American woes by withdrawing the wartime privilege of direct
U.S. trade with Cuba, Puerto Rico, and Hispaniola. In addition, Spain reinstituted its
traditional policy of restricting trade with its possessions, permitting them to import
goods only from Spain. There was an increase in U.S. trade with the French West
Indies, but this was not enough to offset the declines in commercial trade with other
Caribbean islands. Even in its lively trade with the French, the United States was not
allowed to carry sugar from French islands, and only in times of severe scarcity did
the French import American flour. In addition, the French imposed high duties on
U.S. salted fish and meat, and these products were banned entirely from the British
islands.

Restrictions and trade curtailments were not limited to the Caribbean. Now Americans were also cut off from direct trade with the British fisheries in Newfoundland
and Nova Scotia. As a result, the New England states suffered severe losses in trade
to the north in provisions, lumber, rum, and shipping services. To the east and into
the Mediterranean, American shipping faced harassment by the Barbary pirates
because the United States was no longer protected by the British flag and by British
tribute to the governments of Tunis, Tripoli, and Algeria.

While American shipping rocked at anchor, American shipbuilding and the supporting industries of lumber and naval stores also remained unengaged. Britain now
labeled all American-built vessels as foreign, thereby making them ineligible to trade
within the Empire even when they were owned by British subjects. The result was the
loss of a major market for American shipbuilders, and after 1783 U.S. ship production
declined still further because American whale oil faced prohibitively high British
duties. In fact, nearly all of the activities that employed American-built ships (cod
fishing, whaling, mercantile, and shipping services) were depressed industries, and
New England—the center of these activities—suffered disproportionately during the
early years of independence.

The states of the former Middle colonies were also affected. Pennsylvania and New
York shared losses in shipbuilding. Moreover, their trades in wheat, flour, salted meat,

and other provisions to the West Indies were well below those in colonial peacetime years. By 1786 the Middle colonies had probably reached the bottom of a fairly severe business downturn, and then conditions began to improve as these products were reaccepted into the traditional West Indian and southern European markets.

Similar problems plagued the South. For instance, British duties on rice restricted planters of South Carolina and Georgia primarily to markets in the West Indies and southern Europe. As the price of rice declined, further setbacks resulted from the loss of bounties and subsidies on indigo and naval stores. Having few alternative uses of their productive capacity, the Carolinas and Georgia faced special difficulties. Their economic future did not look bright. Similarly, Virginia and Maryland faced stagnating markets for their major staple—tobacco. In Britain, a tax of 15d. sterling was imposed on each pound of foreign tobacco. In France, a single purchasing monopoly, the Farmers-General, was created to handle tobacco imports. Meanwhile, Spain and Portugal prohibited imports of American tobacco altogether.

Offsetting these restrictions were a few positive forces. Goods that previously had been "enumerated" could now be traded directly to continental European ports. This lowered the shipping and handling costs on some items such as tobacco, thereby having an upward effect on their prices. Meanwhile, the great influx of British manufactures sharply reduced prices on these goods in American ports. Although American manufacturers suffered, consumers were pleased: compared to the late colonial period, the terms of trade—the prices paid for imports relative to the prices paid for exports—had improved. This was especially true in 1783 and 1784, when import prices were slightly below their prewar level and export prices were higher. Thereafter, however, the terms of trade became less favorable, and by 1790 there was little advantage in the adjustments of these relative prices compared with the prewar period.

A QUANTITATIVE ANALYSIS OF ECONOMIC CHANGE

To convey these many changes more systematically and in a long-run perspective, it is essential to compare the circumstances of the late colonial period and the years immediately following independence. Of course, this does not entirely isolate the impact of independence on the economy, because forces other than independence contributed to the shifting magnitudes and patterns of trade and to the many other economic changes that occurred. Nevertheless, comparisons of the late colonial period with the early 1790s provide important insights into the new directions and prospects for the young nation.

Table 7-1 on the next page shows that by 1790, the United States had taken advantage of its new freedom to trade directly with northern European countries. Most of this trade was in tobacco to France and the Netherlands, but rice, wheat, flour, and maize (Indian corn) were also shipped there in large amounts. Despite the emergence of this new trade pattern, the lion's share of American exports continued to be sent to Great Britain, including items that were then reexported to the Continent. Many

TABLE 7-1   AVERAGE ANNUAL REAL EXPORTS TO OVERSEAS AREAS FROM
THE THIRTEEN COLONIES, 1768–1772, AND THE UNITED STATES,
1790–1792 (IN THOUSANDS OF POUNDS STERLING, 1768–1772 PRICES)

Destination	1768–1772	Percentage of Total	1790–1792	Percentage of Total
Great Britain and Ireland	1,616	58	1,234	31
Northern Europe	—	—	643	16
Southern Europe	406	14	557	14
British West Indies	759	27	402	10
Foreign West Indies			956	24
Africa	21	1	42	1
Canadian Colonies	n.a.	—	60	2
Other	—	—	59	2
Total	2,802	100	3,953	100

SOURCE: JAMES F. SHEPHERD AND GARY M. WALTON, "ECONOMIC CHANGE AFTER THE AMERICAN REVOLUTION: PREWAR AND POSTWAR COMPARISONS OF MARITIME SHIPPING AND TRADE," *EXPLORATIONS IN ECONOMIC HISTORY* 13 (1976): 397–422.

have speculated on the reasons for this renewal of American-British ties. Part of the explanation may be that Britain offered the greatest variety of goods at the best price and quality, especially woolens, linens, and hardwares. Moreover, British merchants enjoyed the advantages of a common language, established contacts, and a knowledge of U.S. markets. Because American imports were handled by British merchants, it was often advantageous to use British ports as dropping-off points for U.S. exports, even those destined for the Continent.

At the same time, new patterns of trade were emerging in the Caribbean. Before the Revolution, trade with the British West Indies had been greater than trade with the foreign islands, but by 1790 the situation was reversed, largely due to the exclusion of American shipping from the British islands. Undoubtedly, many American ships illegally traversed British Caribbean waters, and Dutch St. Eustatius remained an entrepôt from which British islands were supplied as they had been during the war. Consequently, the statistics in Table 7-1 exaggerate this shift. Nevertheless, it would appear that U.S. trade with non-British areas of the Caribbean grew substantially during these years. This trend had been underway before the Revolution, but postwar restrictions on American shipping undoubtedly hastened it.

Lastly, it is worth noting that no new trades to romantic, faraway places emerged in any significant way during this period of transition. The changes in trade patterns were actually rather modest.

As trade patterns changed, so did the relative importance of the many goods traded. For instance, the most valuable export by the early 1790s was no longer tobacco, but bread and flour. Tobacco production grew slowly, but rising tobacco prices aided the recovery of the tobacco-producing areas of Virginia and Maryland. Other important southern staples, such as pitch, tar, rice, and indigo, fell in value and in quantities produced. The decline of indigo was aggravated by the loss of bounties and by

TABLE 7-2 AVERAGE ANNUAL EXPORTS FROM THE THIRTEEN COLONIES, 1768–1772, AND THE UNITED STATES, 1791–1792 (IN THOUSANDS OF POUNDS STERLING, 1768–1772 PRICES)

Origin	1768–1772			1791–1792		
	Total Exports	Percentage of Total	Per Capita Exports	Total Exports	Percentage of Total	Per Capita Exports
New England						
New Hampshire	46	2	0.74	33	1	0.23
Massachusetts	258	9	0.97	542	14	1.14
Rhode Island	81	3	1.39	119	3	1.72
Connecticut	92	3	0.50	148	4	0.62
Total, New England	477	17	0.82	842	22	0.83
Middle Atlantic						
New York	187	7	1.15	512	14	1.51
New Jersey	2	—	0.02	5	—	0.03
Pennsylvania	353	13	1.47	584	16	1.34
Delaware	18	1	0.51	26	1	0.44
Total, Middle Atlantic	560	20	1.01	1,127	30	1.11
Upper South						
Maryland	392	14	1.93	482	13	1.51
Virginia	770	27	1.72	678	18	0.91
Total, Upper South	1,162	41	1.79	1,160	31	1.09
Lower South						
North Carolina	75	3	0.38	104	3	0.27
South Carolina	455	16	3.66	436	12	1.75
Georgia	74	3	3.17	97	3	1.17
Total, Lower South	604	22	1.75	637	17	0.88
Total, all regions	2,803	100	1.31	3,766	100	0.99

SOURCE: JAMES F. SHEPHERD AND GARY M. WALTON, "ECONOMIC CHANGE AFTER THE AMERICAN REVOLUTION: PREWAR AND POSTWAR COMPARISONS OF MARITIME SHIPPING AND TRADE," *EXPLORATIONS IN ECONOMIC HISTORY* 13 (1976): 397–422.

increased British production of indigo in the West Indies after the war. The most striking change of the period, however, was the increase in the export of foodstuffs such as salted meats (beef and pork), bread and flour, maize, and wheat. Of course, these accompanied the relative rise of the trades to the West Indies. Because the uptrend in food shipments to the West Indies was underway before the Revolution, not all of this shift in commodities can be attributed solely to independence.

Because of these changing patterns and magnitudes of trade, some states improved their economic well-being while others lost ground. Table 7-2 shows exports per capita for each state during this period, after adjusting for inflationary effects. Compared to prewar levels, New England had returned to about the same per capita position by the early 1790s. The Middle Atlantic region showed improvement despite the depression felt so sharply in Pennsylvania in the mid-1780s. As indicated in Table 7-2, the trade of the southern regions did not keep pace with a growing population. Although the South's prewar absolute level of exports had been regained by the early 1790s, its per capita exports were significantly below those in colonial times, with the Lower South most severely affected. However, once again, this decline was caused not so much by independence as by a decline in growth of demand in Europe for southern staples.

The wide variety of changes among the states makes it extremely hazardous to generalize nationally. Overall, there was a 30 percent decline in real per capita exports (per year). Total exports had climbed by 40 percent, but this fell far short of the 80 percent jump in population. Accompanying this change was a slowing in urbanization. The major cities of Philadelphia, New York, and Boston grew only 3 percent over this period, despite the large increase in the total population of the states. Both of these adjustments—the decline in per capita exports and the pause in urban growth—were extremely unusual peacetime experiences. Yet, as emphasized, such aggregate figures hide as much as they reveal. The southern declines were sharp; only New York and the New England states (except New Hampshire) fully recovered from trade disruptions.

How big was overseas trade as a proportion of national income? Was overseas trade large enough to merit the emphasis it has been given here? To answer these crucial questions, some calculations are in order.

Taking 1774 as a benchmark year, we see from Table 2-1 (pages 32–33) that there were about 2.4 million people in the colonies. From Table 5-4 (page 104), we determine that average yearly incomes were about £10.7 (using the 3.5-to-1 capital output ratio). Total income was therefore £25.7 million (£10.7 × 2.4 million).

From Table 4-4 (page 79) we can sum commodity exports, plus ship sales, plus invisible earnings (but excluding British expenditures on military personnel) to show the average yearly values (1768–1772) of incomes from overseas trade and shipping activities. These were probably slightly below 1774's earnings, so we have a lower bound of £2,800,000 (exports) + £140,000 (ship sales) + £880,000 (invisible earnings) equaling £3.82 million. We can conclude therefore that income from overseas trade and shipping was nearly 15 percent of total incomes.

An added argument for stressing overseas economic activities is that these were market activities, ones that led the way in moving resources from lesser- to higher-valued uses. It was this commercial sector—not subsistence farming, hunting, wood-cutting, and the like—that provided the chief stimulus to market expansion, economic specialization, technology transfer, capital accumulation, and advancing productivity and standards of living. Finally, if the coastal intercolonial trades are added to the overseas trade and shipping earnings (15 percent of total income), the combined proportion approaches one-fifth of total income.

The result of this quantitative analysis of the magnitudes of overseas (and coastal) trade, along with the arguments advanced here based on economic growth theory, urge our emphasis on this sector as a leading one for the economic progress of the colonies.

The western movement and the persistence of self-sufficient activities cushioned the downfall of incomes per capita. Undoubtedly, per capita internal trade did not decline to the same extent as per capita exports. (Unfortunately, we have no statistics on domestic trade during that hectic period.) Thus, the external relations probably exaggerated the overall setbacks of the period. It is safe to conclude, however, that the political chaos of the early national era was accompanied by severe economic conditions. Indeed, the problems of government contributed to the weakness of the economy, and economic events in turn clarified government failings under the Articles of Confederation.

These were the circumstances entering 1793, the year in which the Napoleonic wars erupted and Eli Whitney invented the cotton gin. The sweeping consequences of those events could never have been foreseen in colonial times. The colonies, however, had already developed a commercial base that now would prove crucial to further development. Because of its early efforts at overseas trade, the new nation was ready to take quick advantage of the economic opportunities available to a neutral nation in a world at war.

WAR, NEUTRALITY, AND ECONOMIC RESURGENCE

As we have seen, the economic setbacks experienced by the United States throughout the late 1770s and most of the 1780s were followed by years of halting progress and incomplete recovery. Then in 1793, just four years after the beginning of the French Revolution, the French and English began a series of wars that lasted until 1815.[5] During this long struggle, both British and French cargo vessels were drafted into military service, and both nations relaxed their restrictive mercantilist policies. Of all nations most capable of filling the shipping void created by the Napoleonic wars, the new United States stood at the forefront.

Due to these developments, the nation's economy briskly rebounded from the doldrums of the preceding years. The stimulus in U.S. overseas commerce is graphed statistically in Figure 7-1 on the next page. As indicated, per capita credits in the balance of payments (exports plus other sources of foreign exchange earnings) more than

---

[5]The Treaty of Amiens, signed late in 1801, provided a year and a half of uneasy peace.

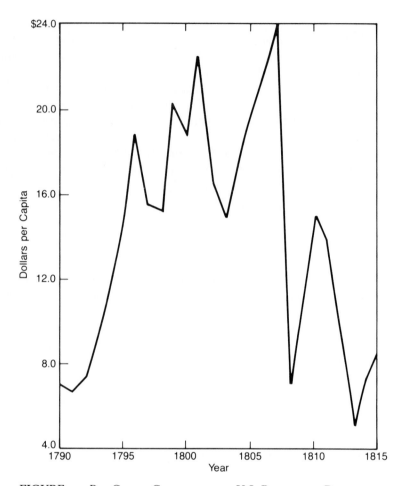

FIGURE 7-1 Per Capita Credits in the U.S. Balance of Payments, 1790–1815

SOURCE: Douglass C. North, "Early National Income Estimates of the United States," *Economic Development and Cultural Change* 9 (1961): 390.

tripled between 1790 and the height of war between the French and English. There can be little doubt that these were extraordinary years for America—a time of unusual prosperity and intense economic activity, especially in the eastern port cities. It was a time characterized by full employment and sharply rising urbanization, at least until 1808. Famed entrepreneurs of New England and the Middle Atlantic region, such as Stephen Girard, Archibald Gracie, E. H. Derby, and John Jacob Astor, amassed vast personal fortunes during this period. These and other capital accumulations added to the development of a well-established commercial sector and eventually contributed to the incipient manufacturing sector.

It is important to recognize the significance of the commercial sector of the economy as well as the role of the merchant class during these decades. The growing mer-

This bustling dockside scene in New York City in 1800 was indicative of the United States' emergence as a center of trade.

chant class, of course, had played an active role in helping to spearhead the move for national independence. Now the merchant class supplied the entrepreneurial talents required to take full advantage of the new economic circumstances. As the spreading European war opened up exceptional trade opportunities, America's well-developed commercial sector provided the needed buildings and ships as well as know-how. In short, both the physical and human capital were already available, and in many ways the success of the period stemmed from developments that reached back to colonial times. It was exactly that prior development that singled out the United States as the leading neutral nation in time of war. Rather than the ports of the Caribbean, Latin America, or Canada, those of the United States emerged as the entrepôts of trade in the western Atlantic.

The effects of war and neutrality on U.S. shipping earnings are shown on the next page in Figure 7-2. In general, these statistics convey the same picture that we saw in Figure 7-1, namely that these were exceptionally prosperous times for the commercial sector.

Although the invention of the cotton gin stimulated cotton production and U.S. cotton supplies grew in response to the growth of demand for raw cotton in English textile mills, commercial growth was by no means limited to products produced in the

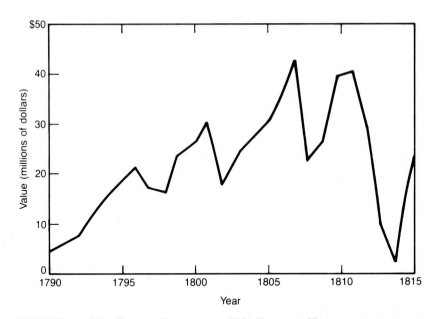

FIGURE 7-2 NET FREIGHT EARNINGS OF U.S. CARRYING TRADE, 1790–1815

SOURCE: DOUGLASS C. NORTH, *THE ECONOMIC GROWTH OF THE UNITED STATES, 1790–1860* (ENGLE-WOOD CLIFFS, NEW JERSEY: PRENTICE-HALL, 1961), PP. 26, 28.

United States. As Figure 7-3 shows, reexports comprised a major portion of the total exports from U.S. ports, especially in such tropical items as sugar, coffee, cocoa, pepper, and spices. Because their commercial sectors were relatively underdeveloped, the Caribbean islands and Latin America depended primarily on American shipping and merchandising services rather than on their own.

Of course, such unique conditions did not provide the basis for long-term development, and (as Figures 7-1, 7-2, and 7-3 all show) when temporary peace came between late 1801 and 1803, the U.S. commercial boom quickly evaporated. When hostilities erupted again, the United States experienced another sharp upswing in commercial activity. This time, however, new and serious problems arose with expansion. In 1805, the British imposed an antiquated ruling, the Rule of 1756, permitting neutrals in wartime to carry only those goods that they normally carried in peacetime. This ruling, known as the Essex Decision, was matched by Napoleon's Berlin Decree, which banned trade to Britain. As a result, nearly 1,500 American ships and many American sailors were seized, and some were forcefully drafted into the British Royal Navy. The Congress and President Jefferson, fearful of entangling the United States in war, declared the Embargo Act of 1807, which prohibited U.S. ships from trading with all foreign ports.

Basically, this attempt to gain respect for American neutrality backfired, and as the drastic declines in Figures 7-1, 7-2, and 7-3 show, the cure was almost worse than the disease. As pressures in the port cities mounted, political action led to the Non-

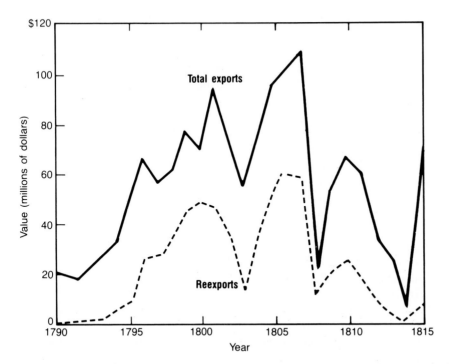

FIGURE 7-3 VALUES OF EXPORTS AND REEXPORTS FROM THE UNITED STATES, 1790–1815

SOURCE: DOUGLASS C. NORTH, *THE ECONOMIC GROWTH OF THE UNITED STATES, 1790–1860* (ENGLE-WOOD CLIFFS, NEW JERSEY: PRENTICE-HALL, 1961), P. 28.

Importation Act of 1809. This partially opened up trade, with specific prohibitions against Great Britain, France, and their possessions.

Nevertheless, continuing seizures and other complications between the United States and Britain along the Canadian border finally led to war—the second with England within 30 years. The War of 1812 was largely a naval war, during which the British seized more than 1,000 additional ships and blockaded almost the entire U.S. coast.

As exports declined to practically nothing, new boosts were given to the tiny manufacturing sector. Actually, stirrings there had begun with the embargo of 1807, which quickly altered the possibilities for profits in commerce relative to manufactures. As prices on manufactures rose, increasing possibilities for profits encouraged capital to flow into manufacturing. From 15 textile mills in 1808, the number rose to almost 90 by 1809. Similar additions continued throughout the war period, but when the Treaty of Ghent in 1814 brought the war to a close, the textile industry faltered badly. Once again, British imports arrived in massive amounts and undercut prices, which had been temporarily inflated by supply shortages resulting from the embargo and the war. Only large-scale U.S. concerns weathered the competitive storm, and there were few of these—most notably the Lowell shops using the Waltham system of cloth weaving (see Chapters 10–11). Nevertheless, the war-related spurts in manufacturing provided an important basis for further industrial expansion, not only in textiles—the main manufacturing activity of the time—but in other areas as well. This marked a time when the relative roles of the various sectors of the economy began to shift. Agriculture was to dominate the economy for most of the century, but to a lesser and lesser degree as economic growth continued.

The economic surge of the early Napoleonic war period (1793–1807) was unique, not so much by comparison to later years as by its striking reversal and advance from the two decades following 1772. Work by Claudia Goldin and Frank Lewis shows that during the decade and a half after the beginning of the Napoleonic wars, the growth rate of per capita income averaged almost 1 percent per year, with the foreign sector accounting for over 25 percent of the underlying sources of growth.[6]

In contrast, during the two decades preceding 1793, per capita exports fell (Table 7-2), and productivity in Pennsylvania agriculture suffered modest declines (see Table 5-1, page 92, for review). Goldin and Lewis estimate that per capita income declined by a rate of 34 percent annually from 1774 to 1793.[7] Wealth holdings per capita also declined substantially over this period.[8]

There is little doubt that the several decades following independence were exceptionally unstable, not merely two decades of bust, and then one and a half of boom. There were ups and downs within these longer bust and boom periods. Because of the importance of foreign trade at the time, export instability had strong leverage effects throughout the economy. Although external forces were always an important factor in determining economic fluctuations, just as the influence of OPEC reminded us in the 1970s, their almost total dominance was now beginning to wane. By the turn of the century, internal developments—especially those in the banking sector—had assumed a more pivotal role in causing economic fluctuations. As we shall see in Chapter 12, both external forces (acting through credit flows from and to overseas areas) and internal forces (acting through changes in credit availability and the money stock) came to bear on the economy during the early nineteenth century. And some of the biggest challenges and opportunities for young Americans were settling and working new lands in the West.

SELECTED REFERENCES
AND SUGGESTED READINGS

Adams, Donald R., Jr. "American Neutrality and Prosperity, 1793–1808: A Reconsideration." *Journal of Economic History* 40 (1980): 713–738.
Beard, Charles A. *An Economic Interpretation of the Constitution.* New York: Macmillan, 1913.

---

[6] Claudia D. Goldin and Frank D. Lewis, "The Role of Exports in American Economic Growth during the Napoleonic Wars, 1793–1807," *Explorations in Economic History* 17 (1980): 6–25, especially p. 22. For an alternative interpretation of the role of neutrality, see Donald R. Adams, Jr., "American Neutrality and Prosperity, 1793–1808: A Reconsideration," *Journal of Economic History* 40 (1980): 713–738.

[7] Goldin and Lewis, pp. 22–23.

[8] Alice H. Jones, *Wealth of a Nation to Be* (New York: Columbia University Press, 1980), p. 82.

Bjork, Gordon C. "The Weaning of the American Economy: Independence, Market Changes, and Economic Development." *Journal of Economic History* 24 (1964): 541–560.

Calomiris, Charles W. "Institutional Failure, Monetary Scarcity, and the Depreciation of the Continental." *Journal of Economic History* 48 (1988): 47–68.

Gilbert, Geoffrey. "The Role of Breadstuffs in American Trade, 1770–1790." *Explorations in Economic History* 14 (1977): 378–387.

Goldin, Claudia D., and Frank D. Lewis. "The Role of Exports in American Economic Growth during the Napoleonic Wars, 1793–1807." *Explorations in Economic History* 17 (1980): 6–25.

Jensen, Merrill. *The New Nation: A History of the United States during Confederation.* New York: Knopf, 1958.

Jones, Alice H. *Wealth of a Nation to Be.* New York: Columbia University Press, 1980.

McGuire, Robert A., and Robert L. Ohsfeldt. "Economic Interests and the American Constitution: A Quantitative Rehabilitation of Charles A. Beard." *Journal of Economic History* 44 (June 1984): 509–519.

———. "An Economic Model of Voting Behavior over Specific Issues at the Constitutional Convention of 1787." *Journal of Economic History* 46 (1986): 79–112.

Nettels, Curtis P. *The Emergence of a National Economy, 1775–1815.* New York: Holt, Rinehart & Winston, 1962. Chapters 3 and 4.

North, Douglass C. *American Economic Growth 1790–1860.* Englewood Cliffs, New Jersey: Prentice-Hall, 1960.

———. "Early National Income Estimates of the United States." *Economic Development and Cultural Change* 9, no. 3 (April 1961).

Shepherd, James F., and Gary M. Walton. "Economic Change after the American Revolution: Pre-War and Post-War Comparisons of Maritime Shipping and Trade." *Explorations in Economic History* 13 (1976): 397–422.

CHAPTER EIGHT

LAND AND THE EARLY WESTWARD MOVEMENTS

CHAPTER THEME The Treaty of Versailles, signed in September 1783, granted the Americans independence and the western lands they claimed by the ancient right of conquest. The western lands, first claimed by individual states but soon ceded to the federal government, were a valuable asset, collectively owned. How to use it best for the collective good was the problem and the challenge.

For the most part, land policy was determined by the great Land Ordinances of 1785 and 1787 through the guiding spirit of Thomas Jefferson. Throughout his career, Jefferson had three main goals for land policy: (1) to provide revenues to the federal government through sales, but not perpetual taxes; (2) to spread democratic institutions; and (3) to assure clear property rights to the land owned by individuals, thereby enhancing their liberty and freedom.

Fearing the potential threat of an excessively powerful, land-rich national government, Jefferson argued that the land should be transferred in a swift but orderly manner to the people. He advocated a process of privatization. First, surveys would be made and boundaries clearly marked. Sales from the federal government to private persons would transfer title completely. The federal government would not tax the land. As populations and settlements spread west, territories would be formed, then through application become states, entering the Union on an equal footing with the existing states. All of this was fundamentally Jefferson's vision, part of his legacy that remains with us today.

THE ACQUISITION OF THE PUBLIC DOMAIN

One of the first truly national issues for the new government, after waging war and financing it, was the disposition of new lands in the West. The Articles of Confederation held that western lands could not be unwillingly taken from the states by the central government, and seven states held claims on western lands. These claims were based on the colonies' original grants from England and from dealings with the Indians. Many people argued, however, that the new western territories should belong to the national government and held or disposed in the national interest. Maryland, a state without western claims, brought the issue to a head by refusing to ratify the Articles until the land issue was resolved. In 1781, Maryland finally signed, after New York voluntarily gave its claims, based on treaties with the Iroquois Indians, to the national government. Virginia promptly followed suit and relinquished its claims on western lands. The other five states having claims soon followed their lead.

What the new nation obtained from the British in 1783 is portrayed in the darkened area of Map 8-1. The United States began with a solid mass of land extending from the Atlantic coast to the Mississippi River and from the Great Lakes to, but not including, Florida.

Between 1802, when Georgia became the last state to relinquish its rights to western land, and 1898, when the formal annexation of Hawaii occurred, the United States very nearly assumed its present physical form as the result of eight main acquisitions (shown in Map 8-1):

1. The Territory of Louisiana, acquired in 1803 by purchase from France.

2. Florida, acquired in 1819 by purchase from Spain. A few years previously, the United States had annexed the narrow strip of land that constituted west Florida.

3. The Republic of Texas, annexed as a state in 1845. The Republic of Texas had been established in 1836 after the victory of the American settlers over the Mexicans.

4. The Oregon Country, annexed by treaty with Great Britain in 1846. Spain and Russia, the original claimants to this area, had long since dropped out. By the Treaty of 1818, the United States and Great Britain agreed to a joint occupation of the Oregon Country and British Columbia; the Treaty of 1846 established the dividing line at the forty-ninth parallel.

5. The Mexican Cession, acquired by conquest from Mexico in 1848.

6. The Gadsden Purchase, acquired from Mexico in 1853.

7. The Alaskan Purchase, acquired from Russia in 1867.

8. The Hawaiian Annexation, formally ratified in 1898.

National acquisition of new land came either by a process of conquest and treaty or by purchase. The right of conquest was part of America's European heritage, rights claimed by the sovereigns of Europe and unquestioned by Christian societies when levied against non-Christian societies. This is seen clearly in early times in Europe,

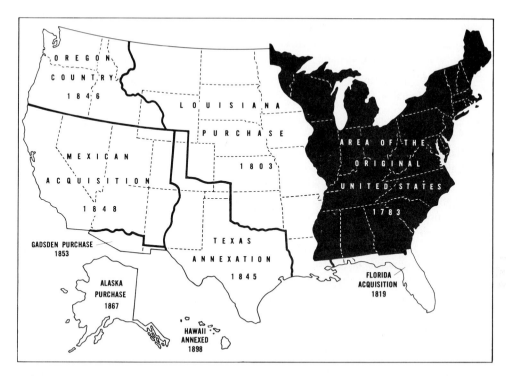

MAP 8-1 LAND GROWTH: *The purchase of Louisiana marked the beginning of the continental expansion of the United States, which culminated in the purchase of Alaska in 1867 and the annexation of Hawaii in 1898.*

repeatedly against the Muslims, through the Crusades, and in Spain in 1492 against the Moors. The European right to conquer, subdue, and rule non-Christian native societies in North America passed into American hands with independence. This legacy was ultimately extended in the nineteenth century, when the remaining Native Americans were forced onto reservations. These acts and their accompanying treaties are targets of continual challenge in the courts by Native Americans today.

In half a century (1803–1853), the United States obtained a continental area of 3 million square miles, of which 1.4 billion acres, or 75 percent, constituted the public domain.[1] In 1862, two-thirds of this vast area was still in the possession of the government, but the process of disposal had been agreed on long before.

DISPOSING OF THE PUBLIC DOMAIN

With rare exceptions, the land was valueless until settled. To give the land value, the Congress of the Confederation had addressed three questions:

---

[1] Of the two later acquisitions, Alaska contained more than 586,400 square miles, most of it still in the public domain, and Hawaii added 6,423 square miles, none of it in the public domain.

1. How were land holdings and sales to be administered?

2. Should the government exact high prices from the sale of land, or should cheap land be made available to everyone?

3. What was to be the political relationship between newly settled areas and the original states?

Two major land systems had developed during the colonial period. The New England system of "township planning" provided for the laying out of townships, for the subdivision of townships into carefully surveyed tracts, and for the auction sale of tracts to settlers. In the eighteenth century, it was usual to establish townships, which often were 6 miles square, in tiers. The opening of new townships proceeded with regularity from settled to unsettled land, gaps of unsettled land appeared infrequently, and no one could own land that had not been previously surveyed. In contrast, the southern system provided for no rectangular surveys. In the South, a settler simply selected what appeared to be a choice plot of unappropriated land and asked the county surveyor to mark it off. Settlers paid no attention to the relationship of their tracts to other pieces of property, and the legal description of a tract was made with reference to more or less permanent natural objects, such as stones, trees, and streams.

THE NORTHWEST LAND ORDINANCE OF 1785

There was no pressure on the Congress of the Confederation to provide a system for regulating public lands until 1784, after Virginia and New York had relinquished their claims to the southern part of the territory lying northwest of the Ohio River. In that year, a congressional committee of five, headed by Thomas Jefferson, proposed a system based on a rectangular survey. It is noteworthy that three of the five members were southerners who, despite their origins, recognized the value of the New England method of settlement. No action was taken, but a year later another committee, composed of a member from each state, reworked the 1784 report and offered a carefully considered proposal. With minor changes, this proposal was passed as the Northwest Land Ordinance of 1785.

Insofar as the ordinance set a *physical* basis for disposing of the public lands, its effects were permanent. Government surveyors were to establish on unsettled land horizontal lines called *base lines* and vertical lines called *principal meridians,* as shown in Map 8-2 on page 158. The first of the principal meridians was to be in what is now the state of Ohio, and the first surveys covered land north of the Ohio River. Eventually, all the land in the United States was included in the surveys except the original thirteen states and Vermont, Kentucky, Tennessee, parts of Ohio, and Texas. These were literally celestial surveys, mappings by the stars.

As the surveys moved westward, other principal meridians were established—the second in what is now Indiana, the third in what is now Illinois, and so on. Map 8-2 indicates the other principal meridians and the base lines perpendicular to them. The insets show how tiers of townships, called *ranges,* were laid out to the east and west of each principal meridian. The ranges were designated by a number and a direction

Thomas Jefferson, the nation's third president, 1801–1809, had an earlier profound influence on the country through his leadership on the great land ordinances of 1785 and 1787.

from the meridian, and the townships within each range were numbered north and south from the base line. Each township, being 6 miles square, contained 36 square miles numbered as shown in Map 8-2. In the Ordinance of 1785, a square mile was called a *lot*, but in later acts the term *section* was used. Each square-mile section contained 640 acres, an acre being about the size of a football field (70 yards by 70 yards).

Two fundamentally different points of view emerged about the terms on which land should be made available, and a debate ensued that was not to end for several decades. Those who advocated a "conservative" policy were in favor of selling the public lands in large tracts at high prices for cash. The proponents of a "liberal" policy were in favor of putting land within the reach of almost everyone by making it available in small parcels at low prices on credit terms.

The Land Ordinance of 1785 reflected the prevalent conservative view that public land should be a major source of revenue, though in fact revenues from land sales never became a major source of federal revenues. Provisions relating to minimum size of tracts, prices, and terms were severe. Alternate townships were to be sold as a whole; the other half of the townships were to be sold by sections. All sales at public auction were to be for a minimum price of $1 per acre in cash. Thus, the smallest possible cash outlay was the $640 necessary to buy a section—an expenditure beyond the means of most pioneers. Moreover, a square mile of land was more than small farmers could normally utilize and work; they could barely clear and cultivate 10 acres in their first year, and a quarter section was the most a settler could handle without the aid of grown children. Only individuals of means and land companies formed by large investors could purchase land under the first law.

THE NORTHWEST ORDINANCE OF 1787

The decision regarding the status of areas to be settled in the future also involved a great political principle. Were these areas to remain in colonial dependence, subject to possible exploitation by the original thirteen states? Or were they to be admitted into a union of states on a basis of equality? The answers to these questions would

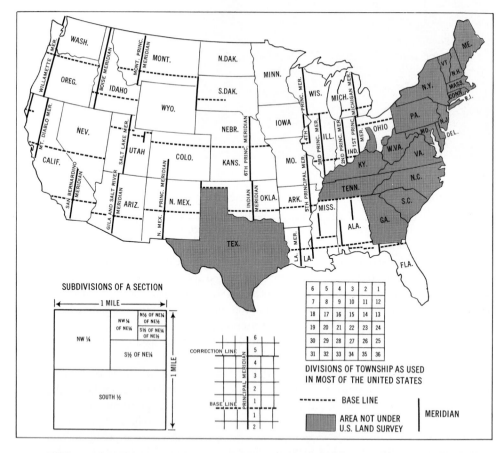

MAP 8-2 LAND SURVEY: *Principal meridians and base lines made possible precise apportioning of newly opened territories into sections, and easily described subdivisions of sections, thus simplifying later property transfers.*

test the foresight and selflessness of Americans, who had themselves escaped the dominance of a ruling empire.

In 1787, the Congress addressed the problems of establishing the *political* principles for western settlement. The Ordinance of 1787 provided that the Northwest Territory should be organized as a district to be run by a governor and judges appointed by the Congress. As soon as it contained 5,000 male inhabitants of voting age, a territorial legislature was to be elected and a nonvoting delegate was to be sent to the Congress. At least three and not more than five states were to be created from this territory; when any one of the established divisions of the territory contained a population of 60,000 inhabitants, it was to be admitted to the Union as a state on a basis of complete equality with the older states. Contained in the ordinance were certain guarantees of civil and religious liberties, together with a prohibition of slavery in the territory.[2] *The main principle, however, was the eventual equality of status for the new areas.* The age-old source of trouble between colony and ruling country was thus removed by a simple, although unprecedented, device—making the colonies extensions of the empire that would be allowed to become socially and politically equal.

THE LATER LAND ACTS, 1796–1862

For a decade after the passage of the Land Ordinance of 1785, pioneering in the area north of the Ohio River was restricted as much by Indian troubles as by the high price of government land. The British, who persisted in maintaining posts on American territory in the Northwest, for years incited the Indians to make war on American settlers. By a treaty of 1794, the British agreed to evacuate the posts in the Northwest, and in August of that year "Mad Anthony" Wayne and his forces defeated the Indians at the Battle of Fallen Timbers. The time was then ripe for the establishment of new land policies by the Congress of the United States.

The Land Act of 1796 represented another victory for the conservatives. A system of rectangular surveys substantially the same as the one established by the Ordinance of 1785 was made permanent. The minimum purchase allowed by the Act of 1796 was still 640 acres, but the minimum price per acre was raised to $2, the only concession to the cheap-land advocates being a credit provision that permitted half of the purchase price to be deferred for a year. Only a small amount of land was sold under this act before Congress changed the minimum acreage to 320 in 1800 and permitted the buyer, after a cash payment of one-half the value, to pay one-fourth the value in two years and the final fourth in four years. A law of 1804 further lowered the minimum purchase to 160 acres. By 1820, the liberal forces had clearly won the battle: the minimum purchase was reduced to 80 acres and the price per acre to $1.25, but the credit provisions, which had resulted in losses to the government, were repealed. Twelve years

[2] Here again it is to Jefferson, who wanted slavery prohibited in all the western territories and states (even south of the Northwest Territory), that we owe these guarantees. See Jonathan Hughes, "The Great Land Ordinances: Colonial America's Thumbprint on History," in *Essays on the Emerging of the Old Northwest*, eds. David C. Klingaman and Richard K. Vedder (Athens: Ohio University Press, 1987).

later, the minimum purchase was reduced to 40 acres, so in 1832 a pioneer could purchase a piece of farmland for $50. By this time, pressures for *free* land, which had been exerted from the first, were beginning to produce legislative results.

Settlers who were brave enough to risk their lives in a pioneering venture were not usually deterred from action by legal niceties. From the beginning, pioneers tended to settle past the areas that had been surveyed and announced for sale. As the decades passed and the West became "crowded," this tendency to pick a tract in an unopened area increased. Unauthorized settlement, or "squatting," resulted from the attempts of the pioneers to find better soils and the hope that they could settle on choice land and make it a going proposition before they were billed for it.

Squatting was illegal, of course, but it was an offense that was hard to police. Moreover, there were those who argued that by occupying and improving the land, a squatter gained the rights to it—"cabin rights" or "corn rights" or "tommyhawk rights," as they were variously called on the frontier. At first, federal troops tried to drive squatters from unsurveyed land, but successes were only temporary. Gradually, the government came to view this pioneer lawbreaking less and less seriously. Against those who would purchase the squatter's land when it became available for public sale, informal but effective measures were taken by the squatters themselves, who formed protective associations as soon as they settled in a particular locality. When the public auction of land in that locality was held, the members of the protective association let it be known that there was to be no competitive bidding for land preempted by them. The appearance of well-armed frontiersmen at the auction ordinarily convinced city slickers and big land buyers that it would be unwise to bid. Even in places where there was no organized action, squatters who found their farms bought out from under them could often charge handsomely for the "improvements" they had made, and frontier courts were inclined to uphold their "rights."

As early as 1820, Congress began to give relief to squatters, and scarcely a year went by after 1830 in which preemption rights were not granted to settlers in certain areas. In 1841, a general Preemption Act, called the "Log Cabin Bill" by its proponents, was passed. This law granted, to anyone settling on land that was surveyed but not yet available for sale, the right to purchase 160 acres at the minimum price when the auction was held. No one could outbid the settler and secure the land, provided the squatter could raise the $200 necessary to buy a quarter section. Technically, squatting on *unsurveyed* land was still illegal; because of this and because there was still no outright grant of land, the westerner (and anyone else who could make money by buying land and waiting for it to rise in value) was not satisfied. Nevertheless, the land policy of the country was about as liberal as could be consistent with the demand that the public domain be a continuing source of revenue.

Pressure remained on Congress to reduce the price of "islands" of less-desirable land that had been passed over in the first surges to the West. In 1854, the Graduation Act provided for the graduated reduction of the minimum purchase price of such tracts, to a point where land that remained unsold for 30 years could be purchased for as little as $12^1/_2$¢ an acre. Settlers quickly purchased these pieces of land, attesting to the fact that people were willing to gamble a little on the probable appreciation of even the most unpromising real estate.

In the 1850s, as agitation for free land continued, it became apparent that the passage of a homestead law was inevitable. Southerners, who had at one time favored free grants to actual settlers, became violently opposed to this as time went on. The 160-acre farm usually proposed by homestead supporters was not large enough to make the working of slaves economical, and it seemed obvious to southern congressmen that homesteading would fill the West with antislavery people. On the other hand, many northern congressmen who might normally have had leanings toward a conservative policy joined forces with the westerners; they too knew that free land meant free states.

In 1860 a homestead act was passed, but President James Buchanan, fearing that it would precipitate secession, vetoed it. Two years later, with the Civil War raging and the southerners out of Congress, the Homestead Act of 1862 became law. Henceforth, any head of a family or anyone over 21 could have 160 acres of public land on the payment of small fees. The only stipulation was that the homesteader should either live on the land or cultivate it for five years. An important provision was that settlers who decided not to meet the five-year requirement might obtain full title to the land simply by paying the minimum price of $1.25 an acre.

Although much land was to pass into private hands under the Homestead Act of 1862, it was not the boon that it was expected to be. Most of the first-class land had been claimed by this time. Furthermore, it was so easy to circumvent the provisions

In the nineteenth century, wagon trains brought a steady stream of migrants to western America and its expansive lands.

of the law that land-grabbers used it, along with the acts that still provided for outright purchase, to build up great land holdings. By 1862, the frontier had reached the edge of the dry country, where a 160-acre farm was too small to provide a living for a settler and his family.

THE MIGRATIONS TO THE WEST

In discussing the colonial period, we noted that pioneers were moving across the Appalachian Mountains by the middle of the eighteenth century. By 1790, perhaps a quarter of a million people lived within the mountain valleys or to the west, and the trickle of westward movement had become a small stream. There were two eighteenth-century routes to the West. The more important one passed through the Cumberland Gap and then into either Kentucky or Tennessee; the other ran across southern Pennsylvania to Pittsburgh and on down the Ohio River. Even as the movement to the West was gaining momentum, pioneers were still settling in Pennsylvania and New York and to the north in Vermont, New Hampshire, and Maine.

An overview of population growth and the distributional impact of western migration and other demographic effects are shown in Table 8-1 and Figure 8-1. In 1812, on

TABLE 8-1   POPULATIONS IN THE TRANS-APPALACHIAN STATES[a]

State	1810	1850	1860
Ohio	231	1,980	2,340
Michigan	5	398	749
Indiana	25	988	1,350
Illinois	12	852	1,712
Minnesota	—[b]	6	172
Wisconsin	—	305	776
Iowa	—	192	675
Kansas	—	—	107
Kentucky	407	982	1,156
Tennessee	262	1,003	1,110
Alabama	9	772	964
Mississippi	31	607	791
Louisiana	77	518	708
Arkansas	1	210	435
Missouri	20	682	1,182
Texas	—	213	604
Total	1,080	9,708	14,831
Total U.S.	7,224	23,261	31,513
Percentage Trans-Appalachia of Total U.S.	15.0	41.7	47.1

SOURCE: *HISTORICAL STATISTICS* (WASHINGTON, D.C.: GOVERNMENT PRINTING OFFICE, 1960), DERIVED FROM SERIES A, PP. 123–180.

[a]FIGURES GIVEN IN THOUSANDS OF PERSONS; EXCLUDES FAR WEST AND WEST COAST.
[b]NO DATA.

the eve of the second war with Great Britain, just over 1 million people (about 15 percent of the nation's total) lived west of the Appalachians. From this 15 percent, the western population grew to almost half of the total by 1860. On the eve of the Civil

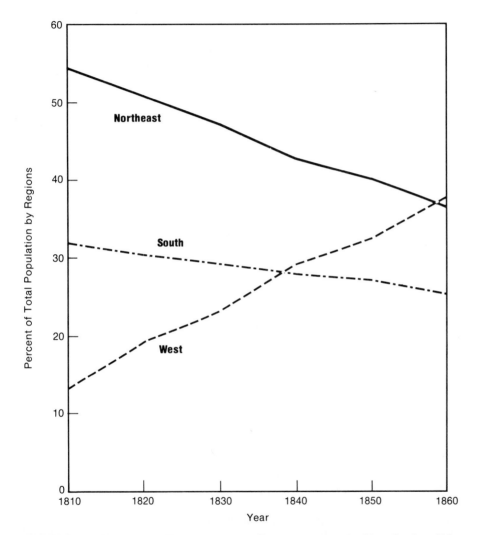

FIGURE 8-1 POPULATION DISTRIBUTION BY REGIONS, 1810–1860 *Note: South—Alabama, Arkansas, Florida, Georgia, Louisiana, Mississippi, North Carolina, South Carolina, Texas, and Virginia; West—Illinois, Indiana, Iowa, Kansas, Kentucky, Michigan, Minnesota, Missouri, Nebraska, Ohio, Tennessee, Wisconsin, California, Nevada, and Oregon; Northeast—Connecticut, Delaware, Maine, Maryland, Massachusetts, New Hampshire, New Jersey, New York, Pennsylvania, Rhode Island, and Vermont.*

SOURCE: U.S. CENSUS BUREAU, *A COMPENDIUM OF THE NINTH CENSUS, JUNE 1, 1870,* BY FRANCIS A. WALKER, SUPERINTENDENT OF CENSUS (WASHINGTON, D.C.: 1872), PP. 8-9. REPRINTED FROM DOUGLASS C. NORTH, *THE ECONOMIC GROWTH OF THE UNITED STATES 1790–1860* (ENGLEWOOD CLIFFS, NEW JERSEY: PRENTICE-HALL, 1960), P. 121.

MAP 8-3 MOVING FRONTIER: *Census data from 1800 onward chronicled the constant westward flow of population. The "frontier," its profile determined by natural attractions and a few man-made and physiographic obstacles, was a magnet for the venturesome.*

War, the center of the population was near Chillicothe, Ohio. The western population grew from 1 to nearly 13 million as the total grew from 7.2 to 31.4 million. In short, the rate of population growth was twice as high west of the Appalachian Mountains as in the East, more than 5 percent annually compared to 2.2 percent.

As the population expanded and pushed westward, the nation's frontier was pressed outward. The frontier, as technically defined in the census reports, was any area containing more than two and less than six people per square mile. In Map 8-3, the frontier lines for 1800, 1820, 1840, and 1860 have been drawn from census data. The line for 1800 indicates a wedge driven into the West, with its point in western Kentucky. Sixty years later, the line ran in a southerly direction from a point in the middle of Minnesota, with a noticeable bulge into the Nebraska and Kansas territories and a definite drift into Texas.

THE NORTHWESTERN MIGRATION AND HOGS, CORN, AND WHEAT

As shown in Table 8-1 and in Map 8-3 on the foregoing pages, during the early 1800s the movement across the top of the country gained momentum and an initial lead over migration from the southern states. During the first quarter of the century, people from the New England and Middle Atlantic states were pouring into the northern counties of Ohio and Indiana and later into southern Michigan. By 1850, lower Michigan was fairly well settled, and the best lands in northern Illinois and southern Wisconsin had been claimed. On the eve of the Civil War, pioneers were pushing the northwestern tip of the frontier into central Minnesota, most of Iowa was behind the frontier line, and the handsome country of eastern Kansas was being settled. Only in Texas did the frontier line of 1860 bulge farther to the west than it did in Kansas. By this time California had been a state for a decade and Oregon had just been admitted, but the

The morning of the opening of the Oklahoma Land Rush.

Land speculation—"holding for a rise"—became a lively offshoot of the westward population surge. Here, a Kansas land office provides a center for speculative activity.

vast area between the western frontier and the coast was not to be completely settled for another half-century.

Southerners moving across the Ohio River were the chief influence in the lower part of the old Northwest. New Englanders, after the Erie Canal made transportation easier, were dominant in the Great Lakes region, but they were joined by another stream that originated in the Middle Atlantic states. For the most part, families moved singly, although sometimes as many as 50 to 100 would move together. As the frontier pushed westward, the pioneers on the cutting edge were frequently the same people who had broken virgin soil a short way back only a few years before. Others were the grown children of men and women who had once participated in the conquest of the wilderness.

Throughout this early period of westward expansion, there was an ever-increasing influx of land-hungry people from abroad. From 1789 to the close of the War of 1812, not more than 250,000 people immigrated from Europe. With the final defeat of Napoleon and the coming of peace abroad, immigration resumed. From 500,000 people in the 1830s, the flow increased to 1.5 million in the 1840s and to 2.5 million in the 1850s. For the most part, the newcomers were from northern Europe; Germans and Irish predominated, but there were many immigrants from England, Scotland, Switzerland, and the Scandinavian countries. Of these peoples, the Germans tended more than any others to go directly to the lands of the West. Some immigrants from the other groups entered into the agricultural migration, but most were absorbed into eastern city populations.

Is there an economic explanation to the timing of the western migrations? Although the absolute numbers of western migrants from the eastern states and from abroad continued to swell, the decades of greatest western expansion, in terms of percentages, were the 1810s and 1830s. In absolute terms, the 1850s were the greatest. From Table 8-1 (see page 162) we can calculate percentage rates of increase of the western population for the five decades from 1810 to 1860: these were 6.9, 4.9, 5.6, 4.2, and 4.1 percent. Also from Table 8-1 we see the greatest increase in absolute numbers coming in the 1850s: nearly 4.3 million people.

As Douglass C. North has argued, in large measure these surges are explained by the exceptional economic opportunities in the West.[3] Hogs, corn, and wheat became the great northwestern staples, and as shown in the figure on the next page, corn and wheat prices were unusually high in these decades. People came to the new lands in response to the profits to be made in the production of these great staples.

Critics of North's "market opportunity response" argument have countered that land sales during these periods were based on pervasive speculation, not settlement and production for market.[4] Much of the land, however, was being put to use. The decades of greatest growth in "improved land" (for grazing, grass, tillage, or lying fallow) were also the 1810s, 1830s, and 1850s. (The percentage rates of change in improved acres from 1810 to 1860, by decade, were 23.5, 6.5, 7.1, 5.4, and 7.8.[5]) In short, North's critics were wrong.

---

[3] See Douglass C. North, *The Economic Growth of the United States 1790–1860* (Englewood Cliffs, New Jersey: Prentice-Hall, 1961).

[4] See, for example, Albro Martin's review of David H. Fischer's *Historians' Fallacies: Toward a Logic Historical Thought* (New York: Harper & Row, 1971).

[5] Eric F. Haites, James Mak, and Gary M. Walton, *Western River Transportation: The Era of Early Internal Improvements* (Baltimore: Johns Hopkins University Press, 1975), p. 113.

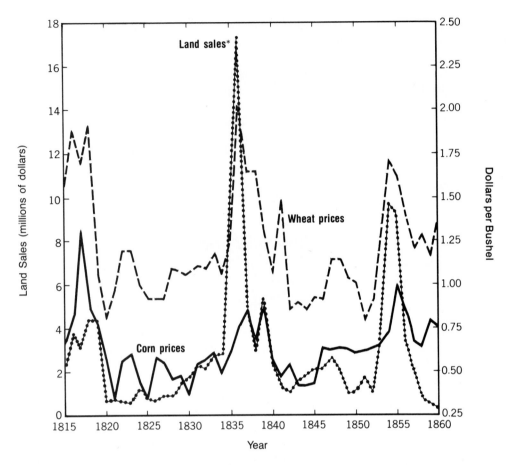

U.S. PUBLIC LAND SALES IN SEVERAL WESTERN STATES* AND WHEAT AND CORN PRICES,
1815–1860

SOURCE: DOUGLASS C. NORTH, *THE ECONOMIC GROWTH OF THE UNITED STATES 1790–1860* (ENGLE-
WOOD CLIFFS, NEW JERSEY: PRENTICE-HALL, 1961), P. 137.

*OHIO, ILLINOIS, INDIANA, MICHIGAN, IOWA, WISCONSIN, AND MISSOURI.

The only variable slightly out of step with North's general argument is the western
population growth *rate* for the 1850s. This slowdown would be expected, however, from
the general slowing of growth for the total population, the rise in the number of
improved acres per person, and the rise in agricultural productivity—all of which
occurred. The supply response to high staple prices is observed in terms of both population and improved acres in the 1810s and 1830s, but the supply response to the boom
years of the 1850s was dominated more by improved acres than by population.

AGRICULTURAL SPECIALIZATION AND REGIONAL DISLOCATION

The resulting surges in production in the Northwest (the Midwest as we know it today) did not immediately dislocate agriculture in the older states. Over the decades, however, the leading producers of hogs, corn, and wheat became western states.

Early in the 1800s, western hog production was greatly limited by high transportation costs; hogs were driven overland from Ohio to the urban centers of the East or were sent south by boat for sale to the plantations. Cattle, too, were driven in great herds to the East, where they were sold for immediate slaughter or for further fattening. But it was not long before pioneer farmers could market their hogs fairly close to home. Slaughtering and meat-packing centers arose in the early West, and by the 1830s Cincinnati, nicknamed Porkopolis, was the most important pork-processing city in the country.

Commercial hog raising required corn growing. For a while, hogs were allowed into the forests to forage on the mast (acorns and nuts that fell from the trees). But regular feeding is necessary to produce a good grade of pork, and corn is an ideal feed crop. Corn can be grown almost anywhere, provided there is adequate rainfall. It had been cultivated in all the original colonies and throughout the South. As late as 1840, Kentucky, Tennessee, and Virginia led the nation in corn production. But within 20 years it was apparent that the states to the northwest would be the corn leaders.[6] On the eve of the Civil War, Illinois, Ohio, Missouri, and Indiana led in corn production, and it appeared that Iowa, Kansas, and Nebraska would one day rank ahead of Kentucky and Tennessee, then in fifth and sixth place respectively.

The attraction of new lands for wheat was also tremendous. Western wheat could not come into its own until facilities were available for transporting it in quantity to the urban centers of the East; even as late as 1850, Pennsylvania and New York ranked first and third, respectively, in its production nationally. Ohio, which had become a commercial producer in the 1830s, ranked second. During the next decade, the shift of wheat production to the West was remarkable. By 1860, Illinois, Indiana, and Wisconsin were the leading producers, and the five states carved from the Northwest Territory produced roughly half the nation's output. The major wheat-growing areas were still not finally established, however; further shifts to the West in the production of this important crop were yet to come.

Ultimately the northern migration forced changes on the agriculture of the northeastern states. For a quarter of a century after the ratification of the Constitution, agriculture in New England, except in a few localities, remained relatively primitive; the individual farm unit produced practically everything needed for the household. With the growing industrialization of New England after 1810, production for urban markets became possible. Between 1810 and 1840, farmers in the Middle Atlantic states continued to grow the products for which their localities had traditionally been suited,

---

[6] For the advantages of corn growing to the western pioneer, see Paul W. Gates, *The Farmer's Age: Agriculture, 1815–1860* (New York: Holt, Rinehart & Winston, 1960), p. 169. A single peck of seed corn, yielding as much as 50 bushels, planted an acre and could be transported far more easily than 2 bushels of wheat seed, which weighed 120 pounds but might bring in only 15 to 18 bushels per acre.

and, as noted, Pennsylvania and New York remained major wheat producers until mid-century. But the arrival of the steamboat in the West in 1811, the opening of the Erie Canal in the 1820s, and the extension of the railroads beyond the Alleghenies in the 1840s meant that products of the rich western lands would flow in ever-increasing amounts to the East. Western competition caused the northeastern farmer to reduce grain cultivation, and only dairy cattle remained important in animal production. Specialization in truck gardens and dairy products for city people and hay for city horses came to characterize the agriculture of this region, and those who could not adapt to the changing market conditions moved to the city or went West.

THE SOUTHWESTERN MIGRATION AND COTTON

As discussed in Chapter 7, the Lower South suffered serious setbacks during the early years of independence. Even the market for tobacco stagnated, especially after the Embargo Act of 1807 and again after the War of 1812 allowed tobacco from other regions to enter and gain greater shares of the world market.

The hope of the South was in cotton. Obtaining their supplies of raw cotton from the Orient, the English had increasingly turned to the manufacture of cotton cloth instead of wool in the late seventeenth century. The inventions that came a century later—the steam engine, the spinning jenny, the water frame, the spinning mule, and the power loom—all gave rise to an enormous demand for cotton fiber. The phase of the Industrial Revolution that made it possible to apply power to textile manufacturing occurred at just the right time to stimulate and encourage the planting of cotton wherever it could be grown profitably. In the southern United States, the conditions for a profitable agriculture based on cotton were nearly ideal. Only some way of separating the green seed from the short-staple "upland cotton" had to be devised. One of the contributions of Yankee genius Eli Whitney was the invention of a gin that enabled a good worker to clean 50 pounds of cotton a day instead of only 1 pound by hand. With the application of power to the gin, the amount of fiber that could be produced appeared almost limitless.

On the humid coasts of Georgia and South Carolina, planters who had grown indigo turned to cotton. Even some rice fields were recultivated to produce the new staple. The culture moved up to North Carolina and Virginia and over the mountains to the beautiful rolling country of middle Tennessee. In the early 1800s, the piedmont of Georgia and South Carolina became the important cotton center; these states were vying for first place by 1820, with South Carolina slightly in the lead.

Beginning with the end of the War of 1812, the really important shift in cotton production was to the west (see Map 8-4). Almost unerringly, the settlers first planted the loamy, fertile soils that extended in an arc from Georgia through Alabama into northeastern Mississippi. A second major cotton-growing area lay in the rich bottom land of the lower Mississippi River and its tributaries. In this extremely fertile soil, the cotton even tended to grow a longer fiber. The culture spread into western Tennessee and eastern Arkansas. A jump into Texas then foretold the trend of cotton production.

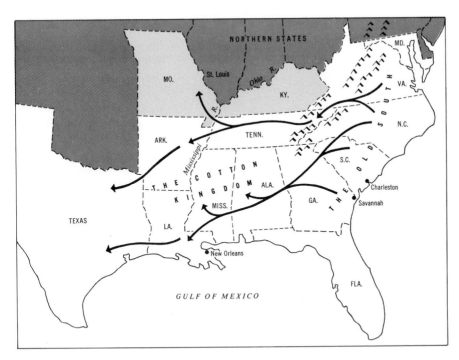

MAP 8-4 SHIFTS IN COTTON CULTIVATION: *The tremendous growth of the world demand for cotton propelled the westward movement of cotton cultivation after the War of 1812 and up to the onset of the Civil War.*

By 1840, the early cotton-producing states had been left behind. In 1860, Alabama, Mississippi, and Louisiana were far in the lead, with Mississippi alone producing more cotton than Georgia and South Carolina combined. This shift in the realm of King Cotton was to have the most far-reaching consequences on the economy of the South.

Just before the Civil War, there could be no doubt that cotton was indeed king. As Douglass North has remarked, it is difficult to exaggerate the role of cotton in American economic growth between 1800 and 1850.[7] The great staple accounted for more than half the dollar value of U.S. exports—a value nearly ten times as great in U.S. foreign trade as its nearest competitor, the wheat and wheat flour of the North. At home, cotton planters furnished the raw materials for textile manufacturers in the North, who by 1860 were selling half again as much cotton cloth as wool cloth. As we will see in Chapter 10, cotton goods were the leading manufacture in the United States in 1860, ranked by value added (second by employment). It was not surprising that even as antislavery forces strengthened in the late antebellum period, southerners could scarcely envisage a North, or even a world, without their chief product.

There was both a slight push and a major pull to the new lands of the South. The push had begun in colonial times, as tidewater lands began to lose the natural fertility

---

[7] See North, *The Economic Growth of the United States 1790–1860.*

that staples grown there required. The small farmer, impelled by hardship, had moved into the piedmont. The shift had been especially pronounced in Virginia and North Carolina, from which struggling families tended to sift through the Cumberland Gap into Tennessee and Kentucky. The frontiersman—the professional pioneer—was then pulled into the rich new cotton country, mostly from Georgia and South Carolina, but partly from Tennessee and even from Kentucky. Following closely came the yeoman farmer; almost simultaneously—and this is what clearly distinguishes the southern migration—came the planter, the man of substance, with his huge household establishment and his slaves.

As with the surges in the Northwest, the 1810s, the 1830s, and the 1850s were the boom decades for the new southwestern areas. It was, of course, the favorable returns expected on cotton cultivation that brought the great, irregular surges of movement toward the southwest. As shown in Figure 8-2, there is close correlation between the price of cotton on the one hand and the volume of public land sales in Alabama, Florida, Louisiana, Mississippi, and Arkansas on the other. Here again, we observe the responsiveness of individuals to favorable economic opportunities.

THE FAR WESTERN MIGRATION

Although of only minor importance when compared with the southern and northwestern migrations, the California Gold Rush was one of the most widely discussed and emotionally charged of all the migrations in response to economic opportunity. On January 24, 1848, just nine days before the war with Mexico ended, James W. Marshall discovered gold while building a sawmill for John Sutter on the South Fork of the American River.

Sutter and Marshall attempted to keep the discovery a secret while trying to secure for themselves stronger property rights on the area. However, a young boy told of the discovery to a man bringing supplies to the mill, and coincidentally the boy's mother gave the driver a small nugget as a present. When the man later used the nugget to buy a drink back at "Fort Sutter," the word was out.

As gold fever swept the land, people poured across the country and "around the Horn." In the first several months of 1849, almost 20,000 left the East Coast by boat destined for California, and nearly 40,000 arrived in San Francisco throughout 1849. From a population of about 107,000 near the end of 1849, California grew to over 260,000 within three years.

Among the most fascinating aspects of the California Gold Rush was the initial absence of property rights to land and of a government capable of enforcing law and order. Despite stiff penalties for desertion, for instance, U.S. soldiers in California left their posts in droves to hunt for gold. (Enlisted men, who typically earned $7 a month plus room and board, numbered almost 1,059 in 1847 but only 660 in 1848.) Yet despite an initial absence of law and order, violence in the gold fields was surprisingly low. As John Umbeck, one of the leading authorities on the Gold Rush, reports:

> During 1848, . . . nearly 10,000 people rushed to mine gold on property to which no one had exclusive rights. Furthermore, although nearly every miner carried a

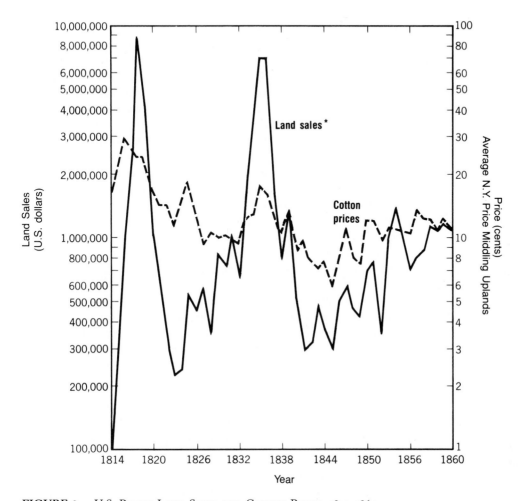

FIGURE 8-2 U.S. Public Land Sales and Cotton Prices, 1814–1860

SOURCE: Douglass C. North, *The Economic Growth of the United States 1790–1860* (Englewood Cliffs, New Jersey: Prentice-Hall, 1961), p. 124.

*Alabama, Florida, Louisiana, Mississippi, Arkansas.

gun, little violence was reported. In July, when Governor Mason visited the mines, he reported that the miners were respecting Sutter's property rights and that "crime of any kind was very infrequent, and that no thefts or robberies had been committed in the gold district . . . and it was a matter of surprise, that so peaceful and quiet a state of things should continue to exist."[8]

Only after new waves of miners entered the fields did gold land become troublingly scarce, thereby urging exclusive property rights or claims. Several first-hand accounts indicate the nature of those rights:

[8] See John Umbeck, "The California Gold Rush: A Study of Emerging Property Rights," *Explorations in Economic History* 14 (1977).

When the mines in and around Nevada City were first opened they were solely in the ravines ... and there was no law regulating the size of a miner's claim, and generally a party that first went into a ravine had the exclusive right there too.... As population increased that rule did not long maintain. The miners saw that something must be done, and therefore a meeting was called and a rule was established that each miner could hold thirty feet square as a mining claim.

All these bars on the Middle Fork of the American River, from Oregon Bar upwards, after the lowest estimate, employed in the summer of 1850 not less than 1,500 men; originally working on shares, and the assessment on the share paid out daily, so that those who had been drunk or absent did not get any part of it; but this after a while caused dissatisfaction and was the reason of breaking up the co-operative work and commencing work on claims. A claim was a spot of ground fifteen feet wide on the river front.

In a comparatively short time we had a large community on that creek, which led to rows and altercations about boundaries, that eventuated in an agreement, entered into by unanimous agreement, that each person should have 10 square feet.

Wood's Creek was filled up with miners, and I here for the first time after the discovery of gold, learned what a miner's claim was. In 1848, the miners had no division of the ground into claims—they worked where it was richest, and many times four or five could be seen at work in a circle of six feet in diameter; but ... here they were now measuring the ground off with tape measures so as to prevent disputes arising from the division.[9]

It was at the "miners' meetings" that contract specifications were determined. Each "field" held its own meetings and afterwards each miner marked his claim boundary with wooden stakes, and frequently a notice such as this:

> All and everybody, this is my claim, fifty feet on the gulch, cordin to Clear Creek District Law, backed up by shotgun amendments.
>
> Any person found trespassing on this claim will be persucuted to the full extent of the law. This is no monkey tale butt I will assert my rites at the pint of the sicks shirter if legally necessary to taik head and good warnin.[10]

In this fashion, property rights first emerged in the gold fields of California, and with them an outpouring of millions of dollars in gold.

The great California Gold Rush had effects far beyond the bossless mass employment and wealth creation it generated. It was a tidal wave of hope to people who no longer were forced to know their place and be resigned to it. And the timing! Ireland's potato famine, China's Taiping Rebellion, political uprisings in France and Germany—all added great numbers to young Americans, many discharged from service at the end of the Mexican War, who sought their fortunes in the gold fields. Not everyone struck it rich like Leland Stanford, formerly a failed lawyer, or Lucius Fair-

---

[9] As quoted in Umbeck, p. 215.

[10] As quoted in Umbeck, p. 216.

child, a store clerk from Wisconsin who returned home rich and became Wisconsin's governor. But the Gold Rush did guarantee dreams and adventure to match the towering Sierras.

SELECTED REFERENCES AND SUGGESTED READINGS

Berry, Thomas. *Western Prices Before 1861.* Cambridge: Harvard University Press, 1943.

Bidwell, Percy, and John Falconer. *History of Agriculture in the Northern United States 1620–1860.* Washington, D.C.: Carnegie Institution of Washington, 1925.

Billington, Ray A. "The Origin of the Land Speculator as a Frontier Type." *Agricultural History* 9 (October 1945).

————. *Westward Expansion: A History of the American Frontier.* New York: Macmillan, 1949.

Bogue, Allan C. "Farming in the Prairie Peninsula 1830–1890." *Journal of Economic History* 23 (March 1963).

————. *From Prairie to Cornbelt: Farming on the Illinois and Iowa Prairies in the Nineteenth Century.* Chicago: University of Chicago Press, 1963.

Bogue, Allan C., and Margaret Bogue. "Profits and the Frontier Land Speculation." *Journal of Economic History* 37 (March 1957).

Carstensen, Vernon, ed. *The Public Lands: Studies in the History of the Public Domain.* Madison: University of Wisconsin Press, 1963.

Cole, Arthur H. "Cyclical and Sectional Variations in the Sale of the Public Lands, 1816–1860." *Review of Economics and Statistics* 9 (1927). Reprinted in Vernon Carstensen, ed. *The Public Lands.* Madison: University of Wisconsin Press, 1963.

Danhof, Clarence. *Change in Agriculture: The Northern United States, 1820–70.* Cambridge: Harvard University Press, 1969.

————. "Farm Making Costs and the Safety Valve, 1855–60." In *The Public Lands,* ed. Vernon Carstensen. Madison: University of Wisconsin Press, 1963.

Freund, Rudolf. "Military Bounty Lands and the Origin of the Public Domain." *Agricultural History* 20 (1946). Reprinted in Vernon Carstensen, ed. *The Public Lands.* Madison: University of Wisconsin Press, 1963.

Gates, Paul W. "Charts of Public Land Sales and Entries." *Journal of Economic History* 24 (March, 1964).

————. *History of Public Land Law Development.* Washington, D.C.: Public Land Law Review Commission, 1968.

————. "The Role of the Land Speculator in Western Development." *Pennsylvania Magazine of History and Biography* 66 (1942). Reprinted in Vernon Carstensen, ed. *The Public Lands.* Madison: University of Wisconsin Press, 1963.

Hughes, Jonathon R. T. "The Great Land Ordinances: Colonial America's Thumb Print on History." In *Essays on the Economic Significance of the Old Northwest,* eds. David C. Klingaman and Richard K. Vedder. Athens: Ohio University Press, 1987, pp. 1–18.

Lebergott, Stanley. " 'O Pioneers': Land Speculation and the Growth of the Midwest." In *Essays on the Economy of the Old Northwest,* eds. David C. Klingaman and Richard K. Vedder. Athens: Ohio University Press, 1987, pp. 37–58.

Merk, Frederick. *History of the Westward Movement.* New York: Knopf, 1978.

North, Douglass C. *The Economic Growth of the United States 1790–1860.* Englewood Cliffs, New Jersey: Prentice-Hall, 1961.

North, Douglass C., and Andrew R. Rutten. "The Northwest Ordinance in Historical Perspective." In *Essays on the Economy of the Old Northwest,* eds. David C. Klingaman and Richard K. Vedder. Athens: Ohio University Press, 1987, pp. 19–36.

Parker, William. "Agriculture." In *American Economic Growth: An Economist's History of the United States,* eds. Lance E. Davis et al. New York: Harper & Row, 1972. Chapter 11.

Parker, William, and Judith Klein. "Productivity Growth in Grain Production in the United States." In *Output, Employment and Productivity in the United States after 1800,* vol. 30, ed. Dorothy Brady. National Bureau of Economic Research, Studies in Income and Wealth. New York: Columbia University Press, 1966.

Primack, Martin. "Land Clearing Under 19th Century Techniques." *Journal of Economic History* 22 (December 1962).

Riegel, Robert E., and Robert G. Athearn. *America Moves West.* New York: Holt, 1964.

Rohrbough, Malcolm. *The Land Office Business: The Settlement and Administration of American Public Lands, 1789–1837.* New York: Oxford University Press, 1968.

Rothenberg, Winifred B. "The Market and Massachusetts Farmers, 1750–1855." *Journal of Economic History* 41 (1981): 283–314.

Steckel, Richard. "The Economic Foundations of East-West Migration During the 19th Century." *Explorations in Economic History* 20 (1983): 14–36.

Treat, Payson J. "Origin of the National Land System Under the Confederation." *American Historical Association Report, 1905.* Reprinted in Vernon Carstensen, ed. *The Public Lands.* Madison: University of Wisconsin Press, 1963.

Turner, Frederick Jackson. *The Frontier in American History.* New York: Holt, Rinehart & Winston, 1921.

Umbeck, John. "The California Gold Rush: A Study of Emerging Property Rights." *Explorations in Economic History* 14 (1977): 192–226.

Wyman, Walker D., and Clifton B. Kroeber, eds. *The Frontier in Perspective.* Madison: University of Wisconsin Press, 1957.

CHAPTER NINE

TRANSPORTATION AND MARKET GROWTH

CHAPTER THEME The economic growth of the United States in the nineteenth century was strategically influenced by the spread of a market economy, by the shifting of resources from lower-valued (subsistence) to higher-valued uses (production for market), and by the growth of specialization and divisions of labor in production. As Adam Smith and early nineteenth-century contemporaries knew, levels of productivity were vitally dependent on the size of the market, especially in manufacturing. Of course, market size was limited by the costs of moving goods and negotiating exchanges. In this early era, transportation costs were the most important component of these costs. For these many reasons, special concentration on transportation, mode by mode, is warranted and indeed vital to our understanding of long-term economic growth and the location of people and economic activity.

THE ANTEBELLUM TRANSPORTATION REVOLUTION

Once the western migrations were unleashed, the demand for improved transportation systems grew dramatically. Investments in steamboats, canals, and railroads were the most important internal transportation developments of the antebellum era. There can be little doubt that the host of improvements in transportation and the precipitous decline in freight rates (as shown in Figure 9-1) were truly revolutionary in impact as well as in form. Not only did they directly propel the process of westward expansion and the relocation of agriculture and mining discussed in Chapter 8, but they also greatly altered various regions' comparative advantages in production. For example, they set the stage for New England to concentrate increasingly in manufacturing and to further the advance and application of new technologies and organizational forms of production in a factory setting (Chapter 10). In turn, these changes set the stage for urbanization and heightening urban problems and labor unrest (Chapter 11). The falling costs of transport—and communication—boosted market size and efficiency and forged a national market for many goods and services. Whereas the pattern of general price declines in the western markets of Cincinnati and St. Louis had followed those in New York and Philadelphia by twelve months near the turn of the century, the lag was reduced to only three or four months by the 1830s. By the 1850s, this lag had fallen even further to a mere week or so. Lastly, the transportation linkage by water and rails between the East and West would prove significant in binding these two regions—politically as well as economically—as interregional tensions mounted in the years preceding the Civil War. The term *transportation revolution* consequently implies far more than a mere series of new technological forms rapidly introduced.

An important part of the transportation story is the role of private versus public initiative during this critical period of growing economic unification. In England railroads and canals were built and operated by private entrepreneurs, and government participation was slight. In the United States, however, there was a mixture of private and public enterprise. Government investments in canals and railroads as a percentage of total investment in these modes were large. Public investments were a smaller proportion in roads, and they were minimal for the natural waterways. A strong, active role in transportation for government had been planned as early as 1807, when Treasury Secretary Albert Gallatin was asked to develop "a plan for the application of such means as are within the power of Congress, to the purpose of opening roads and making canals. . . ."[1] Gallatin's ingenious plan had a projected total cost of $20 million, but questions of legality—and politics, as always—prevented the federal government from undertaking it. Many viewed the Constitution as an agreement among sovereignties (the sovereign states), and "strict constructionism" throughout most of the antebellum period held the federal government to only a few projects, mainly those

---

[1] Carter Goodrich, *Government Promotion of American Canals and Railroads* (New York: Columbia University Press, 1960), p. 27.

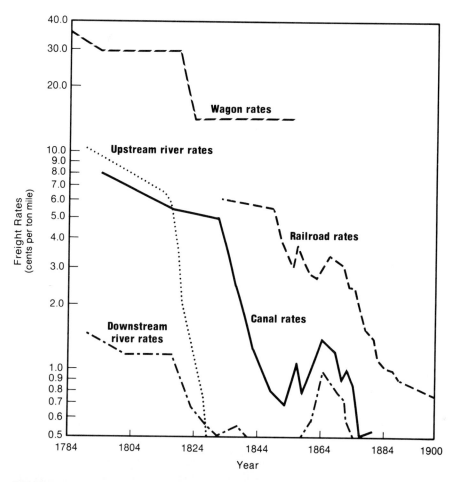

FIGURE 9-1 Inland Freight Rates, 1784–1900

SOURCES: Douglass C. North, *Growth and Welfare in the American Past* (Englewood Cliffs, New Jersey: Prentice-Hall, 1973), p. 108; and Douglass C. North, "The Role of Transportation in the Economic Development of North America," a paper presented to the International Congress of the Historical Sciences, Vienna, August 1965, and published in *Les Grandes Voies Maritimes dans le Monde XVe–XIXe Siecles*, © 1965 by Ecole des Hautes Etudes en Sciences Sociales, Paris.

passing through several states at a time. Nevertheless Gallatin's plan was carried out, not by the federal government, but by private entrepreneurs and by state and local and private enterprise mixtures. Sheer size of the capital requirements often necessitated these collaborations. Both public officials and private citizens promoted government intervention in transport investment. In some cases private operators succeeded in obtaining public credit and special assistance just as special interest groups (such as farmers) do today. In other cases, local politicians who wanted transportation improvements for their town or region took advantage of private entrepreneurs.

THE ROUTES OF WESTERN COMMERCE

During the antebellum period, three natural gateways linked the western territories and states with the rest of the nation and other countries. The first ran eastward, connecting the Great Lakes to New York. The main arteries feeding this Northern Gateway were down the St. Lawrence River or along the Hudson or Mohawk river valleys. Major investments on this route included the opening of the Erie Canal in 1825 and the completion of the New York Central and the New York and Erie railroads in 1852.

The second gateway, called the Northeastern Gateway, was a network of roads, canals, and later rail systems that connected the river launching points at Pittsburgh (on the Ohio River) to Philadelphia, and Wheeling (also on the Ohio River) to Baltimore. The National Road was completed west to Wheeling in 1817, and the Pennsylvania Turnpike—a toll road—reached Pittsburgh the next year. Competing canals on these two links created a rivalry in the 1830s. Then in the 1850s the rivalry of these cities was boosted again through rail linkages.

The Southern Gateway, at New Orleans, was the main southern entrepôt. The key event on the trunk rivers of the Mississippi, Missouri, Ohio, and other western river arteries to this gateway was the introduction of the steamboat in 1811.

Inland shipping points like Cincinnati soon became major markets for an increasing variety of goods and services.

Figure 9-2 (see next page) shows the volume of shipments from the western interior to the East and abroad by each gateway.[2] The growth of total outbound shipments, from 65,000 tons in 1810 to nearly 4.7 million tons in 1860, documents the impressive development that was taking place in the West. We also see that the Northeastern Gateway played only a minor role, typically carrying less than 5 percent of the shipments from the West. The Northern Gateway was far more significant, but not until the late 1830s. Prior to 1825 and the opening of the Erie Canal, this gateway handled no outbound shipments. Even in the early 1830s, most of the shipments on the Erie Canal were from upstate New York. Therefore it was primarily the Southern Gateway that handled western produce shipments, at least until the last few decades of the antebellum period. It was the dominance of the natural waterways, encompassing 16,000 miles of western rivers, that led the contemporary James Lanman to say in 1841:

> Steam navigation colonized the west! It furnished a motive for settlement and production by the hands of eastern men, because it brought the western territory nearer to the east by nine tenths of the distance. . . . Steam is crowding our eastern cities with western flour and western merchants, and lading the western steamboats with eastern emigrants and eastern merchandise. It has advanced the career of national colonization and national production, at least a century![3]

STEAMBOATS AND THE NATURAL WATERWAYS

Before the coming of the steamboat in the West, river travel was especially difficult, hazardous, and costly. Rafts and flatboats allowed downriver passage at reasonable cost, but the return upriver on foot or horseback was time-consuming and dangerous. Typical voyages of 1,000 miles took one month downstream and three to four months to return. The keelboat, which made upstream journeys possible, was based on labor-intensive, back-breaking work. As shown in Figure 9-1 (page 179), upstream costs were typically more than five times downstream costs.

In 1807, Robert Fulton, with the assistance of Robert R. Livingston, built the steamboat *Clermont,* which completed a historic voyage up the Hudson River from New York to Albany, a distance of 150 miles, in 32 hours. Following the initial trip, regular passenger service from New York to Albany was inaugurated and the dependability of the steamboat was quickly demonstrated. A new era of transportation on the rivers of America had begun.

The steamboat's beginning in the West came at the northern terminus of Pittsburgh, where the junction of the Allegheny and the Monongahela forms the Ohio

---

[2]The evidence on inbound shipments is more fragmentary and less complete, but it does not change the relative positions of each gateway in the movement of freight.

[3]James H. Lanman, "American Steam Navigation," *Hunt's Merchants' Magazine and Commercial Review* 4 (1841): 124.

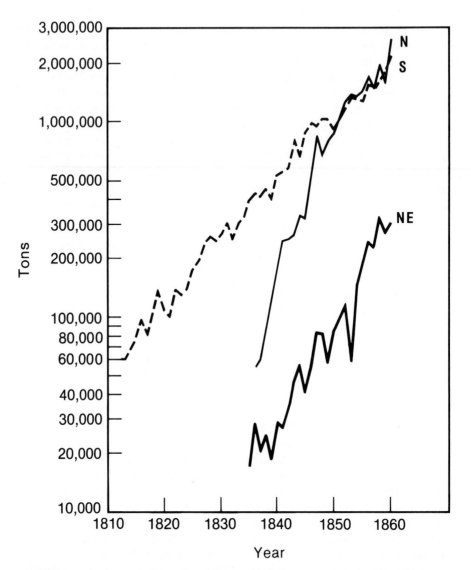

FIGURE 9-2 Freight Shipments from the Interior by the Western Gateways, 1810–1860

SOURCE: Erik F. Haites, James Mak, and Gary M. Walton, *Western River Transportation: The Era of Early Internal Development, 1810–1860* (Baltimore: Johns Hopkins University Press, 1975), p. 7 and Appendix A.

River and where plentiful supplies of timber and the local iron industry fostered a flourishing shipbuilding industry. It was at Pittsburgh that the first steamboat to ply the inland waters was constructed by Nicholas Roosevelt under the Fulton-Livingston patents. Named the *New Orleans*, it left Pittsburgh on October 20, 1811, and completed

Robert Fulton's steamboat the Clermont, built in 1807, started a transportation revolution on America's rivers.

its voyage to the Gulf of Mexico in a little over two and one-half months despite an earthquake en route at New Madrid, Missouri. Six years passed before regular services upstream and downstream were established, but (as shown in Table 9-1 on the next page) by 1819 the tonnage of steamboats in operation on the western rivers already exceeded 10,000. This figure grew to almost 200,000 tons by 1860. The periods of the most rapid expansion were the first two decades following 1815, but significant gains occurred throughout each decade. It was not until the 1880s that steamboating in western rivers registered an absolute decline.

The appearance of the steamboat on inland waterways did not, by any means, solve all problems of travel. Variations in the heights of the rivers still made navigation uncertain, even dangerous. Ice in the spring and sand bars in the summer were ever-present hazards; snags (trees lodged in rivers), rocks, and sunken vessels continually damaged and wrecked watercraft. In addition to these problems, the steamboat exposed westerners to some of the earliest hazards of industrialization; high-pressure boilers frequently exploded, accidentally killing thousands over the decades. This prompted the federal government to intervene: in 1838 and again in 1852, some of the first U.S. laws concerning industrial safety and consumer protection were legislated. The 1852 steamboat boiler inspection law was especially effective, significantly reducing boiler explosions and loss of life. Also, the federal government sporadically engaged in the removal of snags and other obstacles from the rivers. This also reduced losses of cargo, vessels, and people.

TABLE 9-1 ANNUAL CONSTRUCTION (GROSS AND NET) AND TONNAGE OF STEAMBOATS IN OPERATION ON WESTERN RIVERS, 1811–1868

Year	Ships in Operation		Year	Ships in Operation	
	Number	Tonnage		Number	Tonnage
1811	1	400	1840	494	82,600
1812	1	400	1841	504	85,200
1813	2	400	1842	458	76,500
1814	3	700	1843	449	80,000
1815	7	1,500	1844	509	90,300
1816	11	2,300	1845	538	96,200
1817	16	3,000	1846	578	106,300
1818	30	5,800	1847	638	122,400
1819	59	13,000	1848	666	133,400
1820	69	14,200	1849	648	130,100
1821	73	14,500	1850	638	134,600
1822	71	13,400	1851	660	142,900
1823	74	12,500	1852	676	152,900
1824	67	10,500	1853	711	169,300
1825	80	12,500	1854	696	169,000
1826	107	17,300	1855	696	172,700
1827	120	19,700	1856	761	188,100
1828	118	18,900	1857	800	199,600
1829	140	22,300	1858	779	196,400
1830	151	24,600	1859	779	192,800
1831	183	28,700	1860	817	195,000
1832	227	35,200	1861	665	165,100
1833	239	36,800	1862	666	157,300
1834	270	41,000	1863	778	160,200
1835	324	50,100	1864	919	193,200
1836	374	57,400	1865	1,006	228,700
1837	399	63,600	1866	1,028	238,400
1838	391	65,300	1867	976	232,300
1839	480	78,200	1868	874	212,200

SOURCE: ERIK F. HAITES, JAMES MAK, AND GARY M. WALTON, WESTERN RIVER TRANSPORTATION: THE ERA OF EARLY INTERNAL DEVELOPMENT, 1810–1860 (BALTIMORE: JOHNS HOPKINS UNIVERSITY PRESS, 1975), PP. 130–131.

COMPETITION, PRODUCTIVITY, AND ENDANGERED SPECIES

One of the most significant characteristics of western river transportation was the high degree of competition among the various craft. This meant that the revolutionary effects of the steamboat, which were critical to the early settlement of the West, were transfused through a competitive market. Fulton and Livingston attempted to secure a monopoly via government restraint to prevent others from providing steamboat ser-

TABLE 9-2   AVERAGE FREIGHT RATES (PER 100 POUNDS OF CARGO) BY DECADE
BETWEEN LOUISVILLE AND NEW ORLEANS, 1810–1859

	Upstream	Downstream
Before 1820	$5.00	$1.00
1820–1829	1.00	0.62
1830–1839	0.50	0.50
1840–1849	0.25	0.30
1850–1859	0.25	0.32

SOURCE: ERIK F. HAITES, JAMES MAK, AND GARY M. WALTON, *WESTERN RIVER TRANSPORTATION:
THE ERA OF EARLY INTERNAL DEVELOPMENT, 1810–1860* (BALTIMORE: JOHNS HOPKINS UNIVERSITY
PRESS, 1975), P. 32.

vices at New Orleans and throughout the West.[4] Their quest for monopoly rights was ultimately defeated in the courts. These and other associations failed to limit supply and block entry; and without government interference, the modest capital requirements needed to enter the business assured a competitive market.

Following an early period of bonanza profits (30 percent and more) on the major routes, a normal rate of return on capital of about 10 percent was common by 1820. Only on the remote and dangerous tributaries, where trade was thin and uncertain, could such exceptional returns as 35 or 40 percent be obtained.

Because the market for western rivercraft services was generally competitive, the savings from productivity-raising improvements ushered in by the steamboat were promptly passed on to consumers. And the cost reductions were significant, as the evidence in Table 9-2 illustrates.

Of course, a major cause of the sharp decline in freight costs was simply the introduction of steam power. However, the stream of modifications and improvements that followed the maiden voyage of the *New Orleans* provided greater productivity gains than the initial application of steam power. This assertion is verified in the fall of rates. The decrease in rates after 1820 was greater, both absolutely and relatively, than the decline from 1811 to 1820, especially in real terms. For example, in the purchasing power of 1820 dollars, the real cost decline upstream on the New Orleans–Louisville run was from $3.12 around 1815 to $2.00 in 1820 to $.28 in the late 1850s. Downstream, the real cost changes were from $.62 around 1815 to $.75 in 1820 to $.39 in the late 1850s.

Major modifications were made in the physical characteristics of the vessels. Initially resembling seagoing vessels, steamboats evolved to meet the shallow-water conditions of the western rivers. These boats became increasingly lighter in weight, with many outside decks for cargo (and budget-fare accommodations for passengers), and their water depth (or draft) became less and less despite increased vessel size. Consequently, the amount of cargo carried per vessel ton greatly increased. In addition, the season of normal operations was substantially extended, even during shallow-water

---

[4]See Gary M. Walton, "Fulton's Folly," in *Second Thoughts: Learning from American Social and Economic History,* ed. Donald McCloskey (Oxford University Press, 1992).

months. This, along with reductions in port times and passage times, greatly increased the number of round trips averaged each year. It is noteworthy that the decline in passage times was only partially due to faster speeds. Primarily, this decline resulted from learning to operate the boats at night. Shorter stopovers at specified fuel depots instead of long periods spent foraging in the woods for fuel contributed as well. Lastly, as noted earlier, government activity to clear the rivers of snags and other natural obstacles added to the time of normal operations and made river transport a safer business, as evidenced by a decline in insurance costs over the decades.

On reflection, it is clear that most of the improvements did not result from technological change. Only the initial introduction of steam power stemmed from advances in knowledge about basic principles. The host of modifications evolved from the process of learning by doing and from the restructuring of known principles of design and engineering to fit shallow-water conditions. In effect, they are a tribute to the skills and ingenuity of the early craftsmen and mechanics.

In sum, the overall record of achievement gave rise to productivity advances (output per unit of input) that averaged more than 4 percent per year between 1815 and 1860. Such a rate exceeded that of any other transport medium over a comparable length of time in the nineteenth century.[5]

With the steamboat's success, other forms of river transport either evolved or disappeared. The labor-consuming keelboat felt the strongest sting of competition from the new technology and was quickly eliminated from the competitive fray on the main trunk river routes. The keelboat made nearly 90 percent of its revenues on the upriver leg, where men labored to pole, pull, or row with back-breaking effort against the currents. As shown in Table 9-2 (preceding page), the steamboat's greatest impact was on the upstream rates. Only on some of the remote, hazardous tributaries did the keelboat find temporary refuge from the chugging advance of the steamboat.

Surprisingly, quite a different destiny evolved for the flatboat, which showed a remarkable persistence throughout the entire antebellum period. Because the reductions in downstream rates were more moderate, the current-propelled flatboat was less threatened. In addition, spillover effects from steamboating aided flatboating. First, there was the tremendous savings in labor that the steamboat generated by providing quick upriver transport to returning flatboatmen. Not only were they saved the long and sometimes perilous overland journey, but access to steamboat passenger services led to repetitive journeys and thus to the acquisition of skills and knowledge. This led to the adoption of larger flatboats, which economized greatly on labor per ton carried. Because of these gains, there were more flatboats on the western rivers near the middle of the nineteenth century than at any other time.

In combination, these western rivercraft gave a romantic aura to the drudgery of day-to-day freight haulage and commerce. Sumptuously furnished Mississippi riverboats were patronized by rich and poor alike. Yeomen farmers also contributed their adventuresome flatboating journeys. However, such developments were regional in character, and their impact was mainly on the Southern Gateway. On the waterways

---

[5] See Erik F. Haites, James Mak, and Gary M. Walton, *Western River Transportation: The Era of Early Internal Development, 1810–1860* (Baltimore: Johns Hopkins University Press, 1975), pp. 60–63.

of the East or on the Great Lakes, the steamboat never attained the importance that it did in the Midwest. Canals and turnpikes furnished alternative means of transportation, and the railroad network had an earlier start in the East. Steamboats in the East were primarily passenger carriers—great side-wheelers furnishing luxurious accommodations for people traveling between major cities. On the Great Lakes, contrary to what might be expected, sailing ships successfully competed for freight throughout the antebellum years. Where human comfort was a factor, however, the steamship gradually prevailed. Even so, the number and tonnage of sailing vessels on the Great Lakes in 1860 were far greater than those of steamboats.

PUBLIC VERSUS PRIVATE INITIATIVE ON THE NATURAL WATERWAYS

Transportation developments on the natural waterways, especially on the rivers through the Southern Gateway, but along the Northern Gateway avenues as well, were predominantly a product of private initiative. Government investments as a proportion of total investments in vessels and river improvements were minuscule. Private entrepreneurs owned and operated the craft, and state and local government rendered few improvements in the rivers because many of the benefits to users could not be captured within state boundaries. Why should state or local governments appropriate funds for river improvements if most of the benefits went to vessel owners (and users) passing by? Calls for federal action to improve the rivers often went unheeded because of strict constitutional interpretations. With the exception of sporadic but highly beneficial snag-removal programs, the public sector provided very little capital to transportation on the natural waterways, no more than 1 or 2 percent of the total expenditures.

THE CANAL ERA

Although the natural waterways provided a substantial web of transport facilities, many productive areas remained regionally and economically disconnected until the canals were built and other internal improvements were made to link them together. The first major undertaking began in 1816, when the New York legislature authorized the construction of the Erie and Champlain canals. With powerful canal commissioner DeWitt Clinton as its guiding spirit, the Erie Canal was promoted with enthusiasm, and sections were opened to traffic as they were completed. It quickly became apparent that the canal would have great success, and even before its completion in 1825, "canal fever" seized promoters throughout the country. In the tremendous building boom that followed, canals were constructed to link three types of areas. Some ran from the "back country" to the tidewater regions; some traversed, or attempted to traverse, the area between the older states and the Ohio valley; and some, the western canals, linked the Great Lakes with the waterways running to the East. The principal canals of the antebellum period are shown on the next page in Map 9-1. They were vital in developing the Northern and Northeastern gateways.

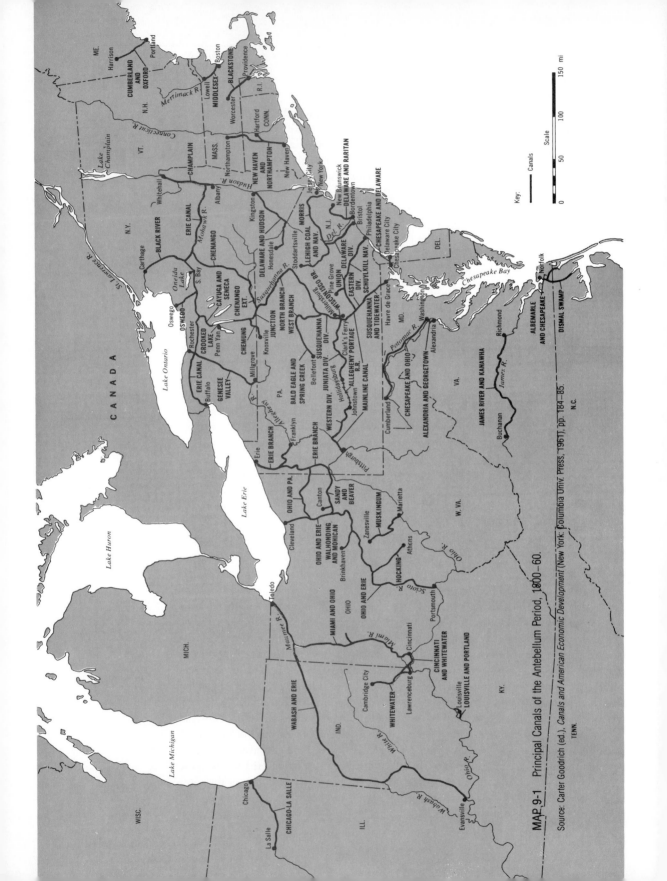

MAP 9-1   Principal Canals of the Antebellum Period, 1800–60.

Source: Carter Goodrich (ed.), *Canals and American Economic Development* (New York: Columbia Univ. Press, 1961), pp. 184–85.

The Erie was the most important of the early canals, though by no means the only profitable one. This system, which still exists in an expanded and improved form as the New York Barge Canal, was a massive undertaking. Beginning at Albany on the Hudson River, it traversed the state of New York westward to Buffalo on Lake Erie, covering a distance of 364 miles. The work cost approximately $7 million and took about nine years to complete. The builders overcame countless difficulties, not the least of which was their own ignorance. Hardly any of the engineers had ever worked in canal construction, and much experimentation was necessary in the process. Some sections of the canal did not hold water at first and had to be lined with clay after work had been completed. The locks presented a special difficulty, but ingenuity and the timely discovery of water-resistant cement helped solve the problems of lock construction.

In its final form, the Erie system reached a fair portion of New York state. The Cayuga and Seneca, the Chemung, and the Genesee extensions connected important territory to the south with the canal. A branch to Oswego provided access to Lake Ontario, and the Champlain Canal gave access to the North. The system not only furnished transportation to much of the state but tapped the Great Lakes areas served by the St. Lawrence route and the vast Ohio Territory as well. Beginning about 1835, a large part of the traffic from the West that had formerly traversed the Ohio and Mississippi rivers to New Orleans was diverted over the Erie Canal to the port of New York. This explains much of the convergence (catching up) of the Northern Gateway with the Southern Gateway revealed in Figure 9-2 (page 182). Lumber, grain, and meat products were the chief commodities to move eastward; textiles, leather goods, machinery, hardware, and imported foods and drugs went west in exchange. Passengers, too, rode the horse-drawn boats in great numbers, with speeds of 100 miles in a 24-hour day compensating in part for the discomfort of cramped and poorly ventilated cabins.

Pennsylvania's answer to the competition of the Erie Canal was the Mainline of the Pennsylvania Public Works—a system of railroads *and* canals chartered in 1826 by the state legislature. But the fate of Pennsylvania's canals stood in sharp contrast to those in New York. A major disadvantage of the Pennsylvania canals was geographic. The terrain traversed by the Erie to reach the western frontier had been difficult enough for canal construction, rising as much as 650 feet above the Hudson at Albany and requiring many locks to raise the water. But the terrain of western Pennsylvania proved to be insurmountable by canal. The Mainline crossed the mountains, lifted passengers and freight to an altitude of over 2,000 feet, and deposited both travelers and goods, westbound from Philadelphia, at Pittsburgh some 400 miles away. All this was accomplished by as fantastic a combination of transport as the country had ever seen. From Philadelphia, at tidewater, to Columbia, 81 miles westward on the Susquehanna River, a horse-drawn railroad carried both passengers and freight.[6] At Columbia the railroad joined the Juniata, or Eastern Division of the Pennsylvania Canal, from which passengers and freight were carried up a river valley by canal 173

---

[6] Although the steam locomotive was not employed in the United States until 1829, rails to permit smooth haulage had been used in both America and Europe for several years.

miles to the Portage Railroad at Holidaysburg. Here intrepid passengers saw their boat separated into front and rear sections, which were mounted on cars and run on underwater rails into the canal. A 36-mile trip on the Portage Railroad then began. The inclined tracks, over which cars were pulled by stationary steam engines winding cables on drums, accomplished a lift of 1,399 feet on the eastern slope to the summit and a descent of 1,172 feet on the western slope to another canal at Johnstown. From Johnstown to Pittsburgh, a distance of 105 miles, the water journey was comparatively easy.

The completion of this colossal work in 1834 was heralded by a celebration at Liberty Hall in Philadelphia. An old print depicts one of the halfboats decked with bunting and flags being drawn away from the hall by teams of prancing horses. In the sense that it carried all the traffic it could, the Mainline was successful, but the bottleneck of the Portage Railroad plus the fact that the system had twice as many locks as the Erie kept it from becoming a serious competitor for western business. Over the years, the Mainline carried 5 to 10 percent of the traffic volume of the Erie Canal, to the great disappointment of the people of a state that had spent more on waterways than any other.

Other states as well expended large sums of money on canals to draw the trade of the new West. The Chesapeake and Ohio Canal was projected up the valley of the Potomac to Cumberland, Maryland, and on to the Ohio River. The canal company was chartered by the state of Virginia with the assent of the Maryland legislature, and the federal government contributed heavily to the venture. But, despite the political blessings of two states and the federal government, the generous financial backing of all three, and the aid of some local governments, due to technical difficulties the project was completed only to Cumberland.

This painting shows the junction of the Champlain Canal and the Erie Canal—an important point on the trade route that was to become the preeminent link between Midwest and East Coast urban centers.

The dazzling success of the Erie Canal and the competitive rivalry among cities and regions for commercial traffic generated many unprofitable investments in canals. The great canal-building era (1815 to 1843) totaled $31 million in investments, nearly three-quarters from government sources, mostly state governments. Despite the lack of profitability, and the arrival and practical demonstration of the railroads, regional competitiveness spurred a second wave of investment in canals totaling $66 million between 1843 and 1860. Nearly two-thirds of the financing was from the government, again mainly from state treasuries. More might have been invested. However, the commercial crises of 1837 and 1839 and the deep depression of the early 1840s caused financial chaos, and nine states had to suspend payments on their debts (mainly bonds, many sold to foreigners). Major canals in Pennsylvania, Maryland, Indiana, and Illinois never recovered.

Although most of the canal investments were not financially rewarding, they did support the natural waterways in opening up the West. Some that have been considered preposterous mistakes might have turned out to be monuments to human inventiveness if the railroad had not developed at almost the same time. The canals posed problems, it is true. The limitations on horse-drawn vehicles for cargo transport were great except with regard to a few commodities. Canals were supposed to provide a *system* of waterways, but as often as not the boats of larger canals could not move through the smaller canals. Floods and droughts often made the movement of the barges uncertain. Yet the chief reason for the eventual failure of the canals was the railroad, which could carry a wide variety of commodities at a much greater speed— and speed was requisite to a genuine transportation revolution.

THE IRON HORSE

Despite the clear-cut technological advantages of the railroad, natural waterways remained the primary means of transportation for nearly 20 years after the first pioneering American railroads were introduced in the early 1830s. Besides the stiff competition of water transport, an important hindrance to railroad development was public antipathy, which had its roots in ignorance, conservatism, and vested interest. People thought that speeds of 20 to 30 miles per hour would be physically harmful to passengers. At least one city in Massachusetts directed its representatives in the state legislature to prevent "so great a calamity to our town as must be the location of any railroad through it." Many honestly believed that the railroad would prove to be impractical and uneconomical and would not provide service as dependable as that of the waterways.

Unsurprisingly, the most vigorous opposition to railroads came from groups whose economic interests suffered from the competition of the new industry. Millions of dollars had been spent on canals, rivers, highways, and plank roads, and thousands of people depended on these transportation enterprises for their livelihood. Tavern keepers feared their businesses would be ruined, and farmers envisioned the market for hay and grain disappearing as the "iron horse" replaced the flesh-and-blood animal that drew canal boats and pulled wagons. Competitive interests joined to embarrass and hinder the railroads, causing several states to limit traffic on them to passengers and their baggage or to freight hauled only during the months when canal operations ceased. One railroad company in Ohio was required to pay for any loss in canal traffic attributed to railroad competition. Other railroads were ordered to pay a tonnage tax to support the operation of canals.

These sentiments, however amusing today, were seriously espoused by national leaders, as seen in this 1829 letter from Martin Van Buren, then governor of New York, to President Andrew Jackson:

To: President Jackson

The canal system of this country is being threatened by the spread of a new form of transportation known as 'railroads.' The federal government must preserve the canals for the following reasons:

One. If canal boats are supplanted by 'railroads,' serious unemployment will result. Captains, cooks, drivers, hostlers, repairment and lock tenders will be left without means of livelihood, not to mention the numerous farmers now employed in growing hay for horses.

Two. Boat builders would suffer and towline, whip and harness makers would be left destitute.

Three. Canal boats are absolutely essential to the defense of the United States. In the event of the expected trouble with England, the Erie Canal would be the only means by which we could ever move the supplies so vital to waging modern war.

As you may well know, Mr. President, 'railroad' carriages are pulled at the enormous speed of 15 miles per hour by 'engines' which, in addition to endangering life and limb of passengers, roar and snort their way through the countryside, setting fire to crops, scaring the livestock and frightening women and children. The Almighty certainly never intended that people should travel at such breakneck speed.

Martin Van Buren
Governor of New York[7]

Despite the opposition of those who feared the railroads, construction went on. In sections of the country where canals could not be built, the railroad offered a means of cheap transportation for all kinds of commodities. In contrast to the municipality that wished to exclude the railroad, many cities and towns, as well as their state governments, did much to encourage railroad construction. At the time, the federal government was restrained by the prevailing political philosophy of strict constitutionalism from financially assisting and promoting railways. It did, however, make surveys to determine rights of way and provided tariff exemptions on railroad iron.

By 1840, railroad mileage in the United States was within 1,000 miles of the combined lengths of all canals, but the volume of goods carried by water still exceeded that transported by rail. After the depression of the early 1840s, rail investments con-

---

[7] As quoted in "No Growth," *The American Spectator*, January 1984, p. 31. Our thanks to R. L. Sexton for bringing this letter to our attention.

TABLE 9-3   MILES OF RAILROAD IN OPERATION, 1830–1860

Year	Mileage
1830	23
1835	1,098
1840	2,818
1845	4,633
1850	9,021
1855	18,374
1860	30,626

SOURCE: *HISTORICAL STATISTICS* (WASHINGTON, D.C.: GOVERNMENT PRINTING OFFICE, 1960), SERIES Q 15.

tinued, mostly government assisted, and by 1850 the country had 9,000 miles of railroads, as shown in Table 9-3. Referring back to Figure 9-2 (page 182) we see that by the late 1840s the Northern Gateway had surpassed the Southern, and by the 1850s the railroad's superiority was clear.

With the more than 20,000 miles of rails added to the transportation system between 1850 and 1860, total trackage surpassed 30,000 miles at the end of the decade, and the volume of freight traffic equaled that of canals.[8] All the states east of the Mississippi were connected during this decade. The eastern seaboard was linked with the Mississippi River system, and the Gulf and South Atlantic states could interchange traffic with the Great Lakes. Growing trunk lines like the Erie, the Pennsylvania, and the Baltimore and Ohio completed construction of projects that had been started in the 1840s, and combinations of short lines provided new through routes. By the beginning of the Civil War, the eastern framework of the present rail-transportation system had been erected, and it was possible to travel by rail the entire distance from New York to Chicago to Memphis and back to New York.

But the United States was still a long way from establishing an integrated railroad system. Although the "Stephenson gauge" of 4 feet $8\frac{1}{2}$ inches (distance between the rails) was preponderant in 1860, its final selection as the "standard gauge" for the country was still a quarter-century away. Because locomotives and cars were built for one gauge only, a multitude of gauges prevented continuous shipment, as did the lack of agreement among companies on such matters as the interline exchange of rolling stock, through bills of lading and passenger tickets, the division of through rates, and standard time.[9]

Many modifications and improvements occurred, however, and, as shown on the next page in Table 9-4, total factor productivity in railroads more than doubled in the two decades before the Civil War. Alternately stated, railroad output grew relative to inputs by a factor of two. Technological advances, according to Albert Fishlow, were

---

[8] Railroads had won from canals almost all passenger business, except that of poor immigrants coming across New York state, and the carriage of nearly all light, high-value goods.

[9] George R. Taylor and Irene Neu, *The American Railway Network, 1861–1890* (Cambridge: Harvard University Press, 1956), pp. 6–7, 12–14.

TABLE 9-4   PRODUCTIVITY CHANGE IN RAILROADS, 1839–1859 (1910 = 100)

			Inputs			
Year	(1) Output	(2) Labor	(3) Capital	(4) Fuel	(5) Total Input[a]	(6) Total Factor Productivity[b]
1839	.08	.3	.8	.07	.5	16.0
1859	2.21	5.0	10.1	1.50	6.6	33.5

SOURCE: ADAPTED FROM ALBERT FISHLOW, "INTERNAL TRANSPORTATION," IN *AMERICAN ECONOMIC GROWTH*, EDS. LANCE E. DAVIS ET AL. (NEW YORK: HARPER & ROW, 1972), P. 499.

[a] Weighted average of labor, capital, and fuel; weights are proportions of costs.
[b] (column 1 ÷ column 5) 100.

reflected in the fact that the average traction force of locomotives more than doubled in these two decades. Freight car sizes also increased, with eight-wheel cars being common by 1859. Most of the productivity rise, however, resulted from increased utilization of existing facilities. The stock of capital—and other inputs—grew, but output grew much faster as the initial inputs became more fully utilized.

TRAILS AND ROADS

Though technologically undramatic, our account of the transportation revolution would be incomplete without the story of trails and roads. Thanks to Hollywood and western movies, we are familiar with the trails followed by western settlers. These "highways" of long-distance land travel are shown in Map 9-2. The routes of westward emigration, settlement, and commerce usually followed the old Indian hunting and war paths, which in turn had followed stream valleys providing the easiest lines of travel. One of the most important was the Wilderness Road, pioneered by Daniel Boone. Penetrating the mountain barrier at Cumberland Gap, near present-day Middlesboro, Kentucky, it then went north and west into the Ohio Territory. Over this road, which in many places was only a marked track, poured thousands of emigrants.[10] Other trails west of the mountains followed the Holston and the Watauga rivers as they flowed from their Appalachian sources into the Tennessee. Thus, geography in part directed the flow of emigration to the Southwest. As a rule, both transport and migration routes followed the natural drainage basins and the easiest, least obstacle-ridden paths overland.

---

[10] This same type of road or marked track appeared during the overland migration to the West Coast. The Oregon Trail, over which travel began in the early 1840s, was 2,000 miles long and carried settlers to the Pacific Northwest and to California. The Mormon Trail, broken by Brigham Young in the late 1840s, paralleled the Oregon Trail along the south bank of the Platte for some distance. Earlier trails marked by the Spaniards, such as the Santa Fe Trail into present-day New Mexico and Arizona and *El Camino Real* (the King's Highway) in California, were valuable to early explorers and traders.

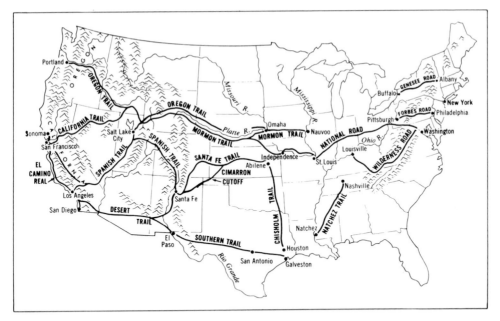

MAP 9-2 WESTWARD TRAVEL *The massive physical barriers faced by the pioneers could be circumvented by following such famous routes as the Oregon Trail and the Santa Fe Trail.*

Although most of the overland roads turned into quagmires in the rainy season and into billowing dust clouds in the dry season, some of them were well constructed and well maintained through portions of their length. The most notable surfaced highway was the Cumberland Road, or "National Pike," built by the federal government after much controversy. Begun at Cumberland, Maryland, in 1811, the road was opened to Wheeling on the Ohio River in 1818 and was later completed to St. Louis.

The national government did not repeat its success with the Cumberland Road, despite Albert Gallatin's 1808 proposed plan for a system of federal roads and support from many progressive people for a comprehensive program of internal improvements. Opposition was based ostensibly on the assertion, repeated endlessly, that federal participation in such an activity was unconstitutional. Sectional rivalries played a major role in blocking the proposed construction. The West in particular persistently and loudly called for a national road system and at first the Middle Atlantic states were inclined to agree. But after New York and Pennsylvania developed their own routes to the West, they did not wish to promote federally financed competition elsewhere. New Englanders, with fairly good roads of their own, were even less inclined to encourage further population drains or to improve the commercial positions of Boston's rivals. The South, although mired in the mud, was bitterly antagonistic to any program that would add to the government's financial needs or facilitate access to non-slave portions of the West. Despite all the opposition, Congress could not avoid appropriating increasing sums for post and military roads, but sectional rivalries over the geographic allocation of internal improvements permitted an incredibly primitive road system to survive well into the twentieth century.

TURNPIKE COMPANIES

In many areas, especially where other transport modes were unavailable, roads were built by private turnpike companies. These companies collected tolls for their use, usually ranging between 13 cents and 20 cents per ton mile. Gates consisting of pikes or spears were turned or lifted to let the tollpayer pass to and from the road at selected points. The turnpike era began in 1789 with the construction of the Philadelphia and Lancaster Turnpike; it ended about 1830, after which date only a few private highways were attempted as business ventures. During this period, Pennsylvania chartered 86 companies that built over 2,000 miles of road. By 1811, New York had 1,500 miles of highways constructed by 135 companies and New England had granted some 180 companies the right to build turnpikes. Despite toll collections, few of the companies that constructed roads for public use were profitable ventures; in fact, it is doubtful that even one earned close to the going rate of return on its capital. Teamsters avoided the tolls if at all possible, and dishonest gatekeepers often pocketed the receipts. But the chief difficulty—one unforeseen by most promoters—was that the only long-distance trade the roads attracted was stagecoach passengers and emigrants. Freight would not, for the most part, stand the cost of land carriage over great distances, and without freight traffic turnpikes simply could not earn a profit. They were eventually faced with extensive competition from steamboats, canals, and railroads, but by this time returns on invested capital had already proved disappointing. Some turnpikes were abandoned and later acquired by the states for the rapidly growing public road system; others were purchased by local governments and made into toll-free highways.[11]

PLANK ROADS

A special kind of toll road was the plank road or "farmer's railroad," developed shortly after the decline in turnpike construction. Plank roads were built by laying wide, heavy planks or "rails" on stringers or ties placed in the direction of travel. They were superior for all-weather use. The first plank road in the United States was built at Syracuse in 1837; within the next 20 years or so, several thousand miles of plank roads were in use throughout the country, the heaviest concentration being in the Middle Atlantic states. So important did they seem that some were subsidized by the states, although most were privately financed.

OCEAN TRANSPORT

Besides the many developments in internal transportation, great strides were being made in the long-traditional merchant marine. Thanks to bold entrepreneurship, the Black Ball line of New York instituted regularly scheduled transatlantic sailings in 1818. Beginning with just four ships, the line had a vessel sailing from New York bound for

---

[11] A few private roads continued into the twentieth century, but all that now remains of them is the name *turnpike* given to some important arteries of the highway system. These throughways differ from the older turnpike in that the modern enterprises are owned by public corporations.

Liverpool in the first week of each month, and a ship began the Liverpool–New York passage at the same time. Considerable risk was involved in pledging ships to sail "full or not full," as the line's advertising declared, because a ship might make three round trips a year (instead of the usual two made by the regular traders) with its hold far from full.[12] But by specializing in passengers, specie, mail, and "fine freight," the packets managed to operate successfully for more than 100 years. In the 1820s, the Black Ball line increased its trips to two a month each way, and other packet lines between New York and European ports were soon established. Henceforth, passengers could count on sailing at a particular hour on a given day, and merchants could book freight with something more than a vague hope that it would arrive in time to permit a profitable transaction. By assuring a set schedule, the Black Ball line reduced risks and uncertainties in overseas commerce.

The transatlantic packets fully established New York as the predominant port in the United States. Coastal packets, running primarily to New Orleans but also to Charleston, Savannah, and Mobile, brought cotton to New York for eastbound ocean shipment and carried southward a considerable portion of the European goods brought from England and the Continent. In fact, trade between the cotton ports and New York was greater in physical and dollar volume than the ocean trade during most of the antebellum period.[13] These packets significantly complemented developments in the western rivers, which funneled produce from the interior through New Orleans, the Southern Gateway.

Between 1820 and 1860, remarkable design changes in sailing ships led to increases in tonnage and efficiency. From an average size of 300 tons in the 1820s, American sailing ships increased to 1,000 tons in the 1850s, and vessels of 1,500 tons burden were not uncommon. There was a marked increase in length-to-beam ratios and spread of sail for the ordinary packet ship, and the centuries-old practice of making the widest part of the vessel forward of the center was abandoned. Borrowing from French designers, Yankee shipbuilders produced a special type of ship that was to dominate the seas for the three decades before the Civil War. This was the famed clipper ship, which, at some sacrifice of carrying capacity, attained unheard-of speeds. The clipper was a graceful ship with three masts, square-rigged but equipped with abundant fore-and-aft sails that gave it a great advantage going into the wind, thus increasing its speed. Manned by fewer hands than vessels of foreign register, a clipper was to be driven 24 hours a day, not put to bed for seven or eight hours at night.

The first American (or "Baltimore") clipper was the *Ann McKim*, launched in 1832. Her builder, Donald McKay, became a legendary figure, and some ships of his design bore names that are remembered even now: the *Flying Cloud*, the *Sovereign of the Seas*, the *Great Republic*, and the *Lightning* were spectacularly beautiful, with concave sides and bow, and sails towering 200 feet above the deck. On its maiden voyage across the Atlantic, the *Lightning* logged a record 436 miles in one day for an average speed of 18 miles an hour. Even today, many ocean vessels do not approach this speed.

---

[12] Robert G. Albion, *The Rise of the New York Port, 1815–1860* (Hamden, Connecticut: Archon Books, 1961), p. 4.

[13] Robert G. Albion, *Square-Riggers on Schedule* (Princeton: Princeton University Press, 1938), pp. 49–50.

Clippers were designed for the express purpose of carrying passengers and high-value cargo long distances. On the Atlantic runs, they were not profitable due to their limited capacity. But they dominated the China trade, and after 1849 they made fortunes for their owners by carrying passengers and freight in the gold rushes to California and Australia. On the New York–San Francisco trip around Cape Horn, a distance of 16,000 miles, the *Flying Cloud* set a record of just over 89 days, at a time when 100 days was about par for the clipper voyage.[14] This represented a time saving over ordinary ocean travel of up to three months, for which some merchants and travelers would pay a good price.

Clippers, however, were not the only vessels in the American merchant fleet. Broad-beamed and full-bowed freighting ships, much slower vessels than the clippers, were the backbone of the nation's merchant marine. Officered by men to whom seafaring was a tradition and a career of considerable social prestige, manned by crews of Americans bred to the sea, and owned by merchants of vision and daring like Stephen Girard of Philadelphia, the cheaply and expertly built ships from the marine ways of New York, Boston, and the Maine coast were the great ocean-freight carriers until the Civil War.

In the meantime, the British were making technical advances that enabled them to challenge American maritime supremacy and finally to overcome it. The major British innovation was the adaptation of the steamboat, originally invented for use on rivers and protected waters, to navigation on the open sea. The two principal changes made by the British were the use of iron instead of wood for the hull and the employment of the Archimedes' screw principle for propulsion instead of paddles. Iron hulls were necessary to transport the heavy machinery of the early steam era safely, but they also had greater strength, buoyancy, and durability than wood. From the 1830s on, the British rapidly solved the problems of iron-ship construction. The composite ship, with a frame of iron and a hull of wood, was tried for a while, but the acid in the oak timber corroded the iron. Once the British had perfected the techniques of riveting and working with sheet iron and steel, they had an absolute advantage in the construction of iron ships—as great an advantage as the United States had enjoyed in the making of wooden ones.

The inefficiency and slow speeds of early steam engines were a source of unending difficulty. For a long time, steamships had to carry a greater weight of coal than of cargo, and low engine speeds made the inefficient paddle wheel necessary despite its theoretical inferiority. After nearly 20 years of development, however, transatlantic steamships were making six voyages a year—twice as many as their sailing-packet competitors. Ten years later, Samuel Cunard's success in starting a line service was not entirely fortuitous; by 1848, engines were designed that could maintain higher speeds. The screw propeller was then rapidly adopted, and fuel consumption was cut greatly. During the 1850s, both the number and registered tonnage of steamships increased by leaps and bounds, and they almost entirely captured the passenger and high-value freight business.

In 1860, sailing ships still carried the greater part of the world's international freight. Yet by this time the shape of the future was clear to all except die-hard American

---

[14]This record was not broken until 1988.

entrepreneurs, who—unable to comprehend the rapid obsolescence of their beautiful wooden ships—failed to take vigorous steps to compete with Britain. Although government subsidies to American steamship builders began as early as 1845, these were both insufficient and poorly administered. Under the most favorable circumstances, however, builders in the United States could scarcely have competed on a cost basis with the vastly superior British iron industry. The signs were there for those who chose to read them. During the 1820s, American ships had carried close to 90 percent of the foreign trade of the United States; by the 1850s, this figure had declined to about 70 percent. The times had changed, and fortune's hand was laid on other shoulders.

A NATIONAL MARKET

These many surges of transportation development solidly linked the interior western regions to the seaboard and abroad. Also contributing to market unification and falling costs of trade was the telegraph, invented by Samuel F. B. Morse in the 1840s. Telegraph wires were strung parallel to the railroads across the nation. By 1852 there were 23,000 miles of wire in operation, speeding communications and reducing uncertainties. In 1866 an undersea cable was laid to Europe, internationalizing further the U.S. and European economies.

Although economic unification was far from complete, dramatic gains had been realized by the eve of the Civil War. As stated earlier, regional price movements portrayed these strides toward economic unification. As Thomas Berry states:

> It is difficult to point to any consistent lag of the West behind the East during this early period (1788–1817) because of such diversity in general behavior; it is safe to state, however, that in such first-magnitude movements as those of 1793–1797 and 1810–1817 there was a lag measuring somewhat more than a year in length. . . . Taking a later interval (1816–1860) weighted general indices of monthly prices in New York, New Orleans, and Cincinnati show agreement with each other to a surprising degree. . . . Cincinnati prices lagged the greater part of a year in their decline in 1819–1820, but they were only three or four months behind the seaboard markets in the turning-point of 1839 and reacted simultaneously at the time of the panic of 1857.[15]

A viable transportation system was vital in perfecting a national market and linking regions. First the steamboats on the western rivers, then the canals, and finally the railroad revolutionized the costs of transport between the West and the seaboard. As Table 9-5 shows (see next page), western prices as a percentage of eastern prices grew dramatically. Farmers gained larger and larger shares of the selling price of their crops. Moreover, consumers paid decreasing shares of the purchase price for transportation and other marketing costs. As freight costs fell, new unsettled areas were profitably cleared and added to the nation's economic activity. As Peter Lindert has shown, average land prices, adjusted for quality, more than doubled and possibly tripled from 1810

---

[15]Thomas S. Berry, *Western Rivers Before 1861* (Cambridge: Harvard University Press, 1943), pp. 97–99.

TABLE 9-5 Cincinnati Wholesale Prices as a Percentage of Philadelphia, New York, and New Orleans Wholesale Prices, 1816–1860

Period	Commodity																	
	Flour (bbl.)			Wheat (bu.)			Corn (bu.)			Mess Pork (bbl.)			Lard (lb.)			Whiskey (gal.)		
	Phil.	N.Y.	N.O.	Phil.	N.Y.	N.O.	Phil.	N.Y.	N.O.	Phil.	N.Y.	N.O.	Phil.	N.Y.	N.O.	Phil.	N.Y.	N.O.
1816–1820	63	66	72	45	48	—	51	48	—	56	58	63	65	69	68	—	—	—
1821–1825	52	52	56	39	38	—	38	32	30	63	67	76	59	65	68	68	70	67
1826–1830	68	67	67	50	48	—	49	41	29	67	68	78	56	65	66	80	79	75
1831–1835	73	74	76	57	56	—	55	49	36	77	77	85	69	71	78	89	89	83
1836–1840	73	73	77	59	61	—	56	51	47	87	85	86	83	82	87	91	91	79
1841–1845	77	73	86	68	65	90	53	47	65	82	79	84	79	83	91	80	77	87
1846–1850	78	71	87	68	63	88	51	48	62	81	90	88	80	86	93	74	73	90
1851–1855	82	79	90	73	61	90	61	59	74	85	90	92	82	93	94	78	78	88
1856–1860	88	95	89	79	70	86	70	66	72	91	94	93	86	96	94	85	83	87

SOURCE: Erik F. Haites, James Mak, and Gary M. Walton, *Western River Transportation: The Era of Early Internal Development, 1810–1860* (Baltimore: Johns Hopkins University Press, 1975), p. 7 and Appendix A.

to 1860.[16] Improvements in transportation increased economic specialization and raised living standards dramatically.

THE ANTEBELLUM INTERREGIONAL GROWTH HYPOTHESIS

A special perspective on the importance of falling transportation costs to the early growth of a national market is provided by the antebellum interregional growth hypothesis. In 1961 Douglass C. North advanced the argument from earlier works with quantitative evidence derived and added theoretical specifications and structure. Briefly stated, North argued that U.S. growth between 1815 and 1843 was propelled primarily by the growth of British demand for southern cotton, which encouraged southern regional specialization in cotton. The interregional trade links by commodity types are illustrated graphically in Figure 9-3 on the next page. The booms in cotton exports to England spurred cotton specialization and raised the demand in the South for western foodstuffs and cheap northeastern manufactures, mainly boots and shoes and coarse-fiber clothing for slaves. Export-led growth, especially cotton, initiated the forces of regional specialization and tied areas together through trade. Reinforcing the growth in the size of the national market were falling transport costs, which realized economies of large-scale productions, and greater regional economic specialization. As the Northeast became more specialized in manufacturing and more urbanized, its growing demand for food added to the South's demand for western foodstuffs. Each region advanced along lines dictated by its respective comparative advantages in production, and each demanded goods produced in the other regions in greater and greater amounts. After 1843, the primary initiating role of foreign demand for cotton diminished, and internal market forces ascended in importance. The railroad, linking the West to the North, also contributed to the lessening initiative forces of the South.

The evidence on the timing and waves of western migrations, land sales, and prices of key regional staples supports North's argument. However, evidence on southern food productions for the years after 1840—the only years providing us with reliable food-production data—suggests that the South was relatively self-sufficient in food.[17]

---

[16] Peter H. Lindert, "Long-run Trends in American Farmland Values," *Agricultural History* (Summer 1988): 60.

[17] Albert Fishlow, "Antebellum Interregional Trade Reconsidered," *American Economic Review* 54 (May 1964): 352–364; also see the "Discussion," by Robert W. Fogel in the same source, pp. 377–389. In addition see Robert E. Gallman, "Self-Sufficiency in the Cotton Economy of the Antebellum South," *Agricultural History* 44 (1970): 5–23.

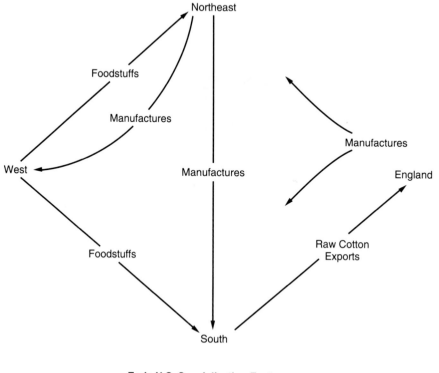

Early U.S. Specialization Features

South	Raw Cotton–Plantations
Northeast	Manufactures–Urbanization
West	Foodstuffs–Family Farms

FIGURE 9-3 Export-Led Growth and the Interregional Growth Hypothesis

And yet, as Lloyd Mercer has shown, pockets of food deficits in the South may have been sufficient to have had a significant impact on western food production for market, especially before 1840.[18] Despite the inconclusiveness of this lively debate, the interregional growth hypothesis provides a useful framework of analysis and an international perspective on the advances and linkages of the regions and of the formation of a national economy in that vital period of the transportation revolution.

[18] Lloyd Mercer, "The Antebellum Interregional Trade Hypothesis: A Reexamination of Theory and Evidence," in *Explorations in the New Economic History*, eds. Roger L. Ransom, Richard Such, and Gary M. Walton (New York: Academic Press, 1982), pp. 71–96.

SELECTED REFERENCES
AND SUGGESTED READINGS

Albion, Robert G. *The Rise of the New York Port, 1815–1860.* Hamden, Connecticut: Archon Books, 1961.

Berry, Thomas S. *Square-Riggers on Schedule.* Princeton: Princeton University Press, 1938.

_____. *Western Rivers Before 1861.* Cambridge: Harvard University Press, 1943.

Chandler, Alfred D., Jr. (1969). *The Railroads.* New York: Harcourt Brace Jovanovich, 1965.

Cootner, Paul. "The Role of the Railroads in the United States Economic Growth." *Journal of Economic History* 23 (1963).

David, Paul. "Transport Innovation and Economic Growth; Professor Fogel On and Off the Rails." *Economic History Review* 22, 2d series, no. 3 (1969).

Fishlow, Albert. "Antebellum Interregional Trade Reconsidered." *American Economic Review* 54 (May 1964): 352–364.

_____. "Internal Transportation." In *American Economic Growth: An Economist's History of the United States,* eds. Lance E. Davis et al. New York: Harper & Row, 1972. Chapter 13.

Gallman, Robert E. "Self-Sufficiency in the Cotton Economy of the Antebellum South." *Agricultural History* 44 (1970): 5–23.

Goodrich, Carter H. *The Government and the Economy, 1783–1861.* Indianapolis: Bobbs-Merrill, 1967.

Goodrich, Carter H., et al. *Canals and American Economic Development.* New York: Columbia University Press, 1961.

_____. *Government Promotion of American Canals and Railroads, 1800–1890.* New York: Columbia University Press, 1960.

_____. "Internal Improvements Reconsidered." *Journal of Economic History* 30 (June 1970): 289–311.

Haites, Erik F., James Mak, and Gary M. Walton. *Western River Transportation: The Era of Early Internal Development, 1810–1860.* Baltimore: Johns Hopkins University Press, 1975.

Hunter, Louis. *Steamboats on the Western Rivers.* Cambridge: Harvard University Press, 1949.

Jenks, Leland H. "Railroads as a Force in American Development." In *Enterprise and Secular Change,* eds. Frederic C. Lane and Jelle Riemersma. Homewood, Illinois: Irwin, 1953.

Lindert, Peter H. "Long-run Trends in American Farmland Values," *Agricultural History* (Summer 1988): 60.

Lindstrom, Diane L. "Demand, Markets and Eastern Economic Development, Philadelphia, 1815–1840." *Journal of Economic History* 25 (1975): 271–273.

Lindstrom, Diane L., and John Sharpless. "Urban Growth and Economic Structure in Antebellum America." In *Research in Economic History,* vol. 3. Greenwich, Connecticut: JAI Press, 1978.

Mak, James, and Gary Walton. "Steamboat and the Great Productivity Surge in River Transportation." *Journal of Economic History* 33 (1972): 619–640.

McIlwraith, Thomas F. "Freight Capacity and Utilization of the Erie and Great Lakes Canals Before 1850." *Journal of Economic History* 36 (December 1976).

Mercer, Lloyd. "The Antebellum Interregional Trade Hypothesis: A Reexamination of Theory and Evidence." In *Explorations in the New Economic History,* eds. Roger L. Ransom, Richard Such, and Gary M. Walton. New York: Academic Press, 1982, pp. 71–96.

Niemi, Albert W., Jr. "A Closer Look at Canals and Western Manufacturing in the Canal Era: A Reply." *Explorations in Economic History* 9 (1972): 423–426.

_____. "A Further Look at Regional Canals and Economic Specialization: 1820–1840." *Explorations in Economic History* 7 (1970): 499–522.

North, Douglass C. *The Economic Growth of the United States, 1790–1860.* Englewood Cliffs, New Jersey: Prentice-Hall, 1961.

_____. "The Role of Transportation in the Economic Development of North America." A paper presented to the International Congress of the Historical Sciences, Vienna, August 1965, and published in *Les Grandes Voies Maritimes dans le Monde XVe–XIXe Siecles*. Paris: Ecole des Hautes Etudes en Sciences Sociales, 1965.

Ransom, Roger L. "Canals and Development, A Discussion of the Issues." *American Economic Review* 54 (1964): 365–376.

_____. "A Closer Look at Canals and Western Manufacturing in the Canal Era." *Explorations in Economic History* 8 (1971): 501–510.

_____. "Interregional Canals and Economic Specialization in the Antebellum United States." *Explorations in Economic History* 5, 2d series, no. 1 (Fall 1967).

_____. "Social Rates of Return from Public Transport Investment: A Case Study of the Ohio Canal." *Journal of Political Economy* 78 (1970): 1041–1060.

Scheiber, Harry. *Ohio Canal Era*. Athens: Ohio University Press, 1969.

Stover, John F. "Canals and Turnpikes: America's Early-Nineteenth-Century Transportation Network." In *An Emerging Independent American Economy, 1815–1875*, eds. J. R. Frese and J. Judd. Tarrytown, New York: Sleepy Hollow Press, 1980.

Taylor, George R. *The Transportation Revolution, 1815–1860*. New York: Holt, Rinehart & Winston, 1951.

Taylor, George R., and Irene Neu. *The American Railway Network, 1861–1890*. Cambridge: Harvard University Press, 1956.

Thompson, Robert. *Wiring a Continent: The History of the Telegraph Industry in the United States, 1832–1866*. Princeton: Princeton University Press, 1947.

Walton, Gary M. "River Transportation and the Old Northwest Territory." In *Essays on the Economy of the Old Northwest*, eds. David C. Klingaman and Richard K. Vedder. Athens: Ohio University Press, 1987, pp. 225–242.

CHAPTER
TEN

MARKET EXPANSION AND
INDUSTRY IN FIRST TRANSITION

CHAPTER THEME Between the adoption of the Constitution and the outbreak of the Civil War, the economy of the United States was structurally transformed, and a solid foundation was laid for the United States to become an industrial power. Beginning with only a few small factories, mostly lumber mills, the new nation emerged by 1860 with a manufacturing sector second only to that of Great Britain. Yet in 1860 the sizes of industrial firms were small by today's standards, and the United States was still predominantly an agricultural country. Nevertheless, many important changes had occurred that marked the advent of industrialization. Most significant was the evolution of new ways of combining factors of production, resulting in the substitution of capital for labor and requiring new forms of business organization. Business interests as a political force became evident, and New England and the Middle Atlantic states led the way in developing the industrial sector. Improvements in transportation played the main role in increasing regional specialization, and in many ways transportation developments were instrumental to economic unification. What made the westward movement, the rise of King Cotton, and industrialization all the more remarkable is that all were unfolding simultaneously.

EARLY CHANGES IN U.S. MANUFACTURING

THE DECLINE OF HOUSEHOLD PRODUCTION

When Alexander Hamilton delivered his *Report on Manufacturers* to Congress in 1791, he estimated that from two-thirds to four-fifths of the nation's clothing was homemade. Most food processing was also done in the home. Water power had not yet been harnessed for textile production and was used mainly for milling grain, cutting lumber, and other uses. Artisans in the towns worked by hand, producing shoes, hats, pots, pans, and tools.

By 1830 household manufacture exhibited a marked decline in the East. Thereafter, home manufacture declined dramatically in all but the least accessible places. The major causes of this decline were the development of industrial organization and modern means of transportation. Wherever steamboats ran or canals, highways, and railroads were built, home manufacture declined quickly. Even on the frontier, most households had access to the products of American or European factories after the middle of the nineteenth century. Map 10-1 shows the influence of transportation on homemade versus factory-made manufactures. The shaded areas in the two maps of New York show the one-third of the counties in the state having the highest per capita output of woolen goods made in the home in two different years, 1820 and 1845. Note that in 1820, no county lying along the Hudson below Albany was in the top third. In 1845, the counties lying along the Erie Canal had similarly dropped in amount of home manufacture. In contrast, as late as 1865, nearly all the country people of Tennessee, especially those living in the mountain areas, wore clothing made at home. Primitive transport prolonged the wearing of homemade clothes.

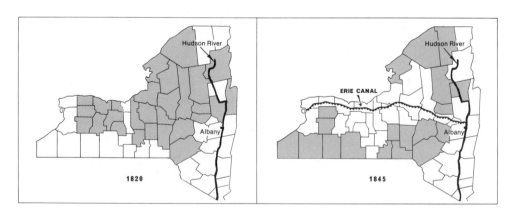

MAP 10-1 CANAL IMPACT: *Household manufacture of woolen cloth (an index of isolation from commercial routes) underwent a drastic change between 1820 and 1845 along the Erie Canal. The shaded areas indicate the one-third of the counties with the highest home production of woolen goods during this period.*

SOURCE: ARTHUR A. COLE, AMERICAN WOOL MANUFACTURE (CAMBRIDGE: HARVARD UNIVERSITY PRESS, 1926), VOL. I.

THE CRAFTSHOP AND THE PUTTING-OUT SYSTEM

Until approximately 1850, the substantial increases in manufacturing output were effected by craftsmen operating independently or in craftshops. Craftsmen did "bespoke" work, making commodities only to order, maintaining the highest standards of quality, and selling through their own small retail outlets. But production by independent craftsmen declined rapidly after 1815. More important at that date and for some time afterward was the craftshop run by a master who employed several journeymen and apprentices. Sometimes, as in the case of the hatters of Danbury, Connecticut, an agglomeration of craftshops sold a quantity output to merchant wholesalers for distribution over wide market areas.

The putting-out or domestic system was a unique form of organization, cutting across the categories of both household and craft production. For example, before 1830, enterprising merchants frequently distributed cotton yarn among families for hand looming but employed skilled craftsmen to weave the yarn for finer fabrics in their shops. Until somewhat later, woolen yarn might be spun in a mill and put out to households for hand weaving: the finishing processes of bleaching and dyeing were finally carried out by workers assembled under one roof. In the boot and shoe industry, the leather might be cut under the supervision of a merchant, the pieces distributed to craftshops for sewing, and the nearly finished shoes returned to the shop for final processing. As people who bought ready-made shoes became more exacting in their demand for quality and fit, and as machinery was developed for making a better product in quantity, the industry slipped easily into factory methods. Straw hats and suspenders, on the other hand, were made by women and children in the home and sold by enterprising merchant employers in a wide market up to 1860.

MILL INDUSTRIES

In the early nineteenth century, as in colonial days, the small mill was to be found in nearly all localities. The census of 1860 reported nearly 20,000 sawmills and 14,000 flour mills in the country. With few exceptions, tanneries, distilleries, breweries, and iron forges also produced for local markets. The decentralization of American industry before 1860, favored by the use of water power and commonly protected by high short-haul transport costs, produced small firms that often constituted effective local monopolies.

Before 1860, however, some mills had achieved large-scale production using methods of manufacture typical of the factory. Furthermore, large mills in two industries tended to concentrate in certain rather well-defined areas. The flour-milling industry, which even in colonial days had been attracted to the Chesapeake area, continued to cluster there as farmers in Maryland and Virginia substituted wheat for tobacco. As cities grew larger and the demand for building materials increased, it became profitable for large lumbering firms to exploit timber areas located some distance from the markets; typical were those situated by 1850 on the upper reaches of streams flowing through New England, New York, and Pennsylvania.

LEADING INDUSTRIES, 1860

By 1860 there was a total manufacturing labor force of nearly 1,530,000 (compared to almost 5,880,000 in agriculture). Over 96 percent of those in manufacturing work engaged in ten industries. These ten leading industries are ranked in Table 10-1 by value added (value of total product minus raw material costs). Cotton goods ranked at the top, having grown from infancy 50 years earlier. Lumbering was a close second to cotton textiles. Looking now at ranking by number of employees, we see that boots and shoes (third by value added) was the top employer, and men's clothing (fifth by value added) was nearly tied with cotton goods as the next highest employer. Note that iron manufactures were underrated due to the narrow definitions of the census; if all iron products and machinery had been combined in a single category, their value added would be the highest. Between 1850 and 1860, the doubling of the output of primary iron products and machinery forecast the shape of America's industrial future.

The rise of these industries was centered primarily in the Northeast. Cotton manufactures were located predominantly in New England, as were boots and shoes. Lumbering moved west and south but stayed strong in New England and the Middle Atlantic states. An overview on the location of industry, given in Table 10-2, testifies to the primacy of the East in early manufacturing. Because the census counted even the smallest sawmills and gristmills as "manufacturing establishments," the large numbers for the West and the South are misleading. By any other criterion, New England and the Middle Atlantic states were the leading regions. The figures for the Midwest reflect in part the rapid antebellum industrial growth of the Ohio Valley and the burgeoning of the Chicago area.

TABLE 10-1   UNITED STATES MANUFACTURES, 1860

Item	(1) Number of Employees	(2) Cost of Raw Material	(3) Value of Total Product	(4) (3)–(2) Value Added by Manufacture	Rank by Value Added
Cotton goods	114,955	$ 52,666,701	$107,337,783	$54,671,082	1
Lumber	75,595	51,358,400	104,928,342	53,569,942	2
Boots and shoes	123,026	42,728,174	91,889,298	49,161,124	3
Flour and meal	27,682	208,497,309	248,580,365	40,083,056	4
Men's clothing	114,800	44,149,752	80,830,555	36,680,803	5
Iron (cast, forged, rolled, and wrought)	48,975	37,486,056	73,175,332	35,689,276	6
Machinery	41,223	19,444,533	52,010,376	32,565,843	7
Woolen goods	40,597	35,652,701	60,685,190	25,032,489	8
Carriages, wagons, and carts	37,102	11,898,282	35,552,842	23,654,560	9
Leather	22,679	44,520,737	67,306,452	22,785,715	10

SOURCE: *EIGHTH CENSUS OF THE UNITED STATES: MANUFACTURES, 1860.*

TABLE 10-2 MANUFACTURING, BY SECTIONS, CENSUS OF 1860

Section	Number of Estab- lishments	Capital Invested	Employment		Annual Value of Products	Value Added by Manu- facture
			Male	Female		
New England	20,671	$ 257,477,783	262,834	129,002	$ 468,599,287	$223,076,180
Middle Atlantic	53,287	435,061,964	432,424	113,819	802,338,392	358,211,423
Midwest	36,785	194,212,543	194,081	15,828	384,606,530	158,987,717
South	20,631	95,975,185	98,583	12,138	155,531,281	68,988,129
West	8,777	23,380,334	50,137	67	71,229,989	42,746,363
Territories	282	3,747,906	2,290	43	3,556,197	2,246,772
Totals	140,433	$1,009,855,715	1,040,349	270,897	$1,885,861,676	$854,256,584

SOURCE: *EIGHTH CENSUS OF THE UNITED STATES: MANUFACTURES, 1860.*

During the period from 1810 to 1860, the total value of manufactures increased from about $200 million to just under $2 billion, or roughly tenfold. Farming was still in first place as a means of earning a livelihood: the value added by manufacture in 1860 was markedly less than the value of three of America's major crops—corn, wheat, and hay—and capital investment in industry totaled less than one-sixth the value of farm land and buildings. However, as already stated, the United States was even then second only to Great Britain in manufacturing.[1] Soon it would be the world's industrial leader as well as its agricultural leader. How was this remarkable achievement accomplished?

PREREQUISITES TO FACTORY PRODUCTION

The development of high-speed mass production required the introduction of machines and technology, standardization of items, continuous-process assembly lines of production, and new sources of power and energy. Advances in these areas increasingly led to the displacement of home manufactures, the putting-out system, and the craftshop. It was an evolutionary process, but in the longer view of history it has been called the Industrial Revolution.

MACHINES AND TECHNOLOGY

Not until after 1845 did it become clear that the old methods of production just described would soon be outmoded. Yet the developments of the 1850s were such that even the most casual contemporary observer could not fail to be impressed by the rapid coming of the "factory system."

---

[1] The *Twelfth Census of the United States*, quoting Mulhall's *Industries and Wealth of Nations*, placed the United States in fourth place after Great Britain, France, and Germany. But Douglass C. North, in *The Economic Growth of the United States, 1790 to 1860* (Englewood Cliffs, New Jersey: Prentice-Hall, 1961), p. v, shows convincingly that the United States ranked second.

The Industrial Revolution that had begun in England in the late eighteenth century by no means guaranteed the immediate establishment of the factory system in America. In fact, the English sought to prevent dissemination abroad of the details of the new inventions. Parliament passed laws in 1774 and 1781 prohibiting the export of new industrial machinery, not unlike later laws that prohibited high-tech exports to Soviet-bloc countries in the Cold War era. In 1782, a law was passed to prevent labor-pirating, the luring abroad of highly skilled British mechanics. Although these efforts possibly slowed the introduction of new machines and technologies in the United States, technology transfers occurred anyway. For example, on the eve of the Napoleonic wars, the Scofield brothers arrived in New England from Yorkshire and built water powered wool-carding machinery. They were preceded by Samuel Slater, who in 1789 came to the United States and in cooperation with Moses Brown and William Almy of Providence, Rhode Island, built the first American spinning mill powered by water. Over a dozen small prototypes of their mill were built during the next decade in New England.

Largely because of the relatively high cost of labor in the United States, American managers always tended to use the most nearly automatic machines available for a particular application. More importantly, they successfully innovated ways of organizing production that saved labor expense per unit of output. Their chief contributions—the two basic ideas that led to American preeminence in nineteenth-century manufacturing—were interchangeable parts and continuous-process manufacture. Both advances were inevitably allied with the development of machine tools and with changes in techniques of applying power.

STANDARDIZED INTERCHANGEABLE PARTS

The idea of standardizing a product and its various parts originated in Sweden in the early eighteenth century and before 1800 had been tried in France, Switzerland, and England. Through standardization, the parts of one product could be interchanged for the parts of a like product, facilitating manufacture and repair. The first permanently successful application of the idea in a nontrivial use was made in the American armament industry. At the turn of the nineteenth century, Eli Whitney and Simeon North almost simultaneously obtained contracts from the government to manufacture firearms by the interchangeable-parts method. Records suggest that North was using the "uniformity principle" as early as 1807 in making his pistols. It has long been customary to credit Whitney with the first successful manufacture by interchangeable parts, but the evidence does not substantiate his claim to priority. Perhaps the first application of the idea in a modern sense was made by John H. Hall, inventor and engineer at the Harper's Ferry Armory, who by 1817 was installing his system using metal-cutting and woodworking machines.[2] In any case, it took more than two gen-

---

[2] See Robert S. Woodbury, "The Legend of Eli Whitney and Interchangeable Parts," *Technology and Culture* II:1 (1960): 235–253. In Professor Woodbury's view, interchangeable-parts manufacture involves four elements: (1) precision machine tools, (2) precision gauges or other measuring instruments, (3) uniform measurement standards, and (4) techniques of mechanical drawing.

erations to make the essential innovations in the arms industry. Captain Hall's pattern-turning greatly reduced the number of man-hours needed to shape unsymmetrical rifle stocks. Drop-forging with dies was successfully introduced about 1827. By 1855, Samuel Colt, who had long since invented his six-shooter, established an armory in which machine work of a high degree of accuracy was accomplished by skilled operators. From approximately midcentury on, the ultimate tool of precision was no longer the hand file.

CONTINUOUS-PROCESS AND ASSEMBLY LINES

Although milling processes did not require assembly operations, continuous-process manufacture—production in which the plant is so arranged that the manufacture is done with facility and as nearly in sequence as possible—had its first successful application in the mills. One of the first to succeed at this was the American inventor Oliver Evans. In 1782 he built a flour mill in Philadelphia run by gravity, friction, and water power that moved grain through its processing with no human intervention other than guiding and monitoring. Continuous-process manufacture in its most significant form today, with motor-driven moving assemblies like those introduced by Henry Ford for automobile production, was an outgrowth of the successful interchangeable-parts production of firearms, clocks and watches, sewing machines, and agricultural implements. In the 1850s, agricultural implement companies actually used conveyor belts to assemble the parts of major subassemblies in sequence, thus foreshadowing the "mass production" techniques of the early twentieth century.

POWER AND ENERGY

During the early years of manufacturing in the United States, water wheels furnished most of the motive power. Plentiful steadily moving rivers and streams assured this dependable source of power, and readily available water power was further enhanced by technological improvements in water wheels.

A water wheel is always placed in a vertical position on a horizontal shaft and is moved at a comparatively low speed by direct action of the water. Wheels are classified by the way water is applied to turn them (see Figure 10-1 on the next page). The kind used in colonial times and for a while thereafter in frontier areas was the *undershot* wheel, which was placed in the stream so that its blades were moved by the water passing underneath it. The undershot wheel, although easy to install, was inefficient, transmitting no more than 40 percent of the power applied to it. The *overshot* wheel was moved by water running from a flume across the top of the wheel into buckets covering its surface; the weight of the water in the buckets moved the wheel in the direction of the stream flow. The overshot wheel was more efficient, easy to install, and satisfactory wherever there was a good head of water, but the power it developed was not great enough for heavy industrial purposes. Consequently, the large manufacturing concerns almost invariably used the *breast* wheel. This type, too, was equipped with buckets, but the water struck the wheel short of its axle so that it rotated in an upstream direction; both the impulse of the water and its weight in the buckets

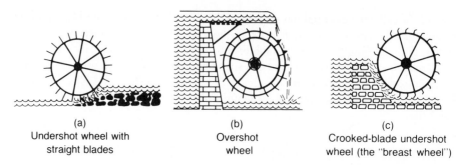

(a)
Undershot wheel with
straight blades

(b)
Overshot
wheel

(c)
Crooked-blade undershot
wheel (the "breast wheel")

FIGURE 10-1 WATER WHEEL DESIGNS: *The three main engineering designs of water wheels that powered early textile and woodworking machinery are displayed here.*

enabled the wheel to utilize up to 75 percent of the power applied to it. Installed in multiples, the breast wheel developed sufficient horsepower to serve the largest early nineteenth-century industrial firms. The machinery of the Merrimack Manufacturing Company, for example, was run by eight breast wheels, each 30 feet in diameter with buckets 12 feet long.

The slow-moving and cumbersome water wheels could develop several thousand horsepower, but they had marked disadvantages. Power from a wheel was transmitted by wooden shafts and cogwheels and was limited by the strength of the entire mechanism. Furthermore, industrial location was restricted to stream sites, and the problem of finding sites, especially in industrialized areas, became a serious one. The first difficulty was partially overcome by making wheels and transmission parts of metal, the second by the improved engineering of dams and canals. The water turbine, which revolved on a vertical shaft, was much more efficient than a wheel and by the 1850s was adding rapidly to the power potential of the country.

Finally came steam power, although its introduction into U.S. manufacturing was slow for several reasons. In the beginning, the steam engine was extremely costly to operate. Breakdowns were frequent, and expert repair technicians were rare. In transportation, the steam engine could pull such heavy loads at such increased speeds that these disadvantages were more than offset, but in industry water power remained cheaper than steam power for a long time. It has been estimated that in 1812 only eleven engines of the high-pressure type developed by Oliver Evans were in use in this country.[3]

During the next two decades, steam engines became more common in the South and West, but most of them were used in ironworks and glass factories that required fuel for other purposes or in mills that could not conveniently be located near water. Around 1840, manufacturers in New England and the Middle Atlantic states estimated the annual cost per horsepower of steam to be five or six times that of water. Within the next 20 years, improvements in metal-working technology lowered the cost of

---

[3] Victor S. Clark, *History of Manufactures in the United States, 1607–1860* (Washington, D.C.: Carnegie Institution of Washington, 1916), p. 409.

This fairly typical overshot water wheel was one of 20,000 sawmills and 14,000 flour mills reported in the 1860 national census.

steam engines and improved both their efficiency and reliability. By the 1850s, steam engines were replacing water wheels in the heat-using industries and wherever stream flows were highly variable, as they were along the Ohio River. In New England, steam engines were being installed to power textile mills due to the serious lack of adequate power sites. As of 1860, water was still the chief source of power, but the years of the water wheel were clearly numbered.

Paralleling the rise of steam power, with a lag, was coal, which eventually became a major new source of energy. Because wood and hence charcoal were so cheap in the United States, however, coal use was slowed by comparison to its rapid adoption in England. Coal, like water, had a major impact on the location of manufacturing. With adequate transportation facilities, coal power increasingly allowed factories to be built in urban centers, and after 1830 coal-powered factories increasingly became a feature of the rise of manufacturing in the United States.

FACTOR PROPORTIONS AND BORROWING AND ADAPTING TECHNOLOGY

Britain's head start in making machines gave the British a great advantage in manufacturing. Their machines typically embodied specific technological forms that reflected their relative costs of labor, capital, and raw materials. The relative costs of these inputs were different in the United States. Nineteenth-century Americans were short on labor and capital but long on raw materials and natural power sources (water). American industrialists, as runners-up to British producers, had not only to copy English machines but to adapt them as well, to economize on labor, perhaps at the sacrifice of raw-material usage. One example of their success is reflected in the comparison of the textile industries in each country. English textile firms averaged 17,000 spindles and 276 looms compared to 7,000 spindles and 163 looms in the United States. Robert Zevin's study of textiles reveals that the American cotton textiles industry had only 20 percent of Britain's spindles and 25 percent of its workers but processed 40 percent as much cotton. Clearly, the Americans had successfully adapted their equipment to save on scarce U.S. labor and capital.

The works of Lars Sandberg and later William Lazonick on the choice of techniques and their adoption reveals that there was not a uniform technology on both sides of the Atlantic. In textiles, the British became increasingly labor intensive and lowered the quality of their raw material inputs. Americans conserved labor, especially scarce unskilled labor, by upgrading machines and adopting higher grades of raw cotton or wool materials. Because Americans did not unionize as did British workers and were more mobile than British workers, American management could more easily substitute new machines to reduce its labor dependence and labor costs. Claudia Goldin and Kenneth Sokoloff add another consideration: early manufacturers depended primarily on women and children. Where the opportunity costs of this labor were low, as in New England where farming produced a poor livelihood, children and women were relatively more available to supply scarce labor. This encouraged the location of manufacturing there and supplied a labor force accepting of technological changes.

In textiles, firearms, clocks and watches, and many other items, the ideas of standardization, interchangeable parts, and division of labor in assembly production processes were being widely applied. In 1851, at the Great Exhibition in London (in many ways like the World's Fair today), American products were a primary attraction. Though simple in design, not elegant or long lasting, they were practical, cheap, and functional. After all, they reflected the characteristics demanded by a population dominated by masses of farmers, pioneers, and workers who were for the most part unpretentious, practical people. In 1855 a British parliamentary committee visited the United States to determine the secret of the success of the "American system," as it became known. This "American system" flourished in America's new factories.

THE EMERGENCE OF U.S. FACTORIES

The word *factory* has been used customarily to designate manufacturing units with the following characteristics:

1. A substantial output of a standardized product made to be sold in a wide, rather than a strictly local, market.

2. Complex operations carried on in one building or group of adjacent buildings. Implied is a considerable investment in fixed plant, the mechanization of processes, and the use of power.

3. An assembly of workers under a definite organizational discipline.

In the United States, the factory developed first in the cotton textile industry. Due to the unusual nature of its founding, we think of the mill of Almy, Brown, and Slater, in operation by 1793, as the first American factory. Moses Brown and William Almy were men of wealth in the New England mercantile tradition. Like many other American enterprisers, they had tried and failed to duplicate English spinning machinery. As noted earlier, in 1789 there came to Rhode Island a young mechanical wizard, Samuel Slater, who had worked for years in the firm of Arkwright and Strutt in Milford, England. Having memorized the minutest details of the water frames, Slater emigrated to the United States, where he hoped to obtain a fortune for his information. Getting

The complexity of mechanized factories and the substantial economies of scale related to them are illustrated here with a cotton manufacturing plant (circa 1839) where cotton is being carded, drawn, and roven (twisted into strands).

in touch with Almy and Brown, Slater agreed to reproduce the equipment for a mechanized spinning mill. Although small, the enterprise served as a training ground for operatives and as a pilot operation for managers.

A number of small mills like the Slater mill soon followed, but most of them failed by the turn of the century because their promoters did not aim for a wide market. Not until the Embargo Act of 1807, and the consequent scarcity of English textiles that stimulated demand for domestic manufactures, did spinning mills become numerous. Between 1805 and 1815, 94 new cotton mills were built in New England, and the mounting competition led Almy and Brown to push their markets south and west. By 1814, 70 percent of all consignments were to the Midwest via Philadelphia. Only two decades after Arkwright machinery was introduced into this country, the market for yarn was becoming national and the spinning process was becoming a true factory operation as it was in England.

THE LOWELL SHOPS AND THE WALTHAM SYSTEM

Two events propelled these changes. One was the successful introduction of the power loom into American manufacture; the other was the organization of production so that all four stages of the manufacture of cotton cloth could occur within one establishment.

After closely observing the workings of textile machinery in Great Britain, Francis Cabot Lowell, a New England merchant, gained sufficient knowledge of the secrets of mechanized weaving to enable him, with the help of a gifted technician, to construct a power loom superior to any that had been built to date. It was as an enterpriser, however, that Francis Lowell made a more significant contribution. He persuaded other men of means to participate with him in establishing a firm at Waltham that had all the essential characteristics of factory production. This was the famed Boston Manufacturing Company, the forerunner of several similar firms in which the so-called Boston Associates had an interest. Specializing in coarse sheetings, the Waltham factory sold its product all over America. Consolidating all the steps of textile manufacture in a single plant lowered production costs. A large number of specialized workers were organized into departments and directed by executives who were not necessarily technical supervisors. The factory, by using power-driven machinery, produced standardized commodities in quantity.

At Lowell, where the Merrimack Manufacturing Company followed the Waltham pattern, and at Manchester and Lawrence, the factory system gained a permanent foothold. In the second leading center of New England textile manufacture—the Providence-Pawtucket region—there was a similar trend, although the factories there were fewer and smaller. The third great district, located about Paterson and Philadelphia, contained mainly small mills that performed a single major process and turned out finer weaves. But by 1860, New England's industry had nearly four times as many spindles as the Middle Atlantic industry and accounted for nearly three-fourths of the country's output of cotton goods. The factory had demonstrated its superiority in the textile field.

It was simply a matter of time until other industries adopted the same organization. Because technological changes were slower, the production of woolen cloth tended to

Technological advances in iron and steel production, like the blast furnace and rolling mill shown here, epitomized the "modern" nineteenth-century factory.

remain in the small mill longer than cotton production did. But after 1830, woolen factories began to adopt the characteristics of the Waltham system, and by 1860 the largest textile factories in the United States were woolen factories. Again, New Englanders far surpassed the rest of the country in combining factors of production in large units; two-thirds of America's woolen output in 1860 was made in New England.

IRON AND OTHER FACTORIES

In most other industries, the decade of the 1830s was one of expansion and experimentation with new methods. In the primary iron industry, establishments by the 1840s dwarfed those of a quarter-century earlier, and even in the pre-steel era some of them had passed beyond what could be called the mill stage. By 1845, for instance, the Brady's Bend Iron Company in western Pennsylvania owned nearly 6,000 acres of mineral land and 5 miles of river front upon the Allegheny. It mined its own coal, ore, limestone, fire-clay, and fire-stone, made its own coke, and owned 14 miles of railway to serve its works. The plant itself consisted of 4 blast furnaces, a foundry, and rolling mills. It was equipped to perform all the processes, from getting raw materials out of the ground to delivering finished rails and metal shapes to consumers, and could produce annually between 10,000 and 15,000 tons of rails. It housed in its own tenements 538 laboring families. This company, with an actual investment of $1,000,000, was among the largest in America before the Civil War, though there were rival works of approximately equal capacity and similar organization.[4]

In the anthracite region to the east, factory operation of furnaces and rolling mills had been achieved by 1850. Also by the 1850s, American factories were manufacturing arms, clocks and watches, and sewing machines.

How one industry could adopt new methods as a consequence of progress in another industry is shown by the fact that, as the sewing machine was produced on a quantity basis, the boot and shoe industry developed factory characteristics. Carriages, wagons, and even farm implements were eventually produced in large numbers. Finally, where markets were more extensive, where there was a substantial investment in fixed plant, and where workers were subjected to formal discipline, some firms in the traditional mill industries other than the textile and iron industries achieved factory status. The great merchant flour mills of Baltimore and Rochester fell into this category, as did some of the large packing plants in New York, Philadelphia, Baltimore, and (after 1840), Cincinnati.

THE QUESTION OF PROTECTION

After the peace of 1815, imports of English manufactured goods reached alarming proportions from the viewpoint of American businesses. Before 1815, duties on foreign goods had been set at rates that, although originally intended to protect, maximized governmental revenues in a hit-or-miss fashion. Growing protectionist sentiment in the Northeast gained enough support from the West and South to secure passage of the Tariff Act of 1816.

The tariff of 1816 levied ad valorem duties of 20 to 25 percent on most manufactured goods and 15 to 20 percent on raw materials. In general, the level of duties on manufactures did not prevent the entry of many goods at that time, although cheap cottons were shut out of the home market by specific duties (that is, duties of so much per yard). Moreover, the tax on raw materials, particularly raw wool, lowered the expansion potential of domestic industries using raw wool inputs.

From 1816 until 1832, the protectionist tide rose; American producers of cottons, woolens, glass, and iron products received the greatest favors, with raw wool and hemp garnering their shares. Figure 10-2 traces the history of U.S. tariffs measured as rates, namely duties collected as percentages of the values of dutiable imports. It shows the

---

[4] Clark, p. 446.

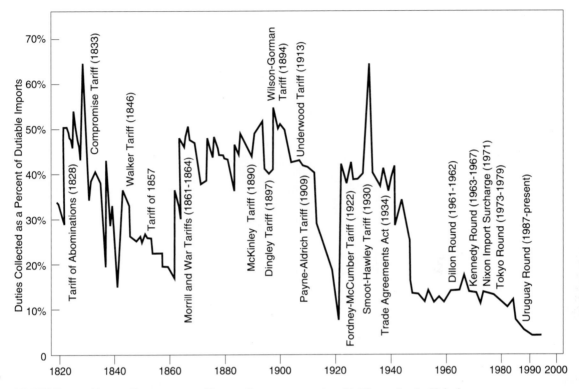

FIGURE 10-2 TARIFF RATES IN THE UNITED STATES SINCE 1820 *Tariff rates in the United States have bounced up and down, suggesting that in Congress tariffs are a political football. Import-competing industries prefer high tariffs. The highest tariffs we have had were the Smoot-Hawley Tariff of 1930 and the "Tariff of Abominations" of 1828.*

SOURCE: U.S. DEPARTMENT OF COMMERCE.

Tariff Act of 1828 realizing a record high, not to be matched again until the Smoot-Hawley Tariff of 1930.

In general, the Northeast and Middle Atlantic states favored high tariffs; the South did not. The political shenanigans leading to the high tariff of 1828—the "Tariff of Abominations"—precipitated agitation in the South and necessitated a compromise within only a few years. In fact, a severe threat to the Union was South Carolina's Nullification Ordinance, which was legislated even after downward revisions in import duties had been made in 1832. The Compromise Tariff of 1833 provided that all duties would be reduced to a maximum of 20 percent ad valorem within a decade. But only two months after the 20-percent maximum level was reached in 1842, the Whigs (who had just gained control of the White House) passed a bill in which rates reverted to about the protective level of ten years before, and President John Tyler, even though a southerner, accepted it because he felt this action would provide more revenue for the government. With the return of the Democrats to power in 1845, more moderate tariffs were rapidly secured, and the Walker Tariff of 1846 set an example that was followed until 1861.

The good times of the 1850s and the consequent increase in imports so swelled the revenues from tariffs that the government achieved great surpluses. The piling up of cash in U.S. Treasury vaults led to a general reduction in rates, and many items were placed on the free list. Just before the Civil War, it appeared that the United States might join the United Kingdom as a free-trade country. As shown on the preceding page in Figure 10-2, tariffs in 1860 averaged less than 20 percent of the value of dutiable imports (15 percent of the value of all imports), levels that had only moderate protective significance.

As indicated by South Carolina's Nullification Ordinance in reaction to the "Tariff of Abominations" (1828), the South had no enthusiasm for high tariffs. They fought against high tariffs just as the Northeast and Middle Atlantic states fought for them, with clear economic gains in mind.

The figure on the next page illustrates the effect of a duty (d) on foreign cotton textiles. First, we derive total supply (S) as the horizontal sum of New England's supply (S_{NE}) and Great Britain's (S_{GB}). Below the price P_o, no supply from New England is forthcoming; at price P, the quantity supplied by New England is Q_{NE}, equal to the line distance ab (= a′b′). Along the price line from P we add a′b′ (= ab) where it cuts S_{GB} (= Q_{GB}) to derive a point on S (b′) to show the total quantity Q supplied at the price P. $Q_{NE} + Q_{GB} = Q$, the total supply. Now we include the demand curve (D) and determine equilibrium at price P and quantity Q, where S and D intersect.

To see the effect of a duty (d) on British cotton textiles, we add it to S_{GB} to get a new higher cost supply curve S_{GBd}, inclusive of the tax. The tax, in effect, adds to the costs of going to the U.S. market for British producers. The end result is a new supply schedule S_d, one above S by the amount of the duty (d). The new equilibrium quantity is Q_d, at price P_d, and the government receives $Q_d \cdot D$ in revenues. Now we shall relate this changed equilibrium to the historical issues.

A tariff is a tax paid in part by consumers on dutiable imported goods. The tariff raises the price of these imported goods (P to P_d) and lowers the real income of consumers of these taxed goods. Since the dutied items were largely imported manufactures like textiles, southern consumers had to pay more for manufactures when tariffs rose. Northeastern manufacturers, however, gained by the higher prices generated; their market shares and profits increased. (Check this by determining along the price line P_d the post-duty quantities supplied by New England and Great Britain.)

There was another way that the South lost because of high tariffs on manufactures. When the United States imported less, substituting American-made items for dutied imports, fewer dollars were exchanged and placed in foreigners' hands. For example, with the English receiving fewer dollars for their textile exports to the United States,

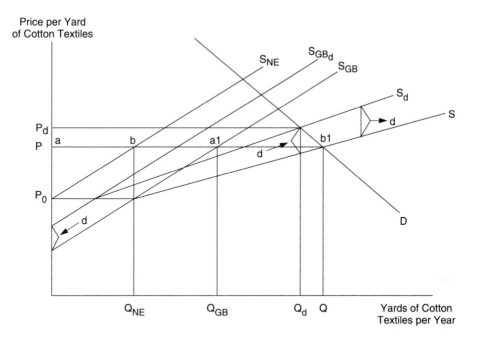

they had less foreign exchange (dollars) to purchase American exports. What was the leading U.S. export, and to whom? Cotton, to England. Sending more cotton to New England only partially offset the reduction to England. Higher-priced cotton textiles meant lower quantities demanded overall (Q_d rather than Q), and that in turn meant lower quantities demanded of raw cotton materials. Southern planters simply lost customers abroad faster than they gained them at home.

We see that the tariff transfers money to the protected industries, helping the owners of capital and the workers employed there. It takes money away from consumers and from foreign producers of dutied items. The government gains from the tax revenues collected. In short, tariffs take money from one group and give it to another. As John James has shown, the high antebellum tariffs redistributed wealth and resources from the South to northeastern industries, a transfer southerners abhorred. From the southern perspective, the terms of trade deteriorated; prices of their exports fell, and the prices of their imports rose.

Besides their transfer features, tariffs are noteworthy for their political popularity. They are often advocated, for example, by politicians to protect American workers from "cheap" foreign labor. But these were not the original arguments for U.S. tariffs. The political economy of tariffs was first expressed in the first Tariff Act in 1789:

> Whereas it is necessary for the support of the government, for the discharge of the debts of the United States, and the encouragement of manufactures, that duties be laid on goods, wares, and merchandise imported. . . .

So the original purposes of the tariff were clear: to generate government revenues and to protect infant American industry.

Initially, tariffs successfully added revenue to government coffers. In 1790, 99.9 percent of total federal revenue was derived from tariffs. In 1860 it was still 94 percent. (Today it is less than 1 percent of federal revenues, and accordingly we never hear this argument, or seldom do.) What about the other purpose, to protect infant industries? Success in that area appears dubious.

When peace came in 1815, ending the protection from foreign competition caused by war, low-grade British textiles flooded U.S. markets. In 1816, Francis Lowell went to Congress asking for a tariff on low-grade textiles competing with the ones his established mills produced. High-grade cotton cloth like that made in the infant firms in Rhode Island received no protection. In short, the Lowell mills gained, Rhode Island's infant industry did not. The protection received was primarily a political matter. Who primarily sought the tariff-protected low-grade cloth? Again, it was the South, with these textiles going to slaves.

Were later higher tariffs a necessary condition for the rise of manufacturing? We note that in 1830, when the nullification controversy raged, the tariff rate on dutied items exceeded 60 percent. By 1860, the tariff rate was just below 20 percent. In short, when manufacturing was growing rapidly (albeit faster in the 1830s and 1850s than in the 1840s) it did so over three decades while tariff protection was falling.[5]

THE RISE OF CORPORATE ORGANIZATION

We must finally consider the changes taking place in the legal concept of the business firm—the change from sole proprietorship and partnership organization to corporate organization. The corporation gained prominence chiefly because some businesses required more capital than one person or a few people could provide. By 1810, the corporate form was commonplace for banks, insurance companies, and turnpike companies; in ensuing decades, canals and railroads could be financed only by tapping various sources of funds, from small merchants and professionals along proposed routes, to English capitalists thousands of miles away.

The corporation, a legal entity with privileges and responsibilities distinct from those of the people associated with it, evolved over centuries. In England, corporations followed two major lines of development. Municipalities and universities were established under corporate charters granted by the sovereign; and the great trading companies, formed for the purpose of exploiting foreign lands, were organized as "joint-stock associations" that borrowed many of the features of the corporation.

So the development of the corporation was in reality the transformation of an instrument of communal service to accommodate the demands of a new industrial age. It is a convention of economic historiography to begin the corporate cycle with Chief

---

[5] Today's arguments for tariffs as a bargaining tool with nations who tax U.S. goods was seldom evoked in the nineteenth century. Our main trading partner, Great Britain, largely adhered to free-trade policies after 1825.

Justice John Marshall's *Dartmouth College* opinion, reading into it the legal foundation of modern capitalism that he implied when he made Dartmouth's royal charter a contract between the college and New Hampshire and, as such, placed it beyond the constitutional power of that state to repeal or amend. Nevertheless, this was only an implication; Marshall's explicit references concerned only municipal bodies and private charities. It is in Justice Joseph Story's concurring later opinion that we find the principle extended to business enterprises. Contemporary opinion, both pro and con, recognized Story's analysis as novel and significant.

This creative revisionism, as a few historians have noted, produced a radical change in traditional analysis. The mere fact that a public authority had granted a charter meant that the corporation had, in some sense, a "public" purpose; taken at face value, this characteristic suggested the ability of the chartering authority to regulate, revise, or even revoke the privilege it had granted. But Story discarded purpose and substituted property as a starting point, achieving a twofold division in result: on the one hand, private corporations holding private property and, on the other, public corporations charged with government or administration. The state could regulate public corporations without restraint; the state could approach private ones only with the deference due vested right and private interest.

An equally significant development was Story's grafting of the ancient law of trusts onto the emerging form of business enterprise. Here the consequence was a separation of ownership and control. Under this division, the capital of a corporation became a trust fund for the successive benefit of creditors and stockholders, the directors became trustees, and the corporation itself increasingly assumed a character and personality distinct from the persons who had provided its resources. The end result was an ideal apparatus of capital formation that involved both permanent contributions of resources and transferable, judicially protected claims.

When it first appeared in the United States, the corporation lacked many of its present-day characteristics. Charters were granted by special acts of legislatures, and the question of the liability of stockholders was far from settled. Nevertheless, the corporation had a number of advantages over the sole proprietorship and the partnership, and its legal status came to be better defined than that of the joint-stock company. Of its unquestioned advantages, the most notable—in addition to the obvious one of attracting greater numbers of investors—were permanence and flexibility. The partnership and the sole proprietorship have one inescapable drawback: if one partner or the proprietor dies, the business is dissolved. The business can go on, of course, under a new partnership or proprietorship, but continuity of operation is contingent on the lives of particular individuals. Furthermore, a partnership is dissolved when one partner's interest is sold. But the shares of a corporation can be transferred, and investors, whether small or large, can enter and leave the business without destroying the structure of the corporation.

Early corporations did not have certain advantages that corporations have today. Take the question of liability, for example. What the liability of the shareholders for the debts of the corporation should be was difficult to determine. Stockholders of the English joint-stock companies had finally come to assume "double liability"—that is, the stockholders were liable to the extent of their investment plus a like amount—

and some states experimented with charters specifying either double liability or unlimited liability. After 1830, however, various states passed statutes providing for limited liability, and by 1860 this principle was generally accepted. Under limited liability, stockholders of a failed corporation could lose only the money they had invested in the venture.

The early requirement that incorporators of banks, insurance companies, canals, and railroads obtain their charters by the special act of a state legislature was not always a disadvantage. For those who had the political connections, this involved little uncertainty and expense, and there was always the possibility of obtaining a charter with exceptionally liberal provisions. Nevertheless, the politically unfavored could spend years lobbying futilely for corporate charters. As early as 1800, those who looked on incorporation by special act as "undemocratic" were agitating to secure "general" acts of incorporation—laws making it possible for any group, provided it observed and met prescribed regulations and requirements, to obtain a charter. Others, fearful that the corporation would spread too rapidly if their elected representatives did not review *each* application for charter, opposed general acts. In 1837, Connecticut passed the Connecticut General Incorporation Act, the first general act that made incorporation the right of anyone.[6] From that date, *permissive* general acts (acts allowing, but not requiring, incorporation under their provisions) were gradually placed on the statute books of most of the chief manufacturing states, and before 1861 the constitutions of thirteen states *required* incorporation under general laws. In those states where permissive legislation had been enacted, incorporators continued until about 1870 to obtain special charters, which enabled the incorporators to secure more liberal provisions than they could under general laws.

After 1837, mercantile and manufacturing firms were organized as corporations with growing frequency. There was, especially during the 1850s, a rapid increase in the number of manufacturing corporations. *Yet in 1860, the greater portion of resources devoted to manufacturing was under the control of proprietorships and partnerships.* At that time, a rolling mill of the most modern design could be built for $150,000 (equal to the selling price of 150 prime field-hand slaves or the yearly income of 300 ordinary workers). Thus the largest textile factory did not require an investment beyond the means of a single very wealthy person, and the course of commerce and industry would not have been very different before 1860 if the privilege of incorporation had been given only to financial and transportation firms. Nonetheless, contemporary observers were aware that the corporate form would be inseparable from the enterprise of the future; bigness obviously lay ahead. For technical reasons alone, the size of the firm had to become larger, and, as the railroad companies had already demonstrated, enterprisers had to choose the corporate type of business organization when huge capital outlays were required.

---

[6] In 1811, New York had passed a law that permitted incorporation, without special act, of certain manufacturing concerns with capitalization of under $100,000.

SELECTED REFERENCES
AND SUGGESTED READINGS

Ames, Edward, and Nathan Rosenberg. "Changing Technological Leadership and Industrial Growth." *Economic Journal* 73 (1963).

Atack, Jeremy. "Fact or Fiction? The Relative Costs of Steam and Water Power: A Simulative Approach." *Explorations in Economic History* 16 (1979): 409–437.

———. "Returns to Scale in Antebellum United States Manufacturing." *Explorations in Economic History* 14 (1977): 337–359.

Atack, Jeremy, Fred Bateman, and Thomas Weiss. "The Regional Diffusion and Adoption of the Steam Engine in American Manufacturing." *Journal of Economic History* 40 (June 1980).

Bateman, Fred, and Thomas Weiss. "Comparative Regional Development in Antebellum Manufacturing." *Journal of Economic History* 35 (1975).

Bateman, Fred, James Forest, and Thomas Weiss. "Profitability in Southern Manufacturing: Estimates for 1860." *Explorations in Economic History* 12 (1975): 211–232.

Brito, D. L., and Jeffrey G. Williamson. "Skilled Labor and Nineteenth Century Anglo-American Managerial Behavior." *Explorations in Economic History* 10 (1973): 235–252.

Chandler, Alfred D. "Anthracite Coal and the Beginnings of the Industrial Revolution in the United States." *Business History Review* (1972): 141–181.

Clark, Victor S. *History of Manufactures in the United States 1607–1860*. Washington, D.C.: Carnegie Institution of Washington, 1929.

Cochran, Thomas. *Frontiers of Change: Early Industrialism in America*. New York: Oxford University Press, 1981.

Cole, A. H. *The American Wool Manufacture*. Cambridge: Harvard University Press, 1926.

David, Paul. "The Horndal Effect in Lowell, 1834–1856: A Short-Run Learning Curve for Integrated Cotton Textile Mills." *Explorations in Economic History* 10 (1973): 131–150.

———. "Learning by Doing and Tariff Protection: A Reconsideration of the Case of the Antebellum United States Textile Industry." *Journal of Economic History* 30 (1970): 521–601.

Davis, Lance E. "The New England Textile Mills and the Capital Markets: A Study of Industrial Borrowing, 1840–1860." *Journal of Economic History* 20 (1960): 1–30.

———. "Sources of Industrial Finance: The American Textile Industry, A Case Study." *Explorations in Economic History*, 1st series, 60, no. 4 (1957).

Field, Alexander James. "Sectoral Shift in Antebellum Massachusetts: A Reconsideration." *Explorations in Economic History* 15 (1978): 146–171.

Goldin, Claudia, and Kenneth Sokoloff. "The Relative Productivity Hypothesis of Industrialization: The American Case, 1820 to 1850." *Quarterly Journal of Economics* 69 (August 1984).

Habakkuk, H. J. *American and British Technology in the Nineteenth Century: The Search for Labor Saving Inventions*. New York: Cambridge University Press, 1962.

Halsey, Harlan I. "The Choice Between High Pressure and Low Pressure Steam Power in America in the Early Nineteenth Century." *Journal of Economic History* 61 (1981): 723–744.

Hughes, Jonathan. *Industrialization and Economic History: Theses and Conjectures*. New York: McGraw-Hill, 1970.

———. *The Vital Few: American Economic Progress and Its Protagonists*. New York: Oxford University Press, 1986.

James, John. "The Welfare Effects of the Ante-Bellum Tariff: A General Equilibrium Analysis." *Explorations in Economic History* 15 (1978): 231–256.

Lazonick, William H. "Production Relations, Labor Productivity, and Choice of Technique: British and U.S. Cotton Spinning." *Journal of Economic History* 41 (1981): 491–516.

Lindstrom, Diane. *Economic Development in the Philadelphia Region, 1810–1850*. New York: Columbia University Press, 1978.

Livesay, Harold. "Marketing Patterns in the Antebellum American Iron Industry." *Business History Review* (1971): 269–295.

Livesay, Harold, and Glen Porter. "The Financial Role of Merchants in the Development of U.S. Manufacturing, 1815–1860." *Explorations in Economic History* 9 (1971): 63–88.

North, Douglass C. *The Economic Growth of the United States 1790–1860.* Englewood Cliffs, New Jersey: Prentice-Hall, 1961.

Passell, Peter, and Marie Schmundt. "The Financial Role of Merchants in the Development of U.S. Manufacturing, 1815–1860." *Explorations in Economic History* 9 (1971): 35–48.

Pope, Clayne. "The Impact of the Antebellum Tariff on Income Distribution." *Explorations in Economic History* 9 (1972): 375–422.

Rosenberg, Nathan. "Factors Affecting the Diffusion of Technology." *Explorations in Economic History* 10 (1972): 3–34.

———. *Technology and American Economic Growth.* New York: Harper & Row, 1972.

Sokoloff, Kenneth L. "Inventive Activity in Early Industrial America: Evidence from Patent Records, 1790–1846." *Journal of Economic History* 48 (1988): 813–850.

———. "Was the Transition from the Artisanal Shop to the Nonmechanized Factory Associated with Gains in Efficiency? Evidence from the U.S. Manufactures Censuses of 1820 and 1850." *Explorations in Economic History* 21 (1984): 351–382.

Temin, Peter. "Manufacturing." In *American Economic Growth: An Economist's History of the United States,* eds. Lance E. Davis et al. New York: Harper & Row, 1972.

———. "Steam and Water Power in the Early 19th Century." *Journal of Economic History* 26 (1966): 187–205. Also reprinted in Robert Fogel and Stanley Engerman, eds. *The Reinterpretation of American Economic History.* New York: Harper & Row, 1971.

Terrill, Tom E. "Eager Hands: Labor for Southern Textiles, 1850–1860." *Journal of Economic History* 36 (1976): 84–99.

Uselding, Paul. "Factor Substitution and Labor Productivity Growth in American Manufacturing, 1839–1899." *Journal of Economic History* 32 (1972): 670–681.

———. "Henry Burden and the Question of Anglo-American Technological Transfer in the Nineteenth Century." *Journal of Economic History* 30 (1970): 312–337.

———. "A Note on the Inter-Regional Trade in Manufactures in 1840." *Journal of Economic History* 35 (1976): 428–437.

Uselding, Paul, and W. Douglas Morgan. "Technical Progress at the Springfield Armory." *Explorations in Economic History* 9 (1972): 269–290.

Williamson, Jeffrey. "Urbanization in the American Northeast." *Journal of Economic History* 25 (1965): 592–608.

Williamson, Jeffrey, and Joseph Swanson. "The Growth of Cities in the American Northeast, 1820–1870." *Explorations in Entrepreneurial History,* 2d series, 4 (Supplement) (1966).

Zevin, Robert B. "The Growth of Cotton Textile Production After 1815." In *The Reinterpretation of American Economic History,* eds. Robert Fogel and Stanley Engerman. New York: Harper & Row, 1971.

———. *The Growth of Manufacturing in Early Nineteenth-Century New England.* New York: Arno Press, 1975.

CHAPTER
ELEVEN

LABOR DURING THE EARLY
INDUSTRIAL PERIOD

CHAPTER THEME Before 1860, most of the U.S. population lived in rural areas and most workers were self-employed on farms and in craftshops. Nevertheless, after the War of 1812, rapid industrialization and urbanization, especially in the Northeast and Middle Atlantic states, transformed the working conditions and living standards of many Americans who depended on their labor for a living. Real wages—money wages adjusted for the cost of living—rose between 1820 and 1860; unskilled workers' earnings fell relative to skilled workers as the supply of unskilled labor swelled through immigration; and working conditions became less personal as more and more workers changed from self-employment to working for an employer. It was a period when the first stirrings of a labor movement began in the United States. These changes occurred as economic growth increased and industrialization advanced and spread.

THE CHANGING LABOR FORCE DISTRIBUTION

A useful starting point in the story of the work force is an overview of the labor force distribution. This is provided by broad categories in Table 11-1, which shows the continued dominance of agriculture throughout the period. It also reflects how markedly different labor was allocated in 1860 compared to 1810. Mining took the biggest jump, largely because of the California Gold Rush; but more important is the twentyfold increase of workers in manufacturing. On the eve of the Civil War there were 1.5 million workers in manufacturing, most of them in the Northeast and Middle Atlantic states. In absolute numbers agricultural workers grew the most, but manufacturing workers grew relatively. The economy was changing its structure from agriculture to manufacturing, a normal pattern of modern economic growth and development.

THE FACTORY AND THE WORKER

As the economy and especially urban centers grew, and as economic unification progressed, output was sold in larger, more integrated markets. As Table 11-2 shows, the size of firms grew, as reflected in the number of employees per firm. For example, the number of workers per firm in cotton textiles nearly tripled, and more than doubled in wool textiles and in hats and caps between 1820 and 1850. Pressures were great to achieve volume at the expense of artistry, and the small artisanal shops were increasingly giving way to the factory. This growth was apparent both in mechanized or mechanizing industries (cotton and wool textiles) and in nonmechanized industries (hats, books, and shoes). So mechanization was only part of the story of this trend toward greater sized production units. Another key change was the greater division of labor, diminishing the proportion and role of workers with general skills. A more intense workplace under careful supervision aimed for standardized products, an early form of quality control on a large scale. Such a transition in a nonmechanized shop is described in a study by B. E. Hazard:

TABLE 11-1   LABOR FORCE DISTRIBUTION, 1810 TO 1860 (IN THOUSANDS)

Year	Total	Agriculture	Fishing	Mining	Construction	Manufactures	Transportation	Trade	Services
1810	2,330	1,950	6	11	—	75	60	—	82
1820	3,135	2,470	14	13	—	—	50	—	130
1830	4,200	2,965	15	22	—	—	70	—	190
1840	5,660	3,570	24	32	290	500	112	350	285
1850	8,250	4,520	30	102	410	1,200	155	530	430
1860	11,110	5,880	31	176	520	1,530	225	890	715

SOURCE: ADAPTED FROM STANLEY LEBERGOTT, MANPOWER IN ECONOMIC GROWTH: THE AMERICAN RECORD SINCE 1800 (NEW YORK: McGRAW-HILL, 1964), P. 510.

TABLE 11-2 NUMBER OF EMPLOYEES PER NORTHEASTERN MANUFACTURING
FIRM, 1820 AND 1850

	1820		1850		Ratio of Firm
	Number of Employees	Number of Firms Observed	Number of Employees	Number of Firms Observed	Size in 1850 to that in 1820
Boots and shoes	19.1	15	33.6	72	1.76
Cotton textiles	34.6	92	97.5	856	2.82
Flour and grist milling	2.4	90	1.8	5,128	0.75
Glass	56.9	8	64.6	76	1.14
Hats and caps	8.4	32	17.0	812	2.02
Iron and iron products	19.5	73	24.2	1,562	1.24
Liquors	2.7	165	5.0	633	1.85
Paper	14.3	33	22.4	12	1.57
Tanning	3.8	126	4.2	3,233	1.11
Wool and mixed textiles	10.6	107	24.5	1,284	2.31

SOURCE: ADAPTED FROM THE 1820 AND 1850 CENSUS OF MANUFACTURES, AS PROVIDED IN KENNETH
L. SOKOLOFF, "WAS THE TRANSITION FROM THE ARTISANAL SHOP TO THE NONMECHANIZED FACTORY
ASSOCIATED WITH GAINS IN EFFICIENCY? EVIDENCE FROM THE U.S. MANUFACTURES CENSUSES OF 1820
AND 1850," *EXPLORATIONS IN ECONOMIC HISTORY* 21 (1984): 354.

He [Gideon Howard, a manufacturer of shoes in South Randolph, Massachu-
setts] had a "gang" over in his twelve-footer who fitted, made and finished: one
lasted, one pegged and tacked on soles, one made fore edges, one put on heels
and "pared them up," and in cases of handsewed shoes, two or three sewers were
needed to keep the rest of the gang busy. . . . These groups of men in a ten-
footer gradually took on a character due to specialization demanded by the markets with higher standards and need of speed in output. Instead of all the men
working there being regularly trained shoemakers, perhaps only one would be,
and he was a boss contractor, who took out from a central shop so many cases
to be done at a certain figure and date, and hired shoemakers who had "picked
up" the knowledge of one process and set them to work under his supervision.
One of the gang was a laster, another a pegger, one an edgemaker, one a polisher.
Sometimes, as business grew, each of these operators would be duplicated. Such
work did away with the old seven-year apprenticeship system.[1]

Another characteristic of this transition to larger firms, at least in most manufacturing firms, was the increase in the proportion of the labor force composed of women
and children. Larger firms typically exhibited a proportionately large share of simple
and relatively narrowly defined tasks, such as machine tending, starting materials in
machines, carrying materials, and other simple tasks. A key problem for many firms

[1]From Kenneth L. Sokoloff, "Was the Transition from the Artisanal Shop to the Nonmechanized Factory
Associated with Gains in Efficiency? Evidence from the U.S. Manufactures Censuses of 1820 and 1850,"
Explorations in Economic History 21 (1984): 357.

was hiring unskilled but able workers, especially before the large waves of immigration in the late 1840s and 1850s.

THE RHODE ISLAND AND WALTHAM SYSTEMS

Mill and factory owners in the textile industry generally solved their employment problems in one of two ways. Under one system, called the *Rhode Island system,* they hired whole families, assigned father, mother, and children to tasks suitable to their strength and maturity, and housed the families in company-constructed tenements. South of Boston, the Rhode Island system was used almost exclusively, partly because child labor was first introduced there in imitation of English methods, and partly because the mule-spinning typical of the area required both heavy and light work. Francis Cabot Lowell and the Boston Associates introduced the *Waltham system,* under which women in their late teens and early twenties were brought together to form the nucleus of a labor force for large factories. Housed in dormitories or boarding houses, they remained under the careful supervision of matrons who kept any taint of disreputability from the young women.

The Waltham system took advantage of the low female wages in agriculture and household service in the New England area, but rapid advances in productivity in the mills raised the value and earnings of the women working there. The initially low female-to-male wage ratio rose as industries dominated by female labor experienced above average productivity increases from 1815 to 1860. During these 45 years, female earnings rose from about a third to nearly half of male wages. In short, low-cost female labor contributed significantly to the initiation of industrialization, and in turn women's earnings in New England rose relative to men's in the antebellum period because of industrialization. Moreover, by drawing women away from agriculture in the North, the Waltham system and other female work opportunities in industry increased the relative value and earnings of women who remained in farming. The weekly wage of farm women and hired farm "girls" more than doubled from 1830 to 1860.

Hours of work in the early factories were unbelievably long. A 12-hour day was not considered at all unreasonable, and half an hour off for meals was standard. From sunrise to sunset, it was possible to operate machinery without artificial light, and in wintertime candles furnished enough illumination to permit operation on into the evening. Because of the slow speeds of the early machines, the work pace was not great; for this reason women and children could work a 72-hour week without physical breakdown.

The life of a New England textile worker was tiresome and drab, although it was not noticeably worse than the life of a poor New England farmer, whose dawn-to-dusk regimen left little time for pleasure and other pursuits. As noted, the factory offered young women an escape from the low pay, boredom, and isolation of farm life. Their next best alternative for work (opportunity cost) was typically farm work or to join their mothers in handweaving or making straw hats, palmleaf hats, or shoes. This lower paying "domestic system" provided part-time or even full-time work for both villagers and farm families in the Northeast right up to the end of the 1850s. Taking

Child labor in spinning was common, especially in areas south of Boston; a family-based labor system known as the Rhode Island system developed there.

another perspective, New England factory workers generally escaped the harshness subjected to English workers during the first decades of the factory system. Undoubtedly, largely because of greater labor scarcity, American manufacturers were compelled to maintain a certain standard of decency to attract and hold the labor they wanted. Nor does evidence show that American factory owners were cruel to children, as some English employers were.

It was in the cities that the most negative aspects of industrialization were first witnessed, both in England and the United States. The worst conditions were in the so-called "sweatshops," where workers worked 14 to 16 hours a day in the garment industries of New York, Philadelphia, and Boston. And common laborers who sold their services to transportation companies, urban building contractors, or factory and mill owners found themselves in an unenviable position when stiff competition from immigrant labor retarded the growth of real wages. For most workers, however, the antebellum period was one of rising wages and higher standards of material well-being.

THE WAGES OF MALE LABOR IN MANUFACTURING

Although female earnings rose relative to men's in the antebellum period, the average wages of adult males working in manufacturing concerns in New England and the Middle Atlantic states grew dramatically between 1820 and 1860. Annual wage earnings of these workers averaged $267 in 1820, $292 in 1832, $341 in 1850, and $360 in 1860.[2] Meanwhile, consumer prices were falling between 1820 and the mid-1830s; then they rose, passing slightly above the 1820 level by the late 1830s. By the mid-1840s prices had fallen below prices of the mid-1830s floor. But then they rose again in the early 1850s. To account for these cost-of-living changes, we must adjust the money wages by a consumer price index; this will show the changes in wages in real constant purchasing power terms. Table 11-3 provides these adjustments and shows indexes of

TABLE 11-3   INDEXES OF REAL WAGES FOR ADULT MALES IN NORTHEASTERN MANUFACTURING BY GEOGRAPHIC AREA, URBANIZATION, AND SIZE OF FIRM, 1820 TO 1860

Weighted[a]	1820	1832	1850	1860	Per Annum Growth Rate, 1820–1860
Middle Atlantic	100	122–143	159–202	157–188	1.2–1.6
Rural	90	118–139	131–166	166–199	1.6–2.1
Urban	111	150–176	165–209	154–185	0.8–1.3
Major urban	115	—	171–217	151–180	0.7–1.2
Small	81	93–108	129–163	140–168	1.4–1.9
Medium	106	128–151	142–180	163–195	1.1–1.6
Large	110	123–144	171–216	159–190	0.9–1.2
New England	101	131–154	149–188	164–197	1.3–1.7
Rural	95	133–156	143–181	156–187	1.3–1.8
Urban[b]	110	130–153	150–190	165–198	1.2–1.5
Major urban	122	170–200	154–195	182–218	1.0–1.5
Small[c]	90	125–147	159–201	172–206	1.7–2.2
Medium	99	127–149	152–193	163–195	1.3–1.8
Large	110	133–157	146–185	164–196	1.0–1.5
Total	101	128–150	155–197	159–191	1.2–1.6

SOURCE: KENNETH L. SOKOLOFF AND GEORGIA C. VILLAFLOR, "THE MARKET FOR MANUFACTURING WORKERS DURING THE EARLY INDUSTRIALIZATION: THE AMERICAN NORTHEAST, 1820 TO 1860," IN STRATEGIC FACTORS IN NINETEENTH CENTURY AMERICAN ECONOMIC HISTORY: A VOLUME TO HONOR ROBERT W. FOGEL, EDS. CLAUDIA GOLDIN AND HUGH ROCKOFF (CHICAGO: UNIVERSITY OF CHICAGO PRESS, 1992), P. 36.

[a] Weighted averages are weighted by number of employees in each group.
[b] Urban firms are those located in counties with a city of 10,000 or more; major urban, the same for 25,000 or more.
[c] Small firms, 1 to 5 workers; medium, 6 to 15; large, 16 or more workers.

[2] See Kenneth L. Sokoloff and Georgia C. Villaflor, "The Market for Manufacturing Workers during the Early Industrialization, the American Northeast 1820–1860," in *Strategic Factors in Nineteenth Century American Economic History: A Volume to Honor Robert W. Fogel*, eds. Claudia Goldin and Hugh Rockoff (Chicago: University of Chicago Press, 1992), p. 36.

real wages for adult males by geographic area, level of urbanization, and firm size. For all workers together (bottom row), real wages grew between 60 percent and 90 percent (101 to 159 or 191) from 1820 to 1860; on average, wages rose between 1.2 and 1.6 percent per year.

Close inspection of Table 11-3 reveals many interesting features of workers' earnings. The period of fastest growth of real wages in all categories was between 1820 and 1832—a range of 2.2 to 3.7 percent per annum depending on place and firm size. Between 1832 and 1850 the pace of advance slowed to between 1.1 and 1.5 percent. There was little gain in real wages in manufacturing during the 1850s.

Wages were at about the same levels in New England as in the Middle Atlantic states, and they grew at about the same rate. This reveals a labor market of responsive workers, and employers who (as sellers and buyers at the margin) moved and/or offered terms that arbitraged away geographical wage differences. In money (not real) terms, annual manufacturing wages in New England were only about 1 percent higher than in the Middle Atlantic states in 1820. This difference was still only 5 percent by 1860.

From Table 11-3, we see that in 1820 manufacturing workers in rural areas earned less than those in urban areas, who in turn earned less than those in major urban areas.

Women, whose wages were far below men's comprised a large portion of the early industrial labor force. Women's earnings began to close that gap by the end of the antebellum era.

A similar relation for 1820 is seen in the earnings among workers by size of firm: the larger the firm, the more pay. But this was no longer true by 1860. Rural manufacturing real wages grew faster than urban wages, and the earnings in smaller firms rose faster than in larger firms.

Here again we see the erosion of wage gaps. Improvements in transportation enhanced labor mobility and made both product and labor markets more competitive. As navigable waterways spread and improved and railroads advanced, markets became more integrated and wage rates converged. These market forces had disproportionately large effects on the rural areas and outlying hinterlands, pulling them into the market and affording them opportunities for specialization.

ENGLISH-AMERICAN WAGE GAPS

Although wage gaps in the industrializing states remained low, market separation sustained significant gaps in wages between England and the United States. When American industry started to develop in the early nineteenth century, the wages of adult laborers were much higher in the United States than in England or other countries. Table 11-4, based on work by Nathan Rosenberg, shows pay differentials classified by various skills for the years 1820 to 1821. Across all skill categories listed, wages were higher in the United States than in England.

By and large, these pay differentials are attributable to the fact that a floor under the remuneration of labor in industry was set by rewards in agriculture. Well into the 1800s, there were no insuperable obstacles, either of distance or expense, to obtaining a fertile farm in the United States. Output per worker in agriculture was relatively high, and the course of agricultural technology in the early nineteenth century increased output per person. Moreover, farmers in America, who ordinarily owned their own land, received, in addition to their own wages and those of their families, elements of rent and profit that in England went to the landlord. American farmers always stood to gain from appreciation in land values as the country's population moved westward and transportation improvements brought more farmlands closer to market.

International labor mobility, at least in the early nineteenth century, failed to close these observed wage differentials. Sharp increases in immigration in the late 1830s and throughout the 1840s and 1850s led to a narrowing of the wage differential between American and British labor; even so, the floor for U.S. industrial wages was, according to a consensus of voluminous testimony, still relatively high in 1860.

SKILLED-UNSKILLED WAGE RATIOS

More importantly perhaps, from the perspective of free American workers, was the change in relative wages among various "grades" or skill levels. During the first decades of the nineteenth century, as throughout most of the colonial period, the premiums paid for artisan skills in the United States were typically less than those paid in England. However, the evidence in Table 11-4 shows that this was not uniformly true.

TABLE 11-4   WAGE DIFFERENTIALS BY SKILL BETWEEN ENGLAND AND THE UNITED STATES, 1820 TO 1821 (ENGLISH WAGE = 100)

Workers	U.S. Wages
Skilled	
Carpenter	150
Mason	147
Best machine makers, forgers, etc.	77 to 90
Ordinary machine makers	114 to 129
Unskilled	
Common laborer	135
Farm laborer	123 to 154
Servant, maid	149 to 224
Common mule spinners in cotton mills	106 to 137
Common mule spinners in woolen mills	115
Weavers on hand looms	122
Women in cotton mills	102 to 153
Women in woolen mills	128
Boys—10 to 12 years old	115

SOURCE: ADAPTED FROM NATHAN ROSENBERG, "ANGLO-AMERICAN WAGE DIFFERENCES IN THE 1820S," *JOURNAL OF ECONOMIC HISTORY* 27 (1967): 226.

By "premiums" we mean the extra compensation paid to skilled labor above earnings to unskilled labor. Skilled American workers typically earned more than skilled British workers, but the skilled-to-unskilled U.S. wage ratio was lower than the skilled-to-unskilled English wage ratios. This is most clearly evident in the machinists skill category when compared to common or farm labor.

The relatively low premium paid for skilled labor in early nineteenth-century America resulted primarily from the greater pulling power of agricultural expansion on unskilled labor and the higher proportion of skilled British migrants entering the United States before mass migration began.[3] By the 1820s, however, this skill premium began to advance, thus significantly widening the U.S. pay differential between skilled and unskilled workers. For example, Table 11-5 on the next page shows the ratio of machinists' daily wages to those of common laborers in urban Massachusetts during the antebellum period. Although these changing pay differentials may have differed somewhat regionally, they were generally representative of a broad pattern of advance.[4]

Such advancing pay differentials disfavoring the unskilled may have contributed to a growing sense of class consciousness. They certainly contributed to a widening in the distribution of income and wealth, as noted in the material featured on the following pages.

---

[3] See H. J. Habakkuk, *American and British Technology in the Nineteenth Century* (Cambridge: Cambridge University Press, 1962).

[4] For further evidence on this point see Jeffrey G. Williamson and Peter H. Lindert, *American Inequality: A Macroeconomic History* (New York: Academic Press, 1980), pp. 70–75. For work challenging this view and based on labor contracts at military installations, see Robert A. Margo and Georgia C. Villaflor, "The Growth of Wages in Antebellum America: New Evidence," *Journal of Economic History* 47 (1987): 837–896.

TABLE 11-5   RATIOS OF DAILY WAGES OF MACHINISTS TO COMMON LABORERS IN URBAN MASSACHUSETTS, 1825–1860

Year	Percent
1825	150%
1831–1840	156
1837	185
1845	169
1841–1850	190
1851–1860	220

SOURCE: C. D. WRIGHT, *COMPARATIVE WAGES, PRICE, AND COST OF LIVING* (BOSTON: WRIGHT & POTTER, 1889), PP. 22, 54, AND 55. AS QUOTED IN JEFFREY G. WILLIAMSON AND PETER H. LINDERT, *AMERICAN INEQUALITY, A MACROECONOMIC HISTORY* (NEW YORK: ACADEMIC PRESS, 1980), P. 71.

Two features of the antebellum labor market beg for more explicit economic reasoning: First, why did the rapid rise in early nineteenth-century real wages in U.S. manufacturing slow to nearly zero in the 1850s (Table 11-3, on p. 232)? Second, why did unskilled wages fall relative to skilled wages between 1830 and 1860 (Table 11-5)? Supply and demand will serve as our analytical guide, and we can add demographic evidence to support the hypotheses empirically.

Figure 11-1 portrays the first hypothesis graphically. The argument is that the demand and supply for manufacturing both grew over the early nineteenth century.

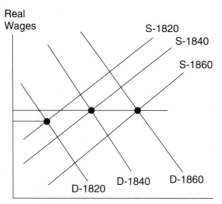

FIGURE 11-1 THE MARKET FOR MANUFACTURING WORKERS

Before 1850, the demand shifts exceeded the supply shifts, and wages rose. By the late 1840s, the supply increase was larger than normal. The supply shift was approximately the same as the change in demand for manufacturing workers, and wages changed little if at all.

Figure 11-2 portrays the second hypothesis; namely, that while both the supply and demand for skilled and unskilled labor grew dramatically over the period, the growth in the supply of unskilled labor (S-1840 to S-1860, Fig. 11-2B) accelerated in the 1840s and 1850s, and grew relative to the supply of skilled labor (S-1840 to S-1860, Fig. 11-2A). This lowered the wages of unskilled workers relative to skilled workers.

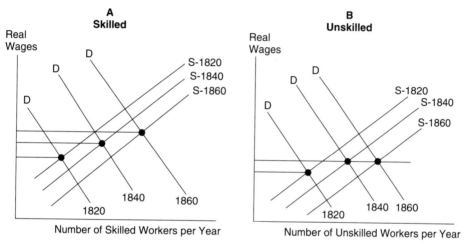

FIGURE 11-2 THE MARKET FOR MANUFACTURING WORKERS SEPARATED BY SKILL

We now turn to the demographic evidence. The population data given on the next page in Table 11-6 reveal dramatic gains. The underlying rate of advance in the totals is 3.3 percent per annum. No European nation at the time showed anything like this rate of advance, not even by half. Birthrates in the United States were 50 to 55 per 1,000 before 1850—compared to 12 per 1,000 today. Death rates remained similar to those in Europe. Hence the birthrate was the key natural source of rapid population growth.

In addition, many new immigrants came to America. In the decade of the 1820s, the influx from abroad was still less than 150,000, but as shown in Figure 11-3 on the next page, immigration grew substantially in the 1830s. Then in the mid-1840s it rose dramatically. While immigration accounted for only 3 percent of the total U.S. population growth from 1820 to 1825, it grew to between 25 and 31 percent from 1845 to 1860.

The combined effects of natural increases and immigration raised the average (median) age of the population from 16 to 19 and swelled the proportion of people in their working years and in the labor force. Between 1820 and 1860, the ratio of gainfully employed to total population grew from 33 to 36 percent—a gain of *nine* percent

TABLE 11-6   BASIC POPULATION DATA, 1790–1860

Year	Population (in millions)			Percentages		Net Immigrants' Share of Population Change in Previous Decade
	Total	White	Nonwhite	Nonwhite	Urban	
1790	3.9	3.2	0.7	17.9	5.2	n.a.
1800	5.3	4.3	1.0	18.9	6.1	n.a.
1810	7.2	5.9	1.3	18.1	7.3	3.3
1820	9.6	7.9	1.8	18.8	7.2	2.1
1830	12.9	10.5	2.3	17.8	11.7	3.8
1840	17.1	14.2	2.9	17.0	10.8	11.7
1850	23.3	19.6	3.6	15.5	15.2	23.3
1860	31.5	26.9	4.5	14.3	19.4	31.1

SOURCE: *HISTORICAL STATISTICS* (WASHINGTON, D.C.: GOVERNMENT PRINTING OFFICE, 1960), SERIES A2, 45, 46, AND 195.

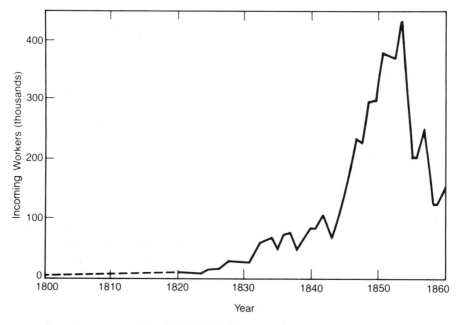

FIGURE 11-3   ADDITIONS TO THE U.S. LABOR FORCE FROM MIGRATION, 1800–1860: *Laborers came in huge numbers during the post-1845 period to a nation rich in land and rapidly increasing its stock of capital. Famine in Ireland and domestic unrest in Germany sent millions of immigrants across the ocean to America.*

(3/33ds). Moreover, the proportion of people living in urban places more than doubled between 1820 and 1850, and nearly doubled between 1840 and 1860 (Table 11-6).

Although the high birthrate dominates the story of rapid total population growth, it was the increase in immigration that so significantly *at the margin* added to the total number of new workers. This rapid build-up was especially apparent after 1840. These were disproportionately unskilled young workers, many from Ireland, with agricultural backgrounds. They flooded the unskilled labor market—again at the margin—depressing unskilled wages relatively.

We conclude that the demographic evidence is consistent with the hypotheses. This empirical consistency, however, is not conclusive proof of causation; other hypotheses, not offered here, may also be consistent with the historical record.

THE CHANGING COMPOSITION OF THE WORK FORCE

The origins of the new immigrants are of special interest. As shown in Table 11-7 on the next page, the large waves that arrived in the 1840s and 1850s came principally from three countries: England, Ireland, and Germany. A steady stream of immigrants from England flowed into the United States until the decade of the Civil War; the Irish and the Germans came in ever-increasing numbers through the mid-1850s, repelled by conditions at home and attracted by economic opportunities in a new land. The tragic potato famine of 1845 to 1847 precipitated the heavy Irish emigration. Fleeing starvation and the oppression of hated absentee landlords, the Irish found employment as common laborers and factory hands. (As many American laborers moved West to join the gold rush, opportunities opened up for the new arrivals.) The census of 1850 reported nearly 1 million Irish in the United States, 40 percent of them in large cities, where their "shanty towns" became the notorious slums of the era. The Germans came a little later, following the failure of the democratic and nationalistic revolutions of 1848. Within 15 years, 1.3 million had arrived. Most Germans, having a little capital, settled on farms in the Midwest, but almost one-third of them swelled the populations of booming cities like Cincinnati, Chicago, Milwaukee, and St. Louis. Immigration was also having its effects on the sexual composition of the labor force. By 1860 women constituted only one-fifth of the manufacturing labor force, indicating the lessening *relative* importance of textile manufacture and the competition of cheap immigrant labor, most of which was male. Like today, this was a period of significant change in women's social roles, but then the trend was toward domestic pursuits. The cotton textile industry still employed the most females (many of whom were children); the clothing and shoe industries were second and third in this respect, ahead of woolen textiles. Nevertheless, as Pamela Nickless has shown, despite the transition in the late 1840s from predominantly women workers to male Irish workers, the advance of labor productivity in the textile mills remained high and steady, averaging 4.5 percent annually between 1836 and 1860.[5]

---

[5]Pamela J. Nickless, "Changing Labor Productivity and the Utilization of Native Women Workers in the American Cotton Textile Industry, 1825–1860," *Journal of Economic History* 38 (1978): 288.

TABLE 11-7   AVERAGE YEARLY IMMIGRATION BY ORIGIN, 1845–1860
(IN THOUSANDS)

Year	Total	Great Britain	Ireland	Germany	Other
1845–1850	233	34	107	66	26
1851–1855	350	47	139	129	35
1856–1860	170	38	44	61	27

SOURCE: *Historical Statistics* (Washington, D.C.: Government Printing Office, 1958), Series C, pp. 88–114.

THE EARLY LABOR MOVEMENT

The rise in the numbers of workers in manufacturing paralleled growing activities by workers to organize for their benefits. Some have argued that the origin of the labor movement and the original labor-management problem sprang from the separation of workers from their tools. It is claimed that artisans, who owned their trade implements, lost their identity and independence when employer capitalists furnished the equipment. Like most generalizations, this one has its uses, but it may lead to false inferences. The Industrial Revolution placed great numbers of laborers in a position of uncertainty and insecurity, making them dependent on the vagaries of economic fluctuations and the mercy of employers. Yet the first impetus to a genuine labor movement was furnished by workers who were by no means separated from their tools. Craftsmen in Philadelphia, New York, and Boston founded craft labor societies in the 1790s, the prototypes of modern unions. Most of these societies were established in the hopes of securing increases in real wages (that is, of pushing up money wages faster than the prices of consumer goods), although attempts were also made to gain shorter working hours, to establish and maintain a closed shop, and to regulate the conditions of apprenticeship. Invariably, there was considerable fraternal motivation as well to these societies, as people who made a living in the same way easily forged a social bond. In nearly all the major cities, shoemakers (cordwainers) and printers were among the first to form "workingmen's societies"; carpenters, masons, hatters, riggers, and tailors also found it worthwhile to organize. Again, these organizations were separated by craft and initiated by skilled workers.

LEGAL SETBACKS AND GAINS

The early craft societies were typically transitory, the longest-maintained union being the Philadelphia Cordwainers (1794–1806). Cyclical economic downturns routinely dissolved worker collective actions, and wage reductions, though resisted, were common during downturns in the economy. A more steady threat to organizing laborers was court actions. Conservative judges, in their instructions to juries, contended that union action per se was illegal. Societies of workers were considered conspiracies under English common law, a conspiracy being defined as "a confederacy of two or more, by indirect means to injure an individual or to do any act, which is unlawful or prejudicial to the community." A doctrine developed in England during the late Middle Ages was thus applied some 500 years later to restrict the unionization of craftsmen. In the famous case of the Pittsburgh Cordwainers in 1815, the judge contended that both the master shoemakers *and* the journeymen were coerced:

> No shoemaker dare receive one who worked under price, or who was not a member of the society. No master workman must give him any employment, under the penalty of losing all his workmen. Moreover, a conspiracy to prevent a man from freely exercising his trade, or particular profession, in a particular place, is endictable. Also, it is an endictable offense, to conspire to compel men to become members of a particular association, or to contribute towards it.[6]

The jury in this case agreed that the master shoemakers, the journeymen, and the public were endangered by the association of journeymen and returned a verdict of guilty of conspiracy, although the court fined the defendants only $1 each, plus prosecution costs.

Judgments against unions in two additional cases, one in the 1830s and one in 1840, confirmed this legal perspective. The first was the trial of the Geneva Shoemakers. The journeymen shoemakers of Geneva, New York, had agreed not to work for any master who did not hire union workers. One master hired a nonunion member at below-union rates, and the other workers in the shop promptly struck. For refusing to work, the journeymen were indicted and convicted of criminal conspiracy. The case was appealed to the state supreme court, where Chief Justice Savage upheld the conviction on the grounds that such union action was harmful to trade. "It is important to the best interests of society," he said, "that the price of labor be left to regulate itself. . . . Competition is the life of trade." Meanwhile, in New York City, the Society of Journeyman Tailors had secured an increase in wage rates for its members, only to have them later reduced by a combination of master tailors. A strike ensued, accompanied by much strife. "Dungs," as scabs were then called, were hired by the masters to break the strike, with violent results. After Justice Savage handed down his decision in the Geneva Shoemakers case, the master tailors charged 20 of the journeymen with conspiracy. Again, the strike was the offense. The judge followed Justice Savage in his charge to the jury, and the journeymen were convicted and fined heavily. As a result of the trial judge's contention that American "trades and tradesmen" had hitherto flourished without the aid of combinations and that the unions must therefore have been "of foreign origin . . . and upheld by foreigners," there was much indignation among labor supporters over the outcome of the trial. In two similar cases union members were acquitted, but the legality of union activity was still very much in question.

A definite turning point came in the now famous case of *Commonwealth v. Hunt.* In the fall of 1840, Hunt and other members of the Boston Bootmakers' Society were hauled into municipal court for attempting to enforce a closed shop. Again, after a strict charge from a judge who felt that such union activities could lead only to a

---

[6] Quoted in Commons, *A Documentary History of American Industrial Society*, vol. 4 (Glendale, California: Arthur H. Clark), pp. 82, 83.

"frightful despotism," the accused were convicted. The case was appealed to the supreme court of the Commonwealth of Massachusetts, and in 1842 Chief Justice Lemuel Shaw handed down a monumental decision that set a precedent on one point and opened the way to more liberal decisions on another. First he held that a combination of union members was not criminal unless the object of the combination was criminal; the mere fact of organization implied no illegal conspiracy. Second, he asserted the doctrine that union members were within their rights in pressing for a closed shop and in striking to maintain union security. Justice Shaw was not a radical, nor was he particularly sympathetic with labor's cause, but he was well aware of the economic realities that were pressing labor to act collectively. This decision did not mean that trade unions were free from further court confrontations, but there were no more serious efforts to make the mere fact of organization a criminal offense, and there would henceforth be some reticence about presuming that the use of any and all weapons of the trade unions were socially harmful.

ORGANIZATIONAL GAINS

Judge Shaw's decision brought no immediate revival of unions, however; the long, deep slump from the late 1830s through the early 1840s had wiped out most of the societies that had formed in the craft union resurgence of 1824 to 1837. Workingmen's societies made a comeback in the 1850s (with setbacks in the recession years of 1854 and 1857), but it is important to remember that before 1860 union members never exceeded 1 percent of the total labor force. Factory workers, field hands, slaves, and domestic workers were almost completely outside the union movement. The primary early beneficiaries of workingmen's organizations were labor's minority elite, the craftsmen. Their unions were important, however, in that they established two concrete organizational advances for labor as a movement, and a series of political advances as well.

First, the technique of bargaining collectively was learned, and aggressive unions began to use the weapons of the strike and boycott with skill and daring. The *closed shop*—an agreement whereby membership in a recognized union is made a condition of employment—was soon tested as an instrument for maintaining union security. The benevolent and protective aims of labor organizations tended to disappear, and militancy replaced early hesitance and reluctance to act.

Second, the rapidly increasing number of individual societies began to coalesce. Local federations and then national organizations appeared. In 1827, unions of different crafts in Philadelphia federated to form a "city central" or "trades' union," the Mechanics' Union of Trade Associations. Six years later the societies in New York established a General Trades' Union. In the next three years, city centrals were formed in several major cities—not, as might be supposed from the modern functions of such organizations, to exchange information or engage in political activities, but for the more pressing purpose of aiding individual unions engaged in battle with employers. Attempts at organization on a national scale followed. In 1834, the General Trades' Union, New York's city central, called a national convention of these city federations, which resulted in the foundation of a National Trades' Union. At the same time, some of the craft societies began to see the advantages to be gained from a national organization along strict craft lines, and in 1835 and 1836 no less than five national unions of this type were established. The strongest of these were formed by the shoemakers and the printers.

POLITICAL GAINS FOR LABOR

SUFFRAGE. One of the most significant political gains for workers was the broadening of suffrage, the right to vote. In the first decades of our history, a person had to own a minimum amount of real property or pay a certain amount of taxes in order to have a voice in political affairs. The struggle for voting privileges took place in the original thirteen states; only four of the new states entering the Union placed no property or tax-payment qualifications on the right for an adult male to vote. By the late 1820s, suffrage had been extended sufficiently to enable working men to participate in the elections of the populous states. First to disappear was the property-owning requirement; by 1821, only five states retained it. Five states still set a tax-paying restriction 30 years later, but it was purely nominal.[7] Generally speaking, by 1860 white male citizens of the United States could vote, black males could vote in New York and New England, and alien males could vote in the agricultural Northwest.

PUBLIC EDUCATION. Although she could not vote herself, Fanny Wright effectively strove for reforms in education. Except in New England, children of the poor received little or no education; and even in New England the early training was of poor quality and exhibited a religious slant that was obnoxious to many. Fanny Wright and her followers proposed that the state establish boarding schools for the education of rich and poor children alike, where class distinction would be eliminated. Others, less radical, proposed a simple plan of free public schools. By the mid-1830s progress had been made to broaden educational opportunity; Albert Fishlow has shown that by midcentury nearly 1 percent of GNP was spent on education (compared to almost 8 percent today). Public common schools were most prevalent in the North, where political concern and efforts were greatest.

DEBTS, MILITARY SERVICE, AND JAIL. In the minds of the working people, the most needed reform, next to that of the educational system, was the abolition of imprisonment for debt. Thousands of citizens were jailed annually for failure to meet obligations of a few dollars, and there was understandably fierce resentment against this injustice. The unfairness of the militia systems of the several states, which favored the rich, rankled in the hearts of the poor who were faced with the alternatives of a term in the service or a term in jail. These and other objectives—removing the

---

[7] Comparing the votes for President with the total population, we find that there were two large jumps in the electorate: from 1824 to 1828 (3.2 percent to 9.3 percent) and from 1836 to 1840 (9.6 percent to 13.6 percent).

competition of convict labor and obtaining the right to file liens on the property of employers for back wages—inflamed the spirits of great numbers of laborers, small businessmen, and professional people with a high degree of social consciousness. The militia system did eventually become less onerous, mechanics' lien laws were passed in many states, and imprisonment for debt was outlawed in most jurisdictions. But this first movement lost momentum after 1832, as labor turned its energies during the ensuing period of prosperity to advancing the cause of unionization, which in turn collapsed in 1837.

THE 10-HOUR DAY. Although later movements and colorful episodes of the 1840s and 1850s were characterized by impractical utopian schemes (proposed and led by Robert Owen, Charles Fourier, and George Henry Evans), one movement of the midcentury gained quick relief for workers: the struggle for the 10-hour day. That goal was set as early as 1835, but there was then no serious prospect of attaining it. Hope rose in 1840 when Martin Van Buren[8] set a 10-hour day for federal employees. Craftsmen in some trades already worked no longer than 10 hours, but factory operatives still labored 12 to 14 hours a day. In the mid-1840s, New England factory workers added to the agitation for shorter hours. In 1847, the New Hampshire legislature passed the first regulatory law setting a 10-hour upper limit for a day's work, but there was a loophole in it. The law provided that if workers *agreed* to work longer hours, the 10-hour limit might be exceeded. Threatened with discharge if they did not agree, factory hands found themselves no better off. Statutes passed by other state legislatures followed the same pattern, except that laws limiting the workday of children to 10 hours did not contain the hated "contract" clause. Perhaps the most important effect of the agitation for regulatory acts was the pressure of public opinion thereby exerted on employers. Many large factories voluntarily established 11-hour days. By 1860, a 10-hour day was standard in all the craft trades, and already a new standard of 8 hours was being timorously suggested.

ECONOMIC GROWTH: A BRIEF OVERVIEW

Both short-term business fluctuations and longer periods of sustained economic growth determined the periods of prosperity or hardship for working people. It should be recalled from Chapter 7 that in the period from the end of the Revolution to the end of the War of 1812, oscillations were frequent and wide, reflecting the changing fortunes of the European belligerents and the vagaries of international politics. The period from 1816 to 1857 contained two crises of great severity: the panics of 1819 and 1837. Each crisis was followed by years of deflation and distress.[9] Yet the boom of 1834 to 1837—with its rapidly rising incomes, full employment, inflation, and investment

---

[8] This is the same man, eleven years older and now President, who had feared the hazards of the railroad. See his letter to President Jackson in Chapter 9.

[9] After the contraction of 1837 to 1838, there was a substantial recovery that peaked in 1839 and then disappointingly vanished.

(in land rather than in securities)—foreshadowed the recurrent upward surges of activity that characterized the growth of the economy. In 1843 a long period of prosperity began, marred only by a brief crisis in 1854 and a short, nasty depression from 1857 to 1858. These years just preceding the Civil War provided evidence of the kind of sustained forward movement of which the economy was capable.

Whereas it was once popularly held that the American economy experienced a unique economic "take-off" from 1843 to 1860, followed by another stage called a "sustained drive to maturity," the evidence on real wages suggests that for labor at least— the source of most income—both decades before 1843 generated substantial income gains.[10] Work by Paul David on measures of national economic growth also shows that the post-1843 advance was only part of a broader pattern of advances in real per capita income.[11] According to David, real gross domestic product (GDP) per capita grew at a rate of nearly 1.3 percent yearly between 1790 and 1860.

By 1840, per capita real GDP was probably 60 percent greater than it had been at the turn of the century. To be sure, growth in per capita income did not proceed steadily during these years. As emphasized in Chapter 7, per capita incomes increased substantially from 1793 to the embargo of 1807. They subsequently fell somewhat, but then at least regained their 1800 levels by the depression of 1818 to 1819. From 1820 to the middle 1830s, per capita real GDP may have grown at an average rate of 2.5 percent, only to fall to an average rate of 0.6 percent per annum from the middle 1830s to the middle 1840s.[12]

TRENDS IN THE DISTRIBUTION OF WEALTH

The advance in real wages from 1820 to 1860 and other gains to labor were not uniformly felt. Unskilled workers in particular lost ground to skilled workers in real wage earnings. Material standards of living advanced for most of the population, but the advance was higher for the relatively well-to-do. According to evidence on wealth trends provided by Jeffrey Williamson and Peter Lindert, we find that between 1774

---

[10] W. W. Rostow's *The Stages of Economic Growth* (Cambridge: Cambridge University Press, 1961) was an extraordinarily influential book, and offered a stage model of growth different from Karl Marx's. Policymakers in many underdeveloped countries were particularly influenced by it.

[11] Paul A. David, "New Light on a Statistical Dark Age: U.S. Real Product Growth Before 1840," *American Economic Review* 57 (1967): 294–306, and "The Growth of Real Product in the United States Before 1840: New Evidence, Controlled Conjectures," *Journal of Economic History* 27 (1967): 151–197. David's estimates, we should note, have not gone unchallenged. Gallman considers David's growth estimates too high, and Diane Lindstrom's regional study of the Philadelphia area reveals that growth was lower there in the pre-1840 period than David's figures show. See Robert Gallman, "The Statistical Approach," in *Approaches to American Economic History*, eds. George R. Taylor and Lucia Ellsworth (Charlottesville: University Press of Virginia, 1971); and Diane Lindstrom, "American Economic Growth Before 1840: New Evidence and New Directions," *Journal of Economic History* 39 (1979): 289–302.

[12] From the evidence of colonial growth in Chapter 5, we recall that incomes per capita in the various regions also revealed different periods of advancing surges and years of stagnation. And there was a modest upward secular trend, probably around 0.5 percent per year overall from 1700 to 1775. Further, in Chapter 7, the evidence indicated economic decline, or at the very best, stagnation, in per capita incomes from the 1770s to the early 1790s.

and 1860 wealth concentrations grew significantly. This growing inequality denotes a sharp break with the stable (but unequal) pattern of aggregate wealth concentration prevalent during the colonial period. In 1774, 12.6 percent of total assets were held by the top 1 percent of free wealth holders, and the richest 10 percent held slightly less than one-half of total assets. By 1860 the wealthiest 1 percent held 29 percent of U.S. total assets, while the top 10 percent held 73 percent.[13] In short, the share held by the richest 1 percent more than doubled, and that of the top decile jumped by almost half again of its previous level. There are no statistical peculiarities to these measures, and Williamson and Lindert emphasize their broad impact: "the movement toward wealth concentration occurred within regions, just as it seems to have occurred within given age groups, among native and foreign born, and within rural and urban populations."[14] Further work by Jeremy Atack and Fred Bateman adds to this perspective, demonstrating that in 1860 wealth was more equally distributed in northern rural areas than in the cities or in the rural South.

Changes in the distribution of wealth and income occurred among regions as well as among people. Table 11-8 shows estimates of income levels by region in 1840 and 1860. It shows the industrializing Northeast growing more rapidly than the other regions. The "old" South was poorer relatively and stagnating. The "new" cotton South, the West South Central area on the table, was the richest region in 1840 but slipping somewhat relative to the new industrializing Northeast. These conclusions hold for comparisons using either the total population or only the free population to determine income per capita.

Thomas Jefferson's egalitarian dream of a strong, free democratic nation of contented individualistic small farmers was a vision shared by others. But the forces of

TABLE 11-8   PER CAPITA INCOME BEFORE THE CIVIL WAR (IN 1860 PRICES)

	Total Population		Free Population	
	1840	1860	1840	1860
National Average	$ 96	$128	$109	$144
North	109	141	110	142
Northeast	129	181	130	183
North Central	65	89	66	90
South	74	103	105	150
South Atlantic	66	84	96	124
East South Central	69	89	92	124
West South Central	151	184	238	274

SOURCE: ROBERT W. FOGEL AND STANLEY L. ENGERMAN, "THE ECONOMICS OF SLAVERY," IN THE REINTERPRETATION OF AMERICAN ECONOMIC HISTORY (NEW YORK: HARPER & ROW, 1971), P. 335.

[13]Williamson and Lindert, American Inequality: A Macroeconomic History, p. 36.

[14]Williamson and Lindert, p. 46.

the Industrial Revolution had leaped the Atlantic from Great Britain. The famed traveler and commentator Alexis de Tocqueville warned in 1839 of the growing concentrations of wealth. He feared that the rise of an industrial elite would destroy the basis of American egalitarianism:

> I am of the opinion . . . that the manufacturing aristocracy which is growing up under our eyes is one of the harshest that ever existed . . . the friends of democracy should keep their eyes anxiously fixed in this direction; for if a permanent inequality of conditions and aristocracy . . . penetrates into [America] it may be predicted that this is the gate by which they will enter.[15]

American egalitarianism in terms of economic end results (income or wealth) was only a dream, then as now. But the Industrial Revolution and advance in the rate of economic growth before the Civil War were engines of opportunity for many, albeit not equally.

SELECTED REFERENCES
AND SUGGESTED READINGS

Adams, Donald R., Jr. "Wage Rates in the Early National Period: Philadelphia, 1785–1830." *Journal of Economic History* 28 (1968): 404–426.

──────. "Wage Rates in the Iron Industry: A Comment." *Explorations in Economic History* 11 (Fall 1973): 89–94.

Craig, Lee A., and Elizabeth B. Field-Hendrey. "Industrialization and the Earnings Gap: Regional and Sectoral Tests of the Goldin-Sokoloff Hypothesis." *Explorations in Economic History* 30 (1993): 60–80.

Crowther, Simon J. "Urban Growth in the Mid-Atlantic States, 1785–1850." *Journal of Economic History* 36 (1976): 624–644.

David, Paul. "The Growth of Real Product in the United States Before 1840: New Evidence, Controlled Conjectures." *Journal of Economic History* 26 (1967): 151–192.

Dawley, Allan. *Class and Community: The Industrial Revolution in Lynn.* Cambridge: Harvard University Press, 1976.

Dublin, Thomas. *Women at Work: The Transformation of Work and Community in Lowell, Massachusetts, 1826–1860.* New York: Columbia University Press, 1979.

Dunlevy, James A., and Henry A. Gamery. "Economic Opportunity and the Responses of Old and New Migrants to the United States." *Journal of Economic History* 38 (1978): 901–917.

Fishlow, Albert. "The Common School Revival: Fact or Fancy?" In *Industrialization in Two Systems,* ed. Henry Rosovsky. New York: Wiley, 1966.

──────. "Levels of Nineteenth-Century American Investment in Education." *Journal of Economic History* 26 (1966): 418–436.

Forster, Colin, and G. S. L. Tucker. *Economic Opportunity and White American Fertility Ratios, 1800–1860.* New Haven, Connecticut: Yale University Press, 1972.

Goldin, C. *Understanding the Gender Gap: An Economic History of American Women.* New York: Oxford University Press, 1990.

Goldin, C., and K. Sokoloff. "Women, Children, and Industrialization in the Early Republic: Evidence from the Manufacturing Censuses." *Journal of Economic History* 42 (1982): 741–774.

Gutman, Herbert. *Work, Culture, and Society in Industrializing America.* New York: Knopf, 1977.

[15] As quoted in Williamson and Lindert, pp. 37–38.

Habakkuk, H. J. *American and British Technology in the Nineteenth Century.* Cambridge: Cambridge University Press, 1962.

Higgs, Robert. "Mortality in Rural America." *Explorations in Economic History* 10 (Winter 1973): 177–196.

Lebergott, Stanley. "Labor Force." In *American Economic Growth: An Economist's History of the United States,* eds. Lance E. Davis et al. New York: Harper & Row, 1972.

_____. *Manpower in Economic Growth: The American Record Since 1800.* New York: McGraw-Hill, 1964.

Leet, Don R. "The Determinants of the Fertility Transition in Antebellum Ohio." *Journal of Economic History* 36 (1976): 359–378.

_____. "Interrelations of Population Density, Urbanization, Literacy, and Fertility." *Explorations in Economic History* (October 1977): 388–401.

Lindstrom, Diane. "American Economic Growth Before 1840: New Evidence and New Directions." *Journal of Economic History* 39 (1979): 289–302.

Margo, Robert A., and Georgia C. Villaflor. "The Growth of Wages in Antebellum America: New Evidence." *Journal of Economic History* 47 (1987): 873–896.

Neal, Larry, and Paul Uselding. "Immigration, A Neglected Source of American Economic Growth: 1790 to 1912." *Oxford Economic Papers,* 2d series, vol. 24 (March, 1972).

Nickless, Pamela J. "Changing Labor Productivity and the Utilization of Native Women Workers in the American Cotton Textile Industry, 1825–1866." *Journal of Economic History* 38 (1978): 287–288.

Pessen, Edward. *Most Uncommon Jacksonians: The Radical Leaders of the Early Labor Movement.* Albany: State University of New York Press, 1967.

Potter, J. "The Growth of Population in America, 1700–1860." In *Population in History,* eds. D. V. Glass and D. E. C. Eversley. New York: Aldine, 1965.

Rosenberg, Nathan. "Anglo-American Wage Differences in the 1820s." *Journal of Economic History* 27 (1967): 221–229.

Ross, Steven J. *Workers on the Edge: Work, Leisure, and Politics in Industrializing Cincinnati, 1788–1890.* New York: Columbia University Press, 1985.

Rostow, W. W. *The Stages of Economic Growth.* Cambridge: Cambridge University Press, 1961.

Rothenberg, Winifred B. "The Emergence of Farm Labor Markets and the Transformation of the Rural Economy: Massachusetts, 1750–1855." *Journal of Economic History* 48 (1988): 537–566.

Smith, Merritt R. *Harpers Ferry Armory and the New Technology: The Challenge of Change.* Ithaca, New York: Cornell University Press, 1977.

Sokoloff, Kenneth L. "Was the Transition from Artisanal Shop to the Nonmechanized Factory Associated with Gains in Efficiency? Evidence from the U.S. Manufactures Censuses of 1820 and 1850." *Explorations in Economic History* 21 (1984): 351–382.

Soltow, Lee. "Economic Inequality in the United States in the Period from 1790 to 1860." *Journal of Economic History* 31 (1971): 822–839.

Steckel, Richard H. "Antebellum Southern White Fertility: A Demographic and Economic Analysis." *Journal of Economic History* 40 (1980): 331–350.

Taylor, George R. "American Economic Growth Before 1840: An Exploratory Essay." *Journal of Economic History* 24 (December 1964).

Uselding, Paul. "Conjectural Estimates of Gross Human Capital Inflow to the American Economy." *Explorations in Economic History* 9 (Fall 1971): 49–62.

Vinovskis, Maris. "Mortality Rates and Trends in Massachusetts Before 1860." *Journal of Economic History* 32 (1972): 184–213.

Williamson, Jeffrey. "American Prices and Urban Inequality Since 1820." *Journal of Economic History* 36 (June 1976).

Williamson, Jeffrey G., and Peter H. Lindert. *American Inequality: A Macroeconomic History.* New York: Academic Press, 1980.

Yang, Donghvu. "Notes on the Wealth Distribution of Farm Households in the United States, 1860: A New Look at Two Manuscript Census Samples." *Explorations in Economic History* 21 (January 1984): 88–102.

THE BIMETALLIC STANDARD

It is one thing to adopt a bimetallic monetary standard of value, and quite another to maintain it. The problem is that the relative values of gold and silver fluctuate. If the mint ratio always corresponded to the valuation placed on the two metals by those who trade in them, there would be no difficulty in maintaining a bimetallic standard. The mint ratio has never prevailed in the open market for long, however, and the experience of the United States and other countries demonstrates the futility of trying to keep mint ratios and market ratios in correspondence. Thus, even though a *mint ratio* of 15 to 1 closely approximated the prevailing *market ratio* in 1792, world supplies of and demands for gold and silver were such that the ratio in the market rose gradually during the 1790s to about 15.5 to 1; by 1808 it was 16 to 1 as silver lost value.

A market ratio of 16 to 1 and a mint ratio of 15 to 1, technically, is a relationship in which silver is overvalued at the mint. Under such circumstances people can get more for silver at the mint than they can by taking their silver "to market." If the market ratio were below the mint ratio—at, say, 14 to 1—we would say that gold is overvalued at the mint. Indeed, if the mint ratio is 15 to 1 and the market ratio is 14 to 1, a profit can be made by melting down silver coins, selling the silver for gold, taking the gold to the mint, and using the newly minted gold coins to repurchase silver at 15 to 1.

For centuries observers had noted that debased coins (those overvalued at the mint) tended to remain in circulation, while full-bodied (or undervalued) coins were either hoarded or exported to pay for imported goods. One naturally paid out debased coins whenever it was possible to pass them off at their nominal value. Popular sayings to the effect that "bad money drives out good money" or "cheap money will replace dear" thus came into various languages. Sir Thomas Gresham, Queen Elizabeth I's master of the mint, is credited with analyzing this phenomenon, which has become known as Gresham's law. For our purposes we may best state the law as follows: *money overvalued at the mint tends to drive out of circulation money undervalued at the mint*, providing that the two monies circulate at face value.

Since silver was overvalued, gold coins soon disappeared from circulation. Oddly, it was also hard to keep American silver coins in circulation even when silver was overvalued at the mint. Merchants engaged in the West Indian trade soon discovered that shiny new American dollars and subsidiary coins could be exchanged abroad for dull Spanish pieces containing a somewhat greater amount of silver. The Spanish money was even presented at the U.S. mint to be recoined into American pieces, which were then exported. The problem became so bad that in 1806 coinage of the silver dollar was suspended by direction of President Jefferson; not until after the legislation of 1834 was the silver dollar again struck at the mint. Thus worn Spanish silver coins, U.S. half dollars, and later French five-franc silver pieces served as the chief "hard money" in circulation before 1834.

In June of 1834, two acts were passed changing the mint ratio to just a fraction over 16 to 1. Gold was then overvalued at the mint, and even though American coinage of silver had never been so high as it was in the years immediately after 1834, gold slowly began to replace silver, which was either hoarded or exported. Finally in 1857 a law was passed that repealed former acts authorizing the use of foreign gold or silver coins as legal tender in the payment of debts.

The international flows of metal under the bimetallic standard were a major nuisance. Often coins in convenient denominations could not be had, and the coins that were available were badly worn. But the bimetallic standard also provided a major, if often overlooked, benefit. A change in the market ratio may reflect the slow growth of one metal, say gold, relative to demand. If the country were tied solely to that metal, the general price level would fall. But under a bimetallic standard the cheaper metal can replace the dear metal, thus helping to maintain the stock of money and the price level.

BANK NOTES AS PAPER MONEY

Although the Constitution forbade the states to issue paper money, the states did retain the power to create corporations by special franchise. After the commercial boom beginning in 1793 a large number of banks were established by special state charters. These were entirely new institutions on the American scene, for commercial banks had not existed in the colonies. From three banks before 1790, there were 28 banks in 1800 and 88 by 1811. All but two of these were private state-chartered banks empowered to issue their own paper money.

The bank notes issued by various institutions came to be accepted at widely varying rates. Notes of established, reputable, "specie-paying" banks were taken at their face value—that is, at par—over wide areas. Bills of other banks were received at discounts ranging from 1 or 2 percent up to 50 percent or more. Distance from the city where the issuing bank was located tended to reduce the acceptability of notes. However, a bank that did not redeem in gold or silver in a period when specie payments were not generally suspended would find its bills circulating at a discount even in the immediate vicinity.

In many ways a bank note was similar to a bank deposit or check. When a bank made loans to its customers, it gave them the proceeds either in the form of its own (bank) notes, which then circulated as cash, or as a deposit credit against which they could draw checks. Nowadays, of course, banks no longer issue notes, and the paper money that passes from hand to hand is issued by the Federal Reserve; moreover, whenever a firm borrows money today it takes the proceeds as a credit to its account. But during the years before the Civil War, and even for some time after that in rural areas, a bank issued notes much more frequently than it made credits to customers' accounts.

In nearly every city there were dealers or brokers who bought and sold bank notes. These note brokers, or "shavers," made profits by exchanging paper that did not circulate at par in a given area for paper that did. The fees they charged were the counterpart of the fees modern banks charge on deposit accounts. Typically the discounts were small. But the note brokers were frequently castigated by prominent citizens, and dissatisfaction with the currency system was widespread.

There is no precise definition of a central bank that all experts would agree to, and hence no exact moment at which a big bank becomes a central bank. Typically, when speaking of central banking economists have one or more of the following criteria in mind: (1) The bank serves as a lender of last resort to other banks or financial institutions by lending them money during crises when no one else will. The idea is that by preventing a few major financial institutions from closing, the central bank can prevent a panic from taking hold. This function was analyzed by Walter Bagehot in his famous book *Lombard Street* (1873), in which he urged the Bank of England to declare its determination to be the lender of last resort and to acquire a gold reserve commensurate with that responsibility. "Bagehot's rule" is that during financial crises the central bank should lend freely but at high interest rates (to encourage prompt repayment after the crisis). (2) The bank has considerable control over the stock of money and uses this control to moderate fluctuations in credit conditions, prices, or other aspects of the economy. If the country is on a metallic standard, the case we are examining here, then the central bank cannot issue as much money as it might like because of the risk to its own metallic reserves. (3) The bank regulates other banks, punishing those whose behavior it considers imprudent. (4) Finally we come to the modern definition of a central bank: the bank lends lots of money to the government.

THE FIRST BANK OF THE UNITED STATES

The first American bank was organized by Robert Morris and established in 1781, with Congress's approval, to help finance the war effort and provide financial organization in those troubled times. However, we usually think of the nation's first central bank as being established ten years later.

Shortly after becoming Secretary of the Treasury, Alexander Hamilton wrote a *Report on a National Bank* in which he argued for a Bank of the United States. Hamilton's report shows remarkable insight into both the financial problems of the young country and the economic implications of banking. He argued that a "National Bank" would augment "the active or productive capital of a country." By this, he meant that the notes issued by the Bank would replace some of the gold and silver money in circulation, which could then be exported in exchange for real goods and services. Normally, moreover, the stock of money must grow from year to year to accommodate

Alexander Hamilton (1755–1804), shown here in a portrait by John Trumbull, was one of the chief architects of the Constitution and the economic policy of the new nation.

increased business activity. With a note-issuing national bank in place, the United States would not be forced in future years to export simply in order to increase its stock of money.

As important to Hamilton as its salutary effects on the economy was the assistance the Bank could give the government by lending money to the Treasury. Moreover, the Bank could serve as a fiscal agent for the government by acting as a depository of government funds, making transfers of funds from one part of the country to another, and (Hamilton hoped) serving as a tax-collection agency. Finally, because the Bank was to be jointly owned by the government and private shareholders, it would cement the relationship between the fledgling government and leading men of business.[2]

The bill creating the Bank followed Hamilton's report closely. There was substantial opposition to it, even in the predominantly Federalist Congress, on the grounds that (1) it was unconstitutional, (2) it would create a "money-monopoly" that would endanger the rights and liberties of the people, and (3) it would be of value to the commercial

---

[2]The federal government bought one-fifth of the $10 million initial capital stock. The government paid for its shares with the proceeds of a $2 million loan extended by the Bank on the security of its *own* stock; the loan was to be repaid in ten equal annual installments. At the start of operations, then, the government participated in the earnings of a privately financed venture without contributing a penny to the original capital.

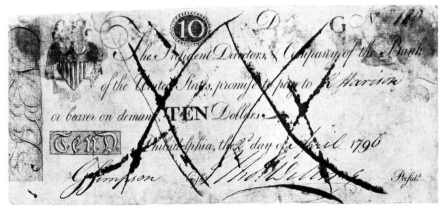

The first Bank of the United States issued these ten-dollar notes, which were canceled by inking three or four x's on their faces after they became worn. They were promises to pay dollars (most likely Mexican or American silver dollars) on demand immediately when brought to an office of the Bank.

North but not to the agricultural South. The bill was carried on a sectional vote, and President Washington signed it on St. Valentine's Day in 1791. But the charter of the Bank was limited to 20 years, so further battles lay ahead.

The notes of the Bank of the United States and its branches were soon circulating widely throughout the country at, or very close to, par.[3] In other words, $1.00 notes of the Bank were always worth $1.00 in gold or silver. Many state banks developed the habit of using notes or deposits issued by the Bank of the United States as part of their reserves, thus economizing on the use of gold and silver as Hamilton had predicted. At all times, the Bank held a considerable portion of the gold and silver in the country; its holdings during the last three years of its existence were probably close to $15 million, which practically matched the amount held by all state banks.

The Bank followed a conservative lending policy compared with the state banks. As a result it continually received a greater dollar volume of state-bank notes than state banks received of its obligations. It became, to put it differently, a creditor of the state banks. The Bank was therefore in a position to present the notes of the state banks regularly for payment in specie, discouraging them from issuing as many notes as they would have liked.

Although there was no obligation on its part, legal or customary, to assist other banks in need, in practice the Bank of the United States (like the Bank of England, which was also a private bank) became a lender of last resort. The Bank also acted as fiscal agent for the government and held most of the Treasury's deposits; in return,

---

[3] By 1800, the Bank had branches in Boston, New York, Baltimore, and Charleston. Branches were added in Washington and Savannah in 1802 and in New Orleans in 1805.

the Bank transmitted government funds from one part of the country to another without charge. After 1800, the Bank helped collect customs bonds in cities where it had branches. It further facilitated government business by effecting payments of interest on the public debt, carrying on foreign-exchange operations for the Treasury, and supplying bullion and foreign coins to the mint.

All in all we can conclude that the Bank was well on its way to being a central bank when Congress refused to recharter it in 1811.

In retrospect, the reasons for the continued operation of the Bank of the United States seem compelling. During the two decades of its existence, there was a well-ordered expansion of credit and a general stability of the currency. Compared to the difficulties before 1791, the money problems of the 1790s and early 1800s were insignificant. The first Bank of the United States helped to give the nation a better monetary system than it had any reason to hope for in 1791.

But political arguments based on economic facts are rarely as effective as those based on appeals to emotion and prejudice. Those who opposed the recharter of the Bank made the same points that had been advanced when the matter was originally debated nearly 20 years earlier. They argued that the Bank was unconstitutional and that it was a financial monster so powerful it would eventually control the nation's economic life and deprive the people of their liberties. To these contentions was added a new objection: the Bank had fallen under the domination of foreigners, mostly Britishers. Foreign ownership of stock was about $7 million, or 70 percent of the shares. This was not unusual; foreigners owned about the same percentage of U.S. bonds. The Bank's charter, moreover, attempted to prevent foreigners from exercising much influence over its policies: only shareholding American citizens could be directors, and foreign nationals could not vote by proxy. Nevertheless, many people felt that the influence of English owners was bound to make itself felt through those American directors with whom they had close business contacts.

Personal politics also mattered. On a number of occasions, Thomas Jefferson had stated his conviction that the Bank was unconstitutional and a menace to the liberties of the people. Although Jefferson was no longer President when the issue of recharter arose, his influence was still immense, and many of his followers doubtlessly were swayed by his view. But the decisive votes were cast against the Bank as a result of personal antagonism toward Albert Gallatin, who, although having served as Jefferson's Secretary of the Treasury, was a champion of the Bank. In the House, consideration of the bill for renewal of the charter was postponed indefinitely by a vote of 65 to 64. In the Senate, Vice-President George Clinton, enemy of both President James Madison and Gallatin, broke a 17–17 tie with a vote against the Bank.

Following the failure to recharter the first Bank of the United States, the number of state banks rose rapidly, from 88 in 1811 to nearly 250 in 1816. This increase was expected. There was an opportunity to take over the business of the big Bank, and investors felt that without its controls bank profits would increase. The rise in the level of manufacturing activity brought about by the War of 1812 made possible the fulfillment of bank promoters' hopes of high earnings. The sharp increase in note issues, together with deficit financing by the government, led to an inflation that was at least temporarily stimulating to business ventures.

President of the second Bank of the United States, archfoe of Andrew Jackson and advocate of central-bank controls, was Philadelphia aristocrat Nicholas Biddle (1786–1844). Some argued that his hauteur cost the Bank its charter; others felt that Wall Street would have done-in Chestnut Street anyway.

THE SECOND BANK OF THE UNITED STATES

Difficulties of financing the War of 1812 and the sharp inflation following the suspension of specie payments in 1814 convinced many people of the need for a second Bank of the United States. It took two years of congressional wrangling and consideration of no less than six separate proposals before a bill to charter such a bank was passed. The Bank was finally chartered in 1816, again for a period of 20 years. And again the renewal clause set the stage for future battles.

The charter of the second Bank of the United States resembled that of its predecessor. The capital was set at $35 million, four-fifths of it to be subscribed by individuals, firms, or states and the remaining one-fifth by the federal government. Most of the capital was to consist of government bonds, but one-fourth of the private subscription ($7 million) was to be paid in gold or silver coin. There were to be 25 directors, 20 elected by private stockholders and 5 appointed by the president. The main office of the Bank was to be located in Philadelphia, with branch offices to be established on the initiative either of the directors or of Congress.

The greatest contributions of the second Bank came after 1823, the time of the appointment of Nicholas Biddle as its third president. Sophisticated, widely traveled,

A bank note issued by a private bank before the Civil War. Notes like this one circulated from hand to hand as money.

and well educated, Biddle typified the early American aristocrat. He had wealth, power, and a mind that enabled him to successfully run the nation's largest enterprise. He was also arrogant and out of touch with the fears and aspirations of the average citizen.

Under Biddle there was a conscious attempt to regulate the banking system according to certain preconceived notions of what ought to be done. In the first place, the Bank soon became the lender of last resort to the state banks. State banks did not keep their reserves as deposits with the Bank of the United States, but they did come to depend on the second Bank in times of crisis, borrowing specie from it to meet their obligations. The Bank was able to meet such demands because it kept a much larger proportion of specie reserve against its circulation than other banks did. The second Bank also assisted in times of stress by lending to business firms when other banks could not or would not. Because of these practices, many came to regard the big Bank as *the holder of ultimate reserves* of the banking system.

In the second place, the Bank developed a policy of regularly presenting the notes of state banks for payment. In the course of business over the years, the Bank always took in more notes from state banks than the state banks received from the Bank. This net redemption against the state banks was no accident. The Bank had to keep its own note issues (including those of its branches) within bounds, so state banks had a reciprocal influence on the institution that was presumably doing the controlling. Nevertheless, the Bank of the United States was definitely in control; by presenting the notes of state banks for payment in specie, it kept their issues moderate. The Bank not only furnished a currency of its own of uniform value over the entire country, but it reduced to a nominal figure the discount at which the notes of state banks circulated. By the late 1820s, the paper money of the country was in a very satisfactory state.

Biddle also tried to affect the general economic climate of the United States by alternate expansion and contraction of the Bank's loans. Furthermore, he made the

Bank the largest American dealer in foreign exchange and was able to protect the country from severe specie drain when a drain would have meant a harmful contraction of monetary reserves. In the 1820s, the problem of making payments over considerable distances within the country was not much different from the problem of effecting remittances between countries. There was a flourishing business in "domestic exchange," and the Bank obtained a large portion of it.

By 1829, the position of the second Bank of the United States seemed secure. It had grown and prospered. In many ways it had become a central bank. It had attained a shining reputation abroad—so much so that when the Bank of Spain was reorganized in 1829, the Bank of the United States was explicitly copied. Although it had made enemies, there was a wide acceptance of the idea of a "national institution" and a grudging admittance even by those who persistently opposed "the monster" that it had been good for business. Congress had made sporadic attacks on the Bank, but these had been ineffective. Yet the apparent permanence of the Bank was illusory. Its fate had already been sealed.

In 1828, Andrew Jackson was elected to the presidency. Beloved by the masses, Jackson had the overwhelming support of the people during two terms in office. Long before taking office he had decided against supporting banks in general and "The Bank" in particular. As a young man in Tennessee, Jackson had taken the notes of a Philadelphia merchant that passed as currency in payment for 6,000 acres. When he tried to use these notes, he found that they were worthless because the merchant had failed. To make his obligations good, Jackson suffered years of financial difficulty in addition to the loss of his land. Later, he and his business partners often found themselves victims of exorbitant charges by bankers and bill-brokers in both New Orleans and the eastern cities.[4] On one occasion, Jackson bitterly opposed the establishment of a state bank in Tennessee, and as late as 1826 he worked against the repeal of a law prohibiting the establishment of a branch of the Bank of the United States in his home state.

In his first annual message to Congress, seven years before the charter of the Bank was to expire, Jackson called attention to the date of expiration, stated that "both the constitutionality and the expediency of the law creating this bank are well questioned by a large portion of our fellow citizens," and speculated that:

> If such an institution is deemed essential to the fiscal operations of the Government, I submit to the wisdom of the Legislature whether a national one, founded upon credit of the Government and its revenues, might not be devised which would avoid all constitutional difficulties and at the same time secure all the advantages to the Government and country that were expected to result from the present bank.

We have the great Democrat's word for it that his statement was toned down by his advisers. It was the beginning of the "Bank War."

---

[4]Claude A. Campbell, *The Development of Banking in Tennessee* (published by the author, 1932), pp. 27–29.

Biddle initially tried to win Jackson's support, but Biddle's efforts were unsuccessful. Henry Clay, charming and popular presidential candidate of the National Republicans (Whigs), finally persuaded Biddle to let him make the question of recharter a campaign issue in the election of 1832. During the summer there was enough support in the Congress to secure passage of a bill for recharter—a bill that Jackson returned, as expected, with a sharp veto message prepared by presidential advisers Amos Kendall and Roger Taney. In the veto the President contended that (1) the Bank was unconstitutional, (2) there was too much foreign ownership of its shares, and (3) domestic ownership was too heavily concentrated in the East. A central theme ran through the message: the Bank was an instrument of the rich to oppress the poor; an institution of such power and so little responsibility to the people could undo democracy itself and should be dissolved.

Agrarians of the West and South felt that the Bank's conservative policies had restricted the supply of credit to agriculture.[5] But there was also opposition to the Bank from Wall Street, which wanted to supplant Philadelphia (where the home office of the Bank was located) as the nation's financial center. Economics makes the strangest bedfellows.

After a furious presidential campaign, Jackson emerged the victor by a substantial margin. He considered his triumph a mandate from the electorate on the Bank question, and the acclaim he was receiving due to his masterful handling of the problem of nullification[6] strengthened his resolve to restrict the Bank's activities at once. In the fall of 1833, the government discontinued making deposits with the Bank, and editor Greene of the Boston *Post* was moved to write its epitaph: "Biddled, Diddled, and Undone."

But Biddle was not through. Beginning in August 1833 and continuing into the fall of 1834, the Bank contracted its loans sharply and continued its policy of presenting the notes of state banks for payment in specie. Biddle maintained that contraction was necessary to prepare the Bank for liquidation, although there was doubtlessly a punitive motive in the vigor of his actions. In any case, his actions contributed significantly to the brief but definite financial stringency of 1834.

The administration, however, remained firm in its resolve to end the Bank, which became a state bank chartered under the laws of Pennsylvania in 1836. Although stripped of its official status, the United States Bank of Pennsylvania remained the most powerful financial institution in America for several years. With its resources alone, Biddle engineered a grandiose scheme to support the prices of cotton and other agricultural staples during the nation's economic troubles of 1837 and 1838. Biddle, in

---

[5] The conviction in the West and South that interest rates are unnaturally high and that the government ought to do something about it is one of the hardy perennials of American politics. It would blossom again during the Populist era, as we will see in Chapter 19. Indeed, politicians have continued to cultivate this issue down to the present day.

[6] The principle of nullification, first enunciated by John C. Calhoun in 1828, was that any state could refuse to be bound by a federal statute it considered unjust until three-quarters of the states had agreed to the statute. South Carolina tried to apply the principle in 1832–1833 during a dispute over a tariff bill. Jackson's strong stand defeated the attempt.

In this cartoon, Andrew Jackson (left) attacks the many-headed serpent (the second Bank of the United States) with his walking stick (his veto). The largest head is Nicholas Biddle, the Bank's president. The remaining heads represent other officials of the Bank and its branches. Jackson is assisted by Martin Van Buren (center).

other words, bet the Bank on a final gamble that the price of agricultural products would rise. If they had, the Bank would have made a tremendous amount of money, farmers would have credited the Bank with raising farm incomes, and Biddle would have been a hero. But this last convulsive effort started a chain of events that led to the Bank's failure in 1841, two years after Biddle's retirement.

ECONOMIC FLUCTUATIONS
AND THE SECOND BANK

During the early years of Biddle's reign, the economy followed a relatively smooth course with no deep recessions or periods of significant inflation. As shown in Figure 12-1 on the next page, during the 1820s, the price level slipped downward as the amount of specie in the economy remained roughly constant and the amount of money (specie

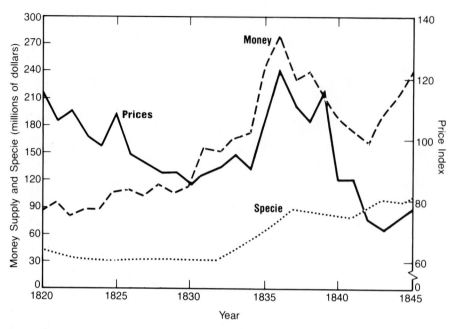

FIGURE 12-1 U.S. Prices, Money, and Specie, 1820–1845

Source: Hugh Rockoff, "Money, Prices, and Banks in the Jacksonian Era," in *The Reinterpretation of American Economic History*, eds. Robert W. Fogel and Stanley L. Engerman (New York: Harper & Row, 1971), Table 1, p. 451.

plus bank notes plus bank deposits) rose modestly. Undoubtedly, the growth in the stock of money was less than the growth of the volume of goods exchanged.

Then entirely new conditions began to prevail: first inflation in the mid-1830s, then the great depression of 1839–1843. At one time historians blamed these disturbances on the demise of the second Bank. The argument was that the absence of the second Bank unleashed irresponsible banking, that increases in the money supply and the price level were a direct result, and that the crashes of the late 1830s and the depression of the early 1840s were the inevitable result of the previous excesses. A glance at the upper two lines in Figure 12-1 seems to support this argument: the stock of money (remember that this includes bank notes and deposits as well as specie) rose sharply as did prices.

Shortly after President Jackson vetoed the Bank's recharter, he began withdrawing government funds from the second Bank and placing them in so-called "pet banks." Allegedly, as Biddle's power to present the notes of state banks for redemption ebbed, many banks began to expand credit and their paper note issues recklessly. New banks were formed by owners interested only in making a quick profit. These disreputable banks came to be called "wildcat banks," and the name stuck. The origin of the term is somewhat obscure. One story, probably apocryphal, is that the banks were located in remote areas, wildcat country, to discourage people from trying to convert their notes into specie.

But subsequent research by George Macesich and Peter Temin showed that Jackson's attack on the second Bank deserves very little of the blame for the inflation. It must be remembered that the United States was still greatly influenced by external events. Coincidentally, at the time of the demise of the second Bank, the United States began to receive substantial amounts of silver from Mexico, which was undergoing its own political and economic turmoil. These and other flows into the United States from England and France sharply raised the amount of specie in the United States. In addition, a steady outflow of specie to China was substantially reduced at this time. Historically, China had run balance of payments surpluses with the rest of the world. But as opium addiction spread in China, China's balance of payments surplus disappeared and Chinese merchants began to accept bills of credit instead of requiring payment in specie.[7]

As shown in Figure 12-1, there was a substantial increase in the stock of specie between 1833 and 1837. Because the amount of money banks could issue was limited mainly by the amount of specie they could keep in reserve, the amount of paper money and deposits increased, step by step, with the new supplies of specie. To a considerable extent, the influx of specie explains the increase in money and prices. The ratio of paper money and bank deposits to specie actually increased only slightly. The banking sector, in other words, does not appear to have acted irresponsibly during the 1830s, even after Jackson's veto.[8]

This episode shows that facts that seem to fit one interpretation on the surface may support an altogether different conclusion when thoroughly analyzed. It seems natural to blame Jackson for the inflation that occurred on his watch, but the real sources of the inflation were very different.

Though the attack on the second Bank was not the cause of the inflation, it did influence the economy in other ways. During Biddle's reign throughout the 1820s and early 1830s, people placed an increasing trust in banks, largely because of the leadership and sound banking practices of the second Bank. As a result, the proportion of money that people normally held in specie declined.[9] Their confidence in paper money reached unusually high levels in the 1820s and early 1830s. Then events changed. First came Jackson's veto in 1832. This was followed by the Specie Circular in 1834, which required that most federal land sales be paid in specie. As prices rose and confidence in paper monies waned, more and more people returned paper for specie at their banks. When large numbers of noteholders attempted to do this, the banks were unable to make the exchanges and banking panics occurred. (A strong second Bank might have

---

[7] China's attempts to restrict foreign trade, particularly the opium trade, led to war with Britain—the Opium War (1839–1842).

[8] For this evidence and a pathbreaking reinterpretation of the Bank War, see Peter Temin, *The Jacksonian Economy* (New York: W. W. Norton, 1969), p. 71.

[9] Temin, p. 159.

According to *Hume's price-specie-flow mechanism* (named after the eighteenth-century Scottish philosopher David Hume), our story makes sense. A sudden increase in the stock of money in one country will raise prices in that country relative to the rest of the world. But it will then set in motion forces that will ultimately drive prices back to where they were. Imports will increase relative to exports as prices rise because imports become relatively cheaper and exports relatively more expensive, and specie will flow to the rest of the world. The loss of specie will reduce the stock of money and prices, and this will continue until prices fall back to a level consistent with balance in international trade.

Since Hume's day economists have developed many qualifications and alternatives to Hume's prediction. Advocates of the *monetary theory of the balance of payments*, for example, believe that prices of internationally traded goods will be kept in equilibrium at all times by commodity arbitrage (buying something where it is cheap and selling where it is expensive). They would expect to find the explanation for the U.S. inflation in a general inflation in countries on the bimetallic standard. They would expect the stock of money to increase during an inflation, but only because a larger stock of money was demanded at a higher price level.

New theories force the historian to look at information that might have been ignored before (here the world price level, and the lags between changes in money and prices). Conversely, the examination of historical episodes can help economists choose among and refine their theories.

been able to nip these panics in the bud by acting as a lender of last resort.) The result was a sharp but temporary recession in 1837 and finally one of the worst depressions of the century from 1839 to 1843.[10]

AN INDEPENDENT TREASURY

When Andrew Jackson and the Democrats were fighting the recharter of the second Bank of the United States, they seemed unconcerned about the prospect of keeping government funds in state banks. In fact, as we noted, Jackson placed these funds in

---

[10] In addition, the Bank of England, concerned over the continuing outflow of specie to the United States, began to call in specie (sell back bonds) in 1837.

certain state institutions—his "pets," according to the President's critics—beginning in September 1833.[11]

In Jackson's view, banks in the hands of those who were "politically friendly" would have preference in receiving government deposits, but "opposition men whose feelings are liberal" might have to do. The first pet chosen was the Union Bank of Maryland, located in Baltimore. Six other selections, ranging from the little-known Moyamensing Bank of Philadelphia to the prestigious Bank of the Manhattan Company in New York, followed during September. By the end of June 1836, 35 pets had been chosen, only one of which (the Bank of Louisville) was clearly an "opposition" bank. Congress then passed a statute limiting the amount of deposits a bank could hold, and the number of pet banks increased to 96; as the favored institutions grew in number, political loyalty became a less-important consideration than the safety of Treasury funds.

The idea was ultimately advanced to separate the federal Treasury from the banking system, and an independent Treasury was established in the 1840s.[12] Henceforth, government officials were "to keep safely, without loaning, using, depositing in banks, or exchanging for other funds than as allowed by this act, all the public money collected by them, or otherwise at any time placed in their possession and custody, till the same is ordered . . . to be transferred or paid out." The federal government was to accept only gold and silver in payment of sums due it. Government funds were to be kept only in the vaults of the Treasury at Washington or in those subtreasuries in various cities.

The difficulties foreseen by the opponents of this method of fiscal separation materialized quickly. During the 75 years or so in which the legislation was in effect, secretaries of the Treasury rarely followed either the spirit or the letter of the law; violations began almost as soon as the law was in force. Frequently, Treasury officials sought the aid of the banks in transferring funds about the country in order to avoid expensive and dangerous shipments of coin.

The transfer of funds was a small problem, however, compared with that occasioned by Treasury surpluses, which became usual during the 1850s. As the Treasury year after year took in more than it expended, there was a withdrawal from the banks of the gold and silver that constituted their reserves. On occasion the secretary of the Treasury would get coin back into the banking system by purchasing obligations of the federal government in the open market, though some restriction was placed on such action by a law preventing repurchase of government stock (in those days the term applied to both equities and bonds) at a figure above par. During the financial stringencies of 1853 and 1857, the secretary had to take vigorous action to assist the banks; these open-market operations were only the beginning of varied kinds of manipulation to be required of secretaries in the next half-century. Within a few years of the passage

---

[11] Frank Otto Gatell, "Spoils of the Bank War: Political Bias in the Selection of Pet Banks," *American Historical Review* 70 (October 1964): 35. See also Harry N. Scheiber, "The Pet Banks in Jacksonian Politics and Finance, 1833–1841," *Journal of Economic History* 23 (1963): 196–214.

[12] The act establishing the Treasury was passed in 1840, repealed (by a coalition of Whigs and eastern Democrats) in 1841, and finally passed again in 1846.

of the law establishing an independent Treasury, it became apparent that independence could *not* be maintained.

EXPERIMENTS IN STATE BANKING CONTROLS

THE SUFFOLK SYSTEM AND THE SAFETY FUND

Though not by conscious design, several important experiments in the states and regions complemented the efforts being made by the second Bank of the United States to provide a more homogeneous currency. Urban banks were persistently confronted with the problem of competing with the circulation of country bank currencies (paper notes). For example, country bank note issues circulated widely in Boston. In 1824, six Boston banks joined with the Suffolk Bank of Boston to create a system for presenting country banks with their notes in volume, thus forcing them to hold higher reserves of specie. Soon after, the country banks agreed to keep deposits in the Suffolk Bank, resulting in the first arrangement of a clearing house for currencies of remote banks.

These deposits, a costless source of funds, helped make the Suffolk Bank one of the most profitable in the country. The other Boston banks shared in this profit through their ownership of Suffolk stock, so the arrangement was hardly altruistic. But as a result the prevailing discounts on country bank notes fell. By 1825, country notes passed through the "Suffolk System" at par. Consequently, New England was blessed with a uniform currency.

The Suffolk Bank continued as the agency for the clearing of New England notes until 1858, when a rival institution was organized by some new Boston banks and by country banks that resented the dictatorial policies of the Suffolk. Shortly afterward, national banking legislation did away with state bank notes and with the need for such regional systems, but the Suffolk System was the predecessor to the modern practice of requiring reserve deposits of member banks in the Federal Reserve System.

In addition to this private regulatory effort, New York in 1827 invoked state regulatory power. To increase protection for depositors and noteholders, the state passed a law holding bank stockholders responsible for debts equal to twice the value of their stock holdings. In 1827, New York passed the Safety-Fund Act, requiring new banks and those being rechartered to hold 3 percent of their capital stock in a fund to be used as reserves for banks that failed. This first state deposit insurance scheme failed in the panic of 1837, but others were tried again and again. State deposit insurance schemes, although generally unsuccessful, were the forerunner of Federal Deposit Insurance initiated in the 1930s.

FREE BANKING

With the demise of the second Bank of the United States, a new era of free banking began. The first important free bank law passed the New York Assembly in 1838. Actually, between the beginning of the agitation for the New York system and final passage of the act establishing it, a Michigan statute provided for a similar plan, but the chief

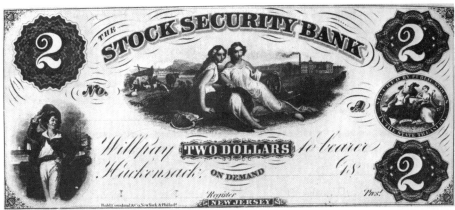

A note issued by one of New Jersey's free banks. Notice that it is "secured by public stocks," probably bonds issued by New Jersey or another state.

influence on American banking derives from the New York law. The adjective *free* indicates the most important provision of the law, under which any individual or group of individuals, upon compliance with certain regulations, could start a bank. (Under the old rule, the *privilege* of starting a bank had to be granted by special legislative act.) Increased competition promised improved services and a reduction of legislative corruption.

To protect noteholders (and sometimes to boost the state's credit), the free banking laws required the banks to deposit bonds, usually federal bonds or bonds issued by the state where the bank was located, with the state banking authority. If a bank refused to redeem a note in specie, the holder could protest to the state banking authority, which would then sell the bonds and redeem all the notes of the bank. The rules governing the amount and type of bonds that had to be deposited had a great deal to do with the success or failure of the system. If too much backing was required for each note issued, no banks would be set up. If too little backing was required, the way might be opened for wildcat banking. But if the required backing protected noteholders while permitting the bankers a reasonable profit, the system worked well.

In New York, to take the most important example, free banking was successful. The system expanded rapidly, and there were few failures. Indeed, the free banking systems of New York and Ohio were probably the models for the national banking system adopted during the Civil War. But Michigan's free banking law of 1837 produced a famous episode of wildcat banking. Despite apparent safeguards, including a safety fund, the law permitted the poorest securities to be put up as a guarantee of note redemption.

Under the Michigan law, all a bank had to do to start operation was to show that it had specie on hand. Enterprising bankers showed an amazing ingenuity in outwitting examiners. Moreover, specie payments at the time were suspended nationwide because of a banking crisis, so the would-be wildcat banker did not even have to fear immediate withdrawals. Two commissioners noted a remarkable similarity in the packages of specie in the vaults of several banks on their examination list and later discovered that a sleigh drawn by fast horses preceded them as they went from place to place. Specie, they said, flew about the backwoods of Michigan with the "celerity of magic." Nearly all banks operating on such a basis failed and disappeared by 1840, but not before a victimized public had been stuck with their worthless notes.

THE FORSTALL SYSTEM

Reasonably sound banking systems usually developed in states that had reached a degree of economic maturity. It was not by chance that Louisiana law of 1842 set up a system, called the Forstall System, that became a model of sound and conservative banking.[13] With a port second only to that of New York, Louisiana had economic ties with both a great productive hinterland and the rest of the world.

The most notable feature of the Louisiana law required banks chartered under it to keep a specie reserve equal to one-third of their combined note and deposit liabilities. Before 1863, several states came to require specie reserves against notes, ranging variously from 5 percent to 33 percent, but except for Louisiana and Massachusetts they did not require reserves against deposit liabilities as well. The notion that deposits as well as bank notes were money was not universally recognized. Partly as a result of the Forstall System, the banks of New Orleans developed a well-deserved reputation for soundness, and their notes circulated widely. According to one popular theory, the South became known as the Land of Dixie because ten-dollar notes issued in New Orleans bore the French word *dix* (ten) on the back.

In many states, then, both practice and legislation were bringing about improved banking. The heterogeneous state of the currency, however, was a matter of continuing concern.

A "CHAOTIC" BANK-NOTE MARKET

By 1860 more than 1,500 state banks were issuing, on an average, six different denominations of notes. Therefore, not fewer than 9,000 different types of notes were being passed. Some were as good as gold; but most were acceptable at a distance from the issuing bank only at a discount, and anyone ignorant of the actual worth of a note was open to loss. Notes of "broken" or liquidated banks sometimes remained in circulation for long periods, and counterfeiting was a continuing problem. Some gangs issued spurious counterfeits that imitated the notes of no particular bank, while others concentrated on careful imitations of genuine bills. Perhaps the most successful way of counterfeiting was to alter the notes of a broken bank to make them appear to be the issue of a solvent bank, or to change bills from lower to higher denominations. Some counterfeiters specialized in the manufacturing end of the business; others, called

---

[13] It was named after Edmund Jean Forstall, the man who proposed it. See George D. Green, "The Louisiana Bank Act of 1842: Policy Making During Financial Crisis," *Explorations in Economic History* 7 (Summer 1970): 399–412; and Irene D. Neu, "Edmund Jean Forstall and Louisiana Banking," *Explorations in Economic History* 7 (Summer 1970): 383–398.

utterers, were adept at passing the bogus money. To combat counterfeiters, banks formed anticounterfeiting associations, hiring men called snaggers to ferret out makers of spurious bills.

It was often difficult to determine the genuineness of a bill and the discount at which a valid note should be accepted. If a bill was much worn, or if it was perforated many times by the bank teller's needle-like staple, one might presume it to be genuine. Anyone who regularly took in paper money, however, usually had more assistance in the form of a "bank-note reporter" and a "counterfeit detector." *Thompson's Bank Note and Commercial Reporter,* a weekly, contained alphabetical listings, by states, of the notes of banks and the discounts at which they should be received, together with descriptions of all known counterfeited bills. *Thompson's Bank Note Descriptive List,* published at irregular intervals, contained word descriptions of genuine bills of banks in the United States and Canada.

Services such as *Bicknall's Counterfeit Detector and Bank Note List* specialized in counterfeit detection. *Nicholas' Bank Note Reporter* at one time listed 5,400 counterfeits. Only a fraction of these were actually in circulation at any one time, but any of them might be. *Hodges' Bank Note Safeguard* contained 360 pages of facsimile reproductions of genuine notes. *Thompson's Bank Note and Commercial Reporter* used facsimiles only for certain bogus bills, and most of the others relied on word descriptions. None of the services achieved complete coverage, but some of them did a remarkably good job. For example, in 1859 *Hodges' Genuine Bank Notes of America* carried a listing of 9,916 notes of 1,365 banks, omitting the issues of fewer than 200 banks.

Although this system seems strange to us today because our currency has the same value everywhere, it is easy to exaggerate the difficulties. Today merchants must still contend with bad checks and stolen credit cards, and some checking accounts carry service charges analogous to the charges once made by note brokers. Indeed, today many individuals rely on check cashing services, which perform an economic service quite similar to that performed by the note brokers before the Civil War. But there can be little doubt that many people of this period were dissatisfied with the currency and hankered for federal action to provide a uniform national currency.

SELECTED REFERENCES
AND SUGGESTED READINGS

Adams, Donald R. "The Role of Banks in the Economic Development of the Old Northwest." In *Essays in Nineteenth Century Economic History, The Old Northwest,* eds. David C. Klingaman and Richard K. Vedder. Athens, Ohio: Ohio University Press, 1975.

Bordo, Michael, and Anna J. Schwartz. "Money and Prices in the Nineteenth Century: An Old Debate Rejoined." *Journal of Economic History* 40 (1980): 61–67.

Buck, Norman S. *The Development of the Organization of Anglo-American Trade, 1800–1850.* New Haven, Connecticut: Yale University Press, 1925.

Catterall, Ralph. *The Second Bank of the United States.* Chicago: University of Chicago Press, 1903.

Davis, Lance E., and Jonathan R. T. Hughes. "A Dollar-Sterling Exchange 1803–1895." *Economic History Review* 13 (August 1960).

Engerman, Stanley. "A Note on the Economic Consequences of the Second Bank of the United States." *Journal of Political Economy* 78 (July/August 1970): 725–728.

Fenstermaker, J. van. *The Development of American Commercial Banking, 1782–1837.* Kent, Ohio: Kent State University Press, 1965.

———. "The Statistics of American Commercial Banking, 1782–1818." *Journal of Economic History* 25 (1965): 400–413.

Ferguson, E. James. *The Power of the Purse: A History of American Public Finance, 1776–1790.* Chapel Hill: University of North Carolina Press, 1961.

Fraas, Arthur. "The Second Bank of the United States: An Instrument for an Interregional Monetary Union." *Journal of Economic History* 34 (1974): 447–467.

Green, George D. "The Louisiana Bank Act of 1842: Policy Making During Financial Crisis." *Explorations in Economic History* 7 (Summer 1970): 399–412.

Hammond, Bray. *Banks and Politics in America from the Revolution to the Civil War.* Princeton, New Jersey: Princeton University Press, 1957.

Hepburn, A. Barton. *History of Currency in the United States.* New York: Macmillan, 1915.

Kahn, James A. "Another Look at Free Banking in the United States." *American Economic Review* 75 (1985): 881–885.

Macesich, George. "Sources of Monetary Disturbances in the U.S., 1834–1845." *Journal of Economic History* 20 (1960): 407–434.

Martin, David A. "The Changing Role of Foreign Money in the United States, 1782–1857." *Journal of Economic History* 37 (1977): 1009–1027.

———. "1853: The End of Bimetallism in the United States." *Journal of Economic History* 33 (1973): 825–844.

———. "Metallism, Small Notes, and Jackson's War with the B.U.S." *Explorations in Economic History* 11 (Spring 1974): 227–248.

Neu, Irene D. "Edmund Jean Forstall and Louisiana Banking." *Explorations in Economic History* 7 (Summer 1970): 383–398.

Ng, Kenneth. "Free Banking Laws and Barriers to Entry in Banking, 1838–1860." *Journal of Economic History* 48 (1988): 877–889.

North, Douglass C. *The Economic Growth of the United States, 1790–1860.* New York: W. W. Norton, 1966.

Olmstead, Alan L. "Investment Constraints and New York City Mutual Savings Bank Financing of Antebellum Development." *Journal of Economic History* 32 (1972): 811–840.

Redlich, Fritz. *The Molding of American Banking: Men and Ideas.* New York: Hafner, 1947 and 1951, 2 vols.

Remini, Robert. *Andrew Jackson and the Bank War.* New York: W. W. Norton, 1967.

Rockoff, Hugh T. *The Free Banking Era: A Reexamination.* New York: Arno Press, 1975.

———. "Money, Prices and Banks in the Jacksonian Era." In *The Reinterpretation of American Economic History,* eds. R. W. Fogel and Stanley Engerman. New York: Harper & Row, 1971, ch. 33.

———. "Varieties of Banking and Regional Economic Development in the United States, 1840–1860." *Journal of Economic History* 35 (1975): 160–181.

Rolnick, Arthur J., and Warren E. Weber. "New Evidence on the Free Banking Era." *American Economic Review* 73 (1983): 1080–1091.

———. "The Causes of Free Bank Failures: A Detailed Examination of the Evidence." *Journal of Monetary Economics* 14 (1984): 267–291.

———. "Explaining the Demand for Free Bank Notes." *Journal of Monetary Economics* 21 (1988): 47–71.

Scheiber, Harry N. "The Pet Banks in Jacksonian Politics and Finance, 1833–1841." *Journal of Economic History* 33 (1963): 196–214.

Smith, Walter B., and Arthur H. Cole. *Fluctuations in American Business 1790–1860.* Cambridge: Harvard University Press, 1935.

Studenski, Paul, and Herman Krooss. *Financial History of the United States.* New York: McGraw-Hill, 1952.

Summer, William G. *A History of American Currency*. New York: Putnam's Sons, 1878.

Sylla, Richard. "Early American Banking: The Significance of the Corporate Form." *Business and Economic History* 14 (1985): 105–123.

Sylla, Richard, John B. Legler, and John J. Wallis. "Banks and State Public Finance in the New Republic: The United States, 1790–1860." *Journal of Economic History* 47 (1987): 391–404.

Taylor, George R., ed. *Jackson and Biddle: The Struggle over the Second Bank of the United States*. Boston: D. C. Heath, 1949.

Temin, Peter. "The Anglo-American Business Cycle, 1820–1860." *Economic History Review* 27 (May 1974): 207–221.

———. "The Economic Consequences of the Bank War." *Journal of Political Economy* 70 (March/April 1968): 257–274.

———. *The Jacksonian Economy*, New York: W. W. Norton, 1969.

Timberlake, Richard C., Jr. *The Origins of Central Banking in the United States*. Cambridge: Harvard University Press, 1978.

Trescott, Paul B. *Financing American Enterprise: The Story of Commercial Banking*. New York: Harper & Row, 1963.

Willett, Thomas D. "International Specie Flows and American Monetary Stability." *Journal of Economic History* 28 (1968): 28–50.

CHAPTER THIRTEEN

THE ENTRENCHMENT OF SLAVERY AND REGIONAL CONFLICT

CHAPTER THEME Slavery, as an economic and social organization, was morally and legally accepted by peoples everywhere for thousands of years. It collapsed in the Americas in approximately a century, between 1776 and 1888. First in the Caribbean and then throughout South America, politicians yielded to abolitionists' arguments and pressures to free the enslaved. In the southern United States, however, slavery based on race became increasingly entrenched in the decades leading up to the Civil War. Investments in slaves had proved profitable, slave labor productivity and plantation efficiency were high, and wealthy planters who dominated southern politics saw clearly the wealth loss implications to them from abolitionists' aims. The clash of abolitionists' moral objectives and southern economic interests persisted, with noted intensity as the country grew westward, until the force of arms resolved the issue on the battlefield.

AFRICAN SLAVERY IN THE WESTERN HEMISPHERE

In the 1860s the African slave trade ended, bringing to a close three and one-half centuries of forced migrations of nearly 10 million Africans across the Atlantic. Their dominant economic activity, overwhelmingly, was sugar production. As Figure 13-1 shows, most of the slaves were destined for Brazil (36 percent) and the Caribbean islands (40 percent), areas economically based on sugar production. The United States received only 6 percent of the total numbers crossing the Atlantic. By 1825 the distribution of slaves was noticeably different from the pattern of arrivals. As revealed in Figure 13-2, in 1825 the United States was the leading slave nation, housing 36 percent of all slaves in the Western Hemisphere. Differences in natural rates of population growth, negative in Brazil and in the Caribbean for long periods and positive and high in the United States, account for this significant demographic adjustment. While only having a peripheral role in the Atlantic slave trade, the United States ultimately became the bulwark of resistance to the abolition of slavery in the Western world. This resistance was almost entirely in the southern United States.

In one sense at least it is astonishing how fast slavery collapsed in the Americas. For thousands of years statesmen, philosophers, theologians, and writers had accepted uncritically the legitimacy and utility of slavery as a "time-honored" form of economic and social organization. Popes and queens and commoners alike accepted it. Early voices against it, such as the Germantown Quakers who in 1688 issued the condemnation of it as a violation of the Golden Rule, were ridiculed. No actions compelling conformity to abolitionist arguments were taken until 1758, when the Quakers in Philadelphia condemned both the slave trade and the owning of slaves. Members in violation were to be excluded from positions of responsibility in the Society of Friends.

Across the Atlantic, the English Society of Friends voted in 1774 to expel any member engaging in the slave trade. As shown in Table 13-1 on page 278, a year later slavery was abolished in Madeira; and the abolition fever strengthened and spread until Brazil, the last American bastion of slavery, abolished it in 1888.

FIRST CONSTRAINTS IN THE UNITED STATES

At the national level, 1787 stands as a landmark year for actions taken to limit the growth of slavery. In 1780, the enslaved populations in the United States equaled nearly 575,000 blacks. Nine percent of these resided north of the Chesapeake; the remainder lived in the South. As part of one of the great constitutional compromises, the nation's forefathers agreed in 1787 to permit the existence of slavery but not to allow the importation of slaves after 20 years. (In 1807, therefore, Congress prohibited the foreign slave trade, effective the following year.) Also in 1787, the Northwest Land Ordinance forbade slavery in the Northwest Territory. In this way, the growth of slavery in the United States was limited and regionally restricted. Of course, the smuggling of human

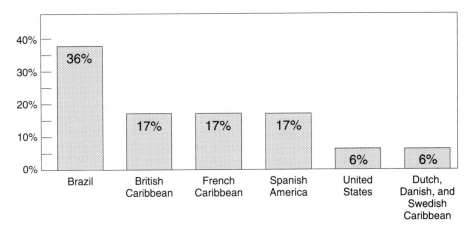

FIGURE 13-1 THE DISTRIBUTION OF SLAVES BROUGHT INTO THE NEW WORLD, 1500–1870

SOURCE: ROBERT W. FOGEL AND STANLEY L. ENGERMAN, *TIME ON THE CROSS: THE ECONOMICS OF AMERICAN NEGRO SLAVERY* (BOSTON: LITTLE, BROWN, 1974), P. 14.

cargo was not uncommon, and various estimates suggest as many as a quarter of a million blacks were illegally imported into the U.S. before 1860. But illicit human importation was only a minor addition to the total numbers held in bondage, and foreign-born blacks comprised a small percentage of the enslaved population by 1860. Indeed, most blacks were third-, fourth-, and fifth-generation Americans. As mentioned on the preceding page, natural sources of population expansion, averaging 2.4 percent per year between 1800 and 1860, were predominant in increasing the number of slaves. In 1863 the slaves numbered almost 4 million—all residing in the South.

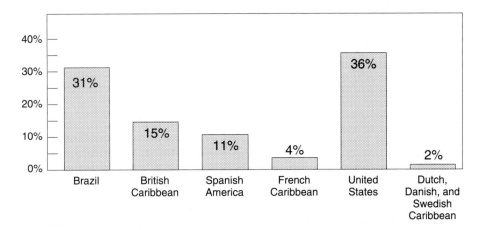

FIGURE 13-2 THE DISTRIBUTION OF SLAVES IN THE WESTERN HEMISPHERE, 1825

SOURCE: ROBERT W. FOGEL AND STANLEY L. ENGERMAN, *TIME ON THE CROSS: THE ECONOMICS OF AMERICAN NEGRO SLAVERY* (BOSTON: LITTLE, BROWN, 1974), P. 28.

TABLE 13-1   A CHRONOLOGY OF EMANCIPATION, 1772–1888

1772	Lord Chief Justice Mansfield Rules that Slavery Is Not Supported by English Law, Thus Laying the Legal Basis for the Freeing of England's 15,000 Slaves.
1774	The English Society of Friends Votes the Expulsion of Any Member Engaged in the Slave Trade.
1775	Slavery Abolished in Madeira.
1776	The Societies of Friends in England and Pennsylvania Require Members to Free Their Slaves or Face Expulsion.
1777	The Vermont Constitution Prohibits Slavery.
1780	The Massachusetts Constitution Declares That All Men Are Free and Equal by Birth; a Judicial Decision in 1783 Interprets This Clause as Having the Force of Abolishing Slavery. Pennsylvania Adopts a Policy of Gradual Emancipation, Freeing the Children of All Slaves Born after November 1, 1780, at Their Twenty-eighth Birthday.
1784	Rhode Island and Connecticut Pass Gradual Emancipation Laws.
1787	Formation in England of the "Society for the Abolition of the Slave Trade."
1794	The French National Convention Abolishes Slavery in All French Territories. This Law Is Repealed by Napoleon in 1802.
1799	New York Passes a Gradual Emancipation Law.
1800	U.S. Citizens Barred from Exporting Slaves.
1804	Slavery Abolished in Haiti. New Jersey Adopts a Policy of Gradual Emancipation.
1807	England and the United States Prohibit Engagement in the International Slave Trade.
1813	Gradual Emancipation Adopted in Argentina.
1814	Gradual Emancipation Begins in Colombia.
1820	England Begins Using Naval Power to Suppress the Slave Trade.
1823	Slavery Abolished in Chile.
1824	Slavery Abolished in Central America.
1829	Slavery Abolished in Mexico.
1831	Slavery Abolished in Bolivia.
1838	Slavery Abolished in All British Colonies.
1841	The Quintuple Treaty Is Signed under Which England, France, Russia, Prussia, and Austria Agree to Mutual Search of Vessels on the High Seas in Order to Suppress the Slave Trade.
1842	Slavery Abolished in Uruguay.
1848	Slavery Abolished in All French and Danish Colonies.
1851	Slavery Abolished in Ecuador. Slave Trade Ended in Brazil.
1854	Slavery Abolished in Peru and Venezuela.
1862	Slave Trade Ended in Cuba.
1863	Slavery Abolished in All Dutch Colonies.
1865	Slavery Abolished in the U.S. as a Result of the Passage of the Thirteenth Amendment to the Constitution and the End of the Civil War.
1871	Gradual Emancipation Initiated in Brazil.
1873	Slavery Abolished in Puerto Rico.
1886	Slavery Abolished in Cuba.
1888	Slavery Abolished in Brazil.

SOURCE: ROBERT W. FOGEL AND STANLEY L. ENGERMAN, *TIME ON THE CROSS: THE ECONOMICS OF AMERICAN NEGRO SLAVERY* (BOSTON: LITTLE, BROWN, 1974), PP. 33–34.

NORTHERN EMANCIPATION
AT BARGAIN PRICES

Even before the writing of the Constitution, some states had progressed toward the elimination of slavery. Between 1777 and 1804, the eight northeastern states individually passed measures to provide for the emancipation of their resident slave populations. In Vermont, Massachusetts, and New Hampshire, vague constitutional clauses left the matter of emancipation to the courts. Unfortunately, little is known about the results of this process; but in any case, these three states domiciled only a very small fraction of the northern blacks—probably 10 to 15 percent in 1780. As shown in Table 13-2, Pennsylvania, Rhode Island, Connecticut, New York, and New Jersey each passed laws of emancipation well before the year prohibiting slave importations. The process of emancipation used in these states was gradual, and the living population of slaves was not freed. Instead, newborn babies were emancipated when they reached adulthood (and were referred to as "free-born").

The form of the emancipation legislation demonstrates that many—perhaps most—of those who were politically dominant were more concerned with the political issue of slavery than with the slaves themselves. Besides not freeing the living slaves, there were no agencies in any of these states to enforce the enactments. In addition, the enactments themselves contained important loopholes, such as the possibility of selling slaves to the South.

The emancipation process, however, did recognize the issues of property rights and costs. These "gradual emancipation schemes" imposed no costs on taxpayers, and owners were not directly compensated financially for emancipated slaves. But curiously

TABLE 13-2   SLAVE EMANCIPATION IN THE NORTH FOR THE FREE-BORN

State	Date of Enactment	Age of Emancipation	
		Male	Female
Pennsylvania	1780[a]	28	28
Rhode Island	1784[b]	21	18
Connecticut	1784[c]	25	25
New York	1799[d]	28	25
New Jersey	1804[e]	25	21

SOURCE: ROBERT W. FOGEL AND STANLEY L. ENGERMAN, "PHILANTHROPY AT BARGAIN PRICES: NOTES ON THE ECONOMICS OF GRADUAL EMANCIPATION," *JOURNAL OF LEGAL STUDIES* 3:2 (JUNE 1974): 341.

[a] The last census that enumerated any slaves in Pennsylvania was in 1840.
[b] All slavery was abolished in 1842.
[c] The age of emancipation was changed in 1797 to age 21. In 1848, all slavery was abolished.
[d] In 1817, a law was passed freeing all slaves as of July 4, 1827.
[e] In 1846, all slaves were emancipated, but apprenticeships continued for the children of slave mothers and were introduced for freed slaves.

enough, owners were almost entirely compensated indirectly for their freed slaves. This was accomplished by maintaining the free-born in bondage until they had repaid their owner for their rearing costs. In most cases, these slaves were freed when they reached their mid-20s. In the first several years after birth, a slave's maintenance cost was determined to be in excess of the value of his or her services (or output). Near the age of 10, the value of the slave's annual output usually just about matched the costs of food, clothes, and shelter. Thereafter, the value of output exceeded yearly maintenance costs, and normally by the age of 25 or 26 the slave had fully compensated the owner.

Most of the political rhetoric of the period was concerned with the problems of suddenly turning an uneducated and unskilled minority out into the world at large, as the ages in Table 13-2 suggest. But results and intentions are two quite different things. Perhaps the intentions of the legal designers were noble; perhaps they were not. In any case, we do know that the slaves themselves bore the lion's share of the costs of emancipation in the North. Newborn slaves who were eventually freed fully paid back their owners for their rearing costs. Owners of males who were born before the dates of enactment suffered no wealth loss. Owners of females who were born before the enactments and who could or eventually would reproduce incurred some minor wealth losses in that they lost the value of their slaves' offspring. About 10 percent of the value (price) of a young female slave was due to the value of her offspring, and perhaps as many as 30 percent of the total enslaved population was comprised of females in their fertile or prefertile years.[1] Consequently only 3 percent (10 percent of 30 percent) of the total slave wealth was lost to northern owners by abiding by these enactments, but the percentage was probably much closer to zero because of the loopholes of selling slaves to the South, working the slaves harder, and reducing maintenance costs.

THE PERSISTENCE OF SLAVERY

Despite the constitutional restrictions on slave imports and the "gradual emancipation schemes" of the northern states, slavery did not die. Table 13-3 profiles the growth of the southern population, showing the slave population increasing slightly more rapidly than the free southern population. The proportion enslaved grew from around 49 percent in 1800 to 53 percent in 1860. Also, the free black population was growing at a faster rate in percentage terms than the total over this period.

After Eli Whitney's invention of the cotton gin in 1793, mechanical means replaced fingers in the separation of seed from short-staple cotton varieties. The soils and climate of the South, especially the new Southwest, gave it a comparative advantage in supplying the massive and growing demand for raw cotton by the British, and later by New England textile firms. Cotton quickly became the nation's highest-valued commodity export, and output expanded as the southwestern migrations discussed in Chapter 8 placed an army of slaves on new southwestern lands. According to estimates by Robert Fogel and Stanley Engerman, nearly 835,000 slaves moved out of the old South (Maryland, Virginia, and the Carolinas primarily), most of them going to the

---

[1] Female slaves of all ages composed 37 percent of the total slave population.

TABLE 13-4   COMPARISONS OF EFFICIENCY IN SOUTHERN AGRICULTURE BY FARM TYPE AND SIZE (INDEX OF FREE SOUTHERN FARMS = 100)

Number of Slaves	Indexes of Output per Unit of Total Input
0	100
1–15	101
16–50	133
51 or more	148

SOURCE: ROBERT W. FOGEL AND STANLEY L. ENGERMAN, "EXPLAINING THE RELATIVE EFFICIENCY OF SLAVE AGRICULTURE IN THE ANTEBELLUM SOUTH," *AMERICAN ECONOMIC REVIEW* 67 (JUNE 1977): 285.

than the small or slaveless farms.[5] Table 13-4 shows these productivity comparisons for southern farms and plantations as well as for plantations worked by different numbers of slaves. By far the most efficient units were those using 50 or more slaves. Small-scale farming was less productive per unit of input employed, and there was little difference in efficiency between southern free-family farms and small farms employing only a few slaves. Therefore, it appears that racial factors had an insignificant effect on productivity. Black workers with their complementary but white-owned capital and land were about as productive in small units as white workers on single-family farms. Alternatively, plantations with sizable numbers of slaves were extraordinarily efficient. Clearly economies of scale, or some other sources of productivity gains, provided advantages for large-sized plantations.

Final answers to why such differences existed still elude us. By and large, however, the main difference appears to be the organization of slaves into production units called gangs, the careful selection of slaves by skill for particular uses, and the intensity per hour with which the slaves were worked.

In many ways, the large antebellum plantations were more like factories than farms. Their organization of slave labor resembled that of assembly-line workers. Even contemporary reports stress these characteristics.[6]

The cotton plantation was not a farm consisting, as the farm does, in a multiplicity of duties and arrangements within a limited scope, one hand charged with half a dozen parts to act in a day or week. The cotton plantation labor was as thoroughly organized as the cotton mill labor. There were wagoners, the

---

[5] For a lively but highly technical debate on the issues of measuring the relative efficiency of slavery, see the exchanges in the March 1979 and September 1980 issues of the *American Economic Review* between Paul David and Peter Temin; Gavin Wright, Donald Schaefer, and Mark Schmitz; and Robert Fogel and Stanley Engerman.

[6] These quotations by contemporaries are in reference to the Canebrake Plantation and the McDuffie Plantation, respectively. See Jacob Metzer, "Rational Management, Modern Business Practices, and Economies of Scale in Antebellum Southern Plantations," *Explorations in Economic History* 12 (April 1975): 134–135, for complete citations and other examples.

An invoice of ten negroes sent this day to John
B Williamson by Geo Kremer named & cost as fol—
lows

To wit - Betsey Hackley . . . . . . $ 410.00
Nancy Aulick 515.00
Harry & Helen Miller . . . 1200.00
Mary Kootz 600.00
Betsey Ott? 560.00
Isaac & Fanny Brent . . 992.00
Lucinda Luckett? 467.50
George Smith . . . 510.00
Amount of my traveling expences & boarding 5 254.50
of lot No 9 not included in the other bills 39.50
Kremers expences transporting lot No 9 to Rich'd 51.00
Carryall hire . . 6.00
$ 5357.00

I have this day delivered the above named negroes
costing includeing my expences and other expences
five thousand three hundred & fifty dollars this May.
26th 1835

John. W. Pittman

I did intend to leave Nancy child but she made
such a damned fuss I had to let her take it I could
of got fifty Dollars for so you must add forty Dollars
to the above

INVOICE OF A SALE OF SLAVES, 1835. *The last two sentences are of special interest.*

plowmen, the hoe hands, the ditchers, the blacksmiths, the wheelwrights, the
carpenters, the men in care of work animals, the men in care of hogs and cattle,
the women who had care of the nursery . . . the cooks for all . . . [n]o industry
in its practical operation was moved more methodically or was more exacting of
a nice discrimination in the application of labor than the Canebrake Cotton
plantation.

When the period for planting arrives, the hands are divided into three classes:
1st, the best hands, embracing those of good judgment and quick motion; 2nd,
those of the weakest and most inefficient class; 3rd the second class of hoe hands.

Thus classified, the first class will run ahead and open a small hole about seven to ten inches apart, into which the 2nd class [will] drop from four to five cotton seeds, and the third class [will] follow and cover with a rake.

The profitable exploitation of slave labor in the antebellum period was made possible principally by speeding up the work and demanding greater work intensity, not longer hours, and the efficiency gains stemmed primarily from worker-task selection and the intensity of work per hour. In fact, slaves on large plantations typically took longer rest breaks and worked less on Sundays than their white counterparts did. Indeed, these conditions were needed to achieve the levels of work intensity imposed on the slaves. It is apparent that these productivity advantages were not voluntary. Essentially, they required slave or forced labor. No free-labor plantations emerged during the period. And as we will see, there was a significant reduction in labor participation, work intensity, and organization after emancipation.

ECONOMIC INSIGHTS

Writing in the first decade of this century, noted historian Ulrich Phillips claimed that antebellum southern slavery had become unprofitable by the 1840s and 1850s. This led some to believe, incorrectly, that slavery eventually would have died out because of market economic forces.

Phillips based his analysis on two time series: the price of prime field hands like that shown in the figure on the next page, and the trend of cotton prices. Cotton prices varied year to year, with 9¢ being typical in the 1840s and 10¢ being the average in the 1850s. With slave prices rising, especially between 1845 and 1859, and cotton prices hardly increasing, Phillips reasoned that investments in slaves increasingly were realizing losses. He further asserted that these losses surely occurred because slaves worked no harder in 1860 than in 1820 or 1830.

These conclusions were widely accepted until two economists, Alfred Conrad and John Meyer, took the pains in the late 1950s to actually measure the rates of return on investments in slaves. Their asset pricing model in its simplest form took into account the yearly expected output values (the price of cotton [P_c] times the marginal physical product of the slave [VMP_s], minus yearly maintenance costs (M) summed over the expected remaining length of life of the slave ($t = 0 \ldots 30$ years). This sum was discounted by (r) to equalize the price paid for the slave (P_s). Expressed as an equation,

$$P_s = \sum_{t=0}^{30} \frac{(P_c \cdot VMP_s - M)_t}{(1 + r)^t}.$$

As the equation illustrates, if the price of cotton should rise, or output per worker rise,

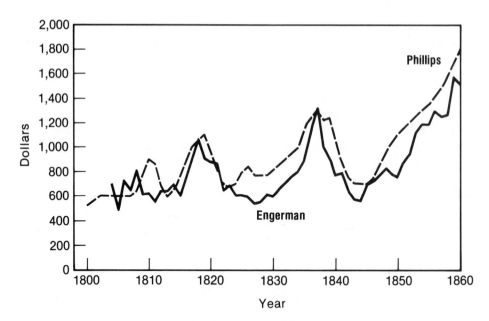

PRICE OF A PRIME MALE SLAVE, NEW ORLEANS, 1800–1860

SOURCE: ROGER L. RANSOM AND RICHARD SUTCH, "CAPITALISTS WITHOUT CAPITAL: THE BURDEN OF SLAVERY AND THE IMPACT OF EMANCIPATION," *AGRICULTURAL HISTORY* (SUMMER 1988): 155. AS REPORTED THERE, THE ORIGINAL SOURCES TO THESE TWO SERIES ARE PHILLIPS AND ENGERMAN. *PHILLIPS:* PRICES FOR 1800, 1801, AND 1812 ARE ESTIMATED VISUALLY FROM ULRICH BONNELL PHILLIPS, *LIFE AND LABOR IN THE OLD SOUTH* (LITTLE, BROWN, 1929), P. 177. ALL OTHER FIGURES ARE FROM ALFRED H. CONRAD AND JOHN R. MEYER, "THE ECONOMICS OF SLAVERY IN THE ANTEBELLUM SOUTH," *JOURNAL OF POLITICAL ECONOMY* 66 (APRIL 1958), REPRINTED IN ALFRED H. CONRAD AND JOHN R. MEYER, *THE ECONOMICS OF SLAVERY AND OTHER STUDIES IN ECONOMIC HISTORY* (ALDINE, 1964), TABLE 17, COLUMN 6, P. 76. *ENGERMAN:* DATA WERE SUPPLIED BY STANLEY ENGERMAN. THEY ARE MEAN VALUES OF THE PRICES INCLUDED IN A SAMPLE OF INVOICES OF SLAVE SALES HELD IN NEW ORLEANS. THE SAMPLE SIZE FOR EACH YEAR RANGED BETWEEN 2.5 AND 5 PERCENT. THE PRICES AVERAGED REFER TO "MALES AGES 18 TO 30, WITHOUT SKILLS, FULLY GUARANTEED AS WITHOUT PHYSICAL OR OTHER INFIRMITY." ENGERMAN "UTILIZED ONLY THOSE CASES IN WHICH THERE WAS AN INDIVIDUAL PRICE LISTED FOR A SEPARATE SLAVE." FOR MOST YEARS THERE WERE ABOUT 15 TO 20 OBSERVATIONS USED IN PREPARING THE AVERAGES GIVEN.

or maintenance costs fall, profits would rise sending the price of the slave upward. These calculations and a host of other estimates that followed showed a range of returns, typically 8 to 12 percent, that were competitive or above normal compared to returns on alternative investments at that time.

But how then did the prices of slaves rise, if cotton prices did not? We now know the answer: more output per slave. Phillips erred in overlooking the productivity gains that arose over the period—from economies of scale as plantations grew, other organizational advances such as assigning tasks, moving into more productive areas (the southwestern migrations), and other sources. Phillips's observation, perhaps correct, that slaves worked no harder in 1860 than earlier and used the same technology, overlooked other sources of productivity advance.

Furthermore, there is no evidence to suggest that slavery would have died out. Not even temporary periods of overcapitalization of slaves—that is, when prices of slaves were being bid too high—would support such a conclusion. Indeed slave prices were apparently overcapitalized in the years from 1818 to 1820 and in the mid-1830s, and prices readjusted to lower levels, reducing losses on "overpriced slaves" to normal rate of return levels. The facts are that slaves produced more, much more, than it cost to rear and maintain them throughout the entire antebellum period. Only if the value of slave output had fallen below subsistence costs would owners have gained by setting slaves free.

ECONOMIC EXPLOITATION

It hardly needs to be stressed that black slaves were exploited. They had no political rights, and the law of the plantation and the whim of the taskmaker was the web of confinement the slave directly faced. Owners did not carelessly mistreat their slaves for obvious reasons. A prime male field hand was worth close to $15,000 in 1993 prices.

Various forms of punishments and rewards pressured slaves to be obedient workers. Few failed to witness or feel the sting of the lash, and fear combined with the hopelessness of escape in maintaining control. Their standards of living were low but self-sustaining; these certainly would have been much higher if the value of their total output had been returned to them. However, because the property rights to their labor and their product resided with the white owner, their output accrued to the owner.

Richard Vedder has attempted to measure the economic exploitation of slaves in the South. His measure is based on the fundamental economic proposition that workers in competitive industries such as cotton production tend to be paid amounts that are equal to what labor contributes at the margin. An additional worker adds a certain value of output. Any sustained difference between the value of output the worker adds and what he or she receives may be reasonably termed economic exploitation. For the average slave, this difference (the value of output added minus maintenance costs) divided by the value of the output added was at least 50 percent and may have been as high as 65 percent.[7]

Of course, there was much more to the exploitation issue than simply taking one-half of each worker's earnings. The mere entrapment of workers blocked their advance materially and otherwise by taking away their incentive for self-improvement and gain.

Perhaps the best thing that can be said about the economic conditions of American slavery is that they were not as bad as the conditions of slavery elsewhere. As emphasized in Figures 13-1 and 13-2 (page 277), the percentage of slave imports to various

---

[7]For further elaboration, see Richard Vedder, "The Slave Exploitation (Expropriation) Rate," *Explorations in Economic History* 12 (October 1976): 453–457. As Vedder notes, in New England cotton textile mills (a sample of 71 firms) in 1820, the comparable exploitation calculation was 22 percent; for iron workers in 1820 (101 firms), the rate was 28 percent. Similar levels of exploitation (24 and 29 percent, respectively) have been computed in Roger L. Ransom and Richard Sutch, *One Kind of Freedom* (Cambridge: Cambridge University Press, 1977), p. 3.

parts of the Western Hemisphere between 1500 and 1825 compared very differently to the ultimate location of slaves in percentage terms in 1825. The drastic relative declines in the slave population in the Caribbean and in Brazil testify to the especially brutal conditions there. By comparison, the southern United States offered treatment that was life-sustaining. Slaves in the antebellum South experienced standards of material comfort that were low by today's standards but well above those of the masses in many parts of their contemporary world.

ECONOMIC ENTRENCHMENT AND REGIONAL INCOMES

Although the slave system proved efficient on the plantation, its economic advantages were not widely applicable elsewhere. As a result of this and other factors—especially its overwhelming comparative advantage in agriculture—the South experienced little structural change during the antebellum years. For instance, the South was slow to industrialize, partly because of the slave system. In pre–Civil War days, some slaves did become skilled craftsmen, and slaves were employed in cotton factories, coal mines, ironworks, lumber mills, and railroads. But there was little point in incurring the costs of training slaves for industrial occupations on a large scale when they could readily and profitably be put to work in agriculture.

In addition, the South experienced very little immigration from Europe or elsewhere. It was not the South's "peculiar institution" that kept European migrants away; immigration did not increase after emancipation. Europeans tended to settle in latitudes where the climate was like that of their former home. The main deterrent to locating in the South was that outsiders perceived a lack of opportunity there; immigrants feared that they would become "poor whites." By 1860, only 3.4 percent of the southern population was foreign-born, compared with 17 percent in the central states and 15 percent in New England.

As stated, as investments of capital, there can be no doubt that plantation slavery was profitable throughout the South. Extremely high net returns in parts of the cotton belt and rewards at least equal to those of alternative employments of capital in most areas of the Deep South were the rule. Nor were there economic forces at work making the slave economy self-destructive. There is simply no evidence to support the contention that slave labor was overcapitalized, and slaves clearly reproduced sufficiently to maintain a growing work force. In addition, internal migration from the older southern states to the new cotton belt areas was on a large scale. The southern economy did show signs of flexibility.

This flexibility, exhibited in the western migrations, was especially important to the South. Table 13-5 shows income figures for various regions in 1840 and 1860. Note that the nearly 44 percent growth in income for the entire free South, from $105 to $150, was higher than the internal growth of any subregion in the South (about one-third for the old South, about 15 percent for the new South). The migrations from poorer to richer areas leveraged up the income growth for the South as a whole. As we shall see, the South was vitally concerned, for apparently sound economic reasons, with the

TABLE 13-5 PER CAPITA INCOME BEFORE THE CIVIL WAR (IN 1860 PRICES)

	Total Population		Free Population	
	1840	1860	1840	1860
National Average	$ 96	$128	$109	$144
North	109	141	110	142
Northeast	129	181	130	183
North Central	65	89	66	90
South	74	103	105	150
South Atlantic	66	84	96	124
East South Central	69	89	92	124
West South Central	151	184	238	274

SOURCE: ROBERT W. FOGEL AND STANLEY L. ENGERMAN, "THE ECONOMICS OF SLAVERY," IN *THE REINTERPRETATION OF AMERICAN ECONOMIC HISTORY* (NEW YORK: HARPER & ROW, 1971), TABLE 8, P. 335.

rights to slavery expansion into western lands. Also noteworthy is the relative position of the West South Central region, where King Cotton reigned supreme. This was by far the highest income region in the country. And these high relative standings remain whether or not slaves are included in the population figures. When the incomes per capita of only the free population are compared, even the older, less wealthy southern

A familiar scene—slaves picking cotton as white overseers look on.

TABLE 13-6   TOTAL VALUE OF SLAVES IN THE U.S., 1810–1860 (IN MILLIONS OF
             DOLLARS)

Year	Total Value
1810	$ 316
1820	610
1830	577
1840	997
1850	1,286
1860	3,059

SOURCE: ROGER L. RANSOM AND RICHARD SUTCH, "CAPITALISTS WITHOUT CAPITAL: THE BURDEN OF
SLAVERY AND THE IMPACT OF EMANCIPATION," AGRICULTURAL HISTORY (SUMMER 1988): 150–151.

areas show levels that were quite high. There can be little doubt that on the eve of
the Civil War, the South was a very rich area indeed.

Yet from the moral, social, and political viewpoints, southern slavery imposed a
growing source of self-destruction on the American people. The system epitomized a
great barrier to human decency and social progress that was contrary to deeply felt
ideals in many quarters. With almost religious fervor, abolitionist elements grew in
strength, and national disunity grew proportionately.

As the antislavery moral arguments gained a louder voice, the economic costs of
emancipation grew as well. Table 13-6 shows the wealth held in slaves in the South
by decade. After 1830 the rise in value was dramatic, reaching almost $1.3 billion in
1850 before more than doubling to $3.1 billion in 1860. According to Ransom and
Sutch, slaves represented 44 percent of the total wealth in the major cotton growing
states in 1859 and real estate comprised another 25 percent.[8] Could $3.1 billion in taxes
be raised to compensate owners for slaves emancipated? Would owners give up such
wealth voluntarily? As an additional consideration, southerners had witnessed, in the
late 1830s, the outcome of rapid emancipation in the British West Indies. There land
values plummeted as the gang system of production disappeared and labor was withdrawn from the fields. The prospect of land value losses adding to the wealth losses
of uncompensated emancipations stiffened the resolve of the South's slaveholding oli-
garchy. Laws were passed in the southern states increasing the punishment for insurrection and for assisting runaways: eleven imposed the death penalty on slaves
participating in insurrection, and thirteen made it a capital crime for free men to incite
slave insurrection. Several states began requiring legislative consent for manumission
on a case-by-case basis. Seven required newly freed slaves to leave their territory. Freedoms to bear arms, assemble in public meetings, and sell liquor were frequently denied
free blacks. In these and other ways, slavery became more entrenched economically
and legally.

---

[8] Roger L. Ransom and Richard Sutch, "Capitalists without Capital: The Burden of Slavery and the Impact
of Emancipation," *Agricultural History* (Summer 1988): 138–139.

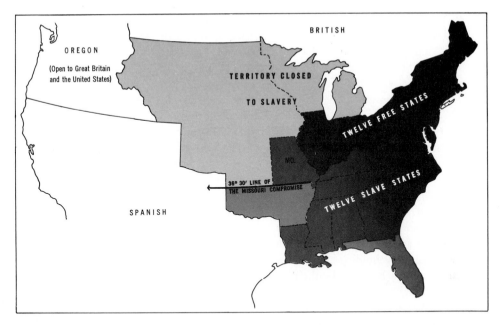

MAP 13-1   THE MISSOURI COMPROMISE OF 1820: *After this enactment, growing sectional acrimony was supposed to be a thing of the past. For a time, a truce did prevail.*

POLITICAL COMPROMISES AND REGIONAL CONFLICT

For a majority of Americans living at the time of slavery, the most significant issue was the containment of slavery, not its eradication. Indeed, the basis of political compromise on this issue was first established in the Northwest Ordinance, passed unanimously by Congress in 1787. Article six reads: "there shall be neither slavery nor involuntary servitude in the said territory . . . provided always, that any person escaping into the same, from whom labor or service is claimed in any of the original states, such fugitive may be lawfully reclaimed and conveyed to the person claiming his or her labor or service as foresaid." The 1787 ordinance, in effect, outlawed slavery in lands that became the states of Ohio, Indiana, Michigan, Illinois, Wisconsin, and Minnesota. This set the stage for controlling the expansion of slavery in other territories, allowing some regions at least to be nonslave, but this important legislation did not provide a final solution.

The western migrations, both north and south, continued to bring the issue of slavery containment to a head. The key problem for the South, as a political unit, was to maintain at least equal voting power in the Senate. The South accomplished this objective and won a series of compromises that enabled it to extend the institution of slavery and counter abolitionist threats.

In 1819, the political balance in the Senate had been even: there were eleven slave and eleven free states. By the Missouri Compromise of 1820 (see Map 13-1 on the preceding page), Missouri was admitted as a slave state and Maine as a free state, on the condition that slavery should thereafter be prohibited in the territory of the Louisiana Purchase north of 36° 30'. For nearly 30 years after this, states were admitted to the Union in pairs, one slave and one free, and by 1850 there were fifteen free and fifteen slave states. As of that year, slavery had been prohibited in the Northwest Territory, in the territory of the Louisiana Purchase north of 36° 30', and in the Oregon Territory—vast areas in which an extensive slave system would not have been profitable anyway. Violent controversy arose over the basis of admission for prospective states contained in the area ceded to the United States by Mexico. The terms of the Mexican Cession required that the territory remain permanently free, yet Congress in 1848 had rejected the Wilmot Proviso, which would have prohibited slavery in the Southwest, where its extension was economically feasible. In the end, California was admitted as a free state in 1850. The territories of Utah and New Mexico were organized, and slaveholding could be permitted there: the final decision on the legality of slavery was to be made by the territorial populations on application for admission to the Union.

Further events of the 1850s for a time appeared to portend ultimate victory for the South in the matter of slavery extension. The Kansas-Nebraska Act of 1854 (see Map 13-2) in effect repealed the Missouri Compromise by providing for "popular sovereignty" in the hitherto unsettled portions of the Louisiana Purchase. The result was gunfire and bloodshed in Kansas. In the Dred Scott decision of a states' rights case, the Supreme Court went even further, declaring that Congress could not prohibit slavery in the territories. And during this time, southerners, desperately eager to inhibit the movement of small farmers into territories where slavery could not possibly flourish, successfully resisted passage of a homestead act that would have given free land to settlers.

Yet legislative successes could be achieved only as long as Democrats from the North and Northwest were willing to ally themselves with the South. Toward the end of the 1850s, the antislavery movement in the North became irresistible. In large part, the movement was led by those who opposed the servitude of anyone on purely ethical grounds, but altruistic motives were reinforced by economic interests. Northwest farmers resisted the extension of the plantation system because they feared the resulting competition of large units with their small ones. And as transportation to eastern centers improved, especially through the Northern Gateway, the products of the Northwest increasingly flowed into the Middle Atlantic states and Europe. In this way, the people of the Northwest found their economic and other interests more closely tied to the eastern industrialists than to the southern planters. The large migrations of Irish and Germans, who had no stake in slavery, added to the shift in economic and political interests near midcentury. The Republican party, founded in the mid-1850s, capitalized on the shift in economic interests. As old political alignments weakened, the Republican party rapidly gained strength, chiefly from those who opposed the extension of slavery into the territories.

In the opening speech of his sixth debate with Stephen A. Douglas on October 13, 1858, in Quincy, Illinois, Abraham Lincoln elaborated on slavery:

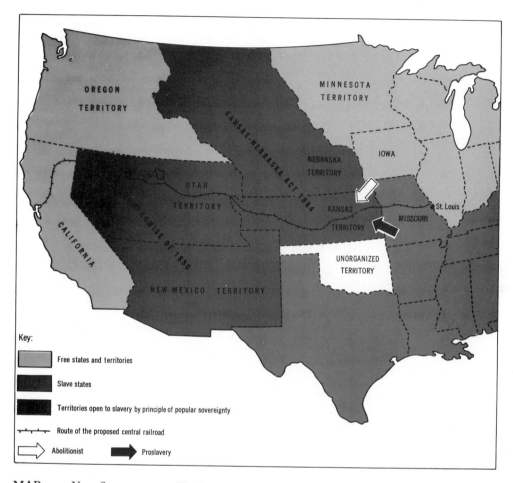

MAP 13-2 NEW SETTLEMENTS: *The Compromise of 1850 and the Kansas-Nebraska Act of 1854 were further attempts to keep sectional strife from erupting into warfare. The concept of "popular sovereignty" introduced in this act led to conflict in Kansas.*

We have in this nation the element of domestic slavery. . . . The Republican party think it wrong—we think it is a moral, a social, and a political wrong. We think it is a wrong not confining itself merely to the persons or the State where it exists, but that it is a wrong which in its tendency, to say the least, affects the existence of the whole nation. . . . I suppose that in reference both to its actual existence in the nation, and to our constitutional obligations, we have no right at all to disturb it in the States where it exists, and we profess that we have no more inclination to disturb it than we have the right to do it. . . . We also oppose it as an evil so far as it seeks to spread itself. We insist on the policy that shall restrict it to its present limits. . . . We oppose the Dred Scott decision in a certain way. . . . We propose so resisting it as to have it reversed if we can, and a new judicial rule established upon this subject.

Lincoln's advocacy of fencing in slavery and keeping it out of the West violated the federal Constitution as the South saw it. Cotton was already flourishing in Texas. California and Arizona bode well for the extension of cotton cultivation. These promising lands had been acquired from Mexico in the 1840s. Were southerners to be excluded from them?

From the southern perspective, the election of Lincoln in 1860 presented only two alternatives: submission or secession. To a wealthy and proud people, submission was unthinkable.[9] To Lincoln, alternatively, the Union had to be preserved. The holocaust that maintained the Union cost the country more lives and human suffering than any other war in the history of the United States. Although initially emancipation was not an objective of the northern war effort, it became, as we know today, a celebrated outcome matched only by the preservation of the Union itself.

SELECTED REFERENCES
AND SUGGESTED READINGS

Aufhauser, R. Keith. "Slavery and Technological Change." *Journal of Economic History* 34 (1974): 36–50.

Blassingame, John. *The Slave Community: Plantation Life in the Antebellum South.* New York: Oxford University Press, 1972.

Canarella, Georgio, and John A. Tomaske. "The Optimal Utilization of Slaves." *Journal of Economic History* 35 (1975): 621–629.

Conrad, Alfred, and John Meyer. "The Economics of Slavery in the Antebellum South." *Journal of Political Economy* 66 (1958): 95–130.

David, Paul, Herbert Gutman, Richard Sutch, and Gavin Wright. *Reckoning with Slavery.* New York: Oxford University Press, 1976.

Douglass, Frederick. *Narrative of the Life of Frederick Douglass.* New York: New American Library, 1968.

Elkins, Stanley M. *Slavery: A Problem of American Institutional and Intellectual Life.* New York: Grosset & Dunlap, 1959.

Engerman, Stanley, and Eugene Genovese. *Race and Slavery in the Western Hemisphere: Quantitative Studies.* Princeton, New Jersey: Princeton University Press, 1978.

Fenoaltea, Stefano. "The Slavery Debate: A Note from the Sidelines." *Explorations in Economic History* 18 (July 1981): 304–308.

Fleisig, Heywood. "Slavery, the Supply of Agricultural Labor, and the Industrialization of the South." *Journal of Economic History* 36 (1976): 572–597.

Fogel, Robert W. "Three Phases of Cliometric Research on Slavery and Its Aftermath." *American Economic Review* 65 (May 1975): 37–46.

_____. *Without Consent or Contract: The Rise and Fall of American Slavery.* New York: W. W. Norton, 1989.

Fogel, Robert W., and Stanley L. Engerman. "Explaining the Relative Efficiency of Slave Agriculture in the Antebellum South." *American Economic Review* 67 (June 1977): 275–296.

_____. "Explaining the Relative Efficiency of Slave Agriculture in the Antebellum South: A Reply." *American Economic Review* 70 (September 1980): 672–690.

_____. "The Relative Efficiency of Slavery: A Comparison of Northern and Southern Agriculture in 1860." *Explorations in Economic History* 8 (Spring 1971): 353–367.

---

[9] Recall the prewar scene from *Gone With the Wind* when eager southern warriors were predicting a short war and a decisive southern victory. Rhett Butler, alone, cautioned to the contrary.

———. *Time on the Cross: The Economics of American Negro Slavery.* Boston: Little, Brown, 1974, 2 vols.

Genovese, Eugene. *From Rebellion to Revolution: Afro-American Slave Revolts in the Modern World.* Baton Rouge: Louisiana State University Press, 1979.

———. *Roll, Jordan, Roll: The World the Slaves Made.* New York: Vintage Books, 1976.

Goldin, Claudia. *Urban Slavery in the American South.* Chicago: University of Chicago Press, 1976.

Gray, Lewis. *History of Agriculture in the Southern United States to 1860.* Washington, D.C.: Carnegie Institution of Washington, 1933, 2 vols.

Gunderson, Gerald. "The Origins of the American Civil War." *Journal of Economic History* 34 (1974): 915–950.

———. "Southern Ante-Bellum Income Reconsidered." *Explorations in Economic History* 10 (Winter 1973): 151–176.

Gutman, Herbert. *The Black Family in Slavery and Freedom.* New York: Pantheon Books, 1976.

Hutchinson, W. K., and Samuel H. Williamson. "The Self-Sufficiency of the Ante-Bellum South: Estimates of the Food Supply." *Journal of Economic History* 31 (1971): 591–612.

Kotlikoff, Laurence J., and Sebastian E. Pinera. "The Old South's Stake with Inter-Regional Movement of Slaves, 1850–1860." *Journal of Economic History* 37 (1977): 434–450.

Metzer, Jacob. "Rational Management, Modern Business Practice, and Economies of Scale in the Antebellum Plantations." *Explorations in Economic History* 12 (April 1975): 123–150.

Olmsted, Frederick L. *The Cotton Kingdom: A Traveler's Observations on Cotton and Slavery in the American Slave States.* New York: Knopf, 1953.

———. *The Slave States.* New York: Capricorn Books, 1959.

Parker, William, ed. *The Structure of the Cotton Economy of the Antebellum South.* Washington, D.C.: Agricultural History Society, 1970.

Passell, Peter. "The Impact of Cotton Land Distribution on the Ante-Bellum Economy." *Journal of Economic History* 31 (1971): 917–937.

Phillips, Ulrich B. "The Economic Cost of Slaveholding in the Cotton Belt." *Political Science Quarterly* (June 1905).

Ransom, Roger L. *Conflict and Compromise: The Political Economy of Slavery, Emancipation, and the American Civil War.* New York and London: Cambridge University Press, 1989.

Ransom, Roger L., and Richard Sutch. "Capitalists without Capital: The Burden of Slavery and the Impact of Emancipation." *Agricultural History* (Summer 1988): 133–160.

Schmitz, Mark D., and Donald F. Schaefer. "Slavery, Freedom, and the Elasticity of Substitution." *Explorations in Economic History* 15 (July 1978): 327–337.

Steckel, Richard H. "Slave Height Profiles from Coastwise Manifests." *Explorations in Economic History* 16 (October 1979): 363–380.

Sutch, Richard. "The Treatment Received by American Slaves: A Critical Review of the Evidence Presented in *Time on the Cross.*" *Explorations in Economic History* 12 (October 1975): 335–438.

Thomas, Robert P., and Richard N. Bean. "The Fishers of Men: The Profits of the Slave Trade." *Journal of Economic History* 34 (1974): 885–914.

Vedder, Richard K. "The Slave Exploitation (Expropriation) Rate." *Explorations in Economic History* 12 (October 1975): 453–458.

Washington, Booker T. *Up from Slavery.* New York: Bantam Books, 1963.

Wright, Gavin. *The Political Economy of the Cotton South: Households, Markets, and Wealth in the Nineteenth Century.* New York: W. W. Norton, 1978.

———. "Slavery and the Cotton Boom." *Explorations in Economic History* 12 (October 1975): 439–452.

Zepp, Thomas M. "On Returns to Scale and Input Substitutability in Slave Agriculture." *Explorations in Economic History* 13 (April 1976): 165–178.

PART THREE

THE REUNIFICATION ERA

1860–1920

ECONOMIC AND HISTORICAL PERSPECTIVES
1860–1920

1. For nearly 100 years following 1815, there were no major wars between national coalitions. The U.S. Civil War, our bloodiest war ever, was a violent exception in this long period of global peace.

2. After the Civil War, rapid industrialization in the North and renewed western expansion sustained a high overall growth rate for the nation. The large absolute fall in output in the South due to the war and emancipation and the slow pace of growth in the cotton belt ushered in an era of southern backwardness and regional disparity.

3. Emancipation redistributed wealth and incomes sharply from white slave-owners to blacks, but a legacy of slavery sustained black poverty in the Deep South.

4. By the mid-1890s, after three decades of falling prices, the United States had become the world's leading industrial power, outproducing by nearly twice the nearest industrial rival, Germany, while England had slipped into third place.

5. Technological change, economies of scale, and mass-production methods became the main engines of modern economic growth.

6. The U.S. population topped 100 million during World War I; 48 states were in the Union; and federal, state, and local expenditures combined reached a record high of nearly 10 percent of GNP.

CHAPTER FOURTEEN

WAR, RECOVERY, AND REGIONAL DIVERGENCE

CHAPTER THEME The Democratic party split in mid-1860, permitting the Republican candidate for President, Abraham Lincoln, to win the November election with a mere 40 percent of the popular vote. Lincoln carried the North and West solidly, but his name did not even appear on ten state ballots in the South. The South's political strategy had been to control the Senate and the presidency. Both were lost in 1860.

By the time of Lincoln's inauguration on March 4, 1861, ten southern states had followed South Carolina's decision to secede. One of Lincoln's first tasks was to counter threats to Fort Sumter in Charleston Harbor. His order to reinforce the fort gave South Carolinians the excuse they sought to begin shooting.

Slavery was the root cause of the Civil War. The United States had equivocated on the slave issue both in 1776 and in 1790. The last "slavery truce," in 1850, was based on popular sovereignty in the western territories and it ended within a decade. By 1860, the South was prepared to fight to save its social order, based on plantation slavery. The North similarly was prepared to fight to save the Union, and to save the Republican victory that "finally had contained the slave power within the political framework of the United States."[1] To allow independence to the southern states would have divided the nation and allowed the South to pursue a separate foreign policy committed to the expansion of slavery.

Lincoln's key miscalculation, like the South's, was his belief that a strong show of force would bring the fighting to a speedy end. The South's victory at Bull Run, the first great battle of the Civil War, added to southern confidence and resolve to maintain the course of rebellion.

The war proved to be longer and more destructive than anyone in power imagined at its start. An estimated 620,000 American soldiers would lose their lives, nearly as many as in all the rest of America's wars combined. By the time the war ended, America's society and economy had been radically transformed. The most important change was the freeing of 4 million slaves. Moreover, nearly every aspect of economic life—including finance, education, land policies, and tariff policies—

---

[1] Roger Ransom, *Conflict and Compromise: The Political Economy of Slavery, Emancipation, and the American Civil War* (New York and London: Cambridge University Press, 1989), p. 177.

was altered in some way. In the North and parts of the South, recovery from the war was rapid. But in parts of the South, the institutional framework that developed after the Civil War prevented the former slaves and poor whites from being rapidly integrated into the mainstream of the American economy.

THE ECONOMICS OF WAR

Despite ample pride, talent, and faith in its cause, the South was woefully unprepared for a protracted war. Figure 14-1 provides a rough portrayal of the available human resources that each side possessed for potential combat. The reality of the situation, moreover, was that the 1.1 million military-aged slaves in the South could not be used for fighting on the front, and probably fewer than 30 percent of eligible whites in the Border States sided with the southern cause.[2] Indeed, the South had to use some of its precious manpower to repress its slave labor force. And, when circumstances permitted, slaves and free blacks joined the Union forces, further tipping the balance in favor of the North. By the end of the war, blacks in the Union army alone outnumbered the Confederate forces. Conventional military wisdom of the day calculated a ratio of two to one for an attacking army to overcome a defending army. Ultimately those calculations proved valid: the North could out-man the South three or more to one.

In industrial capacity the comparisons are even more lopsided. Value added in manufacturing in the North, according to Fred Bateman and Thomas Weiss, totaled $1.6 billion in 1860. It was merely $193 million in the South (half of it in Virginia). Initially neither side had a significant advantage in arms production and both depended heavily on imported arms. But the North was able to increase production quickly. The South was much less able to do this, and the South's lack of domestic manufacturing bore down heavily after the federal naval blockade during 1863 and 1864 shut off foreign supplies.

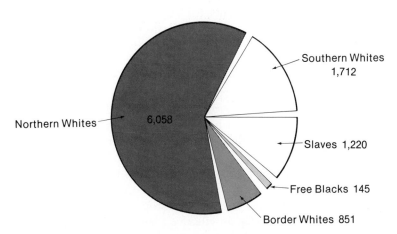

FIGURE 14-1 POPULATION OF MALES 10–49 YEARS OF AGE IN 1860 (IN THOUSANDS)

SOURCE: ROGER RANSOM, *CONFLICT AND COMPROMISE: THE POLITICAL ECONOMY OF SLAVERY, EMANCIPATION, AND THE AMERICAN CIVIL WAR* (NEW YORK AND LONDON: CAMBRIDGE UNIVERSITY PRESS, 1989), FIGURE 6.2.

---

[2] Ransom, p. 196.

Particularly troubling to the South, especially after the North took control of the Mississippi River, was the lack of a transport network sufficient to move food and supplies to the troops. The South's limited rail network was strained to capacity, but the primary shortage was of horses and mules. Because the fighting was largely on southern soil, the South's animal stocks fell relative to the North's as the war wore on.

These comparisons, however, do not mean that the South's decision to fight was irrational. The South's hope was that the North would eventually tire of the enormous human costs of the war and agree to let the South go its own way. The Revolutionary War had provided a forceful example of a nation winning independence from an economically and militarily more powerful foe. (For Robert E. Lee, that example was part of the family history: his father "Light-Horse Harry" Lee had been an outstanding cavalry commander in the Revolution.) In the summer of 1864, even after numerous southern defeats, it still seemed possible that war-weariness might defeat Lincoln in his bid for reelection—indeed, Lincoln himself doubted that he would win—and that a peace which preserved slavery might be negotiated by Lincoln's successor. However, General William Tecumseh Sherman's capture of Atlanta in September rekindled Lincoln's fortunes, and Lincoln's reelection sealed the South's fate.

SOUTHERN POLICIES

With the exception of two new government-built and -operated munitions factories, the South's emphasis on agriculture was maintained. The South's early confidence in the power of King Cotton and the likelihood of a quick end to fighting, moreover, encouraged it to adopt trade policies that reinforced its poor preparation for war.

The northern naval blockade did not become really effective until 1863. Thus for nearly two years the South could produce and export specialty crops, particularly cotton, to England in exchange for munitions and manufactures. The Confederate government, however, discouraged exports in the hope of forcing England to support the southern effort; during 1861 and 1862, only 13,000 bales of cotton from a crop of 4 million bales were exported. The southern government also imposed a ban on sales of cotton to the North. With the advantage of hindsight, it is clear that these policies weakened the southern war effort and helped to maintain a situation of inadequate supply.

Besides production and trade problems, the South also faced financial difficulties. For the most part, foreigners were unwilling to lend to the Confederacy, especially after the North's naval blockade became effective. It also proved difficult, for both political and economic reasons, to develop an effective administrative machinery for collecting taxes. The South's war materials and support, therefore, were financed primarily by inflationary means—by paper note issues. Only 40 percent of its expenditures were backed by taxes or borrowing.

Indexes of prices and money in the South given in Figure 14-2 show clearly that prices rose further and faster than the stock of money, and that the final months were ones of hyperinflation. There were two reasons for the gap that opened up between prices and money: the decline in southern production, and the decline in confidence in the southern currency.

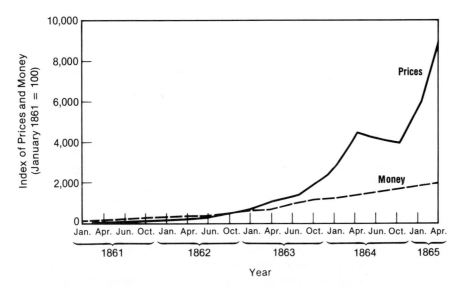

FIGURE 14-2 INFLATION IN THE CONFEDERACY: *The rate of inflation was not very great in the beginning of the Civil War, but the value of a Confederate dollar had depreciated to about 1 percent of its original value by the end of the war.*

SOURCE: E. M. LERNER, "MONEY, WAGES, AND PRICES IN THE CONFEDERACY, 1861–1865," *JOURNAL OF POLITICAL ECONOMY* 63 (FEBRUARY 1955): 29.

A diary account of an exchange in 1864 reveals the decline in confidence in the Confederate paper money:

> She asked me 20 dollars for five dozen eggs and then said she would take it in "Confederate." Then I would have given her 100 dollars as easily. But if she had taken my offer of yarn! I haggle in yarn for the million the part of a thread! . . . When they ask for Confederate money, I never stop to chafer. I give them 20 or 50 dollar cheerfully for anything.[3]

Despite the heroism and daring displayed by the Confederates, Union troops increasingly disrupted and occupied more and more southern territory. By late 1861, Union forces controlled Missouri, Kentucky, and West Virginia; Union forces took New Orleans in the spring of 1862, cutting off the major southern trade outlet. By 1863, thanks to the brilliant campaigning of Ulysses S. Grant, the entire Mississippi River basin was under Union control. Sherman's march through Georgia in 1864, in which he followed a deliberate policy of destroying the productive capacity of the region, splintered the Confederacy and cut off Lee's Army of Northern Virginia from an important source of supplies.

Once a Union victory appeared likely, confidence declined even more sharply, producing the astronomical rates of inflation experienced in the final months of the war.

---

[3] Dated March 7, 1864, from C. Vann Woodward, ed., *Mary Chesnut's Civil War* (New Haven, Connecticut: Yale University Press, 1981), p. 749.

EFFECTS IN THE NORTH

The economic strain of the war was not as severe in the North as it was in the South, but the costs of the war were extremely high even there. A substantial portion of the labor force was reallocated to the war effort, and the composition of production changed with the disruption of cotton trade and the growing number of defaults on southern debts. At the outset, in 1861, there was a sharp financial panic and banks suspended payments of specie. With the federal Treasury empty, the government quickly raised taxes and sold bonds. The tax changes included the first federal taxes on personal and business incomes. But the most significant increases were in tariffs and internal taxes on a wide range of commodities—including specific taxes on alcohol and tobacco (which are still with us) as well as iron, steel, and coal—and a general tax on manufacturing output. Despite these increases, however, bond sales brought in nearly three times the revenues of taxes.

When even these measures proved inadequate, the Union government also resorted to inflationary finance. Paper notes, termed "greenbacks" because of their color, were issued. Unbacked by gold and silver but based on the government's promise to redeem them and their status as legal tender, they circulated widely, but fluctuated in value.[4] In 1864, one gold dollar was worth two and one-half greenbacks, and the northern price level in 1864 in terms of greenbacks was twice what it had been in 1860. Nevertheless, the North escaped the hyperinflation that confounded the South.

THE BEARD-HACKER THESIS

Writing in the years between World War I and World War II, Charles Beard and Louis Hacker provided a captivating economic interpretation of the Civil War, namely that the war spurred industrial expansion. Their thesis emphasized the transfer of political power from southern agrarians to northern industrial capitalists. With new power in Congress, northern legislators passed laws intended to unify markets and propel industrialization. The range of new programs established during the war was remarkable, including the establishment of the national banking system, an increase in tariffs (to protect American industry from foreign competition), the land grant college act, and grants of land to transcontinental railroads. We will discuss the impact of these pieces of legislation at length in later chapters; it is sufficient to note here that subsequent research, while not denying important effects on individuals and regions, has questioned the overall impact of these changes. Total output of the economy would probably have been much the same in any case.

The Beard-Hacker thesis also emphasized that the war stimulated the economy and increased investment. This part of the thesis, too, has been rejected in subsequent research, based on estimates of economic activity that were not available when the thesis was first formulated. Perhaps this is less surprising when we realize that nearly

---

[4]The greenbacks were legal tender for paying private debts (including the obligations of banks to their depositors), but they were not legal tender for paying tariffs—these had to be paid in gold.

1 million men—or almost 15 percent of the labor force of 7.5 million—were normally involved in the fighting each year. Of these working-age soldiers, 259,000 Confederate men and 360,000 Union men were killed and another 251,000 southerners and 356,000 northerners were wounded. One person was killed and another wounded for every six slaves freed and for every ten southerners kept within the Union. These permanent losses of labor and human capital have been assessed by Claudia Goldin and Frank Lewis to have had economic values approaching $1.8 billion ($1.06 billion in the North and $787 million in the South—all lost). In addition, the North spent $2.3 billion directly on the war effort; the South spent $1 billion through direct government outlays. Another $1.5 billion worth of property was destroyed, most of this in the South. These combined sums of $6.6 billion were probably more than twice the size of our national income in 1860, and exceeded eight times the value added of total U.S. manufacturing that year.

The tragedy of the Civil War is compounded by the fact that in 1860 the total market value of slaves was approximately $3.06 billion.[5] The war costs of emancipation exceeded slave purchase costs by more than double. This does not mean that peaceful abolition was realistic before the war. After 1845, peaceful abolition like that undertaken by the British in the West Indies was viewed in the South as a complete disaster. Southerners were convinced that the economy of the West Indies was in shambles and that slaveowners there had lost fortunes in the process of emancipation.

The work of Stanley Engerman and Robert Gallman provides further ground for rejecting the Beard-Hacker thesis that the Civil War stimulated postwar industrialization. For example, the growth rate of total commodity output in the Civil War decade was by far the lowest of any decade of the century after 1820. As shown in Table 14-1, the trends of total commodity production between 1840 and 1860 reveal average yearly growth rates of 4.6 percent. Between 1870 and 1900, these rates were 4.4 percent. The rates during the Civil War decade, however, were only 2.0 percent, less than half those during normal times before and after. This same sharp decline occurred in the growth of manufacturing output in the 1860s, also as shown in Table

TABLE 14-1   AVERAGE ANNUAL RATE OF GROWTH OF COMMODITY OUTPUT, 1840–1899

Years	U.S. Economy	Manufacturing Sector
1840–1859	4.6	7.8
1860–1869	2.0	2.3
1870–1899	4.4	6.0

SOURCE: ROBERT E. GALLMAN, "COMMODITY OUTPUT, 1839–1899," IN *TRENDS IN THE AMERICAN ECONOMY IN THE NINETEENTH CENTURY*, 24, SERIES ON INCOME AND WEALTH (PRINCETON, NEW JERSEY: PRINCETON UNIVERSITY PRESS, 1960).

---

[5] Roger L. Ransom and Richard Sutch, "Capitalists without Capital: The Burden of Slavery and the Impact of Emancipation," *Agricultural History* 62, No. 3 (Summer 1988): 151.

The South could not match the vast amount of munitions produced by northern industry.

14-1. Clearly, the Civil War decade was a sharp and costly break in the nation's long-run growth trend.

Even if the Civil War did not accelerate total output growth, it is still possible that there was in productivity a distinct difference in prewar and postwar trends. Thanks to the efforts of Robert Gallman, such comparisons are possible.[6] Gallman tracked trend rates for the two separate periods 1839–1859 and 1869–1899, respectively. He found that the average decade rates of growth in value added in agriculture were 38 percent before the war and 32 percent afterwards.[7] In manufacturing, they were 133

---

[6] Robert E. Gallman, "Commodity Output, 1839–1899," in *Trends in the American Economy in the Nineteenth Century*, 24, Series on Income and Wealth (Princeton, New Jersey: Princeton University Press, 1960); also see Stanley L. Engerman, "The Economic Impact of the Civil War," *Explorations in Economic History* 3 (Spring 1966).

[7] Gallman, p. 24.

percent and 80 percent; in mining, 112 percent and 99 percent; and in construction, 66 percent and 36 percent. The rates of growth per decade in employment in each of these sectors, except construction, also show much slower advances in the postwar decades than before the war.[8] Finally, taking growth rates per decade of real value added per worker, Gallman observed in agriculture an advance from 7 percent in 1839–1859 to 12 percent in 1869–1899.[9] Alternatively, in mining and manufacturing combined there was little change in the rates of growth of labor productivity, averaging 25 percent and 24 percent. In construction, the rate fell from 27 percent before the war to 5 percent afterward.

Even within the various war industries of the North, there was no great spurt; by and large, the new dimensions of output in the North were modest adjustments in the various sectors. In fact, the most startling aspect of the war years was the minute stimulus to manufacturing. Iron production for small arms increased, but iron production for railroads declined. Although the demand for clothes and boots for servicemen stimulated manufactures, the loss of the southern market more than offset this. For example, in Massachusetts—the center of boot and shoe production—employment and output in that important industry decreased almost one-third during the war. Similarly, without raw cotton, the textile mills were underutilized. True, the enlistment and conscription of men ameliorated unemployment, and speculation offered opportunities for enrichment for a select few. Overall, however, expenditures by the federal government did not spur rapid industrialization or economic expansion.

We have considered the debate over the Beard-Hacker thesis in detail because it illustrates so clearly the importance of quantitative evidence. An argument may be persuasive, and it may be supported by numerous illustrative examples, but it may still be wrong.

THE INEQUITIES OF WAR

Fighting in the Civil War was waged primarily by men from lower income groups. Once the need for mass mobilization was evident, both sides turned to the draft to acquire men, and both sides allowed conscripts to buy out their service by paying another to go in their place. From this time on the war was widely and correctly viewed as a "rich man's war and a poor man's fight." While this policy shifted the burden of fighting to the poor, it arguably had efficiency advantages. The exchanges were voluntary, and if those with higher labor opportunity costs were replaced by those with lower opportunity costs, the overall costs of the war effort were reduced. The inequities, however, remained.

In the North, the most heated discontent was witnessed in the cities, especially in New York where large numbers of immigrants lived. The Irish, especially, felt that the burden of the draft was falling on them. In July 1863, mobs stormed through the streets

---

[8] Gallman, p. 30.

[9] Gallman, p. 31.

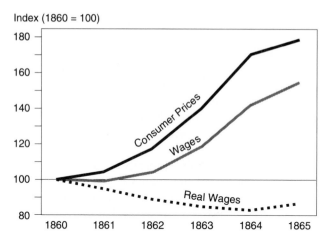

FIGURE 14-3 The Wage Lag in the Civil War

SOURCE: Reuben A. Kessel and Armen A. Alchian, "Real Wages in the North During the Civil War: Mitchell's Data Reinterpreted," in *The Reinterpretation of American Economic History*, eds. Robert W. Fogel and Stanley L. Engerman (New York: Harper & Row, 1971), p. 460.

of New York for four days; 20,000 federal troops were needed to quell the riots, which resulted in 105 deaths.

It might have been expected that the recruitment and drafting of large numbers of men would raise the real wages of those working on the homefront by reducing the available supply of labor. But this did not happen.

As shown in Figure 14-3, prices rose more rapidly than wages in the North. Thus real wages (wages/prices), the amount of goods and services that could be bought with an hour's work, fell. Wesley C. Mitchell, who first studied this problem, thought that workers bargained ineffectively because they (and their employers) were influenced by customary notions about wages. The wage lag, he believed, had produced a surge in profits that could be invested after the war: another reason for thinking that the war accelerated industrialization. Reuben Kessel and Armen Alchian, however, pointed out that the fall in real wages could also be explained by rising taxes, rising prices of imported goods, and other real factors. Subsequently, Stephen DeCanio and Joel Mokyr showed that inefficient bargaining explains about two-thirds of the fall in real wages and real factors about one-third. Northern labor, in other words, would have experienced a substantial decline in its income in any case, but the inability of labor markets to adapt rapidly to the inflation made things a lot worse than they otherwise would have been.

Inequality was even more glaring in the South. In October 1862, the southern draft law was altered to allow an exemption for anyone owning 20 or more slaves. Although the numbers benefiting from this exemption were small, the resentment it created was great. Small farmers were infuriated to see their farms, dependent on their own labor, deteriorate while rich plantations were maintained. R. M. Bradford of Virginia wrote the Confederate Secretary of War in October 1864:

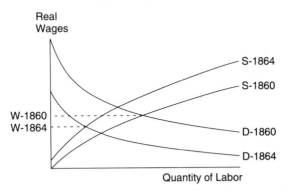

THE LABOR MARKET IN THE NORTH DURING THE CIVIL WAR

The figure above shows why real wages would have declined in the North during the Civil War even if inflation had been held in check. S-1860 is the supply of labor before the war, D-1860 the demand. The expansion of the armed forces reduced the supply of labor to S-1864. Other things equal, this would have raised real wages. But remember that the demand for labor is derived from the demand for final products. Rising taxes on production (excise taxes) and rising costs of imported products reduced profits and the demand for labor from D-1860 to D-1864. The leftward shift in demand was greater than the shift in supply and lowered equilibrium real wages from W-1860 to W-1864.

> The people will not *always* submit to this *unequal, unjust,* and partial distribution of favor and wholesale conscription of the *poor* while able-bodied and healthy men of property are all occupying *soft places.*[10]

Slaves were not used by the South for fighting because both masters and slaves knew the enemy provided a route to freedom.[11] Ironically, the efforts of slaves to grow cotton, spurred on by the exceptionally high prices in the early 1860s, was negated by the South's trade policies to England. Most of this vital labor was simply wasted, as high stockpiles of cotton rotted in the countryside and on the docks.

---

[10] R. M. Bradford to James Seddon, quoted in Paul Escott, *After Secession: Jefferson Davis and the Failure of Confederate Nationalism* (Baton Range: Louisiana State University Press, 1978), p. 119.

[11] At the very end of the war, the South considered plans to employ slaves as soldiers.

THE AFTERMATH OF THE CIVIL WAR

The outcome of the war was a distinct reversal in the relative positions of the North and South. As shown in Table 14-2, in 1860 the South's real commodity output per capita of $77.8 slightly exceeded that of $74.8 in the North. By 1870, the North's per capita output exceeded the South's by nearly two-thirds ($81.5 compared to $47.6). This advantage remained in 1880. The major source of this reversal was not the northern and midwestern advance, but the dramatic absolute decline in southern output during and shortly after the war.

It would be an error, however, to conclude that the entire southern economy remained stagnant. The commodity output per capita figures for 1870 and 1880 show that the South's growth rate was initially rapid, and close to the North's growth rate of almost 2.6 percent yearly. Such high rates were not sustained, however, nor were they distributed evenly across the South. Table 14-3 on the next page shows estimates of the rate of growth of personal income per capita in real terms for the five most cotton-dependent states of the Deep South (Louisiana, Georgia, Mississippi, South Carolina, and Alabama) and for the remaining eight southern states from 1879 to 1899. Clearly there was great variation among the southern states, with several growing more than twice as fast as those comprising the Deep South.

As this evidence would suggest, southern manufacturing rebounded from the war more quickly than southern agriculture. Southern manufacturing output had approached prewar levels by the early 1870s, and the South's transportation network (based on steamboats, roads, and railroads) had been completely revitalized. This revitalization was accomplished with reasonable ease, requiring little more than repairs and replacements and modest additions of capital. In fact, as John Stuart Mill had noted shortly before the Civil War, rapid postwar recoveries have been quite common throughout history:

> An enemy lays waste a country by fire and sword, and destroys or carries away nearly all the movable wealth existing in it; all the inhabitants are ruined, and yet in a few years after, everything is much as it was before. . . . The possibility of a rapid repair of their disasters, mainly depends on whether the country has been depopulated. If its effective population have not been extirpated at the time, and are not starved afterwards; then, with the same skill and knowledge which they had before, with their land and its permanent improvements undestroyed,

TABLE 14-2   COMMODITY OUTPUT PER CAPITA BY REGION (IN 1879 PRICES)

Year	Outside the South	South
1860	$ 74.8	$77.7
1870	81.5	47.6
1880	105.8	61.5

SOURCE: STANLEY ENGERMAN, "THE ECONOMIC IMPACT OF THE CIVIL WAR," *EXPLORATIONS IN ECONOMIC HISTORY* 3 (SPRING 1966): 181.

TABLE 14-3 ANNUAL RATES OF GROWTH IN CONSTANT-DOLLAR VALUES OF PER CAPITA PERSONAL INCOME BY STATE BETWEEN 1879 AND 1899

State	Annual Percentage Rates of Growth per Capita Personal Income
Louisiana	0.44
Georgia	0.81
Mississippi	0.96
South Carolina	0.98
Alabama	1.14
Five cotton states	0.86
North Carolina	1.38
Kentucky	1.42
Arkansas	1.43
Tennessee	1.89
Virginia	2.15
West Virginia	2.26
Texas	2.53
Florida	2.64
Total, 13 southern states	1.54
United States	1.59

SOURCE: DERIVED FROM RICHARD EASTERLIN, "REGIONAL GROWTH OF INCOME: LONG-TERM TENDENCIES, 1880–1950," IN *POPULATION REDISTRIBUTION AND ECONOMIC GROWTH, UNITED STATES 1870–1950, VOL. 2, ANALYSES OF ECONOMIC CHANGE*, EDS. S. KUZNETS, A. R. MILLER, AND R. A. EASTERLIN (PHILADELPHIA: AMERICAN PHILOSOPHICAL SOCIETY, 1960), P. 185.

and the more durable buildings probably unimpaired, or only partially injured, they have nearly all the requisites for their former amount of production.[12]

Rapid regeneration is propelled by eliminating bottlenecks. For example, the South's railroad network almost ceased to function by the war's end, largely due to the lack of rolling stock and partially destroyed track; the roadbed, specialized labor expertise, and considerable track remained in good condition but were unusable. Prompt investment in the essential complementary resources (rolling stock and damaged track) reemployed the other existing resources (labor, roadbed, and usable track). This initiated a regenerative spurt, and other similar spurts in combination led to a temporary high-growth period. When these unusual investment opportunities had been fully exploited, the long-run slower rate of growth resumed.[13]

In agriculture, however, the prospects for southern recovery were quite different. Lincoln's Emancipation Proclamation altered the whole makeup of the South's

[12]J. S. Mill, *Principles of Political Economy*, 1848, Book I, Chapter 5, Section 7.

[13]For elaboration on the theory of regenerative growth, see Donald F. Gordon and Gary M. Walton, "A New Theory of Regenerative Growth and the Post-World War II Experience of West Germany," in *Explorations in the New Economic History: Essays in Honor of Douglass C. North*, eds. Roger L. Ransom, Richard Sutch, and Gary M. Walton (New York: Academic Press, 1982), pp. 171–192.

agricultural society for both whites and blacks. The results were great reductions in agricultural output, especially during the late war years and the immediate postwar years. In the absence of emancipation, the South's agricultural sector surely would have restored itself within a few years; but the political, social, and economic adjustments stemming from emancipation delayed regenerative growth for many years.

The decline in southern output, especially in the cotton states of the Deep South, was much deeper than that precipitated by war destruction alone. As indicated in Figure 14-4, the growth of agricultural output in the Deep South averaged *minus* 0.96 percent per year from 1857 to 1879.

DECLINE IN THE DEEP SOUTH

The five key cotton states of the Deep South—South Carolina, Louisiana, Georgia, Alabama, and Mississippi—have been shown in Table 14-3 (preceding page) and Figure 14-4 to have experienced the greatest setbacks. There were three principal reasons for this precipitous decline.

First, the highly efficient plantation system was destroyed, and attempts to resurrect plantation methods proved futile. Assembly-line methods employing gangs driven

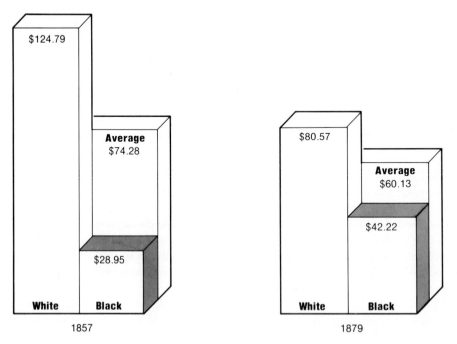

FIGURE 14-4 DISTRIBUTION OF AGRICULTURAL OUTPUT PER CAPITA BY RACE IN THE DEEP SOUTH, 1857 AND 1879

SOURCE: ROGER L. RANSOM AND RICHARD SUTCH, "GROWTH AND WELFARE IN THE AMERICAN SOUTH," IN *MARKET INSTITUTIONS AND ECONOMIC PROGRESS IN THE NEW SOUTH 1865–1900*, EDS. GARY M. WALTON AND JAMES F. SHEPHERD (NEW YORK: ACADEMIC PRESS, 1981), P. 145.

intensively from dawn to dusk were shunned by free blacks, just as they always had been by free whites. In place of the plantations, there arose smaller units—some owned, many rented, and many sharecropped (the owner of the land and the tenant split the crop). Table 14-4 shows the alteration in farm sizes between 1860 and 1870 in the Deep South. Whereas 61 percent of the farms had been less than 100 acres in 1860, 81 percent were under 100 acres in 1870. Economies of scale based on the intense driving of slave labor were lost.

A second closely related reason was the significant withdrawal of labor from the fields, especially labor by women and children. This reallocation of human effort undoubtedly raised household production and improved the quality of life, but it nevertheless contributed to the decline in measured per capita agricultural output in the Deep South by 30 to 40 percent between 1860 and 1870.

Finally, the growth of the demand for southern cotton slowed because of competition from new areas of the world (India, Brazil, and Egypt) and because the growth of world demand slowed. The U.S. South had dominated the world cotton market in 1860, commanding 77 percent of English imports.[14] In the war years, however, when the door to the new competition was opened, only 10 percent of England's cotton came from the South. The South's market share rebounded well in the late 1870s, but even then it never reached its 1860 highmark.

The decline in the Deep South immediately after the Civil War was to be expected. The tragedy was that southern agricultural production remained depressed for decades afterwards. The most puzzling aspect of the decline in the Deep South was the increased concentration on cotton production. Unlike small prewar southern farms, small postwar farms, especially those operated by former slaves, became highly specialized in cotton production. For example, in the five main cotton-growing states, 82 percent of non-slave farms (85 percent of all farms) had grown cotton in 1860 compared

TABLE 14-4 FARM SIZE DISTRIBUTION IN FIVE MAJOR COTTON STATES

Improved Acres	Percentage of Farms in Size Class		Percentage of Land in Size Class	
	1860	1870	1860	1870
3–49	36.9	60.9	7.4	20.2
50–99	24.2	19.8	12.0	19.6
100–499	32.0	17.2	47.6	49.1
500+	6.9	2.1	33.0	11.0

SOURCE: ROGER RANSOM AND RICHARD SUTCH, *ONE KIND OF FREEDOM: THE ECONOMIC CONSEQUENCES OF EMANCIPATION* (CAMBRIDGE: CAMBRIDGE UNIVERSITY PRESS, 1977), P. 71.

---

[14] See Thomas Ellison, *The Cotton Trade of Great Britain* (Augustus Kelley, 1968) cited in Gavin Wright, "Cotton Competition and the Post-Bellum Recovery of the American South," *Journal of Economic History* 34 (1974): 611. Also see Gavin Wright, *The Political Economy of the Cotton South* (New York: W. W. Norton, 1978) and *Old South, New South: Revolution in the Southern Economy* (New York: Basic Books, 1986).

to 97 percent of all farms there in 1870.[15] Moreover, a greater proportion of the land on each farm was devoted to cotton production in 1870 than in 1860. Indeed, whereas many slave plantations had been self-sufficient in food production before the Civil War, the Deep South now became a food importing region. Black farmers were the most cotton dependent, with 85 percent of their crop in cotton compared to 60 to 70 percent for white farmers. White owners placed the smallest proportion of their land in cotton; white tenant farmers produced nearly twice that of white owners, and black tenants nearly four times that of white owners. This increased dependency on cotton occurred despite declining cotton prices in the 1870s.

Concentration on cotton production was not irrational. Stephen DeCanio has shown that the South had a comparative advantage in cotton production and that southern cotton farmers were about as responsive to price changes as northern wheat farmers.[16] Nevertheless, the limited economic alternatives provided by the cotton economy sentenced many of the former slaves to a life of grinding poverty. To see how this happened, we must explore the transition from slavery to freedom, and the new economic institutions that replaced the old.

THE LEGACY OF SLAVERY

The Thirteenth Amendment to the Constitution freed all slaves; the Fourteenth Amendment assured that no "state shall deprive any person of life, liberty or property, without due process of law" and guaranteed that "the right of citizens to vote shall not be abridged." These amendments were passed soon after the war but were not sufficient to assure sustained progress for blacks. The first effects of the new freedoms surely helped blacks dramatically. Just as surely, many southern whites suffered in the late 1860s. Average wealth holdings of whites in the Deep South in 1860 had been $81,400 for plantation owners, $13,300 for slaveowning small farmers, and $2,400 for non-slaveowning farmers. In 1870 the average for all white farmers in the Deep South was $3,200. Resentment against Yankees and blacks reflected the whites' slide in wealth and hatred of the northern occupation.

Land reform that broke up the plantations and gave the land to former slaves was pushed by radical Republicans in Congress. This might have set the South, and ultimately the whole country, on a different course. A bill to give black heads of households 40 acres each was passed by the House and Senate but was vetoed by President Andrew Johnson. Except in a few isolated areas such as the Sea Islands of Georgia— where land reform proved to be a success in promoting stable farming communities— most of the land remained in the hands of the same people who had owned it before the war. Roger Ransom and Richard Sutch show that the wealthiest fifth of the population still owned 73 percent of the land in 1870, a drop of only 2 percent from 1860.[17]

---

[15] These figures are from Roger Ransom, *The House Divided*, Table 7-3, p. 257(s).

[16] Stephen DeCanio, *Agriculture in the Postbellum South* (Cambridge: MIT Press, 1974).

[17] Roger L. Ransom and Richard Sutch, *One Kind of Freedom* (Cambridge: Cambridge University Press, 1977), p. 79.

Moreover, the power of northern Republicans to assure a solid political base in the South by protecting the civil rights of the former slaves was limited by economic conditions nationally and by an absence of effective local support in the South. When President Johnson's executive order of total amnesty to anyone willing to take an oath of allegiance was upheld by the courts, the old Confederates began to take power—aided by violence, including that of the newly formed Ku Klux Klan. The Constitutional amendments protecting black rights were subverted, and blacks ultimately became disenfranchised.

In the immediate aftermath of the war there was considerable interstate migration of former slaves. Much of this movement can be explained by the efforts of former slaves to reunite families broken up during slavery. Perhaps also, many former slaves wanted to see a bit of the country in which they lived, a privilege denied to them by slavery. But from 1870 to 1890 black migration within the South, as shown by Philip E. Graves, Robert L. Sexton, and Richard K. Vedder, was reduced compared with the antebellum period. While slaveowners would generally move or sell slaves whenever economic considerations dictated, the former slave could also weigh the costs of leaving behind family, friends, and familiar institutions. Black migration to the North did not become truly large until after 1910 when a combination of rising northern wages, rising expectations of a better life, and the information provided by earlier generations of migrants encouraged a mass exodus. Instead of heading north after the Civil War, most former slaves settled down to farm the land.

As shown in Figure 14-5, blacks occupied and operated about 30 percent of the land in crops, and whites worked 70 percent. Blacks were close to 70 percent of the

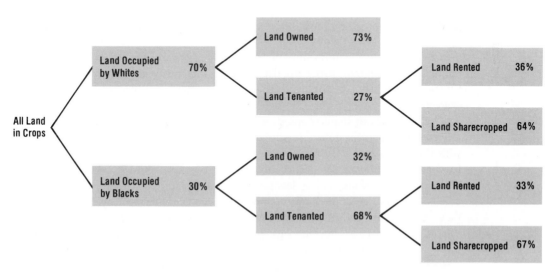

FIGURE 14-5 Ownership and Use of Farm Land in Crops in the Deep South by Race, 1880

SOURCE: Adapted from Roger L. Ransom and Richard Sutch, *One Kind of Freedom: The Economic Consequences of Emancipation* (New York: Cambridge University Press, 1977), p. 84.

Typical of many blacks in the postwar South, the couple in this photograph taken in 1875— twelve years after emancipation—remained entrapped in poverty.

agricultural work force in 1880 but owned less than 10 percent of the land. (As can be seen in the figure: if 30 percent was occupied by blacks and 32 percent of that land was owned by blacks then $.3 \times .32 = 9.6$ percent of all land was owned by blacks.)[18] Given the resistance and hostility of white southerners and the absence of any federal redistribution program, it is a wonder that even this much land was owned by blacks. Of the two-thirds of the land that was tenanted by blacks, two-thirds was sharecropped.

The basic idea of sharecropping, as we noted above, was simple. Instead of paying a fixed annual sum in dollars for the use of the land, the sharecropper split the crop with the land owner after the harvest. Standard yearly contracts gave a fifty-fifty split to owner and tenant; on particularly productive land, however, the owner might demand a greater share, and on less productive land he might settle for a smaller share. The benefits and costs of sharecropping have been hotly debated by economic historians. To Ransom and Sutch tenant farming, and sharecropping in particular, was a disaster that forced the former slaves into dependency on cotton, and in some cases into a condition similar to slavery known as debt peonage.

Other students of sharecropping, however, have concluded that it offered a number of advantages, at least compared with the available alternatives. Former slaves and poor

[18] Philip E. Graves, Robert L. Sexton, and Richard K. Vedder, "Slavery, Amenities, and Factor Price Equalization: A Note on Migration and Freedom," *Explorations in Economic History* 20 (1983): 156–162.

whites were provided independence from day-to-day bossing and a chance to earn a living. The risk of a very bad year—due perhaps to poor growing conditions, or to unusually low prices—was shared with the owner. The sharecropping contract, more-over, as Joseph Reid has pointed out, also gave the owner an incentive to remain inter-ested in the farm throughout the growing season and to share information such as changing crop prices with the tenant.[19] On large plantations where such information sharing was difficult, renting predominated.[20] Just as the sharecropper shares part of the risk of a bad harvest with the owner, he also shares part of any gain from his own hard work. And tenant farmers in general have an incentive to concentrate on the short-run and sleight long-term investments. Competition among tenants, and various incentives built into rental contracts, partially offset the negative effects of renting on long-term investment but it is not known how successful these adjustments were.

In any case, whether sharecropping was a cause of poverty or only a response to it, the sharecropper who grew cotton and bought his food on credit at the local country store became the symbol of southern economic stagnation.

Meanwhile, the credit system added to the cropper's burden. The source of rural credit was the white-owned country store. Here the farmer bought most of his sup-plies, including food. Typically, two sets of prices were common in country stores, one for goods bought for cash and one for goods bought on time to be paid after the harvest. The markups were steep, often implying an interest rate of 40 to 70 percent per annum for buying on time. The cropper who could not pay his debts after harvest often had to mortgage the next year's crop to get continued credit. This transaction was made possible by "crop lien" laws passed in many states. The crop lien was a powerful means of control, and storekeepers (nearly 8,000 throughout the rural South) soon learned that by insisting on payment in cotton they could maintain long-term control over their debtors. The tenant was thus "locked in" to cotton.[21]

High interest rates were the result of the high costs of credit to the storeowner, the risks faced by the storeowner, and the exploitation of any local monopoly power pos-sessed by the storeowner. The slow recovery of southern banking in rural areas after the Civil War contributed to the storeowner's costs of doing business and protected his local monopoly. The National Banking Act had set a minimum capital requirement that made it hard to establish national banks in small towns, and very hard to establish more than one.[22] Banking legislation had also made it impossible for state-chartered banks to issue bank notes, and directed the funds that national banks received by issu-ing notes into federal bonds rather than local loans. After the turn of the century, the development of deposit banking, along with the easing of state and federal banking

---

[19]Joseph Reid, "Sharecropping as an Understandable Market Response: The Postbellum South," *Journal of Economic History* 33 (1973): 106–130.

[20]Lee Alston and Robert Higgs, "Contractual Mix in Southern Agriculture since the Civil War: Facts, Hypotheses, and Tests," *Journal of Economic History* 42 (1982): 327–353.

[21]For further discussion of these and other issues in the postwar South, see Gary M. Walton and James F. Shepherd, eds., *Market Institutions and Economic Progress in the New South 1865–1900* (New York: Academic Press, 1981).

[22]As late as 1880 there were only 42 national banks in the Deep South out of 2,061 in the nation as a whole (126 in the 12 former Confederate states).

regulations, helped bring southern interest rates into line with those in other parts of the country. There is some dispute about how much of the storeowner's high interest charges reflected his monopoly power and how much his own high costs of supplying credit. In either case, the result for the farmer caught in the trap of debt peonage was extreme poverty.

Table 14-5 shows estimates of the real income of slaves in 1859 and of sharecroppers in 1879. Evidently, in terms of real spendable income (available for food, clothing, shelter), emancipation was only a moderate boon. Sharecroppers had more freedom to choose how they would spend their limited income, but between 1859 and 1879 blacks' real disposable income increased at an average rate of only 1.87 percent per year. The 1879 figures, moreover, apply to all black sharecroppers. For some of those caught most firmly in the vise of debt peonage, the gains were even smaller. Only when an allowance is made for the monetary value of increased leisure time (the reduction in hours spent working multiplied by the wage of agricultural labor) does the material gain from emancipation appear to be truly large.[23]

The problem of debt peonage was not endemic to the entire South. To recall the evidence from Table 14-3 (see page 311), such states as Virginia, West Virginia, Texas, and Florida showed remarkable recoveries and sustained advances following the war. Research by Price Fishback has shown that Georgia sharecroppers, on average in the 1880s, were able to pay off their debts after the harvest, and that their debt burdens were declining.[24] Research by Robert Higgs and Robert Margo has shown that in

TABLE 14-5   INCOMES OF SLAVES AND SHARECROPPERS

	Slave on a Large Plantation in 1859	Sharecropper in 1879	Annual Rate of Growth (percent per year)
Income (1879 dollars)	$27.66	$40.24	1.87%
Value of the Increase in Leisure Time	—	33.90[a]	—
Total	27.66	74.14	4.93%

[a] The average of the high and low estimates.

SOURCE: KENNETH NG AND NANCY VIRTS, "THE VALUE OF FREEDOM," JOURNAL OF ECONOMIC HISTORY 49 (DECEMBER 1989): 959.

---

[23] One way to increase our understanding of postbellum southern poverty is to use data and methods drawn from other disciplines. For an excellent example, see Jerome C. Rose, "Biological Consequences of Segregation and Economic Deprivation: A Post-Slavery Population from Southwest Arkansas," *Journal of Economic History* 49 (1989): 351–360. Rose uses skeletal remains to identify disease and nutritional problems in the black population.

[24] Price V. Fishback, "Debt Peonage in Postbellum Georgia," *Explorations in Economic History* 26 (1989): 219–236.

THE MONUMENT TO THE BOLL WEEVIL. *When the boll weevil destroyed their cotton, farmers near Enterprise, Alabama, turned to peanuts, which proved profitable. The partly ironic plaque reads as follows: "In profound appreciation of the boll weevil and what it has done as the herald of prosperity, this monument is erected by the citizens of Enterprise, Coffee County, Alabama, Dec. 11, 1919."*

some areas blacks, despite the enormous difficulties they faced, were able to move up the agricultural ladder and become owners of their own farms.[25]

A variety of factors gradually weakened the grip of debt peonage. One, surprisingly enough, was the boll weevil, an insect that attacked cotton and gradually spread throughout the Deep South after the turn of the century. The boll weevil could be a tragedy for the individual farmer whose crop was ruined and who could not get credit on the basis of his infested land. But in some areas the long-run consequences were favorable: the boll weevil forced farmers to switch to other crops. Improved roads and the automobile also eroded the monopoly power of the local storeowner. And the growth of the great mail-order houses in Chicago provided increased competition in the supply of certain kinds of merchandise.

---

[25] Robert Higgs "Accumulation of Property by Southern Blacks before World War I," *American Economic Review* 72 (1982): 725–735; Robert A. Margo, "Accumulation of Property by Southern Blacks Before World War One: Comment and Further Evidence," *American Economic Review* 74 (1984): 768–776; Higgs, "Reply," *American Economic Review* 74 (1984): 777–781.

More important than these factors, however, was increasing urbanization and industrialization throughout the nation, which provided alternatives to agriculture. Southern industrialization was the goal of the "New South" movement proclaimed by southern politicians, newspapermen, and church leaders. There were some successes—a steel industry developed in Birmingham, the cigarette industry developed in North Carolina, and the cotton textile industry moved to the South—but the southern effort to industrialize progressed slowly.[26] Ultimately, it was northern industrialization and its growing demand for labor that allowed many southern blacks to escape from tenant farming.[27]

Despite the exodus of labor, and industrialization, the southern economy, especially that of the Deep South, remained a distinctive low-wage economy until the 1940s. Gavin Wright's book *Old South, New South* explains the slow pace of progress toward regional parity. In Wright's view, the South remained a separate labor market. Many people left,[28] and few came in, but rapid natural increase kept labor abundant. Cotton became increasingly labor intensive as farm sizes fell in the Deep South. By the late nineteenth century, most southern farms were smaller than northern farms, the reverse of the antebellum years. Mechanization was thereby slowed, and wages and earnings kept low.

Southern whites attempted to protect their position by keeping blacks even lower on the economic ladder. By the turn of the century, "black codes" and "Jim Crow" laws segregated blacks and maintained their impoverishment. Such laws determined where blacks could work, live, eat and drink, ride on public transport, and go to school. Northerners, as Wright emphasizes, shunned investments in the South. The result was that a striking wage gap remained between the North and South.

A considerable part of the South's relative backwardness can surely be attributed to its educational system. Public expenditures per pupil remained a mere fraction of those in the North. Wealthy southerners argued that educating the poor, especially blacks, merely encouraged their migration north in pursuit of higher wages. The Supreme Court held in *Plessy v. Fergusson* (1896) that separate education for blacks was constitutional so long as it was equal. "Separate" was adhered to religiously, but "equal" was not. As Robert Margo shows in his *Race and Schooling in the South*, far more money was spent on white students than black students. Margo found, for example, that in 1910 spending on black pupils relative to white pupils ranged from 17 percent in Louisiana to 75 percent in Delaware.[29] Part of this discrepancy can be explained by discrimination against black school teachers; but other measures of the quality of schooling, such as class size, show similar differentials. Lack of spending on education

[26] Kenneth Weiher, "The Cotton Industry and Southern Urbanization, 1880–1930," *Explorations in Economic History* 14 (April 1977): 120–149.

[27] See Fred Bateman and Thomas Weiss, *Deplorable Scarcity* (Chapel Hill: University of North Carolina Press, 1981).

[28] See Richard Vedder, Lowell Gallaway, Philip E. Graves, and Robert Sexton, "Demonstrating Their Freedom: The Post-Emancipation Migration of Black Americans," in *Research in Economic History* 10 (1986): 213–239.

[29] Robert A. Margo, *Race and Schooling in the South, 1880–1950* (Chicago: University of Chicago Press, 1990), pp. 21–22.

may have served the interest of some wealthy southerners, but the result was a labor force ill-prepared to participate in modern economic growth.

SELECTED REFERENCES AND SUGGESTED READINGS

Aldrich, Mark. "Flexible Exchange Rates, Northern Expansion, and the Market for Southern Cotton, 1866–1879." *Journal of Economic History* 33 (1973): 399–416.

Alston, Lee, and Robert Higgs. "Contractual Mix in Southern Agriculture since the Civil War: Facts, Hypotheses, and Tests." *Journal of Economic History* 42 (1982): 327–353.

Andreano, Ralph, ed. *The Economic Impact of the Civil War.* Cambridge, Massachusetts: Schenkman, 1964.

Bateman, Fred, and Thomas Weiss. *Deplorable Scarcity.* Chapel Hill: University of North Carolina Press, 1981.

Cochran, Thomas. "Did the Civil War Retard Industrialization?" *Mississippi Valley Historical Review* 48 (September 1961).

DeCanio, Stephen. *Agriculture in the Postbellum South.* Cambridge: MIT Press, 1974.

_____. "Productivity and Income Distribution in the Post-Bellum South." *Journal of Economic History* 34 (1974): 422–446.

DeCanio, Stephen, and Joel Mokyr. "Inflation and Wage Lag During the American Civil War." *Explorations in Economic History* 14 (1977): 311–336.

Engerman, Stanley. "The Economic Impact of the Civil War." In *The Reinterpretation of American Economic History,* eds. Robert W. Fogel and Stanley L. Engerman. New York: Harper & Row, 1971.

_____. "Some Economic Factors in Southern Backwardness in the Nineteenth Century." In *Essays in Regional Economics,* eds. John F. Kain and John R. Meyer. Cambridge: Harvard University Press, 1971.

Fishback, Price V. "Debt Peonage in Postbellum Georgia." *Explorations in Economic History* 26 (1989): 219–236.

Fogel, Robert W. *Without Consent or Contract: The Rise and Fall of American Slavery.* New York: W. W. Norton, 1989.

Goldin, Claudia, and Frank Lewis. "The Economic Cost of the American Civil War." *Journal of Economic History* 35 (1975): 294–326.

Graves, Philip E., Robert L. Sexton, and Richard K. Vedder. "Slavery, Amenities, and Factor Price Equalization: A Note on Migration and Freedmen." *Explorations in Economic History* 20 (1983): 156–162.

Hacker, Louis. *The Triumph of American Capitalism.* New York: Columbia University Press, 1940.

Higgs, Robert. "Accumulation of Property by Southern Blacks before World War I." *American Economic Review* 72 (1982): 725–735.

_____. "Accumulation of Property by Southern Blacks before World War I: Reply." *American Economic Review* 74 (1984): 777–781.

_____. *Competition and Coercion: Blacks in the American Economy, 1865–1914.* New York: Cambridge University Press, 1977.

_____. "Patterns of Farm Rental in the Georgia Cotton Belt, 1880–1900." *Journal of Economic History* 34 (1974): 468–482.

_____. "Race, Tenure, and Resource Allocation in Southern Agriculture." *Journal of Economic History* 33 (1973): 149–169.

Kessel, Reuben A., and Armen A. Alchian. "Real Wages in the North During the Civil War: Mitchell's Data Reinterpreted." In *The Reinterpretation of American Economic History,* eds. Robert W. Fogel and Stanley L. Engerman. New York: Harper & Row, 1971.

Lebergott, Stanley. "Through the Blockade: The Profitability and Extent of Cotton Smuggling, 1861–1865." *Journal of Economic History* 41 (1981): 867–888.

Lerner, Eugene. "Money, Wages, and Prices in the Confederacy, 1861–1865." *Journal of Political History* 63 (February 1955).

Mandle, Jay R. "The Plantation States as a Sub-Region of the Post-Bellum South." *Journal of Economic History* 34 (1974): 732–738.

Margo, Robert A. "Accumulation of Property by Southern Blacks Before World War One: Comment and Further Evidence." *American Economic Review* 74 (September 1984): 768–776.

_____. *Race and Schooling in the South, 1880–1950.* Chicago: University of Chicago Press, 1990.

McGuire, Robert A., and Robert Higgs. "Cotton, Corn, and Risk in the Nineteenth Century: Another View." *Explorations in Economic History* 14 (1979): 167–182.

_____. "A Portfolio Analysis of Crop Diversification and Risk in the Cotton South." *Explorations in Economic History* 17 (1980): 342–371.

Ransom, Roger L. *Conflict and Compromise: The Political Economy of Slavery, Emancipation, and the American Civil War.* New York and London: Cambridge University Press, 1989.

Ransom, Roger L., and Richard Sutch. "Capitalists without Capital: The Burden of Slavery and the Impact of Emancipation." *Agricultural History* 62 (Summer 1988): 133–160.

_____. "The Ex-Slave in the Post Bellum South." *Journal of Economic History* 33 (1973): 131–148.

_____. "The Impact of the Civil War and of Emancipation on Southern Agriculture." *Explorations in Economic History* 12 (January 1975): 1–28.

_____. *One Kind of Freedom: The Economic Consequences of Emancipation.* New York: Cambridge University Press, 1977.

Reid, Joseph. "Sharecropping as an Understandable Market Response: The Postbellum South." *Journal of Economic History* 33 (1973): 106–130.

Rose, Jerome C. "Biological Consequences of Segregation and Economic Deprivation: A Post-Slavery Population from Southwest Arkansas." *Journal of Economic History* 49 (1989): 351–360.

Sellers, James L. "The Economic Incidence of the Civil War in the South." *Mississippi Valley Historical Review* 14 (September 1927).

Temin, Peter. "The Post-Bellum Recovery of the South and the Cost of the Civil War." *Journal of Economic History* 36 (1976): 898–907.

Vedder, Richard, Lowell Gallaway, Philip E. Graves, and Robert L. Sexton. "Demonstrating Their Freedom: The Post-Emancipation Migration of Black Americans." *Research in Economic History* 10 (1986): 213–239.

Walton, Gary M., and James F. Shepherd. *Market Institutions and Economic Progress in the New South, 1865–1900.* New York: Academic Press, 1981.

Wright, Gavin. *Old South, New South: Revolutions in the Southern Economy.* New York: Basic Books, 1986.

_____. *The Political Economy of the Cotton South.* New York: W. W. Norton, 1978.

Wright, Gavin, and Howard Kunreuther. "Cotton, Corn, and Risk in the Nineteenth Century." *Journal of Economic History* 35 (1975): 526–551.

CHAPTER FIFTEEN

WESTERN AGRICULTURE'S ADVANCE

CHAPTER THEME During the 25 years following the Civil War, the American frontier moved steadily west. So dense was settlement by 1890 that the frontier had virtually disappeared. Spearheading the drive into the western territories were miners and cowboys. The miners were drawn by discoveries such as the famed Comstock Lode of silver in Nevada and the gold in the Black Hills of South Dakota. Though remembered in legend as hard-drinking tellers of tall tales, the miners were first of all businessmen who were able to evolve precise sets of efficient property rights from their crude mining camp rules.[1]

The cowboys came in vast numbers to spur cattle on the drives to market. Long cattle drives from Texas began in 1866, and by the 1880s cattle baronies of great wealth occupied the territories from Texas to Montana. The cattle drives were destined for the nearest railheads: in the earliest years Sedalia, Missouri, but later Abilene (the destination of the famous Chisholm Trail) and then Dodge City, Kansas (for transport to Chicago). The rise and decline of the great long-distance cattle drives is fascinating history and superb folklore.[2] The long drives ended abruptly in 1885, not because of the advent of barbed wire (as popularly believed) but because of overstocking of the northern ranges and the passage and enforcement of quarantine laws to keep out the distant Texas herds.[3]

However important miners and cattlemen were as path-breakers, the abiding economic pattern of the West was set by the families who settled down to farm. This chapter tells their economic history: how they got title to their land, what they grew and how they grew it, what prices they were paid for their products, and why many farmers became disillusioned with the economic system and demanded help from state governments, and ultimately from Washington.

---

[1] See Gary D. Libecap, "Economic Variables and the Development of the Law: The Case of Western Mineral Rights," *Journal of Economic History* 38 (1978): 338–362.

[2] The movie classic *Red River* starring John Wayne and Montgomery Clift and the 1989 CBS TV special "Lonesome Dove" are recommended. Also see Lewis Atherton, *The Cattle Kings* (Bloomington: Indiana University Press, 1961). Although the scions of wealthy eastern families like Richard Trimble and Teddy Roosevelt could not resist the West, the men who started from scratch and became fabulously successful were for the most part country boys from the Midwest and South or cowboys only a few years away from the hard-drinking, roistering life of Newton or Dodge City.

[3] For an in-depth account of the reasons long drives were abruptly ended in 1885, see David Galenson, "The End of the Chisholm Trail," *Journal of Economic History* 24:2 (June 1974): 350–364.

THE EXPANSION OF LAND UNDER CULTIVATION

Most of the participants in the final opening of new land came from places that only a few years before had been the object of settlement. People who moved into Kansas, Nebraska, the Dakotas, and later Montana and Colorado more often than not traveled only short distances to get there. Some had settled previously in Missouri or Iowa, Minnesota or Wisconsin, Indiana or Illinois; others were sons and daughters of the pioneers of a previous generation. It was not uncommon for settlers to move from place to place within one of the new states. No matter how bitter previous pioneer experiences or how monotonous and unrewarding the life on virgin land, the hope persisted of better times if only new soil could be broken farther west.

Table 15-1 shows the total number of farms and farm acres by decade from 1860 to 1920. The decades of sharpest advance were the 1870s and 1890s. The addition of land input in these decades was extraordinary: total land under cultivation more than doubled between 1870 and 1900.[4] This was made possible by a policy of rapidly transferring ownership of land to farmers and other users—by rapidly "privatizing" ownership of the land, to use the modern jargon.

FEDERAL LAND POLICY

During the Civil War, the absence of southern Democrats allowed the Republican Congress to pass the Homestead Act of 1862. Recall from Chapter 8 that this act, which provided 160 acres per homestead (320 per married couple), continued the liberalization of the federal government's land policy. At the time of the act, prime fertile lands remained unclaimed in western Iowa and western Minnesota and in the eastern parts of Kansas, Nebraska, and the Dakotas; these were soon taken, however, leaving little except the unclaimed lands west of the hundredth meridian in the Great Plains (an area of light annual rainfall) or in the vast mountain regions. Consequently, in most of the plains and mountain regions, a 160-acre homestead was impractical. The land, being suitable only for grazing livestock, required much larger farms. Between 1870 and 1900, less than one acre in five added to farming belonged to homesteads.

Mining and timber interests also pressed Congress to liberalize land policy, winning four more land acts:

1. *The Timber-Culture Act of 1873.* Passed ostensibly to encourage the growth of timber in arid regions, this law made available 160 acres of free land to anyone who would agree to plant trees on 40 acres of it.

2. *The Desert Land Act of 1877.* By the terms of this law, 640 acres at $1.25 an acre could be purchased by anyone who would agree to irrigate the land within three years. One serious defect of this act was its lack of a clear definition of irrigation.

---

[4]During the 1860s the number of farms increased sharply and total acreage not at all. As discussed in Chapter 14, the 1860s were unusual because of the breakup of southern plantations.

TABLE 15-1   TOTAL NUMBER OF FARMS AND ACRES BY DECADE, 1860–1920

Year	Number of Farms (in hundred thousands)	Percent Increase	Number of Acres (in hundred thousands)	Percent Increase
1860	2.0		407	
		35%		0%
1870	2.7		408	
		48		31
1880	4.0		536	
		15		16
1890	4.6		623	
		24		35
1900	5.7		839	
		11		5
1910	6.4		879	
		2		9
1920	6.5		956	

SOURCE: *Historical Statistics* (Washington, D.C.: Government Printing Office, 1975), Series K4 and J51.

3. *The Timber and Stone Act of 1878.* This statute provided for the sale at $2.50 an acre of valuable timber and stone lands in Nevada, California, Oregon, and Washington.

4. *The Timber-Cutting Act of 1878.* This law authorized residents of certain specified areas to cut trees on government lands without charge, with the stipulation that the timber be used for agricultural, mining, and domestic building purposes.

The transfer of public lands into private hands also included purchases at public auctions under the Preemption Act. This act, as noted in Chapter 8, encouraged "squatting" by allowing first rights of sale to settlers who arrived and worked the land before public sales were offered.[5] Furthermore, huge acreages granted by the government as subsidies to western railroads and to states for various purposes were in turn sold to settlers. Nearly 100 million acres from the Indian territories were opened for purchase by the Dawes Act of 1887 and subsequent measures.

During the first administration of Grover Cleveland, steps were taken to tighten up on the disposition of public lands, but Congress did not pass any major legislation for several years. Then, in the General Revision Act of 1891, critical loopholes were closed. The Preemption Act was repealed, and provisions defining irrigation were added to the Desert Land Act of 1877. The Timber-Cutting Act of 1878 was repealed, removing from the books one of the most flagrantly abused of all the land laws. Finally, the President was authorized to set aside forest preserves—a first milestone in the conservation movement, which had been gaining popular support.

After the turn of the century, the Homestead Act itself was modified to enable settlers to obtain practical-sized farms. Beginning in 1904, a whole section (one square mile or 640 acres) could be homesteaded in western Nebraska. A few years later, the Enlarged Homestead Act made it possible to obtain a half section in many areas free

[5] As late as 1891, an individual could buy a maximum of 1,120 acres at one time under the public land acts. Unlimited amounts of land could be purchased from railroad companies and from states at higher, although still nominal, prices.

of charge. Still later, residence requirements were reduced to three years, and the Stock-Raising Homestead Act of 1916 allowed the homesteading of 640 acres of land suitable only for grazing purposes. Whereas only one acre in five added to farming before 1900 came from homesteading, the ratio jumped to nine in ten between 1900 and 1920.

THE DISTRIBUTION OF FEDERAL LANDS

From the findings of a commission that reported to President Theodore Roosevelt on the pre-1904 disposition of public lands, we may see how the land had been distributed. The total public domain in the United States from 1789 to 1904 contained 1,441 million acres. Of this total, 278 million acres were acquired by individuals through cash purchase. Another 273 million acres were granted to states and railroads, about which more will be said in Chapter 16. Lands acquired by or available to individuals free of charge (mostly via the Homestead Act) amounted to 147 million acres. The rest of the public domain, aside from miscellaneous grants, was either reserved for the government (209 million acres) or unappropriated (474 million acres). Between 1862 and 1904, acres homesteaded exceeded cash sales by the government to individuals. If, however, we count purchases from railroads and states, ultimate holders of land bought twice as much between 1862 and 1904 as they obtained free through homesteading.

After 1904, U.S. land policy became less generous, but by that time nearly all the choice agricultural land, most of the first-rate mineral land, and much of the timber land located close to markets had been distributed. Between 1904 and 1920, more than 100 million new acres of land were homesteaded in the dry and mountainous country, more than 90 percent of total new acres added. During this same short period, the government reserved about 175 million acres. Of the original public domain, 200 million acres of land that remained to be disposed of were "vacant" in 1920.[6]

THE IMPACT OF FEDERAL LAND POLICY

The principal goals of federal land policy—namely government revenues, wide accessibility (or fairness), and rapid economic growth—varied in importance over time, with the latter two gaining in importance. Clearly, the most outstanding feature of American land policy was the rapidity with which valuable agricultural, mineral, and timber lands were transferred into private hands. In addition, the goal of making land widely accessible was largely achieved, especially in the second half of the nineteenth century. But by no means was the process, or the result, egalitarian. As we just emphasized, large tracts of lands went to corporations and wealthy individuals. Special interests were favored, and for a time the granting of land to railroads was considered normal public policy. In addition, large grants to the states were rationalized as growth enhancing, either to support transportation ventures or for educational purposes (the land-grant universities).

---

[6] Homestead entries were substantial in the 1920s and 1930s but fell to practically zero by midcentury. Some homesteading continues today in Alaska.

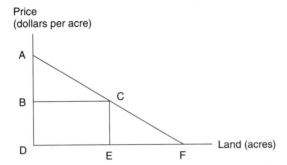

What price for federal land would have maximized real GNP? Surprisingly the answer, in many areas, would have been zero. The figure above shows why. The vertical axis shows the price of land and the horizontal axis the quantity, arranged from high quality to low. The curve ACF is the demand for farmland in a region of new settlement. All the land is initially owned by the federal government. The government might set a relatively high price for federal land, BD, to maximize the government's revenues (BCED). This might seem the best policy because the revenues could then be redistributed fairly to the people—assuming, of course, that special interests did not get there first. But setting a price of BD reduces the land in production from a maximum of DF to DE. How do we measure the loss associated with keeping EF out of production? The distance between a point on the horizontal axis and the demand curve tells us the maximum that some farmer will pay for a piece of land, presumably because the farmer's resources would produce this much wealth in alternative uses. Therefore the triangular area CEF measures the value of the future incomes that are lost if the price for the land is set at BD and EF is kept out of production. Setting the price at zero will eliminate the welfare loss triangle.

Concerns about fairness, about the rationality of farmers, or about the effect on the environment may lead one to reject the real-income-maximizing policy. But one should at least recognize the powerful economic argument that the right policy was the one followed: getting federal land rapidly into the hands of those who could use it productively.

Frequently, good land was obtained fraudulently by mining and lumber companies or by speculators. Aided by the lax administration of the land laws, large operators could persuade individuals to make a homesteading entry or a purchase at a minimum price and then transfer the title. With the connivance of bribed land officials, entries were occasionally made for people who did not even exist. As Gary Libecap and Ronald Johnson have shown convincingly, fraud ultimately served a positive economic purpose: it helped transfer resources to large companies that could take advantage of economies of scale. Resource laws that recognized economic realities and permitted sales of large acreages directly to final users would have reduced fraud and corruption.[7]

For most of the twentieth century, the consensus among American historians has been that federal land policy was economically inefficient and reduced total output. Because people of all sorts and circumstances settled on the land, there was a high rate of failure among the least competent—settlers who eventually lost their holdings and became either poor tenants or low-paid farmworkers. More importantly, it is alleged that the rapid distribution of the public domain laid the groundwork for modern agricultural problems by inducing too much capital and labor into agriculture, thereby impeding the process of industrialization.

There can be little doubt that specific errors were made and inefficiencies were imposed. And, yet, it is difficult to make the case that federal policies were generally inefficient. Partially as a result of this rapid addition of resources, the new West produced crops at such a rate that consumers of foodstuffs and raw materials enjoyed 30 years of falling prices. Furthermore, according to Robert Fogel and Jack Rutner, average rates of return on investments in land improvements, livestock, farm buildings, and machinery equaled or exceeded returns on other contemporary investments, and real incomes in the *new* agricultural areas outside the South grew at rates comparable to those in manufacturing.[8] There were, as we shall see, numerous instances of hard times in rural America, and political unrest characterized certain sections of the Midwest and the Plains in the late nineteenth century, but these should not be permitted to dominate our judgment of federal land policy.[9]

GROWTH AND CHANGE IN AGRICULTURE

NEW AREAS OF CULTIVATION

As various areas became settled, they tended to specialize in certain crops. These areas of geographic specialization are depicted for the principal crops in Map 15-1. The wheat and corn belt continued its western advance over the century, with spring wheat

---

[7] Gary D. Libecap and Ronald N. Johnson, "Property Rights, Nineteenth-Century Federal Timber Policy, and the Conservation Movement," *Journal of Economic History* 39 (1979): 129–142.

[8] For the evidence and more discussion of these issues, see Robert Fogel and Jack Rutner, "Efficiency Effects of Federal Land Policy, 1850–1900," in *Dimensions of Quantitative Research in Economic History*, eds. William Aydelotte et al. (Princeton: Princeton University Press, 1972); and Susan Previant Lee and Peter Passell, *A New Economic View of American History* (New York: W. W. Norton, 1979), pp. 318–322.

[9] For an assessment of the politics of federal land policy see Paul Gates, "An Overview of American Land Policy," in *Two Centuries of American Agriculture*, ed. Vivian Wiser (Washington, D.C.: Agricultural History Society, 1976), pp. 213–229.

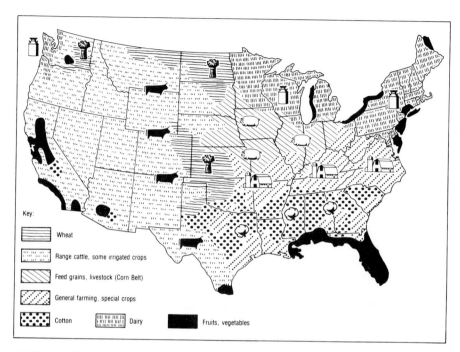

Key:

	Wheat
	Range cattle, some irrigated crops
	Feed grains, livestock (Corn Belt)
	General farming, special crops
	Cotton
	Dairy
	Fruits, vegetables

MAP 15-1 GEOGRAPHIC AREAS OF SPECIALIZATION IN MAJOR CASH CROPS IN THE LATE NINETEENTH CENTURY: *It should be noted that the boundaries between sections did change and that many crops were and still are grown within various belts.*

leading in western Minnesota and the Dakotas and winter varieties dominating the southern Midwest and Nebraska, Kansas, and Oklahoma.[10]

Though tobacco remained tied to the old South, cotton production leapfrogged the Mississippi River. By 1900, Texas was the leading cotton producer as well as a major source of cattle. Farmers around the Great Lakes found it profitable to turn from cereals to dairy farming, following a path traveled previously by farmers in New England. In California, Florida, and other warm climate areas, fruits, vegetables, and specialty crops became important—especially after the refrigerated railcar, introduced in the 1880s, created a national market.

In an era preceding chemical and biological improvements, output advances were approximately proportional to acres added. Table 15-2 on the next page shows the growth of corn and wheat outputs and acreage harvested in each crop between 1870 and 1910. The evidence shows very little, if any, growth in land productivity as measured in bushels per acre. Nonetheless, labor productivity grew dramatically in wheat and corn over these decades. According to Robert Gallman, labor productivity in these two crops grew at a rate of 2.6 percent annually between 1850 and 1900.[11] In the first

---

[10] Winter wheat is sown in the fall and harvested in late spring or early summer, depending on the latitude. Where the climate is too cold, spring wheat is grown. Modern varieties of winter wheat are hardy enough to be grown in the southern half of South Dakota at least as far north as Pierre.

[11] Derived from Robert E. Gallman, "The Pace of Economic Growth: U.S. Experience in the Nineteenth Century," in *Essays in Nineteenth Century History,* eds. David C. Klingaman and Richard K. Vedder (Athens: Ohio University Press, 1975).

TABLE 15-2   CEREALS OUTPUT AND LAND INPUT, 1870–1910

Year	Corn[a]	Land in Corn[b]	Bushels of Corn per Acre	Wheat	Land in Wheat	Bushels of Wheat per Acre
1870	1,125	38.4	29.3	254	20.9	12.1
1890	1,650	74.8	22.1	449	36.7	12.2
1910	2,853	102.3	27.9	625	45.8	13.7

SOURCE: *HISTORICAL STATISTICS* (WASHINGTON, D.C.: GOVERNMENT PRINTING OFFICE, 1975), SERIES K502, K503, K506, K507.

[a] In millions of bushels.
[b] In millions of acres harvested.

half of the nineteenth century, the comparable figure was 0.4 percent. Further evidence of output growth relative to inputs is shown in Figure 15-1, which measures total agricultural output relative to all inputs (land, labor, and capital), weighted respectively by output and input prices. Figure 15-1 clearly shows the "miracles" of the scientific chemical and biological advances that came in the 1920s and after. It also reveals the effects of mechanization that had such important influences, as Gallman's nineteenth-century findings reveal.

In 1848 Cyrus Hall McCormick boldly moved his main implement plant to Chicago, thereby assuring a steady supply of his harvesting machines to the Midwest. The day of the hand scythe and the one-horse plow had passed, as this editorial from an 1857 *Scientific American* suggests:

> Every farmer who has a hundred acres of land should have at least the following: a combined reaper and mower, a horse rake, a seed planter, and mower . . . a thresher and grain cleaner, a portable grist mill, a corn-sheller, a horse power, three harrows, a roller, two cultivators, and three plows.[12]

Increased amounts of capital per worker, along with new technologies embodied in the capital equipment, raised labor's productivity. Even though yields per acre changed little, mechanization allowed farmers to add more acres to their farms, thus expanding output per farm. Mechanized farming, however, did not replace traditional farming instantaneously. Paul David's analysis of the mechanical reaper shows that in 1850 a minimum of 46 acres in grain was needed on a farm to profitably employ a reaper.[13] This was well over the typical acreage per farm in most of the Midwest at that time.[14]

---

[12] Quoted in C. Danhof, "Agriculture," in *The Growth of the American Economy*, ed. H. T. Williamson (New York: Prentice-Hall, 1951), p. 150.

[13] Paul David, "The Mechanization of Reaping in the Antebellum Midwest," in *Technical Choice, Innovation and Economic Growth, Essays on American and British Experience in the Nineteenth Century* (Cambridge: Cambridge University Press, 1945). For an important study showing the dominance of supply-side effects on the relative price of harvesting equipment during this period, see Alan L. Olmstead, "The Civil War Was a Catalyst of Technological Change in Agriculture," in *Business and Economics History*, ed. Paul Uselding, 2d series, vol. 5 (New York: Johnson, 1976), pp. 36–50.

[14] Farmers could hire the services of a reaper, or could buy one with a neighbor, but both solutions to the minimum farm size problem involved potentially high transaction costs.

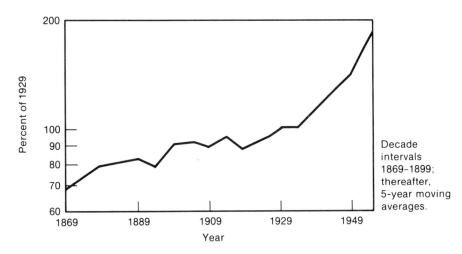

FIGURE 15-1 TOTAL FACTOR PRODUCTIVITY IN AGRICULTURE, 1869–1955

SOURCE: JOHN W. KENDRICK, *PRODUCTIVITY TRENDS IN THE UNITED STATES* (PRINCETON: PRINCETON UNIVERSITY PRESS, 1961), PP. 362–364.

Many inventors tried to market reapers, but McCormick's was the best. The courts didn't always see it that way, but McCormick made a fortune nonetheless.

After the Civil War, wages paid to grain cradlers (hand harvesters) increased and acres per farm devoted to grains increased, hastening the introduction of mechanical reapers.

By 1857, John Deere's new plant in Moline, Illinois, was annually producing 10,000 steel plows, eclipsing the iron plow, which had proved ineffectual in the tough clay-sod of the prairies. Seed drills, cultivators, mowers, rakes and threshing machines, and myriad attachments and gadgets for harvesting machines added to the mechanization of farming in the second half of the century. Between 1860 and 1920, the numbers of mouths fed per farmer nearly doubled, freeing labor for industry, but not without economic dislocations and personal hardships.

HARD TIMES ON THE FARM, 1864–1896

The years from the close of the Civil War to the end of World War I comprise two contrasting periods in agricultural history. The first of these, from 1864 to 1896, was characterized by agricultural hardship and political unrest; the second, from 1896 until about 1920, represented a sustained period of improvement in the lot of the farm population. This improvement is reflected quantitatively in Table 15-3, which traces average annual percentage growth rates in real farm income over the last half of the nineteenth century. Note that real incomes did rise during the first period, but the rate of increase

High horsepower was possible before the advent of steam and gasoline-powered tractors.

TABLE 15-3 TRENDS IN FARM INCOME AND PRODUCTIVITY (AVERAGE ANNUAL PERCENTAGE CHANGE)

Years	Real Income per Capita	Real Income per Worker
1849–1859	2.0%	2.0%
1859–1869	0.8	0.9
1869–1879	0.8	0.3
1879–1889	0.7	0
1889–1899	2.2	2.1
1849–1899	1.3	1.0
1869–1899	1.2	0.7

SOURCE: ROBERT FOGEL AND JACK RUTNER, "EFFICIENCY EFFECTS OF FEDERAL LAND POLICY, 1850–1900," IN *THE DIMENSIONS OF QUANTITATIVE RESEARCH IN HISTORY,* EDS. W. O. AYDELOTTE, A. G. BOGUE, AND R. W. FOGEL, COPYRIGHT © 1972 BY THE CENTER FOR ADVANCED STUDY IN THE BEHAVIORAL SCIENCES. TABLE 2, P. 396, ADAPTED BY PERMISSION OF PRINCETON UNIVERSITY PRESS.

seemed painfully slow, and the averages obscure the hardships suffered by many western farmers: "In God we trusted, in Kansas we busted."

American farmers, from the middle 1860s to the middle 1890s, knew that their life was hard without being shown data to prove it. Conditions were especially hard on the frontier, where the combination of dreary surroundings and physical hardship compounded the difficulties of economic life, which included declining prices, indebtedness, and the necessity of purchasing many goods and services from industries in which there appeared to be a growing concentration of economic power.

All prices were falling between 1875 and 1895, but as Table 15-4 shows, the price of farm products was falling *relative* to other prices. To put it slightly differently, the farmer's terms of trade—the price of the things the farmer sold divided by the price of things the farmer bought—were worsening. This did not mean that real farm income was falling (recall that Table 15-3 shows that it was rising), because the terms

TABLE 15-4 THE FARMER'S TERMS OF TRADE, 1870–1915

Year	Wholesale Farm Prices	Consumer Prices	Terms of Trade
1870	100	100	100
1875	88	87	102
1880	71	76	94
1885	64	71	90
1890	63	71	89
1895	55	66	84
1900	64	66	97
1905	71	71	100
1910	93	74	127
1915	90	80	112

SOURCE: *HISTORICAL STATISTICS* (WASHINGTON, D.C.: GOVERNMENT PRINTING OFFICE, 1975), SERIES E42, E53, E135.

of trade (as defined here) do not take productivity into account.[15] But it does mean that the farmer had to run faster just to avoid losing ground. By 1895, to take the low point in Table 15-4, the farmer had to produce about 16 percent more just to offset the fall in his terms of trade.

Why were the farmer's terms of trade worsening? Part of the explanation is the rapid increase in the supply of agricultural products. All over the world, new areas were entering the competitive fray. In Canada, Australia, New Zealand, and Argentina as well as the United States, fertile new lands were becoming agriculturally productive. In the United States alone (as we saw in Table 15-1 on page 325), the number of acres in farming more than doubled between 1870 and 1900. Reinforcing this trend was the increased output made possible by mechanization.

There were notable changes, too, on the demand side. One favorable influence on the domestic demand was the continued rapid increase in the population. After 1870, the rate of population growth in the United States fell, but until 1900 it was still high. In the decades of the 1870s and 1880s the increase was just over 25 percent, and in the 1890s it was more than 20 percent—a substantial growth in the number of mouths to feed. But there was an offsetting factor: In 1870, Americans spent one-third of their current per capita incomes on farm products. By 1890, they were spending a much smaller fraction, just over one-fifth, and in the next few years this proportion dropped a little more. Thus, although both the money and real incomes of the American population rose during the period, and although Americans did not spend less on food absolutely, the proportion of those incomes earned by farmers declined. (In other words, as incomes increased the amounts spent on food increased, but by a smaller percentage than the income increased. In technical terms, the *income elasticity* of demand was less than 1 for most agricultural crops.)

Offsetting these effects in part was the rise in the demand abroad for U.S. crops after the Civil War. Export demand for farm products increased steadily until the turn of the century. Wheat and flour exports reached their peak in 1901, at which time nearly one-third of domestic wheat production was sold abroad. Likewise, meat and meat products were exported in larger and larger quantities until 1900, when these exports also began to decline. Overall, the value of agricultural exports rose from $297 million in 1870 to more than $840 million in 1900. Exports of farm products during these decades helped expand agricultural markets, but they were far from sufficient to alleviate the hard times on the farm.

Farmers were not inclined to see their difficulties as the result of impersonal market forces. Instead, they traced their problems to monopolies and conspiracies: bankers (some thought that Jewish bankers were particularly to blame) who raised interest rates and manipulated the currency and then foreclosed on farm mortgages, grain elevator operators who charged rates farmers could not afford, industrialists who charged high prices for farm machinery and consumer goods, railroads who charged monopoly rates on freight, and so on.

---

[15] For alternative definitions and more data see John D. Bowman and Richard H. Keehn, "Agricultural Terms of Trade in Four Midwestern States, 1870–1900," *Journal of Economic History* 34 (1974): 592–609.

The slow growth of demand for farm products reflected the slope of the Engel curve, named for nineteenth-century Prussian statistician Ernst Engel. Engel curves are usually based on samples of family budgets and show average expenditures on food (or other goods and services) at each level of income. Economic growth lifts the average family to higher income levels, but expenditures on food rise less rapidly, and the share spent on food falls. The farmer could retain his share of total spending only if the slope of the Engel curve for farm products was equal to the slope of the line bisecting the figure.

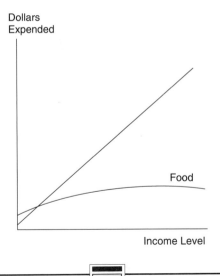

The evidence on these alleged sources of distress is largely unsupportive, suggesting that farmers were responding to symptoms rather than causes. Figure 15-2 on the next page shows that the prices of industrial items in the West fell relative to the prices of farm products; Figure 15-3 shows that freight costs also fell as a percentage of farm prices. This does not mean, of course, that every complaint of every farmer was baseless. Although long-haul railroad rates fell dramatically relative to agricultural prices over the period, for example, certain monopolized sections of railroad permitted discriminatory monopoly pricing on short hauls.[16]

---

[16] For more on this, see Robert Higgs, "Railroad Rates and the Populist Uprising," *Agricultural History* 44 (July 1970).

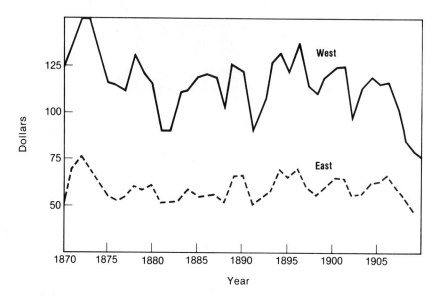

FIGURE 15-2 PRICE OF INDUSTRIAL GOODS IN TERMS OF FARM PRODUCTS, WEST AND EAST, 1870–1910

SOURCE: DERIVED FROM JEFFREY G. WILLIAMSON, *LATE NINETEENTH CENTURY AMERICAN DEVELOPMENT, A GENERAL EQUILIBRIUM HISTORY* (CAMBRIDGE: CAMBRIDGE UNIVERSITY PRESS, 1974), P. 149.

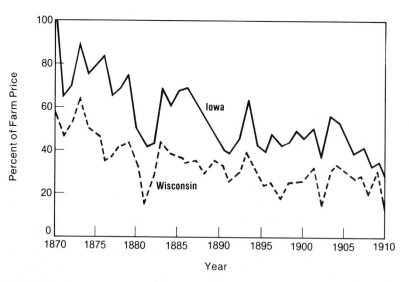

FIGURE 15-3 FREIGHT ON WHEAT FROM IOWA AND WISCONSIN IN NEW YORK AS PERCENTAGE OF FARM PRICE, 1870–1910

SOURCE: DERIVED FROM JEFFREY G. WILLIAMSON, *LATE NINETEENTH CENTURY AMERICAN DEVELOPMENT, A GENERAL EQUILIBRIUM HISTORY* (CAMBRIDGE: CAMBRIDGE UNIVERSITY PRESS, 1974), P. 261.

Populism thus emerged from 30 years of unrest—an unrest that was chiefly agricultural but had urban connections. To its supporters, populism was something more than an agitation for economic betterment: it was a faith. The overtones of political and social reform were part of the faith because they would help to further economic aims. The agitation against monopoly control—against oppression by corporations, banks, and capitalists—had come to a head. Along with the key principle of anti-monopolism ran a strongly collectivist doctrine. Populists felt that only through government control of the monetary system and through government ownership of banks, railroads, and the means of communication could the evils of monopoly be put down. In fact, operation of government-owned firms in basic industries was advocated by some populists, so that the government would have the information to determine whether or not monopolistic prices were being charged. The government-owned firm would, in other words, provide a "yardstick" to measure the performance of private firms.

In older parts of the country, the radicalism of the People's Party alienated established farmers. Had the leaders of the 1896 coalition of populists and Democrats not chosen to stand or fall on the issue of inflation, there is no telling what the future of the coalition might have been. But inflation was anathema to property owners with little or no debt, and when the chips were down, rural as well as urban property owners supported "sound" money.

THE BEGINNINGS OF FEDERAL ASSISTANCE TO AGRICULTURE

Although attempts by farmers to improve their condition through organization were unsuccessful as far as immediate goals were concerned, the way had been opened for legislation and federal assistance. Of course, the land acts of the nineteenth century had worked to the advantage of new farmers, but they can scarcely be considered part of an agricultural "program." Similarly, much regulatory legislation passed in the late nineteenth and early twentieth centuries, although originating in agrarian organizations, produced effects that were not restricted to agriculture. Federal assistance to agriculture before World War I was designed to compile and disseminate information in order to help the individual farmer to increase productivity; it was not designed to alleviate distress, as was later New Deal legislation.

THE DEPARTMENT OF AGRICULTURE

As early as 1839, an Agricultural Division had been set up in the Patent Office. Congress created a Department of Agriculture in 1862, but its head, who was designated the Commissioner of Agriculture, did not have Cabinet ranking until 1889.

Until 1920, the Department of Agriculture performed three principal functions. These were (1) research and experimentation in plant exploration, plant and animal breeding, and insect and disease control; (2) distribution of agricultural information through publications, agricultural experiment stations, and county demonstration work; and (3) regulation of the quality of products through the authority to condemn diseased animals, to prohibit shipment in interstate commerce of adulterated or mis-branded foods and drugs, and to inspect and certify meats and dairy products in inter-state trade. There was always pressure on the department to give "practical" help to the farmers, as evidenced by the fact that throughout this period it regularly distributed free seeds. In retrospect it seems that the chief contribution of the Department of Agriculture in these early years lay in its ability to convince farmers of the value of "scientific" farming.

AGRICULTURAL EDUCATION

Attempts to incorporate the teaching of agricultural subjects into the educational system began locally, but federal assistance was necessary to maintain adequate programs. Although colleges of agriculture had been established in several states by 1860, it was the Morrill Act of 1862 that gave impetus to agricultural training at the university level. The Morrill Act established "land-grant" colleges that gradually assumed statewide leadership in agricultural research. The Hatch Act of 1887 provided federal assistance to state agricultural experiment stations, many of which had already been established with state funds. The Hatch Act also provided for the establishment of an Office of Experiment Stations in the Department of Agriculture in order to link the work of the department with that of the states. After 1900, interest in secondary schools began to develop. The Smith-Hughes Vocational Education Act of 1917 provided funds to states that agreed to expand vocational training at the high-school level in agriculture, trades, and home economics.

These and other measures advanced by reformers nurtured the beginnings of federal involvement in the agricultural sector. As we shall see, such involvement would grow dramatically in the decades after 1920. Similarly, calls to "end the waste" of natural resources advanced the role of government in the control and use of land, timber, and other natural resources.

NATURAL RESOURCE CONSERVATION: THE FIRST STAGES

The waste of natural resources in North America as perceived by Europeans, contemporaries, and others dates as far back as colonial times. For instance, many colonial dirt farmers ignored "advanced" European farming methods designed to maintain soil fertility, preferring to fell trees and plant around stumps and then move on if the land wore out. Because land was abundant, their concern was not with soil conservation, but rather with the shortage of labor and capital.

Similarly, in the early nineteenth century lumber was in great abundance, especially in the eastern half of the nation where five-sixths of the original forests were located. Indeed, in most areas of new settlement, standing timber was often an impediment rather than a valued resource. As late as 1850, more than 90 percent of all fuel-based energy came from wood.

By 1915, however, wood supplied less than 10 percent of all fuel-based energy in the United States, and in the Great Plains and in other western regions timber grew increasingly scarce.[24] The western advance of the railroad (which devoured nearly one-quarter of the timber cut in the 1870s) and the western shift of the population brought new pressures on limited western and distant eastern timber supplies. Moreover, the price of uncut marketable timber on public lands was zero for all practical purposes. This fact and the lack of clear legal rights to timber on public lands provided incentive to cut as fast as possible on public lands. As a result, much waste occurred and various environmental hazards were made more extreme. These included the loss of watersheds, which increased the hazard of floods and hastened soil erosion. More importantly, the buildup of masses of slash (tree branches and other timber deposits) created severe fire hazards. In the late nineteenth century, large cutover regions became explosive tinder boxes. For example, in 1871 "the Pishtigo fire" in Wisconsin devoured 1.28 million acres and killed more than a thousand people. Similar dramatic losses from fire occurred in 1881 in Michigan and in 1894 in Wisconsin and Minnesota. These and other factors, such as fraudulent land acquisitions, demanded legislative action and reform.[25]

LAND, WATER, AND TIMBER CONSERVATION

The first major step toward reform was the General Revision Act of 1891. As noted earlier, this law repealed measures that had been an open invitation to land fraud, making it more difficult for corporations and wealthy individuals to steal timber and minerals. Prevention of theft scarcely constitutes conservation, but one section of the 1891 act, which empowered the President to set aside forest reserves, was a genuine conservation measure. Between 1891 and 1900, 50 million acres of valuable timberland were withdrawn from private entry despite strong and growing opposition from interest groups in the western states. Inadequate appropriations made it impossible for the Division of Forestry to protect the reserves from forest fires and from depredations of timber thieves, but a start had been made.

When Theodore Roosevelt succeeded to the presidency in 1901, there was widespread concern, both in Congress and throughout the nation, over the problem of conservation. With imagination, charm, and fervor, Roosevelt sought legislation

---

[24] For an excellent account of the responsive process in the form and use of natural resources to changes in their costs and supplies, see Nathan Rosenberg, "Innovative Responses to Material Shortages," *American Economic Review* 63 (May 1973).

[25] For further detail see Alan L. Olmstead, "The Costs of Economic Growth," in *The Encyclopedia of American Economic History* (New York: Scribner's 1980), vol. 2, pp. 863–881; and Marion Clawson, "Forests in the Long Sweep of American History," *Science* 204 (June 15, 1979).

during both his terms to provide a consistent and far-reaching conservation program. By 1907, he could point to several major achievements:

1. National forests comprised 150 million acres, of which 75 million acres contained marketable timber. In 1901 a Bureau of Forestry was created, which became the United States Forest Service in 1905. Under Gifford Pinchot, Roosevelt's able chief adviser in all matters pertaining to conservation, a program of scientific forestry was initiated. The national forests were to be more than just preserves; the "crop" of trees was to be continually harvested and sold such that ever-larger future crops were assured.

2. Lands containing 75 million acres of mineral wealth were reserved from sale and settlement. Most of the lands containing metals were already privately owned, but the government retained large deposits of coal, phosphates, and oil.

3. There was explicit recognition of the future importance of waterpower sites. A policy was established of leasing government-owned sites to private firms for a stipulated period of years, while actual ownership was reserved for the government.

4. The principle was accepted that it was a proper function of the federal government to implement a program of public works for the purpose of controlling stream flows. Specifically, storage dams and irrigation works were to be constructed for the benefit of western settlers. The Reclamation Act of 1902 provided for the use of receipts from land sales in the arid states to finance the construction of reservoirs and irrigation works, with repayment to be made by settlers over a period of years. In this way, the idea of "reclamation" entered into the broader concept of conservation.

To students in the 1990s concerned with the environment, such achievements seem modest enough. But in the first decade of the twentieth century, many people bitterly opposed any interference with the private exploitation of the remaining public domain. Much of the growth of government expenditures in water control, dams, and irrigation systems awaited a second Roosevelt in the 1930s. But the precedents set by Theodore Roosevelt's administration set the stage for the engineering marvels of the present era, which freed western agriculture from the shackles of dry-land farming of basic grains and livestock feeding—at considerable cost to the taxpayer. They also set a new direction, however haltingly, toward more prudent conservation of natural space, minerals, forests, and water.

SELECTED REFERENCES
AND SUGGESTED READINGS

Arrington, Leonard. *Great Basin Kingdom.* Cambridge: Harvard University Press, 1958.
Atack, Jeremy. "Tenants and Yeomen in the Nineteenth Century." *Agricultural History* 62, no. 3 (Summer 1988): 6–32.
Bateman, Fred. "Improvements in American Dairy Farming, 1850–1910: A Quantitative Analysis." *Journal of Economic History* 23 (1968): 255–273.

Bogue, Allan. *From Prairie to Cornbelt: Farming on the Illinois and Iowa Prairies in the Nineteenth Century.* Chicago: University of Chicago Press, 1963.

Bowman, John D. "An Economic Analysis of Midwestern Farm Land Values and Farmland Income, 1890 to 1900." *Yale Economic Essays,* Fall 1965.

Bowman, John D., and Richard H. Keehn. "Agricultural Terms of Trade in Four Midwestern States, 1870–1900." *Journal of Economic History* 34 (1974): 592–609.

Carstensen, Vernon. *Farmer Discontent, 1865–1900.* (New York: Wiley, 1974).

Coelho, Philip, and James Shepherd. "Differences in Regional Prices: The United States, 1851–1880." *Journal of Economic History* 34 (1974): 551–591.

David, Paul. "The Agricultural Sector and the Pace of Economic Growth: U.S. Experience in the Nineteenth Century." In *Essays in Nineteenth Century Economic History,* eds. David Klingaman and Richard Vedder.

———. "The Mechanization of Reaping in the Antebellum Midwest." In *Technical Choice, Innovation and Economic Growth, Essays on American and British Experience in the Nineteenth Century* (Cambridge: Cambridge University Press, 1975).

Eichengreen, Barry. "Mortgage Interest Rates in the Populist Era." *American Economic Review* 74 (December 1984): 995–1015.

Galenson, David. "The End of the Chisholm Trail." *Journal of Economic History* 24 (1974): 350–364.

Gallman, Robert E. "Changes in Total U.S. Agricultural Factor Productivity in the Nineteenth Century." *Agricultural History* (January 1972).

Griliches, Zvi. "Hybrid Corn and the Economics of Innovation." *Science* 132 (July 29, 1960).

Harley, C. Knick, "Western Settlement and the Price of Wheat, 1872–1913." *Journal of Economic History* 38 (1978): 865–878.

Hays, Samuel P. *Conservation and the Gospel of Efficiency: The Progressive Conservation Movement, 1890–1920.* Cambridge: Harvard University Press, 1959.

Hicks, John D. *The Populist Revolt.* Lincoln: University of Nebraska Press, 1961.

Higgs, Robert. *The Transformation of the American Economy, 1865–1914: An Essay in Interpretation.* New York: Wiley, 1971.

Jones, Lewis. "The Mechanization of Reaping and Mowing in American Agriculture: A Comment." *Journal of Economic History* 37 (1977): 451–455.

Libecap, Gary D. "Bureaucratic Opposition to the Assignment of Property Rights: Overgrazing on the Western Range." *Journal of Economic History* 41 (1981): 151–158.

———. "Economic Variables and the Development of the Law: The Case of Western Mineral Rights." *Journal of Economic History* 38 (1978): 338–362.

———. "Property Rights in Economic History: Implications for Research." *Explorations in Economic History* 23 (1986): 227–252.

Libecap, Gary D., and Ronald N. Johnson. "Property Rights, Nineteenth-Century Federal Timber Policy, and the Conservation Movement." *Journal of Economic History* 39 (1979): 129–142.

Lindert, Peter H. "Long-Run Trends in American Farm Values." *Agricultural History* 62, no. 3 (Summer 1988): 45–85.

Mayhew, Anne. "A Reappraisal of the Causes of Farm Protest in the United States, 1870–1900." *Journal of Economic History* 32 (1972): 464–475.

McGuire, Robert A. "Economic Causes of Late Nineteenth Century Agrarian Unrest." *Journal of Economic History* 41 (1981): 835–849.

Merk, Frederick. *History of the Westward Movement.* New York: Knopf, 1978.

Olmstead, Alan. "The Mechanization of Reaping and Mowing in American Agriculture, 1833–1870." *Journal of Economic History* 35 (June 1975).

Parker, William. "Agriculture." In *American Economic Growth: An Economist's History of the United States,* eds. Lance E. Davis et al. New York: Harper & Row, 1972.

Petulla, Joseph M. *American Environmental History: The Exploitation and Conservation of Natural Resources.* San Francisco: Boyd & Fraser, 1977.

Rasmussen, Wayne D. "The Impact of Technological Change on American Agriculture, 1862–1962." *Journal of Economic History* 22 (December 1962).

Rothstein, Morton. "Farmers Movements and Organizations: Numbers, Gains, Losses." *Agricultural History* 62, no. 3 (Summer 1988): 161–181.

Shannon, Fred A. *The Farmer's Last Frontier, 1860–1897.* New York: Harper & Row, 1968.

Swierenga, Robert P. *Pioneers and Profits: Land Speculation on the Iowa Frontier.* Ames: Iowa State University Press, 1968.

Turner, Frederick Jackson. *The Frontier in American History.* New York: Holt, 1921.

Williamson, Jeffrey G. "Greasing the Wheels of Sputtering Export Engines: Midwestern Grains and American Export Growth." *Explorations in Economic History* 17 (1980): 189–217.

Winters, Donald L. "Tenancy as an Economic Institution: The Growth and Distribution of Agricultural Tenancy in Iowa, 1850–1900." *Journal of Economic History* 37 (1977): 382–408.

CHAPTER SIXTEEN

RAILROADS AND ECONOMIC CHANGE

CHAPTER THEME Few developments have captured the attention of historians and contemporary observers quite like the railroad. Fast and powerful, reaching everywhere, the railroad came to dominate the American landscape and the American imagination. Trains became the symbol of modern America, epitomizing America's economic superiority in an industrializing world.

To stipulate the many important influences of the railroad would soon generate a list of unmanageable proportions. We will constrain our attentions to four main questions:

1. Were these continent-spanning investments built ahead of demand, or were railroads followers in the settlement process?

2. How did the builders get their capital? Large land grants, both federal and state, and other means of financial assistance were given. Were these land grants needless giveaways or prudent uses of empty spaces? How important were they in the overall picture?

3. Another factor of great importance was the growth of government intervention in the economy as manifested in railroad regulation, both at the state and federal levels. Key legal interpretations paved the way for new economic controls by government. Was there a capture of the regulatory process by railroad management, or did regulation primarily benefit users?

4. Finally, what impact did the railroad have on the overall growth rate of the economy? Was it only marginally superior to other modes of transport, or was it indispensable to American prosperity? Was the pace of productivity advance that we observed for the railroad in Chapter 9 for the antebellum period sustained in the postbellum period?

These questions have been asked by every generation of economic historians since the railroads were built. As we shall see, the answers have sometimes changed as new sources of data have been exploited and as new tools of analysis have been applied.

THE TRANSCONTINENTALS[1]

The Gold Rush of 1849 yielded knowledge about the riches of the Pacific Coast and about the vast spaces that separated East from West. There were three ways to get there, all hard. Wagon trails to California and the Pacific Northwest were beset with blizzards in winter, thirst in summer, and Indian attacks in all seasons. The shorter sea route via the Isthmus of Panama could cut the six-to-eight-month trip around Cape Horn to as little as six weeks. But from Chagres, the eastern port on the isthmus, to Panama City was a five-day journey by native dugout and muleback, and at Panama City travelers might have a long wait before securing passage north. For those who could afford it, the best way to California was by clipper ship, which made the passage around the Horn in about 100 days. (The record between New York and San Francisco was 88 days, set in 1854 by the clipper *Flying Cloud*.[2]) Thus, it is hardly surprising that a safe rail connection with the Pacific Coast was eagerly sought.

From the outset, government participation was viewed as essential. It was assumed that while the profits to the nation would be enormous, the private profits to investors would be insufficient to compensate for the enormous uncertainty surrounding such a project. By 1853, Congress was convinced of the feasibility of a railroad to the West Coast and directed government engineers to survey practical routes. The engineers described five, but years passed before construction began because of rivalry for the eastern terminus of the line. From Minneapolis to New Orleans, cities along the Mississippi River vied for the position of gateway to the West, boasting of their advantages while deprecating the claims of their rivals. The outbreak of the Civil War removed the proponents of the southern routes from Congress, and in 1862 the northern Platte River route was selected because it was used by the pony express, stages, and freighter wagons.

By the Pacific Railway Act of 1862, Congress granted a charter of incorporation to the Union Pacific Railroad, which was authorized to build a line from Council Bluffs, Iowa, to the western boundary of Nevada. The Central Pacific, incorporated under the laws of California in 1861, was at the same time given authority to construct the western part of the road from Sacramento to the Nevada border. The government agreed to furnish financial assistance in two ways: Ten sections of public land (five alternate sections on each side of the right-of-way) were granted for each mile of track laid. The government agreed further to lend the companies certain sums per mile of construction; the loans were to be secured by first-mortgage bonds. Because the act of 1862 failed to attract sufficient private capital, the law was amended in 1864 to double the amount of land grants and to provide second-mortgage security of government loans, thus enabling the railroads to sell first-mortgage bonds to the public. To encourage speed of construction, the Central Pacific was permitted to build 150 miles beyond

---

[1] Astute readers will note that we sometimes use the term loosely to cover railroads that might be better designated as western railroads.

[2] This record was not broken until 1989, when a small, high-tech sailboat named *Thursday's Child* with a crew of two made the passage in 80 days.

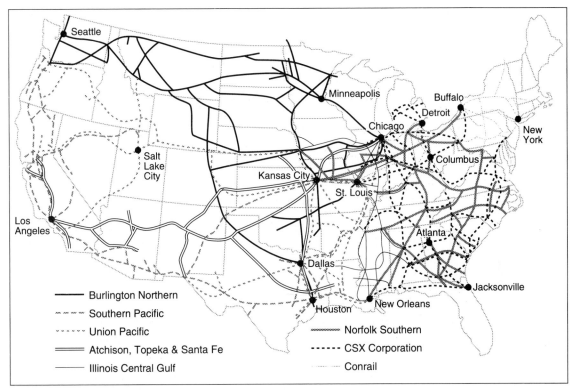

The modern railroad network of the United States reflects the great waves of railroad building that occurred in the nineteenth century.

the Nevada line; later it was authorized to push eastward until a junction was made with the Union Pacific.

The last two years of construction were marked by a storied race between the two companies to lay the most track. With permission to build eastward to a junction with the Union Pacific, the directors of the Central Pacific wished to obtain as much per-mile subsidy as possible. The Union Pacific, relying on ex-soldiers and Irish immigrants, laid 1,086 miles of track; the Central Pacific, relying on Chinese immigrants, laid 689 miles, part of it through the mountains. The joining of the Union Pacific and the Central Pacific occurred amidst great fanfare and celebration on May 10, 1869, at Promontory Summit (commonly called Promontory Point), a few miles west of Ogden, Utah. By telegraph, President Ulysses S. Grant gave the signal from Washington to drive in the last spike. The hammer blows that drove home the golden spike were echoed by telegraph to waiting throngs on both coasts. The hope was expressed that the fruits of the toil of farmer and laborer could now be transported swiftly and cheaply from coast to coast or from the interior to either coast. The continent had at last been spanned by rail; although transcontinental train travel was not without discomfort and even danger, the terrible trials of the overland and sea routes were over.

Yet the thin rails that crossed half a continent could not carry all the traffic to and from a growing West. New lines were quickly projected, but construction, although well underway, was suspended during the depression of 1873. In 1876 southern California was opened to transcontinental traffic by a line from San Francisco to Bakersfield and Los Angeles. Next, the Southern Pacific lines reached eastward from California to El Paso. The Santa Fe and the Texas and Pacific railroads soon provided connections from St. Louis and Kansas City to the Los Angeles area, and the Southern Pacific thrust on eastward from El Paso only a little later. These southern railroads provided the second of the three major transcontinental routes. The third route was the northern one from the Mississippi to the cities of Oregon and Washington. In 1883 the Northern Pacific, chartered nearly 20 years before, connected Portland with Chicago and Milwaukee; three years later it reached Seattle.

TOTAL CONSTRUCTION: PACE AND PATTERNS

As the first transcontinentals pushed toward completion, settled regions were crisscrossed with rails for through traffic. All major lines tried to secure access to New York in the east and to Chicago and St. Louis in the west. On the more northerly routes, the New York Central completed a through line from New York to Chicago by 1877, and the Erie did the same only a few years later. After the mid-1880s, the trunk lines filled the gaps, gaining access to secondary railroad centers and building feeder lines in a north-south direction.

From 1864 to 1900, the greatest percentage of track, varying from one-third to nearly one-half of the country's total annual construction, was laid in the Great Plains states. Chicago became the chief railroad terminus, the center of a web of rails extending north, west, and south. St. Louis, Kansas City, Minneapolis, Omaha, and Denver became secondary centers.

The Southeast and the Southwest lagged both in railroad construction and in the combination of local lines into through systems. Sparseness of population and war-induced poverty accounted in part for the backwardness of the Southeast, but the competition of coastal shipping was also a deterrent to railroad growth. The only southern transmountain crossing utilized before 1880 was the Chesapeake and Ohio, and, except for the Southern, no main north-south line was completed until the 1890s.

Keeping in mind that the rate of growth of the main line railroad network varied in different regions, we turn to Table 16-1, which shows the expansion of total mainline mileage nationally. One feature is unsurprising: the eventual slowing up in percentage jumps in mileage added. Nobel laureate Simon Kuznets and Arthur Burns each revealed this typical feature of rapid industry expansion followed by a tapering off in the growth rate (and speed of productivity advance) in pioneering work done a half century ago.[3] All great innovations and industry growth patterns show these features, as we observed earlier in tobacco production, in cotton, and in steamboating, to

---

[3] Simon Kuznets, "The Retardation of Industrial Growth," *Journal of Economic and Business History* (August 1929); and Arthur F. Burns, *Production Trends in the United States Since 1870* (New York: National Bureau of Economic Research, 1934), Ch. 4, "Retardation in the Growth Industries."

TABLE 16-1   MAIN LINE RAILROAD TRACK IN OPERATION (IN THOUSANDS OF MILES)

Year	Miles	Percentage changes (in five-year intervals)
1860	31	
		13
1865	35	
		63
1870	53	
		42
1875	74	
		26
1880	93	
		38
1885	128	
		30
1890	167	
		8
1895	180	
		15
1900	207	
		15
1905	238	
		12
1910	266	

SOURCE: DERIVED FROM *HISTORICAL STATISTICS* (WASHINGTON, D.C.: GOVERNMENT PRINTING OFFICE, 1960), SERIES Q15, PP. 49–50.

name a few. It is interesting to note, however, that the total absolute mileage doubled in the 25 years preceding 1910. Work by Albert Fishlow reveals three major waves in the late nineteenth-century pattern of main track construction: 1868–1873, 1879–1883, and 1886–1892.[4] These construction booms ended promptly with each of the major financial crises of the period: 1873, 1882, and 1893. As J. R. T. Hughes has argued, this is not terribly surprising when we recall that railroad construction was heavily dependent on borrowed money.[5] Railroad construction had a strong influence on aggregate demand and business cycles. It accounted for 20 percent of U.S. gross capital formation in the 1870s, 15 percent of the total in the 1880s, and 7.5 percent of the total in each of the remaining decades until 1920. These investments reinforced and responded to swings in the business cycle. In 1920 railroad employment reached its peak, about 1 worker in 20.

RAILROAD BUILDING AND RAILROAD DEMAND

Joseph Schumpeter, one of the leading economists of the early twentieth century, argued that many midwestern railroad projects "meant building ahead of demand in the boldest sense of the phrase" and that "Middle Western and Western projects could not be expected to pay for themselves within a period such as most investors care to

---

[4] Albert Fishlow, "Internal Transportation," in *Economic Growth: An Economist's History of the United States*, eds. Lance E. Davis et al. (New York: Harper & Row, 1972), p. 500.

[5] See his elegant and sophisticated book, *Industrialization and Economic History: Theses and Conjectures* (New York: McGraw-Hill, 1970), p. 120.

envisage."[6] The implication of Schumpeter's argument was that government aid to the railroads was necessary to open the West.

To test Schumpeter's assertion, Albert Fishlow analyzed profit rates on railroad investments in the antebellum period. He specified and tested the Schumpeter thesis rigorously, drawing the praise of fellow economists expert in the area.[7] Fishlow reasoned that if railroads were built in unsettled regions, the demand for the railroad's services must have been low initially, with prices below average costs. As settlement occurred, the demand curve would shift upward so that average revenues would eventually exceed average costs. This provided him with three tests: (1) government aid should be widespread; (2) profit rates initially should be less than profit rates in alternative investments, and should grow as the railroad aged; and (3) the number of people living near the railroad should initially be low compared with eastern railroads.

On all three tests, Fishlow's findings failed to support Schumpeter's assertion that the railroads were built ahead of demand. Government aid to the railroads was often minimal, directed more at getting a railroad that was already under construction to go through one particular town rather than another. Profit rates often started out relatively high and then fell over time. And the number of people living near the railroads when they began operations was typically similar to the number living near railroads in eastern rural areas.

What could explain such a paradoxical result? After all, it seems self-evident that farmers wouldn't move into an area before the railroads and that you couldn't build the railroads until you had the farmers in place. How could the market coordinate economic development in the Midwest? Fishlow discovered what he called "anticipatory settlement." Farmers and businessmen were well-informed about the new territories being opened up by the railroads. They moved into a region, cleared the land, planted crops, and opened up ancillary businesses while a railroad was being constructed. By the time it was completed, there was a crop waiting to go to market. Fishlow concluded, however, that "a similar set of criteria casually applied to post–Civil War railroad construction in states farther West suggest that this constituted a true episode of building before demand."[8]

The work to determine whether or not Fishlow's tentative answer was right about the post–Civil War's transcontinentals was done by Robert Fogel and Lloyd Mercer. Using Fishlow's criteria, they showed that indeed the railroads were built ahead of demand; they had relatively low initial profit rates, and their profit rates grew over time. Finally, Fogel and Mercer tested for another interpretation of the notion of the railroads being built ahead of demand. Did the transcontinentals *eventually* earn high enough profit rates on operations to justify private investment without government subsidy? Alternatively stated, was their average rate of return (excluding revenues from

---

[6] Quoted in Albert Fishlow, *American Railroads and the Transformation of the Ante-Bellum Economy* (Cambridge: Harvard University Press, 1965), pp. 165 and 167.

[7] See Robert W. Fogel, "The Specification Problem in Economic History," *Journal of Economic History* 27 (1967): 296; and Meghnad Desai, "Some Issues in Econometric History," *Economic History Review* 21, 2d ser. (1968): 12.

[8] Fishlow, *American Railroads and the Transformation of the Ante-Bellum Economy*, p. 204.

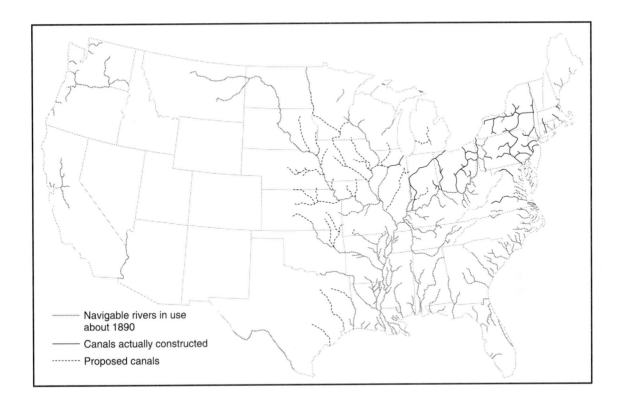

------- Navigable rivers in use
     about 1890
——— Canals actually constructed
------- Proposed canals

land sales) over several decades above or below average rates of return on alternative investments? Mercer's findings showed mixed results. The Central Pacific and the Union Pacific (which formed the first transcontinentals) and the Great Northern (the last) had private rates of return above rates on alternative investments in the long run. Had private investors anticipated this result, they would have been willing to finance the railroads without government assistance. Three others—the Texas and Pacific, the Santa Fe, and the Northern Pacific—did not. These findings show that the postbellum transcontinentals were all built ahead of demand, in the sense that initial profits were low. However, the necessity of government subsidies for the three high-profit railroads could be questioned, since in the long run these railroads made enough extra profits to compensate investors for their low early returns.[9]

LAND GRANTS AND RAILROAD FINANCING

It is noteworthy that before the Pacific Railway Act of 1862, America's largest manufacturing plants rarely had more than $500,000 invested in capital or as many as 1,000

[9]Lloyd Mercer, "Building Ahead of Demand: Some Evidence for the Land Grant Railroads," *Journal of Economic History* 34 (1974): 492–500.

employees. In contrast, five railroads at that time each had over $20 million invested and tens of thousands of employees. Building the transcontinentals was a huge undertaking, and the indivisibility of the fixed plant needed for operation added to the problems of attracting capital.

As we observed with canals and antebellum railroads, subsidies were common for major transportation projects. States and municipalities, competing with one another for lines they thought would bring everlasting prosperity, continued to help the railroads, though on a smaller scale than in the early days. They purchased or guaranteed railroad bonds, granted tax exemptions, and provided terminal facilities. Several states subscribed to the capital stock of the railroads, hoping to participate in the profits. Michigan built three roads, and North Carolina controlled the majority of the directors of three roads. North Carolina, Massachusetts, and Missouri took over failing railroads that had been liberally aided by state funds. Outright contributions from state and local units may have reached $250 million—a small sum compared to a value of track and equipment of $10 billion in 1880, when assistance from local governments had almost ceased.

In contrast to the antebellum period, subsequent financial aid from the federal government exceeded the aid from states and municipalities, although by how much we cannot be sure. Perhaps $175 million in government bonds was loaned to the Union Pacific, the Central Pacific, and four other transcontinentals, but after litigation most of this amount was repaid. Rights-of-way, normally 200 feet wide, together with sites for depots and terminal facilities in the public domain and free timber and stone from government lands, constituted other forms of assistance. But the most significant kind of federal subsidy was the grant of lands from the public domain.

Congress simply gave a portion of the unsettled lands in the public domain to the railroads in lieu of money or credit. Following the precedent set by grants to the Mobile and Ohio and to the Ohio and Illinois Central in 1850, alternate sections of land on either side of the road, varying in size from 6 to 40 miles, were given outright for each mile of railroad that was constructed. The alternate-section provision was made in the expectation that the government would share in the increased land values that were expected to result from the new transportation facilities. Land-grant subsidies to railroads were discontinued after 1871 because of public opposition, but not before 79 grants amounting to 200 million acres, reduced by forfeitures to just over 131 million acres, had been given.[10] This amounted to about 9 percent of the U.S. public domain accumulated between 1789 and 1904 and was slightly less than the amounts granted to the states.

It should be noted, however, that aid to the railroads was not given unconditionally. Congress required that companies that received grants transport mail, troops, and government property at reduced rates. (In 1940, Congress relieved the railroads of land-grant rates for all except military traffic; in 1945, military traffic was removed from the reduced-rate category.) While land-grant rates were in effect, the government obtained

---

[10] Five great systems received about 75 percent of the land-grant acreage. These were the Union Pacific (including the Denver Pacific and Kansas Pacific); the Atchison, Topeka, and Santa Fe; the Northern Pacific; the Texas and Pacific; and the Central Pacific system (including the Southern Pacific Railroad).

ILLINOIS CENTRAL RAILROAD COMPANY

OFFER FOR SALE

ONE MILLION ACRES OF SUPERIOR FARMING LANDS,

IN FARMS OF

40, 80 & 160 acres and upwards at from $8 to $12 per acre.

THESE LANDS ARE

NOT SURPASSED BY ANY IN THE WORLD.

THEY LIE ALONG

THE WHOLE LINE OF THE CENTRAL ILLINOIS RAILROAD,

For Sale on LONG CREDIT, SHORT CREDIT and for CASH, they are situated near TOWNS, VILLAGES, SCHOOLS and CHURCHES.

For all Purposes of Agriculture.

The lands offered for sale by the Illinois Central Railroad Company are equal to any in the world. A healthy climate, a rich soil, and railroads to convey to market the fullness of the earth—all combine to place in the hands of the enterprising workingman the means of independence.

Illinois.

Extending 380 miles from North to South, has all the diversity of climate to be found between Massachusetts and Virginia, and varieties of soil adapted to the products of New England and those of the Middle States. The black soil in the central portions of the State is the richest known, and produces the finest corn, wheat, sorghum and hay, which latter crop, during the past year, has been highly remunerative. The seeding of these prairie lands to tame grasses, for pasturage, offers to farmers with capital the most profitable results. The smaller prairies, interspersed with timber, in the more southern portion of the State, produce the best of winter wheat, tobacco, flax, hemp and fruit. The lands still further South are heavily timbered, and here the raising of fruit, tobacco, cotton and the manufacture of lumber yield large returns. The health of Illinois is hardly surpassed by any State in the Union.

Grain and Stock Raising.

In the list of corn and wheat producing States, Illinois stands pre-eminently first. Its advantages for raising cattle and hogs are too well known to require comment here. For sheep raising, the lands in every part of the State are well adapted, and Illinois can now boast of many of the largest flocks in the country. No branch in industry offers greater inducements for investment.

Hemp, Flax and Tobacco.

Hemp and flax can be produced of as good quality as any grown in Europe. Tobacco of the finest quality is raised upon lands purchased of this Company, and it promises to be one of the most important crops of the State. Cotton, too, is raised, to a considerable extent, in the southern portion. The making of sugar from the beet is receiving considerable attention, and experiments upon a large scale have been made during the past season. The cultivation of sorghum is rapidly increasing, and there are numerous indications that ere many years Illinois will produce a large surplus of sugar and molasses for exportation.

Fruit.

The central and southern parts of the State are peculiarly adapted to fruit raising; and peaches, pears and strawberries, together with early vegetables, are sent to Chicago, St. Louis and Cincinnati, as well as other markets, and always command a ready sale.

Coal and Minerals.

The immense coal deposits of Illinois are worked at different points near the Railroad, and the great resources of the State in iron, lead, zinc, limestone, potters' clay, &c., &c., as yet barely touched, will eventually be the source of great wealth.

To Actual Settlers

the inducements offered are so great that the Company has already sold 1,500,000 acres, and the sales during the past year have been to a larger number of purchasers than ever before. The advantages to a man of small means, settling in Illinois, where his children may grow up with all the benefits of education and the best of public schools, can hardly be over-estimated. No State in the Union is increasing more rapidly in population, which has trebled in ten years along the line of this Railroad.

PRICES AND TERMS OF PAYMENT.

The price of land varies from $7 to $12 and upward per acre, and they are sold on long credit, on short credit, or for cash. A deduction of *ten per cent.* from the long credit price is made to those who make a payment of one-fourth of the principal down, and the balance in one, two, and three years. A deduction of **twenty per cent.** is made to those who purchase for cash. Never before have greater inducements been offered to cash purchasers.

EXAMPLE.

Forty acres at $10 per acre on long credit, interest at six per cent., payable annually in advance; the principal in four, five, six, and seven years.

	INTEREST.	PRINCIPAL.
Cash payment,	$24.00	
Payment in one year,	24.00	
" two years,	24.00	
" three "	24.00	
" four "	18.00	$100.00
" five "	12.00	100.00
" six "	6.00	100.00
" seven "		100.00

Or the same farm, on short credit:

	INTEREST.	PRINCIPAL.
Cash payment,	$16.00	$80.00
Payment in one year,	10.80	80.00
" two years,	5.00	80.00
" three "		80.00

The same farm may be purchased for $320 in cash.

Full information on all points, together with maps, showing the exact location of the lands, will be furnished on application in person or by letter to

LAND COMMISSIONER,

Illinois Central R. R. Co., Chicago, Ill.

Public land granted to the railroads as a subsidy and in turn sold to settlers was a continuing source of capital funds. Ads like this one appeared in city newspapers, luring thousands of Americans and immigrants westward. Note that each region of the state is carefully described so that farmers could buy land suitable for crops with which they had some experience.

estimated reductions of more than $500 million—a sum several times the value of the land grants when they were made and about equal to what the railroads received in land grants with an allowance for the long-run increase in the value of the land. The land grants, moreover, were in some ways a better incentive than alternative subsidies. A railroad could best realize the value of a land grant by quickly building a good track. In contrast, cash subsidies based on miles of track completed or similar criteria encouraged shoddy construction.

Subsidies added to the profits and thus to the incentives of railroad builders until the early 1870s, but the great bulk of both new and replacement capital came from private sources. The benefits of railroad transportation to farmers, small industrialists, and the general public along a proposed route were described in glowing terms by its promoters. Local investors responded enthusiastically and sometimes recklessly, their outlay of funds prompted in part by the realization that the growth of their communities and an increase in their personal wealth depended on the new transportation facility. Except in the industrial and urban Northeast, however, local sources could not provide sufficient capital, so promoters had to tap the wealth of eastern cities and Europe.

Thus, as the first examples of truly large corporations, railroad companies led the way in developing fundraising techniques by selling securities to middle-class investors. Even before 1860, railroads had introduced a wide range of bonds secured by various classes of assets.[11] After the Civil War these securities proliferated as railroads appealed to people who had been introduced to investing through purchases of government debt during the war. Although the common stock of the railroads was avoided by conservative investors, the proliferation of such issues added tremendously to the volume of shares listed and traded on the floor of the New York Stock Exchange.

The modern investment banking house appeared as an intermediary between seekers of railroad capital in the South and the West and eastern and European investors, who could not easily estimate the worth of the securities offered them. From the 1850s on, the investment banker played a crucial role in American finance, allocating capital that originated in wealthy areas among those seeking it. J. Pierpont Morgan, a junior partner in the small Wall Street firm of Dabney and Morgan, joined forces in 1859 with the Drexels of Philadelphia to form Drexel, Morgan and Company. Along with Winslow, Lanier and Company and August Belmont and Company, Morgan's house grew rich and powerful by selling railroad securities, particularly in foreign markets.

European interests eventually owned a majority of the stock in several railroads; English, Dutch, and German stockholders constituted important minority groups in the others. In 1876, European holdings amounted to 86 percent of the common stock of the Illinois Central, and at one time two directorships of the Chicago and Northwestern were occupied by Dutch nationals. By 1914, Europeans, mostly English, owned one-fifth of all outstanding American railroad securities.

---

[11]For a detailed treatment of financial innovation by railroad promoters, see Alfred D. Chandler, Jr., *The Railroads—The Nation's First Big Business* (New York: Harcourt Brace Jovanovich, 1965), pp. 43–94.

UNSCRUPULOUS FINANCIAL PRACTICES

Railroad promoters sometimes indulged in questionable, even fraudulent, practices. Typically, these involved the construction companies that built the railroads.

The railroad contracted with a construction company to build a certain number of miles of road at a specific amount per mile. The railroad then met the costs by paying cash (acquired by selling bonds to the public) and issuing common stock to the construction company. In addition, government subsidies (land grants, state and local bonds, and so on) were passed on to the construction company. Under one complicated but widely used system, common stock was transferred to permit its sale below par value, which was prohibited by law in some states. As long as the railroad corporation originally issued the securities at par, they could be sold at a discount by a second party, the construction company, without violating the law. The contract price was set high enough to permit the construction company, when selling the stock, to offer bargains to the investing public and still earn a profit.[12] This method of financing, although cumbersome, provided funds that might not have been obtained otherwise given the restrictions on the railroads' issue of common stock.

So far so good, but the system was easily abused. The owners of the construction company were often "insiders"—that is, officers and directors of the railroad corporation. The higher the price charged by the construction company, the lower would be the dividends paid to shareholders in the railroad (and the greater would be the risk of bankruptcy), but the greater would be the profits that the insiders made on their investment in the construction company.

Although not all railroad construction was financed through inside construction companies, this device was common—especially during the 1860s and 1870s—and all the transcontinentals made use of it. It was not unusual for the proceeds of security issues, plus the value of the subsidies, to exceed twice the actual cost of constructing a railroad. The most notorious inside company was the Crédit Mobilier of America, chartered under Pennsylvania statutes, which built the Union Pacific. During President Grant's second term this company's operations caused a national scandal. Certain members of Congress bought (at favorable prices) or were given shares. It was a clear conflict of interest. By voting for grants of land and cash for the railroad, they were enriching themselves. Two Congressmen were censured, and the careers of others (including outgoing Vice-President Schuyler Colfax) were tarnished. Representative James A. Garfield was also implicated, but he denied all wrongdoing and was subsequently elected President. Huge profits accrued to the Crédit Mobilier. A congressional committee reported in 1873 that over $23 million in cash profits had been realized by the company on a $10 million investment—and this cash take was over and above a $50 million profit in securities. By inflating the cost of construction, the insider

---

[12] Rank-and-file investors quickly became accustomed to receiving $2,500 or more (at par value) in stocks and bonds for every $1,000 they paid out in cash. For 50 years or more after 1860, it was next to impossible to convince individuals to buy common stock in a new venture without sweetening the deal with a bond or two.

construction companies saddled the railroads with large debt burdens that came back to haunt them, especially in the depressed 1890s.

MONOPOLISTIC AND COMPETITIVE RAILROAD MARKETS

Before 1870, each railroad usually had some degree of monopoly power within its operating area. However, as the railway network grew, adding more than 40,000 miles in the 1870s and 70,000 miles in the 1880s, the trunk lines of the East and even the transcontinentals of the West began to suffer the sting of competition. To be sure, major companies often faced no competition at all in local traffic and therefore had great flexibility in setting prices for relatively short hauls, but for long hauls between major cities there were usually two or more competing carriers. The consequence was a variance in the rates per mile charged between short and long hauls. Increasingly, this brought cries of outrage.

Railroad managers were in charge of firms with high fixed costs, so they tried to set rates in ways that would assure the fullest possible use of plant and equipment. Where it was possible to separate markets, they set rates in a discriminating way. For example, rates were set much lower on bulk freight such as coal and ore than on manufactured goods. If traffic was predominantly in one direction, shipments on the return route could be made at much lower rates, because receiving any revenue was better than receiving nothing for hauling empty cars. And lower charges for hauling carload lots than for smaller shipments were justified on the ground that it cost no more to move a loaded car than one that was half full.

Another form of rate discrimination arose when the same railroad was in a monopolistic position with respect to certain customers (a producer of farm machinery in the Midwest, for example) and a competitive position with respect to others (a favorably located producer of coal who could turn to water transport). Shippers not favored by these discriminatory rates or by outright rebates were naturally indignant at the special treatment accorded their competitors. Railroads also discriminated among cities and towns, a practice especially resented by farmers and merchants of one locality who watched those in another area enjoy lower rates for the same service.

There is a possible economic justification for these practices: by discriminating among customers, the railroad may be able to increase its total output and lower its costs. The low-cost service provided some users, in other words, may depend on the revenues generated by the high prices charged to others. Indeed, if forced to charge one price to all, the railroad may not be able to cover its costs and remain in business. But the person paying the higher price generally doesn't see things that way, and the pressure to regulate such practices grew rapidly.

Opposition to the railroads was heightened by the trend toward price-fixing. By 1873, the railroad industry was plagued by tremendous excess capacity. One line could obtain business by cutting rates on through traffic, but only at the expense of another company, which then found its own capacity in excess. Rate wars during the depressed years of the 1870s led to efforts to stop "ruinous competition" (as railroad owners and managers saw it). Railroads responded by banding together on through-traffic rates. They allocated shares of the business among the competing lines, working out alliances between competing and connecting railroads within a region. More often than not, though, these turned out to be fragile agreements that broke under the pressure of high fixed costs and excess capacity. To hide the rate-cutting, shippers might pay the published tariff and receive a secret rebate from the railroad. Sooner or later, word of the rebating would leak out, with a consequent return to open rate warfare.

To provide a stronger basis for maintaining prices, Albert Fink took the lead in forming regional federations to pool either traffic or profits. The first was the Southern Railway and Steamship Association, which was formed in 1875 with Fink as its commissioner. Then in 1879, the trunk lines formed the Eastern Trunk Line Association. But the federations eventually came unglued, as weak railroads or companies run by aggressive managers broke with the pool and began price-cutting.[13] Shippers and the general public naturally resented pooling, as well as price discrimination. The result was widespread support for government regulation of the railroads.

STATE REGULATION

The first comprehensive railroad regulation came in the early 1870s, largely in response to increasing evidence of discrimination against persons and places. As the decade progressed, agrarian tempers rose as farm incomes declined. As emphasized in Chapter 15, farmers in the Midwest blamed a large measure of their distress on the railroads. Many farmers had invested savings in railroad ventures on the basis of extravagant promises of the prosperity sure to result from improved transportation. When the opposite effect became apparent, farmers clamored for legislation to regulate rates. Prominent in the movement were members of the National Grange of the Patrons of Husbandry, an agrarian society founded in 1867. Thus the demand for passage by the states of measures regulating railroads, grain elevators, and public warehouses became known as the Granger movement, the legislation as the Granger laws, and the review of the laws by the Supreme Court as the Granger cases.

Between 1871 and 1874, regulatory laws were passed by Illinois, Iowa, Wisconsin, and Minnesota. Fixing schedules of maximum rates by commission rather than by statute was a feature of both the Illinois and Minnesota laws. One of the common practices that western farmers could not tolerate was charging more for the carriage of goods over a short distance than over a longer distance in the same direction and by the same line. The pro rata clause contained in the Granger laws, which prohibited railroads from charging short shippers more than their fair share of the costs, was intended to rectify this alleged injustice and was the forerunner of the current long-and-short-haul clause of the Interstate Commerce Act. Both personal and place discrimination were generally outlawed, although product discrimination was not. Finally, commissions were given the power to investigate complaints and to institute suits against violators.

---

[13] Chandler, *The Railroads*, p. 161. Also see Chandler's *The Visible Hand: The Managerial Revolution in American Business* (Cambridge: Belknap Press of Harvard University Press, 1977), especially Chapter 4.

Almost as soon as the Granger laws were in the statute books, attempts were made to have them declared unconstitutional on the ground, among others, that they were repugnant to the Fifth Amendment to the Constitution, which prohibits the taking of private property without just compensation. It was argued, for example, that limitations on the prices charged by the grain elevators restricted their earnings and deprived their properties of value. Six suits were brought to test the laws. The principal one was *Munn v. Illinois,* an action involving grain elevators. This case was taken to the U.S. Supreme Court in 1877 after state courts in Illinois found that Munn and his partner Scott had violated the state warehouse law by not obtaining a license to operate grain elevators in the city of Chicago and by charging prices in excess of those set by state law. From a purely economic point of view the argument made by the grain elevator operators makes some sense. The loss of wealth may be the same whether the government takes a piece of land to build a road (the classic case requiring compensation) or imposes a maximum price.

But the Supreme Court saw the case (and five similar railroad cases also before it) in a different light: the right of a state to regulate these businesses was upheld. Chief Justice Morrison Remick Waite stated in the majority opinion that when businesses are "clothed with a public interest," their regulation as public utilities is constitutional.[14] The Munn case settled the constitutionality of the state regulation of railroads and certain other enterprises within the states—but not between states.

In 1886, a decision in the case of *Wabash, St. Louis and Pacific Railway Company v. Illinois* made a critical delineation of the sphere of state control as distinguished from that of federal control. The state had found that the Wabash was charging more for a shorter haul from Gilman, Illinois, to New York City than for a longer haul from Peoria to New York City and had ordered the rate adjusted. The U.S. Supreme Court held that Illinois could not regulate rates on shipments in interstate commerce because the Constitution specifically gave the power to regulate interstate commerce to the federal government. This view was an extension of the opinion of the Court in the Granger cases, where one contention of the railroads had been that the Granger laws interfered with interstate commerce and therefore with the powers of the U.S. government. In the absence of federal legislation, the Wabash case left a vast area with no control over carrier operation; regulation would have to come at the national level or not at all.

FEDERAL REGULATIONS[15]

Early in 1887, the Act to Regulate Commerce was passed by Congress and signed by President Grover Cleveland. Its chief purpose was to bring all railroads engaged in interstate commerce under federal regulation. The Interstate Commerce Commission,

---

[14] Associate Justice Stephen Johnson Field, in the dissenting opinion, objected to the vague language of the majority; he went on to say that the public is interested in many businesses and that to extend the reasoning of the majority might bring "calico gowns" and "city mansions" within the scope of such regulation. As it turned out, Justice Field was simply ahead of his time.

[15] For an excellent survey of the issues of regulation, see Thomas K. McCraw, "Regulation in America: A Review Article," *Business History Review* 49 (1975): 159–183.

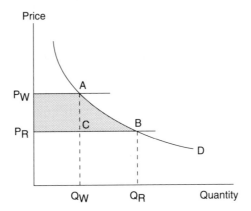

The figure illustrates the measurement of social savings. The quantity of transport (measured, say, in a standardized ton-mile) is measured on the horizontal axis; the price charged is measured on the vertical axis. D is the demand curve. P_W is the price of transport via water, and P_R is the price of transport via the railroad. Q_R is the amount of transport actually supplied with railroads predominant. Q_W is the amount of transport that would be carried by the waterways in the counterfactual world in which railroads did not exist. For simplicity it is assumed that over the relevant range the costs of supplying water transport and rail transport are constant.

The social savings from the railroad are given by the shaded area P_W-A-B-P_R. Why? The area under the demand curve is derived from the demand for goods and services, and represents the value of the transport used in producing those final products. With the higher costs of water transport, some use of transport either must be abandoned (the area A-B-C) or be produced by using more resources and thus reducing output in other sectors (the area P_W-A-C-P_R).

The trick, of course, is to estimate the position and elasticities of the actual curves. Only points near B are likely to be observed directly; others must be estimated in some way. Controversy over the shape of the supply curve of water transport, for example, has been heated. But simply putting the issue in this way takes some of the steam out of the axiom of indispensability. Total railroad revenues were less than 10 percent of GNP in 1890, so it would take some extreme assumptions about the elasticity of demand and the increased costs of water transport to push the social saving to a significant share of GNP.

research, Fogel investigated the effects (in a nonrail world) of an extension of the canal network and improvements in the road network, particularly on the rents on agricultural land. This was possible because the Army Corps of Engineers had made extensive plans to extend the canal network, and similar studies had been made by the Bureau of Public Roads. Fogel did find that the "boundary of feasible agriculture" had been pushed outward by the railroads. Some land would not have been farmed had the rail systems not been developed, but the theoretical reduction in the land under cultivation was much smaller than suggested by some of the rhetoric surrounding the railroads. The prairies would have been farmed even if the railroads had never been invented.

Fogel's "counterfactual" world, in which canals are built and filled with water, roads improved, and the development of trucks and automobiles accelerated, proved to be an especially lively part of the debate and analysis that followed. Traditional historians did not like the idea of historians patiently investigating "imaginary" worlds. But a younger generation of economic historians trained in economics were enthusiastic about evaluating historical developments in terms of the relevant alternatives.

Overall, Fogel found that the railroad had saved about 1.6 percent of GNP in the production and transportation of agricultural products. He did not launch a full-scale effort to measure the social savings for other types of freight or for passengers. His preliminary estimate for total freight, an estimate that did not allow for full adjustment to a nonrail world, was quite similar to Fishlow's measure: about 4.7 percent of 1890 GNP. Subsequently others calculated the social savings of 1890 rail passengers, including the value of their time saved.[25] The total extra costs of having rail passengers travel by water or stage figured to 2.6 percent of 1890 GNP.

This measure of the direct effects of the railroad (which probably overstates the effect) suggests that output per capita would not have reached its 1890 level until 1892 without the railroad. In short, the railroad accounted for about two years of growth, or alternatively stated, failure to build the railroads would simply have postponed growth for two years. Fishlow's and Fogel's pioneering classics debunked long-held myths about the indispensability of the railroad. Though it is difficult to think of any other single innovation that rendered economic gains of a similar magnitude, the railroads were nevertheless merely one among many developments that contributed to America's economic growth.[26] As students of this lively professional debate quickly learn, however, it was not so much the final calculations that were Fishlow's and Fogel's main contributions, significant though these were; rather it was their ability to focus the argument, to specify a testable hypothesis, and bring forth the evidence that narrowed the range of disagreement. In short, they advanced the level of analysis and the profession's understanding of an important issue in economic growth generally and in American economic history in particular.

---

[25] J. Hayden Boyd and Gary M. Walton, "The Social Savings from Nineteenth Century Rail Passenger Services," *Explorations in Economic History* 9 (1972): 233–255.

[26] For a challenge to Fishlow's and Fogel's studies, one that addresses various indirect effects such as greater-scale economics in industry and higher rates of capital formation, see Jeffrey G. Williamson, *Late Nineteenth Century American Economic Development* (Cambridge University Press, 1974), Chapter 9. For Fogel's response, see "Notes on the Social Savings Controversy," *Journal of Economic History* 39 (1979): 1–55.

TABLE 16-2   PRODUCTIVITY IN THE RAILROAD SECTOR, 1870–1910 (1910 = 100)

Year	Output	Labor	Capital	Fuel	Total Input	Total Factor Productivity
1870	7	14	17	5	14	47
1880	14	25	32	12	26	54
1890	33	44	62	29	49	67
1900	55	60	72	46	63	87
1910	100	100	100	100	100	100

SOURCE: ADAPTED FROM ALBERT FISHLOW, "INTERNAL TRANSPORTATION," IN *ECONOMIC GROWTH: AN ECONOMIST'S HISTORY OF THE UNITED STATES*, EDS. LANCE E. DAVIS ET AL. (NEW YORK: HARPER & ROW, 1972), P. 508.

PRODUCTIVITY AND THE RAILROADS

Although the railroads alone do not explain the great surge in American productivity in the nineteenth century, it is worth looking at the pattern of railroad productivity because it is representative of the pattern in other maturing industries. As shown in Table 16-2, total factor productivity of the railroad somewhat more than doubled in the 40 years between 1870 and 1910. As in other maturing sectors and industries, the railroad experienced a continued but slowing advance. As observed in Chapter 9, the pace of total factor productivity advance was so rapid between 1840 and 1860 that it doubled in this early 20-year period.

The sustained rapid growth of output relative to inputs was due primarily to two sources of productivity advance. First, as shown by Fishlow, were additional gains from economies of scale in operation, accounting for nearly half of the productivity advance of the railroads at that time. The other half resulted from four innovations. In order of importance these were (1) more powerful locomotives and more efficient freight cars, which tripled capacity; (2) stronger steel rails, permitting heavier loads; (3) automatic couplers; and (4) air brakes—these latter two facilitating greater speed and safety.[27]

Despite the expected slowing of the railroad's productivity advance, it continued throughout the period up to World War I. It averaged 2 percent annually and exceeded the pace of productivity advance for the economy as a whole, which was approximately 1.5 per unit per annum. The railroads were not, in themselves, the cause of America's rapid economic progress in the nineteenth century, but for several generations of Americans they symbolized the ceaseless wave of entrepreneurial energy and technological advance that was the cause of progress.

---

[27] See Albert Fishlow, "Internal Transportation," pp. 509–510, for a more detailed analysis of these sources of productivity advance.

SELECTED REFERENCES
AND SUGGESTED READINGS

Boyd, J. Hayden, and Gary M. Walton. "The Social Savings from Nineteenth-Century Rail Passenger Services." *Explorations in Economic History* 9 (1972): 233–254.

Chandler, Alfred D. *The Railroads: The Nation's First Big Business.* New York: Harcourt, Brace Jovanovich, 1965.

Cochran, Thomas C. *Railroad Leaders, 1845–1890, The Business Mind in Action.* Cambridge: Harvard University Press, 1953.

David, Paul. "Transport Innovation and Economic Growth: Professor Fogel On and Off the Rails." *Economic History Review* 2, 2d series (1969): 506–525.

Dick, Trevor J. O. "United States Railroad Inventions, Investment Since 1870." *Explorations in Economic History* 11 (1974): 249–270.

Engerman, Stanley. "Some Economic Issues Relating to Railroad Subsidies and the Evaluation of Land Grants." *Journal of Economic History* 32 (1972): 443–463.

Fishlow, Albert. *American Railroads and the Transformation of the Antebellum Economy.* Cambridge: Harvard University Press, 1965.

———. "The Dynamics of Railroad Extension into the West." In *Reinterpretation of American Economic History*, eds. Robert Fogel and Stanley Engerman. New York: Harper & Row, 1971.

———. "Productivity and Technological Change in the Railroad Sector, 1840–1910." In *Output, Employment and Productivity in the United States after 1800, Studies in Income and Wealth*, National Bureau of Economic Research. New York: Columbia University Press, 1966, vol. 30.

Fleisig, Heywood. "The Central Pacific Railroad and the Railroad Land Grant Controversy." *Journal of Economic History* 35 (1975): 552–566.

Fogel, Robert W. "Notes on the Social Saving Controversy." *Journal of Economic History* 39 (1979): 1–54.

———. *The Union Pacific Railroad: A Case of Premature Enterprise.* Baltimore: Johns Hopkins University Press, 1960.

———. *Railroads and American Economic Growth.* Baltimore: Johns Hopkins University Press, 1964.

Fogel, Robert W., and Stanley Engerman. *The Reinterpretation of American Economic History.* New York: Harper & Row, 1971.

Gates, Paul W. *The Illinois Central Railroad and its Colonization Work.* Cambridge: Harvard University Press, 1934.

Greeves, William S. "A Comparison of Railroad Land Grant Policies." *Agricultural History* (1951).

Grodinsky, Julius. *Transcontinental Railway Strategy.* Philadelphia: University of Pennsylvania Press, 1962.

Harbeson, Robert. "Railroads and Regulation, 1877–1916: Conspiracy or Public Interest?" *Journal of Economic History* 37 (1967): 230–242.

Heath, Milton. "Public Railroad Construction and the Development of Private Enterprise in the South Before 1861." *Journal of Economic History* 9 (1949).

Hidy, Ralph, and Muriel Hidy. "Anglo-American Merchant Bankers and the Railroads of the Old Northwest, 1848–1860." *Business History Review* 34 (1960).

Hughes, Jonathan. *The Vital Few: American Economic Progress and Its Protagonists.* New York: Oxford University Press, 1987.

Hunt, E. H. "Railroad Social Savings in Nineteenth Century America." *American Economic Review* 57 (1967): 909–910. Also, P. R. P. Coelho, R. P. Thomas, and D. Shetter, "Comment." *American Economic Review* 58 (1968): 184–189.

Jenks, Leland. "Railroads as an Economic Force in American Development." Reprinted in Thomas Cochran and Thomas Brewer, eds. *Views of American Economic Growth.* New York: McGraw-Hill, 1966, vol. 2.

Kolko, Gabriel. *Railroads and Regulation, 1877–1916*. Princeton: Princeton University Press, 1965.

Lebergott, Stanley. "United States Transport Advance and Externalities." *Journal of Economic History* 26 (1966): 437–461.

MacAvoy, Paul. *The Economic Effects of Regulation*. Cambridge: MIT Press, 1965.

Martin, Albro. *Enterprise Denied: Origins of the Decline of American Railroads, 1897–1917*. New York: Columbia University Press, 1971.

_____. *James J. Hill and the Opening of the Northwest*. New York: Oxford University Press, 1976.

McClelland, Peter D. "Railroads, American Growth, and the New Economic History: A Critique." *Journal of Economic History* 28 (1968): 102–123.

McCraw, Thomas K. *Prophets of Regulation*. Cambridge: Belknap Press of Harvard University Press, 1984.

Mercer, Lloyd. "Building Ahead of Demand: Some Evidence for the Land Grant Railroads." *Journal of Economic History* 34 (1974): 492–500.

_____. "Land Grants to American Railroads: Social Cost or Social Benefit?" *Business History Review* 43 (1969): 134–151.

_____. "Rates of Return for Land Grant Railroads, The Central Pacific System." *Journal of Economic History* 30 (1970): 602–626.

_____. "Taxpayers or Investors: Who Paid for the Land Grant Railroads?" *Business History Review* 46 (1972): 279–294.

Ripley, W. Z. *Railroads: Rates and Regulations*. New York: Longmans, Green, 1912.

Rostow, W. W. *The Stages of Economic Growth: A Non-Communist Manifesto*. New York: Cambridge University Press, 1960.

Stover, John. *American Railroads*. Chicago: University of Chicago Press, 1961.

Ulen, Thomas S. "The Market for Regulation: The I.C.C., from 1887 to 1920." *American Economic Review* 70 (1980): 306–310.

_____. "Railroad Cartels Before 1887: The Effectiveness of Private Enforcement of Collusion." In *Research in Economic History*. Greenwich, Connecticut: JAI Press, 1986.

Weiss, Thomas. "United States Transport Advance and Externalities: A Comment." *Journal of Economic History* 28 (1968): 631–634; and "Reply" by Stanley Lebergott, p. 635.

CHAPTER SEVENTEEN

INDUSTRIAL EXPANSION AND CONCENTRATION

CHAPTER THEME During the half century that lay between the end of one great war and the beginning of another, the American economy assumed many of its modern characteristics. The most impressive change was the shift from an agricultural to an industrial economy. Although this shift had been underway throughout the entire nineteenth century, agriculture remained the chief generator of income in the United States until the decade of the 1880s. The census of 1890, however, reported manufacturing output greater in dollar value than farm output, and by 1900 the annual value of manufactures was more than twice that of agricultural products.

Social and political transformations accompanied the period's industrial and economic progress, but our main concern here is with the primary technological advances of the period, the expanding size and concentration of business enterprises, and the threat of monopoly that spurred new waves of government intervention and legal change. In short, we are looking primarily at changes on the supply side, in production, in business organization, and in the public policy responses. The issues of product distribution, urbanization, and other market changes are assessed in Chapter 20.

STRUCTURAL CHANGE AND ECONOMIC GROWTH

Like the English Industrial Revolution before it, the rise of the industrial (manufacturing) sector in the United States was a key feature of modern economic growth and development. One striking set of numbers is the exact flip-flop between agriculture and manufactures in the percentage distribution of commodities produced in 1869 and in 1899: In 1869 this distribution was 53 percent agriculture, 33 percent manufactures, and 14 percent mining and construction combined. Thirty years later it was 33 percent, 53 percent, and 14 percent.[1]

As emphasized in Chapter 15, agriculture expanded greatly in these years but fell relatively because of more rapid increases elsewhere. Table 17-1 shows the 1910 labor force in several employments as multiples of their 1860 employment level. For example, in 1910, the total labor force of 37,500,000 was approximately 3.4 times the 1860 level of 11,100,000. Agriculture's labor force grew only by a factor of 2, however, from 5,900,000 to 11,800,000 between 1860 and 1910. By comparison, total labor in manufacturing grew by a multiple of 5.4, and in railroads by 23.2 in these 50 years.

Table 17-2 shows comparable multiples of output in several categories. The output expansion multiples are far larger than the labor multiples in comparable categories. For example, total manufactures output in 1910 was 10.8 times that of 1860, whereas the labor force in manufactures had grown by a multiple of only 5.4. The coal and cement multiples suggest the vast devouring of natural resources needed to industrialize the nation; they were far larger than the mining labor multiple. All of these selected categories reveal output multiples higher than the total labor force multiple comparing 1860 and 1910.

TABLE 17-1   LABOR FORCE EXPANSION, 1860–1910: SELECT 1910 MULTIPLES OF 1860

Agriculture	2.0
Cotton textiles	3.0
Total labor force	3.4
Construction	3.7
Teachers	5.2
Total manufacturing	5.4
Trade	6.0
Mining	6.7
Primary iron and steel	7.1
Railroads	23.2

SOURCE: DERIVED FROM STANLEY LEBERGOTT, *MANPOWER IN ECONOMIC GROWTH: THE AMERICAN RECORD SINCE 1800* (NEW YORK: MCGRAW-HILL, 1964), P. 510.

---

[1] Robert E. Gallman, "Commodity Output, 1839–1899," in *Trends in the American Economy in the Nineteenth Century,* National Bureau of Economic Research, Conference on Research in Income and Wealth (Princeton: Princeton University Press, 1960), p. 26.

TABLE 17-2 OUTPUT EXPANSION, 1860–1910: SELECT 1910 MULTIPLES OF 1860

Food and kindred products	3.7
Textiles and their products	6.2
Total manufacturing products	10.8
Iron and steel and their products	25.2
Bituminous coal	46.1
Cement	70.7
Railroad passenger miles[a]	17.1
Railroad freight ton miles[a]	98.1

SOURCES: DERIVED FROM *HISTORICAL STATISTICS* (WASHINGTON, D.C.: GOVERNMENT PRINTING OFFICE, 1960), SERIES M, 178, PART I; FROM EDWIN FRICKEY, *PRODUCTION IN THE UNITED STATES, 1860–1914* (CAMBRIDGE: HARVARD UNIVERSITY PRESS, 1947), PP. 38–43, 54; AND FROM ALBERT FISHLOW, "PRODUCTIVITY AND TECHNOLOGICAL CHANGE IN THE RAILROAD SECTOR, 1840–1910," IN *OUTPUT, EMPLOYMENT AND PRODUCTIVITY IN THE UNITED STATES AFTER 1800*, STUDIES IN INCOME AND WEALTH, NATIONAL BUREAU OF ECONOMIC RESEARCH (NEW YORK: COLUMBIA UNIVERSITY PRESS, 1966), VOL. 30, P. 585.

[a]The railroad multiples are for 1859 to 1910.

Relative to the rest of the world, American gains in manufacturing output were also phenomenal. In the mid-1890s the United States became the leading industrial power, and by 1910 its factories poured forth goods of nearly twice the value of those of its nearest rival, Germany. In 1913, the United States accounted for more than one-third of the world's industrial production.

Productivity gains in agriculture, transportation, manufacturing, and other sectors powered an advance of total national income well above gains in population. Table 17-3 shows the growth of population, real national income, and real income per capita

TABLE 17-3 POPULATION, NATIONAL INCOME (1929 PRICES), AND NATIONAL INCOME PER CAPITA, 1869–1918 (ANNUAL AVERAGES FOR OVERLAPPING DECADES)

Decade	Population (in millions)	Real National Income (1929 prices)	National Income per Capita (in dollars)	Per Capita Percentage Increases
1869–1878	43.5	$ 9.4	$216	30.1%
1874–1883	48.8	13.7	281	16.0
1879–1888	54.9	17.9	326	5.2
1884–1893	61.2	21.0	343	4.4
1889–1898	67.6	24.2	358	13.4
1894–1903	74.0	30.1	406	13.5
1899–1908	81.3	37.5	461	8.5
1904–1913	89.6	44.8	500	3.0
1909–1918	97.6	50.3	516	

SOURCE: SIMON KUZNETS, "CHANGES IN THE NATIONAL INCOMES OF THE UNITED STATES OF AMERICA SINCE 1870," *INCOME AND WEALTH SERIES II* (LONDON: BOWES & BOWES, 1952), P. 30. BY PERMISSION OF THE PUBLISHER.

in overlapping decades. On average, per capita income in real terms increased about 11 percent per decade. As the period progressed, there was a retardation in the rate of growth, but by World War I real per capita income was nearly 2.5 times as great as it had been during the 1869–1878 decade.

According to Robert E. Gallman's estimates, real gross national product (GNP) grew at an average annual rate of somewhat more than 4 percent between 1865 and 1908—an increase of approximately eightfold for the period. A rate of real growth of this magnitude meant that per capita output advanced at an average annual rate of 2 percent. Thus, between the Civil War and the turn of the century, real per capita GNP doubled.[2]

Technological changes, investments in human capital, widening markets bringing new organizational business structures and economies of scale, and structural shifts in resources from lower- to higher-productivity uses (agricultural to manufacturing) combined to cause these exceptional long-run growth rates. They also led to a marked change in the composition of industries and how the world of business operated.

INDUSTRY COMPOSITION: THE LEADERS

Table 17-4 lists the top ten manufactures (by value added) in 1860 and again 50 years later. It is clear from this evidence that the "make-up" of manufactures altered significantly as industrial expansion unfolded over the period. The push and tug of market forces and a high degree of resource mobility rendered such change possible. In addition, the industrial products of the United States were sold in markets that were expanding both at home and abroad, as we shall see in detail in Chapter 20. Most American manufacturers, however, did not aggressively seek major foreign outlets until late in the nineteenth century because the nation itself provided an expanding free trade arena. For every dollar purchase in 1860 there were nearly six (in real terms) by World War I.

A vast social transformation underlaid the changes shown in Table 17-4. We see there that four entirely new industries—printing and publishing, malt liquor, tobacco, and railroad cars—were front-runners by 1910, whereas flour and meal, woolens, wagons and buggies, and leather goods had slipped into lower positions. The low income elasticity of demand for flour products and woolens, plus new technologies (railroad cars instead of wagons) and other sources of productivity advance, explain much of this transition. Also tastes were changing as cottons and linens, cigars and cigarettes, and store-bought alcoholic beverages added to or replaced other items, many previously homemade. As steel became the basic metal of manufactures, new forms and sources of power emerged, like electricity and petroleum, and the scale of production grew to proportions unimaginable in 1860 or 1870.

---

[2] Recalling our doubling time formula, r × t = 70, where r = rate of growth and t = doubling time, we derive t = 35 years (70/2).

TABLE 17-4 THE TEN LARGEST INDUSTRIES, 1860 AND 1910 (BY VALUE ADDED)

	1860 Value Added (in millions of dollars)		1910 Value Added (in millions of dollars)
Cotton goods	$ 55	Machinery	$ 690
Lumber	54	Lumber	650
Boots and shoes	49	Printing and publishing	540
Flour and meal	40	Iron and steel	330
Men's clothing	37	Malt liquors	280
Iron	36	Men's clothing	270
Machinery	33	Cotton goods	260
Woolen goods	25	Tobacco manufactures	240
Carriages and wagons	24	Railroad cars	210
Leather	23	Boots and shoes	180
All manufacturing	815	All manufacturing	8,529

SOURCE: U.S. BUREAU OF THE CENSUS, *CENSUS OF THE UNITED STATES: 1860*, VOL. 3 (WASHINGTON, D.C.: GOVERNMENT PRINTING OFFICE, 1861), PP. 733–742; AND U.S. BUREAU OF THE CENSUS, *CENSUS OF THE UNITED STATES: 1910*, VOL. 8 (WASHINGTON, D.C.: GOVERNMENT PRINTING OFFICE, 1913), P. 40.

TECHNOLOGICAL ADVANCES IN LEADING MANUFACTURES

The technological changes that helped revolutionize industry after industry in this era provide fascinating and often interrelated stories. No single industry is distinctly representative of the whole, but the advance of each was based on invention and innovation, the dual components of technological change. *Invention* signifies the discovery of something new, such as steam power or electricity. *Innovation* denotes the many ways found to use and adapt the new ideas to existing products and services.

The avalanche of technological change, especially in the 1870s and 1880s, was pervasive. The following sample of new technologies during these decades is by no means exhaustive: the roller mill to process oatmeal and flour; refrigerated cars for meatpacking; can sealing for canned meat, vegetables, and soup; steel-bottomed stills, long-distance pipelines, and steel tank cars for the petroleum industry; advances in Bessemer and open-hearth processes for steelmaking; advances in electrometallurgy for aluminum production; new varieties of machines and high-speed tools of all sorts; the typewriter, electrical streetcar, and so on.[3] These new technologies permitted mass production and generated lower per unit costs through economies of scale in production. Adding to these advances in plant size and productivity were the infrastructure of a transcontinental railroad and a national telegraph network. The outcome was a distribution system, by 1880, that was truly national and continental in scope.

[3] For greater elaboration see Anthony P. O'Brien, "Factory Size, Economies of Scale, and the Great Merger Wave of 1898–1902," *Journal of Economic History* 48 (1988): 648–649.

It is important to realize that new technologies often diffuse slowly; that is, their adoption after invention is not immediate but gradual. Here we analyze the steel industry in terms of two new and competing technologies—the Bessemer process and the open-hearth process—and link these to other technological advances raising productivity and reducing per unit costs in steelmaking.

The first successful method of making steel in quantity was invented in the late 1850s and early 1860s almost simultaneously by an Englishman, Henry Bessemer, and by an American ironmaster, William Kelly. Only a little while after Bessemer and Kelly invented substantially the same process, the open-hearth method reached experimental status. Inventors were trying to find a way of making cheap steel without infringing on Bessemer's patents. They were also trying to overcome some of the deficiencies of Bessemer's process—including the fact that the method was so quick there was not sufficient time to test the steel for carbon content, so that the manufacturer could never be certain for what purposes a given batch would be suitable. The best work in this new direction was accomplished by William and Friedrich Siemens in England and Émile and Pierre Martin in France. By 1868, the main features of the open-hearth or Siemens-Martin process had been developed. Instead of a cylindrical converter that could be tipped like a huge kettle, the open-hearth method employed a furnace with a shallow, open container holding a charge of molten pig iron, scrap iron, limestone, and even some iron ore.

Several considerations made the open-hearth process more economical than the Bessemer process. A large charge required about 12 hours, compared to 10 to 15 minutes for a Bessemer "blow," but during the long refining period open-hearth steel could be sampled and its chemical composition could be adjusted to exact requirements. The open-hearth furnace also had a cost advantage over the Bessemer converter in that scrap iron and iron ore could be charged with the more expensive molten pig iron. The regeneration principle, by which the open-hearth furnace made use of hot gases drawn from nearby coke ovens or blast furnaces to melt and refine the charge, was highly efficient.

Increases in furnace size and efficiency of operation followed these changes. In 1860, good blast furnaces produced 7 to 10 tons of pig iron a day; 25 years later, 75 to 100 tons a day was the maximum; and by 1900 a daily output of 500 tons or more, with markedly less coke consumption, was common. During these years, methods of handling material improved greatly, regenerative heating of the blast was developed, blowing equipment was strengthened, and coke entirely superseded anthracite and bituminous coal as a fuel.

Another major accomplishment was the integration of processes that led to great savings in heat. Coke ovens were eventually placed close to blast furnaces to avoid heat loss. Blast furnaces, in turn, were placed near steel furnaces (either Bessemer or open-

mostly in the textile and paper industries—used direct water power, although grist-mills and sawmills were still powered by this source.

But another way of utilizing the force of water flow was to be devised. At the time when steam engines had gained an unquestioned ascendancy, electricity appeared on the scene as a form of power. Like steam, electricity was not a new energy *source;* it was a new *means* of using energy generated either by the flow of water or the burning of fuel. But electricity brought about a remarkable improvement in the utilization of the older sources of energy. Because electric power is flexible and divisible, the power plant could be separated from the manufacturing establishment by long distances, and the cumbersome devices required to change the to-and-fro motion of the steam engine into rotary motion and then to transmit this motion were no longer necessary. Furthermore, the energy required to turn either a small motor or a large one was readily "on tap."

By World War I, one-third of the nation's industrial power was provided by electricity, far more than in any other country. Nearly one-half of all urban dwellings had electric lights, although more than 98 percent of all farm families were burning kerosene lamps after dark.

The growing importance of electricity should not, however, divert our attention from the importance of other fundamental *sources* of energy. Before World War I, the machines that generated power, whether electrical or not, were run either by the flow of water or by the burning of mineral fuels where wood had dominated earlier. In 1890, coal was the source of 90 percent of the energy furnished to manufacturing; in the years just before 1920, coal remained the source of at least 80 percent of all industrial energy. But petroleum was rapidly growing more important, and hydropower was recovering. Within 25 years, petroleum and natural gas would become strategic fuels, although the transportation and manufacturing industries were planted squarely in the age of coal as late as 1920.

MANAGERIAL CHANGES

Technological changes, new power sources, the development of the corporation based on multiple ownership of stock, and other forces brought forth the modern big business firm. Prior to the huge railroad companies, most businesses, even the largest, were typically managed by single owners or partners on a day-to-day basis. Oftentimes supervisors were added, but owners usually oversaw the business operations and made key managerial decisions. The railroads led the way to change all that.

Faced with unmanageable size and complexity, the railroads developed a host of new management practices and concepts. Managerial innovations and organizational changes were essential to better coordinate the activities of thousands of employees who ran the trains, sold the tickets, loaded freight, repaired track and equipment, and performed endless other tasks. In the 1850s, Daniel McCallum of New York, president of the Erie Railroad, proposed a series of new management principles—with wide potential application. First, managers' authority to make decisions should match their level of responsibility. Internal reporting systems (accounting) should be used to identify trouble spots and allow prompt solutions. Performance evaluations, for employees and managers alike, should be routine. Other large businesses in the late nineteenth century soon adopted these and other concepts of better management and control, and today McCallum's concepts are routine in virtually all large business organizations.[6]

Two relatively new ideas spread like wildfire after the Civil War: mass production and scientific management. Mass production implies two basic production procedures: continuous process and interchangeable parts. Scientific management implies business procedures with a laboratory-like exactness. Entrepreneurs were constantly seeking more advanced production methods. Physically, it was necessary to devise mechanical means of systematically transporting materials from one stage of production to another. Intellectually, detailed planning and ordering of the assembly process by the managers was required. It was essential that management's goals be the minimization of the time consumed by workers in assembling a complex product.

Ever since Oliver Evans's first attempts at continuous-flow milling in the 1780s, entrepreneurs had sought new means of minimizing processing time. The concept of stationary assembly was applied successfully to the production of carriages and railroad cars, but it was Henry Ford, the great automobile entrepreneur, who devised the first progressive, moving assembly-line systems for large, complex final products. In 1914, a chassis that had formerly been assembled in 12 hours could be put together along a 250-foot line in a little over 1½ hours. Before 1920, motor-driven conveyors were moving motors, bodies, and chassis at optimum heights and speeds to workers along

Mass production helped change the face of industry in the early part of the twentieth century. This plant tested engines prior to their assembly into machines.

---

[6] For more on the early leadership of the railroads in these areas, see Alfred D. Chandler, *The Railroads: The Nation's First Big Business* (New York: Harcourt, Brace & World, 1965).

greatly lengthened lines. By this time, the moving assembly had spread throughout the automobile industry, the electrical industry, and the budding household-appliance industry, as well as to food processing and cigarette manufacture.

With increases in size of plant and complexity of layout, the problems of efficiently handling a large labor force became apparent. Frederick W. Taylor, ultimately the most famous contributor in this regard, argued that worker efficiency could be improved by (1) analyzing in detail the movements required to perform a job, (2) carrying on experiments to determine the optimum size and weight of tools and optimum lifts, and (3) offering incentives for superior performance. From such considerations, Taylor went on to develop certain principles pertaining to the proper physical layout of a shop or factory, the correct routing of work, and the accurate scheduling of the production of orders.[7]

These productivity-enhancing improvements helped push real wages upward, softening somewhat workers' resentment to change and faster product processing. But competition kept the changes coming and the size of business growing.

FIRM SIZE AND INDUSTRY CONCENTRATION

Before the landmark legal decision of *Munn v. Illinois* (1877), the creation of the Interstate Commerce Commission (1887), and the passing of the Sherman Antitrust Act (1890), business firms were largely beyond the reach of federal government control. There were tariffs, but no income taxes; there were state-chartered corporations, but not federal ones (banks excepted). The federal government imposed no business licenses, nor did it limit the growth of firms. There were no antitrust laws.

Historians have referred to the period from 1880 to 1920 as the "rise of big business" or the "combination movement" or "merger movement." Central to the discussion of the rise of big business has been the debate on whether big business came about in response to technological changes and other advantages of economies of scale, or whether the pursuit of monopoly power and market control was also a fundamental force.[8]

EARLY BUSINESS COMBINATIONS

The first attempts at combination were two simple devices: (1) "gentlemen's agreements," usually used for setting and maintaining prices, and (2) "pooling"—dividing a market and assigning each seller a portion. In pooling, markets could be divided on

---

[7] For a full account of the timing and dimensions of Taylor's influence on the managerial revolution, see the important book by Daniel Nelson, *Frederick W. Taylor and the Rise of Scientific Management* (Madison: University of Wisconsin Press, 1980). For a critical assessment of "Taylorism" see David F. Noble, *America by Design: Science, Technology & the Rise of Corporate Capitalism* (New York: Knopf, 1977).

[8] Firms at this time typically grew in one or both of two ways: *horizontally* by building or acquiring a number of plants that turn out approximately the same product, or *vertically* to control a sequence of processes or all of the sequences from raw materials to the final good. Firm growth through product diversification was not as common as it is today.

the basis of output (with each producer free to sell a certain number of units) or on a territorial basis (with each producer free to sell within his own protected area). Or sellers could form a "profits pool," whereby net income was paid into a central fund and later divided on a basis of percentage of total sales in a given period. Although pools were formed even before the Civil War, they did not come into their own until after 1875. During the 1880s and 1890s, strong pooling arrangements were made in a number of important industries: producers of whiskey, salt, coal, meat products, explosives, steel rails, structural steel, cast-iron pipe, and certain tobacco products achieved great success with pooling agreements, as did the railroads in trunk-line territory. The pool corresponded to the European cartel; it differed from its European counterpart chiefly in the fact that, as a heritage from English Common Law, such agreements were considered illegal in this country and were not enforceable in the courts among the agreeing parties.

Although gentlemen's agreements and pooling both worked temporarily, they typically were not durable for other reasons. First, insofar as they were successful in raising prices and achieving a "monopoly" profit, with price above cost, they encouraged new firms to enter the field. Second, the temptation to violate business agreements was strong. While others might cut output, some individual managers could profit by exceeding their assigned outputs and encroaching on another's territory, and there was no legal recourse against violators.

TRUSTS AND HOLDING COMPANIES

To overcome these deficiencies, a new combination device was created: the trust—a perversion of the ancient fiduciary device whereby trustees held property in the interest of either individuals or institutions. Under a trust agreement, the stockholders of several operating companies formerly in competition with one another turned over their shares to a group of trustees and received "certificates of trust" in exchange. The trustees therefore had voting control of the operating companies, and the former stockholders received dividends on their trust certificates. This device was so successful as a means of centralizing control of an entire industry and so profitable to the actual owners of stock that trusts were formed in the 1880s and early 1890s to control the output of kerosene, sugar, whiskey, cottonseed oil, linseed oil, lead, salt, rubber boots and gloves, and other products. But the trust form had one serious defect: agreements were a matter of public record. Once their purpose was clearly understood, such a clamor arose that both state and federal legislation was passed outlawing them, and some trusts were dissolved by successful common-law suits in the state courts.

Alert corporate lawyers, however, thought of another way of linking managerial and financial structures. Occasionally, special corporate charters had permitted a company to own the securities of another company, such provisions having been inserted to allow horizontal expansion. In 1889, the New Jersey legislature revised its *general* incorporation statutes to allow any corporation so desiring to hold the securities of one or more subsidiary corporations. When trusts were declared illegal in several states, many of them simply obtained charters in New Jersey as "holding companies." The prime objective of centralizing control while leaving individual companies free to operate under their several charters could therefore be achieved by a relatively simple device. Theoretically, the holding company had to own more than 50 percent of the voting stock of its several subsidiaries. In practice, especially as shares became widely dispersed, control could be maintained with a far smaller percentage of the voting stock. The holding company was here to stay, although it would have to resist the onslaughts of Justice Department attorneys from time to time.

THE TWO PHASES OF THE CONCENTRATION MOVEMENT

Whatever the path to combination and whatever the form of organization finally selected, the large firm was typical of the American manufacturing industry by 1905. Why was bigness inevitable? How can we account for the major transformation that occurred in the last few decades of the nineteenth and the early years of the twentieth centuries? We have suggested that one reason for the concentration of industry was a natural movement, encouraged by competitive pressures, toward larger more efficient sizes and that another reason was a conscious aiming for monopoly power. We now have to examine the forces that impelled entrepreneurs toward the control of a large part of the output of many major industries, for it is clear that a rapacious, overweening desire for monopoly profits did not suddenly sweep American entrepreneurs into great combinations.

We find a clue to the motivation toward combination in the reflection that the movement in this period occurred in two major phases. The first phase (1879–1893) was the predominantly *horizontal* combination of industries that produced the old staples of consumption. The second (1898–1904) was the predominantly *vertical* combination, mostly in the producer-goods industries but also in a few consumer-goods industries that manufactured new products for growing urban markets.[9]

PHASE ONE: HORIZONTAL COMBINATIONS (1879–1893)

During the 1870s and 1880s, as the railroads extended the formation of a national market, many existing small firms in the consumer-goods industries experienced a phenomenal increase in the demand for their products. This was followed by an expansion of facilities to take advantage of the new opportunities. Then, in many areas, there was great excess capacity and "overproduction." When this occurred, prices dropped

---

[9]The following analysis is based closely on the path-breaking work of Alfred D. Chandler, Jr., to whom we are indebted for a new interpretation of the concentration movement. For the initial version of the Chandler thesis at various stages and in alternative sources, see "The Beginnings of 'Big Business' in American Industry," *Business History Review* 33 (Spring 1959): 1–31; "Development, Diversification and Decentralization," in *Postwar Economic Trends in the United States*, ed. Ralph E. Freeman (New York: Harper & Row, 1960), pp. 235–288; and *Strategy and Structure* (Cambridge: MIT Press, 1962). For Chandler's more recent interpretation, see *The Visible Hand* (Cambridge: Harvard University Press, 1977), Part 4.

below the production costs of some firms. To protect themselves from insolvency and ultimate failure, many small manufacturers in the leather, sugar, salt, whiskey, glucose, starch, biscuit, kerosene, and rubber boot and glove industries (to name the most important) combined horizontally into larger units.[10] They then systematized and standardized their manufacturing processes, closing down the least-efficient plants and creating purchasing, marketing, finance, and accounting departments to service the units that remained. By 1893, consolidation and centralization were well underway in those consumer-goods industries that manufactured staple household items that had long been in use. Typical of the large firms created in this way were the Standard Oil Company of Ohio (after 1899, the Standard Oil Company of New Jersey), the Distillers' and Cattle Feeders' Trusts, the American Sugar Refining Company, and the United States Rubber Company.

Of the firms that became large during the first wave of concentration, the most spectacular was the Standard Oil Company. From its beginnings in 1860, the petroleum-refining business had been characterized by a large number of small firms. By 1863, there were more than 300 firms in the industry, and although this number had declined by 1870 to perhaps 150, competition was vicious and the industry was plagued by excess capacity. "By the most conservative estimates," write Harold Williamson and Arold Daum, "total refining capacity during 1871–1872 of at least 12 million barrels annually was more than double refinery receipts of crude, which amounted to 5.23 million barrels in 1871 and 5.66 million barrels in 1872. At the same time, total demand approximated crude production at $4 per barrel."[11] An industry with investment in fixed plant and equipment that can turn out twice the volume of current sales is one inevitably characterized by repeated failures (usually in waves of the downswing of the cycle) and highly variable profits in even the most efficient firms.

In the oil industry, John D. Rockefeller's firm—organized in 1869 as the Standard Oil Company of Ohio—was perhaps the best managed, with two great refineries, a barrel-making plant, and a fleet of tank cars.[12] Standard's holdings grew steadily during the 1870s, largely through the acquisition of refineries in Pittsburgh, Philadelphia, and New York, as well as in Ohio. Demanding and receiving rebates on oil shipments (and even drawbacks on the shipments of competitors), Standard made considerable progress in absorbing independent refining competition. By 1878, Standard either owned or leased 90 percent of the refining capacity of the country. The independents that remained were successful only if they could produce high-margin items, such as branded lubricating oils, that did not require high-volume, low-cost manufacture.

To consolidate the company's position, a trust agreement was drawn up in 1879 whereby three trustees were to manage the properties of Standard Oil of Ohio for the

---

[10] As we have already observed, in the various industries, pools and other loose forms of organization often preceded combination into a single large company.

[11] Harold F. Williamson and Arold R. Daum, *The American Petroleum Industry* (Evanston: Northwestern University Press, 1959), p. 344.

[12] John D. Rockefeller got his start in business at the age of 19, when he formed a partnership with Maurice B. Clark to act as commission merchants and produce shippers. Moderately wealthy even before the end of the Civil War, Rockefeller entered the oil business in 1862, forming a series of partnerships before consolidating them as the Standard Oil Company.

John D. Rockefeller, archetype of the nineteenth-century businessman, brought discipline and order to the unruly oil industry, parlayed a small stake into a fortune estimated at more than $1 billion, and lived in good health (giving away some of his millions) until 96 on a regimen of milk, golf, and riverwatching.

benefit of Standard stockholders. In 1882, the agreement was revised and amended; stockholders of 40 companies associated with Standard also turned over their common stocks to nine trustees. The value of properties placed in the trust was set at $70 million, against which 700,000 trust certificates (par value $100) were issued. The agreement further provided for the formation of corporations in other states having the name Standard Oil Company of New Jersey, and of New York, and so on. After the supreme court of Ohio ordered the Standard Oil trust dissolved in a decree in 1892, the combination still remained effective for several years by maintaining closely interlocking directorates among the major refining companies. Threatened by further legal action, company officials changed the Standard Oil Company of New Jersey from an operating to a holding company, increasing its capitalization from $10 million to $110 million, so that its securities might be exchanged for those of the subsidiaries it held. All the advantages of the trust form were secured, and, at least for the time being, no legal dangers were incurred. Thus, as the American Sugar Refining Company had done in 1891, Standard went from a trust to a holding company after successful combination had long since been achieved.

PHASE TWO: THE GREAT MERGER WAVE (1898–1904)

The severe depression of 1893 brought acts of combination of all kinds to a virtual standstill. But with the return of prosperity late in 1896, a new momentum developed. Between 1898 and 1904, more than 3,000 mergers were effected. In the four years before 1903, companies accounting for almost one-half of U.S. manufacturing capacity took part in active mergers, most of them vertically integrating. The underlying forces causing this merger wave, as with the wave of horizontal combinations just discussed, was the growth of the market and urbanization. In addition there was a change in the law. First, how did urbanization affect firm size?

URBANIZATION AND FIRM SIZE. Urbanization led to changes in both the demand for and the ways to supply consumer goods. Whereas in 1860 20 percent of the population resided in cities (or towns of 2,500 and more), by 1900 the figure was 40 percent; by World War I it was almost 50 percent. This changing proportion, coupled with population growth, raised the numbers of city dwellers from 6.2 million in 1860 to 54.2 million in 1920.

As a consequence, there emerged a new kind of consumer-goods industry that produced *new* products (or old products in novel ways) for growing markets composed of city dwellers. Firms in these industries formed large organizations that were vertically integrated (except for the raw-material stage) to achieve economies of production and marketing. These industries included producers of fresh meat, cigarettes, and high-grade flour, as well as manufacturers of sewing machines and typewriters. Thus, Gustavus F. Swift and his brother Edwin, after experimenting with the shipment and storage of refrigerated meat, formed a partnership in 1878 that grew over the next two decades into a huge, integrated company. Its major departments—marketing, processing, purchasing, and accounting—were controlled from the central office in Chicago. Other meatpackers, such as Armour and Morris, built similar organizations, and by the late 1890s the meatpacking industry was dominated by a few firms with highly centralized, bureaucratic managements. In a similar manner, James B. Duke set out in 1884 to establish a national, even worldwide, organization to market his machine-made cigarettes. In 1890, he merged his company with five competitors to form the American Tobacco Company. Less than 15 years later, American Tobacco, after a series of mergers, achieved a monopoly in the cigarette industry.

An even more spectacular result of the growth of the cities was the increased demand for producer goods and the consequent stimulation of output in the heavy industries (such as steel, copper, power machinery, and explosives). Beginning in the 1840s, municipal authorities discovered what immense outlays were required to lay mains for water and sewer systems, which until then had been provided by private companies only for the wealthy. The post–Civil War mushrooming of the cities meant a continually growing demand for such public-health facilities, which was followed by an expanded demand for gas lighting, telephone lines and exchanges, complex electrical lighting equipment, power lines, and street and elevated railways, to say nothing of construction materials to build the steel-skeletoned skyscrapers that first appeared in the late 1880s. These demands led in turn to the formation of large firms that emphasized vertical integration and highly centralized control over vast operations, extending from the mining of raw materials to the purveying of finished products.

In steel, for example, the Carnegie Company had by the early 1890s consolidated its several manufacturing properties into an integrated firm that owned vast coal and iron deposits. As the Carnegie interests grew, other businesspeople were creating powerful steel companies. In 1898, the Federal Steel Company was formed under the auspices of J. P. Morgan and Company. Its integrated operations and products greatly resembled those of the Carnegie Company, but it had the further advantage of having a close alliance with the National Tube Company and the American Bridge Company, producers of highly finished products. The National Steel Company, created by W. H. Moore, was the third-largest producer of ingot and basic steel shapes and was closely connected with other Moore firms that made finished products: the American Tin Plate Company, the American Steel Hoop Company, and the American Sheet Steel Company. When Carnegie, strong in coal and (through his alliance with Rockefeller) iron ore, threatened to integrate forward into finished products, he precipitated action toward a merger by the Morgan interests. The result was the United States Steel Corporation, organized in March 1901 with a capital stock of over $1 billion and, by a substantial margin, the largest corporation in the world. Controlling 60 percent of the nation's steel business, United States Steel owned, in addition to its furnaces and mills,

Andrew Carnegie, a great salesman, built an integrated steel firm that combined with the Morgan and Moore interests to form the United States Steel Corporation in 1901. At that time, he sold out and became one of the world's leading philanthropists.

a large part of the vast ore reserves of the Lake Superior region, 50,000 acres of coking-coal lands, more than 1,100 miles of railroad, and a fleet of lake steamers and barges. While protecting its position in raw materials, the corporate giant was now able to prevent price warfare in an industry typified by high fixed costs.

THE SHERMAN ACT, 1890. Unique to the second wave of the concentration movement was the passage of legislation to control monopoly power. The clamor from agrarian interests for legal action against monopolies is discussed in Chapter 15. Gary Liebcap has persuasively argued that cattlemen's associations provided the political muscle leading to the Sherman Antitrust Act of 1890.[13] Their quarrel was with the "Chicago meat packing monopolists," the Swift brothers and Armour and Morris, who they felt soaked up all their profits from cattle raising. Small slaughterhouses selling fresh meat and other small businesses and farmers joined the cattlemen urging anti-monopoly legislation. A complementary argument to Liebcap's, by Thomas Hazlett, focuses on Senator John Sherman (brother of General William Tecumseh Sherman), a high tariff advocate who "traded" legislative votes with antimonopolists to secure the McKinley Tariff Bill of 1890, with its high average 51 percent rate on dutied goods.[14]

As interesting as the Sherman Act's origins were its effects. As a legal statue, the Sherman Antitrust Act of 1890 seemed simple enough. It declared illegal "every contract, combination in the form of trust, or otherwise, or conspiracy in restraint of trade among the several states." It prescribed punishment of a fine or imprisonment or both for "every person who shall monopolize, or attempt to monopolize, or combine or conspire . . . to monopolize any part of the trade or commerce among the several states." The Attorney General was charged with enforcing the act by bringing either civil or criminal proceedings in the federal courts. Thus, how the law should be interpreted was left to federal judges.

The Supreme Court did much to discourage enforcement of the act by its decision, in 1895, in the case of *United States v. E. C. Knight Company.* The American Sugar Refining Company had acquired the stock of the E. C. Knight Company along with that of three other sugar refiners in the Philadelphia area, raising American's shares of the refining market from 65 to 98 percent. The Attorney General brought an action against the sugar trust; but the Court would not apply the Sherman Act on the grounds that the company was engaged in manufacture—not in interstate commerce—and that Congress intended the prohibitions to apply only to interstate commerce. The business of sugar refining, the Court held, "bore no direct relation to commerce between the states or with foreign nations. . . . Commerce succeeds to manufacture, and is not a part of it." The Court further implied that the Sherman Antitrust Act did not preclude the growth of large firms by purchase of property—that is, *by merger or consolidation.*

---

[13] Gary D. Liebcap, "The Rise of the Chicago Packers and the Origins of Meat Inspection and Antitrust," in a Symposium: Economic and 100 years of Antitrust, eds. George Bittlingmayer and Gary M. Walton, *Economic Inquiry* 30, no. 2 (April 1992): 242–262.

[14] Thomas W. Hazlett, "The Legislative History of the Sherman Act Re-examined," in a Symposium: Economic and 100 years of Antitrust, eds. George Bittlingmayer and Gary M. Walton, *Economic Inquiry* 30, no. 2 (April 1992): 263–276.

This 1890 drawing depicts a meeting of a company's board of directors—perhaps discussing how to deal with the passage of the Sherman Act.

Consequently, after 1895, mergers were widely viewed as legal and as the safer way to effectively eliminate cutthroat price competition. The post-1898 merger wave was launched in part by the 1898 ruling in the case of *United States v. Addyston Pipe and Steel Company.* Here the Court made it clear that the Sherman Act did apply to collusive agreements among firms supposed to be in competition with each other. But mergers were still apparently legal. George Bittlingmayer reports,

> The trade publication for the iron, steel, and hardware industry, *Iron Age,* ran a full-column editorial on the decision and concluded that merger might now replace price fixing. "The new decision is one which may gravely affect some of the arrangements now in force among manufacturers in different lines, in which some control over prices is sought by concerns otherwise acting independently in the conduct of their business. At first sight it looks as though this decision must drive them to actual consolidation, which is really more apt to be prejudicial to public interests than the losses and temporary agreements which it condemns." [February 17, 1898] A month later *Iron Age* reported that "quite a number of meetings of manufacturers have been held during the past week all looking to some scheme to take off the keen edge of unbridled competition." [March 17, 1898][15]

---

[15] George Bittlingmayer, "Did Antitrust Policy Cause the Great Merger Wave?" *Journal of Law and Economics* (April 1985): 90–91.

As this trade publication suggests, the interest of the law and the effect of the law are not always consistent. The law itself, in this instance, was a strong force in bringing about the combinations—through merger—that people abhorred. Ironically, the available evidence strongly suggests that the first phase of the concentration movement (1879–1893), which led to the 1890 Sherman Antitrust Act, was less spurred by monopoly power seeking than was the second phase (1898–1904). As O'Brien informs us, factories grew in size much more rapidly in the 1870s and 1880s than in later decades.[16] This was because the pace of technological change was so exceptional in those decades. Naomi Lamoreaux's research concludes that the great merger wave, the second phase, was propelled mainly by the desire to suppress price competition.[17] O'Brien also concludes: "Increases in concentration during the merger wave were motivated more by the desire to reduce price competition than by the desire to exploit scale economies."[18] Whatever its primary source of motivation, the great merger wave of the turn of the century became an inviting political target.

TRUST BUSTING

TAKING ON AMERICAN TOBACCO AND STANDARD OIL

As early as 1902, Theodore Roosevelt sensed the political value of trust busting, and in the campaign of 1904 he promised vigorous prosecution of monopolies. During his administration, bills were filed against several great companies, notably the American Tobacco Company and the Standard Oil Company of New Jersey. These firms were the archetypes of monopoly in the public mind, and the judgment of the Supreme Court in the cases against them would indicate the degree of enforcement that might be expected under the Sherman Act.

In decisions handed down in 1911, the Supreme Court found that unlawful monopoly power existed and ordered the dissolution of both the Standard Oil Company and the American Tobacco Company. But it did so on rather narrow grounds. First, it gave great weight to evidence of intent to monopolize. The Court examined the predatory practices that had occurred during each company's growth period and the manner in which the companies exercised their monopoly power. The oil trust, so it was asserted, had achieved its powerful position in the market by unfairly obtaining rebates from the railroads and by acquiring refining companies brought to terms after price wars. Similarly, the tobacco trust was accused of bringing competing companies to heel by price wars, frequently closing them after acquisition by purchase. Moreover, the record showed that the old American Tobacco Company exerted a strong monopsonistic (single-buyer) power, beating down the prices of tobacco farmers when the crop was sold at the annual auctions. Second, the Court adopted a "rule of reason" with

---

[16] O'Brien, "Factory Size, Economies of Scale, and the Great Merger Wave of 1898–1902," pp. 639–649.

[17] Naomi R. Lamoreaux, *The Great Merger Movement in American Business, 1895–1904* (Cambridge: Cambridge University Press, 1985), esp. Chapter 4.

[18] O'Brien, p. 649.

respect to restraints of trade; since action against all possible violators was obviously impossible, it became necessary for the Court to exercise judgment:

> Under this principle, combinations which restricted competition were held to be lawful as long as the restraint was not unreasonable. Since there is no precise economic standard by which the reasonableness of a restriction on competition can be measured, the courts examined the practices pursued by a corporate giant in achieving and maintaining its position in the market. Predatory practices were indicative of an intent to monopolize the market, and a corporate combination which achieved dominance by indulging in them might be dissolved. Those which behaved in a more exemplary manner, even though their size gave them power over the market, did not transgress the law.[19]

Standard Oil and American Tobacco were the only companies that the Supreme Court dissolved, but even if the courts had continued ordering dissolution or divestiture, it is unlikely that competition in the classical sense would have been restored. The four major successor companies to the American Tobacco Company constituted a tight oligopoly with respect to cigarette manufacture. Stock in the 33 successor companies of the Standard Oil Company was ordered distributed pro rata to the stockholders of the holding company, but whatever the benefits of dissolution, an increase in price competition was not an obvious outcome.[20]

LEGAL REFINEMENTS

In two decisions handed down at the close of World War I, large companies formed by merger were effectively freed from the threat of dissolution, provided that the actions of the dominant firm were not calculated to exclude competitors from the market. In the case of *United States v. United Shoe Machinery Company of New Jersey, et al.,* Justice Joseph McKenna took as the basis for his decision the finding of the trial court that the constituent companies had not been *competitors*—that they had performed supplementary rather than identical functions in making shoes. The Court did not deny the monopoly power of the United Shoe Machinery Company; it simply held that the company's power was not illegal, because the constituent companies had never been competitive. The decision in *United States v. United States Steel Corporation* made the position of merged companies even safer. Justice McKenna, who again spoke for the Court, found that the corporation possessed neither the power nor the intent to exert monopoly control. The majority of the Court was impressed by the fact that examination of the history of United States Steel revealed none of the predatory practices complained of in the oil and tobacco cases. The Court took cognizance of the splendid relations of the steel company with its rivals, noting that United States Steel's power "was efficient only when in cooperation with its competitors, and hence it concerted with them in the expedients of pools, associations, trade meetings, and finally

---

[19] George W. Stocking, "The Rule of Reason, Workable Competition, and the Legality of Trade Association Activities," *University of Chicago Law Review* 21: 4 (Summer 1954): 532–533.

[20] For an interesting account of growing price rigidity during these decades, see Austin H. Spencer, "Relative Downward Industrial Price Flexibility 1870–1921," *Explorations in Economic History* 14 (1977): 1–19.

in a system of dinners inaugurated in 1907 by the president of the company, E. H. Gary, and called 'The Gary Dinners.' "[21] But the corporation "resorted to none of the brutalities or tyrannies that the cases illustrate of other combinations. . . . It did not have power in and of itself, and the control it exerted was only in and by association with its competitors. Its offense, therefore, such as it was, was not different from theirs and was distinguished from theirs only in the leadership it assumed in promulgating and perfecting the policy. This leadership it gave up and it had ceased to offend the law before this suit was brought.[22]

Justice McKenna held that United States Steel had not achieved monopoly power, despite its control of 50 percent of the industry's output. He decided that the pattern of regular price changes over time, clearly shown by the evidence, could have emerged from a competitive market just as easily as from collusion. The government's assertion that the size of the corporation made it a potential threat to competition in the industry was denied. On the contrary, said the Court, "the law does not make mere size an offense, or the existence of unexerted power an offense." After such a decision, only the most optimistic Justice Department attorneys could see any point in bringing action against a firm simply because it was big.

THE FEDERAL TRADE COMMISSION.

In 1914, during Woodrow Wilson's first term, Congress passed the Clayton Act, which was intended to remove ambiguities in existing antitrust law by making certain specific practices illegal. Price discrimination among buyers was forbidden, as were exclusive selling and tying contracts if their effect was to lessen competition. Firms could not acquire the stock of a competitor, and interlocking directorates among competing firms were forbidden— again, if the effect was to lessen competition. A newly established Federal Trade Commission of five appointive members was to enforce the act, and decisions of the FTC were to be appealed to the circuit courts. The commission could also carry out investigations, acting on its own initiative or on the complaint of an injured party. If a violation was found, the commission could issue a "cease and desist" order; offenders then had the right to appeal to the federal courts.

The Clayton Act was so weakly drawn that it added little to the government's power to enforce competition. Once the existence of listed illegal practices was determined, the courts still had to decide whether their effect was to lessen competition or to promote monopoly. As we have just observed, by 1920 about the only practice the courts would consistently consider in restraint of trade was explicit collusion among independent producers or sellers. "Reasonable" monopoly practices of huge firms on one hand and "weak" forms of collusion on the other were not subject to punishment. The useful functions of the Federal Trade Commission became the compiling of a massive amount of data helpful to economists and the elevation of the ethics of competition by acting against misbranding and misleading advertising. Not until it could take

---

[21] 40 Sup. Ct. 251 U.S. 417, p. 295.

[22] 40 Sup. Ct. 251 U.S. 417, pp. 295–296.

action on the basis of injury to *consumers* instead of on the basis of injury to a *competitor* would the public gain much advantage from the FTC's efforts.

Thus, the one great pre-1920 experiment in the social control of business achieved little. By the time a vigorous enforcement of the antitrust laws was undertaken late in the 1930s, it was too late to do much about the problem of bigness in industry. But by then it was clear that a kind of competition not envisioned by the framers of the Sherman Act protected consumers. The fall in communication and transportation costs wedded regional markets into national and international markets, thereby reducing local monopoly powers.[23] The effectiveness of these new competitive sources is examined in Chapter 20.

SELECTED REFERENCES AND SUGGESTED READINGS

Aduddell, Robert M., and Louis P. Cain. "Public Policy Toward the 'Greatest Trust in the World.'" *Business History Review* 55, no. 2 (Summer 1981).

Allen, Robert C. "The Peculiar Productivity History of American Blast Furnaces, 1840–1913." *Journal of Economic History* 37 (1977): 605–633.

Asher, Ephraim. "Industrial Efficiency and Biased Technical Change in American and British Manufacturing: The Case of Textiles in the Nineteenth Century." *Journal of Economic History* 32 (1972): 431–442.

Atack, Jeremy. "Industrial Structure and the Emergence of the Modern Industrial Corporation." *Explorations in Economic History* 22 (1985): 29–52.

Averitt, Robert. *The Dual Economy: The Dynamics of American Industry Structure.* New York: W. W. Norton, 1968.

Berck, Peter. "Hard Driving and Efficiency: Iron Production in 1890." *Journal of Economic History* 38 (1978): 879–900.

Cain, Louis P., and Donald G. Paterson. "Factor Biases and Technical Change in Manufacturing: The American System, 1850–1919." *Journal of Economic History* 41 (1981): 341–360.

Chandler, Alfred D., Jr. *The Visible Hand: The Managerial Revolution in American Business.* Cambridge: Harvard University Press, 1977.

Chandler, Alfred D., and Louis Galambos. "The Development of Large-Scale Economic Organizations in Modern America." *Journal of Economic History* 30 (1970): 201–217.

Clark, V. S. *History of Manufactures in the United States 1607–1914.* Washington, D.C.: Carnegie Institution of Washington, 1928, 2 vols.

Feller, Irwin. "The Urban Location of United States Invention, 1860–1910." *Explorations in Economic History* 8 (1971): 284–304.

Floud, R. C. "The Adolescence of American Engineering Competition, 1860–1900." *Economic History Review* 37, no. 1 (February 1974).

Frickey, Edwin. *Production in the United States, 1860–1914.* Cambridge: Harvard University Press, 1947.

Galambos, Louis. *The Public Image of Big Business in America, 1880–1940.* Baltimore: Johns Hopkins University Press, 1975.

---

[23] See Jeremy Atack, "Industrial Structure and the Emergence of the Modern Industrial Corporation," *Explorations in Economic History* 22 (1985): 29–52.

Gallman, Robert. "Gross National Product in the United States, 1834–1909." *Studies in Income and Wealth*. National Bureau of Economic Research. New York: Columbia University Press, 1966, vol. 30.

Gallman, Robert, and Edward S. Towle. "Trends in the Structure of the American Economy Since 1840." In *The Reinterpretation of American Economic History*, eds. Robert Fogel and Stanley Engerman. New York: Harper & Row, 1971.

Hughes, Jonathan. *The Governmental Habit: Economic Controls from Colonial Times to the Present*. New York: Basic Books, 1977.

————. *Industrialization and Economic History: Theses and Conjectures*. New York: McGraw-Hill, 1970.

————. "Industrialization: Economic Aspects." *International Encyclopedia of the Social Sciences*, 1968 edition, vol. 7.

————. *The Vital Few: American Economic Progress and Its Protagonists*. New York: Oxford University Press, 1986.

Hurst, James Willard. *The Legitimacy of the Business Corporation in the United States, 1780–1970*. Charlottesville: University Press of Virginia, 1970.

Josephson, Matthew. *The Robber Barons: The Great American Capitalists, 1861–1901*. New York: Harcourt Brace, 1934.

Kirkland, Edward. *Industry Comes of Age: Business, Labor, and Public Policy, 1860–1897*. New York: Holt, Rinehart & Winston, 1961.

Lamoreaux, Naomi R. *The Great Merger Movement in American Business, 1895–1904*. Cambridge: Cambridge University Press, 1985.

Livesay, Harold. *Andrew Carnegie and the Rise of Big Business*. Boston: Little, Brown, 1975.

McCurdy, Charles W. "American Law and the Marketing Structure of the Large Corporation, 1875–1890." *Journal of Economic History* 38 (1978): 631–649.

McGee, John. "Predatory Price Cutting: The Standard Oil (N.J.) Case," *Journal of Law and Economics* (1958): 137–169.

Mulligan, William H., Jr. "Mechanization and Work in the American Shoe Industry: Lynn, Massachusetts, 1852–1883." *Journal of Economic History* 41 (1981): 59–63.

O'Brien, Anthony P. "Factory Size, Economies of Scale, and the Great Merger Wave of 1898–1902." *Journal of Economic History* 48 (1988): 639–649.

Porter, Glenn. *The Rise of Big Business, 1860–1910*. New York: Thomas Crowell, 1973.

Pratt, Joseph A. "The Petroleum Industry in Transition: Antitrust and the Decline of Monopoly Control in Oil." *Journal of Economic History* 40 (1980): 815–837.

Romer, Christina D. "The Prewar Business Cycle Reconsidered: New Estimates of Gross National Product, 1869–1908." *Journal of Political Economy* 97 (February 1989): 1–37.

Rosenberg, Nathan. "American Technology: Imported or Indigenous?" *American Economic Review* 67 (1977): 21–26.

CHAPTER EIGHTEEN

THE EMERGENCE OF AMERICA'S LABOR CONSCIOUSNESS

CHAPTER THEME Between the Civil War and World War I, the conditions of working Americans changed dramatically. The supply of labor grew rapidly because of immigration and natural increase. The demand for labor grew even faster because of capital accumulation and technological advances in industry, agriculture, and the service sector. Real wages rose. But unemployment was high and real incomes fell during the depressions that punctuated the era, and the gains for unskilled workers appeared to be agonizingly slow, bringing demands from labor and from the middle class for legislation to protect and improve the lot of the common worker.

Class consciousness was never as deeply felt in the United States as in Europe. Nevertheless, in the 50 years following the Civil War, American labor slowly developed a high degree of political influence. The first national unions emerged during this period, and "labor's perspective" became an important consideration for both politicians and employers.

DEMOGRAPHIC CHANGE AND THE SUPPLY OF LABOR

One reason that laborers as a group became more important was simple arithmetic. In 1860 there were about three farmers per manufacturing worker; by 1910 the ratio was one to one. Moreover, the number of workers as a percentage of the total population was rising from 33 to 40 percent. Table 18-1 shows this relative growth: the population grew by a factor of 2.7 between 1870 and 1920, and the labor force grew by 3.2. Immigrants, as Table 18-1 shows, added substantially to the population and even more to the labor force since immigrants tended to be concentrated in the prime working years. But the main source of growth was the natural increase of the native and immigrant populations.

BIRTH AND DEATH RATES

Fertility was high by modern standards, but the trend was down, as shown in Table 18-2, continuing the trend that had begun early in the nineteenth century. Live births per 1,000 people fell by almost half over the nineteenth century, from 55 (for whites; data for blacks are not yet available) in 1800 to 30.1 in 1900. By the turn of the century, Americans were beginning to think of two children as the "normal" family.[1] This trend has continued, and in 1990 the birthrate was about half that of 1900. Urbanization has been a major source of this decline because the costs of raising an additional child are much higher in the city. Also playing their part were declining infant mortality (which reduced the number of births needed to reach a desired family size), rising female employment (which increased the opportunity cost of additional children), and compulsory schooling (which lengthened the time in which children were economically dependent on their parents).

Even this list of factors cannot explain the whole story. Urbanization was important, but fertility dropped in rural areas as well as urban areas in the nineteenth century. Rising land prices that forced families to accumulate greater financial reserves or do with less land may be the answer. Fertility was generally lower, moreover, in the United States than in European countries (other than France), a surprising contrast if urbanization and restrictions on child labor were the crucial factors explaining the decline in fertility.[2] There was also a sharp increase in fertility after World War II (the famous "baby boom") despite the continuation of many nineteenth-century trends such as declining infant mortality. All of these changes in fertility seem to have been achieved primarily by women as they tried to gain greater control over their lives.

---

[1] Paul A. David and Warren C. Sanderson, "The Emergence of a Two-child Norm among American Birth Controllers," *Population and Development Review* 13 (1987): 1–41.

[2] Michael R. Haines, "American Fertility in Transition: New Estimates of Birth Rates in the United States, 1900–1910," *Demography* 26 (1989): 137–148; and Haines, "Western Fertility in Mid-Transition: Fertility and Nuptiality in the United States and Selected Nations at the Turn of the Century," *Journal of Family History* 15 (1990): 23–48. These are hard for undergraduates to read, but perusing them will give a taste of demography, an important discipline with many ties to economic history.

TABLE 18-1 POPULATION AND LABOR FORCE (IN MILLIONS), 1870–1920

Year	Population	Population Increase	Total Immigration	Labor Force
1870	39.9			12.9
1880	50.3	10.4	2.8	17.4
1890	63.1	12.8	5.2	23.3
1900	76.1	13.0	3.7	29.1
1910	92.4	16.3	8.8	37.5
1920	106.5	14.1	5.7	41.6

SOURCE: *HISTORICAL STATISTICS* (WASHINGTON, D.C.: GOVERNMENT PRINTING OFFICE, 1975), SERIES A6, C89, AND D167.

Meanwhile death rates—indicated in Table 18-2 by the expectation of life at birth—began a long decline dating from the 1870s. Surprisingly, specific medical treatments were probably not a major quantitative factor until well into the twentieth century. Instead, the key factor in the first phase of mortality reduction was improved

TABLE 18-2 BIRTHRATE AND EXPECTED LIFE, 1800–1990

Year	White Birthrate (per 1,000)	Black Birthrate (per 1,000)	White Expectation of Life at Birth	Black Expectation of Life at Birth
1800	55.0	n.a.	n.a.	n.a.
1830	51.0	n.a.	n.a.	n.a.
1850	43.3	n.a.	38.9	n.a.
1860	41.4	56.8	40.9[a]	n.a.
1870	38.3	55.2	44.1	n.a.
1880	35.2	53.7	39.6	n.a.
1890	31.5	48.1	45.7	n.a.
1900	30.1	44.4	49.6	n.a.
1910	29.2	38.5	51.9	n.a.
1920	26.9	35.0	57.4	47.0
1930	20.6	27.5	60.8	48.5
1940	18.6	26.7	65.0	53.9
1950	23.0	33.3	69.6	60.8
1960	22.7	32.1	70.7	63.6
1970	17.4	25.1	71.7	65.2
1980	14.9	22.1	74.4	68.1
1990	15.0[b]	23.1[b]	76.0	70.3

SOURCES: MICHAEL R. HAINES, "BIRTHRATE AND MORTALITY," IN *THE READERS' ENCYCLOPEDIA OF AMERICAN HISTORY*, EDS. ERIC FONER AND JOHN GARRATY (NEW YORK: HOUGHTON MIFFLIN), P. 104; AND *STATISTICAL ABSTRACT OF THE UNITED STATES*, 1992, PP. 65, 76.

[a] For the total population
[b] 1989

sanitation, especially better water supplies and sewage disposal.[3] America's biggest cities had been particularly unhealthful; but beginning in the 1890s, they began large-scale projects to provide piped water, filtration and chlorination of water, sewer systems, and public health administration. These improvements brought down the death rates from cholera, typhoid fever, gastrointestinal infections, and other diseases.

IMMIGRATION

Figure 18-1 traces the ebb and flow of immigrants. Major waves began in the early 1880s and late 1890s. Between 1880 and 1920, more than 23 million immigrants came to make their homes in the United States. Their impact on labor markets was substantial. In 1920, immigrants accounted for 33 percent of railroad laborers, 22 percent of railroad foremen, 33 percent of jewelers and watchmakers, and 17 percent of police-

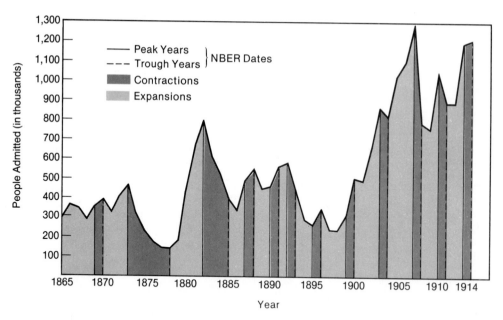

FIGURE 18-1 U.S. Immigration, 1865–1914

SOURCES: Derived from Historical Statistics (Washington, D.C.: Government Printing Office, 1960), Series C88; business cycle dates from: A. F. Burns and W. C. Mitchell, Measuring Business Cycles (New York: National Bureau of Economic Research, 1947), p. 78.

---

[3] Edward Meeker, "The Improving Health of the United States, 1850–1915," Explorations in Economic History 9 (1972): 353–374; Robert Higgs, "Cycles and Trends of Mortality in 18 Large American Cities, 1871–1900," Explorations in Economic History 16 (1979): 381–408; and Michael R. Haines, "Inequality and Childhood Mortality: A Comparison of England and Wales 1911, and the United States, 1900," Journal of Economic History 45 (1985): 885–912.

men. More generally, immigrants accounted for 25 percent of the labor force in manufacturing, 35 percent in mining, 18 percent in transportation, and substantial shares in most other sectors.[4]

As shown in Figure 18-1, the number of immigrants rose in good times and fell in bad times. In times of rising economic activity and employment, the tug on immigrants increased tremendously; as depressions ensued and jobs disappeared, the attractiveness of American opportunity receded. Peak years of inflow coincided with or immediately preceded the *onset* of severe depressions. Peaks were reached in 1873, 1882, 1892, 1907, and 1914. For obvious reasons, immigration declined greatly during the prosperous World War I years, as shipping lanes were cut and people went about sterner business.[5]

The work of Brinley Thomas in the 1950s clarified underlying patterns. The inflow of immigrants—coupled with foreign capital inflows—helped push the American economy in its upswings and slowed the growth phase in the countries of departure. In effect, the growth surges in the United States coincided with slow expansion phases in much of Europe, and growth surges in Europe coincided with slower expansion periods in the United States.

THE CHANGING COMPOSITION OF IMMIGRATION

Table 18-3 shows a striking alteration in the origins of immigrants from 1820 to 1920. In the 1880s, there was a decreasing influx of people from northern and western Europe and an increasing influx from southern and eastern Europe. It is usual to speak of the immigration from Great Britain, Ireland, Germany, and the Scandinavian countries as the "old" immigration, as distinguished from the "new" immigration composed of Hungarians, Poles, Russians, Serbs, Greeks, and Italians. In the 1870s, more than 80

TABLE 18-3   ORIGINS OF IMMIGRANTS, 1820–1920 (IN PERCENT)

	Northern and Western Europe	Central, Eastern, and Southern Europe	Other
1821–1890	82%	8%	10%
1891–1920	25	64	11

SOURCE: *HISTORICAL STATISTICS* (WASHINGTON, D.C.: GOVERNMENT PRINTING OFFICE, 1960), SERIES C88–114.

---

[4] Albert W. Niemi, Jr., *U.S. Economic History,* 2d ed. (New York: University Press of America, 1980), p. 262.

[5] The ratio of foreign born to the total U.S. population rose only from 13.1 in 1860 to 14.6 in 1920. This curious fact is explained by the high rate of increase in the native population, the substantial emigration during depressions, and possibly by a bias in the statistics because persons for whom place of birth was not reported were counted as native born.

percent of the immigrants came to America from northern and western Europe; by 1910, 80 percent of the total was arriving each year from southern and eastern Europe. It is reckoned that 1896 marked the point at which a majority of those arriving annually were of the "new" nationalities.

Much was once made of the presumed economic significance of this geographic shift in the sources of immigration. In cultural characteristics, the Swedes and Germans of the old immigration were not unlike the Anglo-Saxons who colonized America. Slovaks and Magyars, on the other hand, along with Russians and Italians and other people from the new areas, had unfamiliar customs, practiced strange religions, and spoke odd languages—and they looked different. To many native-born citizens of turn-of-the-century America, the new immigrants seemed inferior in skills, in cultural background, and in potentiality. The racism often went undisguised. Each immigrant group in its period of peak arrivals was deemed inferior: the "shanty Irish" and "dumb Swedes" of a previous generation were scorned as much as the "crazy Bohunks" who came later. Twentieth-century Americans seized on the assumed "inferiority" of southern and eastern Europeans as an argument for excluding them.

The new immigrants supplanted the old for two reasons. As economic opportunity grew in England, Germany, and Scandinavia, America became less attractive to the nationals of these countries. Also important was the rapid improvement in transportation during the 1860s and 1870s. The steamship put the Mediterranean much closer to America, and railroads from the interior of eastern Europe to Mediterranean ports gave mobility to southeastern Europeans. There were vast differences between the economic opportunities offered an American laborer—even an unskilled one—and those available to the European peasant at home. The suction created by the removal of transportation barriers was irresistible; railroads, steamship companies, and American mill and factory managers hastened the movement by promotional advertising and financial assistance.

It is probably true that immigrants after 1880 were less skilled and educated than earlier immigrants had been. It may be that their different political and cultural history made their assimilation into American democracy and into the labor force more difficult. Nevertheless, the economic effects of the old and the new immigrations were roughly the same. New arrivals, whatever their national origins, usually filled the ranks of unskilled labor. Slovaks, Poles, and Italians replaced Irish, Germans, and Swedes in the coal fields and steel mills and, like their predecessors, took the lowest positions in the social strata.

FOREIGN WORKERS AND AMERICAN LABOR

What was the impact of these foreigners on the American economy? The great majority of immigrants entered the labor markets of New England, the Middle Atlantic states, and the states of Ohio, Michigan, and Illinois, where they concentrated in the great industrial cities. Working for low wages in crowded factories and sweatshops and living in unsanitary tenements, immigrants complicated such urban social problems as slums, crime and delinquency, and municipal corruption.

Densely packed ships brought millions of workers to America, often under contracts that specified no wage increases during the first year of employment.

Their difficulties did not result from discrimination in hiring or in wages. The relative earnings of native and foreign-born workers were approximately equal after adjusting for differences in schooling, experience, skills, and similar factors. Unskilled immigrants, in other words, earned about the same as unskilled American-born workers, and skilled immigrants about the same as skilled American-born workers.[6]

American business profited greatly from an inexhaustible supply of unskilled and semiskilled workers. The steamship companies that brought these immigrants to America and the railroads that took them to their destinations were the first to benefit.

[6]Martha Norby Frauendorf, "Relative Earnings of Native and Foreign-Born Women," *Explorations in Economic History* 15 (1978): 211–218; Peter J. Hill, "Relative Skill and Income Levels of Native and Foreign-Born Workers in the United States," *Explorations in Economic History* 12 (1975): 47–60; and Peter R. Shergold, "Relative Skill and Income Levels of Native and Foreign-Born Workers: A Re-examination," *Explorations in Economic History* 13 (1976): 451–461.

Manufacturing and mining companies profited most of all: immigration enabled them to expand their operations to supply growing markets. The influx of immigrants also meant more customers for American retailers, more buyers of cheap manufactured goods, and a greatly enlarged market for housing.

The rapidly increasing supply of unskilled labor kept wage levels for great numbers of workers from rising as fast as they would have otherwise. Therefore, some established American workers who could not escape from the unskilled ranks were adversely affected. But supervisory jobs and skilled jobs were given to native white Americans, and the number of better jobs available increased as the mass of unskilled new immigrants grew. As William Sandstrom has shown, by the turn of the century, U.S. firms methodically recruited and trained existing employees for more advanced and skilled positions. Promotion ladders were common, especially in large firms.[7] Moreover, the wages of craftsmen engaged in making equipment to be used by the unskilled and semiskilled masses doubtlessly rose. And native-born American workers gained as consumers of the lower-priced manufactured products made possible by cheap labor.

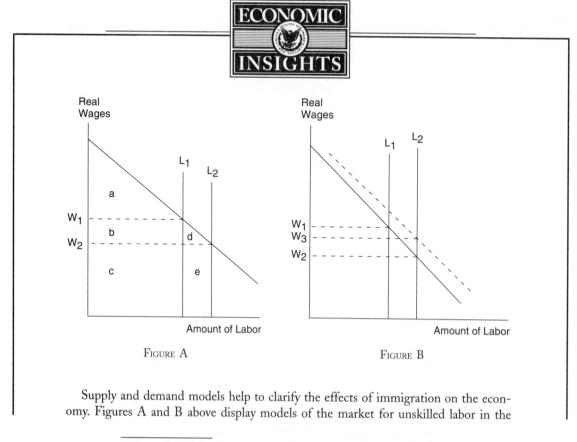

FIGURE A   FIGURE B

Supply and demand models help to clarify the effects of immigration on the economy. Figures A and B above display models of the market for unskilled labor in the

[7]William Sandstrom, "Internal Labor Markets before World War I: On the Job Training and Employee Promotion," *Explorations in Economic History* 25 (1988): 424–445.

late nineteenth century. In Figure A, we assume that all immigrants are unskilled. Immigration shifts the supply of labor to the right, and the real wage of unskilled labor (in the absence of any effect on demand) falls from W_1 to W_2. What happens to Area b, the income (the change in wage rate multiplied by the amount of labor) lost by the existing supply of workers? This is transferred to other factors of production: owners of land and capital and to skilled labor. Total production increases by e+d, and the total income of other factors of production increases by a+b+d.

Is there no way to escape from the logic that immigration reduced the real wage of existing American workers? Figure B shows one possibility. If skilled labor was a complement to unskilled labor, then an influx of skilled immigrants could actually raise the demand for unskilled labor. As drawn in Figure B, this effect raises the real wage of unskilled labor to W_3, partly offsetting the reduction in real wages produced by the immigration of unskilled labor.

RESTRICTING IMMIGRATION

From the Civil War to the end of World War I there was a constant struggle between the proponents and adversaries of immigration restriction. Management was convinced that unrestricted immigration was necessary to the growth of American industry. Labor was equally certain that the influx of foreigners continually undermined the economic status of native workers.

In 1864, at the behest of the manufacturing interests, Congress passed the Contract Labor Law, which authorized contracts made abroad to import foreign workers and permitted the establishment of the American Emigrant Company to act as an agent for the American business sector. The Contract Labor Law had the practical effect of bringing in laborers whose status could scarcely be distinguished from that of indentured servants, their cost of passage being repaid out of their earnings in the United States. The law failed, however, and was repealed in 1868. Few Europeans volunteered to work on contract; ocean passages had become much less costly, and many who did sign contracts left their employment early. Wage earners fought effectively for the repeal of the Contract Labor Law and continued to struggle for additional restrictions on immigration.

The first to feel the effects of the campaign for immigration restriction were the Chinese. Their influence on the labor market was localized on the West Coast, where nearly 300,000 Chinese had arrived between 1850 to 1882. Facing long-distance passage fares four times their annual wage, most of those laborers arrived in debt. Six large Chinese-owned and Chinese-controlled companies held title to most of the debts and used or rented out the immigrants' labor. It was just short of actual indentureship, but no formal contracts existed or were exchanged. These informal but carefully controlled arrangements were legal.[8]

---

[8] For a fascinating account of this labor market, see Patricia Cloud and David W. Galenson, "Chinese Immigration and Contract Labor in the Late Nineteenth Century," *Explorations in Economic History* 24 (1987): 22–42.

Other laborers, especially in California, feared and despised this cheap labor competition, and the Workingman's Party (also known as the "sand lotters") urged the exclusion of all Asians. By the Chinese Exclusion Act of 1882, the first victory of the restrictionists was won. Successful in their first major effort, the restrictionists pressed on to make illegal the immigration of anyone who could neither read nor write English. Acts requiring literacy tests passed Congress, but President Grover Cleveland, and later President William Howard Taft, vetoed them. For many years, labor had to be content with whittling away at the principle of unrestricted immigration. In succeeding laws, further restrictions were imposed on the immigration of the physically and mentally ill, vagrants, and anarchists. In 1917, Congress finally passed a literacy requirement—this time over President Woodrow Wilson's veto—and permanent bars to the free flow of migrants into the United States were erected in 1920.

LABOR'S GAINS IN THE POSTBELLUM PERIOD

HOURS AND WAGES

Despite the rapid growth in the supply of labor, labor made considerable progress between the end of the Civil War and the end of World War I. In 1860, the average number of hours worked per day in nonagricultural employment was close to 10.8. By 1890, the average workday in manufacturing was 10 hours and people normally worked a six-day week.[9] There were, of course, deviations from the average. Skilled craftsmen in the building trades worked a 10-hour day in 1860 and probably no more than an average of 9.5 hours by 1890. On the other hand, in the textile mills outside New England, 12- to 14-hour days were still common in 1890, and workers in steel mills, paper manufacturing, and brewing stayed on the job 12 hours a day, seven days a week.

By 1910, the standard work week was 55 hours in all industries; by 1920, it had dropped to about 50. A widespread standard week consisted of five 9-hour days and 4 to 5 hours on Saturday morning. Again, the skilled trades fared better, having achieved a 44-hour week by 1920. Unskilled laborers, on the other hand, were still working 9-hour days, six days a week, and the 12-hour day persisted in the metal-processing industries.

Both daily wages and annual earnings in manufacturing increased by about 50 percent between 1860 and 1890. Prices rose so rapidly during the Civil War that real wages fell drastically between 1860 and 1865. But from then on, the cost of living declined, not steadily but persistently, eventually returning the dollar to its prewar purchasing power. So *real* wages and earnings also increased by about 50 percent between 1860 and 1890.[10] (Prices and wages, of course, were not independent, because what mattered

---

[9]Clarence D. Long, *Wages and Earnings in the United States, 1860–1890* (Princeton, New Jersey: Princeton University Press, 1960). See especially pp. 3–12 and 109–118.

[10]Data on average wages here and in the remainder of the paragraph are from Long, p. 109. These comments are not intended to imply that prices and wages were independent. What mattered in labor markets was the real wages. If prices had followed a different course, nominal wages would also have followed a different course.

to the labor market was real wages.) Daily wages in manufacturing rose from just over $1 in 1860 to $1.50 in 1890, and annual earnings increased from slightly under $300 in 1860 to over $425 in 1890. In the building trades, both real wages and real earnings rose a little higher, perhaps by 60 percent. If we take into account the shortening of the work week by about 7 percent, the net increase in hourly money or real wages over the 30-year period was about 60 percent, or 1.6 percent compounded annually.

It should be noted that wage differentials among industries were great in both 1860 and 1890: the highest-wage industries paid more than twice as much as the lowest. These differentials reflected differences in skills and differences in the terms and conditions of work. Soft coal miners, for example, earned a higher hourly wage than other industrial workers to compensate for the danger and disagreeable working conditions in the mines.[11]

In the decades after 1890, real wages continued to march upward. The real earnings of manufacturing workers advanced 37 percent (an annual compound rate of 1.3 percent) between 1890 and 1914.[12] Further gains were made during the war years, so that the overall annual growth rate between 1891 and 1920 was only slightly less than that recorded during the preceding 30 years.

WOMEN AND CHILDREN

The role of women in the labor force changed radically after 1880. In that year 2.5 million women, constituting 15 percent of the gainfully employed, were at work outside the home. This number doubled by 1900, when women comprised 18 percent of the work force. By 1920, 8.5 million women, comprising one-fifth of the gainfully employed, were involved in some pursuit other than homemaking.

Sales work in city stores, and professional work, particularly teaching, became attractive alternatives to domestic service. But the main source of additional employment was a technological change. The typewriter was introduced shortly after the Civil War, and the office revolution took hold in the 1890s. By the turn of the century, the typewriter and other office equipment had created a major field of employment for young women. Clerical workers as a percentage of the nonagricultural work force grew from 1.2 to 9.2 percent between 1870 and 1920, while women as a percentage of all clerical workers grew from 2.5 to 49.2 percent over these 50 years.[13]

The office work force, however, remained segregated by sex. Women were confined to routine clerical jobs, while personal secretaries and other decision-making jobs remained a male province. (The new clerical jobs were also segregated by race: black women need not apply.) Segregation of the office work force by sex maintained the norm of the industrial work force. Milliners (hatmakers) were generally women, whereas meatpackers were generally men; in cotton textiles, an industry in which about 50 percent of the work force was female, spoolers (who transferred thread from the

[11] Price V. Fishback, *Soft Coal, Hard Choices* (New York: Oxford University Press, 1992), Chapter 6.

[12] Albert Rees, *Real Wages in Manufacturing, 1890–1914* (Princeton, New Jersey: Princeton University Press, 1961), pp. 3–5.

[13] Elyce J. Rotella, "The Transformation of the American Office: Changes in Employment and Technology," *Journal of Economic History* 41 (1981): 52.

bobbins on which it was wound) were almost all women. The segregation of the labor force had some roots in economic differences between men and women: the labor force attachment of women was often less than for men; so some firms that did not want to invest as much in training workers who would soon leave found it convenient to treat women and men as separate classes, even though they made errors by doing so. But the main sources of sex and race segregation were powerful social norms that dictated the work that women and blacks could do.

These social norms, however, were being gradually eroded by economic forces and political opposition. Typing and sales work, for example, even as they confined women to subsectors of the labor force, changed traditional thinking about the role of women. World War I, moreover, further shook the ideologies that underlay segregated hiring: urged to employ women as replacements for men lost to the armed services, employers discovered that women performed a wide range of occupations as satisfactorily as men and that in some jobs their performance was often superior. It would take another half century, however, for the ideologies that segregated the work place to begin to crumble on a major scale.

Statutes prescribing maximum hours and minimum wages for women were common by 1920. These were motivated in part by growing humanitarian concerns about the physical surroundings in which women worked and the effects on their health and their ability to care for their children. The statutes were also supported by trade-union leaders who hoped that limiting the hours women could work would limit competition with male workers and might limit, in some cases, the hours of male workers whose jobs were complementary with those of female workers. Indeed, empirical studies

In 1886 limited demand and financial difficulties forced Philo Remington to sell his typewriter company. By 1890, the boom was on, remaking the office and bringing large numbers of women into the paid labor force.

When publicized, bad working conditions like these among very young slate pickers in Pennsylvania at the turn of the century won middle-class sympathy for labor's cause.

reveal that wage and hour restrictions for women served to limit the hours worked by both male and female workers. The effect on women's employment, moreover, was negligible: few employers decided not to hire women simply because their hours were regulated.[14]

In the pre–World War I years, humanitarian concerns about the employment of children also increased sharply. In 1880, 1 million boys and girls between the ages of 10 and 15 were "gainfully occupied," and the number rose to a high of nearly 2 million by 1910. In 1910, one-fifth of all youngsters between 10 and 15 had jobs, and they constituted 5.2 percent of the work force. But in 1920, the total number employed in this market was again less than 1 million; children made up only 2.6 percent of the work force, and only one-twelfth of the 10- to 15-year age group was at work. True, the proportion of children who worked was always small, except on the farm, and it was probably lower in the United States than in other industrial countries. But the conditions in which children worked were sometimes brutal.

---

[14]Claudia Goldin, *Understanding the Gender Gap: An Economic History of American Women* (New York: Oxford University Press, 1990), pp. 195–199.

The employment of children decreased primarily because humanitarian groups and trade unions worked to obtain protective legislation at the state level. Massachusetts had had a long history of ineffective child-labor legislation, but the first stringent regulation did not appear until 1903, when Illinois passed a law limiting child labor to an 8-hour day. State laws limiting hours of work, requiring minimum wages, and setting age limits were common by 1920, but additional protection was needed in certain states, such as in the cotton belt and some industrial states in the mid-South and East. In these states especially, the fight against child labor was waged indirectly through increases in compulsory education ages. Federal legislation that outlawed child labor was passed in 1916, but was struck down by the Supreme Court on the grounds that the federal government had no power to regulate intrastate commerce. Child labor would not be effectively controlled by the federal government until the 1930s, when the Supreme Court reversed itself.

THE OVERALL PICTURE

Figure 18-2 on the next page shows how the average real incomes of nonfarm workers—propelled by growing productivity in industry, agriculture, and the service sector—increased after the Civil War. The series beginning in 1870 assumes (for want of information) that the laborer worked a full year; the series beginning in 1900 takes unemployment into account. For that reason, the latter series shows the effects of the business cycle more clearly. But even the pre-1900 series is sharply marked by the severe depressions of the 1870s and the 1890s. The average for all nonfarm workers, moreover, conceals the difficulties of unskilled laborers competing in markets constantly augmented by fresh immigrants. These two factors—unemployment and wage cuts in depressions, and the slow growth of wages for unskilled labor—helped produce one of the most distinctive features of the period: the growth of organized labor.

LABOR UNIONS, 1860–1914

Although the first two years of the Civil War eroded the strength of labor unions, craft unions increased markedly in numbers and membership after 1862. By late 1864 there were about 300 local unions with a membership of 200,000 concentrated in the industrial states of New York, Pennsylvania, and Massachusetts. City centrals reappeared, as did national unions organized along craft lines. At least eleven national unions, some of them having a continuous history down to the present, were formed by 1865.

Business activity slackened after the war, and labor's position was weakened further by the return of soldiers to their jobs. Moreover, the downward pressure exerted on wages by immigrants was not relieved by the westward movement stimulated by the Homestead Act. But the economy (except for agriculture) moved on to good years in the early 1870s, and by 1872 there were 41 national craft unions with a total membership of over 300,000.

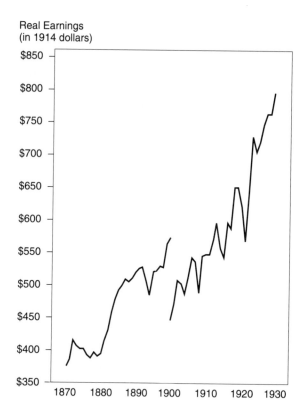

Real Earnings
(in 1914 dollars)

FIGURE 18-2 REAL EARNINGS OF NONFARM EMPLOYEES

SOURCE: STANLEY LEBERGOTT, *MANPOWER IN ECONOMIC GROWTH: THE AMERICAN RECORD SINCE 1800* (NEW YORK: McGRAW-HILL, 1964), P. 524.

A type of craft union had always been advocated by the more conservative labor leaders, who were concerned primarily with wages, hours, and working conditions.[15] These men knew that national organization was essential, for the great improvements in communication and transportation had given labor unprecedented mobility. There was no point in organizing in New York City if Philadelphia workers in the same trade who were not abiding by union rules could come to New York to take the jobs of the strikers. On the other hand, while they recognized the need for a national association of workers in a single craft, these leaders did not advocate an all-inclusive union seeking broad social and political ends.

---

[15] Recommended readings on the relative absence of radicalism in the American labor movement include Gerald Friedman, "Strike Success and Union Ideology: The United States and France, 1880–1914," *Journal of Economic History* 48 (1988): 1–25; Sean Wilentz, "Against Exceptionalism: Class Consciousness and the American Labor Movement," *International Labor and Working Class History* 26 (Fall 1984): 1–24; Werner Sombart, *Why Is There No Socialism in America?* (1906; 1st English ed., White Plains: 1976); Selig Perlman, *A Theory of the Labor Movement* (New York: 1928); and Seymour Martin Lipset, "Radicalism or Reformism: The Sources of Working Class Protest," *American Political Science Review* 77 (March 1983): 1–18.

The depression that followed the downturn of 1873 revealed once more, and with crushing finality, the inherent limits of the pure national craft union. One of the first to collapse was the numerically strongest of them all—the shoemakers' association, known as the Knights of St. Crispin. Of the 41 national craft unions, only 8, greatly weakened, survived six years of hard times after 1872.

Just prior to this collapse, the National Labor Union (NLU) was dissolved after its policies were defeated at the polls in 1872. The NLU is noteworthy as the first manifestation of American labor's yearning to present a solid front against the opposition of the business class. Originally seeking modest, purely economic objectives such as arbitration of disputes and advocating strikes only as a last resort, radical leaders gradually injected more idealistic social reforms into their purpose. Half a million strong and allied with agrarian reformers, the NLU entered politics on a platform that proposed an increase in the money supply, a weakening of the "money monopoly" of the banks, and the establishment of producers' and consumers' cooperatives. This "radicalism" alienated many local craft members, and the NLU splintered in the wake of the 1872 elections.

THE KNIGHTS OF LABOR

Meanwhile, in 1869, the most romantic of all American labor organizations was formed as an association of poor Philadelphia tailors. Under the leadership of a Baptist preacher, Uriah S. Stephens, the Noble and Holy Order of the Knights of Labor had an inauspicious beginning. With all the trappings of a fraternal lodge, including a secret religious ritual, this group offered a new appeal to workers and sought a new type of protection for them. Besides having economic ends in common, the membership was to be held together by bonds of brotherly love (a reference to Philadelphia, the City of Brotherly Love). Because the bitter opposition of property owners had proved so damaging in the past, the new organization extended the protection of anonymity to its members.

The Knights of Labor grew slowly during its first decade. Its real rise began in 1881, when its membership may have been as large as 20,000. Within five years, membership reached the unprecedented total of 750,000—with a huge increase occurring in 1885. Although the Knights were initially opposed to strikes, it was through a series of brilliant strike victories that their great membership was won. In 1884 and 1885, the Knights were successful in a series of work stoppages against the railroads, then the most powerful business firms in the country. The acclaim accorded the union was tremendous. When, in addition, the leadership announced the attainment of an 8-hour day as the next major objective, workers rushed to join.

The peak of membership and power, reached in the spring of 1886, was followed by an almost equally precipitous decline. Stretching their luck too far, the Knights lost a strike against one of Jay Gould's railroads—and with it, much of the prestige they had gained in a victory over Gould the preceding year. When a general strike to achieve an 8-hour day failed to materialize in May 1886, members lost faith. Membership slipped to 100,000 by 1890, the year in which the growing American Federation of Labor won a showdown fight against a group backed by the Knights to organize the cigar trade in New York City. Although the Knights remained in existence until 1917, they were of no importance after 1900.

THE AMERICAN FEDERATION OF LABOR

In 1881, as the Knights of Labor began its rise to short-lived eminence, the leaders of six of the country's strongest craft unions, meeting in Pittsburgh, Pennsylvania, proposed a federation of national unions. The new organization, composed of printers, glassworkers, iron and steelworkers, molders, and cigar makers, was to be known as the Federation of Organized Trades and Labor Unions. Its leaders were Adolph Strasser, then president of the International Cigar Makers Union, and Samuel Gompers, a former radical who rose to prominence as a colleague of Strasser. The original membership of the federation was less than 50,000 and did not begin to increase until the Knights of Labor had expended itself. In 1886, several strong national unions connected with the Knights withdrew in dissatisfaction and founded the American Federation of Labor. It was then a simple matter for the two federations to amalgamate, with the new organization taking the name of the American Federation of Labor (AFL). Samuel Gompers became the first president of the group that was to dominate the labor movement for half a century.

Membership grew slowly during the next twelve years, reaching 250,000 by 1898. Then the first of two pre-1920 periods of remarkable AFL growth followed. By 1905, nearly 1.5 million workers had enlisted in the cause. A decade of gradual increase ensued, and membership numbered approximately 2.4 million by 1917. Then came the second period of rapid additions to the ranks: by the end of World War I, the federation could legitimately claim 4 million workers, or 80 percent of all union members. Of the unions remaining outside the AFL, the most important were the four railroad brotherhoods, which were highly cooperative. The rest contended for jurisdiction with AFL affiliates or had disaffiliated.

Although labor leaders themselves might not place primary emphasis on the fortuitous onset of almost 25 years of good times, prosperity was a major element in the stability of the new organization. Between 1898 and World War I, economic activity on the whole was quite high, exhibiting a rapidly growing rate of industrial output. There were only three depressed periods, and the country emerged from these without experiencing serious deflation or prolonged unemployment. Credit must also be given to those who planned the strategy. After long years of trial and error, labor leaders, including men with radical backgrounds like Strasser and Gompers, had discovered the principle of pushing for concrete gains in good times and strongly supporting what legislative action could be achieved without participating in politics as a labor party. Furthermore, their policy "to defeat labor's enemies and to reward its friends" meant that they played one major political party against the other—a practice that probably maximized the number of bills favorable to labor that were passed by legislative bodies and minimized the risk of shattering defeats at the polls.

Certainly some credit for the American Federation of Labor's prewar success must be attributed to its almost uncanny ability to maintain craft autonomy without permitting one craft to have two unions ("dual" unionism) and to its promotion of the trade or collective-bargaining agreements as a means of stabilizing employer-employee relations. From the experiences of the preceding 75 years, federation leaders were convinced that stable unions had to be organized by self-governing crafts—that is, by workers with the same specific skills, such as printers. The AFL's one unifying principle was to control job opportunities and job conditions in each craft. This principle implied an organizational unit comprised of workers who performed the same job and who, in the absence of collective action, would have competed with one another to their economic detriment. Thus the craft union could act quickly to exert economic pressure on the employer.

Craft organization also meant that there could be no more than one union to a trade or skill. Two unions within a single craft (dualism) was unthinkable; dualism weakened solidarity and destroyed a "united front." After the turn of the century, though, the disadvantages of rigorous adherence to the single-craft ideal became more pronounced. First, there was the perplexing problem of setting the boundaries between different crafts; "demarcation" or "jurisdictional" disputes arose with increasing frequency. Second, problems of common interest to several crafts could not be solved because there was no basis of cooperative action. Finally, mechanization of industry and rapid immigration made it possible for employers to substitute unskilled for skilled workers, thereby weakening the control of single-craft unions.

To solve these problems by a wholesale turning to industrial unionism would have been to deny the principle of craft autonomy. Yet it quickly became apparent that there would have to be *some* exceptions to craft organization. As early as 1902, for example, the AFL granted a charter to an industrial union, the United Mine Workers. An industrial union includes all workers in the industry regardless of their specific skills or craft. In this case, it was readily apparent that the numerical superiority of non-craftsmen in mining made organization on a basis of crafts altogether unrealistic. By 1915, however, only five industrial unions were affiliated with the AFL.

Meanwhile, AFL affiliates were assuring their own continued existence and the general stability of the labor movement by obtaining increased use of the written trade agreement. Written trade agreements were rare before the late 1880s; after 1890, they gradually became an accepted outcome of collective bargaining, on both local and national levels. Such recognition was a great source of strength in the decade of slow growth that followed, and the footholds thus secured made possible a second period of increase in collective bargaining during World War I.

INDUSTRIAL CONFLICT AND EMPLOYER OPPOSITION

Labor's organizational gains were not won without a serious and prolonged struggle, which was still unresolved by 1920. Strikes, though frequent even in the late nineteenth century, were not sanctioned legally; nor were they always instigated by unions. Sometimes strikes erupted as simply the spontaneous responses of unorganized workers, and on certain occasions successful strikes resulted in a union being formed. In any case, employers, supported by middle-class opinion and by government authorities, took the position that their rights and the very institution of private property were threatened by the growing strength of the unions.

The most violent conflicts between management and labor occurred in the last quarter of the century. During the depressed years of the mid-1870s, much blood was shed when strikes were broken by force. The climax of this series of conflicts occurred in 1877, a zenith of turmoil that had begun with railroad strikes in Pittsburgh and had spread throughout the country. In the anthracite regions of Pennsylvania, a secret society of Irish-American miners known as the "Molly Maguires" (named for the leader of an Irish antilandlord organization) was blamed for numerous murders and other outrages. What they did and didn't do is still a matter of heated dispute. Their power was finally broken after a trial that led to the hanging of 20 men on the basis of testimony provided by a Pinkerton agent who claimed to have infiltrated the organization.[16]

The brutality was not all on one side. Generally, however, it was the laborer who had to fend off the physical assaults of paid thugs, state militiamen, and federal troops. Three incidents, purposely spaced over time, it would seem, to do the maximum damage to labor's cause, stand out as symbols of the most severe disputes.

The infamous Haymarket affair on May 4, 1886, was the tragic climax of efforts of the Knights of Labor to secure a general strike of workers in the Chicago area. A

Simultaneous strikes by various Chicago unions were met by strong police action, resulting in the Haymarket Riot of May 4, 1886.

---

[16]This episode was dramatized effectively in *The Molly Maguires,* a movie starring Sean Connery, Richard Harris, and Samantha Eggar.

bomb thrown at police officers attempting to break up a mass meeting at Haymarket Square resulted in several deaths. The authorities and the press demanded action. Seven men, who were probably innocent, were executed for murder. Although the injustice of the punishment aroused great resentment among labor's sympathizers, antilabor agitators used the incident as a horrible example of what radicals and anarchists would do to undermine American institutions by violence.

Six years later, just as antilabor feeling was subsiding, the management of the Carnegie Homestead Works at Pittsburgh decided to oust the Amalgamated Association of Iron and Steel Workers, which was trying to organize the Homestead laborers. A strike was called, ostensibly because the company refused to come to an agreement on wage matters. Henry Frick, a close associate of Carnegie, brought in 300 Pinkerton detectives to disperse the strikers and maintain order. Turning the tables, the striking mob won a heated battle with the detectives, capturing several and injuring many severely. The state militia was called out to restore order, and the union suffered a defeat that set the organization of labor in steel mills back several decades.

The adverse publicity received by the Homestead episode was exceeded only by that of the Pullman strike of 1894. Although the Pullman strike was led by the mild-mannered Eugene V. Debs, who had not yet embraced socialist doctrines, the strife was attributed to the un-American ideology of other radical leaders. Rioting spread over the entire Chicago area, and before peace was restored—this time by federal troops sent on pretext of protecting the U.S. mails—scores of people were killed or injured. Again the seriousness of the labor problem became a matter for widespread concern and the basis of much immoderate opposition to labor's cause. On the other hand, the Pullman strike served as a warning to conservative union leaders that violence would only disrupt unions and damage them in the public regard. Furthermore, the dispatch with which Debs and other labor leaders were jailed on contempt proceedings for disobeying a court injunction against inciting union members to strike was a sobering blow. Any long-run strategy would have to include efforts both to pacify voters and to strengthen labor's position in the courts. Pre-1920 successes along both lines were limited, to say the least.

Beginning in 1902, employers changed their tactics. They began a serious drive to sell Americans on the benefits—to employers, workers, and the public—of the open shop. To further their propaganda, several organizations were formed. The most prominent were the National Association of Manufacturers and the American Anti-boycott Association, both of which were assisted materially by employers' trade associations. So effective were the employers' efforts that even conservative labor leaders experienced increasing pressure from their constituents to fight back.

Perhaps it was inevitable that a radical, activist left should then emerge. Socialism under various labels gained small followings; doctrines ranged from the utopian idealism of novelist Edward Bellamy to marxist insistence on revolutionary seizure by the state of basic industries and services. Yet the only radical group that showed any signs of gaining a permanent place in the labor movement was the Industrial Workers of the World (IWW), which was formed about 1905. From 1909 to 1917, the IWW was a militant organization, preaching the doctrine of direct action: strikes, and if need be, sabotage. The goal of the IWW was first to organize all workers within each industry,

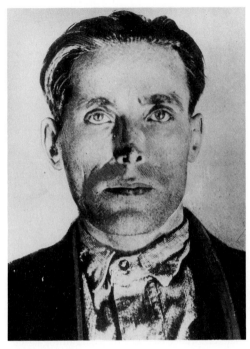

Joe Hill, an organizer for the IWW, was executed for murder at Salt Lake in 1915 at age 36 in an apparent frame-up. Hill was born Hillstrom, in Sweden, emigrating in 1902. He wrote many labor songs such as the union version of "Casey Jones." The fear that many industrialists had of radicals, like Joe Hill, made a good talking point for more conservative labor leaders.

and ultimately to unite all workers in "one big union." A general strike of all labor would then overthrow capitalism. Under the leadership of William D. (Big Bill) Haywood, the IWW led a number of strikes in the East with variable results—a strike by textile workers at Lawrence, Massachusetts, in 1912 was a success, but a strike by silk workers at Paterson, New Jersey, the following year was a failure—and organized successfully among western agricultural, timber, and mine workers. The IWW's emphasis on industrial unionism and direct action, a sharp contrast with both the pragmatism of the AFL and the political orientation of the socialists, appealed to the immigrants in the East and itinerant workers in the West who were its main backers.

The "Wobblies," as they were also called (allegedly because some immigrant members had trouble pronouncing the name of the union), opposed American participation in World War I and struck certain industries deemed to be important to the war effort. The federal government arrested the union's leaders in 1917 for violating espionage and sedition laws, and won convictions in 1918. The Wobblies never recovered. Although the direct economic impact of the IWW was small, its idealism, often communicated through folksongs, inspired later generations of reformers.

> When the Union's inspiration
> thru the worker's blood shall run,
> There can be no power greater
> anywhere beneath the sun;

Yet what force on earth is weaker
    than the feeble strength of one,
For the Union makes us strong.

Solidarity forever, solidarity forever,
    solidarity forever,
For the Union makes us strong.

In our hands is placed a power
    greater than their hoarded gold,
Greater than the might of armies
    magnified a thousandfold;
We can bring to birth a new world
    from the ashes of the old,
For the Union makes us strong.[17]

Samuel Gompers, able young John Mitchell of the United Mine Workers, and others favored a counteroffensive against the employers through education and propaganda. Affiliating with the National Civic Federation—an association that included wealthy eastern capitalists, corporation officers, editors, professional people, and labor representatives—AFL leaders sought to elicit a more favorable attitude from the electorate. The National Civic Federation maintained a division for the mediation and conciliation of disputes, tried to secure wider acceptance of collective-bargaining agreements, and preached the doctrine that greater labor responsibility would mean fewer work stoppages and a better livelihood for all. How much good the National Civic Federation did is hard to say. It doubtlessly served in part to offset the organized efforts of employers, but the alliance may have lulled job-conscious unionists into ultraconservatism at a time when more aggressive policies were called for. At any rate, the core of employer opposition remained almost as solid as ever, particularly among industrialists of the Midwest.

Union activity in the United States, especially in comparison to labor efforts in Europe, was largely apolitical, at least at the national level. No national labor party emerged as a political entity, and unions were seldom united in their stand on national issues. Instead, the main confrontation lay outside the political arena and was predominantly between employers and employees. For that reason, perhaps, strikes were longer in the United States than in Europe, even without the sanction of law.[18]

REACTIONS FROM THE BENCH

The judiciary showed no sign of increasing liberality toward statutory attempts to protect the rights of workers to organize. By the end of the nineteenth century, the right of labor unions to *exist* was established; yet the right of employers to force

---

[17] Words by Ralph Chaplin of the IWW, written to the tune of "The Battle Hymn of the Republic." Quoted in Pete Seeger, *American Favorite Ballads* (New York: Oak Publications, 1961), p. 91.

[18] For an analysis of these and other historical features of strikes in the United States, see Poko Edwards, *Strikes in the United States 1881–1974* (New York: St. Martin's Press, 1981).

employees to enter into antiunion contracts was upheld to the very end of this period. In this way nonunion status as a condition of employment was maintained by many employers. For example, in *Adair v. United States* (1908), the Supreme Court declared unconstitutional a provision of the Erdman Act that made it unlawful for any carrier in interstate commerce to discharge an employee for joining a union. In the case of *Coppage v. Kansas* (1912), the Court overturned a state law passed to outlaw antiunion contracts—called "yellow-dog contracts" because they were as worthless as a mongrel dog. Coppage, a railroad employee, had been fired for refusing to withdraw from a union. Because his withdrawal would have cost him $1,500 in insurance benefits, the Kansas supreme court held that the statute protecting him prevented coercion and was valid. But the U.S. Supreme Court reversed this decision, holding that an employer had a constitutional right to require an antiunion contract from employees; a statute contravening this right, the Court held, violated the Fourteenth Amendment in that it abridged the employer's freedom of contract.

State and federal governments typically stood firmly on the side of business against labor unions. Calling out troops to break strikes was considered a legitimate use of police power. Such actions were condoned by the state and federal courts, which proved to be invaluable allies of management in the struggle to suppress collective

Labor leadership eventually became concentrated in the hands of Samuel Gompers who sat on the first executive council of the American Federation of Labor in 1881.

action on the part of the laboring class. Especially effective as a device for restraining union action was the injunction. Employers could go to court to have labor leaders enjoined from calling or continuing a strike. Failure to comply with an injunction meant jail for the offenders, and "government by injunction" proved to be one of the strongest weapons in the antiunion arsenal.

As late as 1917, the U.S. Supreme Court decided that antiunion contracts, whether oral or written, could be protected by injunction. The Hitchman Coal and Coke Company, after winning a strike, had hired back miners on the condition that they could not be members of the United Mine Workers while in the company's employ. Later, union organizers tried to convince the miners to promise that after a certain time had elapsed they would again join the union. In a U.S. district court, the company asked for and obtained an injunction stopping further efforts to organize. The Supreme Court affirmed the decision, holding that, even though the miners had not yet joined the union, they were being induced by organizers to break a contract with the employer and that the employer was entitled to injunctive protection.

LABOR'S GAINS AND THE UNIONS

In 1920, the American factory worker could look back on 60 years of substantial improvement. Real wages were up, hours were shorter, with laborers, children, and (to some extent) women protected by law. The fundamental ideas of Social Security were being more generally discussed, and clear-cut legislative victories had been won to reduce the hardships caused by industrial accidents. In addition, urban dwellers of all kinds saw vast improvements that brought about sharp long-run reductions in mortality.

How much of these gains should be attributed to the labor movement? Clearly, the unions' ability to control the supply of labor, and thus the conditions and terms of work, was limited throughout the period from the Civil War to the Great Depression by the inability of the labor movement, despite valiant efforts, to organize more than a small fraction of the labor force. The crucial figures are given in Table 18-4. At the nineteenth-century peak in 1886, unions had organized only about 8 percent of the nonfarm labor force. Even at the peak after World War I, unions could only claim 17 percent of the nonfarm labor force. Hence there was little that unions could do directly to raise the average level of real wages or improve the typical conditions of work. Unions could raise wages in unionized sectors; but by restricting the supply of labor in those sectors, they had the undesired effect of increasing the supply of labor and lowering wages in nonunionized sectors.

On the eve of World War I, however, unions could lay claim to some other important gains for their members. As direct owner-supervision declined and management became impersonal, the power of foremen indulging their personal whims increased. Unions helped offset and reduce arbitrariness in hiring and firing and other harsh treatment by supervising personnel. In addition, some particularly strong unions gained substantial wage differentials for their members. For example, a substantial differential was obtained in the bituminous (soft) coal industry, where union workers

TABLE 18-4   UNION MEMBERSHIP, SELECTED YEARS

Year	Total Union Membership (thousands)	Total Membership as a percent of Total Labor Force	Total Membership as a percent of Nonfarm Labor Force
1860	5	.1%	n.a.
1870	300	2.4	4.6
1880	50	.3	.5
1886	1,010	4.8	8.2
1890	325	1.4	2.3
1900	791	2.8	4.7
1905	1,918	5.9	9.3
1910	2,116	5.8	8.6
1917	2,976	7.4	10.0
1920	5,034	12.2	16.7
1929	3,625	7.6	9.7

SOURCES: STANLEY LEBERGOTT, "THE AMERICAN LABOR FORCE," IN *AMERICAN ECONOMIC GROWTH: AN ECONOMIST'S HISTORY OF THE UNITED STATES*, EDS. LANCE E. DAVIS ET AL. (NEW YORK: HARPER & ROW, 1963), P. 220; AND *HISTORICAL STATISTICS* (WASHINGTON, D.C.: GOVERNMENT PRINTING OFFICE, 1975), SERIES D4, D7, D8, D12, D17, D940, AND D943.

received wages some 40 percent above nonunion workers.[19] For most unskilled work, though, the wages of union members were only slightly higher than for nonunion workers, perhaps a few percentage points.

Finally, trade unions had become an important voice for labor in the political system. Labor Day as a national holiday was first celebrated in 1894; in 1913, Cabinet-level status was given to the Department of Labor. A more concrete example of the growing political power of labor was the change in rules governing compensation of workers for injuries received on the job. Historically, an employer who was sued by an injured worker had three, often effective, legal defenses: (1) that the risk had been known and accepted by the worker, (2) that the worker had not been reasonably careful, and (3) that the worker had been injured because of the negligence of a fellow worker. Between 1910 and 1930, labor won changes in state laws that eliminated these defenses. Eventually, insurance programs were established in which employers and employees contributed to a common pool that compensated injured workers. The result was that injured workers received more compensation. But, as Price Fishback has pointed out, the side-effects sometimes differed from what was intended. It was hoped that putting the burden on employers would make for a safer workplace, and often it did. The rate of fatal accidents in bituminous coal mining increased, however, because workers had a smaller incentive to avoid accidents and employers found it cheaper to pay the additional claims than to try to reduce accident rates.[20]

---

[19] H. G. Lewis, *Unionism and Relative Wages in the United States* (Chicago: University of Chicago Press, 1963).

[20] Price V. Fishback, "Workplace Safety During the Progressive Era: Fatal Accidents in Bituminous Coal Mining," *Explorations in Economic History* 23 (1986): 269–298.

The power of organized labor's support for favorable legislation was destined to grow and, as we shall see, flower during the Great Depression. For labor as a whole, however, it is fair to conclude that labor's nineteenth-century progress owed more to economic growth and rising productivity than to the unions' strength.

SELECTED REFERENCES AND SUGGESTED READINGS

Bernstein, Irving. *The Lean Years: A History of the American Worker, 1920–1933*. Boston: Houghton Mifflin, 1960.

Brody, David. *Labor in Crisis: The Steel Strike of 1919*. Philadelphia: Lippincott, 1965.

———. *Steelworkers in America*. Cambridge: Harvard University Press, 1960.

Carlson, Leonard A. "Labor Supply, the Acquisition of Skills and the Location of Southern Textile Mills, 1880–1900." *Journal of Economic History* 41 (1981): 65–71.

Commons, John R., et al. *History of Labour in the United States*. New York: Kelly, 1921.

Dubofsky, Melvyn. *Industrialism and the American Worker, 1865–1920*. Arlington Heights, Illinois: Harlan Davidson, 1975.

Dunlevy, James A., and Henry A. Gemery. "Economic Opportunity and the Responses of the 'Old' and 'New' Migrants to the United States." *Journal of Economic History* 38 (1978): 901–917.

Easterlin, Richard. "Economic-Demographic Interactions and Long Swings in Economic Growth." *American Economic Review* (1966): 1063–1104.

———. "Population." In *American Economic Growth; An Economist's History of the United States*, eds. Lance E. Davis et al. New York: Harper & Row, 1972.

———. "Population Issues in American Economic History: A Survey and Critique." In *Research in Economic History*, ed. Robert Gallman. Greenwich, Connecticut: JAI Press, 1977, supplement.

———. *Population, Labor Force, and Long Swings in Economic Growth: The American Experience*. New York: Columbia University Press, 1968.

Erickson, Charlotte. *American Industry and the European Immigrant 1860–1885*. New York: Russell & Russell, 1967.

Ermisch, John, and Thomas Weiss. "The Impact of the Rural Market on the Growth of the Urban Workforce, U.S., 1870–1900." *Explorations in Economic History* 11 (Winter 1973–1974): 137–154.

Fishback, Price V. *Soft Coal, Hard Choices: The Economic Welfare of Bituminous Coal Miners, 1890–1930*. New York: Oxford University Press, 1992.

———. "Workplace Safety During the Progressive Era: Fatal Accidents in Bituminous Coal Mining." *Explorations in Economic History* 23 (1986): 269–298.

Frauendorf, Martha Norby. "Relative Earnings of Native and Foreign-Born Women." *Explorations in Economic History* 15 (1978): 211–220.

Galloway, Lowell, and Richard Vedder. "Emigration from the United Kingdom to the United States, 1860–1913." *Journal of Economic History* 31 (1971): 885–897.

———. "Population Transfers and the Post-Bellum Adjustments to Economic Dislocation, 1870–1920." *Journal of Economic History* 40 (1980): 143–150.

Galloway, Lowell, Richard Vedder, and Vishwa Shukla. "The Distribution of the Immigrant Population in the United States: An Economic Analysis." *Explorations in Economic History* 11 (1974): 213–226.

Goldin, Claudia. *Understanding the Gender Gap: An Economic History of American Women*. New York: Oxford University Press, 1990.

———. "The Work and Wages of Single Women, 1870–1920." *Journal of Economic History* 40 (1980): 81–88.

Grob, Gerald. *Workers and Utopia: A Study of the Ideological Conflict in the American Labor Movement, 1865–1900.* New York: Quadrangle Books, 1969.

Harber, Samuel. *Efficiency and Uplift: Scientific Management in the Progressive Era, 1890–1920.* Chicago: University of Chicago Press, 1964.

Higgs, Robert. "Cycles and Trends of Mortality in 18 Large American Cities, 1871–1900." *Explorations in Economic History* 16 (1979): 381–408.

———. "Landless by Law: Japanese Immigrants in California Agriculture to 1941." *Journal of Economic History* 38 (1978): 205–225.

———. "Mortality and Rural America, 1870–1920." *Explorations in Economic History* 10 (1973): 177–196.

———. "Race, Skills and Earnings: American Immigrants in 1909." *Journal of Economic History* 31 (1971): 420–428.

Hill, Peter. "Relative Skill and Income Levels of Native and Foreign-Born Workers in the United States." *Explorations in Economic History* 12 (1975): 47–60.

Jenks, Jeremiah, and Jeff Lauck. *The Immigration Problem.* New York: Funk & Wagnalls, 1926.

Jerome, Harry. *Migration and Business Cycles.* New York: National Bureau of Economic Research, 1926.

Kirk, Gordon W., and Carolyn J. Kirk. "The Immigrant, Economic Opportunity, and Type of Settlement in Nineteenth-Century America." *Journal of Economic History* 38 (1978): 226–234.

Kuznets, Simon. "Notes of the Pattern of U.S. Economic Growth." In *The Reinterpretation of American Economic History,* eds. Robert Fogel and Stanley Engerman. New York: Harper & Row, 1971.

———. "Two Centuries of Economic Growth: Reflections on U.S. Experience." *American Economic Review* 67, no. 1 (1977): 1–14.

Kuznets, Simon, and Ernest Rubin. *Immigration and the Foreign Born.* New York: National Bureau of Economic Research, 1954.

Lebergott, Stanley. "The American Labor Force." In *American Economic Growth,* eds. Lance E. Davis et al. New York: Harper & Row, 1972.

Livesay, Harold. *Samuel Gompers and Organized Labor in America.* Boston: Little, Brown, 1978.

McGouldrick, Paul F., and Michael B. Tannen. "Did American Manufacturers Discriminate Against Immigrants Before 1914?" *Journal of Economic History* 37 (1977): 723–746.

Meeker, Edward. "The Improving Health of the United States, 1850–1914." *Explorations in Economic History* 9 (1972): 353–374.

Neal, Larry, and Paul Uselding. "Immigration, A Neglected Source of U.S. Economic Growth, 1790–1913." *Oxford Economic Papers* 24, 2d series, no. 1 (March 1972).

Nelson, Daniel. *Frederick W. Taylor and Scientific Management.* Madison: University of Wisconsin Press, 1980.

———. *Managers and Workers: the Origins of the New Factory System in the United States, 1880–1920.* Madison: University of Wisconsin Press, 1975.

Nevins, Allan, and Frank Hill. *Ford: The Times, the Men, and the Company.* New York: Scribner's, 1954.

Niemi, Albert W. "The Role of Immigration in United States Commodity Production, 1869–1929." *Social Science Quarterly* 52, no. 1 (June 1971).

Rotella, Elyce J. *From Home to Office.* Ann Arbor: UMI Research Press, 1981.

———. "The Transformation of the American Office: Changes in Employment and Technology." *Journal of Economic History* 41 (1981): 51–57.

Taylor, Philip. *The Distant Magnet: European Emigration to the United States.* New York: Harper & Row, 1971.

Thomas, Brinley. *Migration and Economic Growth.* Cambridge: Cambridge University Press, 1954.

CHAPTER NINETEEN

MONEY AND FINANCE IN THE POSTBELLUM ERA

CHAPTER THEME The 50-year span between the Civil War and World War I was one of continuous, intense public controversy over the American monetary system. Two issues—deflation and banking panics—overshadowed all others and produced repeated attempts to reform the monetary system.

The deflation began after the Civil War, when the money supply and prices had doubled, and persisted with brief interruptions for three decades. Debtors suffered from the protracted deflation, and farmers were particularly hard hit. As one popular folksong from the 1880s put it: "The farmer is the man, lives on credit till the fall, with interest rates so high, it's a wonder he don't die, for the mortgage man's the one who gets it all."[1] Farmers and other debtors were vocal in their opposition to deflation, and supported a number of inflationary schemes. For the nation as a whole, though, this was a period of rapid economic growth, which might be threatened by inflationary measures. From the high inflations of Revolutionary times and the Civil War, and from the hyperinflation in the South toward the end of the Civil War, Americans had learned lessons they would not soon forget. With few exceptions, leaders in politics and finance insisted on "sound money" and were generally successful in resisting inflationary changes.

The deflation was punctuated by financial crises in which banks closed, factories and railroads went bankrupt, and millions lost their jobs. The depressions of the mid-1870s and mid-1890s were especially severe. In April 1894, "Coxey's Army" of the unemployed arrived in Washington to vocalize demands for federal relief. It portended a different future for the nation, where the government provided direct aid to the unemployed. Prices began moving upward after the depression of the mid-1890s, but there was another banking panic in 1907.

Although the problems were easy to identify, reaching agreement on solutions was far harder. Special interests, ever watchful, used every means at hand to forestall change or force it in directions favorable to themselves. Silver producers, for example, powerfully represented in the Senate, jumped on the antideflation bandwagon and helped direct its course. And lobbying by country bankers shielded a system of thousands of local banks that were restricted in their growth and prevented from

---

[1] Pete Seeger, *American Favorite Ballads* (New York: Oak Publications, 1961), p. 57.

crossing state boundaries to engage in interstate branch banking, thus perpetuating a system that was vulnerable to banking panics.

These legal restrictions had an important impact on the growth of firms hungry for financial capital. Many firms merged to accommodate their financial needs, and investment bankers, essentially brokerage houses specializing in stocks and bonds, emerged to take positions of dominance in the world of U.S. finance. This was quite different from England, where large banking conglomerates were allowed and grew large enough to meet most of the financial needs of the industrializing nation.

Despite the conflicts among interest groups, by the end of 1913 the nation once again had a central bank, one based on arrangements different from earlier versions. These were codified in the Federal Reserve Act signed by President Woodrow Wilson. But as the Great Depression of the 1930s clarified, the Federal Reserve System was not a foolproof answer to the nation's hard-earned lessons about deflation and panics.

THE CURRENCY AND THE POLITICS OF THE PRICE LEVEL

Figure 19-1 (see next page) traces the different forms of currencies in circulation from 1860 to 1915. The figure does not show bank deposits, the larger part of the money supply. Deposits will be discussed later in this chapter. But it is important to begin with the currencies, because these constituted bank reserves and helped determine the growth rate of the total amount of money. We will summarize the story of each currency.

UNITED STATES NOTES (GREENBACKS)

Before the Civil War, the amount of money in circulation was determined by flows of specie into and out of the country through foreign trade and by flows from American mines. Federal revenues were obtained overwhelmingly from tariff collections, which declined markedly as trade fell when the Civil War began. By 1862, gold was flowing out of the country so fast that the government and banks were obligated to suspend gold specie payments. Silver, which had been undervalued at the mint ever since the Currency Act of 1834, had virtually no circulation.[2]

Because sufficient revenues to wage the war were not obtained from sales of U.S. Treasury bonds (at least at interest rates the government was willing to pay), the Treasury in 1862 issued a new fiat currency, nicknamed "greenbacks." This avalanche of new paper money is shown in Figure 19-1; the results are reflected in Figure 19-2 (page 430), which shows the upward zoom of prices in greenbacks during the war years. People were legally bound to accept greenbacks during the Civil War, and the government accepted greenbacks for all payments except customs duties. Nevertheless, the value of greenbacks did not equal that of gold. In the eastern part of the country, gold ceased to be used for ordinary transactions. Its main use was for paying certain taxes, for foreign exchange to purchase imports, and for speculation. In California, however, where gold had always been widely used, people continued to use it. In California greenbacks were "foreign exchange."

On the New York gold market, the price of gold in greenbacks varied from moment to moment. News from the battlefield would often send the price of gold roaring up or down depending on whether it portended a shortening or lengthening of the war. At its low point, a prewar gold dollar cost $2.86 in greenbacks. On August 31, 1865, four and a half months after Lincoln's assassination, $100 in gold exchanged for $144 in greenbacks or checks drawn on bank deposits. Other types of paper money (such as state-bank notes), which could be redeemed only in greenbacks, depreciated similarly.

---

[2]The mint set a price at which it would convert silver into money. If silver could be sold for a higher price on the bullion market, then the mint was said to undervalue silver. See Chapter 12 for more discussion.

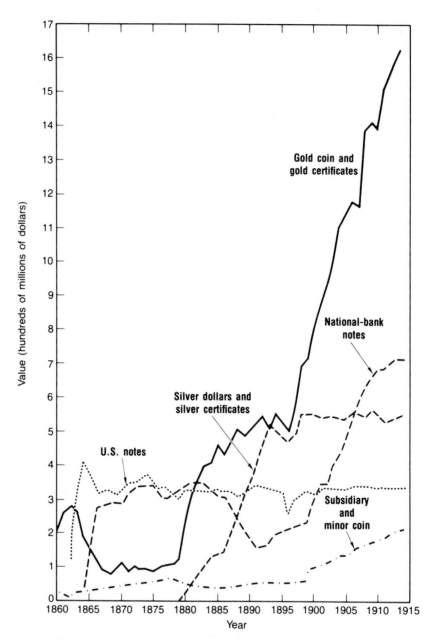

FIGURE 19-1 FORMS OF MONEY IN THE UNITED STATES, 1860–1915 *From the late 1870s to the early 1890s, there were substantial additions to the nation's monetary stocks of gold and silver, but it was not enough to prevent deflation. After 1895, however, the increase in the stock of gold became even more rapid, and deflation became inflation.*

SOURCE: BOARD OF GOVERNORS OF THE FEDERAL RESERVE SYSTEM.

The changing face of the American dollar—it reflected the search for a sound banking system and a stable price level.

RETURNING TO THE GOLD STANDARD

After the Civil War, there was a vigorous national debate about whether the country should return to the prewar gold standard: one dollar in greenbacks or bank deposits equal to one dollar in gold. The problem was that prices in the United States had risen relative to prices in England and other countries on the gold standard. If the United States simply promised to pay one dollar in gold for one dollar in greenbacks, America's stock of gold would quickly dwindle as people rushed to buy relatively cheaper

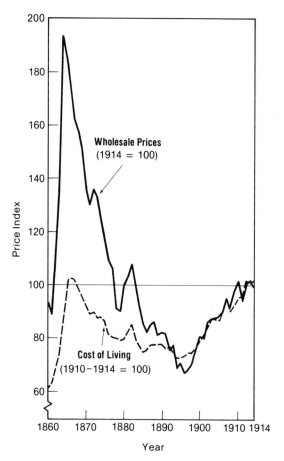

FIGURE 19-2 PRICES, 1860–1914

SOURCE: *HISTORICAL STATISTICS* (WASHINGTON, D.C.: GOVERNMENT PRINTING OFFICE, 1960), SERIES
E1, PP. 101, 157.

foreign goods. Prices in the United States, in other words, had to come down before
the United States could successfully resume the exchange of gold for greenbacks. Many
Democrats, along with members of radical groups such as the Greenback party, argued
that resumption of the gold standard was not worth the economic pain that was sure
to result. Debtors would suffer during the deflation, and working people would suffer
from unemployment.

But Republicans, who held the upper hand politically, argued that resumption was
necessary for several reasons. First, it was only fair that bondholders, who had been
paid interest in gold during the war, get their principal in gold as well. Bond prices
had remained strong during the war and, it was said, this was because bondholders
had received an implicit promise that they would be repaid in gold.[3] Second, to leave

---

[3]This was assured by the Public Credit Act of 1869.

the monetary base tied permanently to paper money would be dangerous, because governments could not be trusted with this power. Third, and perhaps most importantly, returning to the prewar gold parity was necessary to maintain the credibility of the United States abroad and access to foreign capital markets, especially London.

To bring greenbacks and other currencies onto a par with gold, and to eliminate the "gold premium," Treasury officials had recourse to two practical courses of action:

1. The general price level could be forced down rather quickly by contracting the supply of paper money. The greenback price of gold would decline with the general decrease of prices; when the mint price was reached, resumption could be proclaimed.

2. A slower, less painful decline in prices could be achieved by holding the money supply constant and allowing the growth of the economy to bring about a gradual decline in prices. Once again, the market price of gold would fall relatively and ultimately reach the mint price.[4]

Actually, as reflected in Figure 19-1, a severe policy of money contraction was initiated by Hugh McCulloch, Secretary of the Treasury in the Andrew Johnson administration, and this strategy was approved by Congress in December 1865 by passage of the Contraction Act. But the deflationary medicine was too bitter, and Congress ended contraction in February 1868. President Grant's Secretary of the Treasury, George S. Boutwell, followed a much easier policy: a general *easing* of the money markets rather than a tightening of them.[5] After Boutwell's resignation in 1873, his Assistant Secretary, William Richardson, pursued a still more passive policy. The idea was that the price level fell as the country grew up to its currency.

From 1868 to 1874, the Republican administration, while paying lip service to a return to gold, had taken the temperate course of not pressing for this return through severe contraction of the money stock. But after the Democrats won control of Congress in the election of 1874, lame-duck Republicans, fearful of the antipathy of western and southern legislators toward resumption, hurriedly passed an act providing for a return to gold payments in four years. After January 1, 1879, the United States was to maintain strict convertibility between greenbacks and gold. Thanks to a favorable balance of trade in the late 1870s, gold stocks in this country increased at a rapid rate. The government removed the requirements that all customs duties be paid in gold to prevent discrimination against greenbacks, and on the appointed day the United States began to maintain specie payments. For a technical reason to be discussed presently, the United States was not finally and legally committed to a gold standard and would not be for another 21 years. Nevertheless, between 1879 and 1900, the government did

---

[4] Other alternatives included devaluation of metal dollars, abandoning the specie standard, and simply hoping and praying for a fortuitous increase in the supply of the money metals. See Richard H. Timberlake, Jr., "Ideological Factors in Specie Resumption and Treasury Policy," *Journal of Economic History* 24 (1964). See also James K. Kindahl, "Economic Factors in Specie Resumption: The United States, 1865–1879," *Journal of Political Economy* 69 (February 1961): 30–48.

[5] It was Boutwell who broke the dramatic corner on gold attempted by James Fisk and Jay Gould by selling $4 million of the money metal in the "Gold Room" of the New York Stock Exchange. See Larry Wimmer, "The Gold Crisis of 1869: Stabilizing or Destabilizing Speculation Under Floating Exchange Rates," *Explorations in Economic History* 12 (1975): 105–122.

The *quantity theory of money* can be expressed by the following equation:

$$M = kPy$$

M stands for money (greenbacks and bank deposits and so on); k for the proportion of income held as money, usually assumed to be fairly stable; P for the price level; and y for real output. The question during the greenback era was how to lower P to bring it into line with other countries. One policy was to lower M by the necessary amount. The alternative was to hold M constant and allow the increase in y to gradually lower P, letting the "country grow up to the currency."

in fact maintain parity of all other money forms with gold, and during these years America was on a de facto gold standard.

THE CRIME OF '73

During the Civil War and for several years afterwards, silver coins had gone out of circulation, having been replaced at first by ungummed postage stamps and later by fractional currency—paper notes issued by the government in denominations of 5, 10, 25, and 50 cents. It is not surprising, then, that when Congress sought to simplify the coinage in 1873, the silver dollar was omitted from the list of coins to be minted. Some farseeing officials feared an increase in the supply of silver that would flood the mint, increasing the money supply, raising prices, and thus delaying resumption. But most of the Congress took little notice of the omission at the time, because at the mint ratio of approximately 16 to 1, silver was worth more on the market than at the mint. Yet scarcely three years later, the failure to include the silver dollar in the Act of 1873 began a furor that was to last for a quarter century.

The reason for the subsequent agitation over the "demonetization" of silver lay in the fact that the price of silver began falling in international markets. The increasing output of western silver mines in the United States and a shift of the bimetallic countries of western Europe to the gold standard had led to a growing surplus of silver. When the value of the silver contained in a dollar actually fell below the price for a dollar that the government, under the Coinage Act of 1834, had *formerly* paid, silver

When gold fluctuated wildly in 1869, the Gold Room of the New York Stock Exchange was the nerve-center of speculation. In its center, a bronze Cupid sprayed water quietly; on the dais, the secretary of the room had to cup his ears to hear and record transactions.

producers took silver to the mint for coinage.[6] To their dismay they discovered that the government would take only as much silver as the Treasury needed for small subsidiary coins. The cry that went up from the silver producers was horrendous.

A relatively small group like the silver producers would not appear to have much power. But during the 1870s and 1880s, a number of western states were being admitted to the Union, each having two U.S. senators to represent their small populations, and silver producers concentrated in these states acquired political representation out of all proportion to their numbers. The "reflationist" element in the West and South joined the silver producers in a clamor for the free and unlimited coinage of silver at the old mint ratio of 16 to 1. Silver advocates knew that at such a ratio silver would be brought

---

[6] A dollar contained 371.25 grains of pure silver, or a little over three-quarters of an ounce. The *average* bullion value of that amount of silver in 1873 was $1.00368. The next year, the value dropped to $0.98909 and fell consistently from that year on.

to the mint in great quantities and that the monetary reserves of the country, the total money supply, and the general price level would consequently be increased.

The opposition's cry that gold would be driven out of circulation meant nothing to the advocates of free silver except relief to the unemployed and lighter burdens for oppressed debtors. To the supporters of the free coinage of silver, the act that had demonetized silver became the "Crime of '73."

Ultimately, Congress passed a compromise between the positions of the "sound-money" and free-coinage forces. The first of four major silver bills was the Bland-Allison Act of 1878. This law provided for the coinage of silver in limited amounts.[7] The Secretary of the Treasury was directed to purchase not less than $2 million and not more than $4 million worth of silver each month *at the current market price.* The conservative secretaries in office during the next twelve years purchased only the minimum amount of silver, but by 1890 the Treasury's monetary silver (not counting subsidiary coins) amounted to almost $380 million.

The government made a tidy profit (about $70 million) on its silver purchases under the Bland-Allison Act—the difference between the cost of the silver and the value placed on it by the Treasury—but the silver question was by no means settled. In 1878 the average market value of the silver contained in a dollar was just over 89¢. For the next twelve years, silver prices, despite the purchases, consistently fell. Neither the producers of silver, nor the debtors who wanted inflation, were appeased by the Bland-Allison Act.

After 1888, Republicans controlled both the White House and Congress. But to secure the passage of high-tariff legislation, it was necessary to have the votes of the silver senators. In exchange for their affirmative votes on the McKinley tariff bill, the Republican leadership agreed to further silver legislation. A new bill, the Sherman Silver Purchase Law of 1890, was carefully prepared to avoid the veto of President Benjamin Harrison. The Secretary of the Treasury was directed to make a monthly purchase, at the market rate, of 4.5 million ounces of silver. To pay for this quantity of bullion, he was to issue a new type of paper money to be known as Treasury notes, which were to be redeemable in either gold or silver at his discretion. At the silver prices prevailing in 1890, the new law authorized the purchase of almost double the monthly amount of silver taken in under the previous law. But silver supplies kept expanding so rapidly that its market price resumed further sharp declines almost immediately.

Within three years, the dollar amount of silver being purchased was little more than it had been under the old act. In 1893, at the insistence of Democratic President Cleveland—a "sound-money" man at odds with his party on this issue—the Sherman Act was repealed. In over three years of purchasing under this law, more than $150 million of the Treasury notes of 1890 were issued; overall, between 1878 and 1893 (as shown in Figure 19-1, page 428), $500 million was added to the currency by silver purchases. This was a victory of sorts for the silver forces. But the Treasury's silver purchases were

---

[7] According to the Bland-Allison Act and an amendment passed in 1886, the Treasury could keep the actual silver in its vaults and issue silver certificates instead. Nearly everyone except westerners preferred paper currency.

If the Government stamps 412½ grains of silver with the words "One Dollar," and forces them upon the people when they are at 7 per cent. discount with gold and over 4 per cent below greenbacks, it stamps a lie upon the coin, and legalizes a cheat and fraud upon those whom it forces to accept it.—*Times.*

THE CURRENT QUESTION.

SILVER—"*You need not hold yourself so high. I'm as good as you are.*"
GOLD—"*You never were, and never will be, my equal.*"

Friends of silver saw in its monetization relief from depression and persistent grief and agony if gold continued to reign as the sole monetary metal in America.

insufficient to prevent silver prices from falling, and (as shown in Figure 19-2 on page 430) the general price level continued its deflationary spiral. When the Sherman Act was repealed in 1893, the nation was just entering a severe depression.

THE COMMITMENT TO THE GOLD STANDARD

As Figure 19-2 shows, prices continued to fall from resumption in 1879 to the mid-1890s. This was true not only in the United States but also in other countries on the gold standard. Only countries on the silver standard experienced rising prices. Deflation did not mean that economic growth ceased. Quite to the contrary, economic expansion occurred at a rapid rate on average both here and in Europe. This is an important point to remember because many people who know only about the deflation and depression in the 1930s assume that falling prices mean falling output.

Though the economy grew, some people did lose out. Farmers with fixed mortgage payments, for example, suffered because they had to pay back their mortgages with "heavier" dollars. Farm prices fell faster than other prices, but it was hard for the farmer to distinguish relative price effects that were determined by the supply and demand for agricultural products from the absolute price effects that were subject to a monetary remedy. Farmers therefore tended to blame the deflation for problems caused by other economic forces.

Why were prices falling? The basic problem was that the demand for money (and ultimately for gold, which was the base of the monetary system) was growing faster than the supply. The rapid increase in economic activity, growing financial sophistication, and the addition of more countries to the gold standard all increased the demand for gold. Meanwhile the supply, although growing at a good rate by historical standards, could not keep pace.

Although the silver acts of 1878 and 1890 made silver certificates redeemable in *either* gold *or* silver, in practice Treasury authorities redeemed them in gold if it were demanded. After 1879, Treasury secretaries felt that a minimum gold reserve of $100

ECONOMIC INSIGHTS

As debtors, farmers would benefit from inflation, but perhaps not by as much as they hoped. Farm mortgages, particularly on the frontier, were for short durations, often five years or less. If a mortgage was renewed after silver inflation was expected, lenders would demand and get higher interest rates. American economist Irving Fisher published a detailed study of the relationship between price level changes and interest rates in 1894 in response to the debate over silver. He found that interest rates did go up after inflation and down after deflation, but with a long lag. In his honor the tendency of interest rates to reflect inflation is known as the "Fisher effect." It can be expressed by the following equation:

$$i = r + p$$

where i is the market rate of interest, r is the real rate of interest, and p is the rate of price change. Critics of the silverites maintained that an increase in p would just produce an increase in i, leaving r unchanged.

million was necessary to back up the paper circulation. Just at the time when the Treasury notes of 1890 were authorized, the government's gold reserve began declining toward the $100 million mark as the public presented Treasury notes and greenbacks for payment in gold. To meet current expenses, the Treasury had to pay the paper money out again almost as soon as it was received. By early 1893, the gold drain had become serious, and the gold reserve actually dipped below the traditional minimum toward the middle of the year.

Several times during the next three years it appeared certain that the de facto gold standard would have to be abandoned. Two kinds of drains—"external" (foreign) and "internal" (domestic)—plagued the Treasury from 1891 to 1896. Today, abandonment of gold redemption hardly seems ominous, but in the middle 1890s conservatives considered going off the gold standard equivalent to declaring national bankruptcy. The difficulty was that when the danger of abandoning gold became apparent, people rushed to acquire gold, thus making it even more likely that the Treasury *would* have to abandon the gold standard. Chiefly by selling bonds for gold, the administration replenished the government's reserve whenever it appeared that the standard was about to be lost. The repeal of the Sherman Silver Purchase Law of 1893 reduced the number of Treasury notes, which, along with greenbacks, the public was presenting for redemption. Increasing exports at last brought an influx of gold from abroad in the summer of 1896, improving public confidence to the extent that the gold standard was saved.

William Jennings Bryan on the political stump. Bryan was more than just a political leader; he also had a lively awareness of the need for economic and political reform. Although he was defeated on the money issue, Bryan's monetary prescriptions had a solid New Deal ring.

The election of 1896 settled the matter of a monetary standard for nearly 40 years. The Democrats, under the leadership of William Jennings Bryan, stood for free coinage of silver at a ratio of 16 to 1—even though the market ratio was then over 30 to 1. At the Democratic national convention, Bryan inspired the inflationists and won the party's nomination with his famous "Cross of Gold" speech, which ended with this stirring call to arms:

> Having behind us the producing masses of this nation and the world, supported by the commercial interests, and the toilers everywhere, we will answer their demand for a gold standard by saying to them: You shall not press down upon the brow of labor this crown of thorns, you shall not crucify mankind upon a cross of gold.

The Republicans, with William McKinley as their candidate, stood solidly for the gold standard.[8] The West and the South supported Bryan; the North and the East supported McKinley. In the conservative East, industrial employers brought every possible pressure, legitimate or not, to bear on employee voters. One genuine issue was the tariff. Bryan, like many of his supporters in the farm states, opposed a high tariff, but workers may have been persuaded that the tariff protected jobs. In any event, Bryan did not draw the great urban vote, as Franklin Roosevelt was to do 36 years later, and when well-to-do farmers in the older agricultural states deserted Bryan, the cause was lost.[9]

The Republican victory of 1896 was not followed immediately by legislation ending the controversy, because free-silver advocates still held a majority in Congress. But the return of prosperity, encouraged by new supplies of gold, made Congress receptive to definitive gold legislation. The new supplies of gold, although partly the result of the high real price for gold (the price paid by the mint relative to prices in general), were largely unanticipated. New gold fields were opened in many areas of the world, including the immensely rich gold fields of South Africa, and a new method for processing gold through the use of cyanide was developed. Ironically, the increase in the supply of gold accomplished the goal of the silverites—expansion of the money supply and inflation.

Under the Gold Standard Act of 1900, the dollar was defined solely in terms of gold, and all other forms of money were to be convertible into gold. The Secretary of the Treasury was directed to maintain a gold reserve of $150 million, which was not to be drawn on to meet current government expenses. To prevent a recurrence of the difficulties of the 1890s, a provision was made to keep redeemed silver certificates and greenbacks in the Treasury during times of stress for borrowing to meet deficits that

---

[8] McKinley did, however, promise to call a conference to consider an international bimetallic standard, a promise he honored.

[9] The battle over the standards was reflected, it has been argued, in L. Frank Baum's contemporary *The Wonderful Wizard of Oz*. Dorothy represents America; the Scarecrow, the farmer; the Tin Man, the working man; the Cowardly Lion, William Jennings Bryan; and so on. Dorothy seeks wisdom by following the yellow brick road (the gold standard) to the Emerald City (Washington). But in the end she discovers that she had the power to solve her problems with her all the time, her silver shoes (the ruby slippers were added by MGM). See Hugh Rockoff, "The Wizard of Oz as a Monetary Allegory," *Journal of Political Economy* 98 (August 1990): 739–760.

might occur from time to time.[10] The United States had at last committed itself by law to the gold standard.

Who was right, Bryan and the silverites or McKinley and the "gold bugs"? Economist Milton Friedman has provided the most convincing answer. He argues that eliminating the silver dollar in 1873 was a mistake that produced an unnecessary deflation, but that by Bryan's time it was probably too late to do much about it.[11] Friedman and Anna J. Schwartz have also pointed out that a firm commitment to either standard would have been better than the long, drawn-out battle that took place.[12]

The years between 1896 and World War I were the heyday of the gold standard. As seen in Figure 19-2 (page 430), prices rose at a moderate rate, about 2 percent per year. International exchange rates were fixed because most industrial countries were on the gold standard. Indeed, it could well be said that there was really only one international currency, gold; it simply had a different name in each country. Fixed exchange rates and mildly rising prices encouraged the free flow of goods and capital across international borders. London was the financial center of the world. Bonds sold there sent streams of capital into the less developed parts of the world. No wonder that many economists still look to this period as a model for the world's monetary system.

But there were costs to the gold standard. Resources were used to mine gold in South Africa and the Klondike and to dredge gold from the rivers of California. A paper standard would have permitted these resources to be used elsewhere. The rates of growth of the world's money supplies, moreover, were being determined by the individual decisions of miners and chemists and by the forces of nature that had sewn the rare seams of gold into the earth. During the years after 1896, the net result was that the world's stock of monetary gold grew at a satisfactory rate. But this conclusion was not so clear for the years before 1896. During financial crises, moreover, adherence to the gold standard made it difficult to supply additional money to financial markets. In any case, there is always the hope, sometimes betrayed, that central bankers backed up by reams of scientific analysis can do a better job than an automatic mechanism such as the gold standard.

The debate over the net benefits of the gold standard continues unabated. Historical comparisons, however, can narrow the range of debate. Michael D. Bordo has shown that on many dimensions (most importantly, average unemployment), the performance of the gold standard was inferior to modern monetary standards. Only with respect to long-run price stability could the gold standard be declared clearly superior.

NATIONAL-BANK NOTES AND THE TOTAL MONEY SUPPLY

A new set of banking institutions, national banks, were created by the National Bank Act in 1863. Several considerations combined to push the federal government

---

[10]The Treasury notes of 1890 were retired by the Gold Standard Act.

[11]Milton Friedman, "The Crime of 1873," *Journal of Political Economy* 6 (December 1990): 1159–1194.

[12]Milton Friedman and Anna J. Schwartz, *A Monetary History of the United States* (Princeton: Princeton University Press, 1963), p. 134.

into the business of chartering banks. First, and cynics would say foremost, was the need to strengthen the market for government bonds. National banks were permitted to issue notes that could circulate as money. To secure its note issue, each national bank was required to buy U.S. government bonds equal to one-third (later one-quarter) of the dollar amount of its paid-in capital stock, with the provision that no bank would have to buy more than $50,000 worth of bonds. Each bank was to deposit its bonds with the U.S. Treasurer and was to receive notes, engraved in a standard design but with the name of the issuing bank on the obverse side, in the amount of 90 percent of the par or market value (whichever was lower) of the bonds deposited. A national bank could have any amount of government bonds in its portfolio, but the amount of its notes outstanding could not exceed its *capital* in dollar amount.[13]

There were other considerations besides bonds. The national banking system was seen as a reform that would replace the heterogeneous mass of currency issued by state banks with a uniform national currency. Salmon Chase, the Secretary of the Treasury who proposed the national system, had advocated reform of the note issue before the war. The National Banking Act was also seen as a conservative reform. A uniform national currency, the greenback, did exist in 1863, but permanently giving the federal government the power to print money was considered risky. The result might be the sort of wild inflation that had occurred during the American Revolution. It would be better, it was argued, to have a gold-backed currency managed by privately owned banks. Finally, there was a practical consideration: many western banks that had invested heavily in southern bonds had gone bankrupt; something had to be done to replace them.

National-bank notes became important by 1865, grew steadily in amount for a decade, and then began to fluctuate. Originally, the total issue was limited to $300 million, a sum allotted among the states in proportion to the population and to the total national-bank capital within each state. Restrictions were removed by a clause in the Resumption Act of 1875, and from then on national banks kept in circulation whatever amount of notes seemed profitable (again, see Figure 19-1 on page 428). The low point of notes outstanding was reached in the early 1890s. A slow rise followed, which changed in the early years of the century to a sharp increase, and a record high of more than $700 million was reached in 1914.

Collectively, greenbacks, national-bank notes, and silver and gold specie or their certificates, plus small subsidiary coins, made up the currency. As shown in Figure 19-1, first greenbacks (U.S. notes) and then national-bank notes initiated the monetary increases that sent prices skyrocketing during the Civil War years. Later gold and silver provided other notable increases in the supply of hand-to-hand money. These types of currency provided the "dynamic" elements in the *supply of currency*. But as shown in Figures 19-3 and 19-4 on the following pages, most of the increase in the *total money supply* was created by the growth of bank deposits—savings and checking deposits

---

[13]National banks in towns of less than 6,000 population had to have a minimum capital of $50,000; those in towns of more than 6,000 but less than 50,000 a capital of $100,000; and those in cities of 50,000 or more a capital of $200,000.

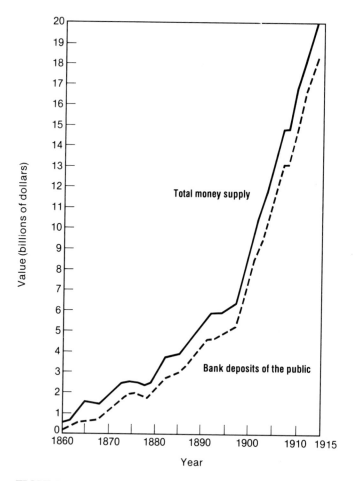

FIGURE 19-3 THE U.S. MONEY SUPPLY, 1860–1915 *The total U.S. money supply grew in three trend surges of increasing speed, 1860–1878, 1879–1896, and 1897–1914, with greater instability before 1897.*

SOURCE: ALBERT G. HART, *MONEY, DEBT, AND ECONOMIC ACTIVITY* (ENGLEWOOD CLIFFS, NEW JERSEY: PRENTICE-HALL, 1948).

created by loans. The currency amounts were critical to the total, however. Cash, except for the national-bank notes, constituted the reserves of the banking system. The growth of these reserves allowed the growth of bank deposits and the total money supply.

A DUAL BANKING SYSTEM

The National Bank Act of 1863 created a new type of bank, a national bank, but it did not eliminate the older institutions chartered by the states. To make the national

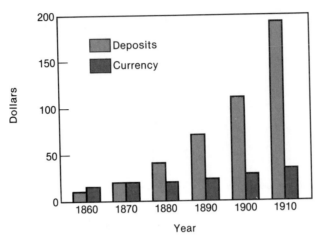

FIGURE 19-4 Per Capita Deposits and Currency in Circulation, 1860–1910

Source: Data from *Historical Statistics of the United States, 1789–1945* (Washington, D.C.: Government Printing Office, 1947), pp. 25, 262, 263, and 274.

banks appear more sound than state banks, legal reserve requirements were mandated and double liability was imposed on the stock of national banks.[14]

The National Bank Act recognized prevailing practice in many states by permitting new national banks to keep their reserves in two forms: cash in their vaults or deposits with a national bank in one of 17 "redemption" cities. Banks located in New York City (later called a "central reserve" city) were exceptions in that they had to keep *all* their reserves as cash in vault. Banks in the 16 other redemption cities (later redesignated "reserve" cities) had to keep half their reserves as cash but could keep the other half as deposits with national banks in New York. Banks in all other cities and towns (country banks) had to keep two-fifths of their reserves as cash but could deposit the remaining three-fifths in a national bank in a redemption city. Reserves, in whatever form they were maintained, were set at 25 percent for banks in redemption cities and at 15 percent for country banks. Originally, reserves were to be calculated as a percentage of notes outstanding plus deposits.

These rules kept in place an "inverted pyramid" of reserves based in New York. The inverted pyramid made the banking system more vulnerable to panics. A demand for cash in rural areas (perhaps because of a high number of bank failures) would be focused on the New York money market. If the New York banks were forced to cut lending and suspend gold payments, the whole system would be brought to a stop.

Because the early pace of conversion from state to national status was slow, a tax of 2 percent was levied against state-bank notes in June 1864, and this was raised to 10 percent in March 1865. Then, as Table 19-1 indicates, the pace of conversion soared.

---

[14]Under double liability, a shareholder in a failed bank lost not only his original investment but also an additional amount equal, if need be, to the par value of his shares.

TABLE 19-1 COMMERCIAL BANKS IN THE UNITED STATES, 1860–1914

Year[a]	State banks[b]	National banks	Year[a]	State banks[b]	National banks
1860	1,562	n.a.	1888	1,523	3,120
1861	1,601	n.a.	1889	1,791	3,239
1862	1,492	n.a.			
1863	1,466	66	1890	2,250	3,484
1864	1,089	467	1891	2,743	3,652
			1892	3,773	3,759
1865	349	1,294	1893	4,188	3,807
1866	297	1,634	1894	4,188	3,770
1867	272	1,636			
1868	247	1,640	1895	4,369	3,715
1869	259	1,619	1896	4,279	3,689
			1897	4,420	3,610
1870	325	1,612	1898	4,486	3,581
1871	452	1,723	1899	4,738	3,582
1872	566	1,853			
1873	277	1,968	1900	5,007	3,731
1874	368	1,983	1901	5,651	4,163
			1902	6,171	4,532
1875	586	2,076	1903	6,890	4,935
1876	671	2,091	1904	7,970	5,327
1877	631	2,078			
1878	510	2,056	1905	9,018	5,664
1879	648	2,048	1906	10,220	6,046
			1907	11,469	6,422
1880	650	2,076	1908	12,803	6,817
1881	683	2,115	1909	13,421	6,886
1882	704	2,239			
1883	788	2,417	1910	14,348	7,138
1884	852	2,625	1911	15,322	7,270
			1912	16,037	7,366
1885	1,015	2,689	1913	16,841	7,467
1886	891	2,809	1914	17,498	7,518
1887	1,471	3,014			

SOURCE: *BANKING STUDIES*, BY MEMBERS OF THE STAFF OF THE BOARD OF GOVERNORS OF THE FEDERAL RESERVE SYSTEM (BALTIMORE: WAVERLY PRESS, 1941), PP. 422–423. SEE ALSO *HISTORICAL STATISTICS OF THE UNITED STATES, COLONIAL TIMES TO 1957* (WASHINGTON, D.C.: GOVERNMENT PRINTING OFFICE, 1958), ESP. PP. 623–632.

[a] All figures as of June 30, or nearest available date.
[b] Excludes unincorporated banks and mutual savings banks.

A majority of the state banks immediately shifted to federal jurisdiction; in 1866, less than 300 state banks remained. For the most part, these state banks were large city banks that had long since discarded the practice of issuing notes when they extended loans. After the Civil War, bank deposits (checking) were far more important than notes in cities; by the mid-1870s, banks in all but the backwoods areas could extend loans simply by crediting the deposit account of the borrower.

By the early 1870s, then, it had become clear that a national charter was not essential. Moreover, for bank organizers who had no aspirations toward national or substantial regional operations, state charters had several positive advantages:

1. Lower amounts of capital were required in most state jurisdictions. Until 1900, the minimum amount of capital required for a national bank was $50,000. In the West and South, state minimum capital requirements of $10,000 were common, and some states prescribed no capital minimums at all.

2. Reserves required against deposits were lower under most state banking laws than under the National Bank Act. Furthermore, national banks had to observe substantially stricter rules regarding the amount of cash held in reserve—and the Comptroller of the Currency was generally more severe in dealing with reserve deficiencies than were state counterparts. Finally, several state laws permitted lower reserves to be maintained against time deposits.[15]

3. In general, national banks operated under much stricter lending and investment policies than did their state-chartered competitors. Before 1913, the National Bank Act for all practical purposes prohibited loans on real estate, which in some areas constituted a major portion of state-bank business. Until 1906, a national bank could not lend to a single borrower more than 10 percent of its paid-up capital—a limitation that became increasingly harmful in competing with other institutions. And although state banks and trust companies frequently had wide latitude in purchasing the stocks of banks and other corporations, national banks were barred from such activities.

4. Standards of bank supervision and examination were much higher in the national jurisdiction.

In summary, the rules governing the entry and operations of banks chartered by the states were far less onerous than those prescribed for national banks. From 1864 to 1914 (and, for that matter, to the present day), a dual banking system developed simply because one set of rules was easier than the other. Bankers weighed the advantages of membership in the national system (prestige that attracted depositors, and the right to issue notes) against the costs (stricter regulations) and chose the charter that promised the most profits.

As Table 19-1 shows (see preceding page), the revival of state banking began in the 1870s; by the early 1880s, the relative growth of the state-bank system was unmistakable. Between 1880 and 1900, the number of national banks increased from 2,076 to 3,731 while the number of state banks jumped from 650 to just over 5,000. In 1900, the resources of national banks were just less than double those of state banks. A few years later, in 1907, state banks outnumbered national banks by nearly two to one, and the resources of state banks were about the same as those of national banks.

---

[15] Time deposits required the depositor to notify the bank in advance if the deposits were going to be withdrawn. Normally banks waived the notification requirement, but during a panic they might insist upon it.

FINANCIAL CAPITAL, INVESTMENT BANKING, AND THE NATIONAL DEBT

The National Bank Acts, as we have seen, were effective in curtailing the growth of state banking in the late 1860s and early 1870s. Barriers formed by high capital requirements of national banks, restrictions on mortgage loans, and limits on their note issues before 1875 also protected many country national banks from new entrants and increased competition. This allowed many rural national banks to effectively price discriminate: rural national banks restricted loans and charged higher interest rates to local borrowers; they also sent their reserves to city banks, usually above required limits. This practice, in combination with slower banking expansion rurally, helped finance urban-industrial growth. As Richard E. Sylla has concluded, the national banking system "raised barriers to entry into banking, and these had differential geographic impact which, when coupled with the increased mobility the National Banking System gave to interbank transfers of funds, worked very much to the advantage of industrial finance."[16]

The discrimination by rural banks created regional differences in lending rates that persisted, narrowing gradually, from the Civil War to 1900. The narrowing took place for a number of reasons. The recovery of the southern financial system after the Civil War gradually brought rates in that region into line with those in other regions. The spread of the commercial paper market (in which short-term business loans were sold directly to private investors) provided additional competition for the state banks. And, as John James has pointed out, the introduction of free banking in a number of states increased competition among the state banks.[17]

THE RISE OF INVESTMENT BANKING

As Lance Davis discovered in his comparative analysis of U.S. and British industrial finance, the American system was very different from the British one.[18] British industrialists could visit their local branch banks—Lloyd's or Westminster of Barclays—and draw capital loans on a huge system, a capital pool built internationally. American firms, on the other hand, faced banks with more restricted capital pools. Typically, theirs were locally based funds plus some additional funds from interbank transfers.

Because of this limitation, a new form of banking—investment banking—emerged to serve the expansion of railroads, mining companies, and large-scale manufacturers. Unlike commercial banks, investment banks did not have the power to issue notes (money) or make deposits. Instead they acted as middlemen, bringing together

---

[16] Richard E. Sylla, "The United States, 1863–1913," in *Banking and Economic Development: Some Lessons of Economic History,* ed. Rondo Cameron (New York: Oxford University Press, 1972), p. 236.

[17] See John James, *Money and Capital Markets in Postbellum America* (Princeton: Princeton University Press, 1978), for a thorough discussion of these issues.

[18] Lance E. Davis, "Capital Immobilities and Financial Capitalism: A Study of Economic Evolution in the United States," *Explorations in Entrepreneurial History* 1, no. 1 (Fall 1963): 88–105.

investors (stock buyers) and borrowers (firms). J. P. Morgan and Company was a pioneer in investment banking, earning $3 million for services in advising and selling stocks for Vanderbilt and his New York Central Railroad in 1879. Charles Schwab, an employee of Andrew Carnegie, carried a note to Morgan in 1900 with an asking price of over $400 million for Carnegie's steel holdings. Morgan promptly replied, "I'll take it"—thus giving birth to the United States Steel Corporation; it was by far the largest merger up to that time. Forty years earlier, when Carnegie had tried to raise financial capital of only a fraction of the sum Morgan promptly gave him, Carnegie had to go to England because no U.S. banks could supply his capital needs.

Investment banking grew up in response to the huge demands for capital, and close links between investment bankers and big business were forged even more strongly by the practice of placing representatives of the large investment houses on the boards of directors of the firms. Critics of the investment bankers complained that this practice stifled competition. Morgan and a few smaller investment banking firms such as Kuhn Loeb and Company in New York and Kidder Peabody and Company in Boston seemed to control both the distribution of securities and (through interlocking directorates) the business decisions of the major industrial firms themselves. In 1912 this "money trust" was subjected to a detailed and highly critical examination in Congress by the Pujo committee. But recent research by J. Bradford De Long has shown that there was also a positive side to Morgan's links with industrial firms: they helped inform investors about how best to invest their funds.

Another important force helping to finance industrial growth was the rapid, steady retirement of the national debt. The federal debt had been retired completely by 1835 (for the first and only time in our history), and only a small debt existed on the eve of the Civil War. By 1865, the debt was $2.32 billion; it was reduced to $648 million by 1877 before increasing for several years. By 1893, $1.73 billion had been retired. High tariffs supplied government with continued surpluses that permitted the debt retirement. This inflow of government funds to buy up old bonds—a type of crowding in, as John James has called it—lowered yields on private assets and stimulated capital formation in the private sector.[19] How different from the 1990s, when huge federal deficits and Treasury bond sales have continually raised interest rates and "crowded out" corporate bond issues.[20]

BANK PANICS AND THE ESTABLISHMENT OF THE FEDERAL RESERVE SYSTEM

Despite the development of state banking and investment banking that increased the flexibility of the banking system, the depression of the mid-1890s was followed by the

---

[19] John A. James, "Public Debt and U.S. Economic Growth," *Explorations in Economic History* 21 (April 1984): 192–217.

[20] A significant minority of economists, however, believe that interest rates, at least in the twentieth century, have not been greatly affected by the deficits because the United States can draw on world capital markets and because people save more when there is a deficit in anticipation of higher future taxes.

severe panic and ensuing depression of 1907. Once again, the American people were aroused to the need for basic reforms.

One of the most painful manifestations of economic crisis before World War I was the rush by individuals and business firms, as they became apprehensive about the economic future, to the banks to convert their deposits into cash. The banks, which operated on the "fractional reserve" principle, could not immediately meet the demands for their total deposit liabilities. A single bank could *gradually* convert its assets into cash; given time, any sound bank could even be liquidated in an orderly fashion, and its depositors and stockholders could be paid in full. But in periods of panic, an orderly shifting of assets into cash was difficult, if not impossible. As harried banks all tried to sell securities (their most liquid assets) at the same time, the prices of securities fell drastically. For some banks, the consequent losses on securities proved disastrous, even though "runs" were stopped. If, instead of selling its securities, a bank called in its loans or refused to renew notes as they came due, pressure was transferred to its customers. And if these customers could not meet their obligations, the banks were forced into insolvency.

A common way of mitigating these difficulties was to *suspend* cash payments during crises. Before the Civil War, suspension meant that banks temporarily refused to redeem their notes or to pay out deposits in specie. After the Civil War, suspension meant that banks ceased to pay out cash in any form: gold or gold certificates, silver or silver certificates, greenbacks, national-bank notes, or subsidiary coins. As another option, instead of suspending payments, a bank might restrict cash payments to a certain maximum sum per day or per withdrawal. During the panic of 1907, such suspensions were more general and for longer time periods (over two months in some cities) than ever before. In the Southeast and Midwest, the resulting shortage of cash was so serious that local clearing houses issued emergency notes against collateral pledged by cooperating banks so that people could carry on business. These small-denomination "clearing-house certificates" were not issued much elsewhere, but large-denomination certificates were used by banks in cities all over the United States to make up balances due one another.

NATIONAL MONETARY COMMISSION

Suspending cash payments and issuing clearing-house certificates were better solutions than allowing the panic to continue, but the public wanted a reform that would prevent suspensions altogether. In response, the Aldrich-Vreeland Act of 1908 provided for the organization of "national currency associations" to be composed of not less than ten banks in sound financial condition. The purpose of these associations was to enable the banks that formed them to issue emergency bank notes against the security of bonds and commercial paper in their portfolios. A secondary provision established a National Monetary Commission. The report of the commission in 1912 blasted the American banking system:

> The methods by which our domestic and international credit operations are now conducted are crude, expensive and unworthy of an intelligent people. . . . The

unimportant part which our banks and bankers take in the financing of our foreign trade is disgraceful to a progressive nation. . . . The disabilities from which our producers suffer in our foreign trade also apply largely to domestic transactions.[21]

The key recommendation was a new central bank. The commission felt that what was needed was a central institution that could create reserves to stretch or contract the money supply, a great central institution with the authority to hold the reserves of the commercial banks and to increase their reserves through its own credit-granting powers. A central bank was also needed to help the Treasury. After the demise of the second Bank of the United States, the federal government had to maintain its own fiscal agent in the form of the Independent Treasury, which was by law required to remain aloof from the banking system. Impossibly antiquated methods of handling government funds resulted. By 1912 the need for a modern, central fiscal agent was too great to be postponed further.

FEDERAL RESERVE ACT

Two days before Christmas in 1913, President Wilson signed the bill that established the Federal Reserve System. The system was composed of twelve Federal Reserve Banks, one in each of twelve districts in the country. Unlike the 20-year charter of the first and second Banks of the United States, the charter of the Federal Reserve was permanent.

The system was to be headed by a Federal Reserve Board composed of seven members, including the Secretary of the Treasury, the Comptroller of the Currency *ex officio,* and five appointees of the President. Each Federal Reserve Bank was to be run by a board of nine directors. Three of the directors, representing the "public," were to be appointed by the Federal Reserve Board; the remaining six were to be elected by the member banks of the district. Three of the six locally elected directors could be bankers; the remaining three were to represent business, industry, and agriculture. Thus the banking community had a minority representation on the Reserve Bank directorates in each district.

The Federal Reserve Act made membership in the system compulsory for national banks; state banks, on compliance with federal requirements, might also become members. To join the system, a commercial bank had to purchase shares of the capital stock of the district Federal Reserve Bank in the amount of 3 percent of its combined capital and surplus. Thus the member banks nominally owned the Federal Reserve Banks, although the annual return they could receive on their stock was limited to a 6-percent cumulative dividend. A member bank also had to deposit with the district Federal Reserve Bank a large part of the cash it had previously held as reserves. The act originally provided that member banks might retain a part of their reserves as cash, but

---

[21]Report of the National Monetary Commission (Washington, D.C.: Government Printing Office, 1912), pp. 28–29.

in 1917 the requirement was changed; after 1917, *all* the legal reserves of member banks were to be in the form of deposits with the Federal Reserve Bank.[22]

It was expected that the Federal Reserve Banks, as a system of control, would operate almost automatically and that, if the Federal Reserve Act were carefully followed, monetary disturbances would be very nearly eliminated. To most people, prudent monetary control and the elimination of monetary disturbances were synonymous with the elimination of business fluctuations. But, as we will see in Part Four, despite the high hopes held for the Federal Reserve System, periods of inadequate leadership and lack of understanding at the "Fed" permitted catastrophic monetary disturbances, bank panics, and sharp business cycles. Indeed, the Great Depression—America's darkest economic period—was partly a result of failure at the Fed. Its remedy left a New Deal legacy that lives with us today.

SELECTED REFERENCES AND SUGGESTED READINGS

Bloomfield, Arthur I. *Short-Term Capital Movements Under the Pre-1914 Gold Standard.* Princeton: International Finance Section, Department of Economics, Princeton University, 1963.

Bordo, Michael D. "The Classical Gold Standard: Some Lessons for Today." *Federal Reserve Bank of St. Louis, Review* 63 (1981): 1–17.

Bordo, Michael D., and Anna J. Schwartz, eds., *A Retrospective on the Classical Gold Standard, 1821–1931.* Chicago: University of Chicago Press, 1984.

Calomiris, Charles, and Glenn Hubbard. "Price Flexibility, Credit Availability, and Economic Fluctuations: Evidence from the United States, 1894–1909." *Quarterly Journal of Economics* 104 (1989): 429–452.

Carosso, Vincent P. *Investment Banking in America, A History.* Cambridge: Harvard University Press, 1970.

———. *The Morgans: Private International Bankers, 1854–1913.* Cambridge: Harvard University Press, 1987.

Davis, Lance E. "Capital Immobilities and Finance Capitalism: A Study of Economic Evolution in the United States." *Explorations in Entrepreneurial History* 1, no. 1 (Fall 1963): 88–105.

———. "The Investment Market, 1870–1914: The Evolution of a National Market." *Journal of Economic History* 25 (1965): 355–399.

De Long, J. Bradford. "Did J. P. Morgan's Men Add Value? A Historical Perspective on Financial Capitalism." In *Inside the Business Enterprise,* ed. Peter Temin. Chicago: University of Chicago Press, 1991.

Friedman, Milton, "The Crime of 1873," *Journal of Political Economy* 6 (1990): 1159–1194.

Friedman, Milton, and Anna J. Schwartz. *A Monetary History of the United States, 1867–1967.* Princeton: National Bureau of Economic Research, Princeton University Press, 1963.

Gorton, Gary. "Clearinghouses and the Origins of Central Banking in the U.S." *Journal of Economic History* 45 (1985): 277–283.

Gurley, J. G., and E. S. Shaw. "The Growth of Debt and Money in the United States, 1800–1950: A Suggested Interpretation." *Review of Economics and Statistics* (August 1957).

Hawtrey, R. G. *The Gold Standard in Theory and Practice.* London: Longmans, Green, 1939.

Hughes, Jonathan, and Nathan Rosenberg. "The United States Business Cycle Before 1860: Some Problems of Interpretation." *Economic History Review* 15, 2d series (1963).

James, John A. "Cost Functions of Post-bellum National Banks." *Explorations in Economic History* 15 (1978): 184–195.

---

[22] All required reserves were held on deposit with Federal Reserve Banks from June 1917 until late 1959, when, after a series of transitional steps, member banks could once again count vault cash as reserves.

_____. "The Development of a National Money Market, 1893–1911." *Journal of Economic History* 33 (1976): 878–897.

_____. *Money and Capital Markets in Postbellum America.* Princeton: Princeton University Press, 1978.

_____. "Public Debt Management Policy and Nineteenth-Century American Economic Growth." *Explorations in Economic History* 21 (1984): 192–217.

Jenks, Leland H. *The Export of British Capital to 1875.* London: Cape, 1938.

Kindahl, James K. "Economic Factors in Specie Resumption: The United States, 1865–1879." In *The Reinterpretation of American Economic History,* eds. Robert W. Fogel and Stanley L. Engerman. New York: Harper & Row, 1971.

Livingston, James. *Origins of the Federal Reserve System: Money, Class, and Corporate Capitalism, 1890–1913.* Ithaca, New York: Cornell University Press, 1986.

Myers, Margaret. *The New York Money Market.* New York: Columbia University Press, 1931.

Officer, Lawrence H. "The Remarkable Efficiency of the Dollar-Sterling Gold Standard, 1890–1906." *Journal of Economic History* 49 (1989): 1–41.

Rockoff, Hugh. "The Wizard of Oz as a Monetary Allegory." *Journal of Political Economy* 98 (1990): 739–760.

Simon, Matthew. "The Morgan-Belmont Syndicate of 1895 and Intervention in the Foreign Exchange Market." *Business History Review* 42 (Winter 1968).

Smiley, Gene. "Interest Rate Movements in the United States, 1888–1913." *Journal of Economic History* 35 (1975): 591–620.

Snowden, Kenneth. "American Stock Market Development and Performance, 1871–1929." *Explorations in Economic History* 24 (1987): 327–353.

Sobel, Robert. *The Big Board: A History of the New York Stock Market.* New York: Free Press, 1969.

Sushka, Marie Elizabeth, and W. Brian Barrett. "Banking Structure and the National Capital Market, 1869–1914." *Journal of Economic History* 44 (1984): 463–478.

Sylla, Richard. "American Banking and Growth in the Nineteenth Century: A Partial View of the Terrain." *Explorations in Economic History* 9 (Winter 1971–1972): 197–228.

_____. *The American Capital Market, 1846–1914.* New York: Arno Press, 1975.

_____. "Federal Policy, Banking Market Structure, and Capital Mobilization in the United States, 1863–1913." *Journal of Economic History* 29 (1969): 657–686.

Tanner, J. E., and B. Bonomo. "Gold, Capital Flows, and Long Swings in American Business Activity." *Journal of Political Economy* 76 (January–February 1968).

Timberlake, Richard. *The Origins of Central Banking in the United States.* Cambridge: Harvard University Press, 1978.

Unger, Irwin. *The Greenback Era.* Princeton: Princeton University Press, 1964.

West, Robert Craig. *Banking Reform and the Federal Reserve 1863–1923.* Ithaca, New York: Cornell University Press, 1977.

White, Eugene N. "The Political Economy of Banking Regulation, 1864–1933." *Journal of Economic History* 42 (1982): 33–42.

Williamson, Jeffrey G. *Financial Intermediation, Capital Immobilities and Economic Growth in Late Nineteenth Century American Development: A General Equilibrium History.* Cambridge: Cambridge University Press, 1974.

_____. "Watersheds and Turning Points: Conjectures on the Long-Term Impact of Civil War Financing." *Journal of Economic History* 34 (1974): 636–661.

Wimmer, Larry T. "The Gold Crisis of 1869: Stabilizing or Destabilizing Speculation Under Floating Exchange Rates?" *Explorations in Economic History* 12 (1975): 105–122.

Zecher, J. Richard, and D. N. McCloskey. "How the Gold Standard Worked, 1880–1913." In *The Monetary Approach to the Balance of Payments,* eds. Jacob A. Frenkel and Harry G. Johnson. London: Allen & Unwin, 1976. Reprinted in B. Eichengreen, ed. *The Gold Standard in Theory and History.* London: Methuen, 1985.

_____. "The Success of Purchasing Power Parity: Historical Evidence and Its Implications for Macroeconomics." In *A Retrospective on the Classical Gold Standard 1821–1931,* eds. Michael Bordo and Anna J. Schwartz. Chicago: University of Chicago Press, 1984.

CHAPTER TWENTY

COMMERCE AT HOME AND ABROAD

CHAPTER THEME Between 1880 and 1920 the United States became the leading manufacturer in the world in terms of both total production and output per worker. Quality as well as quantity increased. Rather than buying commodities in bulk for further processing within the home, as they had done in an earlier and simpler time, Americans increasingly relied on finished products. Dependable brand-name products, heavily promoted through advertising, played an increasingly important role in the distribution of goods. These developments resulted from underlying trends in urbanization, transportation, and the exploitation of America's comparative advantage in the production of goods dependent on non-reproducible natural resources.

URBANIZATION

The percentage of the total population that resides in cities has grown persistently since the nation's beginning. The long march to city dominance is revealed in Table 20-1, which shows that the percentage of the population living in urban centers nearly doubled between 1800 and 1840, again between 1840 and 1860, and again from 1860 to 1900. By 1910, nearly 10 percent of the total population lived in three cities—New York, Chicago, and Philadelphia—each having a million-plus residents.

Before 1860, the rapid pace of urbanization resulted primarily from the rapid growth of interregional trade spurred by the transportation revolution. Urban centers emerged as "entrepôts" of trade, and trade more than industry was the magnet pulling people into cities and towns. Early industrial progress in the United States was largely a matter of "carrying labor to raw materials."[1] As Eric Lampard has shown, the 15 greatest cities in the nation in 1860 employed relatively small shares of their population in manufactures. For the period from 1840 to 1860 he concluded, "It would be misleading to suggest that this explosion to American cities was due entirely to the growth of urban manufactures. It was much more the outcome of a continental development carried out with railroads—colonialism on a continental scale."[2] What the cities in this early period provided was primarily transport, commercial, and banking services for expanding long-distance trades.

Urbanization after the Civil War was different. Early industrial complexes, which had been tied to primary resources in city hinterlands, shifted to the city. The railroad and other advances in transportation and communication made factories and cities nearly synonymous by the late nineteenth century.

People poured into the centers of industrial activities, many from abroad. Between 1860 and 1910, over half of *new* city residents came from overseas. About 10 percent of the urban growth resulted from natural increase, and a little over one-third came from domestic rural areas.

TABLE 20-1   URBAN PROPORTIONS OF THE POPULATION, 1800–1910

Year	Population in Towns over 2,500	Population in Towns over 100,000
1800	6%	0%
1840	11	3
1860	20	8
1880	28	12
1900	40	19
1910	46	22

SOURCE: *HISTORICAL STATISTICS, 1975* (WASHINGTON, D.C.: GOVERNMENT PRINTING OFFICE, 1976), SERIES A2 AND A57–72.

---

[1] V. S. Clark, *History of Manufactures in the United States* (New York: McGraw-Hill, 1929), vol. 2, p. 2.

[2] Eric Lampard, "The History of Cities in the Economically Advanced Areas," *Economic Development and Cultural Change* 3 (January 1955): 119.

Cities in the Midwest and the South, long established as distributing centers for the manufactures of the East and now developing industry of their own, grew phenomenally as industrial workers flocked to them. Chicago and Detroit, Cleveland and Cincinnati, St. Louis and Kansas City, Memphis and New Orleans, and Atlanta and Birmingham originated shipments that went far beyond their own trade areas. By 1910, the West and the South originated half as much railroad tonnage of manufactures as the East. Meanwhile, smaller cities within the trade areas of the metropolises and cities in the thinly populated region west of the Mississippi specialized in the mercantile functions. As automobiles came into common use after 1910, large towns and cities gained business at the expense of small towns and villages; by 1920, retailers in urban centers were attracting customers from distances that had been unimaginable just a few years earlier. This change was reflected in new ways of distributing goods and in new marketing institutions.

MARKETING AND SELLING

On the eve of the Civil War, the typical store was more devoted to processing sales orders than to promoting and selling goods. Advertising was limited largely to local newspapers and some national magazines, with occasional outdoor ads in a few large cities. "Business getting" was not a part of advertisements; the information conveyed was simple and direct. Newspaper ads wasted no space, listing the items for sale and the location, but usually not prices. Installment buying was known but rare. Cyrus McCormick sold his reaper "on time" at 20 percent down and four months to pay. Edward Clark of the Singer Sewing Machine Company innovated consumer credit in 1856, selling $125 sewing machines for $5 down and $3 per month. But McCormick and Singer, who pioneered direct sales to consumers before the Civil War, were rare exceptions. Most manufacturers sold directly to wholesalers or to commission agents who marketed the wares. Many wholesalers, in turn, hired "drummers," traveling salesmen who "drummed up" trade and solicited orders in the towns and countryside.

WHOLESALING

The full-service wholesale houses that evolved after 1840 bought goods on their own account from manufacturers and importers to sell to retailers, frequently on credit. In the growing cities of the Midwest, successful retailers began to perform some wholesale functions along with the business of selling to consumers. As these houses grew, they sometimes dropped their retailing activities altogether and concentrated on handling the output of manufacturing centers in the East. A few wholesale firms, especially those located in major distributing centers such as Chicago and St. Louis, offered several lines of merchandise, but more often they specialized in a single "full line," such as hardware or dry goods.

From 1860 to 1900, full-line, full-service wholesale houses were without serious competitors in the business of distributing goods from manufacturers to retailers. But beginning in the 1880s and increasingly after 1900, they faced competition from the marketing departments of large manufacturers.[3] Wholesale houses did not decline absolutely between 1900 and 1920—in fact their sales continued to increase—but they handled an ever-smaller proportion of goods in the channels of distribution.

The reason for the relative decline in wholesaling lay in the structure of emerging large-scale producers. Firms in many different industries were adopting "continuous-process" technologies, in which raw materials moved in a steady flow through the factory rather than being processed in separate batches. This meant that any interruption in the distribution of the final product would cause a steep increase in production costs. These firms then sought to gain control over their distribution channels in some cases by dealing directly with retailers. James B. Duke's marketing of cigarettes illustrates the point. In 1884 Duke installed two Bonsack cigarette-making machines in his factory. Each machine could turn out 120,000 cigarettes per day, compared with the 3,000 that a skilled worker could produce by hand. Duke's machines, working continuously, easily could have saturated the cigarette market that existed in 1884. To create and maintain the market for these cigarettes, and to assure that his output moved steadily to the consumer, Duke built an extensive sales network that kept an eye on local advertising and worked closely with other departments in the firm to schedule the flow of cigarettes from machine to consumer.

BRAND NAMES. The marketing departments of firms like Duke's also helped to establish and maintain the brand name of the product, particularly by stressing better quality or unique services. For example, producers requiring controlled temperatures during shipment, such as the Chicago meatpackers Armour and Swift, wanted to be certain that consumers would identify their product as the one that reached the market at the right temperature. Others, such as John H. Patterson, founder of National Cash Register, needed to make sure that consumers knew NCR provided adequate instruction in how the product worked, proper service, or credit. Manufacturers urged buyers to ask specifically for their brand. Brand names were the way the market protected consumers, far removed from producers, from inferior merchandise. They were an alternative, although one found by critics to be sadly lacking, to consumer-protection legislation.

RETAILING

In rural areas, where retail units characteristically remained small and independent, the wholesale house kept its customers. The "general store" was rapidly disappearing elsewhere, however, as retailers in towns with a surrounding trade area began to specialize in particular lines. But, interestingly, this specialization of retail functions did not bring about a reduction of the traditional wholesaler's business. What transpired instead was the development of new types of retail outlets, usually large ones, and the increasing ability of manufacturers to establish strong consumer preferences through advertising.

---

[3] For further discussion see Alfred D. Chandler, Jr., *The Visible Hand: The Managerial Revolution in America* (Cambridge: Belknap Press of Harvard University Press, 1977); and Harold Livesay and Glenn Porter, *Merchants and Manufacturers* (Baltimore: Johns Hopkins University Press, 1971).

Measurements of American male sizes for Civil War uniforms marked the beginning of standardized clothing, and U.S. manufacturers of boots and shoes steadily improved the quality and fit of their product. Economies resulting from mass-production techniques drove down the cost of clothing, and mail-order solicitation helped to broaden markets.

DEPARTMENT STORES. Of the new retailing organizations that gained definite acceptance by World War I, the department store ran counter to the trend of greater specialization in handling merchandise. As cities became bigger and more congested, the convenience of being able to shop for all personal necessities in a single store had an increasing appeal. Furthermore, department stores offered delivery services and credit. The early department stores in large cities evolved after the Civil War from the efforts of dry-goods stores to replace business lost to the growing ready-to-wear trade. There was a definite division of the store into separate departments, each with its own manager, buyers, and clerks; the separation was once so distinct that departments were frequently leased to individuals or companies.

At first, department stores bought merchandise through wholesalers. However, larger stores such as Macy's in New York, John Wanamaker's in Philadelphia, and Marshall Field in Chicago took advantage of their growing size to obtain price reductions by going directly to manufacturers or their selling agents. Because of the size of their operations, large stores with numerous clerks had to set one price for all customers, and the old practice of haggling with merchants over the price of an article was soon a thing of the past. So successful was the department store concept that by 1920 even small cities could usually boast one. Small department stores purchased merchandise through regular wholesale channels, and their departmentalization was so indistinct that they were very similar to the general store of an earlier day.

CHAIN STORES. It soon became apparent to some enterprisers that the costs of distributing goods in certain lines could be reduced by performing agency and brokerage functions in their own departments and by buying directly from manufacturers and processors. But to achieve the bargaining power to enable them to buy directly, enterprisers had to have retail sales of considerable magnitude. Such sales could be obtained by combining many spatially separate outlets in "chains" with a centralized buying and administrative authority. Additional savings could be made by curtailing or eliminating the major services of credit and delivery.

One of the early chains, still with us today, was the Great Atlantic and Pacific Tea Company, founded in 1859. From an original line restricted to tea and coffee, the company expanded in the 1870s to a general line of groceries. In 1879, F. W. Woolworth began the venture that was to make him a multimillionaire when he opened variety stores carrying articles that sold for no more than a dime. By 1900, tobacco stores and drugstores were often organized in chains, and hardware stores and restaurants soon began to fall under centralized managements. By 1920, grocery, drug, and variety chains were firmly established as a part of the American retail scene. A few companies then numbered their units in the thousands, but the great growth of the chains was to come in the 1920s and 1930s—along with innovations in physical layout and the aggressive selling practices that would incur the wrath of the independents.

MAIL-ORDER HOUSES. It is difficult for the modern urban resident to imagine the thrill of "ordering by mail." Yet for many American families in the decades before World War I, the annual arrival of a catalog from Montgomery Ward or Sears, Roebuck was an event anticipated with pleasure. Although Montgomery Ward started

F. W. Woolworth—a pioneer in chain-store merchandising—opened his first store in 1879 in Lancaster, Pennsylvania. At 1994 prices, it would be a $1.50 and $3.00 store.

his business with the intention of selling only to Grangers, he soon included other farmers and many city dwellers among his customers. Both Montgomery Ward and Sears, Roebuck and Company experienced their great growth periods after they moved to Chicago—a vantage point from which they could sell, with optimum economies of shipping costs and time, to eager Midwestern farmers and to both coasts as well. Rural free delivery and the establishment of a parcel post system were godsends to mail-order houses. By 1920, however, towns were readily accessible to farmers, who could now make their own purchases. If the mail-order houses were to remain important merchandisers, they would have to modify their selling methods.

PRODUCT DIFFERENTIATION AND ADVERTISING

Merchants had advertised long before the Civil War, but as long as durable and semidurable goods were either made to order for the wealthy or turned out carelessly for the undiscriminating poor, and as long as food staples were sold out of bulk containers, the field of the advertiser was limited. In fact, the first attempts at advertising on more than a local level were directed largely toward retailers rather than consumers. Notable exceptions were patent-medicine manufacturers, the first sellers in America to advertise on a national scale.[4]

After the Civil War, advertising on a national scale finally became a widely accepted practice. With the trusts came truly national firms whose brand names and trademarks

Advertising helped to expand the consumer demand for new products like this all-purpose potion.

---

[4]There is a suspicion that the popularity of patent medicines resulted in good part from their high alcohol content. Many, if not most, customers would not have touched liquor, and they may not have realized that the immediate sense of well-being derived from such medicines arose from alcohol instead of from other "beneficial ingredients."

became impressed on the minds of consumers. Wherever products such as tobacco, whiskey, kerosene, or shoes could be differentiated in terms of buyer thinking, the trusts attempted an institutional advertising designed to reassure householders about the quality of the goods being purveyed. And as the quality of nondurables improved, particularly in the case of clothing, manufacturers of leather shoes, hosiery, underwear, and men's suits and overcoats found that a loyal, nationwide following could be won through brand name advertising.

By 1920, advertising was a billion-dollar industry. In some fields, the increasing size of a firm was an important factor in the growth of its national advertising, but advertising itself helped many firms to attain large sizes.

It became a well-accepted fact that a firm had to advertise to maintain its share of an industry's sales. It was also realized that as competing firms carried on extensive campaigns, the demand for a product might increase throughout the entire industry. Yet only a beginning had been made. Two changes were to loom large in the future of American advertising. One was the radio, which within a decade was to do the job of advertising far more effectively than it had ever been done before. The second was the change in the kind of consumer durables people bought. In 1869, half the output of consumer durables consisted of furniture and house furnishings; 30 years later, the same categories still accounted for somewhat more than half of the total. But after 1910, as first the automobile and then electrical appliances revolutionized American life, the share of furniture and household furnishings in the output of consumer durables declined rapidly. Household furnishings were articles that could not be differentiated in people's minds with any remarkable degree of success, although efforts were continually made to do so. On the other hand, automobiles and household appliances could be readily differentiated, presenting a wonderful challenge to the American advertising account executive.

THE FIRST STEPS TOWARD CONSUMER PROTECTION

The Meat Inspection Act and the Pure Food and Drug Act of 1906 were dramatic interventions into the economy by the federal government to ensure quality standards of products for unwary customers. In 1906, Upton Sinclair's novel *The Jungle* was published and received the personal attention of President Theodore Roosevelt. Sinclair's descriptions of unsanitary production facilities for meat and his allegations of occasional processing of diseased animals stirred up sensational media and public reactions.

Sinclair's book was timely, coming on the heels of the 1898 "embalmed beef" scandal, an event of the Spanish-American War in which adulterated beef was allegedly provided to the army. Although Sinclair's allegations and those from the scandal ultimately were found baseless in congressional testimony, the acts were promptly passed.

The Pure Food and Drug Act was initially trivial in effect, calling simply for federal regulation of the content and labeling of certain food and medicinal products. The sum of $174,180 was allocated to the Bureau of Chemistry for its enforcement. In

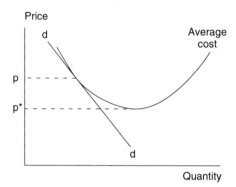

The growth of brand names, advertising, and product differentiation led economists to develop a new theory: monopolistic competition. In 1933, two books were published describing the new theory, Edward Chamberlin's *The Theory of Monopolistic Competition: A Re-orientation of the Theory of Value* and Joan Robinson's *Economics of Imperfect Competition.* The figure above illustrates the famous "Chamberlinian tangency solution." The demand curve facing the firm, dd, is downward sloping, showing that the firm has some monopoly power. Even if it raises its price, it will not lose all of its customers because it produces a differentiated product. Some customers will remain loyal, for example, to Levi Strauss's overalls or Dr. C. V. Girard's ginger brandy even when the prices of these products are raised relative to alternatives. But these firms will not be able to earn extraordinary profits for long. New entrants to the industry will capture some of the market, reducing demand, and force the existing firms into more advertising, raising costs. The long-run equilibrium price will be at P. Price will be equal to average cost, which includes only a normal profit.

There is, in one sense, excess capacity in a monopolistically competitive industry. If product differentiation could be eliminated, say by prohibiting advertising and requiring firms to produce a simple standardized product, the resulting competitive price would be lower, approximately at P* (only approximately because cost curves would be affected as well as demand). There would be fewer firms in the industry, each producing more output. Critics of the theory of monopolistic competition have pointed out, however, that variety may be of real value to consumers. Although it is easy to make fun of Dr. Girard's ginger brandy, Levi Strauss's riveted overalls are another matter. For economists, moreover, the theory has fallen somewhat from favor for another reason: it has not proved fruitful in producing testable hypotheses.

contrast, the Bureau of Animal Husbandry had its budget increased by the 1906 Meat Inspection Act for inspection purposes from $0.8 million to $3.0 million.

The 1906 meat act was not new. It was merely an amendment to the Meat Inspection Act of 1891, which had been passed in response to allegations by small local butchers and their organizations that dressed meat sent to distant markets by refrigerated railroad cars was unwholesome.[5] Chicago meatpacking companies such as Armour, Swift, Morris, and Hammond dominated the interstate dressed-beef trade. In 1890 their market shares of cattle slaughtered in Chicago were 27, 26, 24, and 12 percent, respectively. Because the new refrigeration technology dramatically lowered the costs of shipments (dressed beef was roughly one-third of the weight of whole beef), local butchers' prices were vastly undercut. To fight back, local butchers attempted to discredit refrigerated beef, claiming it was unwholesome. Although these claims were unfounded, the big packers welcomed the governmental response.

The large Chicago packers had private quality controls for dressed beef and a substantial stake in protecting their brand name reputations. They welcomed federal inspection of beef in interstate markets, first because federal inspection augmented their own quality assurances, and secondly because it gave each firm clear and accurate public information on the shipments of every other firm. This publicly provided inspection system allowed the firms to engage in pooling and market-sharing arrangements with excellent assurances that no firm could cheat on sale-share agreements.

The 1891 Meat Inspection Act for interstate trade was similar to an 1890 act on meat for export. Both acts largely benefited the producers by reinforcing each firm's quality-control standards for shipment to markets at home and abroad. Whether or not consumers benefited from the acts is unsubstantiated, but the grounds and precedents for consumer protection were established by these first inspection acts, ostensibly on the consumers' behalf.

FOREIGN TRADE

By 1900 the United States had become the leading manufacturing country in the world in terms of total production. Great Britain (the world's first industrial nation) was second and Germany was third. By 1913 the U.S. lead had increased, and Britain had fallen to third. The United States forged to the front in iron and steel production, and Germany and the United States became leaders in the electrical, chemical, and machine-tool industries. This does not mean, we hasten to add, that output had declined in Britain. To the contrary, British output continued to increase. In terms of industrial output per capita Britain was still the leader in 1900 and was only slightly below the United States in 1913 when the United States took over the lead. What had happened to Britain was simply that two large nations, well-endowed with natural resources and possessing economic systems conducive to growth, had expanded their output more rapidly.

---

[5] Gary D. Libecap, "The First Consumer Quality Guarantees by the Federal Government: The Meat Inspection Acts of 1890 and 1891," Working Paper 88-12, Karl Eller Center, University of Arizona, 1988.

During this period the network of international trade assumed its modern characteristics. From the industrial countries—the United States, Germany, Great Britain, and a few others—went the manufactured and semimanufactured products. In exchange, the less-industrialized nations sent an ever-swelling flow of foodstuffs and raw materials to support the growing industrial populations and feed the furnaces and fabricating plants of industry.

Rapid improvement in methods of communication and transportation was the key to this system. To cite several examples: the first successful transatlantic cable began operations in 1866, a railroad line spanned the American continent in 1869, the Suez Canal was opened in the same year, and dramatic productivity gains in ocean transportation occurred over the last half of the nineteenth century. An extremely important improvement was the development of railroads in various parts of the world, making possible a flood of cheap grain from Canada, Australia, Argentina, Russia, and the Danube valley, as well as from the midlands of the United States. In the late 1870s and early 1880s, refrigeration on vessels made possible the shipments of meats, then dairy products, and lastly fruits. To these were added the products of the tropics: rice, coffee, cocoa, vegetable oils, and tapioca. However, the shipment of grains was also of great importance in stimulating the worldwide distribution of foods.

CHANGING COMPOSITION OF EXPORTS AND IMPORTS

Figure 20-1 shows the changing composition of U.S. foreign trade between 1850 and 1900. This transition portrays the shift in U.S. comparative advantage internationally, away from agriculture and toward manufactures. On the export side, Figure 20-1 shows that the most striking change was the decline of raw materials (such as cotton) from three-fifths to one-fourth of the total. Crude foodstuffs, which had swelled from about 1 percent in 1850 to nearly one-quarter of all exports in the late 1870s (reflecting the piercing of the West by the railroad), declined to 17 percent by 1900 and continued to fall until 1915. Manufactured foodstuffs, which also had climbed to about 25 percent of the total, held fairly steady. As shown, another important trend was the rise of semimanufactures and finished manufactures. (By the period between 1915 and 1920, these would account for almost half the total value of exports.)

Opposite movements, although not as remarkable, can be seen on the import side. Crude materials rose from one-twelfth the value of imports in 1850 to one-third the value of imports by 1900. The chief crude materials imported—those that were necessary to a great industrial structure but could not be found in the United States—were rubber, tropical fibers, and metals such as nickel and tin. Crude foodstuffs showed uneven ups and downs but did not change materially over the half-century as Americans imported coffee, tropical fruits, and olive and coconut oils, which could be produced domestically only at great cost, if at all. Imports of semimanufactures increased somewhat, but finished manufactures declined greatly in importance as American productive capacity grew.

Trade linkages altered as well. Although Europe became a more important customer of the United States after the Civil War than ever before, American exports to

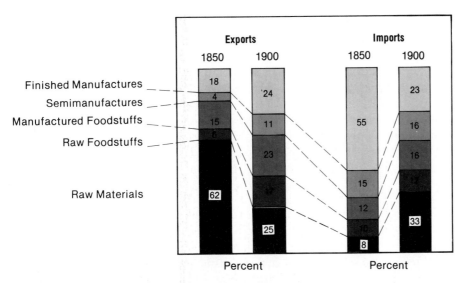

FIGURE 20-1 COMPOSITION OF U.S. FOREIGN TRADE, 1850 AND 1900

SOURCE: U.S. DEPARTMENT OF COMMERCE.

Europe began to decline relatively about 1885. During the 1870s and 1880s, Europeans were the recipients of more than four-fifths of all U.S. exports; by 1920, this share had dropped to three-fifths. In the meantime, the United States remained Europe's best customer. The sharp decline in the proportion of American imports from Europe between 1915 and 1920, a result of wartime disruption, permanently injured this trade.

In the first 20 years of the twentieth century, Americans found new customers in Asia and Canada, and an interest in the Latin American market was just beginning. On the import side, the Asian countries and Canada were furnishing a great part of the crude materials that were becoming typical U.S. imports. South America had already achieved a substantial position as a purveyor of coffee and certain key raw materials to the United States.

What was the source of the American preeminence in manufacturing achieved by 1900? As Gavin Wright has shown in recent research, America's preeminence resulted not so much from a relative abundance of capital or skilled labor or technological knowledge, but rather from the relative abundance of nonreproducible natural resources.[6] In 1913 the United States produced 65 percent of the world's petroleum, 56 percent of the copper, 39 percent of the coal, 37 percent of the zinc, 36 percent of the iron ore, and 34 percent of the lead, and was the world's leader in the production of each of these materials. It was the leader, or among the leaders, in the production of many other minerals. America's abundance of nonreproducible resources did not result from a series of lucky accidents of nature. The large and stable internal market for manufactures, combined with a flexible system for establishing property rights, promoted intensive exploration for and exploitation of natural resources.

---

[6]Gavin Wright, "The Origins of American Industrial Success, 1879–1940," *American Economic Review* 80 (September 1990): 651–668. The data on mineral output that follow are from p. 661.

To look ahead a bit, we can contrast this era of American preeminence with the period of relative decline after 1965. America's resources were not exhausted after 1965. Indeed, in many cases production and proven reserves exceeded those available at the turn of the century. Instead, declining transport costs and trade barriers led to the rapid exploitation of mineral resources in other parts of the world (petroleum being the most dramatic example) and to their use by manufacturing firms in emerging industrial countries. To some extent, America's relative decline after 1965 was a mirror image of Britain's relative decline at the turn of the century. Like Britain after 1885, America after 1965 grew richer, but others grew richer faster.

CHANGES IN BALANCE OF TRADE

A good way to summarize the history of American foreign trade is to examine a series of international balance-of-payments statements to see what changes occurred in the major accounts. As Table 20-2 shows, the United States had a slightly unfavorable trade balance between 1850 and 1873. (America was importing more than it was exporting.) Between 1874 and 1895, the balance of trade shifted to favorable, becoming markedly favorable between 1896 and 1914 and enormously favorable between 1915 and 1919.[7] As we have learned, however, items other than merchandise enter into the international balance of payments. A persistently favorable balance of trade may be offset by "importing" the services, the securities, or the gold of other nations. It is important to understand how, as years went by, the people of the United States offset their constantly favorable balance of trade.

Table 20-2 shows that a net total of $1.8 billion (columns 2 + 3) was paid out by Americans between 1850 and 1873. Residents of the United States could enjoy this net

TABLE 20-2   UNITED STATES INTERNATIONAL PAYMENTS, BY PERIODS (IN BILLIONS OF DOLLARS)

(1) Period	(2) Net Goods and Services	(3) Net Income on Investment	(4) Net Capital Transactions	(5) Unilateral Transfers	(6) Changes in Monetary Gold Stock[a]	(7) Errors and Omissions
1850–1873	−0.8	−1.0	1.6	0.2	0.0	
1874–1895	1.7	−2.2	1.5	−0.6	−0.4	
1896–1914	6.8	−1.6	− 0.7	−2.6	−1.3	−0.6
1915–1919	14.3	1.4	−14.1	−1.8	1.2	−1.0

SOURCE: HISTORICAL STATISTICS, COLONIAL TIMES TO 1970 (WASHINGTON, D.C.: GOVERNMENT PRINTING OFFICE, 1971), PP. 865–869.

[a]A minus sign indicates an addition to the U.S. monetary gold stock. Why?

---

[7]The terms *favorable* and *unfavorable* are somewhat arbitrary. After all, if you give me 10 apples and I give you 8 in return, you are unlikely to call it a favorable balance of trade. The terms date from mercantilist times, when an increase in the stock of gold was considered important.

inflow of goods and services and pay interest and dividends on existing foreign investments largely because foreign nationals continued to make new investments in American businesses (column 4), especially in railroads. Another balancing item during this
period was the $200 million in foreign currencies brought or sent to the United States
and changed into dollars by immigrants and their families. Such payments are called
unilateral transfers (column 5).

From 1874 to 1895, American agricultural commodities were available to the world
market in rapidly increasing quantities. When we consider that the manufacturing
industries of the United States were also becoming progressively more efficient, reflecting America's growing comparative advantage in the production of goods dependent
on mineral resources, it is hardly surprising to find that exports increased as they did.
During these years, the favorable *trade* balance was reduced by the growing tendency
of Americans to use the *services* of foreigners. Even so, Americans had net credits on
current account of $1.7 billion (column 2), and foreign investors poured another $1.5
billion into this country (column 4). Offsetting the credits were more than $2 billion
in interest and dividend payments to foreigners, and on balance unilateral transfers
began to reverse themselves as immigrants sent substantial sums back to friends and
relatives in their countries of origin. To make up the balance, the United States
imported $400 million in gold (column 6).

During the prosperous years of 1896 to 1914, the United States came into its own
as an economic power. The favorable balance of trade shot up to over $9 billion,
although this figure was cut to less than $7 billion by purchases of services from for-
eigners. Interest and dividend payments to foreign investors, remittances of immigrants to their families, a slight reversal of the capital flow, and an inward gold flow
secured a balance of payments. The reversal in the international capital flows, though
small compared with domestic investment in the United States, nevertheless had considerable symbolic value. The United States was now a lender rather than a borrower,
a sign of economic maturity.

Finally, World War I brought considerable change in the U.S. balance of payments.
The last rows of Table 20-2 show the great jump in the favorable balance of trade
created by the prodigious demand for American war materials. Until the United States
entered the war in 1917, European nations financed their purchases here by selling their
American securities and by shipping gold. When the United States finally took its
position on the side of the Allies, continued large purchases of American goods were
made possible by U.S. government loans to the Allies of nearly $10 billion. At this
stage in the progress of international relations, the United States did not think of
giving assistance to its friends. It was expected that one day the loans would be repaid,
but just how Europeans would earn the dollar exchange to repay the loans was not
made clear. During the war, Americans, as private citizens, began to invest heavily in
the fortunes of other countries; in these few years they received more income in the
form of interest and dividends than they paid out. At last, the United States had
shifted from a debtor position to the position of a major creditor. Although the capital
flow reversal had preceded World War I, the effect was to involve the United States
in world matters on an unprecedented scale. As we will see in the following sections,
to some we appeared to be a new imperialist power.

THE ACCEPTANCE OF PROTECTIONIST
DOCTRINES

The United States, which had long been protectionist (like most of Europe, although unlike Great Britain), became more so beginning with the Civil War. Setting up ever-higher tariff walls, Americans sought to control trade with other countries in the interests of national policy. To observe these changes systematically, Figure 20-2 traces a 100-year history of tariffs, or customs duties, as a percent of the value of (1) total imports and (2) dutiable imports. As revealed there, compared to earlier times, on the eve of the Civil War the nation traded in an atmosphere of limited protection.

In 1861, maximum U.S. tariffs were not more than 24 percent and averaged less than 20 percent on dutiable commodities. The national prosperity of the last 15 years before the Civil War seemed to refute protectionists' arguments that a healthy economy required high duties. Yet by 1864, the trend of nearly three decades was reversed so sharply and positively as to put the United States on a high protective-tariff basis for nearly three-quarters of a century. There was no widespread demand for such a change in policy; only in the manufacturing centers were the old arguments for protection advanced with enthusiasm. To win the votes of the industrial East, the Republicans advocated higher tariffs during the campaign of 1860. After the returns were in but before Lincoln's inauguration, Congress passed the Morrill Act of 1861, the first in a long series of laws levying ever-higher taxes on imports. Thus the first step was actually taken before the war, but after the southern opponents of the tariff had left the Congress. The requirements of Civil War financing, at a time when import duties

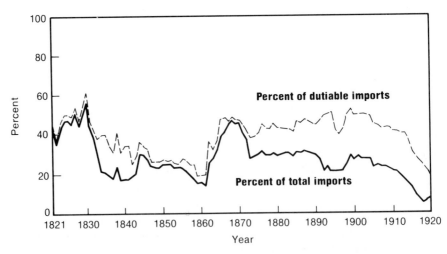

FIGURE 20-2 Customs Duties as a Percent of (1) Total Imports and (2) Dutiable Imports, 1821–1920 *Tariffs slid steadily until the Civil War, then the new politics set forth a sharp increase and new level that was maintained until the turn of the century.*

SOURCE: *Historical Statistics, Colonial Times to 1970* (Washington, D.C.: Government Printing Office, 1971), p. 888.

and domestic excises furnished the principal revenues, provided an excuse for raising tariffs to unprecedented highs. By 1865 the *average* level of duties was 48 percent, and protection was granted to nearly any commodity for which it was requested.

For 25 years after the war, a few leaders in both political parties attempted to reduce the "war tariffs." In 1872, to ward off drastic downward reductions that appeared imminent, protectionist forces in Washington agreed to a flat 10-percent decrease in all protective duties. In 1875, however, the earlier levels were restored, and it appeared for a time that consumers and the electorate were resigned to permanently high import rates. Yet people were increasingly persuaded that protective tariffs were, in effect, a tax that raised consumer-goods prices—and there was a growing suspicion that high levels of protection fostered the rapid growth of business combinations. During his first administration, President Grover Cleveland placed the Democrats squarely on the side of greater freedom of trade, but two Democratic assaults on the protective system produced disappointingly modest results. Cleveland's defeat in 1888 blasted hopes of genuine reform. The McKinley tariff of 1890 raised the average level of protection to 50 percent, increased the articles on the dutiable list, and reaffirmed the Republican commitment to the support of high tariffs. Following insignificant reductions during Cleveland's second term (1893–1897), the Dingley Act of 1897 raised duties above 50 percent. More goods, by value, were now taxed as imports than were admitted free. As might be expected, free goods were mostly raw and semifinished commodities requiring further processing, but even some farm products, raw wool, and hides were placed in a protected category.

The prosperity between 1897 and 1914 made it easy to defend high-tariff policies. Protectionists argued that the country was experiencing a high level of employment and economic activity *because* tariffs were high. Yet by 1900, American industry had obviously come of age. American manufacturers were competing in the markets of Europe; it was apparent, especially in the metal-processing industries, that most American firms needed no protection. The textile industries, which had enjoyed the benefits of high tariffs for a century, paid the lowest wages, had the highest unemployment, and suffered from the rigors of competition more than any other class of producers. Moreover, it was readily demonstrable by this time that import duties usually raised the prices of protected articles to consumers. As the populace felt the pressures of rising living costs in the first decade of the century, voters blamed the tariffs, and Democratic politicians exploited this political unrest. When the Payne-Aldrich bill of 1909 failed to bring any relief from high tariffs, there was widespread political protest.

In the campaign of 1912, the Democrats promised a downward revision of import duties, a revision that was carried out in the Underwood-Simmons bill of 1913. Iron and steel were placed on the free list, and duties on cost-of-living items like cotton and woolen textiles were sharply reduced. The result was a simplified tariff structure, still of protective significance, with average duties about one-half of what they had been for several decades. During President Woodrow Wilson's administration, the average level of the tariffs was slightly below 25 percent—almost the level that had prevailed just before 1860.

Economists have long accepted the idea that protection may be beneficial in the case of an "infant" industry. When a firm is first starting out, its productivity will be low because workers and managers do not have much on-the-job training, and the firm may not be able to survive competition from experienced foreign firms. Tariff protection will buy the domestic firm time to mature. Eventually, tariff protection can be removed. In the long run, the gains to the consumer from having a vigorous domestic producer may offset the short-run costs of protection.

The problem with the infant-industry argument, revealed in the long history of tariff protection after the Civil War, is that the "infants" never grow up. As Bennett Baack and Edward Ray have shown, the structure of tariffs and subsequent levels of protection throughout the late nineteenth century were explained largely by the profit motives of established special interest groups rather than by a scientific determination of which infants needed protection based on costs and benefits to the economy as a whole.[8]

Although we are justified in criticizing tariff protection for established industries, we should not exaggerate the costs to the American people. In many protected industries, vigorous domestic competition was a close substitute for foreign competition. At the turn of the century, imports were a little over 6 percent of GNP, and it is hard to imagine that this figure would have increased dramatically even if all tariffs had been removed. Indeed, it was because the costs to individual consumers were relatively small that Congress was so open to persuasion by special interests seeking tariff protection.

THE UNITED STATES IN AN IMPERIALIST WORLD[9]

In the early 1880s, western Europeans became obsessed with a desire to own more of the earth's surface. Africa's interior, which before 1875 had been almost entirely unexplored and unmapped by Europeans, was partitioned among the major European powers, with only Liberia and Ethiopia remaining independent. In Asia, the French took over all of Indochina, British India annexed Burma, and Britain extended its hold over the Malay states. China, although it avoided physical disintegration, nevertheless had to make humiliating economic concessions to the major European powers. By the end of the nineteenth century, there was not much of the world left to colonize.

A detailed study by Lance Davis and Robert Huttenback has shown that the costs of the British Empire to the British people outweighed the economic benefits, although some citizens and enterprises benefited.[10] Nevertheless, a combination of special interests, fears of other European powers, and exaggerated claims about potential economic gains kept the competition for colonies going full tilt.

---

[8] Bennett D. Baack and Edward J. Ray, "The Political Economy of Tariff Policy: A Case Study of the United States," *Explorations in Economic History* 20 (1983): 73–93.

[9] For a most interesting reinterpretation of the issue of American imperialism, see Stanley Lebergott, "The Return to U.S. Imperialism, 1890–1929," *Journal of Economic History* 40 (1980): 229–252.

[10] Lance Davis and Robert Huttenback, *Mammon and the Pursuit of Empire: The Economics of British Imperialism* (New York: Cambridge University Press, 1988).

Through most of the nineteenth century, the United States remained apart from the race to acquire colonies in other parts of the world. Before the Civil War, southern politicians had looked to Central and South America for colonies that might be incorporated as slaveholding areas within the United States, but these efforts came to naught. Americans concentrated on westward expansion in North America, wresting control when necessary from the European powers and from the Indians. It was imperialism, to be sure, but not what Americans of that day had in mind when they debated the merits of an empire.

The only territory outside the continental limits that the United States acquired before 1898 was Alaska, which was presumed at the time to be almost worthless. In 1893 agitation to annex Hawaii began, but the American people balked at the high-handed methods used to depose the existing Hawaiian government, and the islands were not finally annexed until 1898. As explained at the end of this chapter, business interests generally were opposed to the needless and tragic Spanish-American War, despite the chauvinist campaign of the Hearst and Pulitzer newspapers, and there was little popular enthusiasm for the conflict until a martial spirit was whipped up by the destruction of the U.S. battleship *Maine* in Havana Harbor on February 15, 1898. But the quick and favorable outcome of that "splendid little war" (as Secretary of State John Hay described it to Theodore Roosevelt) forced Americans to make decisions regarding expansion outside their continental borders.

The first decisions concerned disposition of the former Spanish colonies of Cuba, Puerto Rico, and the Philippines. Cuba was given nominal independence, and Puerto Rico received territorial status, but the Platt Amendment of 1901 so restricted Cuban independence that Cuba, in effect, became a protectorate of the United States. Instead of granting independence to the Philippines, the United States claimed them as a colonial possession. An insurrection followed, which the United States put down with brutal force. With these islands in the Pacific and a growing interest in trade with the Orient, the United States insisted on an "open-door" policy in China and, in general, on economic opportunities in East Asia equal to those of the European powers. In the western hemisphere, the United States in 1903 acquired a perpetual lease of the Panama Canal Zone from the newly independent Republic of Panama, and the completion of the canal in 1914 assured a lasting American interest in the Caribbean and Central America.

Indeed, two years before construction of the canal began, the policy known as the "Roosevelt Corollary" to the Monroe Doctrine had been pronounced. In a message to Congress in 1904, President Theodore Roosevelt enunciated a principle that was to make the Monroe Doctrine an excuse for intervention in the affairs of Latin American countries. Roosevelt argued that because chronic weakness of a government might require some "civilized" nation to restore order and because, according to the Monroe Doctrine, European interference would not be tolerated, the United States might be forced to exercise police power in "flagrant cases of wrongdoing or impotence." Europeans were not disturbed by such an assumption of international police power, but Latin Americans were—and they had reason to be apprehensive.

The United States did not wait long to apply the Roosevelt Corollary. When the Dominican Republic could not meet its financial obligations, certain European states threatened to collect payments by force. Roosevelt's new doctrine required American intervention to forestall such moves. A treaty was signed in 1905 giving the United States authority to collect customs duties, of which 55 percent was to be paid to foreign creditors. In 1916, the Dominican government tried to escape American domination, and U.S. marines were sent in to quell the rebellion. In 1914, Haiti was made a protectorate of the United States, again with the aid of the marines. American forces landed so often in Nicaragua that the succession of episodes became a standing joke.

After the 1910 Mexican revolution against the country's dictator, Porfirio Diaz, American and other foreign investors, who were heavily committed in railroads and oil, pressed for intervention and the restoration of order. For a time, President Wilson encouraged Latin Americans by declining to invade Mexico. But "watchful waiting" could last just so long amid the cries of outrage at the destruction of American property, and U.S. politicians were unable to tolerate these repeated affronts to American honor. Troops crossed onto Mexican soil in 1914 and 1917—the second time, under the leadership of General John "Black Jack" Pershing—to seize the "bandit" Pancho Villa. With the adoption of the Mexican constitution in 1917, the turmoil subsided temporarily, only to begin again in the early 1920s.

Economic motives have been invoked to explain America's imperialist adventures. America sought foreign colonies, it is said, to provide an outlet for American capital and a cheap source of raw materials. But there is little evidence to back up such an explanation. Only a small fraction of U.S. foreign investment went to areas under U.S. political control, and only a small fraction of raw materials imported from the rest of the world came from these areas.[11] J. P. Morgan and other leaders of big business and finance opposed the Spanish-American War. Among other things, they were worried about the value of Spanish securities held by American banks and the value of American investments in the Cuban sugar industry. A more satisfying economic explanation could be based on the role of special interests anxious to collect debts or protect other interests.

But clearly, noneconomic motives were the prime movers of U.S. imperialism. It was widely believed that the United States had to play a role in the "great game" of international power politics, and that to do so the United States needed overseas bases and colonies, especially coaling stations for its fleets. Racism was also important, urging America to do its part in taking on the "white man's burden" and bringing civilization to the benighted peoples in other parts of the world.

Many Americans remained unconvinced. The years from 1898 to 1918 were marked by an uncomfortable conviction that euphemisms such as "manifest destiny" and "extending the areas of freedom" could not long cover up the high-handed methods used to acquire America's growing empire. Nor would it be possible to maintain approval for a diplomacy that was devoted largely to promoting or protecting private financial or commercial interests. Critics of imperialism contended that investors seeking profits in the countries of Central America and the Caribbean should be willing to take the risks of venturing under unstable governments.

---

[11]Robert B. Zevin, "An Interpretation of American Imperialism," *Journal of Economic History* 32 (March 1972): 316–370; and Stanley Lebergott, "The Return to U.S. Imperialism, 1890–1929," *Journal of Economic History* 40 (June 1980): 229–252.

The economic consequences of America's imperialistic ventures were relatively small, but the diplomatic consequences were important. These adventures forced the United States to turn its attention outside itself and increase its military strength. Offsetting these gains were the fears and hatreds built up among natural allies in Central and South America, with whose aspirations Americans should have been in sympathy. It would take a new generation of Americans and a second world war to remove part of this emotional conflict. Even so, the harm of two decades of harsh diplomacy could not be easily undone. As the fires of world revolution were kindled among the disadvantaged peoples of the world in the 1950s, it was not hard to perceive the long-run injury to U.S. international relationships that was inflicted by America's early experiments with imperialism.

SELECTED REFERENCES
AND SUGGESTED READINGS

Ashworth, William. *A Short History of the International Economy 1850–1950.* London: Longmans, Green, 1952.

Baack, Bennett D., and Edward John Ray. "The Political Economy of Tariff Policy: A Case Study of the United States." *Explorations in Economic History* 10 (1983): 73–93.

———. "Tariff Policy and Comparative Advantage in the Iron and Steel Industry, 1870–1929." *Explorations in Economic History* 11 (1973): 3–24.

Chandler, Alfred D., Jr. *The Visible Hand: The Managerial Revolution in America.* Cambridge: Belknap Press of Harvard University Press, 1977.

Clark, V. S. *History of Manufacturers in the United States.* New York: McGraw-Hill, 1929, vol. 1.

Davis, Lance, and Robert Huttenback. *Mammon and the Pursuit of Empire: The Economics of British Imperialism.* New York: Cambridge University Press, 1988.

Galloway, Lowell E., and Richard K. Vedder. "The Increasing Urbanization Thesis: Did 'New Immigrants' to the United States Have a Particular Fondness for Urban Life?" *Explorations in Economic History* 8 (1971): 305–320.

Hawke, G. R. "The United States Tariff and Industrial Protection in the Late Nineteenth Century." *Economic History Review* 28 (1975).

Lebergott, Stanley. "The Return to U.S. Imperialism, 1890–1929." *Journal of Economic History* 40 (1980): 229–252.

Libecap, Gary D. "The First Consumer Quality Guarantees by the Federal Government: The Meat Inspection Acts of 1890 and 1891." Working Paper 88-12, Karl Eller Center, University of Arizona, 1988.

Lipsey, Robert. "Foreign Trade." In *American Economic Growth: An Economist's History of the United States,* eds. Lance E. Davis et al. New York: Harper & Row, 1972.

Livesay, Harold, and Glenn Porter. *Merchants and Manufacturers.* Baltimore: Johns Hopkins University Press, 1971.

Simon, Matthew. "The United States Balance of Payments, 1861–1900." In *Studies in Income and Wealth.* National Bureau of Economic Research. Princeton: Princeton University Press, 1960, vol. 24.

Smolensky, Eugene. "Industrial Location and Urban Growth." In *American Economic Growth: An Economist's History of the United States,* eds. Lance E. Davis et al. New York: Harper & Row, 1972.

Taussig, Frank W. *The Tariff History of the United States.* New York: Putnam's Sons, 1932.

Weiher, Kenneth. "The Cotton Industry and Southern Urbanization, 1880–1930." *Explorations in Economic History* 14 (1977): 120–140.

Weiss, Thomas. "The Industrial Distribution of the Urban and Rural Workforces: Estimates for the United States, 1870–1910." *Journal of Economic History* 32 (1972): 919–937.

———. "Urbanization and the Growth of the Service Workforce." *Explorations in Economic History* 8 (1971): 241–259.

Williamson, Jeffrey G. *American Growth and the Balance of Payments.* Chapel Hill: University of North Carolina Press, 1964.

Wright, Gavin. "The Origins of American Industrial Success, 1879–1940," *American Economic Review* 80 (1990): 651–668.

Zevin, Robert B. "An Interpretation of American Imperialism." *Journal of Economic History* 32 (March 1972): 316–370.

PART FOUR

THE INTERWAR ERA

1914–1946

ECONOMIC AND HISTORICAL
PERSPECTIVES
1914–1946

1. Two world wars engulfed the industrial nations with enormous costs in terms of labor, capital, and human suffering. The United States emerged from each conflict with its domestic capital intact, and with an enhanced position relative to its economic rivals.

2. The stock market boom of the late 1920s was based on widespread expectations that a new age of continuous prosperity had dawned. The great crash of 1929 dashed those hopes and ushered in a severe economic contraction.

3. The Great Depression of the 1930s was a cataclysm of unparalleled magnitude. The banking system collapsed, farm prices fell, and industrial production plummeted. At the lowest point in 1933 one worker in four was unemployed.

4. As a result of the depression, the federal government took a much larger role in the economic life of the nation. Regulation of the private sector, and expenditures for social welfare, increased. In 1929 federal spending amounted to 3 percent of GNP; in 1947 it amounted to 15 percent.

5. The nation's financial system was changed radically as a result of the depression. Deposit insurance was introduced, the payment of interest on deposits was prohibited, and the Securities and Exchange Commission was set up to regulate the stock market.

6. The world's monetary system was radically altered. The gold standard disappeared, and at the end of World War II a new system was established in which the dollar was given the central role.

CHAPTER TWENTY-ONE

WORLD WAR I

CHAPTER THEME Although the United States was actively engaged in World War I for only a short time, labor and capital were quickly mobilized on an impressive scale. The armed forces were increased from 180,000 in 1916 to nearly 3 million in 1918. Over 100,000 would die in military service. To an unprecedented degree mobilization was managed by the federal government. Scores of new agencies attempted to regulate prices, set priorities, and allocate resources. When the war ended, most wartime controls were abandoned and most wartime agencies were dismantled abruptly. Nevertheless, the war proved to be a dress rehearsal for the increased role of the federal government that emerged in the 1930s; the lesson that the government could play a powerful positive role in meeting crises would be remembered when the nation faced the Great Depression.

MOBILIZING FOR WAR

Europe was ready for war in 1914: Her armed forces had been built up in a sustained arms race, and her states had been linked together in military alliances. Nationalistic and imperialistic rivalries had combined to produce a dangerous state of affairs. In France, for example, many still sought revenge for the territory and reparations that France had been forced to give Germany as a result of the Franco-Prussian War of 1870–1871. In Austria-Hungary, fear of the restive Slavic minorities had increased. In Britain, Germany's attempt to challenge British naval supremacy had produced heightened tensions. This list of conflicts and fears could be greatly expanded.

Even on the eve of war, there was still considerable optimism that the peace would hold. Europe had experienced several decades without a major war, and in the meantime industrialization and relatively free international trade had produced rapidly rising standards of living. A war that would destroy the fruits of this progress seemed irrational. Many people believed, moreover, that the rising international solidarity of the labor movement would undermine support for a war entered into by imperialistic capitalist powers. But the optimists were wrong.

The assassination of Austrian Archduke Ferdinand by a Serbian on June 28, 1914, set off a chain reaction that soon engulfed Europe in the bloodiest war the world had ever seen. On one side were the Allies: Britain, France, Russia, and several smaller nations. On the other side were the Central Powers: Germany, Austria-Hungary, and their associates. Some believed that the war would end quickly, as the Franco-Prussian War had done. But on the western front a German advance into France became bogged down in trench warfare, producing a stalemate that could not be broken even with the loss of incredible numbers of lives. By one conservative estimate, 10 million people died in the war and another 20 million were wounded.

The first economic reaction in the United States was a financial panic. The stock market was temporarily closed, and there was considerable pressure on the banks as depositors tried to convert their money into gold. But the crisis soon passed. Under the Aldrich-Vreeland Act, passed after the crisis of 1907, banks had been authorized to issue emergency currency as a temporary substitute for gold, and the issue of this currency put an end to the crisis. At one point, this currency amounted to nearly one-quarter of the currency in the hands of the public.[1]

As the period of American neutrality continued (it lasted from the outbreak of the war in 1914 until America's entry in April 1917), it became clear that this would be an immensely profitable period for American business. German imports from the United States fell to practically nothing because of the successful British naval blockade; but Britain, France, and other European countries began to purchase large amounts of munitions and food at ever-rising prices from the United States, the only industrial power not involved. A wide gap opened up between America's soaring exports to Europe and her declining imports. The Europeans paid for these exports by extinguishing holdings of American debt, by shipping gold, and by incurring new debts.

---

[1] Milton Friedman and Anna J. Schwartz, *A Monetary History of the United States* (Princeton: Princeton University Press, 1963), p. 172.

When the war began the United States was a debtor, the normal status for a developing country. When the war ended, the United States was a creditor who not incidentally held much of the world's stock of monetary gold. Before the war, the world's financial center was London; after the war, it was New York.

With the fighting so far away and so bloody, sentiment in the United States initially favored keeping out of the war, but eventually many forces and events combined to push the United States toward active involvement on the side of the Allies. Partly it was the close cultural and linguistic ties between Britain and the United States. But the crucial factor in turning public opinion against Germany was Germany's use of submarine warfare. In 1915, after the sinking without warning of the British ship *Lusitania* (with the loss of 1,198 lives, including 124 Americans), President Woodrow Wilson sent a series of strongly worded warnings to Germany. For a time, Germany moderated her use of submarines. In early 1917, though, the Germans returned to a policy of unrestricted submarine warfare in a desperate gamble to starve Britain into submission before intervention by the United States could turn the tide.

America's involvement in the war would be brief but decisive. The United States declared war on April 17, 1917. General John J. Pershing arrived in Paris in June 1917 to direct the American Expeditionary Force; the armistice with Germany was signed on November 11, 1918, seventeen months later. American forces were instrumental in winning a number of important victories. But it was not the victories themselves so much as the prospect of enormous American reinforcements that forced the Germans, exhausted by years of war and blockade, to come to terms. Indeed, when the war ended, the Central Powers still controlled large amounts of territory from France to Crimea.

The armed forces of the United States, as noted in the chapter introduction, grew from 179,000 in 1916 to nearly 3 million in 1918. Some 2 million served overseas in the American Expeditionary Force, and about three-quarters of these saw combat. A military draft was instituted in April 1917, with a system of deferments for skilled workers. Americans took part in bitter fighting, and 117,000 Americans died in military service, more than half from disease. Vast amounts of arms and weapons were produced, and a great shipbuilding program was launched.

The financial reflection of the military effort was a tremendous increase in spending by the federal government, from 1.5 percent of GNP in 1916 to 24.2 percent in 1918. American involvement began with the country operating at close to full employment: the unemployment rate in 1916 was 5.1 percent. (This was in marked contrast to World War II, which America entered with reserves of underutilized labor and capital.) Therefore it was not possible to increase the production of weapons and other military supplies greatly without reducing civilian consumption.

FINANCING THE WAR

There are four basic ways of financing a war: (1) taxation, (2) borrowing from the public, (3) creating money, and (4) drafting soldiers and other resources. The United States relied on all four. On October 3, 1917, after considerable wrangling, Congress passed the War Revenue Act. This act increased corporate and personal income taxes (the rate in the top bracket was raised to 70 percent) and established excise, excess profits (for business), and luxury taxes. Table 21-1 shows the total financial cost of the war (excluding the cost of the draft) and how this was distributed among various sources of finance. Taxation was clearly an important source of revenue, but borrowing was far more important, accounting for 61.4 percent of total financing.

It is not hard to see why Congress preferred borrowing to taxation. When taxes are raised, it is altogether too clear who is doing what to whom. Borrowing produces less obvious costs. If interest rates rise as a result of government borrowing, those hurt may blame the market or other private-sector borrowers.

It could also be argued that the war was an investment—"to make the world safe for democracy," in President Wilson's phrase. Since future generations would benefit, why should the current generation bear all the burden of the war? A numerical example will clarify the simple sense in which people probably thought that relying on bond finance would shift the burden of the war. If a middle-aged man was taxed $100 in 1918 to pay for the war, that would have been the end of the story; in later years his son would have to pay no additional taxes. But if the same man bought a bond for $100, then his son would later be taxed to pay back the interest and principal on the bond. How the two generations actually fared is a more complex question that depends on issues that economists have not resolved. If the older generation, for example, increased its savings in order to leave the same real after-tax bequests to the next generation, then the burden might not have been shifted.

Wilson's Secretary of the Treasury William Gibbs McAdoo had studied the financing of the Civil War and concluded that Salmon Chase, the Treasury Secretary in that conflict, had erred in not linking the purchase of war bonds more closely to patriotism. McAdoo launched an aggressive program to market bonds in World War I, to "capitalize patriotism."[2] Huge bond rallies were held, and the crowds were exhorted to buy

TABLE 21-1   FINANCING WORLD WAR I, 1917–1919

	Total (in billions of dollars)	Percent
War expenditures	$31.0	100.0
Taxes	7.6	24.5
Borrowing from the public	19.0	61.3
Creating new money	4.4	14.2

SOURCE: *Historical Statistics* (Washington, D.C.: Government Printing Office, 1976), Series Y336 (expenditures), Y335 (taxes), X594 (U.S. government obligations held by commercial banks), and X800 (U.S. government obligations held by the Federal Reserve).

NOTE: Total wartime expenditures were calculated as the sum of federal government expenditures in 1917 through 1919 less three times average expenditures in 1916.

[2]David M. Kennedy, *Over Here: The First World War and American Society* (Oxford: Oxford University Press, 1980), p. 105.

war bonds by celebrities such as Mary Pickford and Douglas Fairbanks. Charlie Chaplin even made a film showing how the purchase of war bonds helped the government finance the war. Thrift stamps (costing 25¢ each) were sold in schools, post offices, and factories. How much all of this helped is open to question. Despite all the hoopla and the considerable, often vicious anti-German propaganda, the government found that it could not sell bonds that paid much below the going market rate.[3]

As in wars past and wars to come, the government relied on a third means of financing the war: creating new money. In earlier wars the mechanism had been simple, and easy for the public to understand. In the Revolutionary War the government had printed Continental dollars; in the Civil War, greenbacks. Now the mechanism was more complicated. When the Federal Reserve bought bonds on the open market, it did so by creating deposits that had not existed before. When lodged in the banking system, these new deposits became the basis for a further expansion of money and credit by the banks. All told, as Table 21-1 shows, the Federal Reserve and the commercial banking system acquired over $4 billion worth of government bonds, about 14 percent of total war finance. Even this figure understates the effect of money creation to some extent, because the banks made personal loans, secured by government bonds, to purchasers of bonds. Although this transaction appeared on the books of the bank as a personal loan, it was really the indirect purchase of a government bond.

The net result of financing part of the war by creating money was a tremendous increase in the stock of money and the price level. As Table 21-2 shows, the stock of money about doubled during the war, and with it the level of prices. Note, however, that prices did not rise in the exact proportion as money per unit of real output, as a naive version of the quantity theory of money would predict. Prices rose faster than money per unit of output (velocity rose) between 1915 and 1918, more slowly from 1918 to 1919, and then more rapidly from 1919 to 1920. This pattern can be given a fairly

TABLE 21-2 MONEY AND PRICES IN WORLD WAR I, 1914–1920

Year	Stock of Money (in billions of dollars)	Money per Unit of Real NNP (1914 = 100)	Implicit NNP Deflator (1914 = 100)
1914	$16.39	$100.0	$100.0
1915	17.59	104.1	103.1
1916	20.85	105.2	116.5
1917	24.37	126.3	143.9
1918	26.73	126.1	165.5
1919	31.01	140.5	168.0
1920	34.80	166.0	191.7

SOURCE: MILTON FRIEDMAN AND ANNA J. SCHWARTZ, *MONETARY TRENDS IN THE UNITED STATES AND THE UNITED KINGDOM* (CHICAGO: UNIVERSITY OF CHICAGO PRESS, 1982), PP. 123–124.

[3]Margaret G. Myers, *A Financial History of the United States* (New York: Columbia University Press, 1970), pp. 280–283; and Schultz and Caine, *Financial Development of the United States* (New York: Prentice-Hall, 1937), pp. 533–539.

straightforward explanation. During the years of threatened and actual war, the fear of inflation (along with expanding economic activity) encouraged people to spend their money rapidly—thus causing the very thing they feared. The end of the war created expectations of a return to price stability, which worked against rapid turnover of money balances. Finally, an unexpected postwar boom rekindled real economic activity and expectations of inflation, thus adding to the flow of spending.

Inflation is analogous to a tax on money: the cash in your pocket goes down in value while the government acquires real resources. Like deficit financing, though, inflation due to money creation has the attractive political property of being a hidden tax: the public may blame profiteers rather than monetary policy for the inflation. This was probably true in earlier wars as well as this one. But here the complex ways in which the government could finance itself through money creation may have hidden the tax even better. All of this does not mean that there is no justification for finance through money creation. If the government can tax houses and tobacco, automobiles and alcohol, why not tax money? But it does suggest that, because policymakers will not have to bear direct responsibility for the "tax," money creation is likely to be overused.

THE HUMAN COSTS OF THE WAR

In adding up dollars we should not forget that federal spending paid only part of the cost of the war. The major part of the cost was borne by the soldiers themselves. To some extent we can think of these costs in monetary terms. The draft can be thought of as another kind of tax: the tax paid is the difference between what the country would have had to pay a soldier to get his services voluntarily and what it actually paid him. Offsetting this tax were veterans' benefits paid after the war. In all, as noted earlier, 117,000 died while in military service. Another 204,000 received non-mortal wounds.[4] In the end, it is impossible to put dollar signs on all of the human costs.

CENTRAL CONTROLS

During World War I (unlike the Civil War), a real attempt was made to direct the economy from the top, down. To a large extent this effort arose from the ideological temper of the times. The battle between those who favored and those who opposed organizing the economy through the market was particularly sharp in the Progressive Era just prior to the war, and there were strong antimarket factions both in the Democratic and Republican parties. There was also the example of Germany, which was widely perceived to be both powerful and organized along centralizing lines. Perhaps the most daring departure from the tradition of laissez-faire was the nationalization of the nation's railroads, as noted later in the chapter. By the end of the war, Washington was bulging with agencies set up to cope with a vast array of new economic

---

[4] *Historical Statistics*, (Washington, D.C.: Government Printing Office, 1976), series Y879, Y880, Y882.

A battlefield hospital near the front lines in World War I.

problems. There was a Capital Issues Committee designed to limit issues of securities by the private sector; a War Trade Board, with powers over imports and exports; a War Shipping Board and an Emergency Fleet Corporation designed to produce ships and to control their use; and perhaps 150 others. Existing agencies, moreover, were often given new powers. A closer look at a few of these agencies will show how the government tried to manage the war economy.

THE FOOD ADMINISTRATION AND THE FUEL ADMINISTRATION

In August 1917, Congress passed the Lever Food and Fuel Control Act, establishing a wartime Food Administration and a Fuel Administration. Herbert Hoover was appointed the Food Administrator. Hoover enjoyed a reputation as a brilliant administrator—he was then serving as the director of the Commission for the Relief of Belgium—and his reputation grew with his performance as Food Administrator. His job was to maintain an adequate supply of food to the domestic market and to our allies while at the same time preventing excessive increases in prices. The tools given to Hoover were limited, and his philosophy of government—which emphasized voluntary cooperation—discouraged him from seeking greater authority. Direct control of prices, with penalties for violation, was generally avoided, as was formal rationing. But the Food Administrator was given the power to license food dealers. This license could be revoked if the dealer failed to go along with Food Administration price policies.

In place of formal rationing, Hoover called for various voluntary conservation measures. "Meatless Mondays" and "Wheatless Wednesdays" were promoted as ways of reducing domestic demand and leaving more for exports. Retailers were encouraged (or permitted, depending on how you look at it) to sell wheat flour along with less-desirable substitutes such as rye or potato flour. The resulting mixture could be baked into a loaf of "Victory bread." Of course, this was really a hidden price increase. The true price of the wheat flour was the direct amount paid plus the difference between what the buyer paid for the less-desirable flour and what he would voluntarily have paid for it. By such half-measures, food prices were controlled and output rationed.

Harry A. Garfield, the U.S. Fuel Administrator, was not as successful as Hoover. In the extremely cold winter of 1917–1918, parts of the country ran short of coal. There were a variety of reasons for the shortage: unusual cold, unusual demands on the rail network, perhaps even the Fuel Administration's price and allocation policies. After eastern factories were shut down briefly to reduce coal demand and give the railroads time to move the coal, the problem abated, but the Fuel Administration came in for considerable attack, adding to already widespread discontent with Wilson's management of the wartime economy.

THE WAR INDUSTRIES BOARD

In March 1918, responding to the mounting criticism of the war effort, Wilson reorganized the most ambitious of the war agencies, the War Industries Board, and placed at its head Bernard Baruch. Baruch was a successful Wall Street speculator, but as a southern Jewish Democrat he was something of an outsider on the Street and an ideal candidate to manage the War Industries Board in a Democratic administration. Baruch went to work immediately negotiating prices of key industrial products. Other industrial prices were set by a separate Price-Fixing Committee, which used a system called bulkline pricing. Under this system, firms reported their costs of production, and the committee then set a price that would bring forth the "bulk" (say 80 percent) of the maximum possible output. This system was designed to balance the need for raw materials against the need for overall price stability while limiting the profits of low-cost producers. Baruch also set up a system of priorities to guide business in filling the mounting volume of war contracts. Each contract was given a government priority rating: AA, A, B, C, or D. If a conflict arose, a producer had to fill an AA order before an A order and so on. It sounds good. Why rely on the market when a government planner could determine priorities in line with national values? But when firms were given their own power to set priorities in order to save administrative resources, industry soon became choked with high-priority contracts. The natural tendency was to give everything the highest priority. (In World War II, "priorities inflation" nearly wrecked the system.)

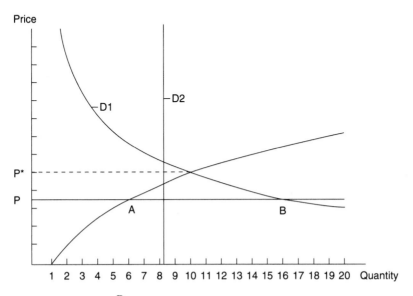

RATIONING IN A COMPETITIVE MARKET

The figure illustrates the role of rationing. The government has fixed the price at P. But at this price the quantity demanded exceeds the quantity supplied by AB. This reduces output (compared with letting the price rise to the free market equilibrium P*. Some consumers will be frustrated by empty shelves. Time may be wasted waiting in line. The scramble among consumers may lead to bribes and various forms of concealed price increases such as reductions in quality.

Instead, consumers can be issued ration tickets. With each purchase a consumer must turn over a ration ticket along with the money price. The ration tickets in this case reduce the effective demand curve from D1 to D2. Since the government has guessed exactly right in this example (issued neither too few nor too many tickets), there is no excess demand, and the problems created by price controls are reduced. Formal rationing was used for sugar (after long waiting lines became intolerable), but in many cases the government permitted "socially desirable" forms of hidden price increases, such as the tie-in sales intended to promote the baking of Victory bread described in the text. The result was to move the true price toward the free market equilibrium, P*.

Baruch's stint at the War Industries Board was brief—about eight months—but he drew strong conclusions from his experience. In subsequent years he repeatedly argued that the example of the War Industries Board pointed the way toward cooperation between business and industry in peacetime and centralized administration (doing away with the market) in wartime.

LABOR DURING THE WAR YEARS

The war tightened labor markets. The demand for labor was increased by government contracts that were financed in part by borrowing and by creating new money. The supply of labor was reduced by the cutoff of immigration and by the drafting of men into the armed forces. By 1918, as Table 21-3 shows, real earnings were considerably above the level of 1914. Adjustments in the labor market, however, were far from smooth. In 1917 in particular, money incomes were up 14.5 percent over 1916, but consumer prices were up 16.1 percent—real wages had fallen. The situation was reminiscent of the Civil War. In the long run we expect real wages to be determined by the productivity of labor, but in the short run some wages may prove to be sticky. It is not surprising, then, that 1917 was a year of strikes—4,450 of them, a record. Strikes were particularly acute west of the Mississippi, where a combination of low wages, harsh working conditions, uncompromising employers, and radical unions spelled bitter labor disputes.

The Wilson administration's response was pragmatic. In a few cases it threatened strikers through the draft and in other ways, but in most cases it was more accommodating. War contracts generally included provisions calling for higher wages and better working conditions, though they did not provide the goal dearest to the heart of organized labor: the closed shop. When a strike of railroad workers threatened to disrupt the industry that was at the heart of the war effort, the administration nation-

TABLE 21-3   ANNUAL EARNINGS, 1914–1920

Year	Money Earnings of All Employees After Deduction for Unemployment	Real Earnings of All Employees After Deduction for Unemployment (1914 dollars)
1914	$ 555	$555
1915	547	541
1916	647	595
1917	748	586
1918	972	648
1919	1,117	648
1920	1,236	619

SOURCE: *HISTORICAL STATISTICS*, (WASHINGTON, D.C.: GOVERNMENT PRINTING OFFICE, 1976), SERIES D723, D725.

alized the railroads. Under government control, the railroads provided improved working conditions and higher wages while raising shipping costs only modestly. The result was an operating deficit made up by the government. The railroads were finally returned to private ownership in 1920.

As you can see in Table 21-3, money earnings leaped upward in 1918 by some 22.6 percent, outrunning the cost of living (although this is hard to be certain about because price controls distorted the meaning of price indexes); real earnings probably reached an all-time high. Organized labor was extremely optimistic in the immediate postwar period. Labor union membership was up, and the public's view of the conservative wing of the labor movement (under the leadership of Samuel Gompers, who had served on a government board during the war) was also high. But the hopes of many labor leaders for a new era in labor relations soon came to an end. An industrial conference called by the President in 1919—with representatives from labor, management, and the public under Baruch's leadership—ended in failure. More importantly, an attempt to organize the steel industry, then the bellwether of American industry, was beaten back after a long and bitter strike.

Women were one potential source of labor tapped during the war. Some women served with the armed forces in Europe, usually as nurses or telephone operators. Women also made important contributions in industry, with about a million taking up war work. However, the war did not mean a breakthrough in the economic role of women. Few took jobs in heavy industry. First-time hires were relatively few. Many married women who entered the labor force had been previously employed while single; they returned temporarily to help their families cope with war. When the war ended, the role of women in the labor force returned to what it had been before the war. Partly this was the result of pressure from labor unions and other sectors for women to make room for returning veterans; partly it was the result of older economic pressures. The labor-force participation rates for married and single women were both a bit lower in 1920 than they had been in 1910. On the political front, the Wilson administration strongly supported the right of women to vote, calling their contributions "vital to the winning of the war."[5] As a result, the Nineteenth Amendment to the Constitution, giving women the right to vote, was finally adopted in 1920.

Perhaps no group of workers seized the opportunities provided by the war more eagerly than African-Americans. With factories operating at full capacity and deprived of a steady stream of immigrants from Europe, northern industry at last looked to African-Americans for a supply of labor. Beginning in 1914, agents for northern industries fanned out across the South to recruit workers, who were often given free transportation north. There began a mass exodus of African-American workers from the rural South: New York, Detroit, St. Louis, Cleveland, Chicago, and other industrial cities saw a steady stream of newcomers. In a few places in the South, the new shortage of labor actually led to improved race relations; but elsewhere the South reacted in the old way, with harassment, detentions, and beatings. Some southerners also tried to prevent northern agents from recruiting black workers, but nothing could stem the tide. Northern industry provided higher wages, and northern cities greater freedom.

---

[5] As quoted in David M. Kennedy, *Over Here*, p. 284.

Competition between African-American and white workers soon exploded in violent race riots: in East St. Louis in July 1917, nine whites and a larger but undetermined number of African-Americans were killed; in Chicago in July 1919, thirteen whites and twenty-three African-Americans were killed.

AFTER THE ARMISTICE

Demobilization followed the simplest possible path after the Armistice. Soldiers were mustered out of the army as fast as possible. War contracts were canceled. Government bureaus were closed down. The War Industries Board was closed down so fast that Baruch ended up paying out of his own pocket for transportation home for some of his employees. It is tempting to argue that this was not the best way, that a more gradual winding-down of affairs would have eased the transition to a peacetime economy. But this is far from obvious. The problem resembles that faced by modern-day countries trying to liberalize their economies: should they do it all at once or only gradually? Individuals can be helped by a gradual transition; life is a lot easier for a government bureaucrat, for example, if he can look for permanent employment while holding on to his old job. On the other hand, the longer resources are held in unproductive uses, the greater the loss of output for the economy as a whole.

THE TREATY OF VERSAILLES AND ITS CONSEQUENCES

Despite the rapid demobilization, things never returned to where they had been before. Some of the most important changes were in the international sphere. In January 1918 President Wilson announced his famous Fourteen Points, describing the basis for peace in Europe, before a joint session of Congress. These points defined in broad terms the territorial adjustments that should occur in postwar Europe, the structure of international relations ("Open Covenants, openly arrived at"), the extent of compensation for damages that should be paid by the Central Powers to the Allies, and in the fourteenth point "a general association of nations" to guarantee each nation's sovereignty. These points, amplified in subsequent statements, became the basis for Germany's agreement to sign the Armistice. Shortly after the war ended, Wilson sailed for Europe to take part in the Paris peace conference that would negotiate the Treaty of Versailles to end the war. Ultimately, a treaty was hammered out by the Big Four: Britain, France, the United States, and Italy. The United States, however, never ratified the treaty. It was bottled up in the Senate, where Republicans insisted on changes that Wilson would not agree to.

John Maynard Keynes, who attended the conference as part of the British delegation, wrote a brilliant analysis of the Treaty of Versailles in *The Economic Consequences of the Peace*.[6] Keynes showed that the Allied demands for reparations went far

---

[6]John Maynard Keynes, *The Economic Consequences of the Peace* (New York: Harcourt, Brace & World, 1919).

beyond any that could be reasonably calculated on the basis of the understanding that had produced the Armistice. He also argued that Germany lacked the capacity to pay the reparations and would have to run a large surplus of exports over imports in order to pay them. Moreover, Keynes's close study of Germany's prewar exports and imports, and of the prospects for expanding those exports and diminishing imports, convinced him that changes on the order implied by the treaty were impossible. Keynes's argument started a long debate among economists over the "transfer problem," as it came to be called, a debate that has still not been resolved. Perhaps Germany did have the capacity to make the required transfers if sufficient political will could be mustered. But few would argue today with Keynes's plea for a more magnanimous peace, for the German belief that the peace was unjust contributed to what then seemed unthinkable—a second world war.

THE WAR'S DOMESTIC LEGACY

The war also left many domestic legacies, as shown by Robert Higgs in his challenging book *Crisis and Leviathan.*[7] Some were financial, such as increased federal spending for interest on the national debt, veterans' benefits, and other long-term costs. More important was the ideological legacy. Though most Americans were more than willing to return to the old patterns after the war, some, such as Bernard Baruch, concluded that the economy would work better if the government played a major role in coordinating economic activity. In retrospect, we can see that American involvement in the war was too brief to draw strong conclusions about the short-run effects of government interventions, let alone the long-run effects.

But the glow of success that surrounded wartime government programs made them powerful examples in the debate over the appropriate role of government in the economy. The idea that an activist government could improve the functioning of the economy lay dormant during the prosperous twenties but would become important in the depressed thirties. The New Deal's National Recovery Administration, for example, was modeled on Baruch's War Industries Board. The New Deal's Commodity Credit Corporation was modeled on the United States Grain Corporation. The controls exercised under the Agricultural Adjustment Acts, passed in the 1930s, were modeled on those exercised by the Food Administration. The Bituminous Coal Division of the Interior Department, established in the 1930s, took its cue from the Fuel Administration. These are only a few examples; the complete list is much longer. Many of the individuals who were chosen to run New Deal programs, moreover, had worked for government agencies during the war. General Hugh S. Johnson, for example, who headed the National Recovery Administration in 1933, had served under Baruch at the War Industries Board.

Reformers undoubtedly would have pushed for and won many changes in the economy in the 1930s even if World War I had never occurred. After all, many of the wartime interventions had been introduced without the benefit of thoroughgoing

---

[7] Robert Higgs, *Crisis and Leviathan: Critical Episodes in the Growth of American Government* (New York: Oxford University Press, 1987), Chapter 7.

rehearsals. But the perception in the 1930s that federal programs controlling and regulating markets had been a success in World War I increased the pace and depth of reform.

The immediate effect of the Armistice was a slowdown in the economy. Although price controls had disappeared abruptly, there was no postwar burst of inflation. Instead, prices remained roughly level for some months. Then, in 1919, a vigorous boom got underway and prices began to rise rapidly. The Federal Reserve realized that the policy of holding its discount rate below market rates was adding to inflationary pressures: banks found it profitable to borrow from the Federal Reserve and then expand their own lending. The Federal Reserve, however, was reluctant to raise its rates. One reason was that higher interest rates might have depressed the values of the large amount of government war loans in the market.

Finally, possibly because its own reserves of gold were becoming depleted, the Federal Reserve acted. In late 1919 and early 1920, the Federal Reserve raised its discount rate. The increase in January 1920 from 4.75 percent to 6 percent was the sharpest single increase in the short history of the system. On June 1 the discount rate was raised again, to 7 percent. These increases sent a strong signal to the market that credit would soon be tight. In addition, there were sharp breaks in other sectors of the economy. Agricultural prices, for example, fell throughout much of the world as European production recovered. As a result, the economy went into a severe recession. From 1920 to 1921, nominal net national product fell 18 percent and real net national product fell 4 percent. But the recession was also very brief: it resembled what has come to be called a "V-shaped" recession, straight down and straight back up again. One reason, perhaps, is that even though the number of bank failures rose substantially, there was no financial panic. (As we shall see, the sharp contraction during 1929 to 1930, which appeared at first to be a repeat of that in 1920 to 1921, produced a financial panic that drove the economy far deeper into depression.)

After the economy recovered from the recession of 1920 to 1921, it entered a long period of economic expansion. So vigorous was this expansion that many people came to believe that a new age of continuous prosperity had arrived. The "roaring twenties" are the subject of the next chapter.

SELECTED REFERENCES
AND SUGGESTED READINGS

Clark, John Maurice. "The Basis of War-Time Collectivism." *American Economic Review* 7 (1917): 772–790.

———. *The Costs of the War to the American People*. New Haven: Yale University Press, 1931.

Clarkson, Grosvenor B. *Industrial America in the World War*. Boston: Houghton Mifflin, 1923.

Coit, Margaret L. *Mr. Baruch*. Boston: Houghton Mifflin, 1957.

Cuff, Robert D. *The War Industries Board: Business-Government Relations During World War I*. Baltimore: Johns Hopkins University Press, 1973.

———. "We Band of Brothers—Woodrow Wilson's War Managers." *Canadian Review of American Studies* 2 (1974): 135–148.

Cuff, Robert D., and Melvin I. Urofsky. "The Steel Industry and Price Fixing During World War I." *Business History Review* 44 (Autumn 1970).

Friedman, Milton. "Price, Income, and Monetary Changes in Three Wartime Periods." *American Economic Review* 42 (May 1952). Reprinted in *The Optimum Quantity of Money and Other Essays.* Chicago: Aldine, 1969.

Friedman, Milton, and Anna J. Schwartz. *A Monetary History of the United States.* Princeton: Princeton University Press, 1963.

Fussell, Paul. *The Great War and Modern Memory.* New York: Oxford University Press, 1975.

Gilbert, Charles. *American Financing of World War I.* Westport, Connecticut: Greenwood, 1970.

Higgs, Robert. *Crisis and Leviathan: Critical Episodes in the Growth of American Government.* New York: Oxford University Press, 1987.

Himmelberg, Robert F. "The War Industries Board and the Antitrust Question in 1918." *Journal of American History* 52 (June 1965): 378–402.

Johnson, James P. "The Wilsonians as War Managers: Coal and the 1917–1918 Winter Crisis." *Prologue* 9 (1977): 193–208.

Kennedy, David M. *Over Here: The First World War and American Society.* Oxford: Oxford University Press, 1980.

Koistinen, Paul A. C. "The 'Industrial-Military Complex' in Historical Perspective: World War I." *Business History Review* 41 (1967): 378–403.

Kuznets, Simon. *National Product War and Prewar.* New York: National Bureau of Economic Research, Occasional Paper 17, 1944.

Leuchtenburg, William E. "The New Deal and the Analogue of War." In *Change and Continuity in Twentieth-Century America.* John Braeman et al., eds. New York: Harper & Row, 1966.

Litman, Simon. *Prices and Price Control in Great Britain and the United States during the World War.* New York: Oxford University Press, 1920.

Mullendore, William Clinton. *History of the United States Food Administration, 1917–1919.* Stanford: Stanford University Press, 1941.

Myers, Margaret G. *A Financial History of the United States.* New York: Columbia University Press, 1970.

Rockoff, Hugh. *Drastic Measures: A History of Wage and Price Controls in the United States.* New York: Cambridge University Press, 1984.

Samuelson, Paul A., and Everett Hagen. *After the War, 1918–1920: Military and Economic Demobilization in the United States.* Washington, D.C.: Government Printing Office, 1943.

Scheiber, Jane Lang, and Harry N. Scheiber. "The Wilson Administration and the Wartime Mobilization of Black Americans, 1917–1918." *Labor History* 10 (1969): 433–458.

Stein, Herbert. *Government Price Policy in the United States During the War.* Williamstown, Massachusetts: Williams College, 1939.

Taussig, Frank W. "Price Fixing as Seen by a Price Fixer." *Quarterly Journal of Economics* 33 (1919): 205–241.

Urofsky, Melvin. *Big Steel and the Wilson Administration: A Study in Business Government Relations.* Columbus: Ohio State University Press, 1969.

CHAPTER TWENTY-TWO

THE ROARING TWENTIES

CHAPTER THEME After World War I the public hoped for a "return to normalcy," as Warren G. Harding put it. Wartime controls were removed quickly, taxes were gradually cut back, and the Republican administrations of the 1920s generally relied upon market forces to produce economic growth. After a severe but brief recession in 1920 and 1921, the economy moved into a long expansion. The stock market surged and the belief took hold that the economy had moved into a new era of continuous growth and prosperity that would eventually eliminate poverty. But the stock market crash in October 1929 and the fall into the depths of an unprecedented depression in the early 1930s made pessimists out of the most determined optimists.

The central question faced by economic historians is whether the disasters of the 1930s were the inevitable outcome of the prosperity of the 1920s and its reliance on a free-market economy, or whether they were the result of shocks and policy mistakes in the 1930s. Was there, to put it differently, a fatal cancer growing in the economy of the 1920s that brought disaster ever closer, even as the economic physicians of the day continued to pronounce the patient in good health? Economic historians have suggested numerous problems and sectors that might have caused the Great Depression—changes in the distribution of income, the ongoing problems in agriculture, the stock market boom and bust, and so on—but it is easier to propose connections than to prove them. In any event, the prestige of the market economy peaked with the stock market. In the depression, the nation turned from the free-market model of 1920s to the central planning model of the war years to restore prosperity and growth.

SOCIAL CHANGES IN THE AFTERMATH OF WAR

When World War I ended, a promising young song writer named Harry Donaldson cast his lot with the just-organized Irving Berlin Music Company. His smash 1919 hit was at once a question and a prophetic answer: "How ya gonna keep 'em down on the farm after they've seen Paree?" How indeed? Millions of young Americans had been wrested from the boredom of country life to serve in the war, marking the beginning of the end of an agrarian society. To be sure, only a fraction of them ever saw Paris, and some got no farther than Camp Funston. But country boy, small-town bookkeeper, and city millworker alike developed a taste for travel and adventure.

Lured by the availability of jobs, the excitement of city life, and advances in transportation, nearly 15 million people were added to the number of American urbanites between 1920 and 1930. Sometime near the end of World War I, the number of Americans living in urban centers of 2,500 people or more passed the 50 million mark. As the census of 1920 was to report, for the first time more than 50 percent of the population, over 54 million people, were urban dwellers. Leading the flight to the city were southern blacks, who had begun migrating northward in large numbers during the war. Especially magnetic to blacks were New York, Philadelphia, Washington, Chicago, St. Louis, and out west, Los Angeles. By 1930, Harlem was the concentration point of nearly 300,000 New York blacks.

In a dreadful intrusion on the rights of the individual, a moralistic minority secured passage of the Eighteenth Amendment, prohibiting the manufacture, sale, or transport of "intoxicating liquors" and taking away a basic comfort of field hands, factory workers, and others, on the grounds that drinking was sinful and that poor people were not entitled to such a luxury anyway.[1] A swell of fear and hate was rising that would crest in the activities of the Ku Klux Klan, and by 1924 that organization's anti-black, anti-Jewish, and anti–Roman Catholic persecutions had become a national scandal.

The future nevertheless held a bright promise of prosperity and more leisure time. Women had gained the right to vote, but their emancipation was broader than that. Young women in particular began to chisel away at the double standard of morality that had been typical of pre-1914 relations between the sexes; the "flapper" of the 1920s was already emerging in 1919 as the girl who could smoke men's cigarettes, drink men's whiskey, and play men's games.

It might have been expected that these changes would be matched by changes in the workplace, especially among older married women.[2] Increased education, a reduced birthrate and completed family size, the emergence of the clerical sector, and the demonstration effect of World War I all worked toward greater female participation in the labor force. Indeed, looking at the purely economic factors, one might have expected a rapid increase in the number of two-earner households of the sort that actually came in the 1980s. But this development was prevented by "marriage bars," policies followed by public and private employers that prohibited the hiring of married women and

---

[1] The authors confess their prejudice on the issue.

[2] Claudia Goldin, *Understanding the Gender Gap: An Economic History of American Women* (New York: Oxford University Press, 1990), Chapter 6.

forced female employees to leave when they married. In part these bars simply reflected broader social norms maintaining that married women belonged at home with their children. They became more widespread in the 1920s with the growth of large firms that relied on personnel departments to make hiring and firing decisions and that preferred bureaucratic rules for making decisions to individualized hiring and firing.

BUSINESS IN THE 1920s

In the 1920s, the administrations of Presidents Warren G. Harding and Calvin Coolidge were openly dedicated to the principle that business should be free to grow without government meddling or interfering. With little hindrance from government, the processes of mass production and marketing accelerated, and businesses became even more consolidated than in earlier decades. Secretary of Commerce Herbert Hoover, among others, encouraged consolidations for reasons of efficiency; competing firms were allowed to form trade associations, not just to standardize tools and share technical information but also to set prices. Both Harding and Coolidge appointed men to the Federal Trade Commission who had little intention of enforcing the antitrust laws, either in letter or in spirit. As the years passed, banking, manufacturing, distribution, electronics, iron and steel, automobiles, and mining all became increasingly controlled by large conglomerates. Such policies added to an environment that produced unparalleled business prosperity. Spectacular advances in the production of consumer durables, electric power, new appliances, suburban housing, and city skyscrapers highlighted the decade.

THE AUTOMOBILE

In many ways the automobile was the economic symbol of the 1920s. Annual automobile production rose from 1.5 million cars in 1921 to 4.8 million in 1929, while prices fell steadily. By 1929, one American in six owned an automobile. The indirect effects of the automobile were very important for production in general. It provided important demands for steel, rubber, plate glass, and petroleum, not so much to spur them as to cushion and replace the fall in demand from cutbacks in railroad rolling stock, wagons, streetcars, and sleighs. Perhaps the automobile's main impact was on the landscape. It not only changed the location of residences, portending the heyday of suburbia, but also ushered in the activity of commuting to work. In addition, there were the recreational features of weekend trips and access to the country. The automobile combined travel with entertainment and spotted the countryside with motels, hot dog stands, road signs, and gas stations.

The automobile also enlarged the demands on government for paved roads, as automobile clubs and especially farmers pressed for assistance to get out of the mud. With the passage of the Federal Aid Road Act of 1916, the development of a nationwide highway system began in a halting, timorous fashion. Under the 1916 act, the government committed itself to spending $75 million to build rural post roads, with the money to be expended by the Department of Agriculture over a period of five years. The national contribution was not to exceed 50 percent of the total construction cost,

Henry Ford began mass production of the Model T in 1908; by 1916 he was producing 2,000 per day. In the late 1920s, however, the Model T lost market share to more stylish, although more expensive, competitors. Production of the Model T was discontinued in 1926.

exclusive of bridges and other major structures, and was conditional on the organization of state highway departments with adequate personnel and sufficient equipment to initiate the work and carry out subsequent maintenance. The Federal Highway Act of 1921 amended the original law by requiring the Secretary of Agriculture, in dispensing aid, to give preference to states that had designated a system of highways to receive federal aid. The designated system was to constitute the "primary" roads of the state and was not to exceed 7 percent of the state's total highway mileage. Incidentally, in the Highway Act of 1921, Congress appropriated as much money for a single year's construction (1922) as it had for all of the preceding five years.

Although state appropriations for roads were sporadic and uneven, these also increased, from $70 million in 1918 to nearly $750 million by the end of the 1920s. Along with this stimulus to government activity came the need for the bureaucracies to administer licensing, titles and registrations, and, of course, traffic courts.

ELECTRICITY AND APPLIANCES

A second major growth sector was the electric power industry, whose influence on residential living was dramatic. In the 1920s, there was a remarkable growth of electric appliances such as ranges, vacuum cleaners, and refrigerators. Over the decade, annual refrigerator production expanded by almost 50 times, reaching nearly 1 million units in 1930.

You will always be glad you bought a Glenwood

THREE times a day, year in and year out, you'll find that a Glenwood range really does "make cooking easy."

This Gold Medal model is ready for anything, it gives you a choice of three fuels, coal, wood or gas; it will do a week's baking all at once, if need be; and if you want to attend to something else, the Thermostat oven-heat control will take charge of your baking while you are gone.

It offers you all the facilities of two complete ranges in less than four feet of space. In two minutes you can

clean and polish its all-over finish of porcelain enamel with just a damp cloth. (The Gold Medal is also made with the regulation black finish.)

Send for booklet No. 250, which describes and illustrates the many helpful features of the Gold Medal Glenwood.

National Glenwood Week—October 7-14—will be observed by Glenwood dealers everywhere.

WEIR STOVE COMPANY, TAUNTON, MASS.

WESTERN BRANCH: 208 North State Street, CHICAGO

Makers of the Celebrated Glenwood Coal, Wood and Gas Ranges, Heating Stoves and Furnaces.

Gold Medal **Glenwood** Pearl Gray

Makes Cooking Easy

Mass production of consumer durables, often purchased with credit, characterized the boom of the 1920s.

Accompanying these new items were marked changes in mass advertising and installment buying, which together created both a greater desire for goods and a greater ease of buying them. Whereas in 1910 advertising expenditures of all types amounted to nearly $1 billion, the figure was $2 billion by 1920 and over $2.5 billion by 1929. The age of consumer goods had arrived.

THE RADIO AND ENTERTAINMENT. In 1922, 3 million homes had radios; by 1930, ownership reached 10 million. Mass entertainment (and advertisement) expanded still further through movie ticket sales, which doubled over the decade to almost 80 million tickets per week. In response to this vast and expanding market, the National Broadcasting Company (NBC) was formed in 1926, one year before the formation of the Columbia Broadcasting System (CBS). Predictably, a proliferation of radio stations resulted. Polling systems by telephone were used to determine program ratings, with low ratings leading to program abandonment. Certain goods became tied to particular programs, as producers sought any and all means to market their products and address the desires, fads, and fancies of the American public. For these and other reasons, the age of mass consumption, mass production, and the giant corporations became the trademark of the 1920s.

THE LABOR FORCE

The 1920s also profoundly affected Americans at work. During World War I, the 48-hour work week was accepted in many manufacturing industries, and by 1920 some agreements granted a half-holiday on Saturday. It was not until the very end of the decade, however, that a 48-hour week was standard for most occupations. Nevertheless, there was a fall in average hours worked by several hours per week. The implied advance in leisure for many American workers was one of the gains of the period.

Another gain was the relative absence of cyclical unemployment. Except for the hard years of 1921 and 1922, the 1920s were generally free of mass joblessness. In 1929, fairly typical of many years in the decade, the percentage of the civilian labor force that was unemployed was 3.2 percent. In short, the threat of unemployment was usually low, thereby contributing, along with added leisure, to the growing sense of prosperity.

THE PAYCHECK

Real annual earnings of nonfarm employees rose between 1919 and 1929, as shown in Table 22-1, by about 23 percent; the increase over 1914 was about 33 percent. More-

TABLE 22-1   Annual Earnings of Nonfarm Employees, 1914–1929[a]

	Money Earnings			Real Earnings (in 1914 dollars)		
Year	When Employed	Income Loss from Unemployment	After Deduction for Unemployment	Consumer Price Index (1914 = 100)	When Employed	After Deduction for Unemployment
1914	$ 696	$ 65	$ 613	100.0	$696	$613
1915	692	93	597	101.1	684	591
1916	760	59	706	108.7	699	649
1917	866	76	805	127.7	678	631
1918	1,063	25	1,041	150.0	709	694
1919	1,215	26	1,174	172.5	704	681
1920	1,426	104	1,343	199.7	714	672
1921	1,330	230	1,105	178.1	747	620
1922	1,289	129	1,148	166.9	772	688
1923	1,376	44	1,313	169.7	811	774
1924	1,396	98	1,284	170.3	820	754
1925	1,420	61	1,336	174.8	812	764
1926	1,452	33	1,411	176.2	824	801
1927	1,487	64	1,399	172.8	861	810
1928	1,490	80	1,394	170.9	872	816
1929	1,534	74	1,462	170.9	898	855

SOURCE: Stanley Lebergott, Manpower in Economic Growth: The American Record Since 1800 (New York: McGraw-Hill, 1964), p. 526. Used with the permission of McGraw-Hill Book Company.

[a] Excludes armed forces.

over, the losses of income from unemployment, which averaged only 3.3 percent between 1923 and 1929, were comparatively small throughout the period, except from late 1920 to 1922.[3] Overall, labor's advance, at least for those in the city and in industry, was substantial.

UNION DECLINE

Despite the general economic surge, the 1920s were not years of advance for organized labor. As Table 22-2 shows, the number of workers holding union membership fell from over 12 percent of the civilian labor force in 1920 to less than 8 percent at the end of the decade. This fall is especially surprising in light of the rapid growth of manufacturing and the concentration of the population in urban areas. It is true that throughout the 1920s, employers continued their effective use of the antiunion instruments developed before World War I. They discriminated, in hiring and firing, against employees who joined or organized unions. They used the hated yellow-dog contract, judged constitutional by the Supreme Court, to prevent union membership and to serve as a basis of civil suits against unions that persuaded employees to violate the contract. But the employers' most useful weapon was the injunction, by which a court could forbid, at least temporarily, such practices as picketing, secondary boycotts, and

TABLE 22-2   UNION MEMBERSHIP, 1919–1929

Year	Total Union Membership (thousands)	Total Membership as a Percent of Total Labor Force	Total Membership as a Percent of Nonfarm Labor Force
1919	4,046	10.2%	14.8%
1920	5,034	12.2	16.3
1921	4,722	11.2	15.0
1922	3,950	9.3	12.4
1923	3,629	8.4	11.1
1924	3,549	8.0	10.6
1925	3,566	7.9	10.3
1926	3,592	7.9	10.3
1927	3,600	7.8	10.0
1928	3,567	7.6	9.7
1929	3,625	7.6	9.7

SOURCE: *HISTORICAL STATISTICS* (WASHINGTON, D.C.: GOVERNMENT PRINTING OFFICE, 1975), SERIES D4, D7, D8, AND D940.

---

[3] These unemployment rates from Stanley Lebergott, *Manpower in Economic Growth: The American Record Since 1800* (New York: McGraw-Hill, 1964) were challenged and revised upward to 5.1 percent by R. M. Coen, "Labor Force Unemployment in the 1920's and 1930's: A Re-examination Based on Postwar Experience," *Review of Economics and Statistics* 55 (1973): 46–55. Such an adjustment, if accepted, would alter the level but not the trend in the progress of labor in the 1923–1929 period.

the feeding of strikers by the union. During the 1920s, except for legislation applying to railroads, government generally did not interfere with labor relations. Although such policies slowed organized labor's progress, it is difficult to accept such actions as the primary cause of an absolute decline in union membership.

It seems most likely that the upsurge in membership associated with World War I had not been firmly established. The wartime increase in membership resulted in part from agreements by the unions to a nonstrike pledge in return for lessened opposition to union organization. The sharp recession of 1921 and 1922, which raised levels of unemployment to 11 percent, undermined labor's bargaining power. In addition, beginning with the important strike against U.S. Steel in 1916, a host of postwar strikes failed—except perhaps to anger employers. It is pertinent to note in Table 22-2 that most of the membership decline had occurred by 1923, after which there was only minor further attrition. Company welfare programs designed to entice workers away from their own organizations also took their toll. But the inertia between 1924 and 1929 must be attributed primarily to two other causes: First, the increase in real wages left the greater part of the labor force generally satisfied. More importantly, the powerful AFL unions, whose members especially benefited from the building boom, took no interest in organizing the growing mass-production industries. Added to this was a generally tired and unimaginative leadership.

THE END OF FREE IMMIGRATION

Labor did, however, finally achieve one of its most cherished objectives in the 1920s—limiting immigration. Partially this was the result of growing hostility to the "new immigrants" from southern and eastern Europe who had constituted the bulk of the large influx of immigrants in the years leading up to the war. Racism, including the activities of the venerable Ku Klux Klan, was on the rise. Sometimes racism was given a pseudo-scientific veneer by writers who claimed that the new immigrants were less able and intelligent than native-born Americans. In rejecting racism, however, we should not overlook labor's basic economic point that increasing the supply of labor, other things equal, tends to lower the real wage.

In the years preceding World War I, the economy of central Europe had developed rapidly. Now it lay in ruins, saddled for years to come with heavy reparation payments. Farther east, the Russian economy, starting from a lower base, had also been exhausted by years of war and revolution. The war, moreover, had created a vast new supply of shipping that was now coming on line and could easily bring immigrants to the United States from Europe. Would not America, American policymakers wondered, if it continued a policy of unlimited immigration, be swamped by immigrants from continental Europe once the war was over? And would they not be arriving just when the recession of 1920 and 1921 was throwing millions of Americans out of work? These fears seemed to be confirmed by the resumption of a high level of immigration immediately after the war. Slightly more than 800,000 immigrants entered the United States between June 1920 and June 1921.

The Emergency Immigration Act of 1921 restricted the number of people to be admitted from any country each year to 3 percent of the number of people of that nationality resident in the United States in 1910. In 1924 a new law limited immigration to 2 percent of a nationality's 1890 U.S. population. This change further restricted immigration from southern and eastern Europe. Immigration from East Asia, moreover, was completely eliminated, reinforcing President Theodore Roosevelt's earlier "gentleman's agreement" with the Japanese. The law also set a maximum limit of slightly over 150,000 immigrants with quotas based on 1920 to become effective in 1929. The effects of these restrictions on the flow of immigrants can be seen in Table 22-3. The contrast between the prewar years (the war in Europe began in 1914) and the 1920s is obvious. The limit on immigration was clearly effective in cutting down the number of legal immigrants.

How much did limiting immigration contribute to the rise in real wages, reduction in hours of work, and other benefits realized by labor in the 1920s? No one, as far as we know, has attempted the difficult task of answering this question. To answer it we would have to identify, among other variables, the elasticity of the supply of immigrants and of domestic labor as well as the elasticity of the demand for labor in the United States.

THE ECONOMIC POSITION OF THE AMERICAN FARMER

For a quarter of a century before 1920, agriculture was moving to a stronger position in the American economy. Indeed, the period between 1896 and 1915—sometimes nostalgically called "Agriculture's Golden Era"—was one of rapid improvement in the economic position of the American farmer. Although farm production slackened its rate of increase to approximately one-half of 1 percent per annum over these years, farm prices and gross farm income rose steadily. The agricultural population remained constant at 32 million, as the natural rate of increase (650,000 per year toward the

TABLE 22-3 IMMIGRATION, 1910–1929

Year	New Arrivals	Year	New Arrivals
1910	1,041,570	1920	430,001
1911	878,587	1921	805,228
1912	838,172	1922	309,556
1913	1,197,892	1923	522,919
1914	1,218,480	1924	706,896
1915	326,700	1925	294,314
1916	298,826	1926	304,488
1917	295,403	1927	335,175
1918	110,618	1928	307,255
1919	141,132	1929	279,678

SOURCE: *Historical Statistics* (Washington, D.C.: Government Printing Office, 1976), series C89.

close of the period) was offset by the movement of farmers to the city. Consequently, from 1911 to 1915, income per person employed in agriculture was approximately two-thirds that of those employed in industry—a remarkably favorable ratio that was not achieved again until World War II. Moreover, farmers' assets—land, buildings, and livestock—continually appreciated in value.[4] Many people on the land were still abysmally poor, but the economic position of large-scale producers was much improved. Then the wartime surge in international demand for American farm products stimulated farm production, boosted prices, and amplified the rise in incomes even beyond that which had been underway for the previous 20 years. In short, the agrarian sector was extraordinarily prosperous in the years just preceding the 1920s.

ECONOMIC DISTRESS IN AGRICULTURE

During 1919 and the early months of 1920, hopes for the future of farming continued to be bright. But in mid-1920, farm prices began a precipitous drop. By the end of 1921, despite a slight recovery, wheat that 18 months previously had sold for $2.58 a bushel was selling for $0.93, and corn was down to $0.41 from $1.86. Many commodities did not suffer quite so severe a decline, but prices seriously decreased in all lines of production. From an index of 234 in June 1920 (1909–1914 = 100), prices received by farmers fell to an index of 112 a year later. A gradual recovery followed, and the farm index stood at 159 in August 1925. After a small decline during 1926 and 1927, prices remained stable until the end of 1929.

The deflation of 1920 and 1921 was severe in the industrial sector and overall economy too, but not as great as in the agriculture sector. Prices *paid* by farmers fell until the end of 1921 and then remained stable until the close of the decade. The terms of trade (the ratio of the prices received by farmers to the prices they paid) ran against agriculture during the break in prices and then recovered, so that by 1925 they were not much below the 1920 level. This index fell a little during the next few years, but in 1929 it was still not far from the level of prosperous prewar years. On the whole, then, it does not seem that agriculture should have suffered much in the middle and late 1920s. Moreover, research by Charles F. Holt suggests a rise in income for the average farmer in the 1920s. Yet there was great agitation for remedial farm legislation during these years. Why?

The answer seems to be that many farmers, especially in the Midwest, had incurred fixed indebtedness at what turned out to be the wrong time. Land values had risen sharply between 1910 and 1920; at the height of the boom, the best lands in Iowa and Illinois sold for as much as $500 an acre—a fantastically high figure for the time. In those ten years, many high-grade farms doubled in value. To buy such high-priced properties, farmers often borrowed heavily, and farm mortgage debt increased rapidly. Long-term debt rose from $3.2 billion in 1910 to $8.4 billion in 1920 and reached a high of nearly $11 billion in 1923. Deflation in the early 1920s turned farm debts into

---

[4] See Theodore W. Schultz, *Agriculture in an Unstable Economy* (New York: McGraw-Hill, 1945), pp. 114–116.

crushing burdens. Although a majority of American farmers may not have been burdened with fixed debt payments during these years, such charges undoubtedly pushed a large and extremely vocal minority toward bankruptcy. In any case, the number of farm mortgage foreclosures advanced sharply at the turn of the decade and then remained high throughout the entire 1920s. According to H. Thomas Johnson, the rate increased from 2.8 per 1,000 mortgaged farms foreclosed in 1918 to 3.8 in 1920, to 6.4 in 1921, to 11.2 in 1922, and to between 14 and 17 per 1,000 for the remainder of the decade.[5]

FIRST EFFORTS AT FARM LEGISLATION

As early as 1919, Secretary of Agriculture David Franklin Houston (who was not as optimistic as most agricultural leaders) called for a conference to discuss possible agricultural problems, but not until disaster struck in the form of sharply falling prices and incomes was this proposal seriously considered. Violent protests from farmers in late 1920 led Congress to create the Joint Commission of Agricultural Inquiry in 1921. The commission reported the obvious—that farm troubles were the result of general business depression and a decline in exports—and recommended measures to help cooperative marketing associations, improve credit facilities, and extend research activities by the Department of Agriculture.

More important was the National Agricultural Conference, convened early in 1922 by Secretary of Agriculture Henry C. Wallace. Despite the administration's attitude, expressed by President Harding, that "the farmer must be ready to help himself," many radical proposals were heard at this conference. In its report, the idea of *parity* for agriculture was first made explicit, and the slogan "Equality for Agriculture" was offered. There was recognition of the fact that in times of a decreasing demand for goods, manufacturers reduced production and lowered prices slowly, if at all, whereas farmers maintained or even increased production and took the consequences in the form of sharply falling prices. It was argued that agriculture as a whole was entitled to its fair share of the national income and that justice would be achieved if the ratio of the prices farmers received to the prices they paid was kept equal to the ratio that had prevailed from 1910 to 1914.

Throughout the 1920s, various ideas were proposed aimed at securing parity prices or "fair-exchange values" for agricultural products. Most readily acceptable to professional farm supporters and politicians were the McNary-Haugen bills, which sought to determine the fair-exchange value of each farm product. The fair value was to be a price that would have pre–World War I purchasing power and was to be maintained in the domestic market in two ways: First, a tariff was to protect the home market from imports. Second, a private corporation chartered by the federal government was to buy a sufficient amount of each commodity to force its price up to the computed fair value. The corporation could in turn sell the acquired commodities. Obviously, if

[5]H. Thomas Johnson, "Postwar Optimism and the Rural Financial Crisis of the 1920s," *Explorations in Economic History* 11 (Winter 1973–1974): 176.

the purchases had been necessary to raise prices, the commodities could not be sold in the domestic market; therefore it was proposed that they be sold abroad at the world price, which would presumably be lower than the supported American price. Administrative expenses and operating losses would be shared among the producing farmers. For every bale of cotton or bushel of wheat sold, a tax called an "equalization fee" would be charged to the grower. These taxes would be used to defray all expenses of operating the price-support plan. The farmer would gain insofar as the additional amount of income resulting from higher prices exceeded the tax expense.

The McNary-Haugen bills were twice passed by Congress and twice vetoed by President Calvin Coolidge. Despite this setback, the agitation of the 1920s did secure some special privileges for agriculture. For one, the Capper-Volstead law of 1922 exempted farmers' cooperatives from the threat of prosecution for violation of antitrust laws. The following year, the Federal Intermediate Credit Act provided for twelve intermediate credit banks that would rediscount agricultural paper maturing within three years for commercial banks and other lending agencies.[6] To achieve the broader aims of price and income maintenance, there were two major efforts. A naive belief in the tariff as a device to raise the prices of farm products (which had been traditionally exported, *not* imported) led to "protection" for agriculture, culminating in the high duties of the Smoot-Hawley Act of 1929. More significant was the Agricultural Marketing Act of 1929, which was passed to fulfill Republican campaign promises of the previous year. The first law committing the federal government to a policy of stabilizing farm prices, the 1929 act worked as much as possible through nongovernment institutions. The act established a Federal Farm Board to encourage the formation of cooperative marketing associations and to establish "stabilization corporations" to be owned by the cooperatives, which would use a $500 million fund to carry on price-support operations.

But the supply of farm output was highly elastic. Without the means to control output, or without greatly increased financial backing, such price-support legislation was doomed to failure. Nevertheless, the policy discussions of the 1920s set the stage for the massive government interference in agriculture that was to follow in the 1930s.

CONSERVATION POLICY

Unlike new government interventions in agriculture, but consistent with the "hands-off" policy toward business, the 1920s witnessed a reduction in the role of the federal government in the control of natural resources. The best known example occurred during the administration of Warren G. Harding. In 1915, President Wilson had set aside Naval Oil Reserve No. 3 in Wyoming. The reserve was named Teapot Dome after a butte located on it, and its supervision and that of previously established Cal-

---

[6]Nonemergency farm credit needs were fairly well taken care of with the passage of this act; the Federal Farm Loan Act of 1916 had already established twelve Federal Land Banks to provide long-term loans to farmers through cooperative borrowing groups.

ifornia reserves were entrusted to the Secretary of the Navy. President Harding transferred the administration of these reserves to Secretary of the Interior Albert B. Fall. Fall then granted leases on each reserve to a single private oil company. At Teapot Dome the lease was given to Mammoth Oil in exchange for a royalty, a pipeline to be constructed to Kansas City, and other considerations.

There was considerable economic logic to Fall's plan to lease each naval reserve to a single firm. The oil reserves were already being drained by many small lease holders on the reserves and on nearby federal and private lands. The situation is known to economists as the *common-pool problem*.[7] Each small producer has an incentive to drill wells and drain the reservoir as fast as possible, and to ignore the long-run costs of rapid production because they are spread over all of the firms pumping oil. Too many wells are drilled, the underground pressure is released prematurely making it hard to recover all of the oil, and unnecessary oil storage facilities are built. Fall's plan would have reduced these costs because a single firm would have taken into account the long-run effects of, for example, an early release of natural gas pressure.

This is not to say, of course, that Fall was motivated by altruism. When word of Fall's action leaked out, a hue and cry was raised by small lease holders who wanted their share of the action and by conservation groups who wanted to eliminate all exploitation of the reserves. A Senate investigation revealed that Fall had received some $400,000 in bribes. He was later fined and spent a year in jail. The Teapot Dome scandal proved to be a major embarrassment to the Harding and Coolidge administrations. It is worth noting, however, that in 1930 federal legislation implicitly vindicated Fall's idea of consolidating leases on federal land, and that in 1938 the navy obtained permission to consolidate the Teapot Dome reserve and lease it to a single firm, Standard Oil.

The trend away from federal conservation activities continued under Herbert Hoover. Both the President and his Secretary of the Interior, Ray Lyman Wilbur, flatly supported the transfer of all unappropriated and unreserved lands to the western states. A commission, appointed by President Hoover to make recommendations regarding future land policies, supported the proposal of ceding the remaining public domain to the states. But even westerners, including those with powerful livestock interests, were opposed to the idea, and Congress refused to enact a bill containing the commission's recommendations.

The development of the Forest Service did gain impetus during the 1920s, along with a policy of cutting and selling only mature timber from the national forests. Efforts were made to introduce the most up-to-date methods of cutting and planting so that a substantial future supply of timber would be assured. There was also a remarkable improvement in the administration of the range lands within the national forests. Essentially, however, nothing new was added to the conservation policy that Theodore Roosevelt had enunciated and practiced early in the twentieth century— and much of the spirit of Roosevelt's policy was lost.

---

[7] Gary D. Libecap, "The Political Allocation of Mineral Rights: A Reevaluation of Teapot Dome," *Journal of Economic History* 14 (1984): 381–393.

THE DISTRIBUTION OF INCOME

Our image of the wealthy during the 1920s is not a kind one. We see them as self-satisfied and self-indulgent, drinking champagne and ignoring the growing misery around them. Some historians, moreover, have seen a direct link between the growing concentration of income during the 1920s and the depression of the 1930s. All the money, goes the argument, was going to the rich, who were not spending it fast enough to maintain aggregate demand. Early studies of the distribution of income to some degree confirmed that the rich had grown relatively richer. In his pioneering work published in 1953, Simon Kuznets shows that the share of disposable income received by the top 1 percent of the population increased from 11.8 percent in 1920 to 18.9 percent in 1929.[8] Charles Holt, working from Kuznets's data, argues that all of the increases in real income in the 1920s went to upper-income groups.[9]

More recent research, however, muddies the waters. Gene Smiley points out that the upward trend in the share of income going to the richest fractions of the population was biased upward because it was based on tax returns.[10] Tax rates for the rich were lowered substantially in the 1920s, encouraging people to shift their wealth into assets yielding taxable income and to report income that had previously gone unreported. Kuznets was aware of these problems but was unable to adjust his data to account for them. Jeffrey Williamson and Peter Lindert, in a landmark study of American inequality, draw attention to the long-run dimension of the problem.[11] A long trend toward increased inequality had been interrupted by World War I, so some increase in inequality in the 1920s was to be expected. Whatever the increase in inequality, it probably represented a return to conditions that were prevalent before the war.

Stanley Lebergott, in an imaginative study, shifts the emphasis to the standard of living. He makes a strong case that whatever the changes in the distribution of income, it is nevertheless clear that increases in the standard of living were widespread in the 1920s. Here are three of Lebergott's many homely examples: the percentage of families with electric lighting increased from 35 to 68 during the 1920s, the percentage of families with washing machines increased from 8 to 24, and the percentage of households with inside flush toilets increased from 20 to 51.[12] The distribution of income was far from equal in 1929, but there is little evidence that something drastic and unexpected had occurred that could explain the depression that was to follow.

---

[8] *Historical Statistics* (Washington, D.C.: Government Printing Office, 1975), series G341. These series are drawn from Simon Kuznets, *Shares of Upper Income Groups In Income and Savings* (New York: National Bureau of Economic Research, 1953). Kuznets, the father of national income accounting, was later awarded the Nobel Prize.

[9] Charles Holt, "Who Benefitted from the Prosperity of the Twenties?" *Explorations in Economic History* 14 (1977): 277–289.

[10] Gene Smiley, "Did Incomes for Most of the Population Fall from 1923 through 1929?" *Journal of Economic History* 42 (1983): 209–216.

[11] Jeffrey Williamson and Peter Lindert, *American Inequality: A Microeconomic History* (New York: Academic Press, 1981), Chapter 12.

[12] Stanley Lebergott, *The American Economy: Income, Wealth and Want* (Princeton: Princeton University Press, 1962), pp. 248–299.

The shares of large well-established companies were traded indoors at the New York Stock Exchange. Curbstone brokers specialized in riskier stocks and bonds.

THE GREAT BULL MARKET

The premier economic event in the 1920s, at least in the mind of the general public, was the great stock market boom. Stock prices rose steadily in the 1920s, but in 1928 and the first three-quarters of 1929 they rocketed upward. Table 22-4 shows what happened to two price averages between 1922 and 1929: In seven years, prices more than tripled. Between 1928 and 1929 the average stock (column 1) rose 26.5 percent in value. It seemed that getting rich was easy—just put money in the stock market and sit back

TABLE 22-4 THE STOCK MARKET, 1922–1929

Year	(1) Standard & Poor's Common Stock Index (all stocks)	(2) Standard & Poor's Common Stock Index (industrials)	(3) Ratio of Stock Price to Dividend
1922	100	100	18.62
1923	102	103	18.52
1924	108	108	19.05
1925	133	137	21.05
1926	150	158	19.08
1927	182	197	21.19
1928	237	266	26.18
1929	309	336	27.40

SOURCE: *HISTORICAL STATISTICS* (WASHINGTON, D.C.: GOVERNMENT PRINTING OFFICE, 1976), SERIES X495, X496, X480.

and wait. Typical of the times was an article by financier John Jacob Raskob in the *Ladies Home Journal* with the optimistic title "Everybody Ought to Be Rich."[13]

What caused the great bull market? Various economic factors have been suggested. Earnings and dividends paid by corporations rose in the late 1920s, but stock prices rose even faster. Consider column 3 of Table 22-4, which shows the ratio of stock prices to dividends. In 1922 an investor had to pay $18.62 for each dollar of current dividends; by 1929 that figure had climbed to $27.40.

Of course, people do not invest on the assumption that dividends will remain the same forever. One of the favorites of the bull market was Radio Corporation of America (RCA), which had never paid a dividend. People bought RCA stock on the assumption (a valid one) that it would pay great dividends in the future. George Sirkin,

Economic theory concludes that if investors are rational, the value of a share of stock will equal the discounted value of expected future dividends. Under the assumptions that the dividend, D, is expected to grow at a constant rate g, and that the rate of interest will remain constant at the current level i, the present value formula for the price of a share, P, becomes

$$P = D/(i-g)$$

In other words, the lower the rate of interest paid on alternative assets and the faster the dividend is expected to grow, the higher will be the value of the share. Many observers of the stock market, however, believe that stock prices are not always priced in this way. "Bubbles" may develop that reflect fads or irrational waves of optimism and pessimism.

The issue is hard to resolve because even in a rational world investors must forecast dividend growth, and it is hard to determine what constitutes a rational forecast.

This point can be illustrated by applying the above equation to 1929. The ratio of dividends to prices was about 3.65 percent, and BAA corporate securities paid about 5.87 percent, so the implicit expected growth rate of dividends as calculated by the equation was 2.22 percent per year. Sirkin's point is that this rate of growth was reasonable given the rapid growth of dividends observed in the 1920s; White's point is that it was out of line with long-term dividend growth rates.

---

[13] As quoted in John Kenneth Galbraith, *The Great Crash of 1929* (Boston: Houghton Mifflin, 1961), p. 57.

in an interesting comment on the bull market, argues that if earnings growth in the years immediately preceding the stock market crash were projected forward, then only relatively few stocks could be considered overvalued at the market's peak. But Eugene White points out that Sirkin's result depends on projecting earnings from a very favorable period of years.[14] In White's view, this begs the question: Why did the market choose to base its projections on the most favorable years?

If earnings did not drive the market, did credit conditions do so? At that time, much stock was bought on margin. The buyer would put down, say, 50 percent of the value of the stock in cash and borrow the remaining 50 percent from the broker.[15] Leveraging in this way means that when stock prices go up by, say, 20 percent, the speculator makes 40 percent on his initial investment. But what is true going up is also true going down. If stocks fall 20 percent, the speculator loses 40 percent. Where did the brokers get the money to lend to speculators? The brokerage houses borrowed the money from banks in the form of *call loans*—loans that had to be repaid on demand, when "called."

Some historians have argued that it was the willingness of the banks to supply call loans that caused the bull market. But Eugene White's sophisticated study of the supply and demand for loans shows that the supply of loans to the market did not shift outward.[16] Instead, the increasing demand for loans moved the market along the supply curve for loans. Credit was pulled into the stock market from other sectors by the rising interest rates being paid on call loans. The call loan rate rose dramatically during the boom, from 4.36 percent in 1922 to 7.74 percent in 1929, showing that the demand for loans grew faster than the supply.[17]

The true explanation for the boom, if there ever is one, will have to be provided by social psychologists. It was an optimistic age. Business was booming. There seemed to be no reason why it could not keep on booming, providing an ever-higher standard of living for the average American. The stock market reflected that optimism. Even for the skeptical, there was always the assumption that they would be able to beat the crowd out the door when the market began to tumble.

INTERNATIONAL DEVELOPMENTS

During the 1920s, the problems of Europe seemed far away to most Americans. Two problems dominated the international scene: German war reparations (and Allied war debts to the United States), and the re-establishment of the international gold standard.

The Treaty of Versailles, which formally ended World War I, called for Germany to make large payments to France and the other Allies to compensate for damages

---

[14] Eugene White, "When the Ticker Ran Late: The Stock Market Boom and Crash of 1929," in *Panics and Crashes in Historical Perspective*, ed. Eugene N. White (Homewood, Illinois: Dow Jones-Irwin, 1989).

[15] It is sometimes assumed that margin requirements were extremely low in the boom, but most brokers required 45 to 50 percent down. See Galbraith, *The Great Crash*, p. 37.

[16] White, "When the Ticker Ran Late."

[17] *Historical Statistics* (Washington, D.C.: Government Printing Office, 1975), Series X447.

caused by German forces during the war. It quickly became apparent that Germany lacked the economic strength and political cohesion to make its payments on schedule. Part of the problem was that Germany would need to run large surpluses in order to make the reparations payments, but tariffs and other economic policies in the United States and elsewhere were not helpful. Germany did benefit, however, from the surge in the stock market and the related willingness of Americans to buy foreign debt—Americans lent heavily to Germany in the twenties. In 1924, under the Dawes plan, German debts were scaled down and a large loan, mostly from the United States, was floated to help Germany restore its currency following its disastrous hyperinflation of 1923. Further reductions in payments were made under the Young plan of 1929. Most historians now agree that trying to extract reparations from Germany was a mistake and that a wiser policy would have aimed at restoring the German economy as rapidly as possible,[18] as indeed it did after World War II.

It was taken for granted in the 1920s that restoration of the gold standard was necessary to achieve lasting prosperity. If each country made its currency convertible into gold, exchange rates would be fixed, the free flow of capital across international borders would be assured, monetary authorities would be forced to be circumspect in the amount of money they created (to avoid an outflow of gold), and inflation would be prevented. British bankers were particularly anxious to return to the gold standard at the prewar parity (that is, the prewar price of pounds in terms of dollars) in order to help restore the position of London as the world's leading financial center. Britain finally did return to the gold standard in 1924, but it appears that the pound was overvalued at the prewar rate. (The new rate was $4.86 per £1, but the equilibrium price where supply and demand for pounds would balance was probably less, say $4.40.) The high rate made it hard to export British goods and contributed to a long period of hard times in Britain.[19] The pressure on British exports would have been lessened had the United States been willing to let the resulting influx of gold increase its price level, but the Federal Reserve chose instead to sterilize the gold inflows.

In retrospect, considerable difficulties might have been avoided had American policymakers seen the importance of taking into account the international repercussions of their actions. American monetary and fiscal policies during the 1920s, however, were influenced primarily by domestic considerations, and (except in the agricultural sector) things seemed to be moving smoothly.

MONETARY AND FISCAL POLICY

The twenties were a period of growing prestige for the Federal Reserve System. It is not hard to see why. Table 22-5 shows that after the sharp but brief recession of 1920 and 1921 the economy advanced smoothly. Real income rose steadily year after year, as did the stock of money. Prices, judging by the NNP deflator, were stable.

---

[18] John Maynard Keynes warned of the dangers of trying to extract reparations from Germany in *The Economic Consequences of the Peace* (New York: Harcourt, Brace & World, 1920).

[19] Once again Keynes warned against a mistaken policy. See *The Economic Consequences of Mr. Churchill* (London: L. & V. Woolf, 1925).

TABLE 22-5   MONEY, PRICES, AND REAL INCOME, 1920–1929

Year	Stock of Money (in billions of dollars)	Implicit Price Deflator (1929 = 100)	Real National Income (in billions of 1929 dollars)
1920	$34.80	121.7	$62.208
1921	32.85	103.7	59.567
1922	33.72	98.6	63.859
1923	36.60	100.9	73.460
1924	38.58	99.6	75.559
1925	42.05	101.6	77.343
1926	43.68	102.1	82.807
1927	44.73	99.4	83.623
1928	46.42	100.1	84.918
1929	46.60	100.0	90.308

SOURCE: MILTON FRIEDMAN AND ANNA J. SCHWARTZ, *MONETARY TRENDS IN THE UNITED STATES AND THE UNITED KINGDOM* (CHICAGO: UNIVERSITY OF CHICAGO PRESS, 1982), P. 125.

What influenced the Fed's policy during these years? Surprisingly, one fact that did not influence policy was the large number of bank closings. Suspensions numbered in the hundreds each year, reaching a peak of 975 banks suspended in 1926. The Federal Reserve concluded that these banks (mostly in rural areas) were inefficiently run and plagued by bad management, unrealistic loans to farmers made during the war boom, and increased competition due to the rise of the automobile. (The automobile increased the ability of borrowers and depositors to shop for favorable terms.) It followed that simply allowing these banks to close strengthened the banking system as a whole. Although it is hard to imagine the Fed taking such a callous position in today's political climate, there was probably a good deal of truth in its analysis. Unfortunately, this analysis was carried into the 1930s when high rates of bank failures under very different economic conditions undermined confidence in the banking system as a whole.

An important series of papers by Eugene White clarifies the nature of the weakness in the rural banking system and its role in the breakdown of the banking system in the early 1930s. To a large extent, the problem stemmed from legislation that prohibited branch banking. Small unit banks were unable to diversify their loan portfolios and had no resources to draw on during periods of temporary illiquidity. The states tried various deposit insurance schemes to protect their systems, but these ended in failure. Eventually, most states began to eliminate crippling prohibitions against branch banking, but by then the damage had been done.[20]

---

[20] Eugene N. White, "State-Sponsored Insurance of Bank Deposits in the United States," *Journal of Economic History* 41 (1981); "A Reinterpretation of the Banking Crisis of 1930," *Journal of Economic History* 44 (1984); and "Before the Glass-Steagall Act: An Analysis of the Investment Banking Activities of National Banks," *Explorations in Economic History* 23 (1986).

The Fed, however, was deeply concerned about the growing speculation on Wall Street. Speculation diverted capital from more-productive investments, the Fed believed, and the inevitable retrenchment might cause widespread disturbances in the economy. But it was not clear how to slow the flow of funds to the stock market without simultaneously restricting the total supply of credit, thus risking a recession. At first the Fed tried "moral suasion," pressuring the New York City banks into making fewer call loans. This policy was partly effective, but other lenders quickly moved into the gap left by the banks.

Finally, frustrated by its inability to cool the market in any other way, the Fed raised its discount rate from 4.5 to 5.5 percent on August 9, 1929. The discount rate was still well below the call loan and other bank lending rates, so the increase itself did not remove the incentive to borrow, but it signaled the Fed's intention to restrict the supply of credit. Other central banks were taking similar actions: the Bank of England raised its discount rate from 5.5 to 6.5 percent in September. Perhaps as a result of these widespread harbingers of tighter credit, American stock prices reached their peak early in September. The exact role of the Fed's policy in subsequent events is a matter of considerable debate, as we will see in the next chapter. But during the 1930s the Fed was given the power to set margin requirements because it was recognized that the Fed's policy had been distorted in the late 1920s by its efforts to control the stock market.

Fiscal policy in the late 1920s is best viewed as a long, drawn-out postwar readjustment. Although certain costs of the war, such as veterans' benefits and interest on the increase in the national debt, continued into the postwar period, demobilization nevertheless created considerable scope for cutting the high level of taxes imposed during wartime.[21] The White House favored reducing taxes by removing the steep pro-

TABLE 22-6   GOVERNMENT SPENDING AND DISTRIBUTION OF EXPENDITURES BY LEVEL OF GOVERNMENT, 1922 AND 1927 (IN PERCENT)

	1922	1927
Share of GNP		
Total government	12.6%	11.6%
Federal	4.9	3.5
State and local	7.7	8.1
Expenditure distribution by level		
Federal	39.2	30.4
State	11.7	12.9
Local	49.1	56.7

SOURCE: ALBERT W. NIEMI, *U.S. ECONOMIC HISTORY* (CHICAGO: RAND MCNALLY, 1975), P. 117; AS DERIVED FROM *HISTORICAL STATISTICS* (WASHINGTON, D.C.: GOVERNMENT PRINTING OFFICE, 1960), PP. 484–516.

[21]Taxes could have been maintained at a high level and the resulting surplus could have been used to pay off the national debt. But that had little political appeal, since the people who benefited, the bondholders, might attribute their good fortune to someone other than Congress.

gression in rates introduced during the war. Secretary of the Treasury Andrew Mellon argued that reducing high rates would encourage the wealthy to shift their assets from tax-exempt municipal bonds to taxable assets, thus minimizing the effect on total revenues. (Similar arguments would be made in the 1980s under the banner of supply-side economics.) Liberals in Congress, however, favored reducing taxes by increasing exemptions for those in lower-income groups. The outcomes of this fight—the revenue acts of 1924, 1926, and 1928—swept away the system of wartime excise taxes, reduced the rates for personal and corporate taxes, and reduced estate duties. On the whole, the pride in their fiscal policies taken by successive administrations during the 1920s is understandable. A federal budget system was introduced in 1921. Tax rates were cut, but revenues grew, and a budget surplus was maintained.

Table 22-6 shows that federal spending was relatively small compared with the whole economy in the 1920s. Indeed, in 1927 the federal government was spending less than half of what was being spent by state and local governments. Table 22-7 shows how the federal and state and local budgets were divided among different categories. At the federal level, most of the spending was accounted for by the traditional categories of national defense, the postal service, veterans' services, and interest on the national debt. Although more funds were being spent on the health and welfare of the people, these were still minor categories. The revolution in the budget was yet to come.

TABLE 22-7   DISTRIBUTION OF DIRECT EXPENDITURES, 1922 AND 1927
(IN PERCENT)

	1922	1927
Federal		
National defense	24.0%	18.1%
Postal service	15.2	20.9
Education	0.2	0.2
Public welfare	0.2	0.3
Natural resources	2.2	3.3
Veterans' services	11.7	17.0
Interest	27.1	22.4
Other	19.4	17.8
State and local		
Education	30.2	28.6
Highways	22.9	23.2
Public welfare	2.1	1.9
Hospitals and health	4.6	4.6
Police, fire, sanitation	9.5	10.1
Natural resources	2.6	3.2
General control	5.5	5.3
Utility and liquor store	6.4	6.3
Other	15.2	16.8

SOURCE: ALBERT W. NIEMI, *U.S. ECONOMIC HISTORY* (CHICAGO: RAND MCNALLY, 1975), PP. 118–119; AS DERIVED FROM *HISTORICAL STATISTICS* (WASHINGTON, D.C.: GOVERNMENT PRINTING OFFICE, 1960), PP. 484–516 AND 547–574.

SHOULD THEY HAVE KNOWN BETTER?

In the uncommonly pleasant summer of 1929, Americans were congratulating themselves for having found a way to unending prosperity. The flow of U.S. goods and services had reached an all-time high, industrial production having risen 50 percent in a decade. Most businesses were satisfied with their profit positions, and workers were content with the gains in wages and earnings that enabled them to enjoy the luxury of automobiles and household appliances. Farmers grumbled about price weaknesses in agricultural products, but it was traditional that they should; anyone could see that mechanical inventions had made life on the farm easier and more productive than ever before. Besides, anyone who really wanted to become rich had only to purchase common stock. The political climate was favorable to the business venturer, then held high in public esteem as the provider of material well-being. Herbert Hoover, a successful businessman and a distinguished public servant, had been elected to the presidency, and although some people considered him a bit inclined to the liberal side, it was generally felt that he would be a temperate and judicious leader. Equally reassuring was the stability of the economies of western Europe. War damage had been repaired, the gold standard had been restored, and the problem of reparations seemed to be near solution. Hope was high for a return to the freer international movement of goods and capital that had characterized the rapid economic growth of the two decades before the war.

The greatest American economist of the day was Irving Fisher. A remarkable figure, Fisher made important theoretical and empirical contributions in areas of economics ranging from index numbers to monetary theory. His invention of a card index system made him a fortune, and his book on how to eat a healthy diet was a best-seller. When journalists wanted to know whether the popular song title "Yes, we have no bananas" was good English, they asked Irving Fisher.[22] Fisher was not shy about making predictions about the stock market. Just weeks before the crash, he argued that "stock prices have reached what looks like a permanently high plateau," adding that "there might be a recession in stock prices, but not anything in the nature of a crash." Even after the crash, Fisher wrote that for "the immediate future, at least, the outlook is bright."[23]

It is easy now to laugh at such optimism. But should Fisher and others have known better? Were there signs of the impending disaster that should have been heeded? The long history of panics and crises in U.S. history (which Fisher knew well) should, perhaps, have given pause. And there were, of course, weaknesses in the economy such as the banking system and the agricultural sector. But the economy had expanded rapidly for years despite these weaknesses. Ultimately, whether we believe that Fisher and other optimists were unwise or merely incredibly unlucky depends on what we believe caused the Great Depression, the subject of the next chapter.

---

[22] The answer was yes, if the question was "Have you no bananas?"

[23] As quoted in John Kenneth Galbraith, *The Great Crash*, pp. 91, 99, 151.

SELECTED REFERENCES
AND SUGGESTED READINGS

Coen, R. M. "Labor Force Unemployment in the 1920's and 1930's: A Re-examination Based on Postwar Experience." *Review of Economics and Statistics* 55 (1973): 46–55.

Field, Alexander J. "A New Interpretation of the Onset of the Great Depression." *Journal of Economic History* 45 (June 1984).

Galbraith, John Kenneth. *The Great Crash of 1929*, reissued with a new introduction. Boston: Houghton Mifflin, 1961.

Hawley, Ellis W. *The Great War and the Search for a Modern Order: A History of the American People and Their Institutions, 1917–1933.* New York: St. Martin's Press, 1979.

Holt, Charles. "Who Benefited from the Prosperity of the Twenties?" *Explorations in Economic History* 14 (1977): 277–289.

Hughes, Jonathan. *The Vital Few.* New York: Oxford University Press, 1986.

Johnson, H. Thomas. "Postwar Optimism and the Rural Financial Crisis of the 1920's." *Explorations in Economic History* 11 (Winter 1973–1974): 173–192.

Keller, Robert. "Factor Income Distribution in the United States During the 1920's: A Reexamination of Fact and Theory." *Journal of Economic History* 33 (1973): 252–273.

Lampman, Robert. *The Share of Top Wealth-Holders in National Wealth, 1922–1956.* Princeton: Princeton University Press, 1962.

Lebergott, Stanley. *The American Economy: Income, Wealth and Want.* Princeton: Princeton University Press, 1976.

Leuchtenberg, William E. *The Perils of Prosperity, 1914–1932.* 1958.

Libecap, Gary D. "The Political Allocation of Mineral Rights: A Reevaluation of Teapot Dome." *Journal of Economic History* 14 (1984): 381–393.

Lorant, John H. "Technological Change in American Manufacturing During the 1920's." *Journal of Economic History* 27 (1967): 243–246.

Mercer, Lloyd, and Douglas Morgan. "Alternative Interpretations of Market Saturation: Evaluation for the Automobile Market in the Late 1920's." *Explorations in Economic History* 9 (Spring 1972): 269–290.

———. "The American Automobile Industry: Investment Demand, Capacity, and Capacity Utilization 1921–1940." *Journal of Political Economy* 80 (November–December 1972): 214–231.

———. "Housing Surplus in the 1920's: Another Evaluation." *Explorations in Economic History* 10 (Spring 1973): 295–304.

Metzer, Jacob. "How New Was the New Era? The Public Sector in the 1920s." *Journal of Economic History* 45 (March 1985): 119–126.

Sirkin, Gerald. "The Stock Market of 1929 Revisited: A Note." *Business History Review* 49 (Summer 1975): 223–231.

Smiley, Gene. "Did Incomes for Most of the Population Fall from 1923 Through 1929?" *Journal of Economic History* 42 (1983): 209–216.

Soule, George. *Prosperity Decade: From War to Depression, 1917–1929.* New York: Holt, Rinehart & Winston, 1947.

Swanson, Joseph, and Samuel Williamson. "Estimates of National Product and Income 1919–1941." *Explorations in Economic History* 10 (Fall 1972): 53–73.

Vatter, Harold G. "Has There Been a Twentieth-Century Consumer Durables Revolution?" *Journal of Economic History* 27 (1967): 1–16.

White, Eugene N. "Before the Glass-Steagall Act: An Analysis of the Investment Banking Activities of National Banks." *Explorations in Economic History* 23 (1986): 33–53.

———. "A Reinterpretation of the Banking Crisis of 1930." *Journal of Economic History* 44 (1984): 119–138.

———. "State-Sponsored Insurance of Bank Deposits in the United States, 1907–1929." *Journal of Economic History* 41 (September 1981): 537–557.

———. "When the Ticker Ran Late: The Stock Market Boom and Crash of 1929." In *The Stock Market Crash in Historical Perspective*, ed. Eugene Nelson White. Homewood, Illinois: Dow Jones-Irwin, 1989.

Williamson, Jeffrey, and Peter Lindert. *American Inequality: A Macroeconomic History.* New York: Academic Press, 1981.

CHAPTER TWENTY-THREE

THE GREAT DEPRESSION

CHAPTER THEME As the decade of the 1920s drew to a close, Americans were confident in their well-being and in the prospects of even better times ahead. On the election trail in the summer of 1928, presidential candidate Herbert Hoover boasted of America's optimism with the words:

> We in America today are nearer to the final triumph over poverty than ever before in the history of any land. The poorhouse is vanishing from among us. We have not yet reached the goal, but, given the chance to go forward with the policies of the last eight years, we shall soon, with the help of God, be in sight of the day when poverty will be banished from this nation.

Hardly a voice in the wilderness, Hoover's words were typical of the confidence of the times; nearly everyone missed the emerging signs of a faltering economy. Indeed, many failed to recognize the magnitude of the decline even after the Great Depression was erupting in full force.

The Great Depression was the most important economic event of the twentieth century. Between 1929 and 1933 the economy of the United States collapsed. It is almost impossible to convey the sheer terror and misery that the depression produced, but numbers can suggest the dimensions. Unemployment rose from 3.2 percent of the labor force in 1929 to 24.9 percent in 1933. Hunger and fear paralyzed the nation.

The central questions for economic historians are what caused this unprecedented collapse, why did the economy remain depressed for so long, and how could a repetition be avoided. As we shall see, scholars are still far from full agreement on all the issues. But a consensus has been reached on the key factors that contributed to the severity of the crisis, in particular the breakdown of the financial system. In this chapter we will concentrate on the dimensions and causes of the crisis. In the next chapter we will concentrate on the response of the Roosevelt administration to the depression, and on the long-run consequences, particularly the emergence of the modern "mixed" economy in which the central government plays a major role in the allocation of resources.

DIMENSIONS OF THE DEPRESSION

It is utterly remarkable, even in hindsight, that an economic catastrophe of such magnitude could have occurred. But in the four years from 1929 to 1933, the American economy (and a number of other industrialized economies) simply disintegrated. The U.S. gross national product in current prices declined 46 percent, from $104.4 billion to $56 billion. As shown in Figure 23-1, in constant (1929) prices, the decline was 31 percent. Industrial production declined by more than one-half, and gross investment, as indicated in Figure 23-2, fell to practically nothing. By 1933, gross investment was below levels of capital depreciation. The nation's capital stock was actually declining. In the process, wholesale prices dropped one-third and consumer prices one-quarter. But the most horrible statistics were those of unemployment. Figure 23-3 (page 518)

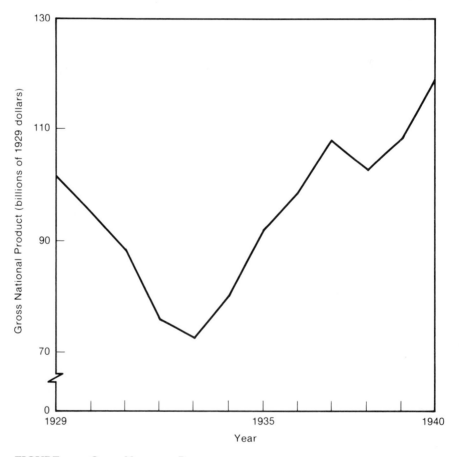

FIGURE 23-1 GROSS NATIONAL PRODUCT, 1929–1940

SOURCE: JOHN W. KENDRICK, *PRODUCTIVITY TRENDS IN THE UNITED STATES,* NATIONAL BUREAU OF ECONOMIC RESEARCH, NO. 71 (PRINCETON: PRINCETON UNIVERSITY PRESS, 1961), P. 291.

graphically illustrates how unemployment soared. Civilian employment dropped by almost 20 percent, and unemployment rose from 1.5 million to at least 13 million. One-quarter of the civilian work force was unemployed in 1933. The figures do count workers employed by government emergency programs as unemployed. But extensive part-time employment and underutilization of skills probably brought the real unemployment rate close to one-third. Fully one-half the nation's breadwinners were either out of work or in seriously reduced circumstances.

The profile of durable goods production (as shown in Figure 23-4 on page 519) also reveals the magnitude of the decline in business in the early 1930s. From a peak of nearly 25 in 1929 (1967 = 100), the index of durable-goods output fell to 6 in 1932. At the trough of the depression in March 1933, the durable-goods index stood at 5; output of durables had fallen 80 percent. Nondurables dropped much less—from an index of slightly over 40 to about 28.

The intensity of the Great Depression was distressing, and its seeming endlessness brought frustration and despair. Forty years had passed since the long depression of the 1890s. The depression of 1920 and 1921 had been sharp and nasty, with a decline in durables output of 43 percent. But it had behaved as a depression should: it had come and gone quickly, with complete recovery of manufacturing production in less than two years. In the Great Depression, on the other hand, manufacturing output did not reach the 1929 level until late 1936; it stayed somewhat above the 1929 level

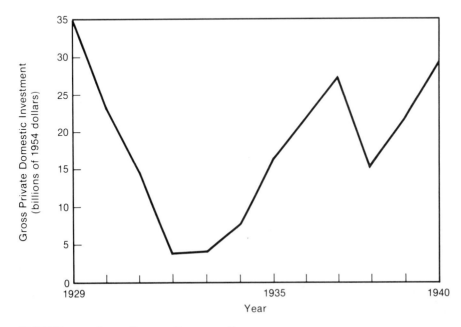

FIGURE 23-2 GROSS PRIVATE DOMESTIC INVESTMENT, 1929–1940

SOURCE: U.S. OFFICE OF BUSINESS ECONOMICS, *U.S. INCOME AND OUTPUT, 1958* (WASHINGTON, D.C.: GOVERNMENT PRINTING OFFICE, 1959), P. 118.

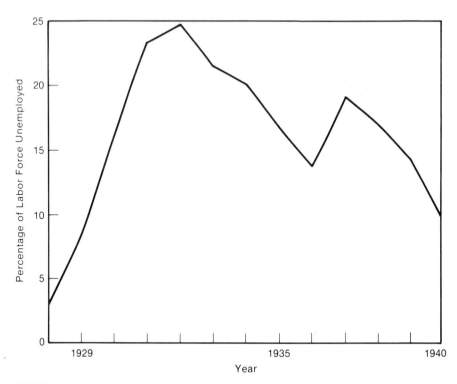

FIGURE 23-3 PERCENTAGE OF LABOR FORCE UNEMPLOYED, 1929–1940

SOURCE: *ECONOMIC REPORT OF THE PRESIDENT* (WASHINGTON, D.C.: GOVERNMENT PRINTING OFFICE, JANUARY 1955), P. 153.

for nearly a year but dropped again and did not climb back to the pre-depression peak until late 1939. Durable-goods production did not regain the 1929 peak until August 1940, more than 11 years after the beginning of the depression.

It is difficult to overemphasize the deep imprint registered by the duration and depth of the collapse. Overall, the revolutionary impact—economically, politically, socially, and psychologically—of the events of that fateful decade were matched only by those of the Civil War decade.

CAUSES OF THE GREAT DEPRESSION

A satisfactory explanation of the Great Depression requires us to distinguish between the forces that brought a downturn in economic activity and those that turned a business recession into an utter disaster.

Hindsight enables us to detect two drags on the economy that prepared the way for a decline in economic activity. The most important was the decline from 1925 onward in both residential and nonresidential construction. The boom in building activity that began in 1918 had doubtlessly helped the economy out of the slump of

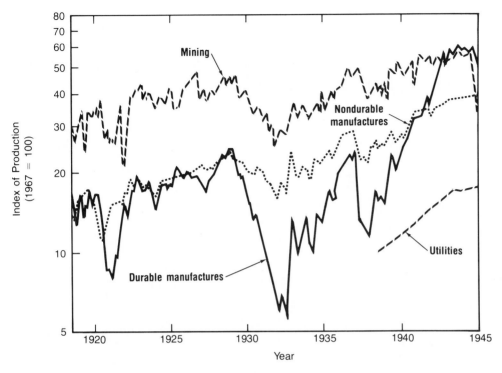

FIGURE 23-4 U.S. Industrial Production, 1920–1945

1920 and 1921; the downward phase of the same building cycle, coinciding as it did with other economic weaknesses, was a major depressing influence. What began as a gentle slide in construction from 1925 to 1927 became a marked decline in 1928.

The second drag on the economy came from the agricultural sector, which was still important enough in the 1920s to exert a powerful influence on the total economy. During the 1920s, the trend of world agricultural prices was downward. As noted in Chapter 22, in the farm belts, where indebtedness incurred for the purchase of land remained high, there were widespread complaints among businesses that sales to farmers were falling. In the great agricultural midlands, few manifestations of boom psychology appeared after 1926. A mild downturn in durables output in the spring of 1929 and a drop in nondurable production in the summer of that year could well have been expected. But nothing catastrophic was portended. The economy, however, was then hit by a series of devastating blows that turned a recession into the Great Depression.

THE STOCK MARKET CRASH

The first blow was the break in the stock market during the last week in October. Normally, economists do not consider fluctuations in the stock market to be a *cause* of business fluctuations, although many recognize the indirect effect of market swings

Wall Street on Black Thursday, October 24, 1929: Investors and the curious milled around in con-fusion in the planked street (subway construction was going on) as the extent of the disaster inside the New York Stock Exchange (at right) became clear.

on the attitudes of entrepreneurs and consumers; others consider the market an important leading indicator of the health of the economy. The 1929 break, however, must be viewed as an exception to the general rule due to the catastrophic magnitude of the decline and to the uncertainty it created about the future course of the economy.

The *New York Times* index of 25 industrial stocks, which early in 1924 had stood at 110, by January 1929 had climbed to 338 and by September to 452. It was almost impossible to buy a common stock that did not rise rapidly in value, and investors quickly accumulated paper fortunes that many of them converted into real ones. The optimism engendered by these gains permeated the business community and led to the conclusion that permanent prosperity had arrived. But many investors had become uneasy about the dizzying heights to which prices had risen. President Hoover and officials at the Federal Reserve worried about excessive speculation and the danger of a crash. In August the Federal Reserve raised the discount rate (the rate at which it lent to member banks) to 6 percent in an attempt to stem the flow of credit into the stock market. Similar actions were being taken by the Bank of England and other central banks. For a short time, at least, these actions had no effect: prices continued upward.

v York Times.

THE WEATHER
Rain today and probably tomorrow; somewhat colder tomorrow.
Temperatures Yesterday—Max. 54, Min. 47.
U. S. Weather Forecast—For details see Page 63.

pyright, 1929, by The New York Times Company.

YORK, TUESDAY, OCTOBER 29, 1929. TWO CENTS In Greater New York | THREE CENTS Within 200 Miles | FOUR CENTS Elsewhere Except 7th and 8th Postal Zones

Memory Honored Day Fete on Ships

ea and in port offi- ted Navy Day yester- igh major land cele- e held on Sunday, the of the birth of Theo- lt, similar ceremonies were reserved for

e was kept by ships he public was invited . Flags appropriate were broken out on all ships, and even some craft in the harbor ennants in honor of

ngeles and the new irigible and other air craft at Lake- were ordered out and h along the Atlantic g over this city and

T. E. BURTON, DIES AT 77

man Had Served in r 41 Years—First to the House.

VOCATE OF PEACE

EUROPE IS DISTURBED BY AMERICAN ACTION ON OCCUPATION DEBT

London Urges an Explanation of Move for Direct Payments by Germany.

BANK'S PRESTIGE INVOLVED

Britain and Continent Feel That We Do Not Have Faith in Young Plan Institution.

SCHEME IS LAID TO HOOVER

President Is Said to Wish to Avoid Clash in Congress Over Linking of Reparations and War Debts.

By EDWIN L. JAMES.

Special Cable to THE NEW YORK TIMES.

LONDON, Oct. 28.—There appears to exist in London a certain absence of understanding as to the significance of the conversations between Washington and Berlin which now are about to ripen into diplomatic negotiations in the German capital for the preparation of a treaty deal

STOCK PRICES SLUMP $14,000,000,000 IN NATION-WIDE STAMPEDE TO UNLOAD; BANKERS TO SUPPORT MARKET TODAY

Sixteen Leading Issues Down $2,893,520,108; Tel. & Tel. and Steel Among Heaviest Losers

A shrinkage of $2,893,520,108 in the open market value of the shares of sixteen representative companies resulted from yesterday's sweeping decline on the New York Stock Exchange.

American Telephone and Telegraph was the heaviest loser, $448,905,162 having been lopped off of its total value. United States Steel common, traditional bellwether of the stock market, made its greatest nose-dive in recent years by falling from a high of 202½ to a low of 185. In a feeble last-minute rally it snapped back to 186, at which it closed, showing a net loss of 17½ points. This represented for the 8,131,055 shares of common stock outstanding a total loss in value of $142,293,446.

In the following table are shown the day's net depreciation in the outstanding shares of the sixteen companies referred to:

Issues.	Shares Listed.	Losses in Points.	Depreciation.
American Radiator	10,096,289	10⅜	$104,748,997
American Tel. & Tel.	13,203,093	34	448,905,162
Commonwealth & Southern	30,764,468	3⅛	96,138,962
Columbia Gas & Electric	8,477,307	22	186,500,754
Consolidated Gas	11,451,188	20	229,023,760
DuPont E. I.	10,322,481	16⅞	109,030,625
Eastman Kodak	2,229,703	41⅞	93,368,813
General Electric	7,211,484	47½	342,545,490
General Motors	43,500,000	6¾	293,625,000
International Nickel	13,777,408	7⅞	108,497,088
New York Central	4,637,086	22½	104,311,071
Standard Oil of New Jersey	24,843,643	8	198,749,144
Union Carbide & Carbon	8,730,173	20	[illegible]

PREMIER ISSUES HARD HIT

Unexpected Torrent of Liquidation Again Rocks Markets.

DAY'S SALES 9,212,800

Nearly 3,000,000 Shares Are Traded In Final Hour—The Tickers Lag 167 Minutes.

NEW RALLY SOON BROKEN

Selling by Europeans and "Mob Psychology" Big Factors in Second Big Break.

Newspapers reported in sterile statistics the painful details of Wall Street's collapse.

On September 5 investment adviser Roger Babson warned that a crash was coming, and the market staggered through the "Babson break." Prices declined through September, but as yet there was no sign of panic. But a sharp break occurred on October 23 and October 24 ("Black Thursday"), when a record 13 million shares traded (3 million was normal). Massive organized buying by banks and investment houses prevented a complete rout. But on October 28 ("Black Monday") and October 29 ("Black Tuesday"), the panic resumed. The slide continued until mid-November. By that time stock prices had fallen to about one-half of what they were in August.

Using a broader measure of stock prices and over a longer period, Figure 23-5 on the next page outlines the "Great Crash" in full force. Much of the panic selling of stocks resulted from brokers selling stocks that had been purchased on margin. On Black Tuesday, 16.4 million shares were sold in record amounts generated by sheer panic. On Black Monday and Black Tuesday, an average stock lost almost 25 percent of its value. But note that even well into 1930, share prices remained above the levels

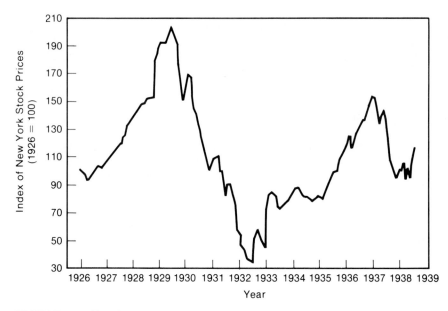

FIGURE 23-5 THE STANDARD STATISTICS INDEX OF NEW YORK STOCK PRICES, 1926–1938
The rise and fall in stock prices shows the magnitude of speculative activity and the market crash. From a level of 100 in 1926, the market index soared to a high of 206 in September 1929, before collapsing to 34 in June 1932.

SOURCE: CHARLES KINDLEBERGER, *THE WORLD IN DEPRESSION, 1929–1939* (BERKELEY: UNIVERSITY OF CALIFORNIA PRESS, 1973), PP. 110–111. REPRINTED BY PERMISSION OF THE UNIVERSITY OF CALIFORNIA PRESS.

reached a few years earlier. The unique psychological trauma produced by the crash was more significant for the economy than the direct effects of the loss of wealth. Purchases of consumer durables, in particular, declined as consumers took an increasingly pessimistic view of the future. Within a year industrial production was down more than 25 percent.

THE BANKING CRISES

The devastating impact of the stock market collapse and other faltering aspects of the economy came in the early stages of the depression. Public morale might have improved and the market and the economy might have regained some buoyancy had it not been for the structural weaknesses of the banking system and the international economy. Three waves of bank failures, each timed to have a particularly unsettling effect, shook the economy.

Bank failures had been frequent in rural parts of the country throughout the 1920s, so the high rates of failure that occurred in early 1930 did not strike observers as unusual. But in October 1930 a wave of bank failures concentrated in the South and Midwest produced something new: a general alarm about the banking system spread

In It's a Wonderful Life, *Jimmy Stewart and Donna Reed coped with a familiar problem during the depression, a run on a savings and loan association.*

across the country, and people began converting bank deposits into currency.[1] Sometimes this produced runs on banks, the classic sign of a panic. A rumor that a bank was in trouble would literally send people running to the bank to try to get their money out before it closed. The crisis continued in November and December, and on December 11, the Bank of the United States in New York failed. This failure was significant for several reasons. It was the largest failure, measured by deposits, in the history of the United States up to that time. And, although it was an ordinary bank (chartered by the state of New York), its name may have led some people to believe that a bank having a particularly close association with the government had failed.

The Fed at this point, most historians agree, should have acted as a *lender of last resort*. It should have lent generously to the Bank of the United States and other failing banks to break the cycle of fear that was undermining the banking system. But for a

---

[1]Although the response to the crisis was new, a sophisticated study by Eugene White has shown that the banks that failed were similar to those that had failed previously. See Eugene N. White, "A Reinterpretation of the Banking Crisis of 1930," *Journal of Economic History* 44 (1984): 119–138.

variety of reasons that we will discuss in detail later in the chapter, it did not do so. It still seemed to the Fed that the banks that were failing were simply badly managed banks that should be eliminated to make the system more efficient. In retrospect we can see that with the economy in a downward spiral, permitting bank failures only made matters worse, but this was not evident to the Fed at the time.[2]

For a few months things seemed to be calmer, but a second, more intense crisis began in March 1931. This time events abroad reinforced the sense of crisis. In May 1931 the Kreditanstalt, a major bank in Vienna, failed. Since gold was the root of the money supply in most of the industrial countries, failures such as this one convinced people worldwide that now was the time to convert paper claims to gold into the real thing. In September 1931 Britain left the gold standard: the British pound would no longer be convertible on demand into gold. This in turn increased the pressure on currencies such as the dollar that were still convertible into gold.

The final banking panic began in 1933. Between 1930 and 1932 over 5,000 banks containing over $3 billion in deposits (about 7 percent of total deposits in January 1930) had suspended operations. In 1933 another 4,000 banks containing over $3.5 billion in deposits would close. The weakened condition of the banks after years of deflation, uncertainties about how the new administration of Franklin D. Roosevelt would handle the crisis, and the general atmosphere of distrust and fear—all contributed to the final crisis. By the time that Roosevelt took office on March 4, 1933, the destruction of the financial system that had taken place was incredible.

One of President Roosevelt's first acts was to announce a nationwide bank holiday beginning on March 6, 1933. This action, which followed a number of state bank holidays, closed all of the banks in the country for one week. How could such an action improve things? The public was told that during this period the banks would be inspected and only the sound ones allowed to reopen. Questions have been raised about the way this was handled. Probably many sound banks were closed, and unsound ones allowed to remain open. But the medicine seemed to work, even if it was only a placebo; the panic subsided.

In addition to the bank holiday, the federal government took a number of other actions that helped to restore confidence in the financial system. Gold hoarding was ended by the simple expedient of requiring everyone to turn monetary gold over to the Fed in exchange for some other form of currency. Perhaps most important, the Federal Deposit Insurance Corporation (FDIC) was established to insure bank deposits. The insurance took effect on January 1, 1934, and within six months almost all of the nation's commercial banks were covered. Deposit insurance dramatically changed the incentives facing depositors. No longer would a rumor of failure send people rushing to the bank to try to be first in line, because they now knew that they would eventually be paid their deposits in any case. All of these factors together drastically changed the rate of bank failures. The number of bank failures fell from 4,000 in 1933

---

[2] An excellent example of how to handle a run on a bank (in this case a savings bank) occurs in the popular 1946 movie *It's a Wonderful Life*, which stars Jimmy Stewart as the president of a small savings bank. There is a run on the bank. But at the height of the panic the wife of the bank's president (played by Donna Reed) acts as a lender of last resort and offers the family's personal savings to allay the fears of depositors.

to 61 in 1934, and remained at double-digit levels through the rest of the 1930s. (By way of contrast, the lowest number of bank failures in any year from 1921 to 1929 was 366 in 1922.) Although the Great Depression was to drag on for the remainder of the decade, the banking crisis had been surmounted.

THE ROLE OF MONETARY FORCES IN THE GREAT DEPRESSION

To monetarists such as Milton Friedman and Anna J. Schwartz, the primary cause of the Great Depression was the decline in the money stock produced by the withdrawal of currency from the banking system and by the decisions of banks to hold more reserves. According to the quantity theory of money, when the money supply contracts people try to restore the relation between their money balances and their incomes by spending less. The result is a fall in net national product.

Even monetarists do not claim that the fall in the stock of money was the only factor at work. In Table 23-1, note that the ratio of net national product to money (the velocity of money) also fell. During the first year of the depression, the ratio of net national product to money fell dramatically (perhaps because of the stock market crash) while the money supply fell only slightly. Nevertheless, monetarists insist that any decline in the money supply is significant. The decline in the money supply itself might explain part of the decline in the ratio of income to money. People normally spend less freely in recessions, and if prices are falling people have another incentive not to spend because their money is worth more the longer they hold on to it.

It is hard to believe that the financial collapse did the economy any good, and most economic historians now follow the monetarists in assigning a major role to the financial collapse in causing the Great Depression. There has been some controversy, however, over exactly how much weight to assign to the financial crisis compared with other causes such as the stock market crash. The most skeptical view has been expressed by Peter Temin, whose interpretation of the figures in Table 23-1 is just the

TABLE 23-1 MONEY AND INCOME, 1929–1933

Year	(1) Money Supply (billions)	(2) Net National Product (billions)	(3) Ratio of Money to NNP	(4) Commercial Paper Rate (percent)	(5) Real Rate of Interest (percent)
1929	$46.6	$90.3	1.94	5.78%	5.88%
1930	45.7	76.9	1.68	3.55	8.15
1931	42.7	61.7	1.45	2.63	15.46
1932	36.1	44.8	1.24	2.72	14.99
1933	32.2	42.7	1.32	1.67	3.03

SOURCE: MILTON FRIEDMAN AND ANNA J. SCHWARTZ, *MONETARY TRENDS IN THE UNITED STATES AND THE UNITED KINGDOM* (CHICAGO: UNIVERSITY OF CHICAGO PRESS, 1982), P. 124.

reverse of that proposed by the monetarists.[3] Net national product fell, according to Temin, because spending collapsed. (Temin believes that there was a sudden and unexplained collapse in consumer spending.) As a result profits fell, workers were laid off, and many firms and individuals could no longer repay their bank loans. This triggered the waves of bank failures and the decline in the money stock shown in column 1 of Table 23-1. This was a tragedy, to be sure, but it was a *symptom* of the depression analogous to the problems in agricultural, consumer durables production, and other sectors of the economy.

The key piece of evidence, according to Temin, is the behavior of the rate of interest. He contends that if the decline in the money stock were the initiating factor, we would have seen interest rates rising. People would have begun selling financial assets to acquire money, and the prices of those assets would have fallen while the returns they yield (relative to their prices) would have risen. But we observe just the opposite: short-term interest rates fell from 5.78 percent in 1929 to 1.67 percent in 1933. If there is a shortage of wheat we expect the price of wheat to rise, and if there is a shortage of money we expect the rate of interest to rise.

Temin's view, however, remains the minority opinion. The monetarists countered forcefully that the interest rate is the price not of money but of credit. The demand for credit declined because of the general decline in economic activity caused by the decline in the money supply. To the monetarists, the price of money is the inverse of the price level, the purchasing power of money. That variable rose from 1929 to 1933, showing that the supply of money was contracting faster than demand.

Recent research, moreover, has identified additional channels, besides the effect on demand, through which the financial crisis contributed to the decline in economic activity. The seminal research was done by Ben Bernanke, who argued on the basis of a wide range of evidence that bank failures made it difficult for firms, particularly smaller firms, to get the credit they needed to remain in operation.[4] When a bank failed, long-term relationships between the bank and its borrowers were shattered. These borrowers could approach other lenders, but the new lenders would lack the information about the borrower possessed by the failed bank. In addition, the ongoing deflation reduced the value of a business's assets and raised the value of its debt burden, further reducing its ability to qualify for additional credit.

In short, while controversy continues over the exact role of the financial crisis in the Great Depression, there is agreement that the Federal Reserve deserves considerable blame for the disastrous path along which events unfolded.[5]

---

[3] Peter Temin, *Did Monetary Forces Cause the Great Depression?* (New York: W. W. Norton, 1976).

[4] Ben Bernanke, "Nonmonetary Effects of the Financial Crisis in the Propagation of the Great Depression," *American Economic Review* 73 (1983): 257–276.

[5] Even Peter Temin, in his later work, assigned some blame to the Federal Reserve for the tight money regime it initiated in the late twenties. Peter Temin, *Lessons from the Great Depression* (Cambridge: MIT Press, 1989).

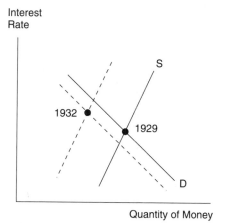

A: If the monetarists were right

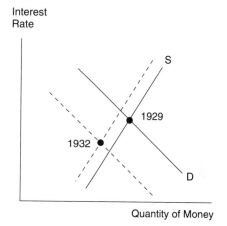

B: If the Keynesians were right

The figures above illustrate Peter Temin's famous critique of the monetarist interpretation of the Great Depression. They depict the supply of and demand for money, with the interest rate as the price of holding money. (Monetarists, incidentally, accepted this model, although they insisted that interest paid on deposits should be deducted from the interest rate to get the cost of holding deposits, and that the stock of money should be deflated by the price level to get the real stock of money.) Figure A depicts Temin's rendering of the monetarist interpretation, Figure B his rendering of the Keynesian interpretation. If the monetarists were correct (according to Temin), the dominant shift would have been the supply curve to the left (Figure A). If the Keynesians were right, the dominant shift would have been the demand curve to the left (Figure B). Because interest rates fell during the depression—as shown in column 4 of Table 23-1 (page 525)—Temin concluded that the Keynesians were right.

Monetarists countered that Temin's argument neglected intermediate and longer-term effects of the decline in the quantity of money on the demand for money. Falling real income and prices (caused by the effect of money in other markets) reduced the demand for money. So part of the shift in the demand curve in Figure B could be attributed to the fall in the stock of money. Moreover, to the extent that these effects were anticipated they would influence the path of interest rates even in the short run.

WHY DIDN'T THE FEDERAL RESERVE SAVE THE BANKING SYSTEM?

There appear to have been several reasons why the Fed remained relatively passive in the face of an unprecedented collapse of the banking system. In its own defense, the Federal Reserve Board maintained in its 1932 Annual Report that its use of open-market purchases of bonds (which pumps reserves into the banking system) was inhibited by the requirement that Federal Reserve notes be backed by either gold or eligible paper (loans sold by the banks to the Federal Reserve). The Federal Reserve Board argued that if the Federal Reserve purchased government bonds in the open market, member banks would reduce their indebtedness, and consequently the Fed's holdings of eligible paper; but this meant that more gold would be required as collateral for Federal Reserve notes at a time when only $416 million of gold was not committed to some legal reserve purpose. This was the so-called "free gold" problem. Had the Fed made a determined effort to get the rules changed, it undoubtedly could have done so. But this technical constraint, and the prestige of the gold standard that lay behind it, probably had some influence on the Fed.

Technical constraints, however, are only part of the story. In his diary entries during August 1931, Charles S. Hamlin, then a member of the Federal Reserve Board, tells us that the Open Market Committee voted 11 to 1 against open-market purchases of $300 million, substituting $120 million instead. The governors of the regional banks, who were still in control of monetary policy, simply could not grasp the extent of the catastrophe, and Governor Meyer of the Federal Reserve Board was even worried about inflation.

Part of the failure to appreciate the magnitude of the collapse was due to the tendency of officials at the Fed to look at the wrong indicators of monetary policy. Many felt that low interest rates were a certain sign of easy money, and concluded (look again at column 4 of Table 23-1) that financial markets were awash with money, and that trying to pump in more would do little good. Had they looked at real interest rates (market rates plus expected deflation), they would have reached a different conclusion. The last column of Table 23-1 shows a simple measure of the real rate of interest: the rate on commercial paper minus the percentage change in prices since the previous year. Real rates, which are likely to influence investment decisions by businesses, clearly were very high in the early years of the depression.

A power struggle within the Federal Reserve system identified by Friedman and Schwartz was another important factor. In the 1920s the Federal Reserve Bank of New York, under its charismatic president Benjamin Strong, had dominated the system. After Strong's death in 1928, the Federal Reserve Board in Washington tried to assert its authority by resisting pressures from New York. This power struggle took its toll in the 1930s, when the New York bank pushed for more expansionary monetary policies and the Federal Reserve Board in Washington resisted for internal political reasons.

The precise weight to be put on each of these factors is a matter of some debate, but the important point is that the Federal Reserve system, although created in 1913 to protect the nation's banking system, failed 20 years later to stop the greatest banking crisis in American economic history.

FISCAL POLICY IN THE EARLY 1930s

The popular belief that the Hoover administration did nothing to combat the depression is erroneous. Within the limits of economic orthodoxy, which called for trying to balance the budget, steps were taken to restore economic equilibrium. In January 1932, the Reconstruction Finance Corporation was set up to borrow money by issuing securities guaranteed by the federal government and to relend it to banks, insurance companies, railroads, and other businesses experiencing financial difficulties. The very formation of such an agency in peacetime (it was a revival of the War Finance Corporation of World War I) marked a sharp break with tradition. Support of agricultural prices with production controls by the Federal Farm Board was equally revolutionary. The major deficiencies of the Hoover administration were its persistent refusal to establish a federal program of work relief and its failure to carry out an aggressive fiscal policy of large deficits financed by borrowing from the banking system. Too much reliance was placed on maintaining confidence through the public testimonials of

Farm and home foreclosures and unemployment created a growing mass of homeless people during the depression. Shantytowns, like this one in New York's Central Park, were called Hoovervilles.

TABLE 23-2   GOVERNMENTAL EXPENDITURES AND REVENUES, 1927–1940
(IN MILLIONS)

| Year | Federal | | State and Local | | Private Investment |
	Expenditures	Revenues	Expenditures	Revenues	
1927	$2.9	$4.0	$ 7.8	$ 7.8	$14.5[a]
1932	4.8	2.0	8.4	7.9	3.4
1934	6.5	3.1	7.8	8.4	4.1
1936	7.6	4.2	8.5	9.4	7.2
1938	7.2	7.0	10.0	11.1	7.4
1940	9.6	6.9	11.2	11.7	11.0

SOURCE: HISTORICAL STATISTICS (WASHINGTON, D.C.: GOVERNMENT PRINTING OFFICE, 1976), SERIES F53, Y335, Y336, Y339, Y340, Y652, Y671.

[a]This is the 1929 figure.

business and government leaders, and not enough was placed on measures to raise incomes and correct the deflation.

It is true, as shown in Table 23-2 above, that the Treasury began running small but growing deficits by the early 1930s. But these deficits were not the result of bold spending programs (or cuts in tax rates) by government. Rather they were primarily due to the decline in tax revenues as incomes fell, and they occurred despite efforts to prevent them.

Indeed, in 1932 a tax increase was enacted, partly over concern about the deficit and its effects on bond values. It should be remembered that declining bond values were contributing to the deteriorating capital holdings of banks, and this was especially important to those facing possible "runs." Of course, this policy move was counterproductive, not unlike taking a steambath to reduce a fever. What Hoover should have done was cut taxes, vastly increase spending, and demand that the Fed buy bonds in great volume to finance the deficit, bolster bank reserves, and ease credit.

Franklin D. Roosevelt and his staff were not entirely comfortable with the idea of deficits. During the campaign of 1932, Roosevelt promised to cut spending 25 percent and balance the budget. But once in office, the Roosevelt administration was willing to run fairly large deficits by historical standards to finance its many new programs. How large were these deficits? Why did they not lift the country out of the depression, as Keynesian economic theory predicts?[6] Some evidence is given in Table 23-2. The federal budget was steadily in deficit during the depression. Relative to the traditional size of the federal government, the level of spending and the deficits seemed large indeed. Note that by 1938 federal spending was two and a half times as high as it had been in 1927.

---

[6]The famous book by John Maynard Keynes, The General Theory of Employment, Interest and Money, was not published until 1936. Many economists, however, favored increased government spending financed by deficits. Some thought that increased spending would "prime the pump" and stimulate the natural expansionary powers of the economy.

Campaign promises to balance the budget and cut spending met head-on with the economic realities of the Great Depression. Some in the media chastised FDR for deficit spending to pay for his new programs.

Compared with other parts of the economy, however, the federal government was still rather small. In 1938 the federal deficit was $0.2 billion ($7.2 − $7.0), but this was more than offset by a surplus at the state and local levels of $1.1 billion ($10.0 − $11.1). Remember, too, that tax revenues were down because of the depression. At full employment, the same tax rates would have produced much higher revenues.[7] Keynesian theory suggests that the role of government spending is to offset decreases in autonomous private spending such as investment or consumption. It is clear that the fall in investment spending, $7.1 billion between 1929 and 1938, was far greater than the increase in federal spending or the federal deficit. No wonder then that Keynesian economist E. Cary Brown concludes that "fiscal policy . . . seems to have been an unsuccessful recovery device in the thirties—not because it does not work, but because it was not tried."

In retrospect this should not surprise us. Orthodox economic opinion, although far from unanimous, still looked skeptically at large-scale federal deficits as a remedy for depression. Political constraints on spending, moreover, were significant; research by

---

[7] This point was first made in the 1950s by E. Cary Brown. More work by Larry Peppers in 1973 has strengthened Brown's original conclusions.

Gavin Wright shows that New Deal spending was carefully allocated to maximize political support for the Roosevelt administration.[8]

MONETARY AND FISCAL POLICY, 1934–1939

Net national product rose from a low of $42.7 billion in 1933 to $75.1 billion in 1937, still well below the level of 1929 but sufficient to alleviate much hardship and to indicate the potential of the economy to recover. Over the same period the implicit price deflator rose from 73.3 to 81.0 (1929 = 100). This boom was stimulated partly by the expansion of government spending for the relief and other programs discussed above and partly by the expansion of the money stock from $32.2 billion in 1933 to $45.7 billion in 1937. The latter resulted not from a deliberate Federal Reserve policy of increasing the money stock to fight the depression, but from an increase in confidence in the banking system and an increase in the monetary base (currency in circulation, currency held by banks, and the deposits of banks in the Federal Reserve).

As measures aimed at restoring confidence in the banking system (such as federal deposit insurance) took hold, people began to redeposit currency in the banking system. This process led to an increase in the money stock because banks would create several dollars of loans and deposits on the basis of each additional dollar of currency redeposited. The fractional reserve system that had worked to destroy the monetary system from 1930 to 1933 now ran in reverse. Even more important was an increase in the monetary base, primarily because of purchases of gold by the U.S. Treasury.

THE PRICE OF GOLD AND THE MONEY SUPPLY

During the bank holiday and the weeks that followed, the Roosevelt administration prohibited transactions in gold; on April 5, 1933, it took the extraordinary step of ordering all holders of gold to deliver their gold (rare coins, and other specialized holdings were exempt) to the Federal Reserve. These actions took the United States off the gold standard. For several months the price of gold, and therefore of foreign currencies linked to gold, fluctuated according to the dictates of supply and demand. The federal government, however, made a determined effort to increase the price of gold (and of related foreign currencies) by purchasing gold. The idea was to raise the dollar price of commodities, particularly agricultural commodities, set on world markets. To this extent the policy was successful; some of the inflation that occurred in this period, otherwise surprising because of the depressed state of the economy, can be attributed to the manipulation of the exchange rate.

On January 31, 1934, the United States recommitted itself to a form of the gold standard by fixing a price of $35 per ounce (the pre-depression price had been $20 per ounce) at which the Treasury would buy or sell gold. The new form of the gold standard, however, was only a pale reflection of the classical gold standard, because ordi-

---

[8] Gavin Wright, "The Political Economy of New Deal Spending: An Econometric Analysis," *Review of Economics and Statistics* 56 (1974): 30–38. For a less-cynical view see Don Reading, "New Deal Activity and the States, 1933 to 1939," *Journal of Economic History* 33 (1973): 792–810.

nary citizens were not allowed to hold gold coins or use them in day-to-day transactions. The United States in effect set a floor under the world price of gold. Production of gold in the United States and much of the rest of the world soared in the thirties. World production rose from 25 million ounces in 1933 to 40 million ounces in 1940. After all, costs of production such as wages had fallen, but the price at which gold could be sold (to the U.S. Treasury) had risen. The result was a rapid increase in the Treasury's stock of gold. In addition, the rise of fascism in Europe created a large outflow of capital, including gold, seeking a safe haven, further augmenting U.S. gold holdings.

When the Treasury purchased gold it created gold certificates that it could use as cash or deposit with the Federal Reserve. In effect, if the Treasury bought gold it was allowed to pay for it by printing new currency. The result was a rapid increase in the monetary base, which, in conjunction with the redeposit of currency in the banking system, produced a rapid increase in the money supply.

PARTIAL RECOVERY, THEN A NEW DOWNTURN

By early 1937 total manufacturing output had exceeded the rate of 1929, and the recovery, though not complete, seemed to be going well. But at that point the expansion came to an abrupt halt. Industrial production reached a post-1929 high in May 1937 and then turned downward. Commodity prices followed, and the weary process of deflation began again. Retail sales dropped off, unemployment increased, and payrolls declined substantially. Adding to the general gloom, the stock market started a long slide in August that brought prices in March 1938 to less than half the peak of the previous year. The important setbacks of 1937 are revealed graphically earlier in this chapter in Figures 23-1 through 23-5.

What had happened? Then, as now, many attributed the renewed onslaught of depression to the reform measures introduced and passed in 1935 and 1936. Social Security and the new freedom granted labor came in for some harsh words. But most of the criticism was directed toward the antibusiness political climate created by the Roosevelt administration, which, it was asserted, made vigorous business expansion impossible. In his state of the union message of 1936, President Roosevelt had castigated "the royalists of the economic order" who, he said, opposed government intervention in economic affairs and received a disproportionate amount of national income. Tax legislation in 1935 and 1936, directed at preventing tax avoidance and making the tax structure more progressive, was especially resented by people of means. In addition, estate and gift taxes were increased, as were individual surtaxes and taxes on the income of large corporations. The undistributed profits tax of 1936—a surtax imposed on corporations to make them distribute profits instead of holding them so that individual stockholders could avoid personal taxation—was also resented. Why would business undertake long-term investments, critics of the administration wondered, when the profits might all be taken away by future legislation?

Whatever merit there is in this argument, it is clear that fiscal and monetary policy also played a role in causing the downturn. Government officials were convinced in early 1937 that full employment and inflation were just around the corner. Expenditures for relief and public works were cut, and new taxes (those discussed previously and the Social Security tax, to be discussed in the next chapter) were imposed. The result was that the projected deficit for 1937 dropped significantly. Keynesian economists would not be surprised to find a recession.

Monetary policy also worked to create a recession. The excess reserves of the banks, as noted, had risen steadily after the banking crises of the early 1930s. The Federal Reserve interpreted these reserves simply as money that could not be profitably invested at the low rates then prevailing. Money, the Federal Reserve reasoned, was just piling up because the banks didn't know what to do with it. The Federal Reserve then decided to raise legal reserve ratios to lock up the excess reserves and prevent them from being put into use during the anticipated not-too-distant inflation. This proved, however, to have been a disastrous mistake. In fact these reserves were not unwanted by the banks. The banks had been deliberately building up a cushion in the event of a replay of the banking crises. Their response to the Federal Reserve's decision to raise legal reserve ratios was to restore their margin above the legal reserve ratio. To do this they had to reduce their loans and deposits. The money supply fell once again, although only slightly, in 1937.

The contraction from 1937 to 1938 was not as deep or as persistent as the contraction from 1929 to 1933. One reason is that the banking system did not collapse. The protection created by deposit insurance, along with the cautious behavior of the banks that survived the debacle of the early 1930s, prevented a repetition. Only 82 banks suspended operations in 1937 and only 80 in 1938, compared with 1,350 in 1930 and 2,293 in 1931. Nevertheless, the result of the "recession within the depression" was that the economy was still far from fully employed in 1939.

CAN IT HAPPEN AGAIN?

No one, unfortunately, can say for certain that it cannot happen again. But there are many reasons for thinking that a collapse on the scale of the Great Depression is a remote possibility under modern circumstances.

One reason is that we are not likely to repeat the same mistakes. The Federal Reserve, with better data at hand and with the experience of the Great Depression laid out in many books and articles, is unlikely to permit a complete collapse of the banking system. Moreover, because we are no longer on a gold standard, the Fed's ability to create dollars during a crisis is virtually unlimited.

The same is true of fiscal policy, although here we cannot be quite so confident. Faith in a balanced budget seems to be hard to shake even under very dire circumstances. Nevertheless, it seems likely that conditions similar to those of the early 1930s would be met today with tax cuts and increased spending on a substantial scale. Many sorts of spending, such as unemployment benefits, would increase even without specific congressional actions—the so-called automatic stabilizers.

The private economy, too, may be less vulnerable to economic collapse. The industrial sector, particularly producers of consumer durables, seems to be the most vulnerable to sudden shifts in demand that lead to massive layoffs. But this sector is now relatively much smaller compared with the service sector than it was in the 1930s. The rapid increase in two-earner households has reduced the probability for many families that an economic downturn will completely deprive them of an income.

Lastly there exists a vast network of government programs that would alleviate suffering and, simply by being there, reduce the chance of a paralyzing fear. These include the Federal Deposit Insurance Corporation, the Pension Guarantee Corporation, and others. But however much we may be aware of these facts, it is nevertheless true that the nightmare of the Great Depression comes back to haunt us time and again when conditions in one sector or another take a turn for the worse.

THE GREAT DEPRESSION AND LAISSEZ-FAIRE

Rexford Tugwell, a member of President Roosevelt's "brain trust" (a group of advisers who suggested many new programs to combat the depression) remarked,

> The Cat is out of the Bag. There is no invisible hand. There never was. If the depression has not taught us that, we are incapable of education. . . . We must now supply a real and visible guiding hand to do the task which that mythical, nonexistent, invisible agency was supposed to perform, but never did.[9]

Tugwell's forthright remark addresses the fundamental question raised by the Great Depression: doesn't the depression prove that unguided by government a free-market economy has the potential to run off the rails and produce an economic disaster? And furthermore, doesn't the depression prove that there is something wrong with Say's Law (the theory, named for French economist J. B. Say, that the balancing of supply and demand creates a tendency toward full employment)? And if the market cannot accomplish the simple task of balancing the supply and demand for labor, why should we trust it to allocate resources at the micro level? Should we leave the allocation of capital to a stock market that goes through ridiculous boom-and-bust cycles? Should we leave the allocation of agricultural products to Adam Smith's "invisible hand" when it drives farmers off the land while people in cities go hungry? To many thoughtful observers in the 1930s, the clear answer to these questions was the one given by Tugwell: do not leave things to the free market; common sense tells us that government regulation can make things better.

Most mainstream economists and economic historians, however, have not been entirely persuaded. John Maynard Keynes, who agreed that the depression revealed fundamental weaknesses in the economic system, nevertheless concluded that it did not justify across-the-board intervention in the market. He believed that the depression was a problem of aggregate demand and that this was separate from the problem of individual markets. As he wrote,

> To put the point concretely, I see no reason to suppose that the existing system seriously misemploys the factors of production which are in use. There are, of course, errors of foresight; but these would not be avoided by centralizing decisions. When 9,000,000 men are employed out of 10,000,000 willing and able

---

[9] Quoted in Rebecca Gruver, *An American History* (New York: Appleton-Century-Crofts, 1972), p. 936.

to work, there is no evidence that the labour of these 9,000,000 men is misdirected. The complaint against the present system is not that these 9,000,000 men ought to be employed on different tasks, but that tasks should be available for the remaining 1,000,000 men. It is in determining the volume, not the direction, of actual employment that the existing system has broken down.[10]

Monetarists have given the most negative answer to Tugwell. In their view, the Great Depression was a monetary crisis. Government regulation had produced a weak, crisis-prone banking system. The Fed, the agency created to prevent banking crises, failed to save it when confidence in the banking system collapsed. Eliminate these weaknesses, by allowing the banking system to strengthen itself through competition and by forcing the Fed to maintain the stock of money, and a recurrence of the Great Depression could be prevented. But during the 1930s it was Tugwell's position that prevailed. As we shall see in the next chapter, the depression led to a vast increase in the extent to which the federal government attempted to influence individual markets.

SELECTED REFERENCES
AND SUGGESTED READINGS

Bernanke, Ben. "Non Monetary Effects of the Financial Crisis in the Propagation of the Great Depression." *American Economic Review* 73 (1983): 257–276.

Boughton, James, and Elmus Wicker. "The Behavior of the Currency-Deposit Ratio During the Great Depression." *Journal of Money, Credit and Banking* 1 (1979): 405–418.

Brown, E. Cary. "Fiscal Policy in the Thirties: A Reappraisal." *American Economic Review* 46 (December 1956).

Brunner, Karl, ed. *The Great Depression Revisited.* Boston: Martinus Nijhoff, 1981.

Eichengreen, Barry. "Central Bank Cooperation under the Interwar Gold Standard." *Explorations in Economic History* 21 (1984): 64–87.

———. *Golden Fetters: The Gold Standard and the Great Depression, 1919–1939.* New York: Oxford University Press, 1992.

Eichengreen, Barry, and Jeffrey Sachs. "Exchange Rates and Economic Recovery in the 1930s." *Journal of Economic History* 45 (1986): 925–946.

Epstein, Gerald, and Thomas Ferguson. "Monetary Policy, Loan Liquidation, and Industrial Conflict: The Federal Reserve and the Great Contraction." *Journal of Economic History* 44 (1984): 957–984.

Field, Alexander. "Asset Exchanges and the Transactions Demand for Money, 1919–1929." *American Economic Review* 74 (1984): 43–59.

———. "A New Interpretation of the Onset of the Great Depression." *Journal of Economic History* 44 (1984): 489–498.

Fisher, Irving. *Booms and Depressions.* New York: Adelphi, 1932.

———. "The Debt Deflation Theory of Great Depressions." *Econometrica* 1 (1933): 337–357.

Friedman, Milton. "Why the American Economy Is Depression-Proof." In *Dollars and Deficits.* Englewood Cliffs, New Jersey: Prentice-Hall, 1968.

Friedman, Milton, and Anna J. Schwartz. *A Monetary History of the United States.* Princeton: Princeton University Press, 1965, pp. 299–545.

---

[10]John Maynard Keynes, *The General Theory of Employment, Interest and Money* (1936; reprint, New York: Harcourt, Brace & World, 1964), p. 379.

Galbraith, John Kenneth. *The Great Crash.* Boston: Houghton Mifflin, 1972.

Gandolfi, Arthur, and James Lothian. "Review of '*Did Monetary Forces Cause the Great Depression?*'" *Journal of Money, Credit and Banking* 9 (1977): 679–691.

Kindleberger, Charles P. *Manias, Panics, and Crashes.* New York: Basic Books, 1978.

Mayer, Thomas. "Consumption in the Great Depression." *Journal of Political Economy* 86 (1978): 139–145.

_____. "Money and the Great Depression: A Critique of Professor Temin's Thesis." *Explorations in Economic History* 15 (1978): 127–145.

Meltzer, Allan H. "Monetary and Other Explanations of the Start of the Great Depression." *Journal of Monetary Economics* 2 (1976): 455–471.

Muchmore, Lynn. "The Banking Crisis of 1933: Some Iowa Evidence," *Journal of Economic History* 30 (September 1970).

Peppers, Larry C. "Full Employment Surplus Analysis and Structural Changes: The 1930s." *Explorations in Economic History* 10 (Winter 1973): 197–210.

Romer, Christina. "The Great Crash and the Onset of the Great Depression." *Quarterly Journal of Economics* 105 (1990): 597–624.

Stauffer, Richard. "The Bank Failures of 1930–1931." *Journal of Money, Credit and Banking* 13 (1981): 109–113.

Temin, Peter. *Did Monetary Forces Cause the Great Depression?* New York: W. W. Norton, 1976.

_____. *Lessons from the Great Depression.* Cambridge: MIT Press, 1989.

Trescott, Paul. "The Behavior of the Currency-Deposit Ratio During the Great Depression." *Journal of Money, Credit and Banking* 16 (1984): 362–365.

_____. "Federal Reserve Policy in the Great Contraction: A Counterfactual Assessment." *Explorations in Economic History* 19 (1982): 211–220.

White, Eugene N. "A Reinterpretation of the Banking Crisis of 1930." *Journal of Economic History* 44 (1984): 119–138.

Wicker, Elmus. "Interest Rate and Expenditure Effects of the Banking Panic of 1930." *Explorations in Economic History* 19 (1982): 435–445.

_____. "A Reconsideration of the Causes of the Banking Panic of 1930." *Journal of Economic History* 40 (1982): 435–445.

CHAPTER TWENTY-FOUR

THE NEW DEAL

CHAPTER THEME The presidential campaign of 1932 was fought in an atmosphere of fear and discontent. Herbert Hoover, nominated for a second term, blamed events in Europe for the nation's troubles and promised that prosperity would soon return. Tampering with our basic economic institutions, Hoover argued, could only lead to even worse disasters. Franklin D. Roosevelt, the warm and yet forceful Democratic candidate, was generally not specific about what measures he would take if elected, though he did promise to balance the budget. But there was no mistaking his willingness to use the power of the government directly to try to solve the nation's problems. In his acceptance speech at the Democratic convention Roosevelt promised a "New Deal" if he was elected. Few people at the time realized how fully these words would be put into practice in the years to come.

Between the time of his election and the time he took office, economic conditions deteriorated. No president since Abraham Lincoln had faced a greater crisis at the moment he assumed power. Industrial production was at about 40 percent of full potential, and one-quarter of the nation's workers were unemployed. But in his inaugural address, delivered on March 4, 1933, Roosevelt rallied the nation's spirits, declaring, "Let me assert my firm belief that the only thing we have to fear is fear itself—nameless, unreasoning, unjustified terror which paralyzes needed efforts to convert retreat into advance." In the famous "hundred days" that followed, the Roosevelt administration proposed many new—and, for the time, radical—pieces of legislation. Thus was born the New Deal. Although it occupied only a brief span of time in the context of our history, we must consider it in detail, because it is the origin of many of the institutions and ideas that shape our daily lives today.

RELIEF AND REFORM

The most pressing problem for the new administration was to provide relief for destitute families; the administration responded with legislation on this and a host of related problems. The Federal Emergency Relief Agency (FERA), directed by Harry Hopkins, pumped a half billion dollars into bankrupt state and local relief efforts. In 1935 the federal government set up the Works Progress Administration, later the Works Projects Administration (WPA), also under Hopkins's direction. This agency employed millions of people in road building, flood-control projects, and similar programs. Its most famous and controversial projects employed writers, photographers, and other creative artists. Critics complained, with some justice, that these projects often had strong left wing political messages. But some of the projects, such as recording the recollections of the last generation of former slaves, also had lasting value. Under Hopkins's direction the main emphasis of the WPA was creating employment; the contribution of these projects to the infrastructure of the economy was secondary. Another well-known agency with a similar purpose was the Civilian Conservation Corps (CCC), which hired young men to work on planting trees and other outdoor conservation projects.

The Civilian Conservation Corps provided work for unemployed young men. At its peak in 1935, the corps employed 500,000 men in building national park facilities, planting trees, cleaning and enlarging reservoirs, and similar activities.

Larger construction projects were undertaken by the Public Works Administration, which spent more than $6 billion over the course of the depression on dams, low-cost housing, airports, warships, and other projects. Its director, Harold Ickes, earned an enviable reputation for honesty and for his efforts to secure employment for African-Americans, but he was sometimes criticized for taking too much time to plan projects.

The overall impact of the emergency relief measures is shown in Table 24-1. In 1933, the first year of the New Deal, over 2 million workers (4.3 percent of the labor force) were employed by federal, state, and local emergency work programs. The peak year was 1936, when 3.7 million people (7 percent of the labor force) were employed in such programs. To put the point somewhat differently, had the relief programs not existed, and had the workers not been able to find employment in the private sector, then the unemployment rate would have been not 9.9 percent in 1936 (in itself a very high rate) but 16.9 percent. Indeed, the official figures, the ones you are likely to see quoted in history textbooks or the newspaper, listed 16.9 percent of the workforce as unemployed in order to stress the seriousness of the problem.

The emergency work agencies were merely one facet, albeit a very important one, of a myriad of federal agencies created to deal with the Great Depression. Critics of the New Deal complained that this "alphabet soup" was turning the United States into a bureaucratic state. But there can be no doubt, as revealed by Roosevelt's over-whelming reelection victories in 1936 and 1940, that a majority of the public approved of the administration's active and experimental response to the crisis.

TABLE 24-1   EMERGENCY WORKERS DURING THE GREAT DEPRESSION

Year	Unemployed (in thousands)	Unemployed (percent of labor force)	Emergency Workers (in thousands)	Emergency Workers (percent of labor force)
1929	1,550	3.2%	0	0.00%
1930	4,320	8.7	20	0.04
1931	7,721	15.3	299	0.6
1932	11,468	22.5	592	1.2
1933	10,635	20.6	2,195	4.3
1934	8,366	16.0	2,974	5.7
1935	7,523	14.2	3,087	5.8
1936	5,286	9.9	3,744	7.0
1937	4,937	9.1	2,763	5.1
1938	6,799	12.5	3,591	6.6
1939	6,225	11.3	3,255	5.9
1940	5,290	9.5	2,830	5.1
1941	3,351	6.0	2,209	3.9
1942	1,746	3.1	914	1.6
1943	985	1.8	85	0.2

SOURCE: MICHAEL DARBY, "THREE AND A HALF MILLION U.S. EMPLOYEES HAVE BEEN MISLAID: OR, AN EXPLANATION OF UNEMPLOYMENT, 1934–1941," *JOURNAL OF POLITICAL ECONOMY* 84 (1976): 7, 8.

The New Deal did not merely supply temporary relief. It reformed the economic system to try to prevent a recurrence of depression and to redress the imbalance between rich and poor that had existed even before the contraction.

Reform of the financial system was an obvious and popular place to start. One of the first pieces of New Deal legislation was the Truth-in-Securities Act of 1933, which required issuers of new securities to register them with the Federal Trade Commission. Later this power, along with far more general regulatory authority, was transferred to the newly created Securities and Exchange Commission (SEC). The power to set margin requirements on stock purchases, however, was given to the Fed. The stock market boom had been attributed, in part, to the buying of stock on margin with very little money down. The Fed had argued that its inability to stop the boom in time to prevent a collapse was due to the lack of an instrument aimed directly at the stock market.

Inevitably, much of this legislation was based on ill-conceived theories of what caused the depression and on the pleadings of special interests. The prohibition of interest payments on bank deposits is an example. Until the 1930s, commercial banks had been free to compete for deposits by offering to pay interest on them. But many bankers argued that this forced them to take unnecessary risks in order to maintain their deposits. It is not hard to see why Congress responded to this argument during the Great Depression by prohibiting interest payments on checking accounts. But the long-run effect of this legislation was simply to help some less-competitive banks maintain their share of the market at the expense of consumers.

A fundamental readjustment of the industrial wage and price structure was attempted with the National Industrial Recovery Act (NIRA). The chief purposes of the act were to raise prices and wages, spread out work by reducing hours, and prevent price cutting by competitors trying to maintain volume. A National Recovery Administration (NRA), under the direction of General Hugh Johnson, supervised the preparation of a "code of fair practice" for each industry. Deputy administrators, presumably assisted by representatives of employers, labor, and consumers, prepared the codes,

Roosevelt's broad grin, in evidence above, center, at the 1936 Democratic convention, made his theme song, "Happy Days Are Here Again," believable to a shaken nation. His charm and buoyancy did much in itself to soften the Great Depression's psychological impact.

which were really agreements among sellers to set minimum prices, limit output, and establish minimum wages and maximum hours of work. Pending the approval of basic codes, the President issued a "blanket code" in July 1933. Sellers signing the blanket code agreed to raise wages, shorten the maximum work week, and abstain from price cutting. In return, they could display a "blue eagle" and avoid being boycotted for not doing their part. By 1935, 557 basic codes had been approved. In practice, labor representatives participated in the construction of fewer than 10 percent of the codes, and consumer representation was negligible. Employer representatives found it convenient to work through their national trade associations and manufacturers' institutes, with the consequence that prices were set with a view toward profit maximization in the manner of a European cartel. The possibility of such an outcome was recognized in the NIRA by suspending the antitrust laws.

The effectiveness of the NIRA and other New Deal measures, especially in the early phase of development, will forever be debated. For the most part, however, they

Agricultural poverty sent thousands fleeing from the Midwest to California, with belongings piled in the family jalopy. A nation that "drove to the poor house in an automobile," as Will Rogers said, had to change some of its babies' diapers on the miserable highways of the time.

redistributed rather than expanded incomes. Manufacturing output jumped after the institution of the NRA, as merchants added to their inventories in anticipation of price increases. But industrial production lapsed again, and by mid-summer of 1935 the index was no higher than it had been after the first NRA spurt. Unemployment, although reduced, was still incredibly high, and most manufacturing firms were operating at far less than capacity.

Early in 1935, there was a growing awareness that the lift the economy had experienced had come chiefly from income injections via deficit spending and money creation. It was with little regret, then, that New Dealers saw the passing of the NRA, which was declared unconstitutional by the Supreme Court—in *Schecter Poultry Corp. v. United States,* affectionately known as the "sick chicken case"—on the grounds that Congress had illegally delegated legislative powers to the President.

THE TENNESSEE VALLEY AUTHORITY

A more conventional approach to the depression was the construction of large-scale public works through a variety of agencies. The most ambitious and controversial of all the New Deal public works was the Tennessee Valley Authority (TVA). This was a multifaceted project designed to promote economic development in a large region that had been poverty-stricken for decades. The TVA built dams in a seven-state area (see Map 24-1), supplied low-cost electric power to farmers (a policy that created considerable opposition from private power companies), engaged in flood control, created inland navigation routes, and promoted farmer education and related projects.

Any judgment about the overall effect of the TVA would be hotly debated, but there is agreement that in the area of conservation it has been a success. First, major floods are a thing of the past in the Tennessee Valley; this means that much of the bottom land in the valley is protected from the periodic dumping of erosion debris. Second, the TVA has done much to prevent upland erosion. Although a unified system of dams and reservoirs can prevent *major* floods and their consequent destruction of bottom land, the problem of erosion on the uplands remains. Silting from the uplands is the enemy of the reservoirs and the navigable channel; it must be stopped at the source—where the raindrop strikes the ground. Thus, TVA authorities have had no choice but to work hard to secure the general adoption of conservation practices. Their program includes reforestation and afforestation, the substitution of cover crops for row crops, contour plowing, and the building of check dams to prevent rapid runoff. Technical assistance and demonstration, in cooperation with other federal agencies and with state universities, has been the chief help to the landowner, but free seedlings and fertilizers have frequently swung the balance in securing the farmers' cooperation.

AGRICULTURE AND THE NEW DEAL

It is worth considering the case of agriculture in detail, because it illustrates clearly the strengths and weaknesses of the New Deal. With the onset of the Great Depression, farm people began to suffer a severity of economic distress that only a few old-timers

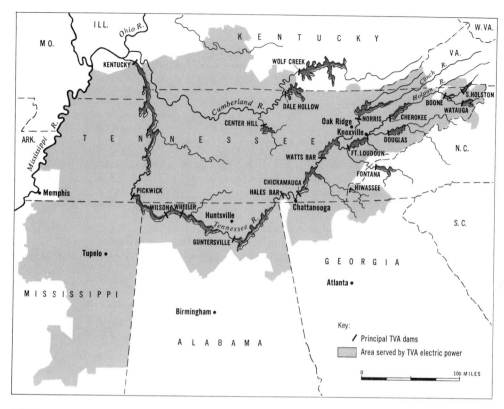

MAP 24-1 PUBLIC POWER: *The Tennessee Valley Authority—the New Deal's major experiment in publicly financed power—ranges through portions of seven states. Its supporters call the TVA a splendid monument to "regional planning"; its foes denounce it as a noxious example of "creeping socialism."*

would have believed possible. Yet in many ways the rural communities, which had suffered through hardship and waves of bank failures in the 1920s, were perhaps the best prepared psychologically for the crisis.

The first signs of depression reality came with the downturn and then tumble of agricultural prices. In three years the average price of corn at central markets fell from $0.77 to $0.19 per bushel, and the average price of wheat dropped from $1.08 to $0.33 per bushel. At many local elevators, the selling point for farmers, 10-cent corn and 25-cent wheat were common, and 5-cent cotton similarly burdened southern planters. From an overall farm price index of 147 in January 1930, there was a drop to 57 in February 1933 (1909–1914 = 100).

Gross farm income, which had reached a postwar high of almost $14 billion in 1929, slipped to $11 billion in 1930 and fell drastically to about $6.5 billion in 1932. Production expenses also declined during these years, but gross income fell more. In 1932 net realized income in agriculture was less than one-third of what it had been in 1929; indeed, it was only one-half of that recorded in the exceptionally bad year of 1921.

Farmers with fixed indebtedness were particularly hard hit: in 1932, 52 percent of all farm debts (45 percent of all farm debtors) were in default. The threat of foreclosure reached an all-time high and marred the lives of rural people everywhere. From the previous record high level of 17 farm foreclosures per thousand farms in 1926 (14.9 in 1929), foreclosures jumped to 18.0 per thousand farms in 1930 and 27.8 per thousand in 1931, finally peaking at 38.1 per thousand in 1932.[1] Many states responded with moratoriums on foreclosures.

Most devices to help farmers in earlier years had centered on the notion of price parity or "fair exchange" values, as Senator George Norris had called them. Most acceptable to politicians had been the traditional devices of high tariffs, and high duties were imposed with the Smoot-Hawley Act of 1929. Far more important, however, was the passage of the Agricultural Marketing Act of 1929, which was the outcome of Republican campaign promises of 1928. This pre-depression law committed the government to a policy of farm price stabilization and established a Federal Farm Board to encourage the formation of cooperative marketing associations. The board was also authorized to establish "stabilization corporations" to be owned by the cooperatives and to use an initial fund of $500 million for price-support operations.

With the onset of serious depression in 1930, the Federal Farm Board strove valiantly to support farm prices, but between June 1929 and June 1932 the board's corporations bought surplus farm products only to suffer steadily increasing losses as prices continued to decline. The board itself took over the operation and accepted the losses, expending in three years some $676 million in stabilization operations and loans to cooperatives. While all this was going on, however, farmers faced with catastrophically falling prices increased output. At the time it seemed that prices could not be supported in a sustained fashion without production controls.

THE CRYSTALLIZATION OF A FARM POLICY, 1933–1941

By the date of Franklin D. Roosevelt's inauguration, theories about farm policy had undergone fundamental changes. Proponents of dumping American farm products abroad were successful in securing the dollar devaluation of 1933 and 1934, which made dollars cheaper in terms of foreign currencies and thereby stimulated demand for U.S. commodities traded in world markets. But this solution to the farmers' dilemma was not satisfactory either, because the worldwide depression was accompanied by extremely low world prices, and other countries devalued their currencies, too. American policymakers wished to devise a plan to raise farm prices substantially in the home market. It soon became clear that supports through purchases and loans, like those attempted by the Federal Farm Board, would require enormous outlays. Consequently, a scheme evolved that took the central idea of the domestic-allotment plan, a plan that had been widely discussed in the 1920s.

The Agricultural Adjustment Act, passed in May 1933, provided for an Agricultural Adjustment Administration, the AAA, which was given the responsibility of raising

---

[1] H. Thomas Johnson, "Postwar Optimism and the Rural Financial Crisis of the 1920s," *Explorations in Economic History* 11 (Winter 1973–1974): 176.

farm prices by restricting the supply of farm commodities. The most important weapon of the AAA was the "acreage allotment." The AAA would determine a total acreage of certain major crops to be planted in the next growing season. The total acreage would then be subdivided into state totals, which were in turn to be allotted to individual farms on the basis of each farm's recent crop history. For example, the base acreage for each wheat farm was to be the average acreage in wheat from 1928 to 1932. To secure the cooperation of the individual farmer, a direct "benefit payment," later called an "adjustment payment," was made. The payment was made by check from the federal Treasury, but in these early New Deal days it still seemed a little too much to expect the general taxpayer to foot the bill—at least directly. The benefit payments were financed, therefore, by processing taxes paid by the first processor of any product (millers, for example, had to pay a tax for each bushel of wheat that was ground into flour), although it was assumed that the processing tax would be shifted forward and be paid by the consumer.

The original AAA scheme experienced a setback in 1936 when the Supreme Court, in the Hoosac Mills case, declared the Agricultural Adjustment Act unconstitutional because it attempted to regulate agricultural production—a power reserved to the states. The adverse decision did not force a discontinuance of acreage allotments, but only changed the *basis* on which these allotments were made to one that presumably encouraged soil conservation.

The drought of 1936, with its attendant dust-bowl conditions, provided the needed loophole, focused attention on the need for vigorous soil-conservation measures, and prompted passage of the Soil Conservation and Domestic Allotment Act of that year.[2] Under this act, the Secretary of Agriculture could offer to make benefit payments to anyone who would reduce acreage of soil-depleting crops and take steps to conserve or rebuild the land withheld from production. But production in 1937 was very high, and there was pressure to supplement acreage reduction with even more vigorous measures.

In 1938 Congress passed a new Agricultural Adjustment Act, which placed more emphasis on giving direct support to prices. Since 1933, the Commodity Credit Corporation (CCC) had operated as an independent agency, performing the minor function of "cushioning" the prices of corn, wheat, and cotton by making loans to farmers on the security of their crops. Most of these loans were made "without recourse." Nonrecourse loans were a heads-you-win, tails-I-lose proposition. If the CCC extended an advance against a commodity and the price of that commodity fell, the farmer could let the CCC take title to the stored product and cancel the debt together with the accumulated interest. If the price of the commodity rose, the farmer could sell the commodity, pay back the loan with interest, and keep any profit. Thus, loan rates became, in effect, minimum prices.

The Agricultural Adjustment Act of 1938 greatly increased the power of the CCC by making it mandatory that the directors extend loans on corn, wheat, and cotton at

---

[2] The migration of the "Okies" from the dust bowl of the Midwest to California is eloquently described by John Steinbeck in *The Grapes of Wrath*. A superb 1940 movie based on the novel stars Jane Darwell and Henry Fonda.

Adding to the farmer's woes during the depressed 1930s were several years of unprecedented heat and drought. The subsequent blowing of previously eroded land created dust storms like this one in the Texas panhandle.

favorable rates. From this point on, Congress was to specify support prices at a certain percentage of parity prices, parity prices being defined as farm prices adjusted to have the same purchasing power as those prevailing in a favorable base period. In 1938 and for many years thereafter, the base period for most products was 1910–1914, a time when farm prices relative to other prices were exceptionally high.

From 1939 to 1941, the CCC accumulated great quantities of wheat, corn, cotton, and tobacco. Strengthened demand following the outbreak of World War II enabled the government to sell these stocks at a profit, but large holdings of wheat were stored into the war years, and vast amounts of low-grade, short-staple cotton were not disposed of until even later.

Two other means of restricting the supply of farm products came into use during the 1930s. One of these, the *marketing agreement,* became important in the production of certain fruits and vegetables and in the chief milk areas. Marketing agreements are contracts between an association of producers of a raw product and the processors of that product; the contractual agreement is reviewed by a Department of Agriculture representative. Producers and processors may set minimum prices, total quantities to be marketed, and allotments of marketings among processors. Milk producers and the city milk companies, in addition to controlling the amounts of milk marketed, have made a profitable enterprise of establishing different prices in different markets for milk uses with different elasticities of demand—that is, by becoming discriminating monopolists.

Marketing quotas became important after 1936, when Congress empowered the Secretary of Agriculture to set an upper limit to the quantities that growers of certain crops could sell. Before such controls could be instituted, the Secretary had to determine that the current supply of a basic commodity exceeded a "reserve supply." A referendum was then held, and if two-thirds of the qualified producers approved, a quota was assigned to each grower. Any farmer who marketed amounts in excess of the quota was subject to a fine on the excess sold.

The Roosevelt administration also introduced a number of "surplus removal" programs. The more acceptable operations have been the nutrition or direct-distribution programs. Nutrition programs have taken the form of food-stamp plans, low-cost milk distribution plans, and school lunch programs. The Food Stamp Plan, in operation from 1939 to 1942, won enthusiastic support.[3] Stamps given to low-income families were (and indeed, still are) used to purchase food from regular retail outlets. Thus, surplus commodities were given to those who presumably had the greatest need for them. In addition to using up the excess stocks, they helped offset the effect on the poor of artificially high prices created by the crop restrictions.

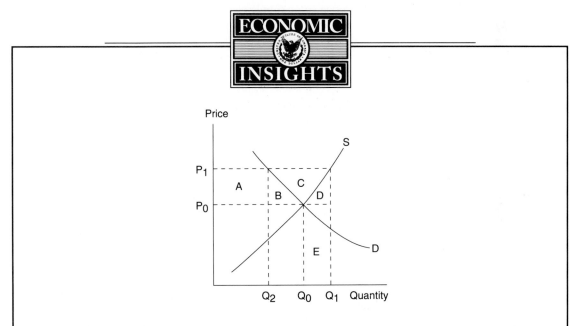

The figure above illustrates the effects of CCC price supports. In the absence of government intervention, the price would be P_0 and the quantity produced Q_0. Intervention raises the price to P_1 and the quantity produced to Q_1. The higher price reduces consumption to Q_2 and leads to the accumulation of $Q_1 - Q_2$ stocks by the government. Farm incomes (net of production costs) are raised by the sum of areas $A+B+C$. Area $D+E$ is also paid to farmers, but this amount simply covers increased production costs; this may be considered socially desirable since it may, in part, reflect

---

[3] In 1961, advocates finally secured reactivation of this program. The fiscal 1971 appropriation for the national food-stamp program was just over $1.4 billion. In 1989, the food-stamp program costs were about $13.6 billion, about $55 per capita.

higher wages for farm labor. Area A is paid directly by consumers in the form of higher prices. B+C are paid by consumers indirectly through taxes. Total expenditures by the government are $(Q_1-Q_2)\times P_1$. The change in expenditures by consumers is $(Q_2\times P_1)-(Q_0\times P_0)$. (Whether consumers spend more or less than before depends on the elasticity of demand.)

There are a number of losses associated with this program. First, the resources used to produce Q_1-Q_2 are wasted. Storage costs for the surplus (not shown) are also incurred. Second, consumers are deprived of farm products that they value more than the costs of production. Their loss on this account is measured by area B. The attempt to minimize these losses then leads to other programs described in the text: production quotas, surplus removal programs, and export subsidies.

Economists often recommend direct income supplements to farmers combined with a free market in agricultural products as a way of helping farmers without incurring these losses. For a number of reasons, however, farmers usually prefer price supports. Three are worth noting: (1) Direct income supplements may be viewed as demeaning. (2) Direct income supplements may go mostly to poor farmers, and are therefore opposed by rich and influential farmers. (3) Direct income supplements tend to remain fixed over time. The subsidy delivered through price supports may grow as technological advances lower production costs.

Another type of surplus removal operation has been the *export subsidy*. This method of increasing the sales of farm commodities originated with the Agricultural Adjustment Act of 1933, but not until the passage of an amendment in 1935 (commonly referred to as Section 32) did sales become significant. In that year, the amendment provided that as much as 30 percent of annual customs revenues might be used to finance the disposal of farm surpluses at home and abroad. The subsidization of exports by payments of bounties did not reach alarming proportions before World War II.[4] In the fiscal year 1939, bounties for wheat and cotton amounted to $26 million and $38 million, respectively. In the postwar period, however, expenditure of public funds on export subsidies would become an effective, if somewhat dubious, means of adding to American farm income. This kind of interference with international trade can be defended on the grounds that it offers the rest of the world an enhancement of real income. But it adversely affects the income and marketing positions of producers of competing commodities.

THE IMPACT ON FARMERS

The price-support programs and other New Deal legislation in agriculture succeeded in improving the relative price and income positions of farmers. Farm prices began to rise in April 1933, more than doubling and ultimately climbing to an index

---

[4]For further details, see D. Gale Johnson, *Trade and Agriculture* (New York: Wiley, 1950).

of 131 early in 1937. The recession of 1937 and 1938 affected the agricultural sector, and the index of farm prices reverted back to 100, where it stood in both the first and last months of 1940. Meanwhile, prices *paid by* farmers recovered somewhat from a 1933 low and then remained almost stable through 1940; because farm prices recovered more than industrial prices, the terms of trade (parity ratio) were definitely improved. From the low of 1932, gross farm income moved steadily upward to $11 billion in 1937, declined slightly for two years, and then rebounded to the $11 billion mark in 1940— about where it had been a decade earlier.

Clearly, Roosevelt's New Deal for farmers was far removed from President Harding's policy advice that "the farmer must be ready to help himself." The most concrete step taken by government was its advance into production controls. To restrict output in agriculture and raise prices on food and fiber when the major national problems were economic depression, massive unemployment, and hunger must certainly be viewed with suspicion if not outright alarm. As with other types of New Deal legislation aimed at helping particular groups, the primary outcome was to redistribute income. Never again, except in temporary short periods, did agricultural production become guided by "free market" forces. The acceptance by the American people of the principle that the government ought to bolster the economic fortunes of particular occupational groups or classes was of momentous importance. Farmers have not been the only beneficiaries of this philosophy; but we cannot find a better example of the way in which legislation, passed at first in an effort to relieve emergency distress, has become accepted as a permanent part of the economic system.

LABOR AND THE NEW DEAL

Besides the advance of government relief agencies, further bonding between government and workers came about as new powers were given to unions. Most important of these were the right to strike and to organize, free of employer interference.

Union membership had declined sharply in the early 1920s, falling from over 5 million in 1920, to 3.5 million in 1923. It remained steady around this level until 1930, when it began falling again before reaching bottom in 1933. By this time, and before the new administration had been in power a year, the more vigorous union leaders sensed that the government would encourage organization and that the attitude of the nation toward unions had changed as people became disillusioned with business. Especially successful in their organizational efforts were the powerful and able leaders of the industrial unions that had evolved within the AFL: John L. Lewis of the United Mine Workers, Sidney Hillman of the Amalgamated Clothing Workers, and David Dubinsky of the International Ladies Garment Workers.

By the mid-1930s, a conflict within the union movement had grown to major proportions. The move to organize the new mass-production industries (steel, automobiles, rubber, and electrical equipment) was inevitable, but the older unions hampered such organization by insisting that their craft jurisdiction remain inviolate and by raiding the membership of the new industrial unions. In 1935, eight industrial unions formed the Committee for Industrial Organization within the AFL, and in 1936 these

TABLE 24-2   UNION MEMBERSHIP, 1930–1955

Year	Number (in thousands)	Percent of Labor Force	Year	Number (in thousands)	Percent of Labor Force
1930	3,401	6.8%	1943	13,213	20.5%
1931	3,310	6.5	1944	14,146	21.4
1932	3,050	6.0	1945	14,322	21.9
1933	2,689	5.2	1946	14,395	23.6
1934	3,088	5.9	1947	14,787	23.9
1935	3,584	6.7	1948	14,300	23.1
1936	3,989	7.4	1949	14,300	22.7
1937	7,001	12.9	1950	14,300	22.3
1938	8,034	14.6	1951	15,900	24.5
1939	8,763	15.8	1952	15,900	24.2
1940	8,717	15.5	1953	16,948	25.5
1941	10,201	17.7	1954	17,022	25.4
1942	10,380	17.2	1955	16,802	24.7

SOURCE: *HISTORICAL STATISTICS* (WASHINGTON, D.C.: GOVERNMENT PRINTING OFFICE, 1975), P. 178, SERIES D948–949.

unions were suspended from the federation. Three years later, the CIO became a separate entity, the Congress of Industrial Organizations.

Conflict continued between these two great federations throughout the 1930s. CIO leaders made no secret of their contempt for the AFL's lack of militancy and its failure to participate aggressively in political activities, and AFL leaders viewed the CIO's violent break with conservative unionism with concern. But complacency and inertia no longer beset the labor movement.[5]

As shown in Table 24-2, union membership increased rapidly in the 1930s. The new pro-labor attitude of government clearly revealed in the labor legislation of the New Deal, played an important role. Between 1930 and 1939 union membership increased from 6.8 to 15.8 percent of the labor force.

THE NORRIS-LaGUARDIA ACT

Except for legislation that applied only to the railroad industry, Congress had refused to interfere by statute with labor relations until 1932. The Norris-LaGuardia Act of 1932, however, created a first step toward removing the barriers to free organization. Largely procedural in character, the act had the effect of eliminating or modifying the worst abuses of the labor injunction. The yellow-dog contract (an agreement not to join a union) was eliminated by making it nonenforceable in the federal courts, and the issuance of injunctions was greatly restricted. Moreover, boycotting and pick-

---

[5] In 1955, the AFL and the CIO, prodded into unity by hostile public opinion and primitive labor legislation, merged to form the AFL-CIO. Roughly 50 percent of the total membership was in AFL affiliates, 30 percent in CIO unions, and the remainder in unaffiliated unions.

eting by nonemployees was permitted. The act granted to workers the opportunity to organize but did not positively intercede to assure that they could secure the benefits of collective bargaining.

The first positive assertion of the right of labor to bargain collectively was contained in Section 7a of the National Industrial Recovery Act, but no means of enforcing the statement of principle were provided. Two years later, when the NIRA was declared unconstitutional, Congress replaced Section 7a with a much more elaborate law of labor relations. This was the National Labor Relations Act, usually called the Wagner Act after its sponsor, Senator Robert F. Wagner of New York.

THE WAGNER ACT

The Wagner Act proceeded from the explicit premises that inequality of bargaining power between employees and large business units depresses "the purchasing power of wage earners in industry" and prevents "stabilization of competitive wage rates and working conditions," and that denial of the right to self-organization creates industrial strife. The act established the principle of collective bargaining as the cornerstone of industrial relations and stated that it was management's obligation to recognize and deal with a bona fide labor organization in good faith. The act further guaranteed workers the right to form and join a labor organization, to engage in collective bargaining, to select representatives of their own choosing, and to engage in concerted activity. In addition, the Wagner Act outlawed a list of "unfair" managerial practices. Henceforth, employers could *not:*

1. Interfere with, restrain, or coerce employees in the exercise of their rights of self-organization and collective bargaining.

2. Dominate or interfere with the formation or administration of any labor organization or contribute financial or other support to it.

3. Encourage or discourage union membership by discrimination in regard to hiring or tenure of employment or condition of work, except such discrimination as might be involved in a closed-shop agreement with a bona fide union enjoying majority status.

4. Discharge or otherwise discriminate against an employee for filing charges or testifying under the act.

5. Refuse to bargain collectively.

The Wagner Act was no mere statement of principles. It established a National Labor Relations Board (NLRB) with genuine powers of enforcement. After hearings regarding a union complaint, the board could issue cease-and-desist orders to employers who were judged guilty of unfair labor practices. If employers did not comply with these orders, the NLRB could turn to a U.S. Circuit Court of Appeals for enforcement. The board also had the power, on its own initiative or at the request of a union, to supervise a free, secret election among a company's employees to determine which union, if any, should represent the workers.

When the Supreme Court declared the Wagner Act constitutional in 1937, there were no remaining barriers to the rapid organization of labor. But before the question of constitutionality was settled, many employers openly violated the act, producing increasing turbulence in labor relations. Animosity between the suspended CIO unions and the AFL grew, leading to jurisdictional conflicts that the NLRB had to spend much time settling. As industrial strife seemed to be increasing rather than decreasing, there were public demands for amendments to the act, and employers complained bitterly of the one-sidedness of the law. From labor's view, however, the Wagner Act was its Magna Carta.

The Wagner Act was never intended to be a comprehensive code of labor relations. It did not even define "collective bargaining," nor did it cover the problems of jurisdictional disputes, "national emergency" disputes, or secondary boycotts. If World War II had not intervened, basic amendments to the act would doubtless have been made sooner, but the war placed the national problem of labor relations on hold.

THE FAIR LABOR STANDARDS ACT

The Fair Labor Standards Act of 1938, which replaced and extended provisions of the National Industrial Recovery Act, was the beginning of federal regulation of the workplace. The law, among other provisions intended to protect labor, set a minimum wage of \$.25 per hour (scheduled to rise eventually to \$.40—average hourly earnings in manufacturing were then about \$.62 per hour), fixed a maximum work week of 44 hours (scheduled to fall to 40) with extra pay for overtime work, and prohibited the employment of children under 16 years old. The Wages and Hours Division of the Department of Labor was created to enforce the act. Agriculture was exempt, and other exemptions reduced the share of nonagricultural workers initially covered by the law to about 44 percent. The goal was to protect workers and to increase employment of heads of households. It was hoped, for example, that requiring extra pay for overtime would encourage firms to hire more workers at the 44-hour rate.

Any assessment of the direct effects of even individual provisions of the act would be controversial. The minimum wage provision, for example, has been criticized for increasing unemployment among low-skilled workers; even today economists have not reached agreement on the employment effects of the minimum wage law. What is clear is that the law left an enduring imprint on the institutional structure of the labor market and created a presumption that the federal government would help to set the terms and conditions of work.

FURTHER QUESTS FOR SECURITY

Before 1932, loss of income from any cause other than industrial accident posed a great hardship, because workers had no economic protection except the buffer of their savings, help from friends and relatives, help from organized charity, and payments from the relief agencies of states and their subdivisions. The burden of relief during the

Great Depression overwhelmed charitable organizations and local government units, and the federal government, largely through the WPA and other emergency agencies, took over the job. This experience with federal relief convinced the majority of Americans, on both economic and ethical grounds, of the necessity of a permanent plan for coping with severe losses in income.

A few leaders in government, business, and academia had long argued that a comprehensive program of social security was requisite to the adequate functioning of a modern industrial economy. Such programs had long been common in Europe. Yet as late as 1930, there was little public sentiment in favor of social security legislation. Americans believed that the individual ought to be self-reliant and objected to compulsory supportive action by the government. In agriculture, where the need for social insurance was not so pronounced, there was understandable opposition to additional taxes for such insurance. The astonishing fact is that organized labor itself did not support social insurance (except worker compensation) before the Great Depression: as late as 1931, a national AFL convention refused to endorse unemployment-insurance legislation. Not inconsequential opposition was also voiced by private insurance companies, which sought to prevent, or at least modify, government insurance of social risks.

Four years of economic disaster removed all serious obstacles to major legislation. Whatever the philosophical objection to a social security program may have been, certain hard facts of life were undeniable. Almost four out of every five income receivers depended on paid employment for their livelihood. There were many hazards to continuity of income, some of which seemed to be increasing in severity as the economy became more specialized. Income interruptions included being laid off, getting sick, being injured on the job, and becoming too old to meet the demands of modern industrial life. Finally, the incidence of income interruptions, although uncertain and uneven, fell most heavily on low-income people, who were the least able to prepare for them.

THE SOCIAL SECURITY ACT OF 1935

The Social Security Act of 1935 provided for a federal old-age and survivors' insurance program based on payments from workers of 1 percent of earnings up to $3,600, with the employers paying an equal share.[6] It further provided for *assistance* to the needy aged, needy and dependent children, and needy blind. Subsequent amendments have added other groups.

Under continuing pressure for ever-higher employee benefits, Congress has further increased substantially both individual and employer contributions and benefits. This

---

[6] It should be emphasized that the premium payment by the employer is part of the wage cost to the employer. Therefore, this results in a lower wage being paid to the worker. It is an unfortunate but common misconception that the employer pays half the premiums; actually, the worker pays almost the entire amount. It is also important to understand that these payments are not saved or placed in a fund. Rather, they are promptly spent by those receiving Social Security checks.

fact reflects its strong appeal to Americans generally and to those who remember when social insurance first emancipated millions of workers from the fear of one day being "on the county."

The program of unemployment insurance was less extensive in its aim than Social Security, but it has been a powerful short-run help to discharged workers. Largely to circumvent legal difficulties, unemployment insurance is provided through state systems. The Social Security Act of 1935 secured state action by levying a 3-percent tax on the first $3,000 of wages paid by employers in all except a few business occupations. Similar to changes in Social Security, recent trends have been to make unemployment insurance laws more liberal—partly in recognition of the fact that unemployment compensation is a highly dependable automatic stabilizer. This automatic stabilizing effect occurs through the timely increase in unemployment compensation payments when unemployment increases. This lowers the fall in income and expenditures of displaced workers, thereby helping to stabilize the economy "automatically."

THE LEGACY OF THE NEW DEAL

The New Deal, as we have seen, was a mélange of (sometimes conflicting) programs, some aimed at relieving distress, others aimed at preventing a recurrence of the Great Depression. In retrospect it might have done better had it aimed at maximizing the aggregate monetary and fiscal stimulus and paid less attention to reforming individual markets. But in any case, the New Deal left an indelible imprint. First, it created a wide array of institutions and programs that continue to regulate our economic life: the Securities and Exchange Commission, the Federal Deposit Insurance Corporation, the Employment Standards Administration within the Department of Labor, Social Security, and so on. Second, it created an idealistic spirit among young New Dealers that would bear fruit in the form of additional legislation passed during the Kennedy-Johnson years. Third, it created the presumption that people could look to Washington for solutions to their economic difficulties. True, people had often turned to Washington for help before 1929: to reduce foreign competition, to subsidize railroad construction, to relieve the victims of fire, and so on. But all potential reforms had to overcome the presumption that the existing political and economic institutions, including the free market, were fundamentally sound. The Great Depression and the New Deal reversed, or at least distributed more evenly, the burden of proof. Now it was up to defenders of the status quo to show that market forces could solve a problem to which the attention of the public had been drawn. The fourth and perhaps most important legacy of the New Deal is, paradoxically, what it did not do: it did not try to overthrow capitalism. With the nation in turmoil and its economy in ruins, socialism or at least widespread nationalization of commerce and industry might have been instituted in 1933. But the basic instinct of the New Deal was to reform and preserve the system. Americans like to think of themselves as good poker players. In 1932 they did not want to stop playing, they just wanted to change the rules a bit, and to get a New Deal.

SELECTED REFERENCES
AND SUGGESTED READINGS

Allen, Frederick Lewis. *Since Yesterday: The Nineteen Thirties in America.* New York: Harper & Brothers, 1940.

Alston, Lee J. "Farm Foreclosures in the United States during the Interwar Period." *Journal of Economic History* 43 (1983): 885–903.

_____. "Farm Foreclosure Moratorium Legislation: A Lesson from the Past." *American Economic Review* 74 (1984): 445–457.

Bernstein, Michael. *The Great Depression: Delayed Recovery and Economic Change in America.* New York: Cambridge University Press, 1988.

_____. "A Reassessment of Investment Failure in the Interwar American Economy." *Journal of Economic History* 44 (1984): 479–488.

Brunner, Karl, ed. *The Great Depression Revisited.* Boston: Martinus Nijhoff, 1981.

Chandler, Lester V. *America's Greatest Depression, 1929–1941.* New York: Harper & Row, 1970.

Darby, Michael. "Three and a Half Million U.S. Employees Have Been Mislaid: Or, an Explanation of Unemployment, 1934–1941." *Journal of Political Economy* 84 (February 1976): 1–16.

Hawley, Ellis W. *The New Deal and the Problem of Monopoly: A Study in Economic Ambivalence.* Princeton: Princeton University Press, 1966.

Higgs, Robert. *Crisis and Leviathan: Critical Episodes in the Growth of American Government.* New York: Oxford University Press, 1987, Chapter 8.

Jones, Jesse H. *Fifty Billion Dollars: My Thirteen Years with the RFC.* New York: Macmillan, 1951.

Kindleberger, Charles P. *The World in Depression 1929–1939.* Berkeley: University of California Press, 1973.

Leuchtenberg, William E. *Franklin D. Roosevelt and the New Deal, 1932–1940.* New York: Harper Colophon Books, 1963.

_____. "The New Deal and the Analogue of War." In *Change and Continuity in Twentieth Century America,* eds. John Braeman, Robert H. Bremner, and Everett Walters. Columbus: Ohio State University Press, 1964.

Margo, Robert. "The Microeconomics of Depression Unemployment." *Journal of Economic History* 51 (June 1991): 333–342.

Mitchell, Broadus. *Depression Decade: From New Era through New Deal, 1929–1941.* New York: Harper Torchbooks, 1969.

Reading, Don. "New Deal Activity and the States, 1933 to 1939." *Journal of Economic History* 33 (1973): 792–810.

Smiley, Gene. "Recent Unemployment Rate Estimates for the 1920s and 1930s." *Journal of Economic History* 43 (1983): 487–493.

Wallis, John Joseph. "The Birth of the Old Federalism: Financing the New Deal, 1932–1940." *Journal of Economic History* 44 (1984): 139–159.

Wallis, John Joseph, and Daniel K. Benjamin. "Public Relief and Private Employment in the Great Depression." *Journal of Economic History* 41 (1981): 97–102.

Walton, Gary M., ed. *Regulatory Change in an Atmosphere of Crisis: Current Implications of the Roosevelt Years.* New York: Academic Press, 1979.

Weinstein, Michael M. "Some Macroeconomic Impacts of the National Industrial Recovery Act, 1933–1935." In *The Great Depression Revisited,* ed. Karl Brunner. Boston: Martinus Nijhoff, 1981.

Wright, Gavin. "The Political Economy of New Deal Spending: An Econometric Analysis." *Review of Economics and Statistics* 56 (1974): 30–38.

CHAPTER TWENTY-FIVE

WORLD WAR II

CHAPTER THEME Just 21 years after the end of World War I, the world was once more engulfed in war. America's goal was to supply the arms necessary to defeat the Axis (Germany, Japan, and their allies), to become, as contemporaries put it, the "Arsenal of Democracy." This goal was achieved brilliantly. In a few short years the factories of the United States were turning out more weapons than any other nation and more than all the Axis powers combined, even though the Axis had begun converting to a war footing years before the United States.

In the short run, the war effort alleviated the need for many of the New Deal's emergency measures. Work relief was no longer necessary because the nation's factories were humming at full capacity; emergency funds were no longer needed to bail out firms faced with bankruptcy because profits were surging. In the long run, the war effort reinforced the restructuring of the economy that had taken place in the 1930s. The association of large federal deficits and low unemployment convinced economists, and the public at large, of the effectiveness of Keynes's cure for unemployment. And the government's management of the mobilization convinced economists, and the public at large, that the federal government had the ability to successfully manage large-scale projects.

MOBILIZING FOR WAR[1]

World War II began in September 1939, when German forces attacked Poland. Britain and France, who had guaranteed Poland's independence, then declared war on Germany. In the United States there was a brief surge in industrial production as manufacturers anticipated a repeat of the heady days of 1916, when a neutral America had made enormous profits by supplying a Europe at war. But industrial production sagged during the "phony war," when it appeared that Britain, France, and Germany, although officially at war, would avoid a major clash of arms. The phony war ended in May 1940, when Germany launched a *blitzkrieg* (lightning war) attack against the Low Countries, swept around France's supposedly impenetrable Maginot Line, and conquered France. American manufacturers began building up inventories in anticipation of future shortages, Britain and her remaining allies began placing large orders for American war materials, and the United States launched a vastly expanded program of military procurement.

Initially, Britain was asked to pay for arms on a "cash and carry" basis. It paid by transferring gold and by requisitioning American bank deposits and securities owned by British nationals. (This policy, by the way, stripped Britain of much of its overseas investment.) When these sources of funds began to run out, President Roosevelt succeeded in establishing the Lend-Lease program in March 1941. The term "Lend-Lease" was calculated to deflect attention from the simple fact that the United States government would now be paying for the arms sent to Britain and our other allies.

At first, prices remained relatively stable because there were still millions of unemployed and underemployed American workers and much underutilized industrial capacity. The United States had not yet reached the production possibilities curve, to use the economist's term (see boxed material on page 563). By the autumn of 1940, however, supply had become inelastic in many sectors and wholesale prices had begun to rise. In 1941 the American economy was moving into high gear, despite some pockets of unemployment. Production of steel ingots and castings, for example, had already reached 59.8 million long-tons in 1940, exceeding the previous peak of 56.4 million reached in 1929; in 1941 production reached 74.0 million long-tons. Sulfuric acid, a chemical having a wide variety of industrial applications, was also being produced in unprecedented quantities: 6.8 million short-tons in 1941 compared with 5.3 million in 1929. The Federal Reserve Board's index of industrial production reached a level of 139 in 1941 compared with 100 in 1929.

Although American industry was moving into high gear, many Americans still doubted the wisdom of aid to Britain and its allies. But all doubts vanished on December 7, 1941. To quote President Roosevelt's famous war message:

> Yesterday, December 7, 1941—a date which will live in infamy—the United States of America was suddenly and deliberately attacked by the naval and air forces of the Empire of Japan. . . . The facts of yesterday speak for themselves.

---

[1]The best general survey of the American economy during the war is Harold G. Vatter, *The U.S. Economy in World War II* (New York: Columbia University Press, 1985).

The people of the United States have already formed their opinions and well understand the implications to the very life and safety of our nation.

America was now fully committed to war against the Axis powers (Germany had quickly declared war against the U.S. after the Japanese attack), but many military and economic questions still had to be answered.

Under President Roosevelt's leadership, the United States adopted a bold plan of economic mobilization. America would use its vast industrial might to mass-produce arms and overwhelm the Axis with sheer firepower. Characteristically, President Roosevelt called for the unheard-of total of 50,000 airplanes, although at the time no one knew how such a vast number of planes could be produced. Economic mobilization involved many trade-offs. The most obvious and most important was how far to reduce civilian consumption—the choice, as it was often put, between "guns and butter."[2] America entered the war, as we have noted, with considerable reserves of unemployed resources, so to some extent the nation could divert those resources to the war effort without actually reducing civilian consumption. But as the economy reached full employment, it was possible to achieve further increases in military production only by diverting resources from the civilian sector.

Table 25-1 shows, in very broad terms, how America allocated its resources to the war effort: In 1929, the federal government was spending only a small fraction of GNP, 2.6 percent. Even in 1940, after years of expansion in the role of the federal government under the New Deal, the federal government was spending only about 8.2 percent of

TABLE 25-1   REAL GROSS NATIONAL PRODUCT (IN BILLIONS OF 1982 DOLLARS)

Year	GNP	Total Federal Purchases of Goods and Services	Previous Column as a Percentage of GNP	Total Civilian Purchases of Goods and Services[a]	Previous Column as a Percentage of GNP
1929	$ 709.6	$ 18.3	2.58%	$ 691.30	97.42%
1939	716.6	53.8	7.51	662.80	92.49
1940	772.9	63.6	8.23	709.30	91.77
1941	909.4	153.0	16.82	756.40	83.18
1942	1,080.3	407.1	37.68	673.20	62.32
1943	1,276.2	638.1	50.00	638.10	50.00
1944	1,380.6	722.5	52.33	658.10	47.67
1945	1,354.8	634.0	46.80	720.80	53.20
1946	1,096.9	159.3	14.52	937.60	85.48
1950	1,203.7	116.7	9.70	1,087.00	90.30

SOURCE: *ECONOMIC REPORT OF THE PRESIDENT, 1987* (WASHINGTON, D.C.: GOVERNMENT PRINTING OFFICE, 1987), PP. 246–247.

[a]Includes state and local government spending.

[2]Civilian consumption of butter did fall during the war, but this appears to have been simply part of a long-run trend toward lower consumption. Consumption of ice cream, on the other hand, was higher during the war than it had been before, also part of a long-run trend.

GNP. But the war changed things dramatically. The maximum effort occurred in 1944, when the federal government spent some $722.5 billion (at 1982 prices), about 52.3 percent of total GNP.

Another way of analyzing these figures is also of interest. Between 1940 and 1944, total real federal spending increased by $658.9 billion (722.5 − 63.6), while total real GNP increased by $607.7 billion (1,380.6 − 772.9). Thus 92.2 percent of the increase in military spending (607.7 ÷ 658.9) can be accounted for by the increase in real GNP; only 7.8 percent of the increase had to be offset by a decline in production for the civilian sector. The great bulk of the resources for the war effort were obtained by employing previously unemployed resources and by using already-employed resources more intensively. Remarkably enough, Germany was also able to sustain civilian consumption well into the war, although not throughout. In other countries, though, where the capacity to expand was less, the need to sacrifice current consumption or investment to make available resources for the military effort was correspondingly greater.

INDUSTRIAL SAFETY, PRODUCT QUALITY, AND OTHER QUESTIONS OF WARTIME PRODUCTION

While the decision of how much to reduce civilian consumption and investment was the most important, there were other and more subtle trade-offs involved in wartime economic mobilization. One was in the area of industrial safety. Industrial accidents, often resulting in serious injury or death, increased dramatically during the war. To some extent this was to be expected with so many more men and women working so many more hours in dangerous jobs. But it also appears that the rate at which accidents occurred increased, at least in manufacturing. The official figures show an increase in the number of disabling injuries per million hours worked in manufacturing from 15.3 in 1940 to 20.0 in 1943, the all-time peak.

Should greater efforts have been made to maintain safety? Possibly, but the problem was always one of the trade-off between safety and production. Well-rested workers are safer workers, but more rest breaks may mean lower output. More work space in shipping yards reduces the risk of accidents, but more work space means higher construction costs and fewer resources available to build other facilities.

Another subtle trade-off lay between the quality of arms produced and the quantity. Changing technology and battlefield experience were constantly suggesting modifications of existing weapons. But making these modifications often meant tearing down and rebuilding an assembly line, thereby losing valuable production time. This trade-off was often a bone of contention between military leaders, who would argue for the most sophisticated weapon possible, and the civilians in charge of military production, who were more mindful of the potential loss in production. When Hitler's troops attacked the allied invasion force in the Battle of the Bulge, Germany's tanks, the famous panzers, were as good or better than any tank in the hands of the Allies, but they were vastly outnumbered.

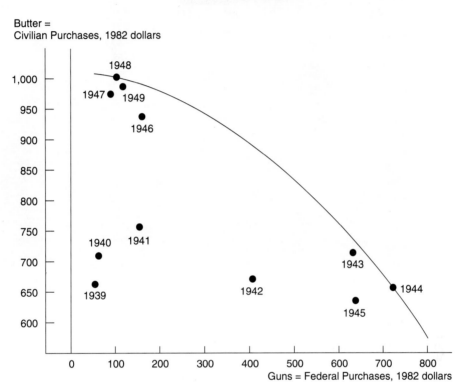

The production possibilities curve shows the trade-off between guns (military spending), measured on the horizontal axis, and butter (civilian spending), measured on the vertical axis. The figure shows the actual combinations of guns and butter produced annually during the war years, and a hypothetical curve drawn through the combinations achieved in 1944 and 1948. Some of the combinations lie inside the production possibilities curve (1939, 1940, 1941, and 1942 in particular); these points indicate that the economy was still operating below its maximum possible output. Thus, in general, the United States increased its war output mainly by moving horizontally toward the production possibilities curve rather than moving along it.

Production of automobiles for civilian use was ended in February 1942. The industry then turned to the mass production of tanks, machine guns, aircraft engines, and other weapons of war, including the jeep, shown here on a Ford assembly line.

On the whole, America's decision to mass-produce the weapons of war turned out to be a brilliant success. America by itself produced more arms than the Axis combined. Not only were supplies such as small arms and ammunition mass-produced, but also planes and even ships to carry the arms to the theaters of war. At Henry Kaiser's shipyards in Portland, Oregon, where some of the most innovative techniques were used, one of the famous Liberty ships was produced in a record eight days. To some extent, as Henry A. Gemery and Jan S. Hogendorn have shown, mass-production techniques were even used in producing destroyers.[3]

Table 25-2 shows the annual production of munitions (cumulatively for 1933–1939) by the five major powers. The United States lagged behind Germany through 1941, but surged past in 1942. Despite surprisingly successful efforts by Germany and Japan to increase their production in the face of heavy naval and air attacks, the final outcome was not in doubt.

Several agencies, the most important being the War Production Board, worked to manage the vast expansion of munitions production. One tool was the priority, essen-

[3] Henry A. Gemery and Jan S. Hogendorn, "The Microeconomic Bases of Short-Run Learning Curves: Destroyer Production in World War II," in *The Sinews of War: Essays on the Economic History of World War II*, eds. Geofrey Mills and Hugh Rockoff (Ames: Iowa State University Press, 1993).

The Liberty ship, mass produced during World War II, helped the United States multiply the total tonnage of its merchant marine fleet by a factor of five.

tially a rating placed on contracts to guide manufacturers in scheduling production. But so rapid was the reallocation of resources, and so huge was the volume of new contracts—at one point the total value of outstanding contracts was said to exceed the gross national product—that munitions production was reaching its peak when the War Production Board finally solved the problems such as "priority inflation" (too

TABLE 25-2 COMBAT MUNITIONS PRODUCED BY THE MAJOR BELLIGERENTS (IN BILLIONS OF DOLLARS AT 1944 U.S. MUNITIONS PRICES)

	1933–1939	1940	1941	1942	1943	1944
U.S.	1.5	1.5	4.5	20	38	42
U.K.	2.5	3.5	6.5	9	11	11
U.S.S.R.	8	5	8.5	11.5	14	16
Germany	12	6	6	8.5	13.5	17
Japan	2	1	2	3	4.5	6

SOURCE: MARK HARRISON, "RESOURCE MOBILIZATION FOR WORLD WAR II: THE U.S.A., U.K., U.S.S.R., AND GERMANY, 1938–1945," *ECONOMIC HISTORY REVIEW* 41 (1988): 172.

When the war began, the United States was producing only small amounts of synthetic rubber for specialty uses. By 1944, plants like this one in Baton Rouge assured the nation an adequate supply.

many contracts having the highest priority) that had developed soon after mobilization began. In the end it was the profit motive that was the primary allocator of resources.[4]

MONETARY AND FISCAL POLICY

There are, as noted in previous chapters, four basic ways to obtain the resources needed to fight a major war: (1) simply confiscating the resources, (2) taxing income or wealth, (3) borrowing, and (4) printing money. In World War II, the U.S. government relied on all four. The draft was the most important example of confiscation. A draft is analogous to a tax, the tax being the difference between what a soldier would need in pay to serve voluntarily and what he is actually paid.

The government also relied on more conventional forms of taxation. Indeed, it financed a larger part of the war effort through taxation than it had during the Civil War or World War I. The income tax was radically changed by the war. The exemption for single persons was lowered from $750 to $500, and the exemption for married persons was lowered from $1,500 to $1,200. Inflation, moreover, was proceeding apace, so the exemptions measured in real terms (divided by the price level) were falling even faster. These steps meant that many more low-income workers owed income tax for the first time. In 1943 the payroll deduction system for collecting income taxes was

---

[4] See Robert Higgs, "Private Profit, Public Risk: Institutional Antecedents of the Modern Military Procurement System in the Rearmament Program 1940–1941," in *The Sinews of War*, eds. Geofrey Mills and Hugh Rockoff, on the profitability of wartime contracts and the unfortunate persistence of lavish profits for military contractors after the war.

introduced, and the term "take-home pay" entered the language. Together these innovations meant that the income tax had become a mass tax for the first time. Corporate tax rates were also increased, and an excess profits tax was introduced. (Some scholars have seen increased taxes as the basis of the continued expansion of government after the war. Because the government could now skim off vast amounts of revenue without causing any one group of taxpayers to complain too bitterly, the total amount of spending could be increased.)

Getting Congress to raise taxes is never easy, not even during a major war. Congressmen complained that high tax rates discouraged work, they objected to the distribution of burdens implicit in legislation offered by the Roosevelt administration, and in general they supported only partial financing of the war through increased taxation. The gap between expenditures and tax revenues then had to be covered by selling government bonds. When the war started in 1941, the federal debt stood at $49.0 billion; by 1945, it had reached $258.7 billion. To get a better perspective on the debt, compare it with GNP in 1945: $213.6 billion; the debt had reached 121 percent of the gross national product. This fact is often cited as evidence that an economy can survive a huge debt, and this evidence is highly relevant. For example in 1990 the national debt, although the subject of many dire predictions, was only 44 percent of GNP. This does not mean that the debt created by World War II had no effect on the economy. Work and savings are discouraged when taxes must be kept higher than they would otherwise be in order to pay the interest costs on a large debt. But the point that the United States entered a period of rapid economic growth saddled with a debt much larger relative to GNP than our current debt warns us that some of our fears about the evil consequences of the current debt may be exaggerated.

Conceivably, all of the wartime deficits could have been financed by sales of securities to the general public, but (despite highly publicized war bond drives) it is likely that the interest rates required to market those bonds would have been very high by historical standards. Therefore the Federal Reserve took the extraordinary step of "pegging" the rate of interest on government securities. It accomplished this by pledging to buy government securities whenever their price fell below predetermined support levels.[5]

On the surface, selling bonds to the Federal Reserve seems like a free ride because it minimizes the future interest costs that the government incurs in raising a given sum of money. The fly in the ointment (or rat in the soup, depending on one's view of things) is that the Federal Reserve must create new money to purchase these securities, and this adds to the inflationary pressures facing the economy.

By 1945, about $24.3 billion in bonds were owned by the Federal Reserve system, and some $84.1 billion by commercial banks. During the Civil War, the system by which the government created money had been straightforward: it simply printed greenbacks and spent them. During World Wars I and II, the system was more complex, but the results were similar. Instead of printing paper money, the Federal Reserve enlarged the Treasury's deposit balances. In either case, creating new money added to

---

[5]The interest rate paid on a government security is determined by the relationship between the fixed annual payments on the security and its market value; low market values imply high interest rates.

inflationary pressures. When bonds were sold to commercial banks, the situation was potentially more complex. To the extent that commercial banks financed their acquisition of bonds by reducing their lending to the private sector, the effect was similar to sales to the general public. However, to the extent that the banks financed their acquisitions by reducing their reserve ratios (reserve ratios were unusually high throughout the late thirties), then the effect was much like sales of bonds to the Federal Reserve.

Table 25-3 shows the relative importance of each form of finance. Although more reliance was placed on taxation than in the Civil War or World War I, considerable reliance was still placed on borrowing and creating new money.

Reliance on money and debt (largely short-term debt) created strong upward pressures on demand in all sectors of the economy. By 1944, the civilian unemployment rate had fallen to 1.2 percent, one of the lowest on record. This experience helped convince economists and policymakers that the Keynesian cure for depression, government deficit-financed spending, would work. To see why, consider Table 25-4, which shows the key figures.

Unemployment, as Table 25-4 shows, remained at a stubbornly high level of 17.2 percent of the labor force in 1939. Even if we use Michael Darby's figure, which counts federal and state emergency workers as employed (the official figures counted emergency workers as unemployed in order to stress the lack of meaningful jobs in the private sector), the figure is 11.3 percent. Keynesians claimed that unemployment could be cured with a *sufficient* increase in government spending, particularly deficit-financed spending. True there was a federal government deficit in 1939, and true there was a great hubbub about it. But, as Keynesians were quick to point out, the deficit was only 3.07 percent of GNP, an even lower percentage than during the worst year of the depression, 1933. What was needed was simply a much larger increase. By 1944, that had been accomplished. The deficit had been vastly increased, up to 22.5 percent of GNP, and unemployment was virtually gone. Most economists, particularly those of the younger generation such as future Nobel Prize winners Paul Samuelson and James Tobin, found this demonstration of the effectiveness of the Keynesian remedy convincing.

TABLE 25-3   FINANCING WORLD WAR II

	Billions of Dollars, 1941–1946	Percent of Expenditures
Total federal expenditures for war[a]	$320.2	100.0%
Tax revenues	129.8	40.5
Borrowing from the public	115.8	37.0
Creating new money	74.6	22.5

SOURCES: *HISTORICAL STATISTICS* (WASHINGTON, D.C.: GOVERNMENT PRINTING OFFICE, 1960), P. 711; AND MILTON FRIEDMAN AND ANNA J. SCHWARTZ, *MONETARY STATISTICS OF THE UNITED STATES* (NEW YORK: NATIONAL BUREAU OF ECONOMIC RESEARCH, 1970), PP. 33–37.

[a]Total expenditures 1941–1946, less six times 1940 expenditures.

TABLE 25-4   DEFICIT SPENDING AND THE FALL IN UNEMPLOYMENT

Year	Unemployment (percent of the labor force)	GNP (in billions of dollars)	Federal Budget Deficit (in billions of dollars)	Deficit as a Percentage of GNP	Stock of Money (in billions of dollars)
1929	3.2%	$103.9	$ .7	−0.67%	$ 46.6
1933	24.9	56.0	−2.6	4.64	32.2
1939	17.2	91.3	−2.8	3.07	49.2
	(11.3)				
1944	1.2	211.4	−47.6	22.52	106.8

SOURCES: *ECONOMIC REPORT OF THE PRESIDENT, 1987* (WASHINGTON, D.C.: GOVERNMENT PRINTING OFFICE, 1987), PP. 244, 280, AND 331; AND MICHAEL R. DARBY, "THREE AND A HALF MILLION U.S. EMPLOYEES HAVE BEEN MISLAID: OR, AN EXPLANATION OF UNEMPLOYMENT, 1934–41," *JOURNAL OF POLITICAL ECONOMY* 84 (1976): 8. THE LAST COLUMN IS DERIVED FROM MILTON FRIEDMAN AND ANNA J. SCHWARTZ, *MONETARY TRENDS IN THE UNITED STATES AND THE UNITED KINGDOM* (CHICAGO: UNIVERSITY OF CHICAGO PRESS, 1982), PP. 124–125.

A number of economists at the time, and a growing number since, were skeptical. For one thing, the data are also consistent with the monetarist claim that a large increase in the money supply would cure the depression. Consider the last column of Table 25-4. The stock of money in 1939 was only slightly above the level of 1929, but by 1944 it had more than doubled. Some economists have also pointed out that the drafting of large numbers of young men into the armed forces removed many individuals with a high probability of being unemployed from the labor force. As in so many cases, the lessons of history are ambiguous, because in the natural experiments of history other factors are seldom as constant as we would like.

Whatever reservations economists may now entertain about this demonstration of the Keynesian message, there is no doubt that it had a profound impact on economic policymaking in the United States. Even at the time, however, some Keynesians worried that the inflationary pressures produced by wartime policies of deficit spending had been checked only by a set of wage and price controls that would be unacceptable in peacetime.

WAGE AND PRICE CONTROLS

Early in the war, the Roosevelt administration decided that in addition to relying on taxation to control prices it would combat rising prices with direct controls. It would try to persuade firms not to raise prices by appealing to their patriotic instincts; and if persuasion failed, it would simply make price increases illegal.

In May 1940, President Roosevelt set up the National Defense Advisory Committee and chose Leon Henderson, a crusty, cigar-smoking New Dealer, to head its Price Stabilization Division. Henderson sought voluntary agreements from producers in key areas of the economy not to raise prices, a policy that met with very limited success. Prices continued to rise, although severe inflation was still concentrated in a few sectors. In April 1941, Roosevelt strengthened Henderson's hand by creating the Office of Price Administration and Civilian Supply. Eventually OPA would become the civilian agency most familiar to the average American because it set the prices and determined the quantities of the goods and services consumed every day. Of special interest to economists was the creation of the Price Division of OPA under the direction of John Kenneth Galbraith. In the postwar period, the tall, urbane, and articulate Galbraith would become a leading advocate of the liberal view that America's social and economic problems could be solved by expanding the role of the federal government. Undoubtedly, his experience at the OPA, with its enormous (and, in his view, favorable) effect on the economy, profoundly influenced his thinking.

Initially, the OPA hoped to control the general price level by applying controls only in selected sectors, but uncontrolled prices continued to rise and at an increasing pace. In April 1942, OPA issued the General Maximum Price Regulation, affectionately known as General Max, which put a ceiling on most prices. But even this measure was only partially successful. One problem was that each seller was responsible for setting his own prices according to the rules set up by the government. It was altogether too easy for a firm to justify the price it charged by pointing to an unusually high base period price or an unusually high price set by a competitor. Effective price control required that the OPA set specific dollar and cents prices that its employees or its boards of volunteer price watchers could check.

In April 1943, President Roosevelt issued his famous "Hold-the-Line" order requiring OPA to refuse all requests for price increases except in very limited circumstances. This approach, economically suspect because it did not provide for the adjustment of relative prices but easy to defend in the court of public opinion, worked surprisingly well for the remainder of the war. The official consumer price index rose at only 1.6 percent per year from April 1943 until February 1946, when the Hold-the-Line policy began to come apart. Perhaps the main positive result of this policy was that it encouraged people to save rather than spend their high wartime earnings by creating expectations of future price stability. People who bought government bonds felt confident that the real value of their interest payments and principal repayments (which were fixed in dollars) would not be eroded by a near-term inflation.

But the official index alone does not tell the whole story. It is a basic proposition of economics that if a price ceiling is set below the free-market equilibrium, there will be a scramble for supplies that will very likely result in attempts to evade the ceiling. There were innumerable examples during the war. In some cases evasion took the form of quality deterioration: fat was added to hamburger, coarse fabrics were substituted for finer ones, maintenance on rent-controlled apartments was reduced or eliminated. Quality deterioration could be limited by regulations that specified the exact content of a product, such as the specified butterfat content of milk. But such regulations tended to get longer and longer, and became a problem in themselves. In one famous case, Lou Maxon, an OPA official, resigned in 1943, complaining about what he saw as the antibusiness atmosphere at OPA. Many of Maxon's charges were exaggerated, but the six-page regulation specifying the content of fruit cakes, which he used to dramatize his charges, spoke to a real problem.

Quality deterioration was just one in a long list of techniques available to people who wanted to evade the controls. "Forced uptrading" was the term used to describe the problem caused by the elimination of lower-priced lines of merchandise. Before the war, manufacturers often offered buyers a choice between low-priced, low-quality items and high-priced, high-quality items. Typically, the high-priced lines carried higher profit margins but were sold in smaller volumes. With wartime demand in all lines exceeding supply, manufacturers eliminated the lower-priced lines. This was fine for those consumers who wished to move up to the higher-priced item anyway, but for those who were forced to trade up, the difference between what they would have voluntarily paid for the high-priced line and what they were forced to pay because the low-priced line was eliminated was a hidden price increase.

The most startling form of evasion, although not the most frequent, was the black market. Here buyers willing to pay more than the official price and sellers willing to sell for more would meet away from the prying eyes of the OPA. The black market took many forms, depending on the product and the enforcement effort being made by the OPA. In New York there were "meat-easys," much like the speakeasys that had flourished during prohibition, where one could buy extra meat but at prices much higher than those being set by the OPA. After production of automobiles resumed at the end of the war, evasion of automobile price controls was widespread. Some of it occurred in the dealer's showroom, where cash payments were often made on the side while official documents showed that the car had been sold at the OPA ceiling. But a true black market also developed. At Leesville, South Carolina, for example, there was a huge lot where cars recently purchased from dealers were brought from all over the country to be sold at black-market prices.

RATIONING

Rationing is one way to reduce evasion when prices are being held below their free-market equilibrium. A consumer who is assured at least a bare minimum is less likely to enter the black market than a consumer who is in danger of being left without anything in a mad scramble for supplies. Moreover, a company that must be able to show the authorities ration tickets corresponding to the output it has sold will find it harder to divert supplies to the black market. Rationing was often necessary even when supplies were adequate by prewar standards; demand had increased and the price was being held below the new equilibrium. In other cases rationing was undertaken to achieve particular policy goals. Gasoline was rationed, for example, to reduce the use of automobile and truck tires, which were in short supply due to the rubber shortage.[6]

The simplest form of rationing was a ticket entitling the holder to buy a certain quantity of a certain good, surrendering the ticket when the good was purchased. Tires, the first commodity rationed, were rationed in this way.[7] More-complicated

---

[6] In a few cases the goals of the rationing program were debatable. A well-publicized fat-salvage program led consumers to believe that the fat was needed to make a chemical crucial to the war effort. But the real motive was the fear on the part of soap manufacturers that a shortage of fat would lead to the rationing of soap, and that consumers accustomed to economizing on soap during the war would continue to buy less afterwards.

[7] The largest part of the tire supply consisted of tires already on automobiles. These could not be rationed. But tire wear was controlled indirectly by rationing gasoline, and this was one of the main purposes of the gasoline rationing program in areas of the country where gasoline was abundant.

systems were used for certain food groups. Under the red point system for meats and fats, the consumer was periodically supplied with a certain number of points. Each good was assigned a point price, and the consumer could choose among rationed items as long as he had enough ration points.

Balancing the supply of goods and the number of ration tickets or points outstanding was no easy matter. In order to make the red point system operate more smoothly, the OPA issued red point tokens that could be taken as change and stored for use at a later date. By late 1944, surveys showed that consumers had stored up large quantities of these tokens, and the OPA feared a run on the stores that would leave shelves bare and confidence in the rationing program shaken. In order to regain control, OPA canceled all outstanding ration tokens, a move that cost the agency a great deal of public support. In 1945, as the war came to a close, most of the rationing programs were discontinued, a highly popular decision. But few people understood the intimate connection between rationing and price control, or the problems that would soon afflict the price-control system.

When legislation authorizing price controls came to an end in June 1946, Congress passed a new law. But it was so riddled with loopholes that President Truman vetoed it in hopes that a strong dose of inflation would force Congress to pass a stiffer price-control measure. Eventually legislation was passed that permitted the recontrol of selected prices. When meat prices were recontrolled, ranchers withheld their animals from the market—after all, it was clear that price controls were on the way out and that prices could only go higher—and the result was a meat shortage. Faced with outraged consumers on one hand and recommendations that he nationalize the nation's cattle herds on the other, Truman decided to terminate price controls for good.

LABOR IN THE WAR

The war took an enormous human toll. The United States suffered 405 thousand deaths in World War II, 292 thousand in battle. In addition, 671 thousand suffered nonmortal wounds. The death toll was four times that of World War I and two-thirds that of the Civil War. For the other belligerents, the tolls were much higher. All told, about 40 million people died in World War II. One could try to analyze these losses in economic terms, but there comes a point at which economic analysis fails to go to the heart of the matter.

As noted in Chapter 24, the war put normal labor relations on hold. The Roosevelt administration had been evolving a policy that would support labor's efforts to organize, bargain collectively, and strike; now labor was expected to cooperate with the effort to maximize production. And on the whole labor did so. Labor took a no-strike pledge, paralleling management's no-lockout pledge. The major exception was the United Mine Workers, under their charismatic leader John L. Lewis. As the result of public indignation over strikes in the coalfields, Congress passed the Smith-Connally War Labor Disputes Act in 1943, which provided for government takeover of plants in essential war industries that were hampered by strikes. Despite this case, however, the conflict between labor and management was generally kept in check during the war by labor's patriotism and by the government's extraordinary powers.

The real crunch came at the end of the war. As workers' overtime disappeared and real earnings were eroded by rising prices, labor leaders were under pressure to secure wage increases, which were not to be forthcoming without a struggle. Meanwhile, the widespread work stoppages of 1945 and 1946, shown vividly in Figure 25-1, alienated large segments of the electorate.

During this period of unusual strike proneness, employers complained loudly that they were being caught in the jurisdictional disputes of rival unions and that labor itself was guilty of unfair practices. There was a growing belief that union power was being used to infringe on the rights of individual workers.

In fact, employers often used strikes during the transition to their own advantage, putting pressure on the OPA to grant a price increase to make possible a wage increase. Labor, of course, realized that this avenue was open to employers, and this entered their strike calculations. The OPA, in many cases, claimed that higher wages could be paid without granting higher prices. But the path of least resistance was often to grant a round of wage and price increases in an industry experiencing a strike. The end result was that it was increasingly difficult for OPA to maintain its line on prices.

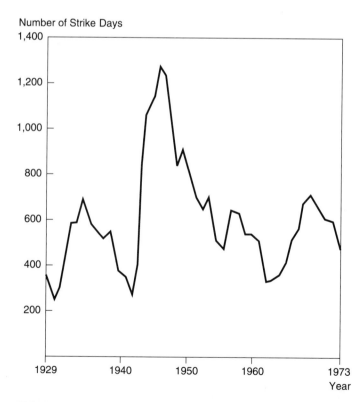

FIGURE 25-1 FIVE-YEAR MOVING AVERAGE OF NUMBER OF STRIKE DAYS PER THOUSAND NONAGRICULTURAL EMPLOYEES, 1929–1973

SOURCE: P. K. EDWARDS, *STRIKES IN THE UNITED STATES, 1881–1974* (NEW YORK: ST. MARTIN'S PRESS, 1981), P. 18.

After the Republicans won control of Congress in 1946, they lost no time in drawing up a long, technical bill that significantly amended the Wagner Act. The new law, passed in 1947 over President Harry S Truman's veto, was officially called the Labor-Management Relations Act but became known familiarly as the Taft-Hartley Act. The act reflected the belief that individual workers should be protected by public policy not only in their right to join a labor organization but also in their right to refrain from joining. The closed-shop agreement, under which the employer hires only union members, was outlawed. Union-shop agreements, which permit nonunion members to be employed but require them to join the union within a certain time period after starting to work, were permitted. However, the enforcement of union-security provisions was limited to cases of nonpayment of dues; more importantly, the law permitted the states to outlaw *all* forms of union security, including the union shop.

The Taft-Hartley Act, unlike the Wagner Act, assumed that the interests of the union and individuals in the union are not identical, taking the view that many union members are "captives" of the "labor bosses"—a position especially offensive to a great part of organized labor. For example, the act provided that a union could not negotiate a union-shop provision in collective-bargaining agreements unless a majority in the union voted for it. In 1951, after 46,000 separate polls in which security provisions won 97 percent of the time, the requirement of NLRB-conducted union-security elections was dropped, and a large number of doubters became convinced that union leaders commonly reflect the wishes of their memberships.

The most important features of the Taft-Hartley Act were those purporting to regulate unions in the "public" interest. A union seeking certification or requesting an investigation of unfair labor practices had to submit to a scrutiny of its internal affairs by filing statements, and its officers were required to sign affidavits stating that they were not Communists. The right to strike was modified by providing a "cooling-off period" after notice of termination of contract, and the President was given authority to postpone strikes for 80 days by injunction. More significant in "evening up" the one-sidedness of the Wagner Act was the outlawing of certain unfair union practices. Since 1947, it has been unfair for a union to

1. restrain or coerce *employees* regarding their right to join or refrain from joining a labor organization, or restrain or coerce *employers* in the selection of employer representatives for purposes of collective bargaining or adjustment of grievances.

2. cause or attempt to cause an *employer* to discriminate against an employee.

3. charge, under a valid union-shop agreement, an "excessive" initiation fee.

4. refuse to bargain collectively with an employer when the union involved is the certified bargaining agent.

5. "featherbed" the job—that is, to cause an employer to pay for services that are not performed.[8]

6. engage in, or encourage employees to engage in, a strike where the object is to

---

[8] Featherbedding continued to be a scandal in the railroad industry, which is not subject to the Taft-Hartley Act.

force one employer to cease doing business with another employer. This provision banned the secondary boycott.

After twelve years of almost complete freedom, labor found the Taft-Hartley Act harshly restrictive. Dire warnings were voiced about the coming decline of trade unionism in America. Labor's leadership was incensed at the offensive language and punitive spirit of the act. But many of the provisions looked worse in print than they proved in practice. The injunction clause, for example, stirred memories of the days when the courts granted injunctions at the request of private parties; however, in the hands of a President of the United States, acting in an emergency, the injunction was no longer a destructive weapon. Moreover, although union problems persist, they have come primarily from sources other than the Taft-Hartley Act.

ROSIE THE RIVETER

One of the most dramatic developments during the war was the change in the role of women in the labor force. Some 200,000 women entered the military services. Mainly they served in the Women's Army Corps (WAC) and Women Accepted for Volunteer Emergency Services (WAVES), with smaller numbers in the Marine Corps, Coast Guard, and the Women's Auxiliary Ferrying Service. Women also entered the civilian labor force in large numbers. Many entered jobs that women had filled before the war, but many others, as symbolized by "Rosie the Riveter," entered jobs traditionally filled by men. Women became toolmakers, crane operators, lumberjacks, and stevedores. About 14 percent of the women who had been out of the paid labor force before Pearl Harbor went to work.[9]

Women were encouraged to take jobs by high wages and by a desire to serve their country. Government propaganda urged women to work in industry and to help supply the weapons needed to defeat the Axis. This propaganda also encouraged women to think of these jobs as temporary, to be turned back to returning soldiers after the war was over.

There had been a long-term upward trend in women's participation in the labor force throughout the twentieth century, but (as Table 25-5 on the next page shows) the war decade stands out as a period of especially rapid growth. In 1940, only 13.8 percent of married women participated in the paid labor force. In 1950 that figure stood at 21.6 percent, an increase in the participation rate of 5.65 percent per year, a higher rate of increase than in any other decade. Partly, this was the result of changes in attitudes brought about by the war. Women who went to work temporarily (or so they or others may have thought) developed a taste for working in the paid labor force, as well as useful skills, which encouraged them to remain in the labor force after the war was over. Some employers, moreover, after seeing women performing well in jobs traditionally reserved for men only, may have revised their ideas about the productivity of working women.

---

[9] Interestingly, about 34 percent of the women who had been working prior to Pearl Harbor left the labor force during the war. Increased wages earned by husbands, or other family members, and a decline in the availability of household workers may explain this phenomenon.

TABLE 25-5   LABOR FORCE PARTICIPATION OF WOMEN, 1890–1980

Year	Single Women (over 15 years old)	Percent Increase (per year)	Married Women (over 15 years old)	Percent Increase (per year)
1890	40.5%		4.6%	
1900	43.5	0.74	5.6	2.17
1920	46.4	0.33	9.0	3.04
1930	50.5	0.88	11.7	3.00
1940	45.5	−0.99	13.8	1.80
1950	50.6	1.12	21.6	5.65
1960	47.5	−0.61	30.6	4.17
1970	51.0	0.74	39.5	2.91
1980	61.5	2.06	50.1	2.68

SOURCE: CLAUDIA GOLDIN, *UNDERSTANDING THE GENDER GAP* (OXFORD: OXFORD UNIVERSITY PRESS, 1990), P. 17.

Before the war, many firms had "marriage bars." These firms would simply not hire married women, and forced women who married while on the job to leave. Marriage bars became particularly widespread during the Great Depression as a way of rationing scarce jobs. One rationale was that it was unfair for a married woman who might already have a breadwinner in the family to work and thus take a job away from a man who was the sole support of his family. By 1950, marriage bars had virtually dis-

"Debbie the Driller" helped keep production lines moving during the war.

appeared (except for flight attendants), and some personnel managers were singing the praises of married women.

Recent research by Claudia Goldin has shown that fundamental changes in the labor market were even more important than the changes in attitudes brought about by the war.[10] Investigating a sample of women workers over the war decade, Goldin found that more than half of the Rosies who had entered the paid labor force between 1940 and 1944 (the peak year) had dropped out by 1950. Many lost their jobs as a result of seniority rules and social pressures that favored returning servicemen. Others chose to leave because changed economic circumstances permitted them to do so.

Although many of the Rosies left the labor force after the war ended, many other women decided to enter in the late 1940s. Overall, Goldin found that about half of the women who entered the labor force between 1940 and 1950 were Rosies who had entered during the war and continued to work afterwards, and about half were women who had not worked during the war but who had entered the labor force between the end of the war and 1950.

What factors brought these women into the labor force? One was the growing demand for women workers. Full employment meant more demand for all types of labor, and the clerical sector, which employed many women, was growing especially rapidly. This can be seen in Table 25-6, which lists the jobs held by women and the number working in them in 1940 and 1950. As you can see, about 37 percent of the new jobs came in the clerical sector.

Increased education also helped fit women for more jobs. The supply of younger unmarried women was shrinking as a result of low birthrates of the 1930s, and the supply of younger married women was also declining due to the increase in family formation in the postwar period. These changes opened the market for older married

TABLE 25-6   Jobs Held by Women in 1940 and 1950 (in thousands)

Occupation	1940	1950	Increase	Percent of Total Increase
Professional, technical	1,608	2,007	399	8.25
Managers, officials, proprietors	414	700	286	5.91
Clerical	2,700	4,502	1,802	37.26
Sales	925	1,418	493	10.19
Manual	2,720	3,685	965	19.95
Craftswomen, forewomen	135	253	118	2.44
Operatives	2,452	3,287	835	17.27
Laborers	133	145	12	0.25
Service workers	3,699	3,532	−167	−3.45
Farm workers	508	601	93	1.92

SOURCE: *Historical Statistics* (Washington, D.C.: Government Printing Office, 1975), p. 132.

---

[10] Claudia D. Goldin, "The Role of World War II in the Rise of Women's Employment," *American Economic Review* (1991): 741–756.

women. By 1950, these fundamental forces had pushed the labor force participation of women, and especially that of older married women, above the wartime peak.

THE MINORITY EXPERIENCE

The wartime boom accelerated the long-term movement of blacks out of southern agriculture. Even if one intends eventually to move to a new location, the ideal time to move is when unemployment is low in the area you are headed for. This reduces the risk of a long and costly search for a new job once you arrive. Altogether almost a million blacks moved from southern farms to industrial centers in the South, the Northeast, the Midwest, and the Pacific Coast.[11] The movement of poor whites out of southern agriculture was also massive during the war, as whites and blacks responded to similar economic facts of life, but the movement of the black population had the most dramatic political and social consequences.

The urbanization produced by the war is illustrated in Table 25-7. In 1940 the black population was about evenly divided between urban and rural areas; in 1950 it was predominantly urban.

Although discrimination against blacks remained the norm in the United States, there were some beginnings of progress. The military forces remained segregated for the duration of the war, but in 1940 officer's candidate schools (except those for the air force) were desegregated. Moreover, the outstanding record compiled by black troops and pilots, along with the growing demand by the black community for equal justice, contributed to President Harry S Truman's decision to issue an executive order desegregating the armed forces in 1948. There was also some progress on the home-

TABLE 25-7   URBANIZATION, 1920–1940

Year	Percentage of the Population Living in Urban Areas	
	Black	White
1920	34.0	53.4
1930	43.7	57.6
1940	48.6	57.5
1950	62.4	64.3
1960	73.2	69.5
1970	81.3	72.4

SOURCE: U.S. Bureau of the Census, *Historical Statistics* (Washington, D.C.: Government Printing Office, 1960), p. 12.

NOTE: The definition of urbanization changed over these years. With a constant definition, the trends would be even more dramatic.

[11]Harold G. Vatter, *The U.S. Economy in World War II*, p. 127.

front. In February 1941 A. Philip Randolph, head of the Brotherhood of Sleeping Car Porters, organized a march on Washington to protest discrimination in defense industries. The Roosevelt administration prevailed on the Randolph group to call off the march in exchange for an executive order forbidding discrimination in defense work and the establishment of the federal Committee on Fair Employment Practices. The committee, although lacking in enforcement powers, worked with employers to end discrimination.

White-black violence was not as frequent in World War II as in World War I, but in the early summer of 1943 a violent outburst near Detroit left 25 blacks and 9 whites dead.

One of the worst examples of racial bigotry occurred in 1942. Some 110,000 Japanese-Americans (75,000 of them citizens) were forced to leave their homes on the West Coast and were placed in internment camps until 1945. Many were forced to sell farms and other businesses at "fire-sale" prices, thus being deprived of property built up over decades. Meanwhile, Japanese-Hawaiians and Japanese-Americans distinguished themselves in the armed forces, fighting valiantly on the Italian front and serving as interpreters and translators in the Pacific theater. In 1988, Congress formally apologized and granted each of the survivors of the internment $20,000 as compensation.

AGRICULTURE DURING THE WAR

As demand expanded to meet Lend-Lease agreements and growing domestic requirements, agricultural production, aided by exceptionally good weather, climbed at the remarkable rate of 5 percent per year. This figure may be compared with the average in World War I, when agricultural production increased at 1.7 percent per year. Price controls during the war were purposely made less effective for agricultural than for nonagricultural commodities; consequently, the prices of farm products rose more rapidly during the war than the prices of the things that the farmer had to buy. To encourage such expansion, Congress passed three laws in May, July, and December of 1941. The first of these directed the Commodity Credit Corporation (CCC) to support the basic crops of wheat, corn, cotton, tobacco, rice, and peanuts at 85 percent of parity. The second, the Steagall Amendment, gave the Secretary of Agriculture authority to support the price of any nonbasic commodity at not less than 85 percent of parity if, in the opinion of the secretary, support was necessary to increase the production of a crop vital to the war effort. The third law guaranteed the 85-percent loan rate on basic crops for the years 1942 through 1946, putting price floors into effect for six crops well into the future.

During 1942 emphasis was placed on the necessity for stimulating particular kinds of output, notably meats and the oil-bearing crops, and avoiding a repetition of the price collapse that followed World War I. Legislation of October 1942 set final policy for the war period and for two postwar years. The 1942 act provided minimum support rates of 90 percent of parity for both basic and Steagall commodities; the supports were to remain in effect for two full years, beginning with the first day of January following the official end of the war. Finally price ceilings on farm products were set at a maximum of 110 percent of parity.

There were two other provisions in the 1942 legislation of special interest. Cotton supports were set at 92.5 percent of parity. And draft exemptions were provided for workers producing long-fiber cotton, which was demanded for a number of war-related uses.[12] The Secretary of Agriculture, at his discretion, could leave wheat and corn supports at 85 percent of parity if he felt that higher prices would limit available quantities of livestock feed. It is not entirely beside the point to note that cotton and beef interests were strongly represented by Congressmen, some of whom had reached powerful positions through their seniority.

Over the war period and during the first two postwar years, price supports were not generally required. Because of the great demand for most products, agricultural prices tended to push against their ceilings, but the secretary found it necessary to set floors for some needed nonbasic commodities that were above minimum levels. Surplus supplies of eggs and certain grades of hogs created a problem for part of 1944, but farm prices on the whole were subject to upward pressure. For some meats and dairy products it was even necessary to roll back retail prices in an effort to "hold the line" against inflation. In such cases, to prevent a reduction in the floor prices received by farmers, meatpackers and creameries were paid a subsidy equal to the amount of the rollback on each unit sold.

The war enabled the CCC to unload heavy inventories that had built up between 1939 and 1941. From 1944 to 1946, loans extended by the CCC were small. Beginning in 1944, however, egg purchases became so great as to cause embarrassment, and support to the production of eggs and potatoes received a fantastically unfavorable press in 1945 and 1946. But foreign demand through the United Nations Relief and Rehabilitation Administration (UNRRA) and military governments, an unexpectedly high domestic demand, and the removal of price ceilings led to highly favorable postwar prices and lightened CCC loan and purchase commitments. Indeed, contrary to the predictions of many experts, the demand for food, feed, and fiber was exceptionally high after the war. The removal of price controls in the summer of 1946 permitted all prices to shoot up, but similar to the war years, the rise in agricultural prices was steeper than the price rise in other areas. Most production restrictions on crops were canceled before or during World War II, and by the spring of 1948 only tobacco and potatoes were still controlled.

DEMOBILIZATION AND RECONVERSION

It was widely expected that the Great Depression would return once the war was over. After all, it seemed as if enormous levels of government spending during the war were the only thing that had gotten the country out of the depression. Many, perhaps most,

---

[12] Rachel Maines, "Twenty-nine Thirty-seconds or Fight: Goal Conflict and Reinforcement in U.S. Cotton Policy, 1933–1946," in *The Sinews of War*, eds. Geofrey Mills and Hugh Rockoff.

economists agreed with this analysis. They pressed for a commitment by the government to maintain the high level of employment after the war. The result was the Employment Act of 1946.

In 1945, Congress had considered a bill that would guarantee full employment by placing a $40 billion "annual investment fund" at the disposal of the Secretary of Commerce. Senator Murray, its author, said that the bill was a "legal acknowledgment that the national government assumes the responsibility for prosperity in peacetime. The federal government is the instrument through which we can all work to accomplish full employment and high annual income." After much argument and semantic juggling, a revised version of the original "full-employment" bill was passed as the Employment Act of 1946. Full employment was no longer explicitly required; instead it was to be the federal government's responsibility to "promote maximum employment, production and purchasing power." The adjective *maximum* was purposely ambiguous, but the entire statement was generally understood to mean that the government would act quickly to shore up the economy if a severe recession threatened. A Council of Economic Advisers, with an adequate professional staff, was added to the Executive Office of the President. The President, assisted by the council, was directed to submit to Congress at least annually a report on current economic conditions, with recommendations for legislative action. The statute further provided that the House and the Senate were to form a standing Joint Economic Committee on the Economic Report (later simplified to the Joint Economic Committee), which would study the report of the President and the Council of Economic Advisers, hold hearings, and report in turn to Congress. Although no "investment fund" was provided, a watchdog agency was established to keep Congress and the President systematically informed of economic change. A compromise piece of legislation, the act acknowledged the government's role in maintaining full employment but did not say how the government would prevent depressions.

The expected depression did not materialize. During the war, people had accumulated large stores of financial assets, especially money and government bonds. They did so partly because they could not buy consumer durables during the war, and partly because they were saving for the bad times they thought lay ahead. Once the war was over, these savings were released and created a surge in demand that contributed to a postwar rise in prices and to the reintegration of workers from the armed forces and from defense industries into the peacetime labor force. Government policy also played a role in smoothing the transition. The so-called "G.I. Bill of Rights" (the Servicemen's Readjustment Act of 1944) provided returning servicemen with a number of benefits including hospitalization, unemployment compensation, job placement, and subsidies for attending college. This legislation delayed the reentry of many former servicemen into the labor force and provided them with improved skills.

The postwar surge in demand ushered in a new consumer-oriented society that to some represented the fulfillment of the American dream and to others represented the creation of an unthinking, materialistic culture. Builders like Levitt and Sons utilized mass-production techniques developed during the war to provide housing for war workers, adapting them to mass-produce suburban homes, even creating entire new communities such as Levittown, New York. Aided by advances from the Federal

Housing Administration and the Veterans Administration, the Levitts offered attractive terms to returning servicemen and other buyers.

Balladeer Malvina Reynolds expressed the feelings of many critics of the new tract housing in a popular folksong:

Little Boxes on the hillside, little boxes made of ticky tacky,
Little Boxes on the hillside, little boxes all the same.
There's a green one and a pink one and a blue one and a yellow one,
And they're all made of ticky tacky and they all look just the same.[13]

Defenders of the new construction techniques could have argued that by achieving the economies of long production runs, builders were able to lower the unit cost of hous-

TABLE 25-8   THE BIRTHRATE, 1929–1959 (SELECTED YEARS)

Year	Live Births per 1,000	
	Total Population	Women, Age 15–44
1929	21.2	89.3
1930	21.3	89.2
1936	18.4	75.8
1939	18.8	77.6
1940	19.4	79.9
1941	20.3	83.4
1942	22.2	91.5
1943	22.7	94.3
1944	21.2	88.8
1945	20.4	85.9
1946	24.1	101.9
1947	26.6	113.3
1948	24.9	107.3
1949	24.5	107.1
1950	24.1	106.2
1951	24.9	111.5
1952	25.1	113.9
1953	25.0	115.2
1954	25.3	118.1
1955	25.0	118.5
1956	25.2	121.2
1957	25.3	122.9
1958	24.5	120.2
1959	24.0	118.8

SOURCE: U.S. BUREAU OF THE CENSUS, HISTORICAL STATISTICS (WASHINGTON, D.C.: GOVERNMENT PRINTING OFFICE, 1960), P. 49.

[13] Malvina Roberts, "Little Boxes," in The Ballad of America: The History of the United States in Song and Story, ed. John Anthony Scott (Carbondale and Edwardsville: Southern Illinois University Press, 1983), pp. 378–380.

ing, and permit people to buy homes who could not otherwise afford them. No one, however, was able to put that into an enduring folksong.

These years witnessed the beginning of the "baby boom," as birthrates surged in the late 1940s and 1950s. The image of a baby boom following shortly after the reuniting of soldiers with their loved ones is romantic, and undoubtedly valid in many individual cases. But as Table 25-8 shows, the baby boom was a much broader phenomenon that owes its existence, sad to say, as much to economics as to romance. The birthrate had plunged during the Great Depression, reaching a low point in 1936. It then recovered somewhat during the war years and in 1943 reached a level higher than any year since 1927. There was a substantial leap in the birthrate in 1946 and 1947, as the romantic theory predicts, but the boom continued long beyond the late 1940s. The rate of live births per 1,000 women in the 15-to-44 age range actually peaked in 1957. The baby boom was a complex phenomenon, but economic conditions undoubtedly played a role. The 1950s were the economic reverse of the 1930s: a strong economy and optimism about the future encouraged many Americans to start families.

The war, in short, ushered in a period in which millions of Americans could take part for the first time in a middle-class lifestyle. Government programs for veterans such as the G.I. bill helped, but the key factor was the thing that did not happen— a return to the depressed economic conditions of the 1930s.

SELECTED REFERENCES
AND SUGGESTED READINGS

Arnow, Kathryn Smul. "The Attack on the Cost of Living." In *Inter-University Case Program, Cases in Public Administration*, Vol. 1. Washington, D.C.: Committee on Public Administration Cases, 1951.

Blum, John Morton. *V Was for Victory: Politics and American Culture During World War II*. New York: Harcourt Brace Jovanovich, 1977.

Bowles, Chester. *Promises to Keep*. New York: Harper & Row, 1971.

Bronfenbrenner, Martin. "A Theory of Price Control-Review." *Journal of Political Economy* 62 (1954): 68–70.

Bureau of the Budget, War Records Section. *The United States at War: The Development and Administration of the War Program by the Federal Government*. Washington, D.C.: Government Printing Office, 1946.

Burns, James MacGregor. *Roosevelt: The Soldier of Freedom*. 1970.

Cain, Louis, and George Neumann. "Planning for Peace: The Surplus Property Act of 1944." *Journal of Economic History* 41 (March 1981): 129–135.

Campbell, Colin Dearborn, ed. *Wage-Price Controls in World War II, United States and Germany: Reports by Persons Who Observed and Participated in the Programs*. Washington, D.C.: American Enterprise Institute, 1971.

Catton, Bruce. *War Lords of Washington*. Washington, D.C.: Government Printing Office, 1948.

Chandler, Lester Vernon. *Inflation in the United States, 1940–1948*. New York: Harper & Brothers, 1951.

Chandler, Lester V., and Donald Wallace, eds. *Economic Mobilization and Stabilization: Selected Materials on the Economics of War and Defense*. Washington, D.C.: Government Printing Office, 1951.

Clinard, Marshall B. *The Black Market: A Study of White Collar Crime.* New York: Rinehart, 1952.

Clive, Allan. "Women Workers in World War II: Michigan as a Test Case." *Labor History* 20 (1979): 44–72.

Conrat, Maisie, and Richard Conrat. *Executive Order 9066: The Internment of 110,000 Japanese-Americans.* 1972.

Davis, Kenneth S. *Experience of War: The United States in World War II.* 1965.

Dunlop, John T., and Arthur Hill. *The Wage Adjustment Board: Wartime Stabilization in the Building and Construction Industry.* Cambridge: Harvard University Press, 1950.

Friedman, Milton. "Price, Income and Monetary Changes in Three Wartime Periods." *American Economic Review* (May 1952): 612–625.

Friedman, Milton, and Anna J. Schwartz. *A Monetary History of the United States, 1867–1960.* Princeton: Princeton University Press, 1963. Chapter 10, pp. 546–585.

Galbraith, John Kenneth. *A Life in Our Times.* Boston: Houghton Mifflin, 1981.

———. *A Theory of Price Control.* Cambridge: Harvard University Press, 1952.

Gemery, Henry A., and Jan S. Hogendorn. "The Microeconomic Bases of Short-Run Learning Curves: Destroyer Production in World War II." In *The Sinews of War,* eds. Geofrey Mills and Hugh Rockoff. Ames: Iowa State University Press, 1993.

Glenn, Norval D. "Changes in the American Occupational Structure and Occupational Gains of Negroes During the 1940's." *Social Forces* 41 (1962): 188–195.

Goldin, Claudia D. "The Role of World War II in the Rise of Women's Employment." *American Economic Review* 81 (1991): 741–756.

Gordon, David L., and Royden Dangerfield. *The Hidden Weapon: The Story of Economic Warfare.* New York: Harper, 1947.

Gordon, Robert J. "45 Billion of U.S. Private Investment Has Been Mislaid." *American Economic Review* 59 (June 1969): 221–238.

Higgs, Robert. *Crisis and Leviathan: Critical Issues in the Emergence of the Mixed Economy.* New York: Oxford University Press, 1986.

———. "Private Profit, Public Risk: Institutional Antecedents of the Modern Military Procurement System in the Rearmament Program 1940–1941." In *The Sinews of War,* eds. Geofrey Mills and Hugh Rockoff. Ames: Iowa State University Press, 1993.

Hoopes, Roy. *Americans Remember: The Homefront: An Oral Narrative.* New York: Hawthorne Books, 1977.

Hughes, Jonathan. *The Governmental Habit: Economic Controls from Colonial Times to the Present.* New York: Basic Books, 1977.

Janeway, Eliot. *The Struggle for Survival: A Chronicle of Economic Mobilization in World War II.* New Haven: Yale University Press, 1951.

Klein, Lawrence R. "The Role of War in the Maintenance of American Economic Prosperity." *Proceedings of the American Philosophical Society* 65 (1961): 507–516.

Kuznets, Simon. "National Product, War and Prewar." New York: National Bureau of Economic Research, Occasional Paper 17, 1944.

Lane, Frederick C. *Ships for Victory: A History of Shipbuilding Under the U.S. Maritime Commission in World War II.* Baltimore: Johns Hopkins University Press, 1951.

Maines, Rachel. "Twenty-nine Thirty-seconds or Fight: Goal Conflict and Reinforcement in the U.S. Cotton Policy, 1933–1946." In *The Sinews of War,* eds. Geofrey Mills and Hugh Rockoff. Ames: Iowa State University Press, 1993.

Mills, Geofrey, and Hugh Rockoff, eds. *The Sinews of War: Essays on the Economic History of World War II.* Ames: Iowa State University Press, 1993.

Millward, Alan S. *War, Economy and Society, 1939–1945.* Berkeley: University of California Press, 1977.

Nelson, Donald M. *Arsenal of Democracy: The Story of American War Production.* New York: Harcourt Brace, 1946.

Novick, D., M. Anshen, and W. C. Truppner. *Wartime Production Controls.* New York: Columbia University Press, 1949.

CHAPTER TWENTY-SIX

THE GROWTH OF THE FEDERAL GOVERNMENT

CHAPTER THEME Perhaps the most profound change in the American economy in the postwar period was the continued growth in the size and role of government at all levels, especially at the federal level. Government grew not only in dollars spent but also in power to control the private sector through legal regulations and bureaucratic decisions. This growth was sustained, although the trend was by no means steady, until the late 1970s, when growing dissatisfaction with big government led to calls for reduced spending and deregulation. This chapter discusses the dimensions of the growth in government, the causes, and in broad terms, the consequences. The next chapter explores this issue further by looking closely at several specific examples.

INCREASES IN FEDERAL SPENDING

Let us begin by looking at a very simple measure of the size of government: total spending by government relative to the size of the economy (GNP). Table 26-1 tells what appears to be a simple story. Inexorably, decade after decade, government spending has grown relative to the size of the economy. By 1990, spending at all levels of government was equal to 40 percent of GNP. This is the most commonly used measure of the size of government. But even though it appears straightforward, it contains many ambiguities.

Government spending includes not only purchases of goods and services (such as paper clips, tanks, dams, and the salaries of Senators, Supreme Court Justices, and army privates) but also transfer payments (such as welfare expenditures and subsidies for state and local governments). Transfer payments, at least in the first instance, do not actually use up GNP. People on welfare can buy more goods and services, but people who pay more taxes buy less. Indeed, because most of us receive subsidies and pay taxes, there is really no upper limit to the ratio of government spending to GNP; it could exceed 100 percent. In any one year, the government could tax and transfer the same dollar many times over.

But that is not the end of the story. Each time the government imposes a tax, it affects incentives to work and invest, and that in turn affects GNP. People who receive as much in government subsidies as they pay in taxes nevertheless have an incentive to reduce their taxes. If they do so by working less hard or by investing their capital in less-productive uses, the total product of the economy will be reduced.

Economists generally agree with this analysis of the *direction* of the effects of tax and transfer policies; but one of the major controversies of the postwar period concerned the *magnitude* of these disincentive effects. Many of the experts who argue that the disincentive effects are not that great point out that total taxes in the United States, measured as a fraction of national product, appear relatively low compared with other developed countries where work effort and savings seem to be high. For example, one

TABLE 26-1   GOVERNMENT SPENDING RELATIVE TO GNP, 1949–1990

| Year | Percentage of GNP | | |
	Federal	State and Local	Total
1949	16.1	7.8	23.0
1959	18.5	9.5	26.6
1969	19.8	12.4	30.1
1979	20.8	13.1	30.6
1990	25.2	17.7	40.2

SOURCES: *Economic Report of the President, 1987* (Washington, D.C.: Government Printing Office, 1987), pp. 256, 335; and *Statistical Abstract of the United States: 1992* (Washington, D.C.: U.S. Bureau of the Census, 1992), pp. 279, 431.

NOTE: Federal expenditures include grants to state and local governments. These are deducted before computing total government expenditures in order to prevent double counting.

comparison showed that total taxes at all levels of government in the United States in 1989 were 30.1 percent of gross domestic product.[1] This was about the same as in Australia (also 30.1 percent), Japan (30.6 percent), and Switzerland (31.8 percent); but it was lower than in Canada (35.1 percent), West Germany (38.1 percent), and France (43.8 percent).[2] Such comparisons are never conclusive, however, because so many other things are not held constant.[3] Perhaps the most important point to be learned from such comparisons is simply that the trend toward big government was not unique to the United States. It was common to all developed nations.

Let us exclude transfer payments and consider simply government's purchases of goods and services relative to GNP. These figures are shown in Table 26-2. This table tells a different story. There was a marked upward trend in the shares of government in the first postwar decade, but then a leveling off, and an actual decline at the federal level. In terms of this measure, one could make the argument that the federal government was relatively smaller in recent years than in the 1950s. Transfer payments, particularly at the federal level, were clearly the dynamic element in the growth of public spending in the postwar period.

The big winners in the budget process in the postwar period were income security (Social Security, federal employee retirement and disability insurance, housing assistance, food and nutrition assistance, and so on), which grew at 11.6 percent per year between 1949 and 1989; education, which grew at 13.0 percent per year; and health (Medicare, health care services, health research, and so on), which grew at an astounding 16.3 percent per year. During the same period, consumer prices rose about 4.2 percent per year, so all of these categories grew rapidly in real as well as nominal terms.

TABLE 26-2 GOVERNMENT PURCHASES OF GOODS AND SERVICES RELATIVE TO GNP, 1949–1990

| Year | Percentage of GNP | | |
	Federal	State and Local	Total
1949	8.1	6.9	15.0
1959	11.0	8.7	19.7
1969	10.4	11.1	21.5
1979	7.1	11.6	18.7
1990	7.7	11.2	18.9

SOURCES: *ECONOMIC REPORT OF THE PRESIDENT, 1987* (WASHINGTON, D.C.: GOVERNMENT PRINTING OFFICE, 1987), PP. 244–245; AND *STATISTICAL ABSTRACT OF THE UNITED STATES: 1992* (WASHINGTON, D.C.: U.S. BUREAU OF THE CENSUS, 1992), P. 428.

[1] Gross domestic product is similar to gross national product, but it includes factor payments to the rest of the world (such as profits) and excludes receipts of such items. For the United States, the difference between GDP and GNP is too small to make a difference in the percentages.

[2] *Statistical Abstract of the United States: 1992* (Washington, D.C.: U.S. Bureau of the Census, 1992), p. 836.

[3] Why does Table 26-1 show 40 percent of GNP being spent by government when the figure in the comparisons is only 30 percent? Part of the difference is due to government deficits: the federal government spends more than it takes in. A larger part of the difference is due to nontax revenues of governments, such as user fees.

Indeed, in all the major budget categories, only veterans' benefits and international affairs, which were high in 1949 due to the aftereffects of the war, failed to grow faster than prices in the postwar period. The expansion of spending for income security, health, and education has been the result of new programs designed (partly) to protect and expand the choices of the less-well-off.

Figure 26-1 provides a bird's-eye view of how budget priorities changed in the postwar period. Military spending increased primarily in three major buildups. The first was associated with the Korean War in the early 1950s, the second with the Vietnam War in the late 1960s, and the third with the Reagan administration's buildup in the 1980s. Spending on health and education accelerated in the period of liberal activism in the mid-1960s. As late as 1959, spending in each of these categories was less than $1 billion.[4] Health, which includes Medicare, took another leap forward in the 1970s

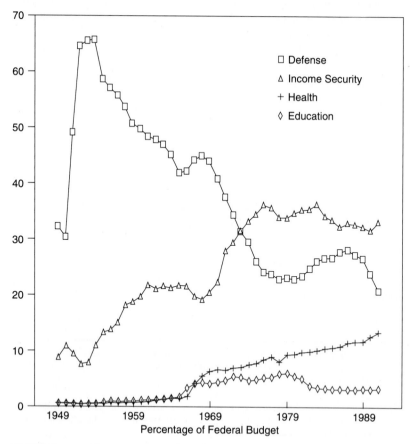

FIGURE 26-1 THE FEDERAL BUDGET, 1949–1991

---

[4]Although, as the late Senator Everett Dirksen of Illinois is credited with saying, "A billion here, a billion there, and pretty soon you are talking about real money."

and 1980s as eligibility for various benefits expanded. Finally, although there were some fluctuations, expenditures for income security grew steadily throughout the period, accelerating (along with health spending) in the 1970s as eligibility for benefits expanded.

In looking at Figure 26-1, one should keep in mind that the total budget was expanding, so the long-term fall in the share of defense spending in the budget was not equivalent to a fall in real defense spending. In dollars of constant purchasing power (1982 dollars), defense spending fell from $166 billion in 1953 to $137 billion in 1960; then, after recovering to $204 billion in 1970, it fell to $152 billion in 1980, the eve of the Reagan military buildup. By 1991, real defense spending was up to $251 billion. These enormous expenditures (in 1991, they were about 5.7 percent of GNP) were the legacy of the *Cold War*, America's ultimately successful attempt to contain communism within its immediate postwar boundaries.

These expenditures obviously reduced the flow of goods and services that could satisfy consumer demands. It makes sense for welfare comparisons, as Robert Higgs has pointed out, to exclude defense spending from GNP. A more difficult question to answer is whether defense spending came at the expense of private consumption or private investment. A careful study by Michael Edelstein shows that private investment spending was largely untouched by changes in defense spending. Instead, it appears that increases in defense spending came at the expense of private consumption, and that the dividend from decreases in defense spending went to civilian government spending.[5]

To see why individual categories such as defense or health rose or fell during the postwar period, we will examine how the political ideologies of the occupants of the White House were translated into budget realities.

PRESIDENTIAL POLITICS, 1945–1969: THE RISING LIBERAL TIDE

During the first three postwar decades, a period of unprecedented prosperity, liberal Democrats pressed hard for an expansion of New Deal reforms; conservatives fought a rear guard action, delaying the advance of the welfare state when they could and retreating to new positions when they could not. The first postwar President, Democrat Harry Truman, favored a major expansion of the New Deal. Truman's program, which he called the Fair Deal, called for a wide range of economic legislation including repeal of the Taft-Hartley Act, increased Social Security benefits, a higher minimum wage, federal subsidies for housing, compulsory federal health insurance, and authority to build industrial plants to overcome "shortages."[6] Some parts of his program, those

---

[5] Michael Edelstein, "What Price Cold War? Military Spending and Private Investment in the US, 1946–1979," *Cambridge Journal of Economics* 14 (1990): 421–437.

[6] The tradition for each administration in the postwar period to sum up its legislative programs in a single grand phrase reflects the tendency of people to look toward Washington for a solution to their problems. Dwight D. Eisenhower gave us the Great Crusade, John F. Kennedy gave us the New Frontier, and Lyndon B. Johnson gave us the Great Society.

that were extensions and modifications of existing programs, were enacted—Social Security benefits were extended, and the minimum wage was raised—but new programs were blocked by a congressional coalition of Republicans and southern Democrats. Special interest groups played an important role in lobbying Congress to oppose legislation they considered contrary to their interests. The American Medical Association, for example, lobbied vigorously against Truman's health insurance proposals, which they denounced as the forerunner of "socialized medicine."

The philosophy of Republican Dwight Eisenhower's administration was generally opposed to new initiatives in the economic sphere. The administration's motto, "less government in business and more business in government," summed up its philosophy. But existing programs around which a consensus had formed continued to expand. For example, Social Security benefits were increased and extended to more workers, the minimum wage was raised from $.75 to $1.00 per hour, and more money was provided for housing.

LEGISLATION AND SOCIAL CHANGE

The breakthrough in welfare legislation occurred during the presidencies of Democrats John F. Kennedy and Lyndon B. Johnson. Kennedy's New Frontier was similar to Truman's Fair Deal, but in many ways it did not go as far; Kennedy's narrow victory over Vice-President Richard Nixon had hardly seemed a mandate for radical change. The program called, among other things, for federal medical insurance for the elderly, aid to education, and more federal money for housing and "urban renewal." As in previous administrations, existing programs were expanded. Social Security benefits were increased, the minimum wage was raised from $1.00 to $1.25 (over a four-year period) and was made applicable to more workers, and more money was made available for federal housing projects.

There were also new initiatives. Concern over poverty in Appalachia and other depressed areas led to the Area Redevelopment Act, which provided low-cost loans for businesses and money for training workers. Other legislation provided aid for medical education, college construction projects, and relief for areas adversely affected by federal projects. But Kennedy's proposals for medical care for the aged and federal aid for public schools were defeated.

Events were moving rapidly, however. The civil rights movement accelerated, drawing attention to the plight of blacks and other disadvantaged groups. On college campuses, students were drawn to the liberal faith in government. For a time it seemed that Joseph Schumpeter's prediction that capitalism would be undermined by the children of the bourgeoisie, who would lose faith in the system that had created the basis for their own high standard of living, had at last begun to come true.[7] When Lyndon B. Johnson took office in 1963 after the assassination of President Kennedy, the prospects for enacting economic legislation were very different from when Kennedy had entered office. Johnson proclaimed his intention of fighting a "War on Poverty." The result was the Economic Opportunity Act of 1964, which established training camps

---

[7]Joseph Schumpeter, *Capitalism, Socialism, and Democracy* (New York: Harper & Row, 1950), pp. 415–424.

in rural and urban areas, provided grants for farmers and small businesses, and helped communities fund their own antipoverty programs. In 1964, President Johnson was reelected by a large majority; this mandate, and Johnson's long experience in Washington, helped him in pushing for the programs that now were referred to as the basis for the "Great Society."[8]

A wide range of important legislation followed. Indeed, there had been nothing like it since the New Deal, and in some respects it was even more radical. A medical care program (Medicare) for those aged 65 or over was at last added to Social Security. A billion dollars was voted for Appalachia to improve land and highways and to provide health centers. A Department of Housing and Urban Development was created, and its head was made a Cabinet-level secretary. A new Housing Act provided, among other things, for federal rent subsidies for the poor, a new departure in welfare legislation. The minimum wage, a familiar part of liberal Democratic programs, was raised and extended to cover farm laborers, workers in small retail shops, and hospital workers. A Mass Transportation Act provided money to improve rail transportation, and the Department of Transportation, the twelfth Cabinet-level department, was created. This list of reforms could be extended, as the role of government extended into more aspects of American life.

THE NEW REGULATION

During the nineteenth century, and with a few exceptions until World War II, federal regulation was designed to deal with specific problems in specific industries. The Interstate Commerce Commission was concerned mostly with regulation of prices charged by railroads, trucks, and water carriers; the Federal Reserve system regulated the banks; and so on. In the postwar period, however, that emphasis changed. Regulatory agencies were set up with broad powers to interfere with decision making in a wide range of industries, and in relation to a broad array of problems. For example, in 1970 Congress established the Occupational Safety and Health Administration (OSHA) to set standards for working conditions throughout the workplace. This agency's penchant for issuing irritating (to business) regulations was later used by presidential candidate Ronald Reagan as a main example of how "government is the problem."

One of the most dramatic developments of the postwar period was the passage of major pieces of legislation designed to protect the consumer from the purchase of dangerous or otherwise unsatisfactory goods and services. Consumer protection is by no means unique to the postwar period. As early as 1838, Congress created the Steamboat Inspection Service to check the safety of steamboats and reduce the risk of explosions. But as Table 26-3 (see next page) makes clear, the rate of passage of such legislation has accelerated in the postwar period. Why this should have been so is not entirely clear.

---

[8] One critical couple preferred a different term: "Roosevelt gave us the New Deal, Truman gave us the Fair Deal, but Johnson gave us the Ordeal." William Morris and Mary Morris, *Morris Dictionary of Word and Phrase Origins* (New York: Harper & Row, 1971), p. 397.

Some pieces of legislation can be traced to particularly dreadful events. Our first example, the Steamboat Inspection Service, was enacted after a series of explosions killed many passengers and crew. The Food, Drug, and Cosmetic Act of 1938 followed

TABLE 26-3   MAJOR CONSUMER SAFETY LAWS OF THE UNITED STATES

Year	Law	Main Provisions
1906	Food and Drug Act	Prohibits misbranding and adulteration of foods and drugs. Requires listing of medicine ingredients on product labels.
1906	Meat Inspection Act	Provides for federal inspection of slaughtering, packaging, and canning plants that ship meat interstate.
1938	Food, Drug, and Cosmetic Act	Defines as "adulterated" any food or drug that contains a substance unsafe for human use. Requires application for introduction of new drugs supported by tests of safety.
1938	Wheeler-Lea Amendment to Federal Trade Commission Act (1914)	Extends prohibitions of FTC Act to "unfair or deceptive acts or practices."
1953	Flammable Fabrics Act	Prohibits manufacture, import, or sale of products so "flammable as to be dangerous when worn by individuals."
1958	Food Additives Amendment to Food, Drug, and Cosmetic Act (1938)	Prohibits use of food additives shown to cause cancer in humans or animals.
1960	Hazardous Substances Labeling Act	Requires labeling of hazardous household substances.
1962	Kefauver-Harris Amendments to Food, Drug, and Cosmetic Act (1938)	Requires additional tests of both safety and efficacy for new drugs.
1965	Cigarette Labeling and Advertising Act	Requires use of health warnings on cigarette packages and in advertising.
1966	Fair Packaging and Labeling Act	Requires listing of product contents and manufacturer.
1966	Child Protection Act (Amendment to Hazardous Substances Labeling Act of 1960)	Prohibits sale of hazardous toys and other items used by children.
1966	National Traffic and Motor Vehicle Safety Act	Provides for establishment of safety standards for vehicles and parts, and for vehicle recalls.
1967	Amendments to the Flammable Fabrics Act (1953)	Extends federal authority to establish safety standards for fabrics, including "household" products.
1970	Public Health Cigarette Smoking Act	Prohibits broadcast advertising of cigarettes.
1970	Poison Prevention Packaging Act	Provides for "child-resistant" packaging of hazardous substances.
1972	Consumer Product Safety Act	Establishes the Consumer Product Safety Commission, with authority to set safety standards for consumer products and to ban products that present undue risk.
1977	Saccharin Study and Labeling Act	Requires use of health warnings on products containing saccharin; postpones saccharin ban.

the Elixir Sulfonamide tragedy. The particular form in which this drug was sold proved to be toxic and left over 100 dead, many of them children. But the producer was held under existing law to be guilty of no more than mislabeling his product. The Kefauver-Harris Amendments to the Food, Drug, and Cosmetic Act (1962) followed in the wake of the Thalidomide tragedy. It was found in Europe that this drug produced severe birth defects when given to pregnant women. Silimar outcomes were largely avoided in the United States. But it appeared to legislators that this was mainly because of the resolute behavior of one public official, Dr. Ann Kelsy of the Food and Drug Administration, who had resisted enormous pressure to license the drug. It was felt that without additional legal safeguards future situations might emerge in which an absence of such a resolute regulator would lead to tragedy.

The Flammable Fabrics Act of 1953 is still another example. This act also followed in the wake of a number of accidents. The industry, it should be noted, did not resist this legislation. By being able to show that their fabrics met federal safety standards, manufacturers hoped to increase demand and provide a basis for defense in legal suits.

But such events are not the whole story. The passage of consumer protection legislation also seems to have been related to swings in public opinion between liberal and conservative views. Notice in Table 26-3 that eight major pieces of consumer-protection legislation were passed between 1965 and 1972, including the Fair Packaging and Labeling Act, the National Traffic and Motor Vehicle Safety Act, and the Consumer Product Safety Act. This burst of legislative activity was related not so much to individual tragedies as to a general lack of faith in the market. In recent years, however, the liberal faith in government's ability to improve on the outcome of market forces has been on the defensive. The "Reagan Revolution" consistently opposed such extensions of federal authority, and there were no major pieces of consumer legislation during the administrations of Ronald Reagan or George Bush.

Weighing the costs and benefits of such legislation is a difficult task, and economists are still far from agreed on even individual regulations, let alone the whole trend. The benefits of regulation are relatively easy to see: consumers may be protected from consuming a dangerous food, using a dangerous drug, or driving a dangerous car. But there are also costs. Regulation may well raise prices by requiring expensive additions to a product or by requiring the firm to amass evidence that its product is safe, limit competition by preventing price competition, or stifle innovation by raising the costs of introducing new products. It has been contended, for example, that regulation of the drug industry has limited the number of new drugs being brought to market.[9]

PRESIDENTIAL POLITICS, 1969–1993: THE TURN TOWARD THE CONSERVATIVES

The 1960s were exciting times. To liberals it seemed that at last the promise of the New Deal would be realized, that a rapidly growing economy would provide the resources to solve the problems of poverty and inequality of opportunity. The 1960s

---

[9] See Peter Asch, *Consumer Safety Regulation* (New York: Oxford University Press, 1988), Chapter 7, for a fair-minded review of the literature on this question.

were especially exciting times for liberal economists: the economy would be managed according to Keynesian full-employment policies. But even though new welfare and regulatory legislation would continue to be passed for the remainder of the decade and into the early 1970s, there were signs, as early as 1966, that the "Little New Deal" was losing momentum. Though few observers realized it at the time, subsequent administrations, while making efforts to expand government in certain areas, would never return to the optimistic "social engineering" of the 1960s.

For two decades after Richard Nixon's reelection in 1972, new federal initiatives would be few and far between. The underlying reasons were a disillusionment with government produced by the long and futile war in Vietnam, along with a deterioration in the performance of the economy. Productivity growth slowed, inflation accelerated, and unemployment remained at high levels. The belief that the economy could easily generate a large surplus with which the government could do good works began to appear naive.

THE NEW DEREGULATION

In previous years, the 1976 election of Democrat Jimmy Carter would have signaled a new round of New Deal–type legislation. But the Carter administration, though it supported many traditional Democratic programs, emphasized economy and efficiency in government and, surprisingly, deregulation of a number of areas of the economy. The administration argued that these regulations were no longer needed or that the original intent of the legislation had been subverted by the very groups that the legislation was intended to control.

It had long been recognized in academic circles that regulatory agencies were often "captured" by a regulated industry. The public would get aroused by the revelation of an abuse in a certain industry, and a regulatory agency would be created, staffed initially by people representing the public interest. But only the regulated industry itself would maintain an interest in who was appointed to the agency and what decisions it rendered after the initial crisis passed. The result, naturally enough, would be that in the long run people sympathetic to the regulated industry would be appointed to the regulatory agency, and rulings would be made in the interest of the industry rather than that of the general public. Partly as a result of such ideas, President Carter supported decontrol of natural gas prices, deregulation of the airlines, trucking, and railroads, and deregulation of the financial services industry (including the elimination of deposit ceilings on interest rates).

Alfred E. Kahn, whom Carter chose to deregulate the airlines, was both symbolic of the new era and a major player in it.[10] Kahn was a liberal Democrat by upbringing and sentiment, but he had come to believe that the general interest would best be served if regulators put more emphasis on increasing competition and marginal cost pricing. (Marginal cost pricing held, to take a simple example, that airline seats should be priced at the cost of actually carrying one more passenger rather than at a high

---

[10] See Thomas K. McCraw, *Prophets of Regulation* (Cambridge: Harvard University Press, 1984), Chapter 7, for an absorbing account of Kahn's role in the regulatory revolution. McCraw's accounts of earlier regulators (Charles Francis Adams, Louis D. Brandeis, and James M. Landis) are also well worth reading.

average cost.) At a time when many airline seats were going unfilled, Kahn's emphasis on marginal cost pricing was welcomed by important segments of the industry.

REVISED BUDGET PRIORITIES

But it was Republican Ronald Reagan, first elected in 1980, who attempted to alter the basic ideological thrust of government in the postwar period. Reagan put it simply in his inaugural address: "Government is not the solution to our problems; government is the problem." His economic policy, often referred to as "Reaganomics," had several elements. One was the reduction in taxes, which we have already discussed in relation to postwar monetary and fiscal policy. An important element in the tax cuts was the reduction of marginal rates (the rates applied to additional income). The Reagan administration claimed that such cuts were necessary to create incentives to work and invest. Its critics complained that such cuts were a giveaway to the rich.

The Reagan administration wanted to alter budget priorities radically, increasing defense expenditures and reducing civilian expenditures. On the military side it had little trouble. Between 1980 and 1983, national defense expenditures rose from $134 billion to $210 billion. But spending cuts on the civilian side, although some were made, were harder to get through Congress. Between 1980 and 1983, all spending other than national defense increased from $457 billion to $598 billion. Prices were rising over the same period (the rise in civilian expenditures was 27 percent, while the rise in the GNP deflator was 19 percent), and certain areas of the civilian budget were hit hard (the budget category of "education, training, employment, and social services" fell from $32 billion to $27 billion). On the whole, however, it was extremely difficult to make cuts, particularly after Reagan's initial "honeymoon" with Congress ended. Reagan's budget director, David Stockman, was in charge of proposing the cuts to be made and selling them to Congress. His book, *The Triumph of Politics*, describes in case after case how difficult it was to cut programs, even those having little justification, once the affected interests and their allies in Congress and the government bureaucracy were alerted for battle.[11]

The 1988 election of George Bush, a moderate Republican, promised a slowdown if not a reversal of the Reagan policies, especially on the regulatory front. Bush did say, in his speech accepting the Republican nomination, "Read my lips: no new taxes," thus laying claim to the most popular part of the Reagan legacy. Two years later, however, under intense pressure to do something about the mounting federal deficit, Bush accepted tax increases. The resulting loss of political capital seemed to far outweigh any effect on the deficit. In 1992 Democrat Bill Clinton was elected President after promising to reverse the Reagan-Bush approach by raising taxes on the wealthy, spending more on the poor and on urban areas, spending less on defense, and increasing the federal government's role in health care. As this book goes to press, it is still too early to say whether this liberal agenda will be adopted, and whether a new era of liberalism has begun.

---

[11]David Stockman, *The Triumph of Politics: How the Reagan Revolution Failed* (New York: Harper & Row, 1986).

THE UNDERLYING ECONOMICS OF GOVERNMENT GROWTH

We have seen that the growth of government in the postwar period was the outcome of an ongoing battle between liberal and conservative political philosophies. Liberal historian Arthur Schlesinger, Jr., has described this as an alternation in the dominant ideology between "public purpose" and "private interest." In the long run, according to Schlesinger, government will tend to grow because programs initiated by liberal administrations are seldom eliminated by the conservatives who follow. The appropriate image is of government as a spiral that widens during periods of liberal dominance but never contracts.[12] In Schlesinger's view, the alternation between liberalism and conservatism is perpetual. Politically active young people adopt the ideology dominant in their formative years. As time goes by they reach higher and higher levels of influence in government, the private sector, academia, and the media. Eventually they take power and attempt to reimpose the liberal or conservative ideology of their youth. The rise of Bill Clinton to the presidency is a clear illustration of Schlesinger's theory: Clinton and many of his close advisers were college students and antiwar activists during the liberal Kennedy-Johnson era. To take Schlesinger's point a step further, we can predict that in about the year 2016 a conservative administration will take power, reflecting the political and economic philosophies dominant in the early 1980s.

Conservative economists Milton Friedman and Rose Director Friedman have also described, in less-favorable language, the tendency of liberal reforms to survive subsequent conservative administrations. In their view, liberal programs resist conservative attempts to eliminate them because of the "tyranny of the status quo." An "iron triangle" of bureaucrats, politicians, and private-sector beneficiaries of government programs protects programs even when it has been shown that they are detrimental to the public interest. Measured across all voters the gain from eliminating a given program may be large; but for each voter separately the gain may be too small to make fighting for it worthwhile.[13]

In his important and influential book, *Crisis and Leviathan*, Robert Higgs agrees that the dominant ideology is the crucial factor determining the growth rate of government but emphasizes the role of economic or social crises in making the liberal interventionist ideology acceptable.[14] A mild recession in 1931 might have led to a Democrat replacing Herbert Hoover, but the Great Depression made people eager to accept a wide range of new programs. John F. Kennedy and Lyndon B. Johnson would have pushed for new programs in any case, but the social and political crises of the 1960s made the public willing to accept a much broader range of new legislation and programs, particularly those designed to solve problems of poverty and racial discrimination.

---

[12] Arthur Schlesinger, Jr., *The Cycles of American History* (Boston: Houghton Mifflin, 1986), Chapter 2.

[13] Milton and Rose Friedman, *Tyranny of the Status Quo* (San Diego: Harcourt Brace Jovanovich, 1983), pp. 41–51.

[14] Robert Higgs, *Crisis and Leviathan: Critical Episodes in the Growth of American Government* (New York: Oxford University Press, 1987). Leviathan was a sea monster in the Bible. The term has come to stand for a totalitarian bureaucratic state.

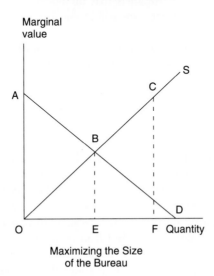

Maximizing the Size
of the Bureau

Why do government bureaucracies often seem so big and inefficient? Why, to put it somewhat differently, does the term "bureaucracy" carry such negative connotations? Economist William Niskanen provides one answer based on the relationship between Congress and the bureaus.[15] The S curve in the figure represents a government bureau's cost of supplying units of "output"—acres of land irrigated, recommendations made to farmers, grants awarded, power plants inspected, or the like. The D curve shows the marginal valuation of each additional unit of output. The efficient output would be OE. At that level of output every unit would be produced for which the marginal value exceeded the marginal cost. At OE the cost of producing the last unit, BE, would exactly equal the value placed on it. This is, of course, what would happen if the product were produced by private firms and sold in a competitive market.

But Niskanen believes that the budget-making process in Congress works differently. Bureaucrats are not interested in minimizing costs or maximizing profits. Their goal is to preside over as large a budget as possible—whence comes prestige in Washington. Because they are likely to be a monopoly and to have all the available information about costs of producing a somewhat hard-to-measure output, they will make it extremely difficult to judge the shape of the S curve. Instead they will provide the congressional committee overseeing the bureau with a single request for the money needed to carry out the bureau's "mission." The congressional committee is also likely

[15] William A. Niskanen, *Bureaucracy and Representative Government* (Chicago: Aldine-Atherton, 1971), Chapter 5.

to be happy with an output larger than OE because the members of the committee will be receiving campaign contributions from the interest groups that benefit from the bureau's work. If, however, the agency's total costs were to grow to the point where they exceeded the total benefits, questions would be raised by other Congressmen on other committees, by the press, and by the executive branch, which takes the heat when total taxes are raised. The result is that the bureau will produce output OF at a total cost of OCF, and that these costs will be equal to total benefits of OACF. The bureau will be too big.

This is not, strictly speaking, a theory of the *growth* of government. But it may explain why, when new bureaus are created, they grow so large and add so much to federal spending.

Beneath the changing tides of politics, a number of economists have discerned deeper currents that determine the size of government. Writing in the 1880s, German economist and economic historian Adolph Wagner wrote that the growth of modern industry would produce increasing political "pressure for social progress" and thereby continuous expansion of the public sector. In part this would happen because competitive nation-states would find it in their interest to appease labor and to meet, at least partially, its demands for social justice. On the whole, Wagner's prediction has proved remarkably accurate, and the idea that the public sector will inevitably expand relative to the private sector has come to be known as Wagner's Law.

A number of American economists have accepted Wagner's Law but emphasized a different underlying force: the increase of real per capita income. Governmental programs that help the disadvantaged, protect the environment, and the like may be luxury goods: we buy proportionately more of them when our income rises. The slowdown in the growth of the demand for government after 1969 is consistent with this thesis. To the extent that voting patterns reflect views about long-run incomes, the belief that productivity growth had slowed produced a substantial decrease in the demand for government expenditures. Other long-run trends may also influence the demand for government. Population growth and urbanization, for example, may have increased the demand for programs to preserve the environment or provide mass transportation.[16]

But what about pure transfer payments? A poor person would naturally vote for heavy taxes on the rich. We might expect that in a democracy in which the rule of one adult/one vote was followed, income tax rates would be highly progressive and after-tax incomes would tend toward equality. Indeed, the surprising thing about most industrial countries is not that they have progressive income taxes but that those taxes are not *more* progressive. Economists Allan H. Meltzer and Scott F. Richard have

---

[16] See Solomon Fabricant, *The Trend in Government Activity in the United States since 1900* (New York: National Bureau of Economic Research, 1952), for an early statement of this view of the growth of government.

attempted to devise a rational theory of transfer payments. In their model, people vote for programs that redistribute income in their favor but take into account the disincentive effects of higher taxes. The poor do not automatically vote for "soak the rich" taxes because they think that as a result the whole economy will be less productive and that they will end up with less than they had before.[17] The Meltzer-Richard theory accurately captures the thrust of Ronald Reagan's argument for cutting marginal tax rates (the tax on an additional dollar of income): total output would increase to the benefit of the poor as well as the rich.

Economist Sam Peltzman has developed a related theory. Based on international comparisons, Peltzman argues that a more-equal distribution of income generated by the market paradoxically, accelerates the growth of government because it increases the political strength of the group that favors further redistribution through the government. When the poor are very poor, they are not able to perceive and effectively articulate their interests. Economic growth empowers the poor and makes them a political force to be reckoned with.[18]

It is common for academic writers to push their own theory as if the factor they stress was the one and only cause of the trends observed. Product differentiation is as useful to academics as it is to producers of automobiles, insurance policies, and chickens. But it seems to us that the theories of the growth of government we have examined complement each other. Schlesinger's emphasis on the nostalgia of political leaders for the ideologies of their youth, Higgs's emphasis on the role of crises, and Meltzer and Richard's emphasis on the rational voter's concern about the disincentive effects of high taxes can all contribute to our understanding of the complex process that has led to the expansion of the role of government in the postwar era.

In this chapter we have had space to discuss the trends in the role of government in only the broadest terms. In the next chapter we will examine the relationship between government and three sectors that have been a major concern throughout this book: agriculture, transportation, and foreign trade.

SELECTED REFERENCES AND SUGGESTED READINGS

Aaron, Henry J. *Politics and the Professors: The Great Society in Perspective.* Washington, D.C.: Brookings Institution, 1978.

Asch, Peter. *Consumer Safety Legislation: Putting a Price on Life and Limb.* New York: Oxford University Press, 1988.

Bennett, James T., and Manuel H. Johnson. *The Political Economy of Federal Government Growth, 1959–1978.* College Station, Texas: Center for Education and Research in Free Enterprise, 1980.

Bernstein, Barton J., and Alan I. Matusow. *The Truman Administration: A Documentary Record.* New York: Harper & Row, 1968.

---

[17] Allan H. Meltzer and Scott F. Richard, "A Rational Theory of the Size of Government," *Journal of Political Economy* 89 (October 1981): 914–927.

[18] Sam Peltzman, "The Growth of Government," *Journal of Law and Economics* 23 (October 1980): 220–285.

Borcherding, Thomas E. "The Sources of Growth of Public Expenditures in the United States, 1902–1970." In *Budgets and Bureaucrats: The Sources of Government Growth*, ed. Thomas E. Borcherding. Durham: Duke University Press, 1977.

Break, George F. "Issues in Measuring the Level of Government Activity." *American Economic Review* 72 (May 1982): 288–295.

Buchanan, James M. *Public Finance in Democratic Process: Fiscal Institutions and Individual Choice*. Chapel Hill: University of North Carolina Press, 1967.

Edelstein, Michael. "What Price Cold War? Military Spending and Private Investment in the US, 1946–1979." *Cambridge Journal of Economics* 14 (1990): 421–437.

Fabricant, Solomon. *The Trend of Government Activity in the United States since 1900*. New York: National Bureau of Economic Research, 1952.

Friedman, Milton, and Rose D. Friedman. *Tyranny of the Status Quo*. San Diego: Harcourt Brace Jovanovich, 1983.

Galbraith, John K. *The Affluent Society*. Boston: Houghton Mifflin, 1969.

Glasner, David. *Politics, Prices, and Petroleum: The Political Economy of Energy*. Cambridge, Massachusetts: Ballinger, 1985.

Heller, Walter. *New Dimensions of Political Economy*. Cambridge: Harvard University Press, 1969.

Higgs, Robert. *Crisis and Leviathan: Critical Episodes in the Growth of American Government*. New York: Oxford University Press, 1987.

Hughes, Jonathan. *The Governmental Habit*. New York: Basic Books, 1977.

Lilley, William III, and James C. Miller III. "The New 'Social Regulation.'" *Public Interest* 47 (1977): 49–61.

Lowery, David, and William D. Berry. "The Growth of Government in the United States: An Empirical Assessment of Competing Explanations." *American Journal of Political Science* 27 (November 1983).

McCraw, Thomas K. *Prophets of Regulation*. Cambridge: Harvard University Press, 1984.

Meltzer, Allan H., and Scott F. Richard. "A Rational Theory of the Size of Government." *Journal of Political Economy* 89 (October 1981): 914–927.

———. "Tests of a Rational Theory of the Size of Government." *Public Choice* 41 (1983): 403–418.

———. "Why Government Grows (and Grows) in a Democracy." *Public Interest* 52 (Summer 1978): 111–118.

Niskanen, William A. *Bureaucracy and Representative Government*. Chicago: Aldine-Atherton, 1971.

Peltzman, Sam. "The Growth of Government." *Journal of Law and Economics* 23 (October 1980): 220–285.

Roberts, Paul Craig. *The Supply-Side Revolution: An Insider's Account of Policymaking in Washington*. Cambridge: Harvard University Press, 1984.

Schlesinger, Arthur M., Jr. *The Cycles of American History*. Boston: Houghton Mifflin, 1986.

Schumpeter, Joseph. *Capitalism, Socialism, and Democracy*. 3d ed. New York: Harper & Row, 1950.

Stockman, David A. *The Triumph of Politics: How the Reagan Revolution Failed*. New York: Harper & Row, 1986.

Stone, Alan. *Economic Regulation and the Public Interest: The Federal Trade Commission in Theory and Practice*. Ithaca, New York: Cornell University Press, 1977.

Vatter, Harold G. *The U.S. Economy in the 1950s*. New York: W. W. Norton, 1963.

Wildavsky, Aaron. *The Politics of the Budgetary Process*. Boston: Little, Brown, 1964.

CHAPTER TWENTY-SEVEN

GOVERNMENT AND THE ECONOMY: AGRICULTURE, THE ENVIRONMENT, AND TRANSPORTATION

CHAPTER THEME To see how government intervention in the economy proceeded during the postwar period, it is not sufficient to look solely at the aggregate statistics on government spending that were the focus of Chapter 26. Intervention often took the form of rules and regulations that were only dimly reflected in those statistics. In some areas of the economy, the regulatory framework laid down or expanded during the New Deal continued to be increased after the war; but in other areas a reaction to government regulation set in, and this led to some dramatic experiments with deregulation. In this chapter we will consider the changing role of government in three sectors of the economy that have been covered in detail in earlier chapters: agriculture, the environment, and transportation.

AGRICULTURE

At one time agriculture might have been the model of the economist's concept of perfect competition: Agriculture was characterized by numerous competitors, each too small to significantly influence total supply, acting as price-takers. In the nineteenth century, American farmers operating in this kind of market vastly expanded the land under cultivation, adopted a wide range of technological improvements, and generated an unprecedented increase in total output. In many ways the system worked well, although the farmer's life, subject as it was to the vagaries of the weather and world markets, was often bitter.

This characterization is, admittedly, overly simple. The nineteenth-century politicians who had wrestled with questions such as land policy, Indian policy, banking, and usury laws—all policies of great interest to farmers—would have been surprised to hear that the government had little to do with farmers. Nevertheless, in the nineteenth century and well into the twentieth, market forces were the primary determinant of farm prices and farm income. By the end of World War II, the situation was very different. The farmer, the cynic might say, had become a ward of the state. Farm life was still far from easy, but prices and output were now determined as much by politicians in Washington as by world supplies and demands for agricultural products.

THE POSTWAR SURPLUS PROBLEMS

Farm prices and income began a downward trend in July 1948, and as a result of the high support prices required by the Agricultural Acts of 1948 and 1949, payments to farmers by the Commodity Credit Corporation (CCC) and government surplus stocks rose. By 1950, corn stocks owned by the CCC or pledged to it as collateral were greater than they had been at any previous time. Wheat inventories were about the same as those held in the previous peak year of 1942. Although cotton holdings did not approach the massive inventories of 1938 to 1941, they were not far below those of 1942, another high year.

To understand why CCC inventories increased so markedly in years of mild recession, it is helpful to review postwar farm legislation. Although it had been amended, the basic farm law was still the Agricultural Adjustment Act of 1938, which was generally felt to be in need of revision. Extensive discussion of the farm problem went on during 1947 and the first half of 1948. The result was the Agricultural Act of 1948, which maintained price-support levels through 1949 at the magical 90 percent of parity (the ratio of farm prices to prices paid by farmers in the "golden" years 1910 to 1914) for a wide range of commodities.

The contribution of the midwestern farm states to the Democratic victory of 1948 led to a lengthy reconsideration of the policy laid down by the Republican-controlled Eightieth Congress in the 1948 act. It seemed for a while that a novel and imaginative method of subsidizing agriculture might be implemented. In the spring of 1949, Secretary of Agriculture C. F. Brannan announced the plan of compensatory payments to which the press and public quickly attached his name, although its central ideas had been developing for many years in academic writings. The Brannan plan would have allowed prices to seek their own level in the marketplace, with the difference between the market price and a "modernized" parity price to be paid to the farmer (up to a certain maximum number of "units") by a check from the Treasury. The advantages of the Brannan plan were substantial. Surpluses would be eliminated, saving storage costs. And the public, the poor in particular, would be able to buy food cheaply.

After months of heated argument, during which the National Grange and the American Farm Bureau Federation aligned themselves against such an unconcealed payment of subsidies, the House of Representatives refused to give the Brannan plan a trial run. Opponents of the Brannan plan won the day by castigating such a straightforward subsidy as "socialism."

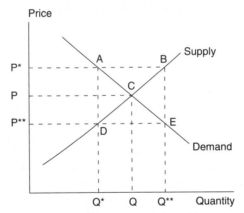

Price supports vs. the Brannan plan

The figure above illustrates the economics of the Brannan plan. In a free market the price would be P and output produced would be Q, determined as usual by the intersection of the supply and demand curves. This price is considered, however, to be unfair to farmers.

Under the traditional system the government wishes to raise the price to P*, the modernized parity price. At this price, consumers are willing to buy only Q*; but farmers produce Q**. To hold the price in the market at P* the government must purchase the excess supply, Q** − Q*. This will cost the government (the taxpayer) P* × (Q** − Q*). The surplus, Q** − Q*, will have to be stored, so storage costs will be incurred in future years. The gain to farmers (compared with the free-market equilibrium) will be the area P*BCP.

Under the Brannan plan, the government simply allows the surplus to be sold in the marketplace. The price falls to P**, the price at which Q** can be sold. The Treasury then writes a check to each farmer for the difference between the modernized parity price P* and the new market price P**. In this case the total cost to the government is given by the area P*BEP**.

Consumers clearly benefit from switching to the Brannan plan: they pay a lower price for farm products. No resources are wasted simply producing food and then storing it in government warehouses. Even under the Brannan plan, however, there is an efficiency loss given by the triangle CBE. Resources are employed in farming that could better satisfy consumer demands elsewhere in the economy.

The impact on the government budget depends on whether area P*BEP**, the costs under the Brannan plan, exceed or fall short of area Q*ABQ**, the costs under the traditional purchase-for-storage system plus the storage costs. In general this will depend on the elasticities of the supply and demand curves. The more elastic the supply and demand curves, the less costly will be the Brannan plan compared with purchase-for-storage.

Financially, farmers fare the same under the two plans. They produce Q** output and receive P*Q** total income. Under the Brannan plan, however, farmers receive a part of the income in the form of a "welfare" check. Some farmers will find this demeaning. And direct payments will be obvious to the public and make it harder for farmers to defend and increase their subsidies.

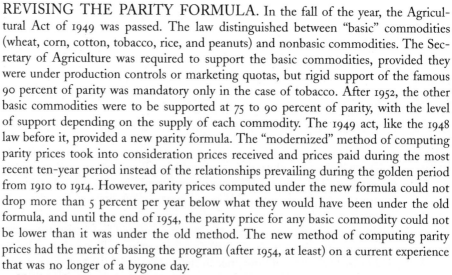

REVISING THE PARITY FORMULA. In the fall of the year, the Agricultural Act of 1949 was passed. The law distinguished between "basic" commodities (wheat, corn, cotton, tobacco, rice, and peanuts) and nonbasic commodities. The Secretary of Agriculture was required to support the basic commodities, provided they were under production controls or marketing quotas, but rigid support of the famous 90 percent of parity was mandatory only in the case of tobacco. After 1952, the other basic commodities were to be supported at 75 to 90 percent of parity, with the level of support depending on the supply of each commodity. The 1949 act, like the 1948 law before it, provided a new parity formula. The "modernized" method of computing parity prices took into consideration prices received and prices paid during the most recent ten-year period instead of the relationships prevailing during the golden period from 1910 to 1914. However, parity prices computed under the new formula could not drop more than 5 percent per year below what they would have been under the old formula, and until the end of 1954, the parity price for any basic commodity could not be lower than it was under the old method. The new method of computing parity prices had the merit of basing the program (after 1954, at least) on a current experience that was no longer of a bygone day.

Neither flexible supports nor the new parity formula became effective as planned. After the start of the Korean War, Congress amended the law to make 90-percent support of the basics mandatory, and the old method of computing parity prices remained more favorable to farmers than the new one. The war temporarily enabled the CCC to reduce embarrassingly high inventories and loans. The crops of 1952 and 1953 required considerable support, however, and by 1954 CCC loans and inventories of surplus commodities were at an all-time high. Twice during 1954, Congress had to increase CCC authority to borrow for support operations, drawing increasing public attention to the farm problem.

After procrastinating for more than a year, the Eighty-third Congress at last came up with its version of a farm program in the Agricultural Act of 1954. Secretary of Agriculture Ezra Taft Benson was especially insistent on restoring flexible supports, which were finally set for five of the six basic commodities at 82.5 to 90 percent of parity. The 1954 act again postponed changing to the modernized parity price formula for basic commodities; the notion that the period from 1910 to 1914 represented parity ("fairity") was too deeply ingrained to die easily. In an attempt to "insulate" the massive stocks of the CCC from the market, Congress authorized that a portion of CCC stocks be set aside for donation or sale for enumerated worthy causes.

FAILURE OF THE SOIL BANK PLAN. But surpluses showed no signs of lessening. The Soil Bank Act of 1956 was devised to reduce supplies of the six basic commodities by achieving a 10- to 17-percent reduction in plowland through payments to farmers who "voluntarily" shifted land out of production into the "soil bank." The diversion payments were based on the old formula of multiplying a base unit price by normal yield per acre by the numbers of acres withdrawn. Although the soil bank idea had been linked at its creation in the 1930s with the dust bowl in the Plains states, the plan remained what it had always been: an attempt to raise farm prices thinly disguised as a conservation program.

The results were unexpected, but easy to understand in retrospect. Farmers placed their least-productive land in the soil bank and cultivated the remainder more intensively. Surpluses went right on mounting, reaching astronomical heights in 1961 after nine consecutive years of increase. Donald McCloskey has pointed out to us another unintended consequence of the soil bank program: Iowa farms were once wooded on the edge of their fields, but the wooded borders (a place for animals and birds, and a source of lumber) were cut down in an effort to get around the acreage restrictions.

In recent years there has been some improvement in the incentives offered farmers. Under the deficiency payments system used for grains, farmers now receive a subsidy based on the difference between a "target" price and the market price or support price, whichever is higher (in recent years this has been the market price). But the quantity to which this deficiency payment is applied is based on historical yields and acreages under cultivation, so farmers cannot increase their deficiency payment by cultivating their land more intensively.

THE KENNEDY YEARS TO THE PRESENT

The Emergency Feed Grain Bill of 1961 encouraged drastic reductions in acreages devoted to corn and grain sorghums by offering $1.20 a bushel in diversion payments to farmers who reduced their acreage by 20 percent; even higher payments were offered for the diversion of an additional 20 percent of feed-crop acreage. On the whole, the plan worked in 1962 because the reduction was large enough to offset attempts by farmers to minimize its effects. For the first time in a decade, feed grain carryover actually dropped, and a continuing reduction was predicted.

This modest success encouraged the Kennedy and Johnson administrations to attack massive surpluses of wheat with a similar, but incredibly expensive, plan. Wealthy farmers and their organization, the Farm Bureau Federation, although at first opposed, quickly saw the error of their ways and joined wholeheartedly in forging the Food and Agriculture Act of 1965. A monstrous giveaway, this act cost the American taxpayer $5 to $6 billion a year to make rich farmers richer while allowing a little to trickle down to poor farmers.

As consumers and taxpayers became more vocal in the 1970s, Congress found it more difficult to respond unilaterally to farm interests. The Democratic Congress and President Jimmy Carter made a heroic effort to balance these interests by passing the Food and Agriculture Act of 1977. This monument to complication set support prices within specified ranges on wheat, feed grains, cotton, dairy products, sugar, peanuts, and other commodities. In the winter of 1978, however, protesting farmers obtained higher support prices through the Emergency Act of 1978. As in the past, farmers could obtain CCC loans to keep their crops off the market, and acreage controls were imposed by requiring farmers receiving payments to set aside at least 20 percent of their land for "soil conservation uses."[1]

This bill reflected the natural alliances and divisions among farmers. A combination of acreage restrictions and CCC-administered price supports has the support of almost all farmers for at least three reasons. First, it masks the amount and extent of the subsidy to agriculture. Department of Agriculture outlays on the subsidy program, great as they are, do not include the higher prices paid by consumers for food and fiber as a consequence of support operations. Second, it ties price and income maintenance to "conservation," diluting the element of subsidy in the public mind. Third, it seems respectable because the subsidy is provided by a market mechanism, whereas subsidy checks paid at the end of the growing season appear too much like welfare checks.

Within agriculture, the only serious differences arising in recent years have been concerned with the question of rigorous versus mild controls over output. The American Farm Bureau Federation, which speaks for the more-affluent farmers, wants lower support prices and greater freedom to plant, because Farm Bureau membership makes huge profits on large volume. Supporting sharp restrictions on acreage combined with astronomical support prices are the organizations of small farmers, chiefly the National Farmers Union, the National Farmers Organization, and the National Grange.

President Ronald Reagan's Farm Bill, passed in late 1981, exceeded $22.6 billion in expenditures, with more than $10 billion of it being allocated for the food-stamp program; price supports were continued on peanuts, sugar, wheat, feed grains, rice, soybeans, cotton, and wool, though these supports were reduced from their higher levels during the Carter years. As expected, both Democratic and Republican farm interests

---

[1]For more details, see D. Gale Johnson, "The Food and Agriculture Act of 1977: Implications for Farmers and Taxpayers," in *Contemporary Economic Problems*, ed. William Fellner (Washington, D.C.: American Enterprise Institute, 1978), pp. 167–210.

claimed that the cutbacks were dictated by the administration, leaving no effective protection for farmers facing severely depressed incomes.

THE DECLINING ROLE OF AGRICULTURE

Unquestionably, farm programs have helped operators who were well down in the income scale, but it is just as clearly true that the lion's share of assistance has gone to those who were already at the top of the heap. When the government supported farm prices, those with the most bushels or bales to sell received the chief benefits; when acreage restrictions were put into effect, those who were in a position to reduce acreage the most received the largest checks. In 1989, for example, the top 15 percent of farm families by income received 62 percent of all government payments. There has been some recent improvement for the bottom half of the farm population, but mostly due to the relief afforded by some farmers quitting the business.

A decline in the number of farmers, however, should not be viewed as a sign of failure in U.S. farm policy. In a technologically progressive society, resources must be continually reallocated. As our knowledge and capital grow, fewer and fewer resources must be devoted to obtaining the necessities of life, and more and more may be devoted to obtaining conveniences and luxuries. This has been true throughout the entire economic history of the United States. In 1790, nearly 90 percent of the work force was employed in agriculture; in 1960, the figure was less than 10 percent; by 1991, it had fallen to 2.5 percent. The decline has been absolute as well as relative: in 1970 there were 2.5 million farm families; in 1990 there were only 1.4 million. Favorable as the exodus has been, there are still far too many people in agriculture, especially in the South.

Paradoxically, the very decline in the economic role of agriculture has tended to increase its political power. As subsidies are spread out over a larger and larger nonfarm sector, the attention paid to the cost of farm programs tends to diminish. The power of the farmer in the Senate has fallen only slowly, if at all. After all, South Dakota has as many Senators as New York or California.

UPDATED APPROACHES. Many agricultural economists who are sympathetic to agriculture feel that policies followed over the last four decades prevent a satisfactory solution to the farm problem. There has long been an objection to the ideal of "parity," on the ground that no group in society is entitled, by right, to a fixed reward for its efforts. Moreover, successful attempts to maintain prices of farm commodities in the same relative position over time may keep consumers from obtaining the supplies that they want most. Parity prices tend to keep agricultural resources employed in the production of products that people have wanted in the past. If some agricultural prices are not allowed to fall relative to others, the pattern of cultivation will remain too rigid, and the result will be chronic "surpluses" of some crops.

Although economists look with disfavor on present types of agricultural subsidies, many agree that some kind of federal farm program may be necessary because the transition from rural to urban life is exceedingly difficult. Many poor farmers remain on the land simply because they have no other skills with which to make a living. For others the pain of giving up a cherished way of life is too much. So a case can be made for slowing the rate at which family farms disappear and for subsidizing the training of the displaced rural poor. But no one familiar with the facts can advocate the artificial support of prices to aid the wealthy when a plan of compensatory payments would maintain incomes of poor farmers satisfactorily. Unfortunately, consumers are less-effectively represented in Congress than are farmers.

THE ENVIRONMENT

A conflict between economic development and preserving the environment generally erupts when entrepreneurs are not forced to take full account of the costs created by their decision to exploit a natural resource. This is the economist's concept of external costs, and it finds its most frequent application in relation to environmental problems. The failure to take costs into account often results from an incomplete specification of property rights. For instance, a developer building homes on a lake may simply ignore the effects on water quality or wildlife. If the courts recognize the right of users of the lake to good-quality water, the developer will have to be more careful or risk a costly lawsuit.

One historical example familiar to economists was the phenomenon that Garrett Hardin labeled in 1968 as the "tragedy of the commons." For centuries cattle farmers in England had the right to pasture their animals on publicly owned land, the commons. The animals grown on the commons were typically puny, and the land was worn bare. The reason was simply that no individual farmer had to consider the damage to the commons when considering whether it was worthwhile placing another animal there. The costs of the additional damage caused by an additional animal were shared among all users of the commons. The idea is widely applicable to environmental problems. The seas are overfished, and the sky is polluted, because they are "commons."

ENVIRONMENTALISM IN HISTORICAL PERSPECTIVE

Concern about the environment has deep historical roots in the United States. Yellowstone, the first and largest national park, was established in 1872 to preserve its natural wonders.[2] There was little fear at the time that the land in Yellowstone would be exploited for agricultural purposes if transferred to private hands. Rather, the concern in Congress was that if a private entrepreneur controlled access to Yellowstone, its natural beauties would be degraded by access roads and advertising. The conservation movement in the twentieth century began auspiciously with Theodore Roosevelt's policy to involve the federal government in the control and acquisition of natural resources.

The movement languished in the 1920s but surged upward under the administration of Franklin D. Roosevelt. Old methods were carried out with renewed vigor, and two

---

[2] A federal "reservation" had been established at Hot Springs, Arkansas, in 1832 to protect its mineral springs.

new policies were introduced. First, the government took steps to conserve the soil owned by private individuals (although, as noted earlier in the chapter, the overwhelming reason for the "soil bank" plan was to raise farm prices). Second, it insisted that a meaningful program of conservation required the simultaneous protection of many resources within an entire region.

GRAZING LANDS. Along lines of traditional policy, perhaps the most important step was the withdrawal from private entry of the remaining public domain—nearly 175 million acres—until the land could be classified according to its best use. A small portion was later made available for entry, but most was organized into grazing districts under the Taylor Grazing Act of 1934. Before the passage of this act, stockmen let their animals feed on the great public ranges without restraint—the old problem of the commons. Under the new system, permits limited the number of grazing animals to the amount that a given range could accommodate without depleting the forage. By 1950, there were 59 grazing districts that included 145 million acres; in addition, grazing leases were issued on scattered public-domain lands and on Indian reservations.

A generation after passage of the Taylor Act, controversy still smolders over the proper disposition of these lands. Among westerners, there is substantial opinion that the federal government should oversee only those areas that are suitable for recreation, national forests, wildlife refuges, and reclamation and power projects, selling the remainder of the public domain to the highest bidders. But on the east and west coasts, there is resistance to the sale of any part of the public domain.

FORESTATION. During the Great Depression, the government made great expenditures on conservation. Late in 1933, Interior Secretary Harold Ickes could remark, with truth, that the Civilian Conservation Corps had accomplished more reforestation in six months than all federal agencies had in the preceding 15 years. Funds were also made available to expand the national forests by purchasing poorly kept private forest lands, located for the most part in the Southeast. By 1950, national forest acreage had risen to 180 million, and the government controlled some 200 million acres of additional forested land in Indian reservations, wildlife refuges, national parks, and other public holdings.

About 116 million acres, or one-quarter of the U.S. total, was publicly owned commercial forest land divided between federal agencies, which managed 89 million acres, and state and local agencies, which controlled 27 million acres. The very best timber owned by the federal government was located in the West, far from markets and in inaccessible areas, so that investments in roads had to be made before it could be used. Pressure by loggers to build roads into federal timber areas was successful, and much of this timber was cut far sooner than it would have been if the timberland had been in private hands.

SOIL CONSERVATION. Old-line conservation efforts included some incidental preservation of the soil. Not until the New Deal, however, were systematic efforts made to conserve agricultural land. These efforts began in 1933 with the establishment of the Soil Erosion Service in the Department of the Interior. In 1935, the Soil Conservation Service became an agency of the Department of Agriculture. Originally, contracts were made with individual farmers; the service furnished technical assistance and some materials, and the farmers furnished labor and the remaining materials. Early in 1937, President Roosevelt wrote the state governors requesting that their legislatures pass acts enabling landowners and occupiers to form soil-conservation districts. By 1954, about 2,500 soil-conservation districts, including 80 percent of all U.S. farms, had been organized.

WATER CONTROL. Any discussion of new concepts of conservation must contain some mention of what may constitute the ultimate solution to the whole problem: the inclusion of water control and major river valleys in programs of great scope. Some advocates argue that nothing less can produce permanently successful conservation. The evidence is not conclusive, although the Tennessee Valley Authority (TVA)—one outstanding example—has unquestionably done a remarkable job of upgrading an entire region.

Technical advances have made possible the reclamation of arid land that was once considered useless. Only water is needed to transform most desert into croplands. For example, pumps driven by 65,000-horsepower motors have been installed at the Grand Coulee Dam in Washington state to lift water 280 feet from the Columbia River into the Grand Coulee chasm, from which it can then be diverted to irrigate vast areas. In another project, by means of complex systems of dams, reservoirs, pumps, and tunnels, water from northern California has been diverted to southern California. The Bureau of Reclamation estimates that eventually 50 million acres west of the Rockies can be converted to fertile land.

As impressive as these achievements are from a technical point of view, they actually amount to nothing more than outlays to increase present production. These outlays could be made now or 100 years from now and produce no deterioration in our natural resources. Thus, irrigation and drainage projects do not ordinarily prevent diminution of future production. A piece of Arizona desert land can be irrigated at any time in the future, and the resultant increase in production will be just as great as it would if the improvement were made now. However, reclamation is not the same as conservation. Estimates of the full cost of producing crops on irrigated western land show that the effort is seldom worth it. Farmers can stay in business only because the water they use is highly subsidized.

CLEANING UP THE ENVIRONMENT. During the 1960s, the public awakened to the belief that the environment had become polluted with numerous dangerous by-products of industry. Making the environment whole again, many argued, was more important than rapid economic growth. The environmental movement did not represent a sharp break with the earlier emphasis on conservation, but there were differences. The conservationists had emphasized the management of resources to sustain long-term yields of timberland, farmland, water, and mineral resources; the environmentalists put more emphasis on the preservation of natural resources for future aesthetic enjoyment, and they emphasized the interdependence of different parts of the environment.

The growing concern about the environment was not confined to the United States; other industrial countries, particularly those in western Europe, experienced the same phenomenon. A clean and well-preserved environment appears to be what economists call a luxury good: as income rises, consumers wish to spend a larger fraction of their income on it. Public attention in the United States shifted from problem to problem depending on the events of the day. In the early 1960s, Rachel Carson's book *Silent Spring* heightened concern about the danger of indiscriminate pesticide use, and as a result the Department of Agriculture banned the use of DDT in 1969. That same year, a major oil spill off the coast of Santa Barbara, California, raised concerns about the danger of offshore oil drilling, and related fears were raised about the impact of the proposed Alaska Pipeline. The oil spill in Alaska produced by the sinking of the *Exxon Valdez* in 1989 reinforced such fears.

Concern about the "greenhouse effect" illustrates the environmental movement's emphasis on the way in which environmental problems are closely interlinked. The greenhouse effect is produced by the accumulation of certain gases (carbon dioxide, methane, and chlorofluorocarbons among them) in the atmosphere. These gases absorb infrared radiation being reflected from the earth (much as does the glass over a greenhouse) and thus raise temperatures worldwide. The effects to be expected from global warming are uncertain and highly controversial. The effects are likely to be greatest for the developing countries, where agriculture (which is a large share of GNP) might be adversely affected, and where debilitating parasitic diseases might become more widespread. The greenhouse effect is another example of the classic problem of a commons. Individual producers, even entire nations, have no incentive to control the gases they release into the atmosphere, because the costs will be shared worldwide and may be concentrated on the other side of the earth.

Various solutions have been proposed for the problem of global warming. As usual there are two approaches. Liberal economists favor explicit emission targets reached through international negotiations and detailed government plans for reaching those targets. Market-oriented economists favor taxes on emissions, and some favor creating tradeable rights in emissions. Countries would be assigned maximum emission levels, and if they exceeded their assigned level they would have to buy the right to emit more from other countries that had managed to hold their emissions below their targets.

Responding to these and other environmental concerns, Congress in 1970 passed the Clean Air Act and Water Quality Improvement Act and established the Environmental Protection Agency (EPA). Since then the EPA has produced a virtual flood of regulations. Typically, the EPA sets a maximum level of pollution allowed based on the "best available technology." In many cases the EPA must set literally hundreds of standards for each pollutant. For example, EPA works out a separate standard for each model of automobile. Measuring the costs versus benefits of the EPA standards is exceedingly difficult and controversial, but no one doubts that the direct costs of complying with EPA standards are very high. By one estimate these were $100 billion in 1988, about 2 percent of GNP.[3]

THE ENERGY CRISIS. Coming on the heels of the new environmentalism was the "energy crisis" and the increasing fear that the U.S. economy was stagnating. Proposed solutions to the energy crisis often seemed in conflict with programs to improve the environment. Beginning in 1973, the Organization of Petroleum Exporting Countries (OPEC), which at that time controlled a dominant share of the world oil market, began to flex its muscles. The price of a barrel of crude oil quadrupled between 1973 and 1975. Particularly disruptive was the oil embargo that followed the Arab-Israeli war in 1973. The result was long lines at gas pumps—rationing by waiting time rather than by price.

This experience touched off a fundamental debate on how to meet the "energy crisis." Should it be through government actions—rationing, subsidies for the poor, and federal expenditures for new sources of energy—or through the price mechanism? Advocates of the price system held that higher prices would produce the most efficient results: higher prices would reduce demand (by making smaller, fuel-efficient cars more attractive, for example) and increase supplies. Instead, a bureaucratic response was tried. A federal energy administration was established in 1974, and a Cabinet-level Department of Energy followed in 1977. Spending on a wide range of federal energy projects was increased; but in the end much of the painful adjustment was the response to higher prices. Americans cut their energy consumption by buying smaller cars (many of them from foreign producers), insulating their homes, and investing in more fuel-efficient productive processes. On the supply side, higher prices led to a rapid increase in oil production in countries outside of OPEC, undermining its monopoly power. The price system worked much as many of its advocates had suggested it would, although not perhaps as quickly and painlessly as some of them had expected.

LEGISLATION VERSUS MARKET MECHANISMS. The Reagan and Bush administrations tended to resolve conflicts between environmentalists and energy producers in favor of the latter. But America's concern with the environment has been a long one, and it seems likely that policies designed to protect the environment will continue to get a sympathetic hearing. There is, after all, a mocking irony in the fact that the major federal statute designed to rectify environmental abuses, the National Environmental Policy Act of 1969, consists largely of amendments to the Clean Air Act of 1894 and the Refuse Act of 1899.

Concern over the environment has grown throughout the past century and has risen to a fever pitch in recent years. Perhaps the main issue to be resolved in years to come is whether environmental protection will rely more heavily on market mechanisms (taxes and the creation of tradeable rights) or on direct government controls. As this is written, there seems to be some enthusiasm for the market. The Clean Air Act

---

[3] In addition, the government has undertaken a number of other programs to improve the quality of the environment. Perhaps the most famous is Superfund, established in 1980 and charged with cleaning up hazardous waste dumps.

Amendments of 1990 allowed the EPA to create emission rights that could be bought and sold by producers, something that had been tried on a small scale during the Carter administration. But it is too early to say whether the current emphasis on the market is part of a long-term trend or only one phase in an alternating cycle.

THE TRANSPORTATION INFRASTRUCTURE

Unlike agriculture, the provision of transportation services has always been subject to considerable government involvement. Transportation frequently appears to be a natural monopoly. We need a road between Centerville and Middletown, but only one. Regulation through competition is not feasible, so throughout our history government has been involved with many aspects of transportation—the building of roads, harbor improvements, and lighthouses, and the regulation of shipping rates.[4] In the postwar period, the scale and scope of government involvement in transportation increased dramatically.

THE HIGHWAYS

The cry for federal assistance to develop the nation's highways began almost from the first automobile show, held in the old Madison Square Garden in New York in 1900. The American Automobile Club, formed in 1902, joined with the American Road and Transportation Builder's Association and the American Association of State Highway Officials to lobby for an integrated interstate highway system, but it was really the farmers who pressed hardest to get out of the mud.[5] Despite the Federal Aid Road Act of 1916 and the Federal Highway Act of 1921, federal outlays, and state and local outlays too, remained sporadic. As a consequence, the traveler of the 1920s often found a smooth strip of concrete ending suddenly in a sea of mud or terminating at a stream that lacked a ferry or a bridge.

Within the states, the most densely populated areas naturally tended to receive the "primary" road designations and consequently the good roads. In the great agricultural midlands, highways remained in unbelievably poor condition as late as the early 1930s. In Kansas, for example, long after the cities of Kansas City, Topeka, and Wichita were connected by a concrete slab, travelers along the old Pike's Peak Ocean-to-Ocean Highway, designated U.S. Highway 36, were frequently stranded hubcap-deep in mud. The dirt roads of Kansas were connected to Nebraska's major highways, then topped with a magnificent layer of gravel, and the county and township roads had not been noticeably improved for 50 years. Under such conditions, a trip of only a few miles could not be undertaken until favorable weather was certain.

---

[4]This should not be taken to mean that there is no role for the private sector in the provision of the transportation infrastructure. For a brilliant discussion of how the private lighthouse service worked in Britain before 1830, see R. H. Coase, "The Lighthouse in Economics," *Journal of Law and Economics* 17 (1974): 357–376.

[5]F. L. Paxon, "The Highway Movement, 1916–1935," *American Historical Review* 51 (1946): 236–253.

One major outcome of the Great Depression was the impetus given road programs by the relief and recovery agencies. Roads received large shares of public expenditures undertaken to stimulate the economy. Before 1932, federal funds had never amounted to as much as 10 percent of total revenues for highways. They rose to 30 percent in 1932 and climbed to over 40 percent the next year. Federal participation, as a percentage of expenditures, did not drop to pre-depression levels until the beginning of World War II, when federal dollars were directed to sterner activities. Meanwhile the concept of federal aid had expanded, and after 1933, "secondary" roads—that is, roads other than the primary 7 percent—were included in the assistance programs, and money was authorized to improve portions of highways that ran through cities and to eliminate grade crossings.

EARLY POSTWAR REBUILDING. During the war years, proper highway maintenance was not possible, and some major routes deteriorated rapidly. In anticipation of the rebuilding program, Congress passed the Federal Aid Highway Act of 1944, making $1.5 billion available for expenditure in the three years following the end of the war. The law provided for the designation of an interstate highway system of not over 40,000 miles; this system was to receive the largest single portion of the appropriated funds. Secondary and feeder routes, including farm-to-market roads, received specific appropriations. Recognizing the seriousness of the growing congestion in urban areas, the law set aside monies for use exclusively on those segments of the basic interstate system lying within the limits of cities of 5,000 or more.

INTERSTATE HIGHWAY SYSTEM. In the decade following World War II, it became apparent that the narrow two-lane highways that constituted most of the U.S. highway network could no longer meet the nation's transportation needs. Spurred by the "highway lobby," Congress authorized the Interstate and Defense Highway System in 1956. Designed to provide some 41,000 miles of limited-access multilane highways connecting the principal centers of the United States, the project was scheduled for completion in thirteen years and was estimated to cost $27 billion. Fifteen years later, 42,500 miles had been completed at a cost of $43 billion, and 10,500 additional miles were completed by 1977. The interstate system was financed on a grant-in-aid basis; the federal government contributed 90 percent of the money, and the states provided 10 percent. Additional excise taxes on petroleum products, tires, and trucks were to be placed in a highway trust fund to finance the new system on a pay-as-you-go basis—called "paid-before-you-go" by its critics. Into this trust fund poured an increasing stream of earmarked user taxes. In 1991 almost $16 billion was spent by the fund.

AIRWAYS AND AIRPORTS

In 1950 air travel, although used extensively by business and government officials, was still a minor component of the transportation system. In that year airways accounted for only 2 percent of all passenger-miles (the movement of one passenger the distance of one mile), railroads accounted for 6.4 percent, buses for 5.2 percent, and automobiles most of the remainder. In 1990 airways accounted for 17.4 percent, buses for 1.1 percent, and railroads for only 0.6 percent.

For more than a decade after the first flight of a heavier-than-air craft in 1903, the new machines were the playthings of eccentric sports enthusiasts and scientists. World War I gave impetus to the development of airplane engines and structures, but major improvements lay in the future. In 1918, a military airplane was used for a commercial purpose when the Post Office Department and the War Department jointly sponsored an airmail route between Washington and New York. The project was soon dropped, but in the early 1920s the Post Office Department established airmail service between major cities. In 1925, when it appeared that airmail was practical, Congress ordered that all contracts be let to privately owned airlines. Meanwhile, sensational long-distance flights, financed by the rich, caught the public imagination and furnished evidence of the great future of commercial aviation.

IMPROVED AIRWAYS. The U.S. government was expected to assist this infant industry. The Air Commerce Act of 1926 marked the first federal attempt to promote civil aviation, aside from subsidies granted through airmail payments. Among other things, this and other early legislation established an airways system including marked routes and improved navigation facilities, equipped at first with beacon lights and then with radio markers and radio-range beacons. With the growth of private airline companies, route mileage rose from less than 2,000 miles in 1926 to 22,000 miles in 1935, when plans to modernize and improve the airways were drawn up in the interest of airline safety. In 1949, there were 57,000 miles of federally owned air routes operating in the United States and its territories; by 1960, this figure had soared to 220,000. The system was equipped with navigational aids, instrumental approach systems, air-route traffic control centers, an extensive weather-reporting service, and traffic control towers at major airports. Further growth carried the total mileage to 374,000 in 1970, and to a peak of 473,000 in 1980.

AIRPORT CONSTRUCTION. Long after the beginning of commercial aviation in 1926, the federal government assumed no responsibility for airport construction except for the provision of emergency landing fields. Until 1933, airports were built as private business ventures or as projects of municipalities. Financial troubles accompanying the depression made municipal investment in such long-range projects difficult, and the federal government then began to participate in these ventures as a part of the relief program. Between 1933 and 1940, the federal government contributed just over 70 percent of the funds for airport construction, and municipalities furnished most of the rest. Because the main object of government expenditure was unemployment relief, no comprehensive plan of location and design was followed, and much of the construction was wasted. Congress provided for a systematic extension of airport facilities in 1940, but World War II intervened before it could go into effect. During the war years, practically all activity occurred at the federal level, with military objectives being the primary factor in all decisions.

The Federal Airport Act of 1946 attempted to provide long-range planning in airport construction. Of the available funds, 75 percent were apportioned among the states based on population and area, and the remainder constituted a discretionary fund. Federal participation in small airports was limited to 50 percent of construction costs, discounting land acquisition; in large airports, federal participation might be more than 50 percent.

In 1958 the Eisenhower administration tried to prevent the act's extension beyond June 30, 1959. However, Congress did not concur in the view that the government should "begin an orderly withdrawal from the airport grant program," and continued to grant federal aid, although the amount was reduced.

In 1969, several airports were so congested at peak traffic hours that controllers staged slowdowns, and the Federal Aviation Administration imposed air-traffic quotas on the nation's five busiest airports. The result was the Airport and Airway Development Act of 1970, which established an "Airport and Airway Trust Fund" to be fed by user tax revenues. By 1991, that fund was generating some $5.3 billion for airports and airways.

FEDERAL REGULATION OF TRANSPORTATION

THE RAILROADS

Federal regulation of the transportation industries began with the railroads, where it acquired a complexity not found in water, air, or highway transportation. Before 1920, the chief emphasis was on protecting the public from discriminatory railroad rates. After 1920, the competition of trucks and automobiles brought a complete turnabout in the objectives of government control: since then, the railroads—not the public—have obtained the protection of the regulatory authority.

TRANSPORTATION ACT OF 1920. The railroads were nationalized midway through World War I. In 1920, when the return of the railroads to their owners was imminent, major financial problems appeared. The government had to be reimbursed for improvements to the railroads made during federal seizure, funds had to be raised for modernization, and money had to be found to bring together scattered employees and equipment. The Transportation Act of 1920 was a heroic effort to solve both the transitional and long-run problems. The act guaranteed that for six months after the return of the railroads to private operation, railroad owners would receive a net income equal to that of the best six-month period under federal control, along with various forms of debt relief and financial assistance. It was hoped that if the railroads were given this much assistance during the transitional period, permanent policy decisions regarding rates and the consolidation of companies into systems could produce a sound, healthy industry.

Section 15a of the act directed the Interstate Commerce Commission (ICC) to set rates that would enable the railroads, as a whole or in certain groups, to earn "under honest, efficient and economical management a fair return upon the aggregate value of the railway property." A "recapture clause" required that one-half of the earnings of any railroad in excess of a fair return should be paid to the ICC. Half of these payments were to be placed in a fund from which loans could be made to weak lines; the other half was placed in a reserve fund from which interest, dividends, and rentals could be paid in bad years.

Another provision of the act reversed the policy toward pooling agreements, devices for splitting either traffic or profits among colluding companies. Long considered a monopolistic practice, pooling was henceforth acceptable if it was in the "public interest" and was carried out under ICC regulation. Legalization of the practice reflected congressional feeling that highway competition would effectively protect the consumer from monopolistic restrictions of the railroads. Thus, policies once condemned by the muckrakers as outrageous violations of public responsibility now became sanctioned by law. The ICC was finally captured by the railroads.

EARLY CONSOLIDATION PLANS. The ICC was also granted the authority to consolidate railroads into systems and to control the rate of investment and disinvestment. Great hopes were placed in consolidation. The ICC was instructed to devise a plan whereby each individual line would be assigned to a system, and each system would be set up so that a uniform rate scale would yield approximately the same return on the fair value of the property. The ICC was then to publish a final plan and assist in proposed consolidations. Any two companies could combine properties, provided that the merger was in accordance with the master plan and was agreeable to the stockholders and to the ICC.

The grandiose consolidation scheme was supported by provisions giving the ICC numerous additional controls over the railroads. For example, after 1920 no railroad line could cease operation without the permission of the ICC, which could also require the construction of new lines where traffic justified extensions. Because of competition from buses and private automobiles, the railroads' passenger business began to decline in the 1920s. In only one year was the "fair-return" standard of 5.5 percent on the "fair value" of properties actually reached by the railroads as a whole. With the onset of depression in 1929, the financial position of all the companies deteriorated rapidly. By 1931, railroad managements were demanding rate increases, just when shippers could least afford them and when competitors were striving desperately to take away business. The ICC could offer little relief. With 60 percent of their total capitalization in bonds, on which interest was payable regardless of earnings, the railroads were in a critical position. Many were saved from outright collapse only by loans from the Reconstruction Finance Corporation.

TRANSPORTATION ACT OF 1933. Deficits in 1932 and the failure to recover in the first half of the next year led to the Emergency Transportation Act of 1933. The emergency provisions of the act tried to promote cooperation among the lines, elimination of "wasteful competitive practices," and financial reorganizations to reduce fixed charges. But little relief was secured by these means. In addition, the 1920 rule of rate-making was abandoned. Instead of fixing rates on the old "fair-return" standard, the ICC was directed to consider the carriers' need for sufficient revenues to provide an adequate transportation service. Further, the highly controversial "recapture" clause was repealed. Railroads with high earnings had continuously resisted efforts to take away their excesses over a "fair-return" standard, and weak roads that needed loans from recaptured funds could not meet the stringent mortgage requirements. No one argued to retain this foolish law.

The 1933 act tenaciously clung to the idea of consolidation, even though by then it had lost its universal appeal. The combination of strong and weak roads to form large rail systems was resisted, for obvious reasons, by the stockholders of the money-making lines. Labor feared that such consolidations would mean a reduction in jobs. Shippers believed consolidations would result in higher rates. Yet those who dealt with the problem of the financial deterioration of the railroads could cling only to this one hope.

The severity and length of the depression in railroading was bewildering. In 1938, roads controlling one-third of total mileage were in receivership, and only the threat of war in Europe created enough business to keep many lines from bankruptcy. The chief source of difficulty was the Great Depression, but the failure of the railroads to respond to the general improvement in the economy in the mid-1930s must be blamed on other causes. Competition from trucks and automobiles, pipelines, and water carriers produced devastating effects. Coal, the principal commodity carried by the railroads, was losing ground to other energy sources, and shipments of building materials did not recover to pre-depression levels.

WARTIME EFFICIENCY. The railroads were buoyed by World War II. To the industry's credit, it must be said that its handling of traffic was as admirable during World War II as it had been sorry during World War I. Facilities for handling traffic were about the same. Cars and locomotives were fewer in number, but their capacities were greater; railroad mileage was less in 1941 than it had been in 1916, but there were more sidings and more double track. The roads were helped by the fact that traffic did not flow to just one coast, by better port facilities, and by the efficient use of equipment through the car-service division of the American Association of Railroads. An incentive to cooperative effort was the fearsome specter of immediate and probably permanent nationalization of the railroads in the event of a breakdown comparable to that during World War I. Finally, the Office of Defense Transportation, headed by Joseph B. Eastman, did a masterful job of coordinating the entire effort. The expeditious handling of a volume of rail traffic almost twice that of World War I stood as a major achievement.

POSTWAR DECLINE. Shortly after the war, however, it became apparent that the railroads were still in serious trouble. From carrying two-thirds of all intercity freight traffic in 1946, the railroads slid to little more than two-fifths in 1961; in the meantime, rail passenger traffic dropped from just under 20 percent to less than 3 percent of all passenger-miles. In 1961 the industry earned a minuscule 1.9 percent on its total investment, and railroad employment on Class I lines was only 664,000, less than one-third of the total for 1921.

The railroad industry's difficulties were readily attributable to a relative, even absolute, decline in the demand for railroad services. But what caused this catastrophic drop in demand? In part, it resulted from a continuing erosion of bulk-commodity traffic. Much of the railroads' coal business, for example, disappeared as the transmission of electricity over long-distance lines made it possible to burn coal at a mine site or at a generating station along the Ohio River. The St. Lawrence Seaway diverted grain and iron ore from the eastern trunk lines to waterways. Motor carriers skimmed much of the traffic cream by transporting high-priced items swiftly across an ever-improving highway network.

LATER LEGISLATION AND AMTRAK. The growing competitive problems of the railways were recognized by legislators. The Transportation Act of 1958 introduced a new rule of rate-making. The ICC was now directed to stimulate weakened business with rates that would bring back lost customers. Section 15a of the Transportation Act of 1920 was amended by the following paragraph:

> In a proceeding involving competition between carriers of different modes of transportation subject to this Act, the Commission, in determining whether a rate is lower than a reasonable minimum rate, shall consider the facts and circumstances attending the movement of the traffic by the carrier or carriers to which the rate is applicable. Rates of a carrier shall not be held up to a particular level to protect the traffic of any other mode of transportation, giving due consideration to the objectives of the national transportation policy declared in this Act.

This passage written in bureaucratese can be translated (we think) as follows: the ICC can allow the railroads or other carriers to compete by lowering prices, but it does not have to.

In the 1970s and 1980s, the railways held their own, even making something of a comeback. Higher fuel prices made motor carriers and airlines somewhat less-effective competitors than they had been. The formation of the National Railroad Passenger Corporation (Amtrak) in 1970 nationalized a considerable portion of passenger transport and left the private lines with the more profitable freight business.

MOTOR CARRIERS

Improved highways, better trucks, and the large pneumatic tire contributed to the commercial success of the truck line. It was not hard to get into the trucking business. A few hundred dollars would make the down payment on a truck, and one truck was the only piece of equipment many of the early operators owned. When the Great Depression came, many unemployed truck drivers purchased a truck on credit and started an intercity truck "line." In this way, they bought themselves a job that would last as long as they could meet the payments and cover out-of-pocket expenses such as gas and oil. These shoestring operators did not keep books or take out insurance. Thousands of them hauled freight, and the mushrooming industry soon began to suffer all the pangs of oversupply, at least temporarily.

COMPETITION VERSUS CONTROL. There were those who argued that truck lines ought to compete freely among themselves and with rival modes of transportation; but there were many sources of opposition to such a policy. The large, well-established operators in the trucking industry felt their profits being reduced by the undercutting of the small-scale carriers. The market, as they put it, was "chaotic" and needed the quick restoration of order.[6] Some New Dealers even proposed that all of the competing transportation industries should be welded into national systems, with each type of carrier performing the service for which it is best suited. The problem with such forms of central planning, of course, is their rigidity. Had the United States adopted a thoroughgoing central plan for transportation in the 1930s, it is doubtful that the postwar shift from railways to other forms of transport would ever have been permitted.

REGULATING COMMON CARRIERS. Although the idea of forming great regional transportational systems comprised of different types of carriers was abandoned in favor of a plan of interindustry competition, each new transportation industry was regulated by Washington as it approached maturity. The Motor Carriers Act of 1935, which became Part II of the Interstate Commerce Act, was the first major attempt to bring an industry other than the railroads under almost total regulation. (The law did exempt certain motor carriers, such as vehicles used to carry agricultural products, and subjected trucks and buses owned and operated by firms that were not in the transport business to only minor supervision.) The Motors Carriers Act directed the ICC to license carriers and set rates. In general, rates were to be "just and reasonable" and the rate-making rule, like the one applying to the railroads, allowed the ICC to exercise wide discretion. The ICC might fix both maximum and minimum rates for common carriers; for contract carriers, however, only minimum rates might be prescribed, and no undue advantage over any common carriers was to be granted. Other provisions were included to assure total regulation of interstate motor carriers, like that of the railroads.

For a while after 1935, it appeared that the hand of the regulatory authority would weigh as heavily on the trucking industry as it had on the railroads. When the motor-carrier industry boomed after World War II, however, the greatest growth was among private trucks rather than common carriers. The relatively slower growth of the common motor carrier meant that in the 1960s and 1970s only one-third of all truck traffic was regulated.

By keeping new competitors out of the business and setting rates that protected the less-efficient common carriers, the ICC encouraged shippers to maintain their own transportation facilities. Even though private carriers were fully loaded in both directions little more than 7 percent of the time, it was cheaper for many companies to own their own fleets than to hire specialists who were granted monopoly rates by the ICC. ICC regulations, moreover, sometimes produced bizarre results. For example, a carrier that was authorized to ship goods from Cleveland to Buffalo, and then acquired an existing firm with authority to ship from Buffalo to Pittsburgh, was still required

---

[6]To this day, the first argument of regulation advanced by large trucking interests has been that a regulatory authority prevents "chaos," meaning that the big companies are thereby spared certain of the less-pleasant manifestations of a competitive industry.

to ship goods loaded in Cleveland and bound for Pittsburgh the long way around through Buffalo.[7]

MOVE TOWARD DEREGULATION. High prices, along with the absurdities produced by certain ICC regulations, led to persistent calls for a modification of ICC practices, and in some quarters for complete deregulation.[8] Prodded by the Carter administration, which had already appointed some proponents of deregulation to the ICC, Congress passed the Motor Carrier Act of 1980. Although this act did not completely deregulate the industry, it did make it significantly easier for firms in the industry to lower prices and for new firms to enter. The evidence seems to be that trucking deregulation lowered shipping costs and improved service. The American Trucking Association had predicted that service to small towns would decline after deregulation. In fact, it appears that trucking firms became more willing to go to out-of-the-way places to pick up and deliver freight. There have been losers, however, from the deregulation of trucking: the strength of the Teamsters Union has declined, and wages paid to both union and nonunion workers in the industry have fallen relative to comparable wages in other industries.

Deregulation of motor carriers was only partial. Deregulation of the airlines was more thoroughgoing, and the results were more dramatic.

THE AIRLINES

During the 1930s, the public was still thrilling to the new speed records being set by daring aviators. The early commercial airlines did not fail to take advantage of the adventuresome appeal of their service. Flight attendants were also registered nurses, meals were served on a complimentary basis, and attention was lavished on the traveler. Such treatment eased the qualms of passengers who reflected on the unenviable safety records of airlines in the early years of commercial air transportation.

Regulation of the growing air transportation industry had long been under consideration by the government. By the mid-1930s, three administrative agencies were rivals for regulatory authority: the Department of Commerce, the ICC, and the Post Office Department, the last by virtue of its power to fix rates and subsidies for airmail. In 1937, legislation was proposed that would have placed commercial air transportation under the jurisdiction of the ICC. This bill was not enacted, partly because President Roosevelt, himself an aviation enthusiast, wanted a separate commission to be created with promotional as well as regulatory powers.

CIVIL AERONAUTICS ACT OF 1938. The Civil Aeronautics Act of 1938, which created the Civil Aeronautics Authority, established the first effective economic

---

[7] Thomas Gale Moore, "Trucking Deregulation," in *The Fortune Encyclopedia of Economics*, ed. David R. Henderson (New York: Warner Books, 1993), p. 433.

[8] Though few would disagree that the ICC was a failure, there is considerable disagreement as to why it has failed. For one assessment, see Ari and Olive Hoogenboom, *A History of the ICC* (New York: W. W. Norton, 1976).

regulation of commercial air transport. Two years later the aeronautics authority was reorganized; at this time, Congress established within the authority (then an agency in the Department of Commerce) the Civil Aeronautics Administration (CAA) and the Civil Aeronautics Board (CAB). The CAA was to handle all matters pertaining to the airways system, including promotion of airline traffic. The CAB was to be in charge of economic regulation and the determination and issuance of all rules relating to safety.

From its inception, the Civil Aeronautics Board exercised authority over the airlines similar to that of the ICC over land carriers. The CAB issued certificates of public convenience and necessity to domestic carriers and permits to lines operating between the United States and foreign countries. It set minimum and maximum fares. Control over intercompany relationships was complete and final. Provisions of the law permitted a tighter regulation than that exercised over any other kind of transportation facility. Moreover, the CAB was directed to do everything in its power to further the progress of commercial aviation. This provision resulted in a rate-making policy that protected the airlines from continuing losses and in a paternalism that neglected the welfare of competing transportation industries—and the public.

THE AIRMAIL SUBSIDY. For more than a decade, the CAB assured the airlines of profitable operations by means of an airmail subsidy. The Civil Aeronautics Act directed the CAB, in fixing rates, to consider "the need of each such carrier for compensation for the transportation of mail sufficient to ensure the performance of such service and, together with all other revenue of the air carrier under honest, economical, and efficient management, to maintain and continue the development of air transportation to the extent and of the character and quality required for the commerce of the United States, the Postal Service, and the United States." The CAB interpreted the "need" of the airlines in a sense most favorable to them. Any company that was not run dishonestly or inefficiently could obtain sufficient airmail payments to make up any operating losses and provide stockholders with a "fair" return on their investment. Congress had said, in effect, that the airlines could operate on a cost-plus basis.

REGULATION IN THE 1950s AND 1960s. In response to the growing complexity of air traffic, the Federal Aviation Act of 1958 established a Federal Aviation Agency (FAA) to exercise control over the physical facilities of civil aviation, including the safety regulatory functions of the Civil Aeronautics Board. The Transportation Act of 1966, which established the Department of Transportation, kept the acronym FAA while redesignating the agency the Federal Aviation Administration. Although air traffic control is the agency's most time-consuming function, it also conducts an aggressive program of research and development on air safety, maintains training and mechanical facilities, and works in cooperation with the International Civil Aviation Organization (ICAO) to achieve uniformity of standards, practices, and safety rules throughout the world.

The CAB maintained high air fares to keep total returns up, and freely awarded new operating rights on trunk routes. In 1967 and 1968, the CAB allowed American, TWA, and United airlines to increase the number of daily nonstop flights between

New York and Chicago from 102 to 135. Introducing larger planes, the carriers increased average aircraft capacity by 4.4 seats at the same time. Although air traffic rose 10 percent, total capacity increased so much that the average load factor (percentage of seats occupied) dropped from 59 to 47. As load factors and profits dropped, the three companies appealed to the CAB for fare increases, which the agency obligingly granted.[9]

AIRLINE DEREGULATION. Episodes like this, along with evidence provided by economists that fares were too high, prompted Congress to pass the United States Airline Deregulation Act in 1978. In an unprecedented reversal of the trend toward greater government intervention in the economy, the CAB was eliminated and airlines were freed to set their own rates. The effects of deregulation are still hotly debated. On the plus side, average fares (adjusted for inflation) did come down. Between 1976 and 1990, according to one estimate, average fares fell 30 percent. Average fares were falling before deregulation because of the introduction of jets and jumbo jets, but the fall seems to have been accelerated by deregulation. More surprising was the shift to the "hub-and-spoke" system, in which airlines route all of their flights through a few "hub" cities. This system was adopted because it was more efficient. For one thing, it permits airlines to adapt their equipment to the distance traveled: small props and jet props for short distances, big jets for long hauls.

But there has been a minus side to deregulation. Airlines such as Continental and TWA have gone bankrupt, and Pan American, one of the pioneers of commercial aviation, has disappeared forever. Much of the price competition, moreover, has taken the form of discounts for travelers who book ahead and travel at off-peak hours; travelers who are unable to take advantage of discounts often have to pay a stiff fare. Finally, the quality of service has declined in certain ways. Flights to small cities often must be made in small planes, and congestion and delays at hub cities have increased. Although a return to heavy-handed price controls appears unlikely, the future may bring additional efforts by the government in the areas of antitrust, safety regulation, and airport construction.

DOMESTIC WATER CARRIERS

Although water traffic continued to fall in relative importance, it remained important on the Great Lakes, the Ohio River, and the coastal lanes in the early twentieth century. Proponents of inland water use, with the Army Corps of Engineers to abet them, were repeatedly successful in persuading Congress to fund harbors and rivers, especially during the Great Depression.

Like all other transportation systems, domestic water carriers eventually fell under federal regulation. During the 1930s, there was agitation for unified government control over inland water carriers, although the reasons for regulation were less compelling than in the cases of the motor carriers and the airlines. By 1938, the Maritime

---

[9]That CAB-approved rates were often on the high side is evidenced by the California experience of the 1960s and 1970s, where state-regulated fares were 40 percent below those elsewhere in the United States.

Commission required common carriers in the intercoastal, coastal, and Great Lakes trade to fix rates, but contract carriers were excluded from regulation. The ICC had jurisdiction over the common ship carriers owned by the railroads. The railroads, complaining that their water lines were much more restricted than those under Maritime Commission control, lobbied steadily for the inclusion of all lines in a comprehensive regulatory act. The Transportation Act of 1940 transferred jurisdiction over all water carriers engaged in interstate commerce from the Maritime Commission to the ICC. Control provisions regarding water carriers were similar to those previously applied to railroads and motor carriers, and these provisions became Part III of the Interstate Commerce Act. So many exemptions were granted, however, that there was little left to regulate. By 1970, only about 10 percent of inland-waterway traffic was under ICC jurisdiction.

THE MERCHANT MARINE

The Merchant Marine Act of 1920 was designed to remove the federal government from the foreign shipping business. Government-owned vessels were to be sold at low prices to shipping companies, which were to receive tax advantages and construction loans on favorable terms. But even though these ships moved into private hands, the merchant marine continued to dwindle. Tonnage in the foreign trade dropped from 11 million in 1920 to 7 million in 1929; a decade later, tonnage was down to about 3.3 million. By 1935, only one-third of U.S. exports and imports, along with a negligible portion of the remainder of world trade, was carried by American ships. Although in the late 1930s, the American merchant fleet was still second only to that of Britain in tonnage, it was slow and old; within another few years, it would have been almost entirely obsolete.

For reasons of national defense, Congress in 1936 reversed the long-standing policy of not granting direct subsidies to carriers in the foreign service. The Merchant Marine Act of 1936 established a new government bureau, the United States Maritime Commission, which was authorized to grant "construction differential" and "operating differential" subsidies. The purpose of the act was to help American shipbuilders and ship operators compete so that the American merchant fleet would carry a substantial part of U.S. foreign commerce. On application by a qualified concern, the commission would undertake construction of a vessel in an American shipyard, at the same time contracting to sell it to the applicant for a price equal to the cost of building the vessel abroad. If, moreover, certain features especially useful for national defense were incorporated in the ship, the government would absorb their costs.[10]

The principle of the operational subsidy was the same: the Maritime Commission would make up the difference between the cost of operation under U.S. ownership and the cost of operation under a foreign flag. A recapture clause in the contracts enabled the government to claim half of any profits in excess of 10 percent per year over a ten-year period.

---

[10]Through this device, the liner *United States*, which cost an estimated $70 million, was made available to the United States Lines for only $28 million. The great liner was retired in 1969 because it could not cover costs despite the receipt of both construction and operating subsidies.

The assistance rendered to the shipping industry between 1936 and 1941 did not produce a merchant fleet large enough to transport troops and supplies to the fighting fronts in World War II. The Liberty ships and Victory ships of the war years were built on government account, so the construction and operating programs under the Maritime Commission were interrupted. After Pearl Harbor, shipyards that had been acres of weeds, rotting timbers, and rusting iron were refurbished, and new shipyards sprang up along inland waterways, in back channels, and on the Great Lakes. For the first time in the history of shipbuilding, component parts were fabricated at inland points and assembled on the coasts.

Since World War II, the merchant marine has enjoyed indirect benefits that are of greater monetary value than the amounts it has received for construction and operational differential subsidies. In the Merchant Ship Sales Act of 1946, Congress provided for the sale of hundreds of high-quality ships on terms especially favorable to American-flag operators. Several hundred first-rate dry-cargo vessels were sold for as low as one-third their prewar cost. Other indirect benefits included the charter of government-owned vessels under favorable terms, assured loans at low interest rates for ship-construction programs, and the guarantee to U.S. operators of half the business shipped under the European Recovery Program and the military-aid program. Direct subsidy payments were resumed under the Federal Maritime Commission, an independent agency that performs the standard regulatory functions of determining the rates, services, and practices of seagoing vessels serving as common carriers and that executes the subsidy contracts with shipping companies.

In the competitive world of international ocean shipping, the United States lost its leadership more than a century ago, largely because foreign-built and -operated ships produced a service at lower cost per ton-mile than American-built and -operated ships did. Beginning in the mid-1960s, there were signs of a possible revival of American leadership in this field. The innovation was the container ship, with its containers loaded six deep in the holds and three deep above deck. Specially designed vessels such as the Lancer and the SL 7, with top speeds of 24 to 33 knots, had tremendous competitive advantages, but the primary U.S. advantage was the drastic reduction in labor costs that resulted from container loading. The United States did not gain a monopoly in container shipping, which constitutes 60 percent of the shipping on the North Atlantic run, but a few companies such as Sea Land Service and United States Lines at least compete for business outside the constraints of the primitive labor relations that nearly destroyed the American shipping industry.

GOVERNMENT AND TRANSPORTATION TODAY

President Kennedy's plea in 1963 for greater reliance on "unsubsidized privately owned facilities, operating under the incentives of private profit and the checks of competition," has been met in part. Deregulation of airlines and motor carriers, although subject to many criticisms, succeeded in lowering costs. The federal government, however, continues to play a major role in the financing of the transportation infrastructure. In 1970 federal expenditures on transportation, primarily for infrastructure, amounted to $7 billion; by 1980 the corresponding figure was $10 billion in 1970 dollars, about a 40 percent increase. The Reagan and Bush administrations did succeed in cutting transportation expenditures in real terms: in 1990 these were about $9 billion in 1970 dollars. The Clinton administration, however, has promised to increase spending. Robert Reich, the administration's articulate Secretary of Labor and a long-time adviser to President Clinton, has argued that such expenditures would increase the productivity and make U.S. firms more competitive in world markets. We shall see.

SELECTED REFERENCES
AND SUGGESTED READINGS

Armstrong, Ellis L., ed. *History of Public Works of the United States, 1776–1976*. Chicago: American Public Works Association, 1976.

Baker, Gladys, and Wayne Rasmussen. *The Department of Agriculture*. New York: Praeger, 1972.

Benedict, Murray R. *Farm Policies of the United States, 1790–1950*. New York: Twentieth Century Fund, 1953.

Caves, Richard. *Air Transport and Its Regulators*. Cambridge: Harvard University Press, 1962.

Coase, Ronald H. "The Lighthouse in Economics." *Journal of Law and Economics* 17 (1974): 357–376.

Cochrane, Willard W., and Mary E. Ryan. *American Farm Policy, 1948–1973*. Minneapolis: University of Minnesota Press, 1976.

Droze, Walmon H. *High Dams and Slack Waters: T.V.A. Rebuilds a River*. Baton Rouge: Louisiana State University Press, 1965.

Hardin, Garrett. "The Tragedy of the Commons." *Science* 162 (1968): 1243–1248.

Hoogenboom, Ari, and Olive Hoogenboom. *A History of the ICC*. New York: W. W. Norton, 1976.

Howe, Charles W., et al. *Inland Waterway Transportation*. Washington, D.C.: Resources for the Future, 1969.

Johnson, D. Gale. "The Food and Agriculture Act of 1977: Implications for Farmers and Taxpayers." In *Contemporary Economic Problems*, ed. William Fellner. Washington, D.C.: American Enterprise Institute, 1978, pp. 167–210.

Kahn, Alfred E. "Surprises of Airline Deregulation." *American Economic Review, Papers and Proceedings* 78 (1988): 316–322.

Lawrence, Samuel A. *United States Merchant Shipping Policies and Politics*. Washington, D.C.: Brookings Institution, 1966.

Meyer, John R., et al. *The Economics of Competition in the Transportation Industries*. Cambridge: Harvard University Press, 1959.

O'Loughlin, Carleen. *Economics of Sea Transport*. London: Pergamon Press, 1967.

Paxon, F. L. "The Highway Movement, 1916–1935." *American Historical Review* 51 (1946): 236–253.

President's National Commission on Rural Poverty. *The People Left Behind*. Washington, D.C.: Government Printing Office, 1967.

Rasmussen, Wayne D., ed. *Agriculture in the United States*. New York: Random House, 1975, Vol. 4.

Schelling, Thomas C. "Some Economics of Global Warming." *American Economic Review* 82 (1992): 1–14.

Schlebecker, John T. *Whereby We Thrive, A History of American Farming, 1607–1972*. Ames: Iowa State University Press, 1975.

Seneca, Joseph J., and Michael K. Taussig. *Environmental Economics*. 3d ed. Englewood Cliffs, New Jersey: Prentice-Hall, 1984.

Strover, John F. *The Life and Decline of the American Railroad*. New York: Oxford University Press, 1970.

White, Lawrence J. *The Automobile Industry Since 1945*. Cambridge: Harvard University Press, 1971.

CHAPTER
TWENTY-EIGHT

MONETARY AND FISCAL POLICY AFTER WORLD WAR II

CHAPTER THEME In the immediate aftermath of World War II, there was considerable apprehension that the Great Depression might return, but this gave way to optimism when the feared economic collapse did not materialize. Academic economists were particularly optimistic because of the belief that John Maynard Keynes, the famous English economist, had showed how a modern industrial economy could be kept on an even keel through the judicious use of fiscal policy. The confidence of economists that the business cycle could be tamed reached its peak during the Kennedy-Johnson years, but then the weaknesses of the Keynesian regimen (as it was applied in practice) began to make themselves felt.

Depression-level unemployment rates were never approached, even in the most severe postwar recessions. Instead, inflation became the primary problem. Figures 28-1 and 28-2 on the next two pages show that inflation tended to fall and unemployment rise in each recession, but inflation did not fall as much in each recession as it had risen in the previous expansion, so that the core or base rate of inflation moved ever upward. Similarly, the unemployment rate did not fall as much in each expansion as it rose in each recession; the core or natural rate of unemployment, as some called it, also increased steadily. By the late 1970s, "stagflation" seemed to be as troubling an economic problem as depression had been to an earlier generation. By then economists and policymakers were beginning to listen not to Keynes but to Milton Friedman, whose theory that inflation was fundamentally a monetary problem seemed to explain and provide a remedy for stagflation. The attempt to apply monetarist ideas (although not always faithful to the original doctrine) became the basis for monetary and fiscal policy in the 1980s and early 1990s.

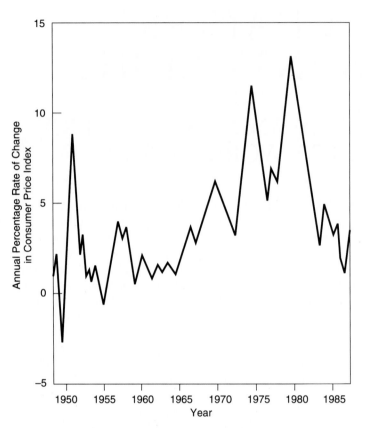

FIGURE 28-1 THE RATE OF INFLATION IN THE UNITED STATES, 1950–1987

SOURCE: U.S. DEPARTMENT OF LABOR.

THE RISE OF KEYNESIAN ECONOMICS

Keynes's masterwork, *The General Theory of Employment, Interest, and Money,* appeared in 1936. It is often listed among the most influential books of the twentieth century, and for good reason. For more than three decades, the ideas advanced in the *General Theory* dominated macroeconomic policymaking in the United States and other industrialized countries. The *General Theory* is a complex book that has generated a large interpretive literature, but several key points come through loud and clear: First, there is no natural tendency for the economy to return to full employment; the basic problem is that investment demand might be insufficient to soak up all of the saving that people wish to do. Second, monetary policy is likely to be ineffective in restoring investment and full employment. And third, to restore full employment, it is necessary to control private investment and supplement it with government spending on public works. The last point—developed further by Keynes's American disciples such as Alvin Hansen,

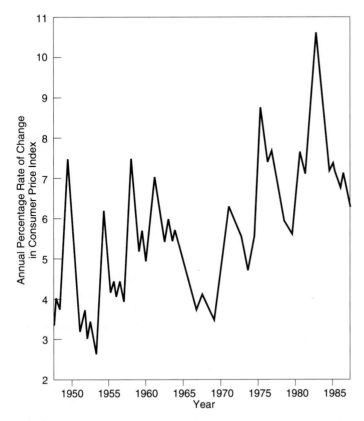

FIGURE 28-2 THE CIVILIAN UNEMPLOYMENT RATE, 1950–1987

SOURCE: U.S. DEPARTMENT OF LABOR.

Abba Lerner, and Paul Samuelson—was taken to mean that the economy could be kept on an even keel by increasing government spending or cutting taxes or both during recessions and by reversing these actions when, after reaching full employment, inflation was threatened.

Thus, in the immediate postwar years, economists grew optimistic that they had finally found the answer to the business cycle. Fiscal policy, flowing logically from Keynesian economics and amply confirmed by the success of deficit spending in World War II, could keep the economy at full employment without causing inflation.

This mood of optimism was strengthened by the handling of the first postwar recession, which came in 1948 and 1949. After industrial production dropped 10 percent and the gross national product fell 4 percent, the Truman administration moved quickly to award military contracts in "distressed areas," and although unemployment rose above 5 percent of the work force for several months, revival came so quickly that public clamor for action never became very loud. Further confirmation for the Keynesian approach came from the handling of the Korean War.

THE KOREAN WAR

On June 25, 1950, North Korean forces crossed the 38th parallel and attacked South Korea. President Harry Truman responded quickly by authorizing the use of U.S. forces to repel the attack. Less than five years after the end of World War II, the United States found itself at war once again. Consumers responded by stocking up on items that had been in short supply during the war years—sugar, consumer durables, and so on. The surge of consumer demand and the anticipation of a wartime economy led to an acceleration of inflation, clearly visible as the first spike in Figure 28-1 (see page 632). This time, as opposed to the World War II years, policymakers responded swiftly with a strong anti-inflation program. The lesson drawn from the experience of World War II was that half-measures do not work.

First, taxes were raised. The Revenue Act of 1950, providing for both higher personal and corporate tax rates, was enacted in September 1950. The Revenue Act of 1951, although less comprehensive than the Truman administration wanted, provided for further increases in individual and corporate taxes.

Second, price and wage controls were adopted. A debate quickly developed within the administration between those who favored a gradual approach to controlling prices and those who favored an immediate across-the-board freeze. This time the advocates of a freeze quickly won their point: an across-the-board freeze was announced in late January 1951. Michael V. DiSalle, the director of the Office of Price Stabilization and a major advocate of a freeze, explained his position by reference to an old maxim. Controlling prices was like "bobbing a cat's tail"—it was better to do it all at once close to the body, otherwise the result would be "a mad cat and a sore tail."

Third, a restrictive monetary policy was imposed. During World War II, as noted in Chapter 25, the Fed followed a policy of pegging interest rates, even though this forced the Fed to purchase more federal debt than it wanted, thus expanding the stock of money. Pegging was continued in the early postwar years at the request of the Treasury despite growing resentment of this constraint by the Fed. The outbreak of the Korean War, and the threat of inflation, brought the conflict into the open. After discussions conducted at the urging of President Truman, the Fed and the Treasury announced that they had reached an agreement on March 4, 1951.

Because the joint statement issued by the two agencies said that they had reached "full accord," this agreement came to be known as the *Treasury-Federal Reserve Accord*. This was essentially a victory for the Fed, although it agreed to certain restrictions desired by the Treasury. Henceforth, the Fed would be free to limit its purchase of government debt and the resulting increase in the stock of money, even if the result was higher interest rates. There were predictions that financial markets would be sent into shock by the emergence of a less-predictable interest rate structure, but financial markets adapted quickly to the new regime. The accord permitted the Fed to follow a noninflationary monetary policy during the war; for the entire period of the war, money per unit of real GNP actually fell slightly.

The anti-inflation program adopted during the Korean War worked well. Consumer prices rose at an annual rate of only 2.1 percent from the price freeze in January

1951 to the termination of controls in February 1953. When controls were terminated many prices were under their ceilings, and there was no post-control price explosion. Consumer prices rose at an annual rate of only 2.6 percent from the termination of controls until the postwar price peak.

The lesson here is that price controls were effective because they were merely a part of the government's response to the fears of runaway inflation produced by the out-break of the war. While they were being used the Fed was following a monetary policy aimed at bringing inflation under control, a policy reinforced with strong efforts to maintain the integrity of the federal budget. As we shall see, controls were used again in the 1970s. But at that time monetary and fiscal policy were set at cross-purposes with the price policy, and controls were a failure.

THE EISENHOWER YEARS

During 1953, the key indicators of economic well-being took an unfavorable turn. Industrial production, the GNP, construction contracts, and manufacturers' new orders dropped and unemployment jumped in the last quarter of the year. The magnitude of the drop was approximately the same as the first post–World War II downturn. In about nine months, industrial production fell 10 percent, the GNP declined 4 percent, and manufacturing employment dropped 10 percent. This second postwar recession was widely forecast by Keynesian economists. National-defense spending and therefore total government spending declined $11 billion between the second quarter of 1953 and the second quarter of 1954. In short, the federal government caused the recession; since there was a $10 billion drop in gross investment—mostly in inventories—the gross product would have declined more than $21 billion if there had not been offsetting expenditures. Fortunately, state and local governments spent more during the year, exports exceeded imports, and personal consumption expenditures increased; the total offset amounted to a little over $7 billion.

This was far from a serious decline. Compared to the full-blown depressions of former years, the recession of 1953 and 1954 seemed small indeed. Nevertheless, it aroused great concern. Unemployment in several areas of manufacturing exceeded 10 percent of the local work force, and many families exhausted their unemployment insurance benefits before any clear signs of improvement were visible. The fact that the economy leveled off for several months during the summer and fall of 1954 was far from comforting to those who knew that output could not stand still if net additions to the work force of about 750,000 people a year were to be absorbed.

The administration, reassured by the Council of Economic Advisers, took no drastic steps to combat the recession by fiscal means. A moderate cash deficit, partly the result of a reduction in federal income-tax rates effective January 1, 1954, had a stimulating effect. A Federal Reserve policy of "active ease" was adopted before most informed people were aware that the business indicators had taken a run for the worse.

It was apparent that there were strong sustaining forces in the economy. A continuing rapid increase in population and a substantial rate of household formation created a demand for consumer goods. To such long-term natural supports were added the *automatic stabilizers:* unemployment insurance payments, a reduction in the total tax bill as the incomes of individuals and corporations declined, the price supports for agriculture, and even some increase in Social Security payments all acted to cushion the decline in aggregate spending.

After a four-year respite from inflationary pressures, prices began a steady rise in mid-1955 that continued until early 1957; the increase amounted to about 8.5 percent during this brief period. Inflation became the pressing domestic problem of the day. The Fed responded with a restrictive monetary policy that continued until well past the point of economic downturn in the late summer of 1957, not reversing itself until November. A recession of substantial proportions followed—the third and deepest of the postwar period thus far. By the spring of 1958, the gap between output and capacity had reached $40 billion, and unemployment at 7.5 percent of the civilian labor force was frightening. The remarkable resilience of the U.S. economy was once again evidenced by a rebound that began in April 1958. But the recovery through 1959 was disappointing, and when the indicators took another adverse turn at the end of the year, the frustration of policymakers was evident.

On average, however, the 1950s were good years: business cycles were modest in amplitude and duration; persistently high levels of unemployment or inflation did not occur, at least by the standard of subsequent periods; and the economy continued to make strong advances in productivity and national output. Nevertheless, policymakers remained sensitive to the threats of inflation and unemployment.

At this time economists began to change their thinking about the relationship between inflation and unemployment. Previously they had considered them opposites: prices would rise after the economy reached full employment. Now they began to think that for a variety of reasons (monopoly power in labor markets, lags in the adjustment process, and so on), continuing inflation could be consistent with fairly high levels of unemployment. In 1958, A. W. Phillips published a path-breaking paper showing that in Great Britain there was an inverse relationship between wage increases (later, economists substituted prices) and unemployment; he showed that only very high levels of unemployment were consistent with perfectly stable wages. The policy implication of the "Phillips curve," as it came to be known, was that a government could choose the combination of inflation and unemployment it wanted from the possible combinations on the curve. It was with this view of the world in mind that the next economic team to assume power attacked the problem of unemployment.

THE KENNEDY-JOHNSON YEARS

The economy was clearly an issue in the election of 1960. Democrat John F. Kennedy promised to get the economy moving, placing more emphasis on full employment and economic growth and (presumably) less on price stability. Although the fourth postwar recession in 1959 and 1960 was mild and short, it was an important factor in Kennedy's narrow 100,000-vote victory over Vice-President Richard Nixon.

The economy began its resurgence in February 1961, but at a rate that disappointed the Kennedy team.[1] In *The Economic Reports of the President* in 1962 and 1963, written by the Council of Economic Advisers under the guidance of Chairman Walter Heller, plans were formed for an experimental tax cut in 1964. After Kennedy's shocking assassination in November 1963, the politically astute Lyndon B. Johnson assumed the presidency and promptly guided the tax-cut legislation through Congress and into law.

This was an historic tax cut. The federal budget was then in deficit; orthodox economic theory called for tax increases to balance the budget. But President Kennedy's advisers believed in the "New Economics" of John Maynard Keynes.[2] They argued that as long as the economy was operating at less than full employment (the rate of unemployment was then about 5.5 percent), a tax cut was justified because it would leave more income in the hands of the public, creating more demand for goods and services. As they pointed out, a budget that was in deficit under current conditions might turn out to be balanced or in surplus at full employment because taxes tend to rise, and certain categories of spending fall, as the economy approaches full employment.

In an often-quoted passage from the *General Theory*, Keynes had written the following:

> The ideas of economists and political philosophers, both when they are right and when they are wrong, are more powerful than is commonly understood. Indeed the world is ruled by little else. Practical men, who believe themselves to be quite exempt from any intellectual influences, are usually the slaves of some defunct economist. Madmen in authority, who hear voices in the air, are distilling their frenzy from some academic scribbler of a few years back. I am sure that the power of vested interest is vastly exaggerated compared with the gradual encroachment of ideas.[3]

Less than 30 years after the publication of the *General Theory*, Keynes's ideas, themselves, were having a profound effect on U.S. fiscal policies.

The Kennedy tax cut was widely acclaimed as a great success. Unemployment fell from 5 percent of the labor force in 1964 to 4.4 percent in 1965 to 3.7 percent in 1966. But the Vietnam War buildup during Johnson's administration that followed closely upon the tax cut had not been part of the calculations when Kennedy's advisers had first planned a cut. The change in economic conditions encouraged Walter Heller and other creators of the tax cut to urge President Johnson to raise taxes. But this advice was not taken. An important political weakness of the Keynesian system was thus

---

[1] Peaks and troughs in the business cycle are dated by the National Bureau of Economic Research, a private research group that initiated much research on the business cycle. The precise date is usually a matter of judgment.

[2] Keynesian ideas, as we have seen, had been growing in influence for some time. But they were still new in the sense that policymakers now felt confident in publicly proclaiming their rejection of balanced-budget orthodoxy.

[3] The passage is quoted, it should not surprise us, mostly by economists. *The General Theory of Unemployment, Interest, and Money* (New York: Harcourt Brace, 1936; first Harbinger ed., 1964), p. 383.

John Maynard Keynes (1883–1946), architect of the theory that full employment could be maintained by appropriate changes in government spending and taxation and through control of private investment. His theories gained increasing acceptance during the 1940s, 1950s, and 1960s.

revealed. Cutting taxes is easy; raising them is hard. Inflationary pressures began to build, and (as Figure 28-1 shows) the rate of inflation turned upward late in 1965.

For a time the Kennedy administration relied on "wage-price guideposts" to control inflation. If labor received wage increases in proportion to increases in labor productivity, then prices and labor's share of income could remain stable.[4] So the Council of Economic Advisers recommended that wage increases be kept within the limits set by productivity increases. In an early test, President Kennedy publicly chastised the steel industry when prices were raised more than the guideposts allowed, threatening a transfer of federal purchases to companies that remained within the guideposts and other sanctions. Eventually the steel industry backed down. But the government could not, of course, treat every price increase that violated the guideposts as a major crisis. When inflation accelerated in 1965 the guideposts fell into disuse.

It was not until the last quarter of 1969 that there was more than a brief pause in the rate of expansion of the economy. Indeed, the expansion from February 1961 to November 1969 was, to that time, the longest sustained rise in the postwar period. The fifth postwar recession, in 1969 and 1970, was brief, with the major indicators showing a trough in the fourth quarter of 1970.

---

[4]An example will make the point clear. There are 10 students in a class, each paying $100 tuition. The professor's wage is $500, 50 percent of total income ($500 ÷ $1,000). Now suppose that class size is increased to 15 (labor productivity has gone up 50 percent!). Even with the same tuition of $100, the teacher's salary can be raised to $750. The share of wages in total income is still 50 percent ($750 ÷ $1,500).

THE NIXON ADMINISTRATION AND WAGE AND PRICE CONTROLS

In 1971 the rate of inflation was around 4 percent per year and the rate of unemployment around 6 percent. Although inflation was down from the pre-recession peak and was probably coming down further, the public was bitter about what seemed a very heavy price for a small reduction in inflation. In addition, the United States now had some reason to be concerned about its international balance of payments. In the second half of the 1960s, the United States began, year after year, to spend more on importing goods and services than it was earning on exports. As a result, foreign central banks were accumulating large amounts of dollars they were not happy about holding. In a few cases they had converted large amounts of dollars into gold, but it was clear that all could not do so since dollars held abroad by foreign central banks far exceeded U.S. gold holdings. One solution was to devalue the dollar (make one dollar exchange for fewer units of foreign currency than before), and so make U.S. exports more attractive and imports less attractive. But the administration was reluctant to take this path, both because it would add to inflation (imports would cost more) and because it would mean a loss of prestige for the United States. The upcoming presidential election in 1972 added to the Nixon administration's anxieties.

So on August 15, 1971, the administration simultaneously "closed the gold window" and imposed a system of wage and price controls. Closing the gold window meant simply refusing to exchange dollars for gold. A brief attempt to reestablish fixed rates, the Smithsonian agreement, was reached in December 1971. It called for fixed exchange rates, with the price of gold raised to $38 dollars (an 8 percent devaluation of the dollar). But the growing worldwide inflation made it difficult to stick to fixed exchange rates, and one country after another began to float its currency against the dollar. The international exchange value of the dollar was now to be determined in the marketplace like the price of wheat or automobiles. The resulting system is frequently described as a "dirty float." Private supplies and demands are the main determinants of exchange rates, but central banks often intervene, buying or selling currencies when the outcome of market forces is not to their liking.

The price controls imposed in 1971 were aimed, of course, at convincing U.S. citizens that something was being done about inflation. But controls also tied in nicely with what was happening to the dollar in international markets. The story was that the balance-of-payments problem was caused primarily by the inflation in the United States because inflation made imports more attractive and exports less attractive. Price controls would buy time while the United States put its house in order. When this was done (presumably sometime after the election), controls could be lifted and a fixed rate of exchange with other currencies based on a fixed price of gold could be restored.

Price controls went through a series of phases. The first three-month period, known as Phase I, was a price freeze. Because prohibiting all price increases would not work for a long period of time and would lead to shortages, evasions, and rationing, a system with greater flexibility had to be introduced. In Phase II, prices were set by the Price Commission and wages by the Pay Board. These bureaus were given considerable latitude in terms of their ability to permit or deny increases, so shortages in individual markets could be addressed. In general the Price Commission aimed at a formula for the economy reminiscent of the Kennedy guideposts—prices could rise by the amount that the Pay Board permitted wages to rise, less the increase in productivity. But unlike the guideposts, the rules were enforced by the government.

Inflation was relatively low during 1972. On a year-to-year basis the rate of inflation was only 3.3 percent, lower than it had been since 1967 and lower than it would be again until 1983. Price controls naturally got much of the credit, although some economists believe that inflation would have slowed in any case. The time seemed right to begin dismantling controls before they became a permanent part of the economy. In Phase III, which began in January 1973, the rules were eased somewhat, and interpretation and administration of the rules were placed in the hands of the businesses themselves. Inflation accelerated from 3.3 percent in 1972 to 6.2 percent in 1973. Worse still, the volatile food index increased at an astonishing 14.5 percent.

The program of price controls came in for considerable criticism. Conservatives complained that inflation was up because the repressed inflation of Phases I and II could no longer be kept in check. Liberals complained that the Nixon administration had deliberately undermined the program because it was working all too well.

In response to the critics, and to the acceleration of inflation, a second freeze was imposed in June 1973 following the imposition of ceiling prices on meats at the end of March. A shortage of meat resulted; grocery meat counters in many cases were literally empty. The shortage was aggravated by the announcement of a date when controls would be lifted; ranchers held their animals off the market in the almost certain knowledge that they would get a higher price later.

With meat shortages, distortions in other sectors, evasions, and rising prices, the control program was in a sorry state. Phase IV replaced Freeze II in August 1973. (It was really Phase V, but by that time no one was counting.) During this phase prices were decontrolled sector by sector. The price controllers tried to prompt producers in sectors that were being decontrolled into promising not to raise their prices too much after controls were lifted. But such promises were mostly face-saving exercises for the controllers.

What was the overall effect on prices of the control program? In 1974 consumer prices rocketed upward at a 12.2 percent annual rate. Some observers have seen this as the release of inflationary pressures built up under controls. Others doubt that there was that much repressed inflation around after Phase III, and look to other factors—such as supply-side shocks in oil and food and the lagged response to previous increases in the stock of money—to explain the acceleration of inflation. Numerous econometric studies analyzed the episode, with varying results. Most studies agree that controls were successful in repressing inflation for a time but differ on how much and for how long.

If the calm created by Freeze I and Phase II had been used to impose restrictive monetary and fiscal policies, the economy might have emerged from this experiment with controls, as it did from the Korean War experiment, with stable prices. This, however, was not to be. The stock of money rose at the unprecedented peacetime rate of 13.5 percent from December 1970 to December 1971 and at 13.0 percent from December 1971 to December 1972.[5] The inflation of 1974 was to some extent the result of these increments to the stock of money working through the economy. Fiscal policy was also not helpful. Deficits of $23 billion and $23.4 billion were run up in 1971 and 1972. In only one previous year in the postwar period had the deficit been larger, and typically it had been far smaller.

It is not clear why monetary and fiscal policies were so expansionary in these years, but it is possible that the controls themselves were partly to blame. By creating the false impression that inflation was under control (and creating a new set of people to blame if it accelerated), the existence of the control system encouraged the Fed to concentrate on reducing unemployment. In any case, it is clear that an opportunity to return to a stable price level, bought at considerable expense, was lost.

Most economists are opposed to the use of controls. Nevertheless, because of their political popularity and bureaucratic support, the advocacy of price and wage controls frequently resurfaced in the 1970s, as testified by President Jimmy Carter's 1978 plan for voluntary wage and price controls.

THE GROWING MENACE OF INFLATION

Although inflation moderated a bit during the recession of 1974 and 1975, it accelerated again between 1976 and 1980. In 1979 and 1980, inflation reached double-digit levels, causing widespread fear of economic disaster. Creditors who had not foreseen rising prices lost, and debtors gained. But even many people who gained or kept pace with inflation were haunted by the fear that if they stumbled and failed to negotiate an adequate wage increase, inflation would quickly and seriously reduce their standard of living.

One of the most troubling aspects of the inflation of 1976 to 1980 was the rise in interest rates. Interest rates moved irregularly upward after 1965, falling in recessions but then more than making up the lost ground during the subsequent expansion. During the remarkably volatile year of 1980, the prime rate (the rate charged by banks to their lowest-risk customers on short-term unsecured loans) tickled 20 percent in April, fell to 11 percent by midsummer, and reached the all-time record high of 21 percent by Christmas. High interest rates, both on bank loans and government borrowings, were maintained throughout 1981 and continued into early 1982.

Inflation was clearly an important factor in the rise of interest rates. Economists have long maintained that in a rational world an inflation premium would be incorporated in the rate of interest. If a lender and a borrower could agree on a rate of 10 percent in a year when no price increases were expected, then they should set a rate of 15 percent if prices were expected to rise 5 percent. In the second case, inflation would wipe out 5 percent of the value of the principal and interest, leaving the lender and borrower in the same real position as the first case. This idea is frequently known

---

[5]There are various definitions of money depending on which financial assets are included. The figures here are for M2.

as the Fisher effect, named after Irving Fisher, the American economist who first studied the relationship between interest rates and inflation.

Historically, the relationship between inflation and interest rates has not always been as exact as this example might suggest. Interest rates have sometimes remained fairly stable despite short bursts of inflation. But as inflation persisted year after year, credit markets learned to pay close attention to inflation signals, and the relationship between inflation and the rate of interest grew closer and closer. Economists were to some extent the teachers in this learning process. So even as economists tried to estimate the relationship between inflation and the rate of interest, the doctrines they professed were altering that relationship.

Looking back, we can see that there were four major bursts of inflation—in 1965 and 1966, 1967 to 1969, 1973 to 1975, and 1976 to 1980—each with increasing duration and magnitude. Either in anticipation of or in response to these four bursts of inflation, the Fed took strong measures to counter the inflationary forces. In 1966, 1969, 1970, and 1974, the Fed substantially lowered monetary growth and accompanied these moves with strong pronouncements (seconded by the White House) that a firm commitment had been made to stem the tide of inflation. On each occasion, however, anti-inflationary policies were abandoned within a year. In each case, both an underestimate of the length of time required to halt the inflation and the political pressures that rapidly built up when the economy showed signs of slowing down combined to produce a reversal in policy. Though strong but temporary measures slowed the inflation for a short time, the reversals produced new price surges and a growing conviction that inflation would not stop because the government lacked the will to stop it.

Such policies contributed to the long-run emergence of higher unemployment and higher inflation. In the 1960s, as we noted, economists had believed that there was a stable Phillips curve: unemployment could be permanently lowered at the cost of permanently higher inflation. Now they began to see that the Phillips curve represented only a temporary trade-off. Once workers and employers began to adjust to the new higher rate of inflation, unemployment would begin moving back to its "natural rate." A number of economists contributed to the new view of the relationship between inflation and unemployment; perhaps most influential was Milton Friedman. His address to the American Economic Association in 1967, "The Role of Monetary Policy," explained that increasing money growth reduced unemployment for a time because prices would initially rise faster than wages, and real wages would fall. But once workers caught on, they would demand wage increases in line with price increases and unemployment would return once again to its "natural rate."[6] The policy implications of this analysis were clear. Governments should not try to reduce unemployment to the lowest possible rate through monetary and fiscal policy because that would lead to ever higher rates of inflation. Better would be a stable monetary and fiscal framework. But as Keynes noted in the passage previously quoted, new ideas are rarely implemented immediately; rather they gradually encroach upon policymakers.

---

[6] Liberal economists preferred the term, *non-accelerating inflation rate of unemployment* (NAIRU) because it did not suggest that there was nothing to be done to improve on this rate of unemployment. (This is an example of the sort of humor that appeals to economists: the Nehru suit was fashionable at this time.)

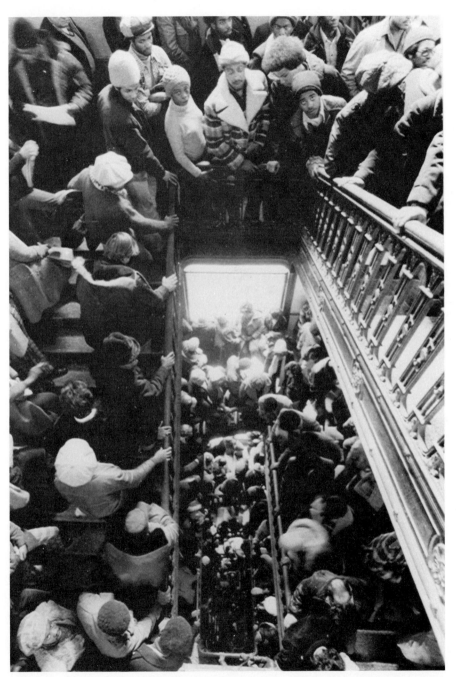

Unemployment was of little public concern throughout the 1960s but had become one of the country's most significant social problems by the 1970s. Scenes like this of applicants for public-service jobs in Chicago in 1975 were commonplace from coast to coast.

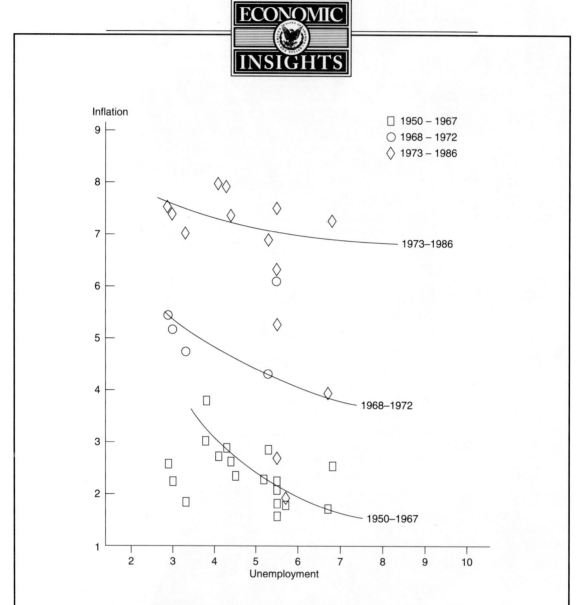

The figure shows the Phillips curve, which describes the relationship between unemployment (on the horizontal axis) and inflation (on the vertical axis). Originally it was believed that the trade-off was stable. Policymakers could choose a low level of unemployment and hit that target through expansionary fiscal policy. The result would be a high rate of wage increase (unions would naturally be militant when demand was strong and replacement workers were few) and, as wage increases were passed along, a high rate of price increase. Policymakers, in the language of the time, were faced with a stable "menu of choices" and could choose the combination of inflation and unemployment that suited their preferences. Republicans, concerned about the value of the dollar, would choose high unemployment and low inflation; Democrats, concerned about the working poor, would choose low unemployment and high inflation.

The figure shows what happened to this tidy view: the Phillips curve shifted steadily upward. (We have drawn the curves freehand, which allows us to ignore "outliers.") Economists responded with new theories about the curve. Initially they looked for a reason that might explain a once-and-for-all shift. Perhaps there were more young workers entering the work force, or perhaps young people were less willing to work. But as the shift appeared to continue, the theory underlying the curve was subjected to a more searching scrutiny. Economists Milton Friedman and Edmund Phelps argued persuasively that it was only a positive gap between actual and expected inflation that increased profits and reduced unemployment. Successively higher Phillips curves were produced by successively higher rates of expected inflation. Moreover, since expectations always adapted in the end to actual inflation, there was no permanent trade-off. Finally, economists led by Robert Lucas argued that because people formed their expectations rationally, the trade-off might not exist even in the short run. What had once appeared to be a stable downward-sloping curve now was seen as a cloud surrounding a long-run vertical line.

THE CARTER YEARS

The brief trial of tight monetary policy under President Gerald Ford in 1974 and 1975 contributed to a sharp recession that pushed unemployment upward and helped Jimmy Carter win the 1976 election. Inflation slowed temporarily, and by the fall of 1976 the rate of inflation had fallen below 5 percent. When Carter took office, his administration had an excellent opportunity to stamp out the long-building inflationary forces. But the Carter team missed the opportunity. Instead it went about the business of stimulating the economy. Political pressure for increases in Social Security benefits, veterans' benefits, farm subsidies, civil service pensions, grants to states, welfare programs, and other spending advances met favor with the Carter administration and with Congress. Meanwhile, and in contrast to the official rhetoric of the Fed, the stock of money advanced sharply. From 1975 to 1976 the stock of money increased at an annual rate of 13.7 percent, and from 1976 to 1977 it increased at 10.6 percent. By the fall of 1978, inflation was advancing at a rate twice that of two years earlier. But unemployment had fallen at a disappointing rate over the same period, from 8.5 percent to 6.0 percent. Greater monetary ease could not be risked.

With the polls repeatedly showing that inflation was "enemy number one," Carter was compelled to act. He named Robert Strauss as his "anti-inflation chief."[7] As a

---

[7] Given ambassador status, Strauss's official title was Special Counselor on Inflation.

gifted lawyer and political strategist, Strauss's influence on the Carter team was large; but as an expert on inflation, his credentials were few. In a speech at the Columbia Business School annual dinner in April 1978, he embarrassed the Carter administration with a speech that blamed most of the inflation on the private sector and the American people. In addition, his remarks suggested the highlights of Carter's new policies that were to be introduced a few months later, in October. Emphasizing that the costs of inaction were high, Strauss listed three options: "a mandatory controls policy, a cooperative approach, and a do-nothing stance." Rejecting the third and noting that the first was inappropriate in the absence of a national emergency, he asked "each American to insure that he make some contribution to lowering inflation rates this year." No mention was made of monetary policy.

VOLUNTARY CONTROLS TO FIGHT INFLATION

Alfred Kahn, the chairman of the Civil Aeronautics Board who had spearheaded the deregulation of the airlines, soon replaced Strauss. But the change came too late to fundamentally alter policy. By the time Kahn took over, Carter's anti-inflation program was comprised of (1) a commitment to *lower the increase* in government spending, (2) a reduction in the federal deficit, (3) a call to increase the labor productivity and efficiency overall, and (4) a set of "voluntary guidelines" for wage and price increases. Within a year it was clear that the program was an act of futility. The voluntary controls proved particularly unsettling and were a bone of contention by labor and business alike. While some large corporations and unions were ignored, other smaller, less politically potent groups were forced by the President's Council on Wage and Price Controls (often with help from the Internal Revenue Service) to conform to the "advised constraints." In effect, the voluntary controls became mandatory controls selectively applied. Meanwhile, inflation continued to rise. By late 1978, inflation was rising at a double-digit annual rate, and throughout 1979 it was rising at a rate above 12 percent.

An atmosphere of confusion prevailed as key members of the Carter team made conflicting public statements. In mid-1979, Charles Schultz, Chairman of the Council of Economic Advisers, said he expected the administration's program to take hold later in the year, moderating inflation generally and especially the rate of increase for food.[8] A month earlier, upon hearing that prices had risen 1.1 percent in one month, Alfred Kahn said, "the government can do some things, but not a helluva lot, for the most part it rests with the consumer." Unlike Nixon, who could justifiably claim that OPEC's (Organization of Petroleum Exporting Countries) price increases in oil and other external shocks were important forces behind inflation during the years between 1973 and 1976, the Carter team could find no one to share the blame other than the nation's private sector.[9]

---

[8] Washington (UPI), May 26, 1979.

[9] Although the large shift in wealth caused by OPEC is beyond dispute, its impact on inflation is less clear. For instance, West Germany and Switzerland were far more vulnerable to the real shocks produced by OPEC and failing agricultural crops than was the United States. Yet they managed, by a determined effort to reduce their monetary growth, to lower their inflations to the vanishing point between 1972 and 1976.

Indeed the political rationale for the wage and price guidelines was precisely for that purpose: it served to shift the blame for inflation from government mismanagement to the private sector. Throughout these years the news media helped to promote this misplaced emphasis. Monthly inflation data were routinely reported in a form that attributed price rises to particular sectors or industries. For example, reporters would say that this month most of the inflation was *caused* by the rise in the price of housing (or food, or energy) or whatever rose the most that month. But such advances were the *result* of inflation; they did not cause it.

PUBLIC DISPLEASURE. By late 1978, the United States and much of the rest of the world were engulfed in an economic and political crisis of growing proportions. The polls repeatedly showed that the majority of Americans lacked confidence in the nation's major institutions. A dramatic and influential illustration of voter outrage over high taxes and perceived government waste was the 1978 landslide passage of Proposition 13 in California.[10] Other states quickly followed suit, and several passed legislation limiting the growth of either state government expenditures and/or taxes. Perhaps the most startling development was the rising call for a constitutional convention to pass an amendment requiring the federal government to balance its budget. By 1980, 31 out of the 34 states required had called for such a convention; in March 1982, President Ronald Reagan announced his support for such a measure. Clearly, fiscal policy and deficit spending were no longer viewed with the favor that had prevailed in the Keynesian era.

GOVERNMENT POLICY AND INCREASED INFLATION

The cumulative effects of government's post-1965 commitment to inflation is shown in Figure 28-3 (see next page) for the major sectors of the economy. Similar to the form of most news media's inflationary reports of the day, the figures may tempt one to single out those sectors revealing the most rapid rise in prices. But clearly, *the general rise of prices* did not stem from any single sector. *All sectors*, albeit with variation, responded to the underlying inflationary forces. As during the Great Depression, many policies were initiated or enlarged in the 1970s to provide relief for needy individuals and families. These were largely redistributive to help correct for the disruptions caused by inflation. For instance, as food prices rose, food stamps were distributed more liberally—thus adding to demand and the rise of prices in that sector. As hospital and medical treatment costs soared, government attempted to assume the medical costs of the needy—who in turn, because of lower personal costs for treatment, increased their demand for services. This increased the costs of medical services and added to inflation in the medical sector. Many communities (such as Berkeley and Santa Monica, California) passed rent controls, which hastened the rate of conversion of apartments to condominiums as owners scrambled to avoid the controls. Though

---

[10]The basic feature of the bill was to reduce property taxes sharply in the state and thereby limit spending.

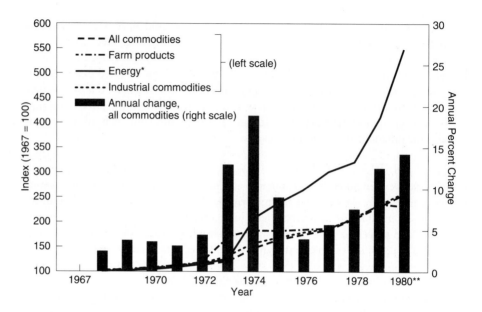

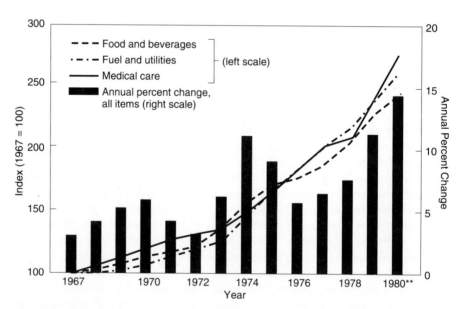

FIGURE 28-3 PRODUCER PRICE INDEXES, 1967–1980 *(1967 = 100)*. *(Upper figure)*

CONSUMER PRICE INDEXES, 1967–1980 *(1967 = 100)*. *(Lower figure)*

SOURCE: CHARTS PREPARED BY THE U.S. BUREAU OF THE CENSUS.

*Fuel, power, and related products.
**Annual rate for five months ending May. For 1980, percent change, May 1979–1980.

growth was being inhibited by high tax rates. Lowering rates would give people more incentive to work, invest, and innovate. Lowering rates would even produce more tax revenue by expanding the tax base, thus helping to balance the budget. The relationship between tax rates and tax revenues became known as the Laffer curve: over some range, raising rates would increase revenues, but at some point further increases would lead to large reductions in work effort and increases in tax evasion; then total tax revenue would fall. Laffer and other supply-side economists believed that the economy had already entered this range. But while most economists agreed that high tax rates tended in some degree to discourage productive effort, many disputed that the effects of cutting rates would be as large as the supply-siders thought. In the campaign for the Republican nomination, George Bush, then Reagan's rival, spoke for many when he denounced the idea of balancing the budget through tax cuts as "voodoo economics," a term that gained wide currency among critics of supply-side theory.

After the election, Congress moved swiftly to reduce income taxes and other taxes by 25 percent over a three-year period. But it should not surprise us that reductions in spending were much harder to achieve. As David Stockman, who was in charge of planning the Reagan spending cuts, tells us in his memoir, even the most common-sense cuts were strongly resisted by an "iron triangle": the direct beneficiaries of government spending in the private sector, the government bureaucrats who administered the program, and the Congressmen who were particularly beholden to the beneficiaries.

Tax cuts, the early recession, failure to make proposed spending cuts, and continued increases in the military budget produced deficits in the federal budget unprecedented in peacetime, although the exact amount to be attributed to each factor is in dispute. Figure 28-4 on the next page shows the deficit (adjusted for inflation) since 1970. It reveals both the long-term nature of the problem—the deficit has been growing for over two decades now—and the acceleration of growth in the deficit under presidents Reagan and Bush.

What were the consequences of such deficits? Neither Keynesian economists (who count on deficits to produce increased demand) nor supply-side economists (who count on tax reductions to spur work effort) were surprised by the long economic expansion that followed the recession of the early 1980s. On the other hand, some economists predicted that large federal deficits would lead to skyrocketing real interest rates (the market rate less inflation) because deficits meant that a much-augmented demand for credit would face the same supply. Although real interest rates were high in the 1980s, the supply of credit proved more elastic than had been anticipated. Foreign lenders rushed into the U.S. market by purchasing government bonds, private securities, real estate, and other assets. Real interest rates did not rocket upward, and the dollar remained strong (worth a large number of units of foreign currency) despite a growing gap between exports and imports.

It was widely believed that there was a close relationship between the "twin deficits." If the federal deficit could be closed, real interest rates would fall and the dollar would decline relative to other currencies, spurring exports and inhibiting imports. The trade deficit would disappear. Even economists who did not take an apocalyptic view of the deficit warned that the taxes necessary to finance the deficit were discouraging

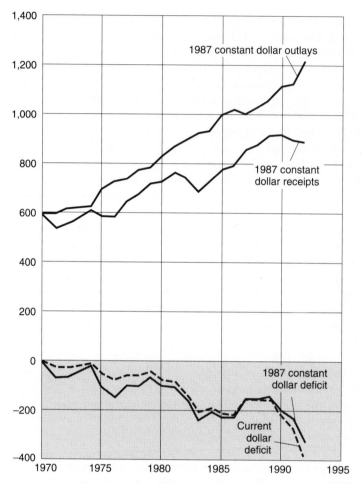

FIGURE 28-4 Federal Budget: Receipts, Outlays, and Deficit, 1970 to 1992

SOURCE: U.S. Bureau of the Census, *Statistical Abstract of the United States: 1992* (Washington, D.C.: Government Printing Office, 1992), p. 314.

Note: Data for 1992 are projected.

capital formation. There was, then, much concern about the budget deficit when President George Bush took office in January 1989. During the campaign, Bush had promised to continue Reagan's policies. He laid down the gauntlet to the Democrats by prefacing his pledge not to raise taxes with the challenging phrase "read my lips." This pledge was abandoned, however, when the recession of 1990 and 1991 helped drive the budget deficit even higher. Despite more than two decades of handwringing, the deficit was larger than ever when President Bill Clinton took the oath of office in January 1993.

SELECTED REFERENCES
AND SUGGESTED READINGS

Blinder, Alan S. *Economic Policy and the Great Stagflation.* New York: Academic Press, 1979.

Brunner, Karl, and Allan H. Meltzer, eds. *The Economics of Price and Wage Controls.* Amsterdam: North Holland, 1976.

Burns, Arthur. *Reflections of an Economic Policymaker.* Washington, D.C.: American Enterprise Institute, 1978.

Eckstein, Otto. *The Great Recession.* Amsterdam: North Holland, 1978.

Friedman, Benjamin M. "Postwar Changes in the American Financial Markets." In *The American Economy in Transition,* ed. Martin Feldstein. Chicago: University of Chicago Press, 1980.

Friedman, Milton. "The Role of Monetary Policy." *American Economic Review* 58 (March 1968): 1–17.

Friedman, Milton, and Anna J. Schwartz. *A Monetary History of the United States, 1867–1960.* Princeton: Princeton University Press, 1963.

Gordon, Robert J. "Postwar Macroeconomics: The Evolution of Events and Ideas." In *The American Economy in Transition,* ed. Martin Feldstein. Chicago: University of Chicago Press, 1980.

———. "Understanding Inflation in the 1980s." *Brookings Papers on Economic Activity* 16, no. 1 (1985): 263–299.

Heller, Walter W. *New Dimensions of Political Economy.* New York: W. W. Norton, 1966.

Holmans, A. E. *United States Fiscal Policy.* Oxford: Oxford University Press, 1961.

Lanzillotti, Robert F., Mary T. Hamilton, and Blaine R. Roberts. *Phase II in Review: The Price Commission Experience.* Washington, D.C.: Brookings Institution, 1975.

Lucas, Robert E., Jr. "Econometric Policy Evaluation: A Critique." In *The Phillips Curve and Labor Markets,* ed. K. Brunner and A. H. Meltzer. Carnegie-Rochester Conference Series on Public Policy. Amsterdam: North Holland, 1976, Vol. 1.

———. "Some International Evidence on Output Inflation Trade-offs." *American Economic Review* 63 (1973): 326–334.

———. "Understanding Business Cycles." In *Stabilization of the Domestic and International Economy,* ed. Karl Brunner and Allan Meltzer. Carnegie-Rochester Conference Series. Amsterdam: North Holland, 1977, Vol. 5.

Okun, Arthur M. "Measuring the Impact of the 1964 Tax Reduction." In *Perspectives on Economic Growth,* ed. Walter W. Heller. New York: Random House, 1968.

Phelps, Edmund S. "Phillips Curves, Expectations of Inflation and Optimal Unemployment Policy Over Time. *Economica* 34 (1967): 254–281.

Phillips, A. W. "The Relation between Unemployment and the Rate of Change of Money Wage Rates in the United Kingdom, 1861–1957." *Economica* 25 (November 1958): 283–299.

Roberts, Paul Craig. *The Supply-Side Revolution.* Cambridge: Harvard University Press, 1984.

Sachs, Jeffrey. "The Changing Cyclical Behavior of Wages and Prices, 1890–1976." *American Economic Review* 70 (1980): 78–90.

Sarget, Thomas, and Neil Wallace. "Rational Expectations and the Theory of Economic Policy." *Journal of Monetary Economics* 2 (April 1976): 241–254.

Schultz, George P., and Kenneth W. Dam. *Economic Policy beyond the Headlines.* New York: W. W. Norton, 1977.

Stein, Herbert. *The Fiscal Revolution in America.* Chicago: University of Chicago Press, 1969.

———. *Presidential Economics.* New York: Simon & Schuster, 1984.

Sundquist, James L. *Politics and Policy: The Eisenhower, Kennedy and Johnson Years.* Washington, D.C.: Brookings Institution, 1968.

Tobin, James. *The New Economics One Decade Older.* Princeton: Princeton University Press, 1974.

CHAPTER TWENTY-NINE

MANUFACTURING, MARKETING, AND INDUSTRIAL PRODUCTIVITY

CHAPTER THEME Although manufacturing has been and continues to be a major force in the U.S. economy, manufacturing employment declined from 24.5 percent of the labor force in 1950 to 14.3 percent in 1992, sparking demands for government policies to protect and encourage this sector. The relative decline in manufacturing was the result of market forces that altered the structure of demands faced by manufacturing firms and the productive techniques with which they met those demands. This chapter discusses the changing role of manufacturing and the changing policies through which government has attempted to direct that role.

THE DECLINE IN MANUFACTURING

Total employment in manufacturing, shown in the second column of Table 29-1, has been stagnant or falling since 1970. New jobs have been produced in other sectors of the economy. The fall in the share of the value of the output of manufacturing industries in total GNP was similar to the fall in the employment share: from about 29 percent in 1950 to about 19 percent in 1989. This does not mean that the actual volume of goods produced fell. From 1980 to 1989, for example, while employment in manufacturing was declining from 19.4 million to 18.2 million, the value of output in manufacturing measured in constant 1982 prices was rising (due to higher productivity) from $674 billion to $929 billion, and in per capita terms from $4,018 to $4,970.

The declining importance of manufacturing in the economy has been the result of the faster growth in the demand for services, the increasing ability of consumers to purchase some manufactured goods more cheaply from abroad, and the increasing productivity in the manufacturing sector. Many economists and policymakers have worried that the decline in manufacturing is bad for the health of the economy because manufacturing is a source of high-paying jobs, new products, and innovative technologies.

In the late 1970s and early 1980s, liberal economists and policymakers began to advocate a collection of policies aimed at reversing the long-run decline in manufacturing, which together came to be known as a "national industrial policy." The proposals that fell under this heading included: (1) national development banks to subsidize crucial industries; (2) government spending to train workers for new industrial jobs; (3) tariffs and quotas to protect American industry from foreign competition; (4) legislation to create an "industrial democracy" providing channels through which workers, residents of nearby communities, and government could influence business decisions on investment and plant closings; and (5) controls on mergers of firms and acquisitions of one firm by another.

The debate over a national industrial policy relied on comparisons with other countries such as Japan. But as Sidney Ratner, James H. Soltow, and Richard Sylla have pointed out, American economic history also provides a useful analogy.[1] For more than a century, and especially since the 1930s, the United States has had a wide range of policies designed to protect and encourage agriculture—that is, a national agricultural policy. Although this policy has undoubtedly had its successes, for example in speeding the dissemination of more-productive farming techniques, the agricultural sector has continued to shrink. One problem was that government agricultural policies often worked at cross-purposes. Policies designed to increase productivity, for example, have undermined attempts to raise prices. But even a perfectly coordinated government policy would have been hard put to preserve agriculture's share of GNP. The relative decline in manufacturing, like the earlier relative decline in agriculture, is the result of fundamental economic forces and is not likely to be reversed by a curious assortment

---

[1]Sidney Ratner, James H. Soltow, and Richard Sylla, *The Evolution of the American Economy*, 2d ed. (New York: Macmillan, 1993), p. 552.

TABLE 29-1 THE CHANGING ROLE OF MANUFACTURING

Year	Employment in Manufacturing (millions)	Employment as a Share of the Labor Force (percent)	Manufacturing Output as a Share of GNP (percent)
1950	15.2	24.5%	29.4%
1960	16.8	24.1	28.7
1970	19.4	23.4	25.8
1980	20.3	19.0	21.3
1989	19.4	15.7	18.6
1992	18.2	14.3	n.a.

SOURCES: (LABOR FORCE) *ECONOMIC REPORT OF THE PRESIDENT, 1993* (WASHINGTON, D.C., 1993), PP. 382, 394; (GNP) *HISTORICAL STATISTICS* (WASHINGTON, D.C.: GOVERNMENT PRINTING OFFICE, 1975), P. 233, AND U.S. BUREAU OF THE CENSUS, *STATISTICAL ABSTRACT OF THE UNITED STATES: 1992* (WASHINGTON, D.C., 1992), P. 429.

of government policies, although government may be able to mitigate the impact of the trend on certain groups of people.

THE RISE AND FALL OF INDUSTRIES

Discussion of the aggregate trend in manufacturing obscures the enormous differences in the experiences of individual firms and industries. Long ago, economist Joseph Schumpeter argued that the true sources of economic development were new products and new methods of production. Capitalism moves forward, according to Schumpeter,

Older manufacturing regions were hard hit by plant closings and job losses in the 1970s and 1980s.

not through small changes in existing products, but through the introduction of new products that destroy the market for older products. "Add as many mail coaches as you please, you will never get a railroad by doing so."[2]

The postwar period provides abundant evidence for Schumpeter's generalization. In the 1940s and 1950s, the antibiotics industry exhibited the highest average growth rate—a phenomenal 118 percent per year. Output of television sets was almost as great; home freezers and clothes dryers were close behind. But at the other end of the spectrum, production of tractors, locomotives, and rayon and acetate showed a definite tendency to slow down. The output of some industries actually declined. Changes in consumer tastes accounted for some of these declines, as in the cases of pipe and chewing tobacco, and lamb and mutton. For the most part, however, the retrogressing industries had fallen victim to the competition of new products. Radiators, convectors, and mechanical stokers were rapidly displaced when better heating systems became popular. And so it was for windmill pumps, soap, steam locomotives, and wood shingles.

It is instructive to observe how growth patterns shift with the selection of a particular time span. Between 1948 and 1960, for example, the list of fast-growth products changed remarkably.[3] Outstanding examples include polyethylene and transistors. But in the last six years of the period, some fast-growth products accelerated their rate of growth, some slowed their rate of growth, and others that averaged more than a 7.5 percent rate of increase for the whole period reached a leveling stage or actually declined during the last six years of the period.

According to a number of studies, a given industry does not usually reach a peak and then level off; once it ceases to grow, it normally begins to decline.[4] When it is first introduced, a product goes through a brief period of slow growth while it is gaining acceptance. If it gains acceptance, output increases for a time at an accelerating rate. As years pass, the growth rate tends to decline. This pattern is partly the result of a mathematical truism: an initial increase in production at a rate of, say, 100 percent per year obviously cannot be maintained forever. Typically, however, there is more to it than that. As Schumpeter emphasized, older products are continually displaced by new ones that satisfy basic consumer demands better or more cheaply.[5] Television hurt the motion picture industry badly, changed radio production altogether, raised problems in the spectator sports industry, and affected book sales and the custom of restaurant dining. Network television, in turn, has been affected by the growth of cable television and videocassettes. Older methods of producing a given commodity may also

---

[2] Joseph Schumpeter, "The Analysis of Economic Change," as reprinted in Readings in *Business Cycle Theory* (Philadelphia: Blakiston, 1944), p. 7. For a critical assessment of Schumpeter's emphasis on major innovations, see Nathan Rosenberg, *Perspectives on Technology* (Cambridge: Cambridge University Press, 1976), Chapter 4.

[3] For the average annual rates of growth of 304 products from 1948 to 1960, see Francis L. Hirt, "New Light on Patterns of Output Growth," *Survey of Current Business* (September 1961): 14–15.

[4] See in particular, Arthur F. Burns, *Production Trends in the United States Since 1870* (New York: National Bureau of Economic Research, 1934); Simon Kuznets, *Secular Movements in Production and Prices* (Boston: Houghton Mifflin, 1930); and J. Paradiso and Francis L. Hirt, "Growth Trends in the Economy," *Survey of Current Business* (January 1953): 5–10.

[5] Cited in Burns, p. xvi.

be displaced by newer methods. Steel-reinforced aluminum cable, which is both stronger and lighter than an electrically equivalent copper cable, captured the high-voltage transmission-line business and is rapidly displacing copper in the so-called secondary distribution field.

Household durables have been a particularly important field for innovators. Before World War I, sales of automobiles and washing machines expanded rapidly. Electric refrigerators and radios got their start early in the 1920s, and sales increased even during the depressed 1930s. After World War II, automatic washing machines, television sets, home freezers, room air conditioners, dehumidifiers, and clothes dryers made their mark. As the 1960s progressed, central air conditioning and electric heating systems, including heat pumps, vied with color television sets for a rapidly increasing share of household outlays. In the 1970s, recreational and avocational expenditures on new designs of old products rose spectacularly as families turned to cameras, stereos, boats, campers, and other leisure-time equipment.

Today, as in the past, American manufacturers endlessly strive to develop new products. Schumpeter believed that the central justification for monopolies and oligopolies is that they develop large research departments that institutionalize the process of industrial research and innovation. In Schumpeter's view, a firm with monopoly power may be able to maintain or increase it by introducing new products, whereas competitive firms or independent laboratories may be hard-pressed to raise capital to invest in research and development. Subsequent research, however, has failed to confirm the central role of monopolies and oligopolies in research and development. For one thing, it appears that firms with market power often focus on minor innovations designed to protect their monopoly power. New products such as Polaroid cameras, personal computers, and intermittent windshield wipers often come from smaller firms or independent inventors.[6]

In recent years, considerable concern has been expressed about the level of research and development expenditures in the United States. This concern has arisen from the belief that more spending in this area would arrest the relative decline in the manufacturing sector. But as Table 29-2 shows (see next page), research and development spending has kept pace with the growth of the economy and has remained relatively stable as a percentage of GNP.

Research and development remains, despite the institutionalization of research, a highly risky affair. Roughly five out of every six items introduced into supermarket channels each year fail to sell. Market testing alone can cost vast sums, and market-tested products can fail even when they are backed by massive advertising campaigns. The example of Ford Motor Company's Edsel is legendary, and other examples abound. No less prestigious a firm than Du Pont lost $100 million on Corfam, simply because people would not accept artificial leather shoes despite their porosity and low-care requirements. General Foods dropped an estimated $15 million on a cereal containing freeze-dried strawberries because children thought the berries were "mushy and soggy."[7]

---

[6] See Frederic M. Scherer, *Innovation and Growth* (Cambridge: MIT Press, 1984), Chapter 11, for a review of the evidence.

[7] "New Products: The Push Is on Marketing," *Business Week* (March 4, 1972): 72–77.

TABLE 29-2   RESEARCH AND DEVELOPMENT, 1953–1990

Year	Total Research and Development (in millions)	Basic Research (in millions)	Total as a Percent of GNP	Basic as a Percent of GNP
1953	$ 5,207	$ 489	1.40%	.13%
1960	13,730	1,326	2.66	.26
1970	26,134	3,531	2.57	.35
1980	62,610	8,432	2.28	.31
1990	145,450	21,920	2.63	.40

SOURCES: (1953, 1960) HISTORICAL STATISTICS (WASHINGTON, D.C.: GOVERNMENT PRINTING OFFICE, 1975), SERIES W109; AND (1970–1990) STATISTICAL ABSTRACT OF THE UNITED STATES: 1992 (WASHINGTON, D.C.: U.S. BUREAU OF THE CENSUS, 1992), P. 586.

There are those, of course, who argue that the constant churning of the marketplace by entrepreneurs seeking to find a niche for a new product wastes resources and raises the costs of supplying accepted products. The alternative is a system in which political commissars make choices for people, a system that failed in other countries in part because it failed to deliver the stream of new products and services provided by market economies in the postwar era.

MARKETING AND THE CONSUMER

As noted in Chapter 20, manufacturers in the late nineteenth century began to bypass the wholesaler and to sell directly to retail outlets. The "general merchandise" wholesaler, with a warehouse of heterogeneous goods in many product lines, declined rapidly before World War I. However, the full-service, full-line wholesale house that furnished goods to retailers in one particular line (such as hardware, groceries, or drugs) over great regions or even nationally was still an important force. This position was maintained primarily in industries where production remained small-scale. Perhaps the major trend in wholesaling over the past 70 to 75 years has been the lessening relative importance of these great houses and the increasing importance of the specialty wholesaler, or "short line" distributor. To a significant extent, this change has been caused by shifting markets. The specialty firm, which confines its selling activity to a portion of the products within a single line of merchandise (coffee, tea, and condiments instead of "groceries," for example, or cutlery instead of "hardware"), has fit into the changing scene by providing expert knowledge from which small retailers can benefit.

The changes in wholesaling were a reflection of changes in retailing. Department stores were well established by 1900 and were popularly accepted in the first decade of the century. Between 1910 and 1920, mail-order companies also began to make great gains. By 1919 the chain stores showed signs of being a potent marketing form, and in the 1920s they became a major force in retailing. How have these types of stores fared since?

During the 1920s and 1930s, department stores maintained a constant proportion of retail sales, indicating that they were just about holding their own. World War II, with its supply shortages and gasoline rationing, restored some of the advantages of shopping under one roof; department-store business increased to about 10 percent of retail sales—a gain of perhaps two percentage points. Since 1947, department stores, although not without a struggle, have moved slowly back to this position, and in 1982 once again accounted for 10 percent of retail sales, a share that they maintained into the late 1980s. Increasing traffic congestion in downtown urban areas, the rise of sub-urban shopping centers, and the expansion of variety chains and mail-order companies into broader fields have been the chief factors working against the independent department store. Yet many large stores have shown unexpected resilience. Ownership groups have bought control of stores in many cities, thereby bringing the advantages of increased buying power to many of the stores that have continued to operate under their old, familiar names. More recently, alert managements have followed the sub-urban trend by establishing branches that serve as "anchors" for suburban shopping malls. To fight the discount houses, which cut costs with plain decor and a minimum of service, department stores have either met discount-house prices in their old loca-tions or opened new and less-pretentious outlets for the purpose of discounting. A final irony of this competition has been the opening of glossy, new central-city stores by the discounters; like every other major retailing form before them, they have finally succumbed to the compulsion to become respectable.

The two great mail-order houses, Sears and Montgomery Ward, were forced to change their sales methods to fit the times. In 1925 Montgomery Ward established its first retail store, and Sears, Roebuck quickly followed suit. At the end of a decade and a half, these retail stores numbered in the hundreds, and more than one-half of the "mail-order" business was conducted over a counter. At the end of World War II, Sears boldly expanded by building great department stores in readily accessible sections of major cities. Montgomery Ward, because it was faint-hearted in carrying out its expan-sion program, lost ground to such an extent that in 1950 its sales were less than one-half those of Sears. During the ensuing decade, Sears became the fifth-largest employer in the United States, with a dollar volume of retailing of more than $4 billion a year—a retail sales figure exceeded only by A&P. In 1971 Sears was still the fifth-largest employer in the country, and its sales of $10 billion were nearly twice the sales of A&P and Safeway, which were second and third on the retailer list, respectively. In the late 1970s Sears' position deteriorated as competition from discounters and small retailers based in malls increased. Management reforms in the 1980s paved the way for a rebound, and by 1987 Sears was the fourteenth-largest company in the country. Despite its success as a retailer, however, Sears was forced to abandon its famous cat-alog in 1993.

But new entrants in the mail-order business have flourished. A number of com-panies specializing in a single line or a few items have sprung up. Two-earner families with high incomes and little time to shop have turned to catalogs, offsetting the decline of the traditional catalog user, the farm family. From 1929 until the mid-1980s, the mail-order business was fairly constant at roughly 1 percent of all retail sales. In 1987 catalog sales were 1.4 percent of total retail sales and climbing.

The past 45 years have witnessed a widespread acceptance of the chain principle of merchandising. Between 1919 and 1929, chain sales rose from an estimated 4 percent of retail sales to slightly less than 25 percent. By 1987, sales of multiunit firms accounted for 57 percent of total sales, and sales of firms with 100 or more outlets accounted for 55 percent of all chain-store sales. The chain-store principle spread to drugs, shoes, toys, women's ready-to-wear, and jewelry among other areas, although only moderate gains have been made in variety merchandise, food, and automobile accessories and equipment.

In 1925 Sears, Roebuck opened its first retail store while continuing its mail-order business. In 1993 the catalog was discontinued.

In concentrating on the spectacular growth of the big merchandisers, we should not forget that many limited-line stores, widely varying in size and under independent ownership, have continued to thrive. Many independents have located in the suburban shopping centers and malls that sprang up after World War II. Although the chains were pioneers in the development of the supermarket, some independents have competed successfully by adopting similar merchandising techniques. Independents have also been successful in metropolitan-area stores selling higher-priced goods such as clothing, appliances, and even automobiles.

In an age in which deference is paid to the specialist, specialists in the retail field have been able to hold their own when they can successfully differentiate their product. Product differentiation may be achieved by adjusting the conditions of the product sale or by varying the quality or appearance of the product itself. Independent retailers have traditionally operated neighborhood stores to reap the rewards of a good location, and some are still able to do so in suburban shopping centers and malls. Retailers may be equally successful in differentiating their establishment by carrying the goods of nationally known manufacturers or "private" lines and appealing to customers who prefer a high degree of personal attention.

The successful differentiation of a product sold in the nationwide market typically requires large advertising outlays. Consumers must be persuaded that there is a reason to buy one brand of cigarettes, cornflakes, or washing machines rather than another. As early as 1910, the annual volume of advertising expenditure reached $1 billion (about 2.8 percent of GNP). By 1929, as shown in Table 29-3, the estimated outlay had reached $3.4 billion (3.3 percent of GNP). Advertising declined greatly during the 1930s. And although expenditures recovered in the late 1930s and 1940s, the share of advertising in GNP never recovered the level apparently reached (the statistics on advertising are not the best) in 1929.

The small and apparently stable share of advertising in GNP does not mean that advertising is unimportant. Most industries are small compared with GNP. To take another comparison, advertising in recent years has averaged about 85 percent of total

TABLE 29-3 EXPENDITURES ON ADVERTISING, 1929–1990

Year	Expenditures on Advertising (in billions)	Percent of GNP
1929	$ 3.4	3.30%
1940	2.1	2.11
1950	5.7	1.98
1960	12.0	2.32
1970	19.6	1.93
1980	53.6	1.96
1990	128.6	2.35

SOURCES: (1929–1950) *HISTORICAL STATISTICS* (WASHINGTON, D.C.: GOVERNMENT PRINTING OFFICE, 1975), SERIES T444; AND (1960–1990) *STATISTICAL ABSTRACT OF THE UNITED STATES: 1992* (WASHINGTON, D.C.: U.S. BUREAU OF THE CENSUS, 1992), P. 558.

spending on research and development, and about 150 percent of the amount spent on research and development by the private sector. Wouldn't we all be better off, critics of advertising have asked, if some of the money being spent to convince us to buy one brand of automobile rather than another were spent instead on developing safer and more efficient automobiles?

Economists have long debated whether advertising, and the product differences it promotes, are socially productive. In the 1920s and early 1930s, Edward Hastings Chamberlin brought this issue to the fore with his theory of monopolistic competition.[8] Despite continuing research, no consensus has been reached. Perhaps it is fair to say that today economists have a better appreciation of the large number of cases in which advertising is informative and of the potential costs of limiting advertising, even if they are not completely reconciled to it.

INDUSTRIAL PRODUCTIVITY

The impact of science on the workplace, particularly through the development of automatic control mechanisms, has been so great that commentators in the early 1960s began to speak of a "new technology" and a "second Industrial Revolution." A generation later, after the computer revolution reached proportions no one could have imagined in the 1960s, social scientists were still debating the consequences of these changes.

In the primary metal industries, for example, almost unbelievable advances have been made in the handling of materials. The continuous rolling of sheet metal, introduced in the steel industry in 1926, is now commonplace. More and more primary metals industries have achieved uninterrupted production in huge integrated plants. In the case of steel, this means that molten iron can be converted into steel beams, sheets, and plates without the great losses of heat that were usual until 1920. And throughout the process, heavy handling is done by all kinds of mechanical conveyors, from forklift trucks to giant cranes.

During the 1920 and 1930s, as the mechanization of industry continued, there was much talk about "technological unemployment." Even in 1962, President Kennedy remarked that the "major domestic challenge of the sixties is to maintain full employment at a time when automation is replacing men." The concern is an old one. In the nineteenth century, David Ricardo, one of the founders of classical economics, argued that the introduction of new machines could lead, at least for a time, to unemployment. And Karl Marx described in eloquent and powerful terms the suffering experienced by hand-loom weavers displaced by machines. Indeed, whenever unemployment rises, demands to limit technological unemployment are sure to follow. To take one recent example of technological unemployment, the number of employees of telephone companies dropped from 742,000 in 1984 to 648,000 in 1990, while the number of calls handled daily rose from 1.2 billion to 9.5 billion. This increase in productivity was made possible by rapid advances in computer-based technologies.

---

[8] Edward H. Chamberlin, *Theory of Monopolistic Competition* (Cambridge: Harvard University Press, 1933).

If the past is any guide, the jobs lost in the telephone industry will be more than made up by new jobs arising elsewhere in the economy. The cost savings that result from technological innovations are passed along to consumers (if competitive pressures are strong) in the form of lower prices. This means that the consumers have more money to purchase more of the good or service whose price has fallen or more of other goods and services. Thus, for the economy as a whole, technological progress need not lead, and has not led, to long-run unemployment. The British economy eventually created jobs to replace those lost by the hand-loom weavers, and the U.S. economy will replace those lost by the telephone operators. The lesson of history is clearly that aggregate unemployment is a short-run phenomenon, frequently exacerbated by mistakes in monetary and fiscal policy.

Our confidence that new jobs will eventually replace old ones should not make us insensitive to the suffering that arises in an industry being mechanized. Workers whose skills once brought a high premium, typically older workers, may find themselves competing with unskilled workers for new jobs. It is little comfort to them to know that the aggregate unemployment rate will eventually recover.

Automation is more than simply the speed-up of production lines. The "revolutionary" feature of automation is control and adjustment through computerized decision making. Modern oil refineries and chemical plants approach the extreme of automation, and more and more products that lend themselves to continuous-process manufacture and assembly-line techniques are being brought under complete automatic control. Because the system is based on the "feedback" principle, the control mechanism operates on a basis of actual performance instead of expected performance.

Steve Jobs, with an early version of the Apple personal computer.

If a part is turned out incorrectly, a sensory device tells the control mechanism, which either allows further time for machining or rejects the part. All feedback devices are tied together in a closed-loop system, so that the assembly or manufacture of a product or of multiple products can be performed without the intervention of a human hand.

This revolutionary approach to manufacturing has required the redesign of products and machines—and even of entire processes. Redesign implies large additions to cost, but the computers that perform the logical tasks of control have rapidly become less costly. As the new technology has become more familiar, broad principles of design have evolved, and something approaching quantity production of the control devices has been achieved. Furthermore, flexibility of both materials-handling mechanisms and machine tools has been attained, so that a given automatic line can be shifted from the production of one product to another. Perhaps the ultimate achievement of automation is the large-scale application of robotics. Robots that not only perform routine production-line chores but also sense their environment and make responses similar to the neurophysiological responses of human beings are currently being introduced in a wide range of manufacturing processes.

A review of the advances in production techniques suggests that aggregate productivity must have risen rapidly in the postwar period. To an extent this is borne out in Table 29-4, which shows the rate of growth of labor productivity for three subperiods between 1948 and 1991. The table is read this way: From 1981 to 1991, output per hour of work in the manufacturing sector, to take one example, increased on average by about 4.7 percent per year. (This means that if workers had produced 100 units of output per hour in a given year, then the next year they would be able to produce 104.7 units.) Of course, the actual increase varied widely from industry to industry. In household furniture the increase was about 2.0 percent per year; in semiconductors it was about 10.1 percent per year.

As the table shows, however, the growth of productivity slowed dramatically and unexpectedly after 1973. Because the economy's ability to generate a rising standard of living depends on its ability to generate productivity increases, this slowdown became a major concern to economists and policymakers.

Why did productivity slow down in this fashion? A number of factors seem to have been at work. (1) The shift of production away from manufacturing toward the service sector has been one important factor slowing aggregate productivity growth. Part of the problem here is that quality improvements are extremely difficult to measure in the service sector, so that output growth may be understated. (2) As Michael Darby has argued, changes in the structure of the labor force can account for much of the slowdown.[9] For one thing, many young and therefore inexperienced workers were entering the labor force for the first time in the 1970s. (3) As oil prices rose sharply, industries and agricultural producers who had relied on cheap and abundant oil suddenly were forced to adjust to higher prices. Large investments were required to replace older equipment with more energy-efficient equipment, even if the new equipment led to the same output per labor hour. (4) The growth of capital per unit of labor input

---

[9] Michael R. Darby, "The U.S. Productivity Slowdown: A Case of Statistical Myopia," *American Economic Review* 74 (June 1984): 301–322.

TABLE 29-4 LABOR PRODUCTIVITY GROWTH RATES BY SECTOR, 1948–1991
(ANNUAL PERCENTAGE CHANGE IN OUTPUT PER HOUR)

Years	Total Business Sector	Nonfarm Sector	Manufacturing
1948–1973	2.8%	2.3%	2.1%
1973–1981	0.7	0.6	1.5
1981–1991	0.8	0.7	4.7[a]

SOURCES: (1948–1981) ECONOMIC REPORT OF THE PRESIDENT, 1987 (WASHINGTON, D.C., 1987), P. 46; AND (1981–1991) STATISTICAL ABSTRACT OF THE UNITED STATES: 1992 (WASHINGTON, D.C.: U.S. BUREAU OF THE CENSUS, 1992), P. 409.

[a] 1980–1991

also slowed in the 1970s. To some extent this may have been the result of rising inflation that disrupted financial markets and discouraged saving. (5) The highly variable rate of inflation in the 1970s may also have distorted price signals and prevented the reallocation of resources to their most efficient uses. When inflation varies dramatically from month to month, it is hard for workers or owners of capital to know whether their real income has fallen because they are in a declining sector or because their nominal income has temporarily lagged behind prices in general. (6) Some blame probably also attaches to the high cost of complying with new government regulations stemming from legislation passed in the 1960s, as perhaps some credit should be given to deregulation for the rebound of manufacturing productivity in the 1980s.

When all is said and done, though, most economists who have studied this issue agree that there still remains a residual that cannot be explained by the factors we have enumerated. Common sense tells us that automation, robotics, and the computer revolution should have spurred a great advance in productivity, yet in both the United States and much of the rest of the industrial world, productivity growth slowed in the 1970s. Some recent evidence (see the last line of Table 29-4) indicates that the slowdown has ended in manufacturing; but low productivity growth rates have persisted in other sectors, despite the alleviation of some of the problems, such as high and unpredictable inflation, that afflicted the 1970s.

CONCENTRATION IN INDUSTRY

It is understandable that observers during the Great Depression era became concerned about the "decline of competition." First, as shown in Figure 29-1 (see next page), the decade of the 1920s had brought a wave of business consolidation that was comparable at least in some respects to the merger movement of 1897 to 1904.[10] Second, a startlingly large proportion of corporate wealth was concentrated in the hands of a few

---

[10] The comparisons are only very approximate for these periods because data limitations prevent the measure of mergers by value for the years 1920 through 1948.

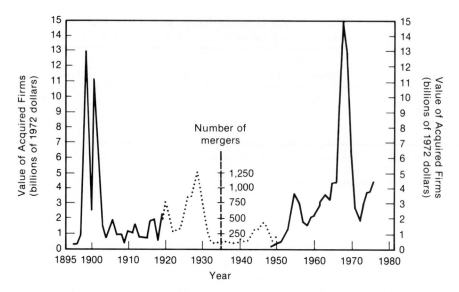

FIGURE 29-1 VOLUME OF MANUFACTURING AND MINING FIRM MERGERS AND ACQUISITIONS, BY VALUE, 1895–1919 AND 1948–1977, AND BY NUMBER OF MERGERS, 1920–1948

SOURCE: BASED ON DATA FROM F. M. SHERER, INDUSTRIAL MARKET STRUCTURE AND ECONOMIC PERFORMANCE, 2D ED. (CHICAGO: RAND MCNALLY, 1980), FIGURE 4.5.

firms. By 1933, well over 50 percent of all corporate wealth outside the financial field was controlled by 200 firms. Third, new and subtle ways of reducing price competition seemed to be gaining popularity and even overt government sanction. Among these, the most effective was to organize all the producers in a field into manufacturers' institutes or trade associations. Finally, and most importantly, it was believed during the depression that prices were stickier and output declines were more severe in those industries where a few firms were dominant.

There was, however, a noticeable difference in character between the mergers of the 1920s and those of the great wave of mergers at the turn of the century. During the earlier wave, mergers typically produced a high degree of control of the industry's output, usually in excess of 50 percent.[11] In the 1920s, mergers continued to be predominantly horizontal, as shown in Table 29-5, but most of the merged firms secured much smaller percentages of an industry's output, because mergers usually took place among companies that were smaller than the dominant company in the industry. As a result, the dominant firm, which had frequently held a partial monopolistic position, gradually came to control a smaller share of the industry's production. The steel industry best exemplified this trend. United States Steel's share of ingot capacity dropped as Bethlehem and Republic sharply incased their shares through mergers. The shift

---

[11]George J. Stigler, "Monopoly and Oligopoly by Merger," American Economic Review 40 (May 1950): 23–33.

TABLE 29-5 PERCENTAGE DISTRIBUTION OF MERGERS BY TYPE IN
MANUFACTURING AND MINING COMPANIES, 1926–1977

Type of Merger	1926–1930	1940–1947	1948–1955	1956–1963	1964–1972	1973–1977
Horizontal	75.9	62.0	36.8	19.2	12.4	15.1
Vertical	4.8	17.0	12.8	22.2	7.8	5.8
Conglomerate	19.3	21.0	50.4	58.6	79.8	78.1
Total	100.0	100.0	100.0	100.0	100.0	100.0

SOURCES: SENATE COMMITTEE ON THE JUDICIARY, SUBCOMMITTEE ON ANTITRUST AND MONOPOLY, *ECONOMIC CONCENTRATION,* HEARINGS PURSUANT TO S. RES. 40, PART 8A (FEDERAL TRADE COMMISSION, *ECONOMIC REPORT ON CORPORATE MERGERS*) (WASHINGTON, D.C.: GOVERNMENT PRINTING OFFICE, 1969), P. 637; AND FEDERAL TRADE COMMISSION, *STATISTICAL REPORT ON MERGERS AND ACQUISITIONS* (VARIOUS ISSUES).

from partial monopoly to oligopolies was also notable in cement, cans, petroleum, agricultural instruments, and glass.[12]

Some industries that had approached the competitive norm, in the sense that they had been composed of large numbers of firms, became oligopolies during the 1920s. Dairy products and packaged foods were the outstanding examples of this kind of rapid change in market structure; liquors and beverages, paper and printing, machinery and machine tools, and even motion pictures were also eventually produced in markets characterized by "few" sellers. In short, the third wave of mergers led primarily to oligopolistic market structures.

MODERN MERGERS

The first waves of post–World War II mergers took a new form. In the past, merger strategy, if not for gains of monopoly power, at least normally followed the logical extension of product lines either to create new demands for existing products or to make new uses of materials developed for existing products. As shown in Table 29-5, the more recent merger type is the conglomerate that combines unrelated commodities and business activities; its fundamental purpose is to maximize the value of the common stock of a firm acquiring companies felt to be underpriced in the market. A characteristic of the conglomerate is its management organization. A small, elite headquarters staff attends to such general matters as financial planning, capital allocations, legal and accounting tasks, and operations research. Operating managers, motivated by handsome stock options, are usually given wide latitude in managing their subsidiaries.

Ling-Temco-Voight (LTV), one of the first and most successful companies of its type, began in 1958 as a small firm called Ling Electronic, with annual sales of less than $7 million. During the next ten years, Ling acquired or merged with Temco Aircraft, Chance-Voight, Okonite, Wilson and Company, Wilson Sporting Goods

---

[12] Stigler, p. 31.

Company, the Greatamerica Corporation, and some 24 other companies. Its revenues in 1968 were close to $3 billion. When LTV acquired the Jones and Laughlin Steel Company in 1969, the merger meant that two corporations in the list of the nation's 100 largest companies were combining to make LTV the fourteenth-largest company in the United States.[13] Comparably spectacular results have been achieved by other conglomerates such as Gulf and Western Industries, International Telephone and Telegraph, Litton Industries, Boise Cascade, and the "Automatic" Sprinkler Corporation. Although these and other conglomerates have been plagued with both financial and managerial difficulties from time to time, they characterize much of the glamour and excitement associated with fast-paced financial action.

In the late 1970s and early 1980s, merger activity intensified. As Table 29-6 shows, the number of merger and acquisition announcements increased by more than 30 percent between 1975 and 1985, and the value of merged firms rose at least by the factor of 15 shown in the table (and possibly by substantially more since the statistics are probably incomplete). New terms such as *junk bonds* and *leveraged buyouts* and new personalities such as T. Boone Pickens, Carl Icahn, and Michael Milken dominated the financial pages.

In the typical case, corporate raiders such as Pickens and Icahn targeted a firm believed to be undervalued. They then issued junk bonds (high-risk and hence high-yield bonds), offering some combination of these bonds and cash to the holders of the stock of the firm being acquired. Milken (of the investment banking firm of Drexel,

TABLE 29-6   RECENT MERGER TRENDS IN THE UNITED STATES, 1975–1987

Year	Total Net Mergers and Acquisitions	Total Value (in billions)[a]
1975	2,297	$ 11.8
1980	1,889	44.3
1981	2,395	82.6
1982	2,346	53.8
1983	2,533	73.1
1984	2,543	122.2
1985	3,001	179.8
1986	3,336	173.1
1987	2,032	163.7

SOURCE: *MERGERSTAT REVIEW 1987* (CHICAGO: W. T. GRIMM, 1988), P. 103. COPYRIGHT © 1988 BY W. T. GRIMM & COMPANY. REPRINTED WITH PERMISSION.

[a] Refers to a subset of the total net mergers for which data were available.

[13] Richard W. McLaren, then Assistant Attorney General for antitrust, obtained an injunction against LTV halting the final merger of the two companies. In 1971 LTV agreed to divest itself of Braniff Airlines and other assets as a condition of merger with Jones and Laughlin.

Burnham, Lambert) was instrumental in bringing together entrepreneurs who wished to use junk bonds in takeovers with buyers. It was Milken's contention, based on the historical record of junk bonds, that these bonds rarely proved to be as risky in the long run as conventional wisdom would have it. What he and his buyers tended to forget was that through his own actions, Milken had so reshaped the market that his crop of junk bonds could not easily be compared with those issued in the past.

How could acquiring firms afford to pay more for common stock than it currently sold for in the market? Ultimately, each leveraged buyout (leverage is the ratio of debt to equity) depended on the belief that income generated by the firm being acquired could be increased by an amount sufficient to cover the interest on the new debt and still leave an ample return for shareholders. The many ways of doing this included replacing incompetent management, exploiting underutilized holdings of natural resources, and reducing "excessive" contributions to pension funds.

Defenders of leveraged buyouts and junk bonds argued that these techniques increased economic efficiency, as control was shifted from lax managements to entrepreneurs who would use resources more profitably. Critics argued that leveraged buyout artists simply stripped firms of valuable assets for short-term gains and gulled foolish purchasers of junk bonds. The critics charged, moreover, that the debt-to-equity ratio for many of the resulting firms was dangerously high, and that they would be unable to meet their interest payments during the next recession.

The fall of the junk bond market was as rapid as its ascent. In 1986 Drexel became a target in the ongoing investigation of insider trading by arbitrager Ivan Boesky.[14] In 1989 Drexel was forced to dismiss Milken, who later served time in jail for his part in the scandal. A few months later Campeau Corporation, a large issuer of junk bonds in the retail field, encountered a liquidity crisis, sending the junk bond market into a tailspin. Legislation prohibiting U.S. savings institutions from holding junk bonds also contributed to the slide, although only a few savings banks had ever acquired large positions in junk bonds. In 1990 Drexel, which itself held a large inventory of junk bonds, declared bankruptcy. The issuing of new junk bonds and their use in corporate takeovers was over at least for a time.

In retrospect, we can see the spectacular rise and fall of the junk bond market as a symptom rather than a cause of the high interest rates and volatile financial markets of the late 1970s and early 1980s, which sent investors in search of new and more flexible forms of finance.

CONCENTRATION AND COMPETITION

In the manufacturing sector, the largest companies produce a substantial portion of total output, although the share of large firms in total output has not been rising as rapidly as the volume of merger activity might suggest. This is illustrated in Table 29-7 (see next page). Here we are confronted with a paradox. By any measure, the U.S.

---

[14] Insider trading occurs when securities are bought or sold based on information from the management of the firm that has not been released to the public.

TABLE 29-7   SHARES OF TOTAL VALUE ADDED IN MANUFACTURING PRODUCED
BY THE 50 AND 200 LARGEST COMPANIES

Year	50 Largest Companies	200 Largest Companies
1947	17	30
1954	23	37
1963	25	41
1972	25	43
1982	24	43

SOURCE: U.S. BUREAU OF THE CENSUS, "CONCENTRATION RATIOS IN MANUFACTURING," *1982 CENSUS OF MANUFACTURERS* (WASHINGTON, D.C.: GOVERNMENT PRINTING OFFICE, 1983), TABLE 1.

consumer's position has progressively improved over the past half-century. How, then, can an economy weighted down with oligopoly so readily make available to consumers such an abundance of the goods and services? The answer to this question rests on the role of new techniques and new products—Schumpeter's gales of creative destruction—often produced by entirely different industries that are sometimes located in other countries. The demand for any particular firm's products, in other words, might not be stable and assured, even if it controls a large fraction of the industry's output, because products of firms in other industries may provide intense competition.[15] Thus, counting only market shares of top firms within a particular "industry" tells us very little.

The competition of aluminum with other materials is one good illustration of interindustry competition. Both copper and aluminum compete as materials for carrying electricity. Which metal is used depends on the job to be done, and on relative prices. Steel-reinforced aluminum cable, both stronger and lighter than an electrically equivalent copper cable, completely displaced copper in the high-voltage transmission-line business. However copper, with its higher electrical conductivity, still has a decided advantage over aluminum where wire of fine sizes is used and space must be conserved. Between these two extremes there is a vigorous, persistent competition. Large motor windings, power and feeder cable, and bus bars in central power stations can be made from either material. In these uses, firms in the copper industry and their copper- and brass-fabricating subsidiaries are direct rivals of the major aluminum companies.

Consider another use: In the field of die castings, aluminum alloys supplanted zinc castings, which had long been dominant. In this field, there is also competition with the brasses and, more and more, with alloys of magnesium and the plastics. If we add sand and permanent-mold castings to this category, we must include almost any metal that can be melted—gray and malleable iron and cast steel being the chief additions

---

[15]The question of interproduct and interindustry competition received considerable attention in the early 1950s. See David E. Lilienthal, *Big Business: A New Era* (New York: Harper & Row, 1952), pp. 47–94; Sumner H. Slichter, "The Growth of Competition," *Atlantic Monthly* (November 1953): 66–70; and A. D. H. Kaplan, *Big Enterprise in the Competitive System* (Washington, D.C.: Brookings Institution, 1953).

to the competition, which is decided (once weight, strength, and finish have been considered) on a basis of costs, including those of dies and machining.

The rivalry between aluminum and the steels is keen in the manufacture of truck, van, and trailer bodies (where magnesium and fiberglass are also alternative materials) and in certain construction uses. In making truck bodies, the competition between aluminum and steel involves a balancing of manufacturing costs and costs in use; the higher cost of aluminum bodies may be much more than offset by the greater average payloads, reduced license fees, greater fuel efficiency, and increased tire mileage that result from the lower weight. In construction uses, the cost advantage may turn on savings in maintenance, as in the case of industrial windows.

As we proceed to examine the main uses of aluminum, the other metals appear and reappear; as unlikely a competitor as lead is an alternate material for at least two uses, collapsible tubes and cable coverings. The plastics also reappear; wood, rubber, fiberglass, and even conventional building facings such as brick and stone enter the system of alternatives. In sum, if we consider interindustry competition, the number of competing firms rapidly moves from "few" to "many." It appears, moreover, that as we cut across industry lines, the conditions of rivalry differ greatly from those of interindustry competition. The managers of firms in one industry usually lack the technological and accounting knowledge that enables them to predict the reactions of other-industry rivals, making collusion difficult. But the reality of interindustry competition should not blind us to the dangers of concentration. In some cases, rivalry may be limited to a few firms even after interindustry competition has been taken into account, and there may be some uses for a material where competition from alternatives is not feasible. The point is simply that defining the appropriate market is an economic, rather than simply a technological, exercise.

ANTITRUST POLICY

After Thurman W. Arnold became head of the antitrust division of the Justice Department in 1938, he began a vigorous program of antitrust prosecution that continued even after his tenure.[16] Between 1937 and 1948, more prosecutions were begun than in the entire previous history of the Sherman Act, and the cases instituted were largely directed toward established oligopolies. Emphasis was placed on dissolution, divorcement, and divestiture cases—that is, on the actual breaking up of industrial concentration in the old "trust-busting" sense.[17] But although the government won most of its major cases, the penalties imposed by the courts were mild—for the simple reason that drastic penalties would have resulted in units of uneconomic size.

The case against the Aluminum Company of America (Alcoa) provides the best example of two major problems that have perplexed the courts in the postwar period: (1) defining the relevant market and deciding whether a firm monopolizes it, and

---

[16] Arnold resigned in 1943, amid criticisms that his antitrust policies were hindering the war effort.

[17] Walter Adams, "The Aluminum Case: Legal Victory—Economic Defeat," *American Economic Review* 41 (December 1951): 915.

(2) deciding how to remedy monopoly without creating economic inefficiency. In 1937, a complaint instituted against Alcoa, *United States v. Aluminum Company of America*, alleged that the company monopolized the manufacture and sale of virgin aluminum and fabricated shapes. In 1942 a U.S. district court found Alcoa not guilty, but in March 1945 this decision was reversed by the Circuit Court of Appeals, with the famous jurist Learned Hand giving the opinion.[18] Judge Hand ruled that Alcoa, which at the time made and fabricated more than 90 percent of the virgin aluminum manufactured in the United States, was a monopoly. Turning away from the idea that "mere size is no offense," Judge Hand ruled that even though the company had engaged in no immoral or predatory practices, it was still in violation of the Sherman Act because it controlled most of the output of the industry. But having pronounced Alcoa a monopoly, the court refused to break it up; instead, the court recommended that no action be taken until the effect on competition of the government disposal of war-surplus aluminum plants could be determined.

Further attempts by the government to break up Alcoa met with little success. In 1950, although Kaiser and Reynolds were firmly established in the industry, the Court held that competition had still not been achieved; but the only change ordered by the Court was to require persons who held stock in both Alcoa and Alcoa's Canadian subsidiary to sell the stock of one corporation or the other. In a number of subsequent cases, the courts followed the Alcoa precedent. In *United States v. United Shoe Machinery Corporation*, for example, Judge C. E. Wyzanski held that United Shoe Machinery had violated the Sherman Act because its control of the shoe machinery market was indisputable even though the company's practices had been neither predatory nor discriminatory between different customers.[19] But he refused to dissolve the company and ordered several small changes that did little to weaken its monopoly.

In the "cellophane case" (*United States v. E. I. Du Pont de Nemours and Company*, 1953), it seemed that the Supreme Court would move in the direction of considering interproduct competition in determining the extent of monopolistic power when the Court defined the relevant market to include all the wraps that competed with cellophane—from brown paper to polyethylene film.

In the field of antitrust, it seems that every time the law appears reasonably certain, the Supreme Court changes direction and charts a new course. Just four years after the cellophane decree, as the result of another action brought against Du Pont, the Court reversed itself, narrowly defining the market for finishes and fabrics to include not the entire market but only the automobile market. Moreover, this case produced the startling realization that any large corporation that had achieved size through stock acquisitions after 1914 (the year the Clayton Act was passed) could be required to sell those holdings, no matter what the cost to the firm.

In the landmark case of *Brown Shoe Company v. United States* in 1962, the Supreme Court greatly strengthened the hand of the Justice Department in merger cases. The Brown Shoe Company and the G. R. Kinney Company were both engaged in the

---

[18] On appeal to the Supreme Court, a quorum could not be obtained because some justices had been previously involved in the case. Consequently, the circuit court decision stood.

[19] *United States v. United Shoe Machinery Corporation*, 110 F. Suppl. 295.

manufacture and retail marketing of shoes. Brown accounted for only about 4 percent of the national output of shoes, Kinney for about 1.5 percent; but the government argued that the relevant lines of commerce were not just "footwear" but rather men's, women's, and children's shoes. The Court also ruled that the "section of the country" within which the anticompetitive effect of a merger is to be judged could be every city with a population of 10,000 or more in which Brown or Kinney shoes were sold. Thus, in Dodge City, Kansas, the combined share of the market was over 57 percent for women's shoes and 49 percent for children's shoes—a dangerous horizontal concentration.

The same definition of markets was used successfully in other cases. Yet little effort was made to arrest the tide of mergers that marked the 1960s, partly because of a lack of resources and the ambivalence of succeeding Attorneys General. Another explanation for limited response of the Justice Department was that, as we have noted, most mergers at that time were conglomerate. Donald F. Turner, Assistant Attorney General for Antitrust in the Johnson administration, took the view that the Clayton Act could not be applied against conglomerate mergers unless the government could demonstrate that anticompetitive results occurred in a specific market. William H. Rehnquist, Turner's successor under President Nixon, took the tougher stance that major conglomerate acquisitions (such as LTV's purchase of Jones and Laughlin) must be offset by the spinoff of an approximately equal amount of other assets.

The consequence has been that attacks on "product extension," such as the one initiated by the Federal Trade Commission against Procter and Gamble's acquisition of the assets of the Clorox Chemical Company, have been few and far between. In this particular case, decided in 1967, Procter and Gamble was required to separate itself from Clorox on the grounds that P&G's tremendous marketing power would give the product a great advantage over the three major competing products and keep Procter and Gamble from entering the market as a separate competitor.

In a series of decisions issued in 1974 the Supreme Court shifted once again, this time toward a more skeptical view of alleged anticompetitive effects of mergers and acquisitions. In *United States v. Marine Bancorporation,* for example, the Court looked at the acquisition of a bank in Spokane by one in Seattle. The Court decided that because there was no other route for the Seattle bank to follow if it wanted to enter the Spokane market, competition had not been hurt. Claims that the Seattle bank would then control a larger share of the state's banking assets were not deemed relevant.

The biggest antitrust cases in recent years were those involving International Business Machines and American Telephone and Telegraph Company. The IBM case *(United States v. International Business Machines Corporation)* was launched in 1969. After years of costly legal proceedings, it was dropped by the government in 1982. Some observers have seen this as simply the result of the Reagan administration's probusiness attitude, but the computer industry had changed dramatically in the 1970s. Although it had been possible to view IBM as an impregnable monopolist in 1969, by 1982 the company faced domestic and foreign competitors in many markets.

The telephone case *(United States v. American Telephone and Telegraph Company)* was launched in 1974 and settled in 1982. AT&T was forced to give up its operating

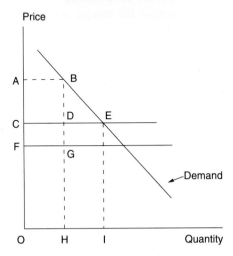

The Economics of Antitrust

The figure above illustrates the dilemma typically faced by the courts in deciding antitrust cases. OC represents the constant marginal costs of production and OI the output in the industry before mergers and acquisitions create a monopoly. Monopoly allows the firm to raise the price to OA by cutting production to OH. But at the same time, costs of production are lowered, by economies of scale, to OF.

The "deadweight loss" caused by monopoly is the area BDE. (The area ABDC is lost to consumers, but it is captured by the monopolist—it is a "transfer" and not a loss to society.) The gain to society from increased efficiency is given by the area FCDG.

In principle, society benefits from the successful prosecution of an antitrust action if the deadweight loss BDE exceeds the efficiency gain FCDG. If BDE is less than FCDG, society would be better off if the courts permitted the monopoly to stand.

In practice, of course, it is extremely difficult to make calculations of this sort, and the courts must take other factors into account. For one thing, although the transfer of ABDC from consumers to the monopolist does not enter the efficiency calculation, it may be important to the public.

It should also be noted that the costs of litigating the case need to be deducted to compute the net gain or loss in efficiency.

companies, but it was permitted to enter new communication and data-processing markets it had previously been barred from. Opinion is divided on whether the breakup of AT&T was in the public interest. Long-distance rates have come down, but there have been some increases in local rates. Over the years, AT&T had developed an outstanding record as a source of scientific and technological innovations. Ultimately, a judgment about the value of this case will depend on how well AT&T and its competitors perform in this area.

As suggested earlier, many economists have long felt that interindustry competition effectively protects consumers and that the Justice Department should stop trying to add one or two more firms to industries that must always remain oligopolistic (and, for that matter, it should stop worrying about the purchase of one company by another when market structure does not change much after the acquisition). Instead, the department might concentrate on detecting products for which there are few alternative suppliers, within or outside of the "industry," and bring actions in these relatively few cases. In 1984 the Justice Department adopted the economists' view and brought a measure of stability to antitrust policy by publishing explicit guidelines on acceptable mergers. The guidelines defined in terms of market shares the level of concentration in a market—and the increase in concentration—that would trigger antitrust actions by the government. These explicit guidelines should enable the Justice Department to root out genuine instances of monopoly while avoiding much useless and costly litigation.[20]

SELECTED REFERENCES AND SUGGESTED READINGS

Asch, Peter, and Rosalind S. Seneca. *Government and the Marketplace.* 2d ed. Chicago: Dryden Press, 1989.

Baumol, William J., John C. Panzar, and Robert D. Willig. *Contestable Markets and the Theory of Industry Structure.* New York: Harcourt Brace Jovanovich, 1982.

Bork, Robert H. *The Antitrust Paradox.* New York: Basic Books, 1978.

Caves, Richard B. "The Structure of Industry." In *The American Economy in Transition,* ed. Martin Feldstein. Chicago: University of Chicago Press, National Bureau of Economic Research, 1980.

Darby, Michael R. "The U.S. Productivity Slowdown: A Case of Statistical Myopia." *American Economic Review* 74 (June 1984): 301–322.

Denison, Edward F. *Accounting for Slower Economic Growth: The United States in the 1970s.* Washington, D.C.: Brookings Institution, 1979.

————. *Accounting for United States Economic Growth, 1929–1969.* Washington, D.C.: Brookings Institution, 1974.

Didrichsen, Jon. "The Development of Diversified and Conglomerate Firms in the United States, 1920–1970." *Business History Review* 36 (Summer 1972): 202–219.

---

[20] See Peter Asch and Rosalind S. Seneca, *Government and the Marketplace* (Chicago: Dryden Press, 1989), pp. 262–271, for a balanced discussion of the pros and cons of various antitrust policies.

Elzinga, Kenneth G. "The Goals of Antitrust: Other Than Competition and Efficiency, What Else Counts?" *University of Pennsylvania Law Review* 125 (1977): 1191–1213.

Fisher, Franklin. *Folded, Spindled, and Mutilated.* Boston: MIT Press, 1983.

Galbraith, John Kenneth. *The New Industrial State.* Boston: Houghton Mifflin, 1967.

Harberger, Arnold C. "Monopoly and Resource Allocation." *American Economic Review* 44 (May 1954): 77–87.

Magaziner, Ira C., and Robert Reich. *Minding America's Business: The Decline and Rise of the American Economy.* New York: Harcourt Brace Jovanovich, 1982.

Manne, Henry G. "Mergers and the Market for Corporate Control." *Journal of Political Economy* 73 (April 1965): 110–120.

Mansfield, Edwin. "Technology and Productivity in the United States." In *The American Economy in Transition,* ed. Martin Feldstein. Chicago: University of Chicago Press, National Bureau of Economic Research, 1980.

Mueller, Willard F., and Larry G. Hamm. "Trends In Industrial Market Concentration 1947 to 1970." *Review of Economics and Statistics* 56 (November 1974): 511–520.

Posner, Richard A. *Antitrust Law.* Chicago: University of Chicago Press, 1976.

———. "A Statistical Study of Antitrust Enforcement." *Journal of Law and Economics* 13 (October 1970): 365–419.

Scherer, Frederic M. *Industrial Market Structure and Economic Performance.* 2d ed. Chicago: Rand McNally, 1980.

———. *Innovation and Growth: Schumpeterian Perspectives.* Cambridge: MIT Press, 1984.

Schumpeter, Joseph. *Capitalism, Socialism, and Democracy.* 3d ed. New York: Harper & Row, 1950.

Steiner, Peter O. *Mergers: Motives, Effects, Policies.* Ann Arbor: University of Michigan Press, 1975.

Stigler, George J. The Economic Effects of Antitrust Laws." *Journal of Law and Economics* 9 (October 1966): 225–258.

Stonebraker, Robert J. "Turnover and Mobility among the 100 Largest Firms: An Update." *American Economic Review* 69 (December 1979): 968–973.

Temin, Peter. *The Fall of the Bell System.* New York: Cambridge University Press, 1988.

Tiffany, Paul A. "The Roots of Decline: Business-Government Relations in the American Steel Industry, 1945–1960." *Journal of Economic History* 44 (June 1984): 407–419.

Williamson, Oliver S. "Economies as an Antitrust Defense Revisited." *University of Pennsylvania Law Review* 125 (April 1977): 699–736.

CHAPTER THIRTY

LABOR'S PROGRESS SINCE WORLD WAR II

CHAPTER THEME The American labor market underwent a profound transformation during the postwar era. On the demand side, the key development was the rise of the service sector. By 1992, two out of three workers were in the private service sector or the government. On the supply side, the key development was the toppling of discriminatory barriers that had confined women, African-Americans, and other minorities to the margins of American economic life. One of the victims of the changes in the labor market was the union movement, which reached a peak of power and membership in the 1950s only to see its influence wane in the following decades.

THE RISE OF THE SERVICE SECTOR

The most important change in the demand for labor was the growth of the white-collar sector, a diverse grouping that includes retail trade, finance, education, medicine, entertainment, and so on. Table 30-1 shows the expansion of this sector. In 1946 the service sector provided about one-third of all jobs; by 1992 it provided more than one-half. The major declining sectors were agriculture, and mining, construction, and manufacturing; their combined share fell from 44.5 percent in 1946 to 20.9 percent in 1992. Agriculture declined most rapidly in the period before 1970; manufacturing, on the other hand, about held its own until 1970 and then began to decline. Indeed, after 1970, the absolute number of workers in manufacturing declined, along with their share of total employment. As Donald McCloskey has put it to us, production of "things" declined relative to production of "words."

To a large extent the pattern of rising and falling sectors was a matter of demand. As real incomes rose, the demand for certain products such as consumer durables increased slowly, while demand for others such as medical care and insurance increased rapidly. Other trends also played a role in the growth of the service sector. For example, rapid improvements in medical technology and increased federal funding produced rapid growth in the number of health-related jobs. Inflation and deregulation encouraged firms in the financial sector to offer an array of new products.

Some people question whether the white-collar sectors are truly productive. There is an ancient prejudice against workers who merely push papers around in favor of those who produce something tangible like wheat or automobiles. Even Adam Smith distinguished between productive labor (used to produce goods) and unproductive labor (to produce services). And recent proposals to "reindustrialize" America derive part of their influence from this prejudice. But clearly the service sector does contribute to our economic welfare. Extra life insurance or a better-diversified portfolio of assets, for example, may contribute as much to the purchaser's sense of well-being as an extra automobile or refrigerator. It is true that mistakes are made; on occasion capital may be invested in a business producing a service that could have been more profitably

TABLE 30-1   DISTRIBUTION OF JOBS, 1946–1992 (PERCENT OF TOTAL EMPLOYMENT)

Year	Agriculture	Manufacturing, Mining, and Construction	Services	Government	Other
1946	14.5%	30.0%	32.7%	9.7%	13.1%
1950	11.5	29.7	33.2	9.7	15.8
1960	7.8	29.3	36.5	12.0	14.3
1970	4.2	28.5	42.0	15.2	10.2
1980	3.1	24.0	45.4	15.2	12.3
1992	2.5	18.4	52.3	14.6	12.1

SOURCE: *ECONOMIC REPORT OF THE PRESIDENT, 1993* (WASHINGTON, D.C.: GOVERNMENT PRINTING OFFICE, 1993), PP. 382, 394–395.

invested in manufacturing. But on the whole, the reason why services have expanded more rapidly in the postwar period is that we valued their output more than the product of other sectors.

Productivity growth in the expanding sectors has been comparatively slow, and this has contributed to the slowdown in the growth of real wages. But this does not mean that the economy would grow faster if we invested more in other sectors. Expansion of some sectors has favorable external effects on others. For example, while productivity growth in education may be relatively slow, the expansion of the education sector contributes to the manufacturing sector by supplying new techniques and better-educated workers.

The growth of the service sector has also contributed to economic stability. In the manufacturing sector, a decrease in demand often leads quickly to unemployment. In the white-collar sector, however, employers are often willing to continue to employ workers even though they do not make a positive contribution to current profits. Service employees often have specialized knowledge or long-term relationships with customers that make them hard to replace. For this and other reasons, the rise of the service sector has tended to dampen the impact of recessions on employment in the postwar period.

THE CHANGING ROLE OF WOMEN IN THE LABOR FORCE

The most dramatic trend in the supply of labor after the war was the increase in the proportion of all women who participate in the paid labor force. Table 30-2 shows the key ratios at decade-long intervals. The proportion of single men participating in the labor force (working or seeking work) has risen slightly since 1960, while the proportion of married men in the labor force has fallen slightly. The overall result has been a slight fall in male participation in the labor force. But the proportion of women, especially married women, in the labor force has increased steadily. The net result was that the proportion of Americans who are participating in the paid labor force rose steadily in the postwar period, reaching an all-time peak in the late 1980s.

TABLE 30-2   LABOR FORCE PARTICIPATION OF MEN AND WOMEN, 1960–1991[a]

Year	Total	Single Men	Married Men	Single Women	Married Women
1960	59.4%	69.8%	89.2%	58.6%	31.9%
1970	60.4	65.5	86.5	56.8	40.5
1980	63.8	72.6	80.9	64.4	49.9
1991	66.0	74.2	77.8	66.5	58.5

SOURCE: *STATISTICAL ABSTRACT OF THE UNITED STATES: 1992* (WASHINGTON, D.C.: U.S. BUREAU OF THE CENSUS, 1992), PP. 383, 387.

[a]Percentage in the work force of each category's total number.

Several trends combined to produce the rapid increase in the labor-force participation of married women: (1) Real wages rose. Real wages of men also rose, which tended to discourage the labor-force participation of married women, but the effect of higher real wages for women dominated. (2) Years of schooling increased dramatically over the course of the century. About 10 percent of the nonwhite women born in 1900 and about 30 percent of the white women would graduate from high school; by 1970 those figures had increased to 80 and 90 percent. The increased incomes made possible by increased schooling naturally encouraged women to join the paid labor force. (3) The average number of children in a family declined from three or four at the beginning of the century to one or two in the 1980s. Over the same period, the average life expectancy of women increased. Together these demographic trends meant that women had many more years to pursue a career after the burdens of rearing a family moderated. The increased rate of divorce also encouraged women to invest in a career outside the home.

We should note, however, that the interaction of these trends was complicated. For example, the rising participation rate of women in the paid labor force encouraged some women to choose divorce who would have been unable to afford it in earlier periods; causation, in other words, ran from the divorce rate to the labor-force participation rate of women, and back again from the participation rate to the divorce rate. We should also remember, as Claudia Goldin has stressed, that factors (2) and (3) both operated with long lags. For some women, for example, the full effects of an increase in education on labor-force participation were not seen until they have passed the years in which child-rearing demands were greatest.[1]

(4) The rapidly growing service sectors, especially the clerical and education sectors, were particularly attractive to women. Until 1950, the growth of these sectors affected mainly the participation rates of white single women due to discrimination against married and minority women. But as discriminatory hiring practices were broken down, the effects of growth in these sectors spread more widely.

(5) Some historians would assign a non-negligible weight to the growing availability and technological sophistication of consumer durables. Electric washing machines and refrigerators, low-maintenance fabrics, telephone answering machines, and other labor-saving devices reduced the labor input in home maintenance.

(6) The feminist movement also helped to overcome discrimination against women workers through moral suasion and political action. Until the 1960s, the postwar period had seen little activity that would predict the feminist movement to come. A key event was President Kennedy's appointment of a Presidential Commission on the Status of Women in 1961, with the venerable Eleanor Roosevelt as its honorary chairwoman.

Partly as a result of the commission's recommendations, Congress passed the Equal Pay Act of 1963, which called for equal pay for equal work. Title VII of the Civil Rights Act, passed in the following year, barred discrimination in hiring, promoting, or firing workers on the basis of race, color, religion, national origin, or sex and set

---

[1]Claudia Goldin, *Understanding the Gender Gap* (New York: Oxford University Press, 1990), pp. 138–149.

up the Equal Employment Opportunity Commission to help enforce the law.[2] In 1965, President Johnson created the Office of Federal Contract Compliance Program to require affirmative action plans from employers doing business with the federal government. Affirmative action is more than a color-blind, sex-neutral labor policy; it requires positive efforts to find workers traditionally discriminated against. In 1966 the National Organization for Women was founded, partly to pressure the government into vigorous enforcement of its new antidiscriminatory legislation.

The 1970s witnessed further successes for the feminist movement. Title IX of the Educational Amendments Act of 1972 extended the Civil Rights Act to educational institutions; one consequence of Title IX was to increase the participation of women in high school and college sports. In the late 1970s and 1980s the feminist movement seemed to lose momentum and was unable to win major legislative victories, but in 1992 (the "Year of the Woman") the women's movement made great gains at the ballot box, winning a number of important House and Senate seats.

THE GENDER GAP

Despite federal legislation, a considerable gap remained between the earnings of men and women in a variety of occupations. Table 30-3 (which is taken from a book by Claudia Goldin, one of the leading experts in the field) shows the gender gap in six broad occupational classifications in 1890, 1930, and 1970. The surprising thing is the persistence of the gender gap and its tendency to increase in every class of occupations except "professional" between 1930 and 1970. It would appear that since 1970 progress has occurred in several sectors, in sales for example, but that in others the gap remains about the same.

The factors that seem to have produced much of the increase in the relative earnings of women between 1890 and 1930 were the increase in the education of women and their greater labor-force experience. What has kept the gender gap from closing is the

TABLE 30-3 THE GENDER GAP

Occupation	Ratios of Female to Male Earnings		
	1890	1930	1970
Professional	.26	.38	.71
Clerical	.49	.71	.69
Sales	.59	.61	.44
Manual	.54	.58	.56
Service	.53	.60	.56
Farm	.53	.60	.59

SOURCE: CLAUDIA D. GOLDIN, *UNDERSTANDING THE GENDER GAP: AN ECONOMIC HISTORY OF AMERICAN WOMEN* (NEW YORK: OXFORD UNIVERSITY PRESS, 1990), P. 64.

---

[2]The word *sex* did not appear in the bill until the day before it was passed. It has been claimed that it was originally inserted with the idea of making the bill unacceptable to a majority, but the matter remains unclear. See Goldin, *Understanding the Gender Gap,* p. 201 and the references cited there.

increase in the participation rate of women. Increasing participation means that women's average years of experience in the labor force remains relatively low because so many have just entered the labor force. Moreover, because discrimination often blocks them from entering or advancing in certain fields, women entering the labor force have crowded into areas open to them, thereby preventing wages in those areas from rising as fast as in the rest of the economy. In the future, as the labor-force participation rate of women stabilizes and the entire array of jobs created by the economy are opened to women, the gender gap should decline.

MINORITIES

Attempts to bring African-Americans, Hispanic-Americans, and other minority workers into the economic mainstream also met with important but limited success in the postwar period. Table 30-4 shows the ratios of black to white and Hispanic to white median family incomes at five-year intervals from 1950 to 1990. For blacks, gains in the ratio appear to have been confined mainly to the period from 1965 to 1970; for Hispanics, on the other hand, there has been some progress in recent years.

Two positive trends might have been expected to produce rapid black progress in the postwar era: (1) the increase in years of schooling, and (2) the geographical redistribution of the black labor force. It may be hard for today's college students, aware of the overcrowding and underfunding of predominantly black schools, to believe that there has been much progress. The reason is that it is hard now to imagine how bad things were in, say, 1940. In that year 80 percent of the black male work force had only elementary schooling and 40 percent had less than five years of schooling.

As shown in Table 30-5, the gap in the amount of schooling obtained by black men narrowed considerably in the postwar period. In 1940 black males aged 26 to 35 had

TABLE 30-4   BLACK-TO-WHITE AND HISPANIC-TO-WHITE MEDIAN FAMILY INCOME RATIOS, 1950–1990

Year	Black	Hispanic
1950	.54[a]	n.a.
1955	.55[a]	n.a.
1960	.55[a]	n.a.
1965	.55[a]	n.a.
1970	.61	n.a.
1975	.62	.67
1980	.58	.67
1985	.58	.65
1990	.60	.71

SOURCES: (1950–1965) *Statistical Abstract of the United States: 1987*, 107th edition (Washington, D.C.: U.S. Bureau of the Census, 1986), p. 436; and (1970–1990) *Statistical Abstract of the United States: 1992* (Washington, D.C.: U.S. Bureau of the Census, 1992), p. 445.

[a] Includes other races.

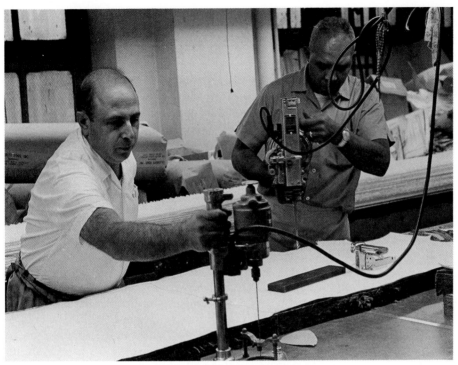

The civil rights movement began the desegregation of the workplace.

only 60 percent as many years of schooling as did whites in that age bracket; in 1980 they had almost 90 percent as many years of schooling. The gap in quality, although harder to measure, probably also narrowed substantially.

Blacks also benefited from the redistribution of the black population. In 1940 a large gap in wages existed between northern and southern wages, for whites as well as blacks, and the gap was much larger for blacks. The rapid northern migration of blacks out of the low-wage South was motivated by this disparity and has tended to lessen

TABLE 30-5 AVERAGE YEARS OF SCHOOLING FOR BLACK AND WHITE MEN (AGES 26–35), 1940–1980

Year	White	Black	White Minus Black
1940	9.89	5.97	3.92
1950	10.77	7.60	3.17
1960	11.49	9.01	2.48
1970	12.87	10.54	1.82
1980	13.56	12.15	1.41

SOURCE: JAMES P. SMITH AND FINIS R. WELCH, "BLACK ECONOMIC PROGRESS AFTER MYRDAL," *JOURNAL OF ECONOMIC LITERATURE* 26 (1989): 531.

it. In 1940, 75 percent of black men lived in the South; by 1980, that figure had fallen to 53 percent.

Despite these trends, gains were slow and halting because of discrimination. The fight against discrimination was long and hard. In 1947 one of the most famous events occurred when Jackie Robinson broke the color barrier in professional baseball. This was important not only for blacks who would earn their living in professional sports in the postwar period, but also for the effect it would have on white stereotypes about black abilities.

In 1954 the Supreme Court ruled in *Brown v. Board of Education of Topeka* that segregated schools were unconstitutional. This decision would have far-reaching consequences for American education. Although many school districts then claimed that they were providing a separate-but-equal education for blacks (a formula laid down by the Supreme Court in *Plessy v. Fergusson* in 1896), this was not the case. As documented by Robert Margo in important recent research, black schools were systematically underfunded, and blacks entered the labor force with a severe handicap.[3] *Brown v. Board of Education* did not bring about change overnight. Many school districts dragged their feet, and it was not until the late 1960s, when courts began to order busing to achieve racial integration, that significant progress was made in many areas.

Other visible signs of discrimination, such as segregated transportation, were also crumbling as a result of the civil rights movement. The culmination of that movement was the march on Washington in August 1963, where the young leader of the Civil Rights movement, Dr. Martin Luther King, gave his memorable "I Have a Dream" speech. Less than a year later, the Civil Rights Act was passed, which among other things, as we noted above, made it illegal to discriminate in employment.

Between 1965 and 1975, as Table 30-4 shows (see page 686), there was a slight increase in the ratio of black to white median family incomes. Some of this gain, although it is hard to say exactly how much, was caused by the breakdown of discriminatory barriers in industries targeted by civil rights activists and federal authorities. Initially, as John H. Donohue III and James Heckman show, federal pressure was directed at the South, where social norms, backed up by state and local legislation, limited employment of blacks. This pressure appears to have been successful. Figure 30-1, showing employment in the South Carolina textile industry, is a dramatic piece of evidence. Notice that the share of blacks (who were confined to the most menial jobs) was low and stable until 1965. To some extent, employers may have welcomed federal pressure. For example, employers in South Carolina who wanted to take advantage of relatively cheap black labor could use the threat of federal sanctions as an excuse for breaking with established racial norms.

Change was brought about by the civil rights movement itself as well as by pressure from the federal government. As Gavin Wright explains in his thoughtful book, *Old South, New South,* southern political and business leaders were trying to attract new businesses to the South; they soon realized that a quick resolution of civil rights turmoil was necessary if they were to continue to compete successfully for outside capital. In 1970 the president of Allis-Chalmers Corporation visited Jackson, Mississippi, and

---

[3] Robert Margo, "Race Differences in Public School Expenditures," *Social Science History* 6 (1982): 9–33; and "Educational Achievements in Segregated Schools," *American Economic Review* 76 (1986): 794–801.

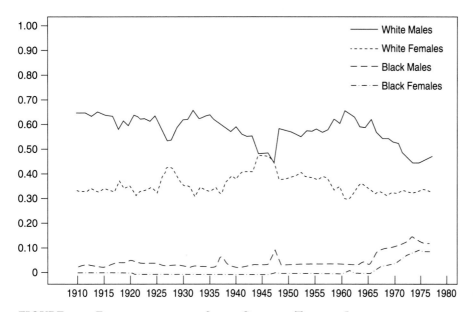

FIGURE 30-1 EMPLOYMENT IN THE SOUTH CAROLINA TEXTILES INDUSTRY

SOURCE: JOHN H. DONOHUE III AND JAMES HECKMAN, "CONTINUOUS VERSUS EPISODIC CHANGE," *JOURNAL OF ECONOMIC LITERATURE* 29 (1991): 1615.

expressed doubts about locating a plant there because of the violent ongoing confrontation between black students at Jackson State University and local police. As a result the deadlock over school integration, then seven years old, was broken and Allis-Chalmers announced plant construction plans.[4] In the late 1970s, however, the ratio of nonwhite to white median family incomes leveled off, as shown in Table 30-4, and in the 1980s it declined. When the fight against discrimination moved outside the South, where the target was informal discrimination rather than explicit laws, progress proved harder to achieve.

THE NEW IMMIGRATION

There was little change in the immigration laws from the establishment of the quota system in the 1920s until 1965. A major exception to this generalization was a program under which Mexican agricultural workers (braceros) could work temporarily in the United States. This program was begun during World War II (although it is doubtful that it contributed to the war effort) and ended in 1965, a casualty of the wave of liberal legislation of the mid-1960s.[5]

---

[4] Gavin Wright, *Old South, New South* (New York: Basic Books, 1986), pp. 266–267.

[5] Lee J. Alston and Joseph P. Ferrie, "The Bracero Program and Farm Labor Legislation in World War II," in *Sinews of War: Essays on the Economic History of World War II*, eds. Geofrey T. Mills and Hugh Rockoff (Ames: Iowa State University Press, 1993).

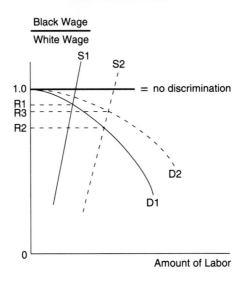

Discrimination in the Labor Market

The figure above shows the supply and demand for black labor in a particular labor market as a function of the ratio of black wages to white wages. It makes two assumptions: (1) all employers have a preference for white labor, although some are more prejudicial than others; and (2) black workers and white workers are equally productive. (The example abstracts, then, from discrimination in education that causes differences in productivity.) The demand curve slopes downward because blacks can compete for jobs only by offering to work at lower wages.

As the supply of black labor increases from S1 to S2, the wage of black workers falls relative to white workers from R1 to R2. Blacks can increase employment only by convincing increasingly prejudiced employers to hire them.

Competition among firms will tend to make the demand curve more elastic over time, shifting it from D1 to D2 and raising the wage relative back to R3. The reason is that firms that discriminate pay a price: they hire more expensive labor than they need to, and in the long run we would expect them to lose out to firms that do not discriminate. The persistence of wage differentials, however, suggests that a number of important countervailing forces continue to be effective: (1) Entry is difficult in some industries, so discriminatory employers might not be threatened by less-discriminatory newcomers. (2) Some firms that discriminate may be reflecting the prejudices of their customers. (3) Firms that discriminate may be responding to the prejudices of their white workers. This is especially a problem if the white workers have an effective, discriminatory union. (4) Employers may be responding to powerful social norms, perhaps backed up by the force of law.

At this time a new immigration system was instituted. President John F. Kennedy and his allies in Congress were strongly opposed to national quotas, which they felt reflected racial and ethnic prejudice. The new law, enacted after Kennedy's death, eliminated quotas based on the ethnic composition of the population in favor of a complex system of priorities that gave very high priority to uniting families. A limit was placed on the total number of immigrants, but that limit did not include spouses, minor children, or parents of American citizens. In 1980 a separate program for admitting political refugees was created. As a result of these changes the number of immigrants increased, many coming from "new" areas—Latin America, Central America, Asia, and the Caribbean. In the 1960s, 37 percent of immigrants came from Europe, 39 percent from Latin America and the Caribbean, and 13 percent from Asia. By 1990, 7 percent came from Europe, 67 percent from Latin America and the Caribbean, and 22 percent from Asia.

Table 30-6 shows total immigration to the United States since 1900. The acceleration of the rate of immigration after the change in the law in 1965 is obvious from the table; the rate increased from 1.5 per thousand between 1951 and 1960 to 2.1 between

TABLE 30-6   IMMIGRATION, 1900–1990

Years	Total (in thousands)	Rate (annual per thousand U.S. population)
1901–1910	8,795	10.4
1911–1920	5,736	5.7
1921–1930	4,107	3.5
1931–1940	528	0.4
1941–1950	1,035	0.7
1951–1960	2,515	1.5
1961–1970	3,322	1.7
1971–1980	4,493	2.1
1981–1990	7,338	3.1
1980	531	2.3
1985	570	2.4
1990	1,536[a]	6.1

SOURCE: *STATISTICAL ABSTRACT OF THE UNITED STATES: 1992* (WASHINGTON, D.C.: U.S. BUREAU OF THE CENSUS, 1992), P. 10.

[a] Includes 880,000 granted permanent residence under the legalization program of the Immigration Reform and Control Act of 1986.

1971 and 1980. Even in the 1980s, however, when the rate reached a post-depression peak of 3.1 per thousand, the rate was still well below the rate of 10.4 averaged between 1901 and 1910.

The figures in Table 30-6 make no allowance for illegal immigration, particularly from Mexico and Latin America. There is evidence that the volume of such immigration, although hard to measure, is large. In 1990, for example, some 1.2 million illegal aliens were apprehended attempting to cross into the United States from Mexico. Some experts believe that the number of illegal immigrants in the 1980s may have totaled as much as 40 percent of the legal immigration. Pressure to do something about illegal immigration led to the Immigration Reform and Control Act of 1986, which put tough new controls on illegal immigration (making it illegal, for example, for employers to hire undocumented workers) while at the same time creating an amnesty program for illegal immigrants who had put down roots in this country. It is still too early to see what the effects of this legislation will be on the volume of illegal immigration and on labor markets. Substantial numbers of people, however, have been granted permanent residence status.

Though labor economists are generally agreed about the direction of various effects of immigration, they are far from a consensus on magnitudes. For the immigrants themselves, migration to the United States is often a major economic boon. Immigrants tend on average to do well after arriving here. After a decade or two, according to Barry Chiswick, the typical male immigrant earns more than a native-born worker with comparable education and experience.[6] The countries from which America receives its immigrants also experience a variety of effects. In recent years considerable concern has been expressed about the "brain drain," the tendency of America to draw down the supply of engineers, scientists, physicians, and similar personnel in developing countries.

Many Americans benefit from immigration: those who own firms that employ immigrants (including many who own firms indirectly through retirement funds), those who possess special skills that become more valuable when unskilled labor is widely available, those who consume the products and services that immigrants help produce, those who provide the services consumed by immigrants, and those who own property in neighborhoods in which immigrants settle. On the other hand, those who compete directly with immigrants in the labor force—particularly unskilled workers in urban areas—face lower real wages and fewer job opportunities. But it is hard to say whether these effects have been large or small. Some labor economists have stressed the substitutability between immigrants and native workers that implies lower wages for native workers.[7] But others have found evidence of complementarity, which implies higher wages for native workers.[8] A sophisticated recent study found evidence of both

---

[6] Barry R. Chiswick, "The Effect of Americanization on the Earnings of Foreign-born Men," *Journal of Political Economy* 86 (October 1978): 897–921.

[7] Jean Baldwin Grossman, "The Substitutability of Natives and Immigrants in Production," *Review of Economic Statistics*, 64 (1982): 596–603; and Vernon M. Briggs, "The Imperative of Immigration Reform," in *Essays on Legal and Illegal Immigration*, ed. S. Pozo (Washington, D.C.: W. E. Upjohn Institute, 1986), pp. 43–71.

[8] George J. Borjas, "The Substitutability of Black, Hispanic and White Labor," *Economic Inquiry* 21 (1983): 93–106.

effects, depending on the group being considered, but stressed that these effects have been small.[9]

If history is any guide, the levels of immigration reached in the late 1980s, like the high rates of the early 1900s, will lead to calls for immigration reform and limitation.

ORGANIZED LABOR SINCE WORLD WAR II

Membership in labor unions increased sharply during the Great Depression and World War II. The percentage of the nonagricultural labor force unionized rose from 14.7 percent in 1933 to 20.4 percent in 1938, and from 22.5 percent in 1940 to 31.6 percent in 1950, stabilizing in the 1950s. At its peak, near 1953, nearly one-third of the nonagricultural labor force was enrolled in labor unions. Since that time, however, there has been a steady decline that has become precipitous since 1970. This can be seen in Table 30-7 on the next page, which shows the percentage of the labor force unionized. By 1991 the percentage of the nonagricultural labor force enrolled in unions had fallen back to the level of the late 1920s.

There have been a number of reasons for the deterioration in the strength of organized labor. The rising service sector, where employee groups are usually small, has proved difficult to organize. Moreover, within the goods-producing sector there has been a steady shift from blue-collar to white-collar employment that has slowed the

Mass labor meetings, like this one, became less important in determining labor's strategy during the postwar era.

---

[9] Francisco L. Rivera-Batiz and Selig L. Sechzer, "Substitution and Complementarity Between Immigrant and Native Labor in the United States," in *U.S. Immigration Patterns and Policy Reform in the 1980s,* eds. Ira Gang, Francisco L. Rivera-Batiz, and Selig L. Sechzer (New York: Praeger, 1991).

TABLE 30-7   Union Membership, 1950–1983

| Year | Union Membership | | |
	Total (thousands)	Percent of Civilian Nonagricultural Labor Force	Percent of Total Civilian Labor Force
1950	14,294	31.6%	23.0%
1955	16,127	31.8	24.8
1960	15,516	28.6	22.3
1965	18,269	30.1	24.5
1970	20,990	29.6	25.4
1975	22,207	28.9	23.7
1980	20,968	23.2	19.6
1983	17,717	19.1	16.7
1991	16,568	14.6	13.2

SOURCES: (1950–1980) LEO TROY AND NEIL SHEFLIN, *U.S. UNION SOURCEBOOK* (WEST ORANGE: INDUSTRIAL RELATIONS DATA AND INFORMATION SERVICES, 1985), PP. A1, A2. (1983, 1991) *STATISTICAL ABSTRACT OF THE UNITED STATES: 1992* (WASHINGTON, D.C.: U.S. BUREAU OF THE CENSUS, 1992), PP. 381, 422. ESTIMATES FROM THE TWO SOURCES ARE NOT STRICTLY COMPARABLE BUT ARE CLOSE ENOUGH TO PERMIT THE GAUGING OF BROAD TRENDS.

pace of union growth, because white-collar workers are less prone to organize. The shift of manufacturing to the South and West, areas traditionally hostile to the labor movement, has also undermined union power. Foreign industrial competition, which has made workers in traditional bastions of union strength (such as automobiles) fearful of layoffs and plant closings, has further undermined organized labor. The high rate of immigration of unskilled workers who tend to be afraid of taking part in union activities, and who may oppose union attempts to control the supply of labor, has also undermined union strength.

In addition to these economic trends, changes in the legal environment have worked against the unions. Because of opportunities for legislation established by the Taft-Hartley Act, numerous states passed "right-to-work" laws. In 1982, 19 states, many of them in the South, had right-to-work laws.[10] By making it illegal to enforce the union-shop provisions of an agreement within the state concerned, "right-to-work" legislation impeded efforts to unionize and were a source of friction between union and nonunion workers.

As the decade of the 1950s closed, labor's public relations continued to suffer. The Labor-Management Reporting and Disclosure Act of 1959 (the Landrum-Griffin Act) tightened restrictions on organized picketing and secondary boycotting, required detailed reports on all financial transactions between unions and their officers and members, and provided for secret-ballot elections of union officers, whose terms of office were restricted. Few could object to the provision preventing felons from being

---

[10] Leo Troy and Neil Sheflin, *U.S. Union Sourcebook* (West Orange: Industrial Relations Data and Information Services, 1985), pp. 7–9.

union officers for five years after conviction, nor could there be serious reservations about the new rules restricting the freewheeling use of union funds. But the effect of the new law, and the congressional hearings that led up to it, was to focus attention on the minority of corrupt or radical union officials and thereby undermine the public's confidence in the union movement.

Intraunion squabbles have also hurt the labor movement. At the peak of union strength, the American Federation of Labor (AFL) and the Congress of Industrial Organizations (CIO) merged in 1955, with George Meany becoming the first president. The radical dream of uniting all workers in one big union seemed near at hand. But harmony could not be maintained. Labor unity suffered a particularly severe blow in 1968 when the United Automobile Workers (UAW), under their dynamic leader Walter Reuther, left the AFL-CIO in a dispute over politics. At the same time, many of the organizational gains were being made by independent unions such as the Teamsters, who had been ousted from the AFL-CIO. Thus, it may well be true that critics who blame mainstream union leadership for part of the decline in labor's influence have a point.

Can organized labor regain some of its former influence? The economic trends we have been examining in connection with the union movement seem likely to continue. On the other hand, it has been noted that in Canada, where the industrial structure is in some ways similar to our own, the labor movement has remained far more influential than in the United States. It is best to remember that unionism in America has traditionally grown in spurts that were never predicted by the experts.

SELECTED REFERENCES
AND SUGGESTED READINGS

Alston, Lee J., and Joseph P. Ferrie. "The Bracero Program and Farm Labor Legislation in World War II." In *Sinews of War: Essays on the Economic History of World War II,* eds. Geofrey T. Mills and Hugh Rockoff. Ames: Iowa State University Press, 1993.

Briggs, Vernon M., Jr. *Immigration Policy and the American Labor Force.* Baltimore: Johns Hopkins University Press, 1984.

Chiswick, Barry R. "The Effect of Americanization on the Earnings of Foreign-born Men." *Journal of Political Economy* 86 (October 1978): 897–921.

Cobb, James C. *The Selling of the South: The Southern Crusade for Industrial Development 1936–1980.* Baton Rouge: Louisiana State University Press, 1982.

Cogan, John. "The Decline in Black Teenage Employment: 1950–1970." *American Economic Review* 72 (1982): 621–638.

Donohue, John H. III, and James Heckman. "Continuous Versus Episodic Change: The Impact of Civil Rights Policy on the Economic Status of Blacks." *Journal of Economic Literature* 29 (1991): 1603–1643.

Freeman, Richard B. "Unionism Comes to the Public Sector." *Journal of Economic Literature* 24 (March 1986): 41–86.

Freeman, Richard B., and James L. Medoff. *What Do Unions Do?* New York: Basic Books, 1984.

Gang, Ira, Francisco L. Rivera-Batiz, and Selig Sechzer, eds. *U.S. Immigration Patterns and Policy Reform in the 1980s.* New York: Praeger, 1991.

Goldin, Claudia. "The Changing Economic Role of Women: A Quantitative Approach." *Journal of Interdisciplinary History* 13 (Spring 1983): 707–733.

_____. "The Female Labor Force and Economic Growth in the United States, 1890–1980." In *Long Term Trends in the American Economy*, eds. Stanley L. Engerman and Robert Gallman (Chicago: University of Chicago Press, 1986).

_____. *Understanding the Gender Gap: An Economic History of American Women*. New York: Oxford University Press, 1990.

Jacoway, Elizabeth, and David R. Colburn. *Southern Businessmen and Desegregation*. Baton Rouge: Louisiana State University Press, 1982.

Lloyd, Cynthia B., and Beth T. Niemi. *The Economics of Sex Differentials*. New York: Columbia University Press, 1979.

Mandle, Jay. *The Roots of Black Poverty*. Durham: Duke University Press, 1978.

Margo, Robert. "Educational Achievement in Segregated Schools: The Effects of Separate But Equal." *American Economic Review* 76 (September 1986): 794–801.

_____. "Race Differences in Public School Expenditures: Disenfranchisement and School Finance in Louisiana, 1890–1910." *Social Science History* 6 (Winter 1982): 9–33.

Marshall, F. Ray. *Labor in the South*. Cambridge: Harvard University Press, 1967.

Masters, Stanley M. *Black-White Income Differentials*. New York: Academic Press, 1973.

Musoke, Moses S., and Alan L. Olmstead. "The Rise of the Cotton Industry in California: A Comparative Perspective." *Journal of Economic History* 42 (1982): 385–412.

Newman, Robert J. *Growth in the American South: Changing Regional Employment and Wage Patterns in the 1960s and 1970s*. New York: New York University Press, 1984.

O'Neill, June. "Trend in the Male-Female Wage Gap in the United States." *Journal of Labor Economics* 3 (January 1984): S91–S116.

Piore, Michael J. *Birds of Passage*. Cambridge: Cambridge University Press, 1979.

Rees, Albert. *The Economics of Trade Unions,* revised ed. Chicago: University of Chicago Press, 1977.

Smith, James P., and Finis R. Welch. "Black Economic Progress After Myrdal." *Journal of Economic Literature* 26 (1989): 519–562.

Street, James H. *The New Revolution in the Cotton Economy*. Chapel Hill: University of North Carolina Press, 1957.

Troy, Leo. "Is the U.S. Unique in the Decline of Private Sector Unionism." *Journal of Labor Research* 11 (1990): 111–143.

Weinstein, Bernard, and Robert E. Firestone. *Regional Growth and Decline in the United States*. New York: Praeger, 1978.

Wilson, William Julius. *The Declining Significance of Race,* 2d ed. Chicago: University of Chicago Press, 1980.

Wright, Gavin. *Old South, New South: Revolutions in the Southern Economy Since the Civil War*. New York: Basic Books, 1986.

CHAPTER THIRTY-ONE

THE FUTURE IN THE LIGHT OF THE PAST

CHAPTER THEME In the years immediately after World War II, Americans were confident of their economic future. The United States appeared to have the richest and most productive economy in the world, and it was assumed that if conflict with the communist powers could be avoided America would grow richer at a rapid rate. It was recognized, of course, that part of America's preeminent position was a result of World War II. The United States emerged from the war with its economy more productive than ever, but its rivals were damaged, some of them severely. Nevertheless, most Americans were confident that their children and grandchildren would be much better off.

By the 1970s, the luster had worn off America's grand vision of the future. The growth rate of productivity had slowed down, inflation had accelerated, and the social problems that Presidents Kennedy and Johnson had attacked seemed to be worse than ever. America's position in foreign trade was challenged by Germany, Japan, and others. The automobile companies were once a symbol of American economic preeminence; now foreign cars increasingly filled the nation's highways. President Ronald Reagan argued that greater reliance on free competitive markets would restore rapid economic growth. But when the economy fell into a recession during the administration of his successor, George Bush, many voters turned to the Democrats. President Bill Clinton won election in 1992 by offering a different prescription for growth: the government should play an active role by investing in education and in the nation's infrastructure.

Hopes and fears about the future are felt with exceptional intensity by college students. Today's students worry about what kinds of jobs will exist in an economy saddled with large federal deficits and in a world where American firms must compete with aggressive foreign rivals. Students from poor families worry that they will never achieve the middle-class standard of living that once seemed to go automatically with a college degree. Students from middle-class families worry that they will never live as well as their parents, and that they will never be able to provide for their own children as well as their parents provided for them.

It is now time to take stock: to ask where we are and where, in the light of our economic history, we might be going.

REAL INCOME

We judge the performance of our economy, first of all, by its ability to generate a rising level of real income for the American people. Figure 31-1, which shows the long-run trend since 1870, should provide some comfort. Although there are several large fluctuations around the trend, the long-run trend is clearly upward. If history is any guide, future generations will be better off than past generations.

Table 31-1 shows real gross domestic product per capita and real consumption per capita since 1960, and the annual rates of growth. The table indicates that real incomes are not falling. Even in the recession year 1991, real per capita gross domestic product was substantially higher than it had been a generation before. Moreover, the figures on real per capita consumption show similar trends. In some ways, real per capita consumption is the best single measure of what the economy is creating for the average citizen. Consumption, after all, is the final end-product of the economy: you are what you eat. Indeed, some economists believe that if full account could be taken of quality improvements—for example, the wide range of electronics that did not exist a generation ago—the current generation would stand even better relative to the past.

However, growth *has* slowed down. The high growth rates achieved between 1960 and 1970 were not repeated in subsequent decades. What if growth now slows down

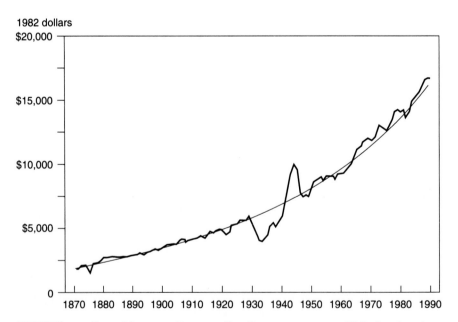

FIGURE 31-1 GROSS NATIONAL PRODUCT PER CAPITA, 1870–1990 *While there have been occasional interruptions, real GNP per capita has been rising since 1870.*

SOURCE: *ECONOMIC REPORT OF THE PRESIDENT, 1993* (WASHINGTON, D.C.: GOVERNMENT PRINTING OFFICE, 1993), P. 74.

NOTE: Trend line represents constant annual growth of 1.7 percent.

TABLE 31-1 PER CAPITA GROSS DOMESTIC PRODUCT AND PERSONAL CONSUMPTION, 1960–1991 (1987 DOLLARS)

Year	Gross Domestic Product	Annual Growth Rate	Personal Consumption Expenditures	Annual Growth Rate
1960	$10,903		$ 6,698	
1970	14,013	2.51%	8,842	2.78%
1980	16,584	1.68	10,746	1.95
1990	19,513	1.63	13,044	1.94
1991	19,077	−2.26	12,824	−1.70

SOURCE: *ECONOMIC REPORT OF THE PRESIDENT, 1993* (WASHINGTON, D.C.: GOVERNMENT PRINTING OFFICE, 1993), P. 355.

and stops altogether, or even becomes negative? We will give our assessment of such a gloomy course of events below. But you might well stop at this point and ask yourself what your study of American economic history tells you about such predictions.

One source of concern is not simply the slowdown in American economic growth, but the perception that other countries are gaining on us. Here again, looking at the relevant statistics can allay some exaggerated fears. Table 31-2 compares the levels of per capita income in the United States and other leading industrial countries. As you can see, other industrial nations still have lower per capita real products than the United States. But it is also true that most of these countries have grown faster than the United States over the last two decades. The largest gain, not surprisingly, was recorded by Japan. If these differences persisted, these countries would eventually overtake the United States.

This is a prospect that worries many Americans. But it is important to remember that our own levels of consumption need not fall just because someone else's are rising. The economy is not like a football game; in the economic game all teams can come out ahead.

TABLE 31-2 GROSS DOMESTIC PRODUCT PER CAPITA OF SELECTED COUNTRIES AS A PERCENT OF THE UNITED STATES

Country	1970	1980	1989
United States	100%	100%	100%
Canada	76	89	90
France	75	83	79
Germany	79	86	83
Italy	63	74	73
Japan	60	70	78
Sweden	81	81	79
United Kingdom	69	70	73

SOURCE: *STATISTICAL ABSTRACT OF THE UNITED STATES: 1992* (WASHINGTON, D.C.: U.S. BUREAU OF THE CENSUS, 1992), P. 833.

THE DISTRIBUTION OF INCOME

Many Americans, and particularly college students, worry that even though the country is growing (albeit at a slower rate than earlier in the postwar period) they may not be able to share in that growth because the distribution of income is becoming less fair; the rich are hogging all the gains made in the economy. Stories about the fabulous incomes of junk bond kings or top sports figures seem to confirm the impression that the rich are getting richer and the poor poorer.

Table 31-3 shows some figures, frequently used by economists, to show changes in the distribution of income. The table can be understood by thinking about a simple numerical example. Suppose there are 100 families in the economy. The total income of those 100 families is $1,000, but the poorest 20 families together earn only $50. Therefore the share of the lowest fifth (20/100) is 5 percent ($50/$1,000).

Evidently, the distribution of family incomes has not changed radically over the postwar period—compare the distribution in 1990 with the distribution in 1947. During the 1980s, however, there was a turn away from the slow progress of the preceding years. Notice that the highest fifth increased its share at the expense of all the others between 1980 and 1990. Figures such as these became extremely controversial during the 1992 election campaign, when Democrats used them to support their claim that Republican policies were enriching only the very wealthy.

Of course, as Republican economists were quick to point out, the figures are dependent on the way things are defined. Changes in family structure (which will be discussed shortly) can affect the final percentages, as can the inclusion of various benefits paid by employers, such as health insurance premiums. Another problem is income that goes unreported because people have earned it in illegal activities or wish to hide it to avoid taxes. Some conservative economists maintained that cuts in the marginal tax rates in the 1980s encouraged wealthy people to report more of their income.

But the main force accounting for the growth in inequality in the 1980s, as economists of all political persuasions acknowledged, was the widening gap between the wages of skilled and unskilled workers. Numerous changes in the workplace, including

TABLE 31-3   THE DISTRIBUTION OF MONEY INCOME AMONG FAMILIES, SELECTED YEARS

Year	Lowest Fifth	Second Fifth	Third Fifth	Fourth Fifth	Highest Fifth	Top 5%
1947	5.0%	11.9%	17.0%	23.1%	43.0%	17.5%
1957	5.1	12.7	18.1	23.8	40.4	15.6
1967	5.5	12.4	17.9	23.9	40.4	15.2
1980	5.2	11.5	17.5	24.3	41.5	15.3
1990	4.6	10.8	16.6	23.8	44.3	17.4

SOURCES: *Current Population Reports,* Series P-60 (Washington, D.C.: U.S. Bureau of the Census), no. 118, Table 13; and *Statistical Abstract of the United States: 1992* (Washington, D.C.: U.S. Bureau of the Census, 1992), p. 450.

the widespread use of computers, placed a premium on education and technical skills, while high levels of immigration maintained the supply of unskilled labor.

The families ranked in Table 31-3 differ in numerous ways: some consist of a husband and wife and children, others are headed by single parents, and so on. Insight into how these different family units fared in recent decades is given in Table 31-4. The biggest gainers over these years were women living separately and households consisting of married couples in which the wife was part of the paid labor force. Single-parent households, whether headed by a man or by a woman, actually lost ground in terms of real money income, although many probably received increases in employer-paid benefits.

Fear of a stagnant or even declining economy radically altered public perceptions of the trade-offs involved in public policy decisions. It is one thing to provide more for disadvantaged minorities or for environmental protection when the additional resources come out of an expanding economy; it is quite another when providing more resources for some purposes means providing absolutely less for others. The economy (to use the term made popular by Lester Thurow) had seemingly become a "zero-sum game."

POVERTY

Perhaps even more important to us as a nation than the relative distribution of income is the number of people living below the "poverty line." This is the number of people who have less income than the amount needed, according to the government, to maintain a decent standard of living. Of course, over time the definition of the minimum amount of income needed to rise above the poverty line changes. We are a much richer society than we were in 1900, and consequently most of us today would define a higher minimum than would have been proposed in those days. The arbitrariness of the definition of poverty in turn sets the stage for politically motivated attempts to manipulate the official poverty line. People who would like to see more money spent on the poor (including government bureaucrats who administer poverty programs) favor adjustments that raise the poverty line. People who would like to see

TABLE 31-4   MEDIAN REAL MONEY INCOME BY TYPE OF FAMILY (1990 DOLLARS)

Families	1970	1980	1990	Growth Rate, 1970–1990
Married-couple families	$35,424	$36,705	$39,895	12.62
Wife in the paid labor force	41,352	42,635	46,777	13.12
Wife not in paid labor force	31,341	30,093	30,265	−3.43
Male householder, no wife present	30,357	27,788	29,046	−4.32
Female householder, no husband present	17,156	16,509	16,932	−1.31
Unrelated male	15,293	17,351	17,297	13.10
Unrelated female	8,364	10,577	12,450	48.85

SOURCE: *STATISTICAL ABSTRACT OF THE UNITED STATES: 1992* (WASHINGTON, D.C.: U.S. BUREAU OF THE CENSUS, 1992), P. 452.

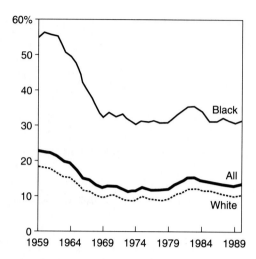

FIGURE 31-2 PERCENTAGE OF PEOPLE LIVING BELOW THE POVERTY LINE *The percentage of people classified as below the poverty line fell dramatically between 1959 and 1969, remained stable between 1969 and 1979, increased between 1979 and 1983, and declined from 1983 to 1989.*

SOURCE: HERBERT STEIN AND MURRAY FOSS, *AN ILLUSTRATED GUIDE TO THE AMERICAN ECONOMY* (WASHINGTON, D.C.: AEI PRESS, 1992), P. 118.

less government spending push for a lower definition. Nevertheless, most of us have at least a vague notion of poverty, and so the government's official statistics are of some interest.

During the 1960s, the percentage of families with incomes below the poverty line decreased sharply, as revealed in Figure 31-2. In the late 1960s, fewer than 25 million Americans were classified as living in poverty. But after leveling off in the 1970s, the percentage of people living in poverty rose substantially. There were a number of causes (including a change in the definition), although it is difficult to determine the relative importance of various factors. The severe recession of the early 1980s was undoubtedly the most important. And the Reagan administration's attempts to check public spending in this area have been criticized. In any case, the failure to maintain the gains of the 1960s has been seen as another sign of a faltering economy.

The stresses and tensions of low-income households have been increasingly mitigated by the intervention of government. This intervention, as we know, spans the whole of economic life, but nowhere has it been as remarkable as in direct outlays for public welfare. In 1890, total social-welfare expenditures were an estimated $318 million, or 2.4 percent of GNP. By 1913, the figure was $1 billion, or 2.8 percent of GNP; by 1929, it had risen to $4.3 billion, or 4.1 percent of GNP.[1] The common impression

---

[1] These data are taken from *Historical Statistics of the United States, Colonial Times to 1957*, Series N1–29, "Social Welfare Expenditures Under Civilian Public Programs: 1890–1956," pp. 189, 193. Included in the category of social-welfare expenditures are all social-insurance programs, public aid, health and medical programs, vocational rehabilitation, institutional care, school lunch programs, child welfare, public housing, and education. A definition of welfare programs that includes education may seem too broad, but the use of this concept is dictated by the need for a generally accepted and continuous time series.

that the "welfare state" began in the 1930s is borne out by the data. Social-welfare programs in 1935 required a $6.7 billion outlay—9.8 percent for that year's GNP and slightly more than one-half of government expenditures at all levels for all purposes in 1935. Although such expenditures declined both absolutely and relatively during World War II, they rose steadily after the war—amounting to $58 billion, or approximately 11.5 percent of GNP, in 1961. In the ensuing decade, federal welfare expenditures soared to $198.3 billion and state welfare funds rose to $133 billion, which together represented 19.6 percent of the 1976 GNP. Public outlays for social-welfare spending in 1971 at all levels of government represented 51 percent of total government spending for all purposes, compared with the 38 percent recorded in both 1950 and 1960. Measured in constant prices, social-welfare expenditures rose slightly more than 80 percent between 1965 and 1971 and continued to climb throughout the 1970s. The growth of such expenditures slowed in the 1980s, but total social-welfare expenditures still reached 18.2 percent of GNP by 1989.

A large number of articulate welfare supporters advocate much greater public expenditures than are presently undertaken. On the other hand, an equally vocal group insists that growing welfare expenditures undermine social progress by destroying incentives to work and invest. The uncontested fact is that nearly 27 percent of GNP was annually appropriated for public and private expenditures on health, education, and welfare in the late 1970s and early 1980s.[2]

Our perception of poverty is undoubtedly highly personal and subjective. What determines a poor person's wants and a rich person's needs? Equally important is our perception of opportunity—the opportunity to move out of poverty. Clearly, poverty is of less concern if it is not viewed as a permanent condition. Indeed, the prospects of advance may generate more happiness for the aspiring poor than for minimally contented individuals in the middle class.

ECONOMIC WELL-BEING AND PERSONAL HAPPINESS

None of the measures of income we have been discussing, of course, is perfectly correlated with personal happiness. One of the difficulties is what economists call the "index number problem." We compute real income by dividing money income by a weighted average of prices. The weights are based on amounts consumed in some base period. This works fine for some commodity that was consumed in about the same relative amounts throughout the period of comparison; but what happens when consumption of one commodity declines because it is replaced by something new and better? In that case, the use of the price index based on the old weights tends to understate the increase in real income. Although government agencies that compute price indexes are well aware of the problem, they can seldom fully take into account the constant flux of the marketplace. In practical terms, this means that the electronic

[2]Wilbur J. Cohen, "Economic Well-being and Income Distribution," in *The American Economy in Transition,* ed. Martin Feldstein (Chicago: University of Chicago Press, 1980) p. 489.

Happiness from the perspective of a second grader.

SOURCE: DEVON WALTON, SECOND GRADE, FLATIRONS ELEMENTARY SCHOOL.

revolution of the past several decades is only partially taken into account in computing the statistics. Pocket calculators, personal computers, VCRs, electronic chess partners, compact discs, video games, and so on have all added to our well-being but are only imperfectly reflected in our measures of price trends and real income, victims of the "index number problem."

Yet our problems in measuring material standards of living pale when compared with trying to determine whether people are happier today than they were several decades ago, a question that cannot be answered even with the help of other social scientists and humanists. So much depends on our perspective. Productivity, for example, has increased so fast that the average American worker produces nearly ten times as much per hour of work as our ancestors did in 1860. And work is clearly less burdensome than it has ever been. One worker with power-driven mechanical equipment can do as much work in a 40-hour week as three could do in a 70-hour week common 100 years ago. Leisure time has at least doubled since 1910, as American workers in the past half-century or so have taken about two-thirds of national productivity gains in the form of goods and services and about one-third in the form of increased leisure.

HEALTH

While life in America was becoming less arduous in the postwar period, it was also spent in better physical health and was certainly longer. When the United States became a going concern in 1789, the life expectancy of a white baby at birth was a

TABLE 31-5   LIFE EXPECTANCY AT BIRTH, 1940–1990 (IN YEARS)

Year	Total			Blacks and Other Minorities		
	Total	Male	Female	Total	Male	Female
1940	62.9	60.8	65.2	53.1	51.5	54.9
1950	68.2	65.6	71.1	60.8	59.1	62.9
1955	69.6	66.7	72.8	63.7	61.4	66.1
1960	69.7	66.6	73.1	63.6	61.1	66.3
1965	70.2	66.8	73.7	64.1	61.1	67.4
1970	70.8	67.1	74.7	65.3	61.3	69.4
1975	72.6	68.8	76.6	68.0	63.7	72.4
1980	73.7	70.0	77.4	69.5	65.3	73.6
1985	74.7	71.2	78.2	71.2	67.2	75.2
1990	75.4	72.0	78.8	72.4	68.4	76.3

SOURCES: *Statistical Abstract of the United States, 1987* (Washington, D.C.: Government Printing Office, 1986), p. 69; and *Statistical Abstract, 1992*, p. 76.

NOTE: Data for 1990 are preliminary.

little more than 30 years. By 1900, a white male child could be expected to live 48.2 years; for blacks the level was lower, but the rate of progress was also very high. As shown in Table 31-5, much progress has occurred since 1940. In 1940 all males on average had a life expectancy at birth of about 61 years; this increased until 1955, then held steady before increasing again in the 1970s and 1980s, reaching 72 by 1990. Females fared even better: they gained life expectancy of more than 13 years over the period. Blacks and other minorities still had shorter life expectancies in 1990 than did whites, but they had made even larger gains. As Table 31-5 shows, for minority males the increase in life expectancy at birth was almost 17 years between 1940 and 1990; for females it was, remarkably enough, more than 21 years.

Infant mortality is another sensitive indicator of well-being. Table 31-6 on the next page shows infant mortality rates between 1940 and 1989. The decline in these rates, particularly in the neonatal rate, has been dramatic, at least until 1980.

Similar gains have been made in the postwar period in reducing the death rates from numerous diseases. Some examples are shown in Table 31-7, also on the next page. Rapid increases in medical technology, improved living standards, and the adoption of more healthful lifestyles have been crucial in producing these improvements. However, as we might expect with an aging population, heart attacks and cancer remain principal causes of death.

Also important in the decline of the infant mortality rate and various adult diseases has been the extension of hospital, surgical, and medical expense coverage. As late as 1940, only 10 million Americans, or about 7 percent of the population, had any kind of hospital insurance (that is, any kind of prepayment of hospital costs that one day must be met by nearly everyone). In 1970, more than 150 million persons, or more than 75 percent of the population had such protection, nearly that many were protected against surgical expense, and perhaps 50 million were protected against the hazards of major medical costs. Moreover, federal old-age, survivors', and disability insurance

TABLE 31-6   INFANT MORTALITY, 1940–1989 (PER 1,000 LIVE BIRTHS)

Year	Neonatal[a]	Postneonatal[b]	Total Infant Mortality
1940	28.8	18.2	47.0
1945	24.3	14.0	38.3
1950	20.5	8.7	29.2
1960	18.7	7.3	26.0
1965	17.7	7.0	24.7
1970	15.1	4.9	20.0
1975	11.6	4.5	16.1
1980	8.5	4.1	12.6
1985	7.0	3.6	10.6
1989	6.2	3.6	9.8

SOURCES: *Historical Statistics* (Washington, D.C.: Government Printing Office, 1975), Series B139, B142; AND *Statistical Abstract of the United States, 1992* (Washington, D.C.: Government Printing Office, 1992), p. 80.

[a] Birth to 28 days.
[b] 28 days to one year.

benefits exceeded $25 billion a year by 1970. And if the number of doctors per 100,000 of population had remained constant for more than a decade, physicians were plainly more efficient (if less personal) in treating patients than they had ever been in the history of medical science.

But, as revealed in Table 31-8 or by some of the entries in Table 31-9, we have seemingly reached a plateau in the 1980s, a plateau that leaves us worse off in some categories than the populations of most other industrialized nations. For example, at the end of the 1980s, the infant mortality rate was about 10 per thousand in the U.S., but only 7.2 in Canada, 6.1 in France, and 4.4 in Japan. Is this a result of government policies or adverse social trends? The widespread use of drugs such as crack, for example, is thought to have influenced the infant mortality rate.

TABLE 31-7   DEATHS FROM SELECTED ILLNESS AND DISEASES, 1940–1990
             (PER 100,000 POPULATION)

Disease	1940	1970	1980	1990
Tuberculosis	45.9	2.6	.9	.7
Cirrhosis of the liver	8.6	15.5	13.5	10.2
Influenza and pneumonia	70.3	30.9	24.1	31.3
Diabetes	26.6	18.9	15.4	19.5
Malignancies	120.3	162.8	183.9	201.7
Major cardiovascular diseases	485.7	496.0	436.4	366.9

SOURCES: *Historical Statistics* (Washington, D.C.: Government Printing Office, 1975), Series B149, B157, B158, B159, B160, B162; AND *Statistical Abstract of the United States, 1992* (Washington, D.C.: Government Printing Office, 1992), p. 82.

TABLE 31-8   CHANGES IN SELECTED SOCIAL INDICATORS, 1950–1990

Year	(1) Births to Unmarried Women[a]	(2) Divorce Rate[b]	(3) Suicide Rate[c]	(4) Murder Rate[d]
1950	3.9	2.6	11.4	n.a.
1955	4.5	2.3	10.2	5.5
1960	5.3	2.2	10.6	5.0
1965	7.7	2.5	11.1	5.0
1970	10.7	3.5	11.6	8.0
1975	14.2	4.8	12.6	8.8
1980	18.4	5.2	11.9	10.2
1985	21.0	4.9	12.3	7.9
1990	27.0	4.7	12.3	9.4

SOURCES: (COLUMN 1) *HISTORICAL STATISTICS* (WASHINGTON, D.C.: GOVERNMENT PRINTING OFFICE, 1975), SERIES B1, B28; *STATISTICAL ABSTRACT OF THE UNITED STATES, 1992* (WASHINGTON, D.C.: GOVERNMENT PRINTING OFFICE, 1992), P. 69. (COLUMN 2) *HISTORICAL STATISTICS*, SERIES B216; *STATISTICAL ABSTRACT*, P. 64. (COLUMN 3) *HISTORICAL STATISTICS*, SERIES B166; *STATISTICAL ABSTRACT*, P. 82. (COLUMN 4) *HISTORICAL STATISTICS*, SERIES H954; *STATISTICAL ABSTRACT*, P. 180.

[a] A percentage of all births.
[b] Per 1,000 population.
[c] Per 100,000 population.
[d] Per 100,000 population.

Other social indicators of well-being reveal "deterioration" in the 1970s. As shown in Table 31-8, births to unmarried women, the divorce rate, the suicide rate, and the murder rate all rose in the early 1970s and 1980s. In some cases we could argue that part of the trend represented an increase in well-being—some people may be happier divorcing rather than remaining married merely because of strong social pressures to do so—but in general the adverse movements in these trends were another reflection of the malaise that engulfed the nation during the second part of the postwar period.

AN AGING POPULATION

One of the major worries intensified by the slow growth of real family income was how the nation was going to take care of an increasingly elderly population. As Table

TABLE 31-9   THE ELDERLY POPULATION, 1960–1990

Age Group	1960	1970	1980	1990
Persons 65 and over (in millions)	16.7	20.1	25.7	31.1
Percent of total population	9.2%	9.8%	11.3%	12.6%
Persons 65 and over per 100 persons aged 18–64	17	17	19	20

SOURCE: *STATISTICAL ABSTRACT OF THE UNITED STATES, 1993* (WASHINGTON, D.C.: GOVERNMENT PRINTING OFFICE, 1993), P. 18, AND PREVIOUS EDITIONS.

31-9 shows, the percentage of individuals over 65 years of age increased steadily. This trend created severe strains for the Social Security system, and doubts about its future. In 1980, 11.3 percent of the population was 65 and older; projections indicate a rise of the age group eligible for Social Security to 12.7 percent in the year 2000 and 19.4 percent in 2030. Whereas in 1980 there were 3.3 covered workers per beneficiary, by 2030 it is projected there will only be 2.0 workers per recipient. Because of the expansion of coverage and benefits, the indexing of benefits to increase automatically with inflation, and this aging trend, the employee-employer tax rate was raised from 2.0 percent in 1935 to 12.26 percent in 1980. The maximum tax payment rose by a factor of 47, from $60 to $2,808. The number of beneficiaries was 220,000 in 1941, and they were supported by 35 million paying workers. In 1980 there were 115 million workers paying into the system to support 36 million beneficiaries.[3] The sharp fall in the ratio of workers to beneficiaries—from more than 100 to 1 in 1941, to 3 to 1 today—has required higher and higher rates. Because this trend will continue, rates must either rise or benefits must be curtailed. The problem, although economic, demands a political solution.[4]

The Social Security system came perilously close to bankruptcy. On April 1, 1982, the system's trustees reported that "Social Security will be unable to pay retirees' and survivors' benefits on time starting in July 1983 unless Congress takes corrective action." Congressman Claude Pepper of Florida, a leading spokesman for the elderly and chairman of the House Select Committee on Aging, said the trustees' report "confirms my belief that the poor performance of the economy is robbing the Social Security trust funds." But it was no temporary matter and no April Fools' joke. For the seventeenth straight year, the combined old age and disability trust funds paid out more than they took in and soon they would be depleted. Legislation based on recommendations of a presidential commission headed by Alan Greenspan rescued the system; today there is a substantial surplus. But the basic problem of an aging population remains. Without continued economic growth, it is hard to see how today's workers can expect to receive the current level of benefits when they retire.

PROPHETS OF CONVERGENCE AMONG NATIONS

As we have seen, there is evidence that sometime, perhaps in the late 1960s or early 1970s, the United States entered a period of deteriorating economic performance. Measurements such as real family income, labor productivity, even measures of physical

---

[3] Initially, the Social Security system was partially an insurance system, one built on the principle of an actuarially sound reserve that would allow payment to potential claims from those who had paid into the system. It was also partially a pay-as-you-go system. Taxes were collected beginning in 1937, but no benefits were paid until 1942, in order to accumulate a reserve. The political temptation to increase benefits became too great, however, and soon the system converted entirely to a pay-as-you-go system, with beneficiaries being supported entirely by those paying in.

[4] For more on this nagging problem see Carolyn L. Weaver, *Understanding the Sources and Dimensions of Crisis in Social Security* (Washington, D.C.: Fiscal Policy Council, 1981).

or social health show evidence of a slowdown in progress or an absolute decline. Comparisons with economies such as those of Germany, Japan, and other Asian rim nations that seemed to do a better job of coping with the economic problems of the 1970s heightened concern about the long-run health of the economy. Not all observers, however, see this period as the beginning of the end. There is a strong current of opinion that an advanced nation like the United States will naturally grow at a slower rate than a latecomer still in the process of industrialization. According to this view, the slowdown of the United States relative to other nations is a natural part of economic maturation.

One of the earliest formulations of this view appeared in Walt Rostow's book, *Stages of Economic Growth.*[5] Rostow argued that all countries tend to go through the same series of stages. Growth is slow or nonexistent in the first phases. Growth is fastest in the stage that Rostow called the "take-off," when rapid economic growth begins; and growth is nearly as fast during the "drive to maturity" when economic growth is made the top priority. Growth becomes slower in the following stage, "the era of high mass consumption," when people turn from making money to enjoying it. If certain countries were growing faster than the United States (today we would point to the Asian rim countries; at the time Rostow had a number of European countries including the Soviet Union in mind), it was because they had only lately entered the "drive to maturity." Later they would slow down when they joined the United States in the "era of high mass consumption." Rostow's theory has been strongly criticized, and important alternatives have been offered. One of the best known is Alexander Gerschenkron's argument that the nature and rate of industrialization depend on the type of society into which the process of industrialization is introduced.[6] Gerschenkron noted that industrialization could occur very rapidly in nations that found a way to quickly adapt technologies developed abroad.

Although Rostow's theory and Gerschenkron's alternative have often been criticized, a key element of them—the notion of a catch-up by latecomers to the industrialization process, and the related tendency of output per capita in different nations to converge—has received wider acceptance. Moses Abramovitz has argued that the catch-up process has been at work, but that for a long time the United States remained far ahead of other nations because of special circumstances.[7] For one thing, new technologies in the nineteenth century tended to conserve labor and require capital and natural resources, a demand pattern that matched American resource endowments. The two world wars, major setbacks for many countries other than the United States, also worked to prolong the American lead.

We can take some comfort in these ideas, which view our current problems as partly the natural consequence of economic maturity. But many other experts warn that without major structural changes in the economy, the United States will tend to spiral downward. The dominant concern has been with the supply of savings in the 1970s and 1980s.

---

[5] W. W. Rostow, *The Stages of Economic Growth* (Cambridge: Cambridge University Press, 1960 and 1971).

[6] Alexander Gerschenkron, *Economic Backwardness in Historical Perspective* (New York: Praeger, 1962).

[7] Moses Abramovitz, "Catching Up, Forging Ahead, and Falling Behind," *Journal of Economic History* 46 (June 1986): 397–398.

SAVINGS, THE GOVERNMENT DEFICIT, AND FOREIGN TRADE

Policymakers in the 1970s and 1980s became concerned (some would say obsessed) with the problem of a decline in the funds available for investment—the funds to build new plants and equipment. The reason for the concern is illustrated in Figure 31-3. The willingness of the United States to build its capital stock lagged behind that of other industrial nations throughout the entire decade of the 1980s. This lag contributed to a deteriorating competitive position for U.S. products in both domestic and world markets. Some observers claimed that low savings was the primary cause of the slow-down in productivity growth. According to this view, more machinery would mean higher productivity. Productivity, moreover, came to be seen as the key to economic and, perhaps, social revival. It was this concern with the savings gap between the United States and its foreign competitors that focused the attention of many economists on the deficit in the federal budget and the excess of imports over exports of goods and services, because the three are closely tied together.

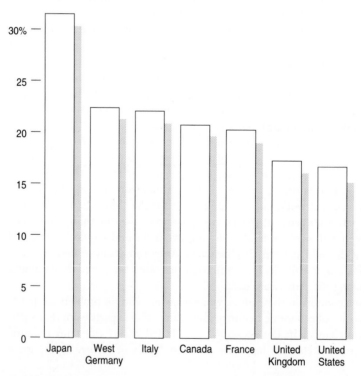

FIGURE 31-3 GROSS SAVINGS AS A PERCENTAGE OF GNP, 1981–1990 *During the 1980s the U.S. lagged behind other industrial nations in the percentage of national income devoted to savings.*

SOURCE: HERBERT STEIN AND MURRAY FOSS, *AN ILLUSTRATED GUIDE TO THE AMERICAN ECONOMY* (WASHINGTON, D.C.: AEI PRESS, 1992), P. 75.

Table 31-10 illustrates the relationship. Column 1 of the table shows the funds available from savings to purchase securities or otherwise invest in the economy. Add to that any funds made available from a government surplus, or subtract the funds used to purchase new government debt when the economy runs a deficit (column 2), subtract any funds used to invest in foreign countries (column 3), and the result is gross private investment in the United States (column 4). The gross savings ratio did not show a distinct trend during this period. But the same cannot be said of gross private investment. First, the decline in governmental surpluses and then the rising deficit caused an alarming drop in the gross investment rate after 1965. In 1975, for example, the gross investment rate was down to 13.6 percent.

The 1980s witnessed something of a turnaround, but the reason was surprising. For most of the postwar period, the United States had been investing abroad. Now the United States was running a current account deficit, and foreigners were investing in the United States. This partial turnaround did mean that Americans would now be experiencing the higher labor productivity growth normally associated with an expanding stock of capital. But considerable future profits would have to be sent abroad: the United States would be forced to export more than it imported. To do so in a highly competitive world market would not be easy.

What could be done about the "twin deficits" and the dangers they create? The basic tool would be the federal budget. And many economists, although not all, recommend some combination of higher taxes or spending cuts to close the budget deficit. Taxes, moreover, could be raised on consumption expenditures and lowered on savings to stimulate further capital formation. Critics of the latter policy note that it would tend to fall more heavily on the poor than on the rich, because the rich typically spend a smaller fraction of their income on consumption. Spending cuts that would be politically acceptable are hard to imagine. Some economists have suggested "means testing" federal transfer expenditures, such as further reducing the net amount of Social

TABLE 31-10   SAVINGS AND INVESTMENT IN THE UNITED STATES, 1950–1991 (PERCENT OF GNP)

Year	(1) Gross Private Savings	+	(2) Government Surplus	−	(3) Net Foreign Investment	=	(4) Gross Private Investment
1950	15.4%		2.8%		−.6%		18.8%
1955	16.1		.8		.1		16.8
1960	15.7		.6		.6		15.7
1965	17.4		.1		.9		16.6
1970	16.2		−1.0		.5		14.7
1975	19.0		−4.1		1.4		13.6
1980	17.5		−1.3		.5		15.8
1985	17.2		−3.4		−2.9		16.7
1991	15.8		−3.4		.2		12.6

SOURCES: *Economic Report of the President, 1993* (Washington, D.C.: Government Printing Office, 1993), p. 378, and previous editions.

Security benefits received by wealthy but elderly individuals. Others have called for a scaling back of defense spending. These issues came to the fore in the presidential election of 1992. Both Democrat Bill Clinton and independent Ross Perot promised to reduce the federal deficit in order to restore savings and growth. As this is written, President Clinton's tax measures are still wending their way through Congress. Even if his proposed tax increases are adopted, it will be many years before we can judge their effect on the economy.

No one can be sure, even if the budget deficit is closed through some combination of policies, that this will solve the nation's savings and trade problems. Economic reactions are often hard to predict. For example, many economists have contended that closing the budget deficit will reduce interest rates in the United States and make U.S. assets less attractive to foreigners, thus producing a decline in foreign investment, a decline in the value of the dollar, and a rise in U.S. exports and a fall in imports. But whether any of this sequence will occur, and certainly to what extent, are hotly debated by economists.

Another group of experts see the budget deficit as more of a symptom of the destructive tendencies of our political and economic institutions than the cause of it. Our failure to make any progress on reducing the federal deficit can be viewed as simply another example of the ability of special interests to block policies that are clearly in the public interest. Japan is often held up as an example of a country where a system worth emulating exists. Labor relations in the United States have traditionally been built on conflict rather than cooperation. If U.S. firms would begin to emulate the Japanese system, where a great effort is made to incorporate the ideas of the worker into the production process, perhaps faster productivity growth could be achieved. We do not have space here to develop these or related ideas in detail. Our point is simply that in recent decades economists and other experts have been offering a wide range of potential medicines to cure the nation's ills. Unfortunately, unlike physicians who can rely on controlled testing to determine which medicines work and which do not, economists have only the ambiguous natural experiments of history from which to draw their conclusions.

PROPHETS OF DECLINE

The slowdown in productivity growth in the 1970s and 1980s, along with the rise in various indicators of social malaise such as the murder rate, brought to center stage a series of pundits who claimed that Americans faced a long-term decline in their living standards if they did not quickly shape up. Some focused on the lack of savings and the government deficit discussed earlier; others stressed America's dependence on oil; still others decried the spoiling of the environment. Paul Kennedy, one of the most thoughtful prophets of decline, stressed the tendency of great empires of the past to decline once they reached a preeminent position because they exhausted their resources in foreign adventures.[8] It was natural for Americans who had witnessed the destructive domestic consequences of the war in Vietnam to see the force of his point.

---

[8] Paul Kennedy, *The Rise and Fall of the Great Powers: Economic Change and Military Conflict from 1500 to 2000* (New York: Random House, 1987).

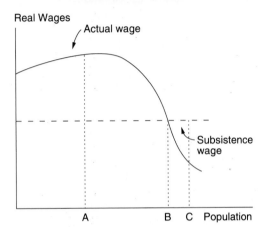

The term *Malthusianism* has entered our language to describe the belief that unchecked population growth will produce widespread poverty and degradation. This was one of the earliest theories of inevitable decline, and it was a model for subsequent theories of decline that stressed limits to mineral resources rather than agricultural land. It is still held to be important by some economists as a model for some less-developed countries. The figure above illustrates Malthus's theory.

The real wage, determined by the food that a worker can buy, is shown on the vertical axis. Population is shown on the horizontal axis. When the population is relatively low, at point A, the real wage is above the minimum needed to sustain life. This leads to rapid population growth—unless checked by moral restraint or explicit government policies. But real wages then fall because each additional worker produces a smaller real output: more labor is being applied to the same, or to a slowly growing, amount of agricultural land. Eventually population rises to level B, and real wages are reduced to the subsistence level. Further increases in population, say to C, are checked by starvation.

One problem with Malthus's analysis, as he himself came to realize, is that improvements in agricultural productivity might shift the wage curve upward. One way that this could (and did) happen is through international trade. British workers could specialize in producing industrial products—over time, technological advances would allow them to do this more easily—and these goods could be traded for food produced in other parts of the world.

We do not wish to argue that the problems addressed by the prophets of decline are not real ones, or that their solutions might not make things better. But it is important to remember that prophecies of decline are not unique to our age. For the British, especially, it is an old story. Writing in 1798, Thomas Robert Malthus predicted that eventually Britain's growing population would run into its declining ability to produce food (after all, the amount of agricultural land was limited).[9] Wages would eventually fall until they reached the minimum necessary to sustain life. Disaster could be avoided only if population could somehow be held in check. Nearly 200 years later, the population of England is far higher than Malthus could have imagined, but the crunch has yet to come.

William Stanley Jevons was another prophet of inevitable decline. In his famous book, *The Coal Question,* written in 1865, Jevons predicted that England would eventually be forced into decline because its reserves of coal (then its chief source of industrial power) would be exhausted. England would face not only economic decline, but also "moral and intellectual retrogression."[10] This catastrophe never came to pass: more reserves of coal were found, technological change permitted other sources of power to be used, and the development of world trade made it possible to escape from the confines of a theory based on the premise that Britain was the only industrial nation.

We cannot say that the Jeremiahs of the current generation are wrong. But the economic historian, looking at the long record of growth achieved by the American economy, is likely to be skeptical. The point was well put long ago by English historian Thomas Babington Macaulay:

> We cannot absolutely prove that those are in error who tell us that society has reached a turning point, that we have seen our best days. But so said all who came before us, and with just as much apparent reason.[11]

SELECTED REFERENCES
AND SUGGESTED READINGS

Abramovitz, Moses. "Catching Up, Forging Ahead, and Falling Behind." *Journal of Economic History* 46 (1986): 385–406.

Blinder, Alan S. "The Level and Distribution of Economic Well-being." In *The American Economy in Transition,* ed. Martin Feldstein. Chicago: University of Chicago Press, 1980. Chapter 6.

Browing, Edgar K., and William R. Johnson. "Taxes, Transfers, and Income Equality." In *Regulatory Change in an Atmosphere of Crisis: Current Implications of the Roosevelt Years,* ed. Gary Walton. New York: Academic Press, 1979.

---

[9] Malthus revised and refined his theory many times over his lifetime. See Thomas R. Malthus, *An Essay on Population,* 2 vols. (London: J. M. Dent, 1914).

[10] Quoted in Stanley Engerman, "Chicken Little, Anna Karenina, and the Economics of Slavery: Two Reflections on Historical Analysis, with Examples Drawn Mostly from the Study of Slavery," *Social Science History* 17 (1993): 163. Engerman points out that both Malthus and Jevons saw the crunch coming far in the future.

[11] "Southey's Colloquies," in *Macaulay's Essays* (1860 ed.; American ed., Boston: 1881; Riverside ed.), Vol. I, ii, p. 186. We thank Donald McCloskey for suggesting this quotation.

Budd, Edward C. *Inequality and Poverty*. New York: W. W. Norton, 1967.

Cherlin, Andrew J. *Marriage, Divorce, Remarriage*. Cambridge: Harvard University Press, 1981.

Clark, Colin. *The Conditions of Economic Progress*. 3d ed. New York: St. Martin's Press, 1981.

Cohen, Wilbur J. "Economic Well-being and Income Distribution." In *The American Economy in Transition*, ed. Martin Feldstein. Chicago: University of Chicago Press, 1980.

Cooper, Richard N. "Dealing with the Trade Deficit in a Floating Rate System." *Brookings Papers on Economic Activity* (1986): 195–207.

Easterlin, Richard A. *Birth and Fortune*. New York: Basic Books, 1980.

———. "Does Economic Growth Improve the Human Lot? Some Empirical Evidence." In *Essays in Honor of Moses Abramovitz*, eds. Paul David and Melvin Reder. New York: Academic Press, 1974.

Gerschenkron, Alexander. *Economic Backwardness in Historical Perspective*. New York: Praeger, 1962.

Joyce, Theodore, Hope Corman, and Michael Grossman. "A Cost-Effectiveness Analysis of Strategies to Reduce Infant Mortality." *Medical Care* 26 (April 1988): 348–360.

Kennedy, Paul. *The Rise and Fall of the Great Powers: Economic Change and Military Conflict from 1500 to 2000*. New York: Random House, 1987.

Lebergott, Stanley. *The American Economy: Income, Wealth and Want*. Princeton: Princeton University Press, 1976.

Levy, Frank. *Dollars and Dreams: The Changing American Income Distribution*. New York: W. W. Norton, 1988.

Madison, Angus. *Phases of Capitalist Development*. New York: Oxford University Press, 1982.

Murray, Charles. *In Pursuit of Happiness and Good Government*. New York: Simon & Schuster, 1988.

———. *Losing Ground: American Social Policy, 1950–1980*. New York: Basic Books, 1984.

Pechman, Joseph. *Who Pays the Taxes, 1966–1985*. Washington, D.C.: Brookings Institution, 1985.

Reich, Robert. *The New American Frontier*. New York: New York Times Publishers, 1983.

Reynolds, Morgan, and Eugene Smolensky. "The Fading Effect of Government on Inequality." *Challenge* 21 (July/August 1978): 32–37.

———. *Public Expenditures, Taxes and the Distribution of Income: The U.S. 1950, 1960, 1970*. New York: Academic Press, 1977.

Rostow, W. W. *The Stages of Economic Growth*. Cambridge: Cambridge University Press, 1960 and 1971.

———. *The World Economy: History & Prospect*. Austin: University of Texas Press, 1978.

Ruggles, Patricia, and Michael O'Higgins. "The Distribution of Public Expenditure Among Households in the United States." *Review of Income and Wealth* 27 (June 1981): 137–163.

Sundquist, James L. *Politics and Policy, The Eisenhower, Kennedy, and Johnson Years*. Washington, D.C.: Brookings Institution, 1968.

Thurow, Lester. *The Zero-Sum Game*. New York: Basic Books, 1980.

———. *The Zero-Sum Solution*. New York: Simon & Schuster, 1985.

Weaver, Carolyn L. *Understanding the Sources and Dimensions of Crisis in Social Security*. Washington, D.C.: Fiscal Policy Council, 1981.

Weitzman, Martin. *The Share Economy*. Cambridge: Harvard University Press, 1986.

Index